IRELAND'S WELCOME TO THE STRANGER

"An eleventh-hour description of life in pre-famine Ireland, endowed with an honesty and an intimacy unrivalled in any travelogue of the nineteenth century. ... Not only a gem of social history, but a monument to courage and to truth."
— Irene Whelan, author of *The Bible War* (2003)

"The most intelligent of all observers." [of A.N. in Ireland]
—Sean O'Faolain

"A Protestant love song to a Catholic people."
—Frank O'Connor

D0920792

IRELAND'S WELCOME
TO THE STRANGER

ASENATH NICHOLSON

Edited by
Maureen Murphy

THE LILLIPUT PRESS
DUBLIN

Copyright © The Lilliput Press, 2002
Editorial matter © Maureen Murphy, 2002

All rights reserved. No part of this publication
may be reproduced in any form or by any means
without the prior permission of the publisher.

First published 2002 by
THE LILLIPUT PRESS LTD
62–63 Sitric Road, Arbour Hill,
Dublin 7, Ireland
www.lilliputpress.ie

A CIP record for this title is available from
The British Library.

1 3 5 7 9 10 8 6 4 2

ISBN 1 901866 67 x

Set by Marsha Swan in 9.5 on 12.75 Hoefler Text
Printed in Ireland by Betaprint of Dublin

CONTENTS

Editor's Introduction vii
Acknowledgments xix
Nicholson's Itinerary xxi

Preface 1
Chapter I Departure from New York ... 5
Chapter II Dialogues with the Poor ... 19
Chapter III Visit to the County of Wicklow ... 31
Chapter IV The Church of Kilbride ... 44
Chapter V The Second Cabin of a Canal-Boat ... 54
Chapter IV Cabin Life – Urlingford Spa ... 67
Chapter VII The spirit of Caste injurious in Ireland ... 84
Chapter VIII Nunnery at Thurles ... 97
Chapter IX Birr – A Miserable Protestant Lodging-House ... 115
Chapter X Walk to Loughrea ... 135
Chapter XI Novel Interior of a Cabin ... 151
Chapter XII Start for another Tour ... 160
Chapter XIII Public Buildings in Wexford ... 170
Chapter XIV Reception from father Mathew ... 180
Chapter XV Cloyne ... 191
Chapter XVI Exploration in Bantry ... 201
Chapter XVII Rambles in Glengariff ... 211
Chapter XVIII Accident at Kenmare ... 222
Chapter XIX Fellow Travellers on the Kerry Mountains ... 235
Chapter XX An Americanized Irishman ... 248
Chapter XXI Rough Road ... 258

Chapter XXII Sunrise on the Kerry Mountains ... 261

Chapter XXIII Tralee ... 269

Chapter XXIV Sail up the Shannon to Limerick ... 281

Chapter XXV Clifden ... 293

Chapter XXVI Misfortunes in Clifden ... 308

Chapter XXVII Sunday Sermons ... 319

Chapter XXVIII Mr. Nangle's Notice ... 336

Notes 341

Bibliography 381

Index 378

EDITOR'S INTRODUCTION

Had you been travelling in Ireland in 1844–5, you might have seen – or heard about – an extraordinary American woman walking through the Irish countryside singing hymns, reading the Bible and distributing religious tracts. She wore a fashionable polka coat, Indian rubber boots that pinched her feet, a velvet bonnet, a black bearskin muff and, when they were not misplaced, silver-rimmed spectacles. She recorded with some indignation that people stared at her.

She was Asenath Hatch Nicholson (1792–1855): teacher, reformer, writer, traveller and social worker. Her travel journal is one of the most valuable documents we have about Ireland on the eve of the Great Famine (1845–52). In *A Short History of Irish Literature* (1967) Frank O'Connor called her account one of the two best descriptions of the period. (His other choice was William Carleton's unfinished *Autobiography*, published with a biographical essay by D.J. O'Donoghue in 1867.) O'Connor's description of Nicholson's work as "a Protestant love song to a Catholic people" suggests that the American's appreciation of the rural Irish may have anticipated the sympathetic descriptions of life in the Irish countryside written a generation later by Anglo-Irish literary revivalists Douglas Hyde and Augusta, Lady Gregory.

O'Connor's contemporary Seán O'Faoláin also turned to Nicholson to furnish a description of the Kerry countryside for his biography of Daniel O'Connell, *King of the Beggars* (1938):

> The pictures of that hard life have been gathered over and over again, but I refuse to regather their misery. One picture alone, and that a happy one, is enough to make the heart pause, and the conscience reject romance; it is from that Darrynane [*sic*] district in the year of 1845, and from one of the most intelligent of all observers, that fine old American lady, Asenath Nicholson, and it is intended to underline what she had so often been delighted to find among the filth and dirt, "the benevolence", "kindness", "patience", even "content" – recurring words in her diaries – of the people among whom O'Connell was reared as a herd's foster child.[1]

Asenath Hatch was born in Chelsea, Vermont. Her parents were devout Congregationalists. She was trained as a schoolteacher and had her own classroom by the time she was sixteen. During the 1820s she moved to New York, where she married Norman Nicholson, a merchant, and started a school of her own. Influenced by the health reformer Sylvester Graham, the Nicholsons in the early 1830s opened a boarding-house that followed Grahamite principles of diet and hygiene; over the coming years they opened further boarding-houses, some of which were devoted to the cause of temperance, and they became close to the founders of the New York Anti-Slavery Society and the American Anti-Slavery Society. Asenath Nicholson pursued an independent course in her social and evangelical work; it was during visits to the Five Points slum that she first encountered the poor Irish of New York.² It was no accident that her first evangelical trip overseas took her to Ireland; shortly after she arrived there, in the summer of 1844, she visited places where she had introductions from New York connections. An Irish woman worried about her mother asked Nicholson to call on her family in Tullamore, and there was great welcome in Johnstown, near Urlingford, Co. Kilkenny, where the families of nine girls whom Nicholson employed in New York held a dance in her honour. These reconnoitering visits and the hospitality extended to her – a potato, a mug of milk and a bed – prepared her for her real purpose: to read the Bible to the Irish poor.

In many ways Nicholson was a typical mid-Victorian Christian evangelist, but her mission was not as straightforward as it might have appeared. She moved in a kind of power vacuum between the predominantly Catholic Irish country people and the Protestant missionary movement actively proselytizing in the countryside. Her position was not enviable: the Catholics were suspicious of Bible-reading strangers and the missionaries suspected her broad tolerance and her democratic ideas. She was ready for the challenge, however; she had prepared for it her entire life by pursuing her own course of independence and active Christian charity.

When she started her Irish journey, Nicholson summoned scripture to explain her self-appointed mission. "The world was before me and all mankind my brethren. 'I have made you desolate. I want you for other purposes. Go work in my vineyard,' was the word. I conferred not with flesh and blood." This suggests something of the legend that describes the call to St Patrick to bring Christianity to Ireland. She alluded to the willingness of Rachel to follow her destiny, the loyalty of Ruth and Timothy's advice to desolate widows to be steadfast.

Nicholson's independent course as a Bible-reader differed from the work of other Bible-readers and Christian evangelists. The rebellion of 1798, which linked Romanism with republicanism, pointed out the necessity for a loyal Protestant yeomanry and provided a rationale for a missionary movement in the evangelical wing of the Church of Ireland. The Presbyterians established a Home Mission for Ireland as well as for foreign missions. There were Methodists, Baptists, Plymouth Brethren, Moravians and independent Bible-readers and preachers.

Nicholson's choice of Bible texts demonstrates a thoughtful ecumenism and a contextualization of the hospitality and generosity shown her by the Irish poor. She regarded John 14:1–2, "In my father's house there are many mansions", as an appropriate choice to introduce the Bible to new listeners who were not of her faith. It conveyed the message that she was not a proselytizer. Her favourite text was Matthew 25:35, "I was a stranger and ye took me in." She also quoted the Old Testament lines from Hebrews 13:1–2, "Be not forgetful to entertain strangers: for thereby some have entertained angels unawares." With parables of charity from Mark 12:41–43 (the widow's mite) and Luke 10:33–37 (the Good Samaritan), Nicholson told the poor that their welcome to travellers was not simply observing the unwritten laws of hospitality in the Irish countryside, but also living the Gospel.

She not only offered more inclusive readings to her listeners, she was also sensitive to texts that might be alienating or offensive to them. She took heed of a young Catholic woman she met in Clifden who advised her to avoid distributing controversial tracts. "'You have,' she said, 'done good here, by showing to the people that you did not come to quarrel with them about their religion, but to do them good by giving such books as they might read; but if you circulate these, it will be said that you are like all others, and the good you have done will be lost.'"

She had the most trouble with her listeners about Catholic doctrine about the Virgin Mary. She found that the Irish considered it a test of her orthodoxy and they interrogated her about her beliefs. "This will cut the garment," she was told in Killarney, where she had been preceded by a Bible-reader with anti-Catholic tracts and found people very suspicious of her. "As ye think of the mother, so ye'd love the Son, and if yer tracts say nothin' of her, we would not read 'em."

Nicholson differed with other Bible-readers and missionaries about matters of literacy and education. There were societies founded to increase Bible literacy in the Irish and English languages. The Association for Discountenancing Vice and Promoting the Knowledge and Practice of

Christian Religion, founded in 1792, was followed by the better-known
Hibernian Bible Society, which distributed Bibles and tracts in English
and Irish. (They supplied Nicholson with Bibles.) The Irish Society (1818)
devoted itself to instructing Irish speakers in their own language as a way
of learning English. They distributed Irish versions of the Bible translated
by Bishop William Bedell (1685) and Archbishop William Daniel's Irish
translation of *The Book of Common Prayer* (1608), and some school books,
while disclaiming any intention of supporting wider education through
Irish.

The use of the Irish language by missionaries and Bible societies had
unhappy consequences for the Irish language. Country people associated
literacy in Irish with proselytizers. In his recollection of his boyhood in
Tipperary, Séamus O'Maolchathaigh recalled that connection:

> B'ait an rud é, ach d'airigh mé go minic é, aon duine sa tuath a
> chuireadh suim i léamh agus scríobh na Gaeilge go mbíodh
> drochamhras air go raibh baint éigin aige leis na "soupers".[3]
> (It was a strange thing, but I often noticed anyone in this place
> who had any interest in reading and writing Irish was regarded
> poorly because it was believed that he had some sort of connection
> with the soupers.)

Believing as she did that only education and a thorough knowledge of
scripture would deliver the Irish countryman from the superstition of
Rome, Nicholson paid particular attention to Protestant educational
societies and to schools organized by these societies. She was especially
interested in visiting the schools in the two missionary colonies that had
attracted great attention in the 1840s, at Dingle and at Achill. Nicholson
used the verse from Matthew 5:14, "Ye are the light of the world. A city
that is set on a hill cannot be hid" to express both her admiration for the
colonies and her caution that such "cities" would be watched carefully.
Her opinions provoked quarrels at both missions when she discovered
that the colonies' conversion efforts were complicated by class and that
literacy and education were limited by attitudes toward the social class of
the converts.

Nicholson visited the Ventry colony first; it had been founded in 1833,
when Lord Ventry appointed the Reverend. Charles Gayer as his private
chaplain and directed him to establish a Protestant colony on his estate.
By 1838, Gayer had 170 converts. Nicholson arrived in the Dingle penin-
sula in April 1845, after there had been trouble between Catholics who

had been evicted from their holdings and converts who had been given those lands and wages of eightpence a day. In December 1844 and February 1845, Catholic tenants tried to reclaim the land they had formerly occupied. When she called on Mrs Gayer, Nicholson was received coldly because she was reputed to have visited Catholics:

> "Do you make a practice of going among the Catholics?"
> "I make it a practice of going among all the poor without distinction, but am sorry to say that 'my own' often reject me, and I should more than once have been without a shelter, if the Catholics had not received me when the Protestants would not."

Nicholson was shown out quickly.

Later, when she visited a Ventry school, Nicholson was bothered by a teacher, probably Miss Rae, the teacher in charge of the mission school, who said that the girls did not learn to read maps because "these are the daughters of the lower order, and we do not advance them".

Her experience at the Achill colony was similar. The colony at Dugort on Achill Island was founded by Edward Nangle in 1834. English travellers' early reports were encouraging. Baptist Noel, a Church of England clergyman turned Baptist minister, paid a visit to the settlement and gave a sympathetic account of progress at Achill in his *Notes on a Short Tour through the Midland Counties of Ireland in the Summer of 1836* (1837). The indefatigable traveller, antiquarian and editor, the Reverend Caesar Otway, also visited Nangle's community in the late thirties. His picture of the prosperity of the Achill Mission is tempered by references to the economic difficulties that plagued the missionaries during what Otway called "this up-hill state of work".

The English publisher Samuel Hall and his wife, the writer Anna Fielding Hall, visited Achill in the autumn of 1842. Favourably disposed to the colony because they "considered every conscientious accession to the Protestant faith as a contribution in aid of the well-being of the state" (III, 398), they were disturbed when they met an orphan boy on the road to Achill. He had been expelled from the colony by Nangle and given three shillings to take him the sixty miles to Sligo. The Halls brought him to Achill and tried unsuccessfully to intercede with Nangle on his behalf. Later, they met five other boys who had been similarly turned out of the colony. The Halls' criticism threatened Nangle, who depended on the support of English subscribers to keep his community solvent; thereafter, he became wary of outsiders.

Nangle's colony was the place Nicholson most wanted to see in Ireland, and her initial impressions were favourable; it was tidy and prosperous-looking, and colonists appeared to be well nourished, but trouble started when Nicholson asked Nangle about the literacy of his adult converts. He responded that converts were not taught to read; it would be too difficult. Nicholson replied briskly that she knew of an adult school in New York where Irish immigrants as old as sixty were taught to read. Nangle dismissed her as "officious", but he was sufficiently bothered by Nicholson to complain about her visit in the pages of his mission paper, *The Achill Herald and Western Witness. A Monthly Journal Exhibiting the Principles and Progress of Christ's Kingdom and Exposing the Errors and Abominations of that Section of the Rival Kingdom of the Anti-Christ commonly called the Papacy; together with a Practical Exposure of the Civil, Social and Political Delinquencies Practiced by the Pope's Emissaries in Attempting to Re-establish his Wicked Usurpations throughout the World Generally and especially in this Kingdom.*

He concluded, "There is nothing in her conduct or conversation to justify the supposition of insanity and we strongly suspect she is the emissary of some democratic and revolutionary society."

For her part Nicholson believed that the Irish poor would abandon their Catholicism only by being able to read the Bible themselves:

> These converts, turned from worshipping images to the living and true God, as they are told, holding a Protestant prayer-book in their hands which they cannot read, can no more be sure that this religion, inculcated by proxy, emanates from the pure Scriptures, than did the prayer book which they held in their hands when standing before a Popish altar.

She gave Nangle his due for building a tidy, self-sufficient community on a rocky island, for cleanliness and for signs of prosperity, but she argued that these were not the things that made permanent converts. History confirms her judgment; in nine years only 92 people of 6392 were converted by Nangle's mission.

If the local people were unresponsive to the Achill Mission, they did not entirely ignore the missionaries among them. Proselytizing efforts, particularly those related to the Great Famine, survive in local folklore. In an Achill ballad called "Na Preachers", a cow escapes from Edward Nangle's Dugort colony because she would rather drown herself than stay in a place where there is heresy.

While her experience with the Ventry and Achill missions was disappointing, Nicholson found other energetic missionaries and Bible-readers who worked among the poor without regard to their willingness to convert. Furthermore, she witnessed Catholic and Protestant clergy frequently co-operating to serve the poor. She described the death of Father McSweeney of Bandon, whose loss was felt by the whole community. A Catholic mourned the death of the Protestant rector of Hyde Park near Killarney, saying: "he was the one that the people loved; he was so kind to the poor and sick, not a hap'orth of a cabin in all the parish but his fut was in, and though he was a Protestant, yet he sarved the Catholics with as many a good turn as he did his own; and when he died, wasn't there the lamentation!" For Nicholson, tolerance and charity counted more than the nominal Christianity of the missions.

Reaction to Nicholson and her Bible-reading mission varied. The Irish were above all curious about her. They wondered why she had come and often ascribed her appearance to one of two traditional notions: the saint's visit or the penitent pilgrim. "It was difficult to make them believe I was not some holy St Brigid going on penance." Both ideas, favourite themes in early medieval literature, are still features of the folklore of the Irish countryside.

Nicholson appears to be as candid and honest about her reception as a Bible-reader as she was fair-minded about what she observed around her. When she met with opposition or rejection, she recorded it, as she did in Galway when a countrywoman, worn down by Nicholson's stubborn argument, sighed, "there's no use in talkin'. She hasn't got sinse; that I see afore, poor thing! She'd never left so fine a country to be walkin' in this, if she'd the right sinse. Aw! she's crack'd."

Nicholson's curiosity about the lives of the Irish poor prompted her to investigate their social institutions, their calendar customs and their everyday lives. The 1840s were a decade of political and social movements that were cut short by the cataclysmic Famine years. Her account includes descriptions of two remarkable men who led those movements: Daniel O'Connell and Father Theobald Mathew.

Near Cappoquin, Co. Waterford, she joined a crowd gathered near the smouldering stump of a bonfire that celebrated O'Connell's release from prison. She noticed, as she did later in Tipperary, that people were patient but tense with anticipation for repeal of the anti-Catholic Penal Laws:

> So anxious are these suffering creatures for the repeal that they cannot let a stranger who speaks to them pass without asking the

question. Such a specimen of self-control as they manifest, though many of them are keenly alive to their privations, is truly unparalleled in any nation. O'Connell now restrains them with a nod. Will he always be able to do so?

Nicholson also observed that the Repeal movement made little difference to the poor. Watching fires blaze on tar barrels celebrating O'Connell's release from prison, the woman next to her said, "It's many a long day that we have been lookin' for that same [man] to do somethin' for us, but not a hap'orth of good has come to a cratur of us yet. We're atin' the pratee today, and not a divil of us has got off the rag since he began his discoorse." While O'Connell was not able to translate political action into economic relief for Ireland's poor, Nicholson as a social reformer noticed with approval his record on abolitionism and religious tolerance.

Repeal was the great political cause of the 1840s; temperance was the great social movement of the decade, and from 10 April 1838 until his death in 1856, the name of the Capuchin friar Father Theobald Mathew was synonymous with it. Father Mathew befriended Nicholson and entertained her when she visited Cork; she tells us coyly that he gave her a gift of a locket. She plunged into his crusade by giving impromptu temperance lectures to punch-drinking coach companions and to whiskey-house barmaids. Watching a fair at Urlingford, Co. Kilkenny, Nicholson's companion told her, "You'll not see such fun, ma'am, now, as you would have seen before the days of Father Mathew. Then we had a power of bloody noses, broken bones and fine work for the police; but ye'll see fine cattle, and fat pigs ...".

The German traveller Johannes Kohl, who visited Ireland in 1842, also noticed the quieting effect of temperance in Tipperary:

"Since temperance," it is said, the unruly people of Tipperary have become more quiet and orderly; and although their unfortunate political condition has a tendency to keep them perpetually in a rebellious mood, yet riots and outbreaks, arising from party hatred and revenge, are much less frequent. But so many changes in Ireland are now dated "since temperance" that if it only continues fifty years longer, this reform will surely mark the commencement of a new era.

Nicholson too had hopes for Ireland "since temperance", but she was concerned about the perilous conditions of the poor. She wrote *Ireland's*

Welcome to the Stranger in the midst of the Great Famine, so she knew the outcome of the conditions she observed: unemployment, underemployment and wages that could not provide shelter, food and clothing for a labourer and his or her family. She saw that the rural poor were seldom rewarded for improvements to their cabins and plots, that evictions were common and that the government failed to encourage economic development. While she professed to have no political opinions, it is likely she would have supported Robert Peel's anti-Corn Law legislation, and the policy of free trade advocated by the radical Quaker John Bright, as the way of promoting world peace and ameliorating social problems.

While she knew the consequences of the poverty she had witnessed before the Great Famine, *Ireland's Welcome to the Stranger* is not a jeremiad. Frank O'Connor said that Nicholson had no interest in culture, but her book is a reliable ethnology of Irish country life before the Famine, a portrayal written with a sharp eye for detail and with great sympathy. Even when she disapproved of a practice like the custom of the funeral *caoine*, she never missed a chance to experience local life.

She documented the seasonal events in the Irish countryside, observing the St Patrick's Day custom of wearing the "crass", a ribbon crossed on the arm, probably the oldest and most truly traditional observance of the day. (Jonathan Swift wrote in 1720 that the Irish in London wore the "crass", and accounts of St Patrick's Day as it was celebrated among the Wild Geese in Austria describe participants wearing the "crass".) She described the Cork and Kerry custom of "sending" bachelors and spinsters to the Skelligs, the celebrated island hermitage off the Kerry coast, at Shrovetide. The Catholic Church permitted no marriages during Lent, so the proper time for marriage in the Irish countryside was "faoi inid", between Christmas and Lent. Shrove Tuesday was the last possible date for marriage before Easter; however, Munster people reasoned that the old later date of Easter must have been valid at the monastic settlement of St Michael the Archangel that was located on the Skelligs. If that were the case, it followed that bachelors and spinsters who had missed their chance to marry on the mainland could still marry if they went to the rocks. Nicholson witnessed the Shrove Tuesday tradition in Cork on 4 February 1845. James Beale's painting "Skellig Night on South Mall 1845" documents that night.

Nicholson did not mention nor would she have approved of the Skellig Lists, songs that mischievously matched ill-sorted couples for the Skellig journey. T.C. Croker's *Popular Songs of Ireland* included twenty-nine titles of Skellig Lists published in Cork in 1836 and an 1834 letter from a

Hugh Driscoll threatening libel to any Skellig list-maker who took liberties with the names of the single ladies in the writer's family. The Skellig
songs continued until about 1920. One of the last lists made in Kenmare
is narrated by a sailor whose ship was sunk by a German torpedo in 1918.
Washed up on the Skelligs, he suddenly sees boats approaching through
the mist. When boats arrive, the "lists" describe incongruous local pairs
disembarking like the animals from the Ark.

It is in *Ireland's Welcome to the Stranger* that we find descriptions of Irish
cabins and of the daily life of the rural poor who were nearly obliterated
during the Famine. Nicholson's account is valuable, because to understand the consequences of those tragic years, one must know what was
lost to families and to communities. And there are unforgettable vign-
ettes: cabin hospitality, witty conversations, the dance held in her honour
in Johnstown, her duet across a Kerry mountainside with a herd boy,
countrywomen gathering seaweed on a Kerry strand and Nicholson's
encounters with schoolchildren.

Nicholson never missed a chance to visit a school. It was not only that
she had been a teacher, but also that she found schools a good measure of
a local community. She visited them everywhere that she went: national
schools, Erasmus Smith schools, estate schools, workhouse schools,
schools run by the Church of Ireland or by religious orders, mission society schools and private schools.

By the time Nicholson visited Ireland, national schools had been
operating in most places for a decade. She noted differences in curricula,
methods and outcomes, and any sign that children's education was limited
by their station in life infuriated her. After visiting the mission school in
Ventry, where girls were not taught to read maps, she praised the nun in
Dingle who said, "Though they are the children of the poor, we do not
know what station God may call them to fill. We advance them as far as
possible while they are with us."

As she travelled around Ireland, even in the most remote parts of the
country, Nicholson was astonished to find the Irish familiar with life in
America. Even when their knowledge was fragmented or confused in its
details, they were keenly interested. She was often questioned about slavery: "I blush for my country when, on every car, and at every party and
lodging house, this everlasting blot on America's boasted history is presented to my eyes."

Nicholson's observations about Irish emigration support contemporary scholarship that argues that the Great Famine did not precipitate
emigration to the United States but that it institutionalized it. She also

described the phenomenon that economists call the "poverty trap". Many Irish she met expressed the desire to emigrate to America but their poverty prevented them from doing so. Nicholson met returned "Yanks", like her own servant girls, who had worked in New York and returned with money saved. She noticed with some satisfaction that women who had worked in America did not work outdoors when they returned. She was outraged to see a beautiful young woman near Cahirciveen, Co. Kerry, carrying a heavy basket of turf. "What a sin, I thought, to take such a finished piece of God's workmanship, and convert it to a beast of burden! Weary and crippled as I was, my real condition called for fresh gratitude, that I was not born in oppressed Ireland, where woman can never be woman if not born to an earthly inheritance."

Her fervent Bible-reading and her lectures on temperance, diet and dirt might lead readers to dismiss her as a crank. She was certainly serious, but she was not solemn. She had a good sense of humour and even enjoyed a little mischief – especially when her co-conspirators were children; on the road to Kilkenny, she waved some little urchins aboard her car while the driver was distracted. She demonstrated the attributes of the true traveller: curiosity, courage, stamina and an openness to experience. She climbed castle walls, throwing her muff and parasol before her, leaped over a mountain stream and stretched out on a wall in Kerry to enjoy the sunshine. She talked to everyone she met: beggars and boatmen, policemen and preachers, shopkeepers and shebeen-keepers. She usually had the last word.

While Nicholson did not dance, she enjoyed making music. She relished an opportunity to play the curate's piano in Clifden, and she expressed her *joie de vivre* especially in song. She sang across a Kerry mountainside with a herd boy; she sang with the birds and the music of the waterfalls; she ran up Diamond Mountain singing. She sang her favourite hymn "Majestic Sweetness Sits Enthroned" joyously on Easter morning in Wicklow, and she sang in Kerry to forget her pains.

Asenath Nicholson wrote her own epitaph in County Galway on a November day in 1844. Walking the road from Oranmore to Loughrea, she rested to ease her blistered feet and thought of her prudent friends who warned her against this reckless adventure. Did she wish to be in her own parlour in New York? She did not. She said, "Should I sleep the sleep of death, with my head pillowed against this wall, no matter. Let the passer-by inscribe my epitaph upon this stone, fanatic what then? It shall only be a memento that one in a foreign land loved and pitied Ireland, and did what she could to seek out its condition."

She never forgot Ireland, but the world forgot about Asenath Nicholson. After leaving Ireland in 1845, she travelled in England and Scotland until the news of Famine brought her back to Ireland, where she worked until the autumn of 1848. Excerpts from *Ireland's Welcome to the Stranger* were published in the Quaker monthly *The Friend* (London), and the book was reviewed in William and Mary Howitt's radical weekly *Howitt's Journal of Literature and Popular Progress* (1847–9), where it was called "one of the most extraordinary books which has appeared in years". The Howitts also published Nicholson's letters from Templecrone, Co. Donegal, and Belmullet, Co. Mayo, which provided readers with eye-witness accounts of famine conditions.

In 1850 she published *Lights and Shades of Ireland*, a book in three parts: a historical narrative from the coming of the Milesians to Daniel O'Connell, an examination of early Irish saints and poets drawn from archaeological sources, and an account of her work among the poor during the Great Famine. *Lights and Shades* was published in London by Houlston and Stoneman in 1850; Part III of *Lights and Shades*, the Famine account, was published in New York in 1851, under the title *Annals of the Famine in Ireland, in 1847, 1848 and 1849*, by E. French. After she returned from Europe in 1852, Nicholson published a collection of her travel writings entitled *Loose Papers or Facts Gathered During Eight Years' Residence in Ireland, Scotland, England, France and Germany* (1853). She was apparently working on a memoir when she died in Jersey City on 15 May 1855.[4] Her friend William Goodell delivered the eulogy and Simeon Jocelyn the final prayers at her funeral.

Nicholson enjoyed a revival beginning in 1925, when Hodder and Stoughton published an abridged edition of *Ireland's Welcome to the Stranger*, edited by Alfred Tresidder Sheppard. (The American edition was published by The John Day Company in 1927.) In his biographical and critical introduction, Sheppard compared Nicholson to George Borrow (1803–81), the linguist and traveller who described his adventures bringing Spanish and Basque translations of the New Testament in *The Bible in Spain* (1843). *The Bible in Ireland*, as Nicholson's abridged work was called, was praised by the reviewers of the time. Joseph Hone, biographer of George Moore and W.B. Yeats, wrote an appreciation of Nicholson for *The Dublin Magazine* in 1934.

Some seventy years after publication of *The Bible in Ireland*, during the 150th commemoration of the Great Famine, historians revisited Nicholson's books and gained new appreciation of her value as a witness to those troubled times. Margaret Kelleher devoted a section of *The Feminization of*

Famine (1997), her study of female representation in famine literature, to Nicholson's account. Seamus Deane included some Nicholson famine sections from *Annals of the Famine* in *The Field Day Anthology of Irish Writing* (1991). Patricia Craig selected passages from both *The Bible in Ireland* and *Lights and Shades of Ireland* for *The Oxford Book of Ireland* (1998). Realizing the value of having Nicholson's work available to the specialist and to the general reader, The Lilliput Press published a new edition of *Annals of the Famine* in 1998, and now publishes its complement, the present edition of *Ireland's Welcome to the Stranger*.

ACKNOWLEDGMENTS

It was Roger McHugh, Professor of Anglo-Irish Literature at University College, Dublin who suggested I might consider the work of the American teacher, temperance advocate and traveller Asenath Nicholson as a thesis topic. In doing so, he gave me a singular companion for my own three decade ramble through Ireland and Irish Studies. She has been a researcher's delight. She led one down byways and detours, but never disappointed. Following her along Irish roads, I realized the truth of the words of Quaker printer and abolitionist Richard Davis Webb, who said of her in 1847, "I know no more impartial-minded, scrupulous, truth-loving person than Mrs. Nicholson."

Many have helped me trace Nicholson's travels through Ireland. Hofstra University Presidential and School of Education Research Grants provided opportunities for me to consult the American Antiquarian Society Library, the American Irish Historical Society Library, the Archives of the South Presentation Convent, the Boston Public Library, the British Library, the Clare County Library (Ennis), the National Archives of Ireland, the National Library of Ireland, the New Britain (Connecticut) Library, the New Haven Historical Society, the New York Historical Society Library, the New York Public Library, and the libraries of the Society of Friends in Dublin, London, New York and at Swarthmore College. I am grateful to those institutions for their assistance. I wish to thank Hofstra University librarians Domenica Barbuto, Eleana Cevallos, Joan Cooney and Janet Wagner for their help with reference questions.

Jean Hatch Farnham, a descendant of Nicholson's brother, David Hatch, supplied me with details of Hatch family history and the staff of the Chester Library and Archives shared information about local history. Connie Hendren Fitz and Margaret Kelleher's pioneering work on Nicholson were valuable resources.

I have benefited from the advice of Diana Ben-Merre, Anne Francis Cavanagh, Francis and Janet Carroll, Adele Dalsimer, Mary E. Daly, James S. Donnelly, Joann Krieg, Emmet Larkin, Robert Lowery, Lawrence J. McCaffrey, James MacKillop, Augustine Martin, Don Murphy, Anraí Ó Braonáin, Caoimhín O'Danachair, Seán O'Suuilleabháin, Robert and Norma Rhodes, Roger and Ginny Rosenblatt, Catherine Shannon, Alan Singer, Máire and Jack Sweeney, Mary Helen Thuente and Maryann Valiulis. Friends who joined me on the Nicholson trail include Joan De-Staebler, Henry and Louise Farrell, Margaret MacCurtain, Éilís McDowell and Donla Uí Bhraonáin.

The Hofstra Office of Special Secretarial Services and the University's Academic Computer Center helped produce the manuscript. Karin Spencer served as my editorial advisor. Antony Farrell and Brendan Barrington of The Lilliput Press prepared this edition of *Ireland's Welcome to the Stranger*, companion volume to Nicholson's *Annals of the Famine* (1998).

My family, the O'Rourkes, have seen me through this project as they have shared and supported all that I have done.

MAUREEN MURPHY, *Sea Cliff, New York, October 2002*

NICHOLSON'S ITINERARY

1844

16 May: Departs on the *Brooklyn* from New York

5 June: *Brooklyn* arrives in the English Channel

12 June: Arrives in Liverpool

14 June: Leaves Liverpool by packet

15 June: Arrives in Kingstown, Ireland. Goes on to Dublin

2 July: Dublin to Tullamore via Grand Canal fly-boat

5 July: Tullamore to Barrack Street, Dublin, by coach

10 July: To Kilbride, Co. Wicklow, by coach

11 July: Walks to Arklow, Co. Wicklow

13 July: By coach to the Vale of Avoca, Rathdrum

21 July: Kilbride

23 July: Glendalough

27 July: Dublin via Radical (Repeal) coach

1 August: Dublin to Kilkenny via fly-boat to Athy, coach

2 August: Kilkenny via coach to Johnstown, Co. Kilkenny

4 August: Dance in AN's honour in field near Johnstown

10 August: Johnstown to Urlingford by kish

17 August: Urlingford Spa (Ballyspellin)

19 August: By baker's cart to the Colliery, New Birmingham

20 August: Grainge (Grangehill, Co. Tipperary)

21 August: Kilcooley, Co. Kilkenny

27 August: By car to Thurles, Co. Tipperary

29 August: By car to Cashel, Clonmel, Dungarvan, Cappoquin

30 August: Mt Melleray, Cappoquin

2 September: To Youghal and back via Blackwater steamer

3 September: To Lismore, Co. Waterford

18 September: Leaves Lismore by car for Cappoquin via Dungarvan, Clonmel

19 September: From Cappoquin to Clonmel

30 September: Clonmel to Urlingford via Thurles

1 October: Walks from Thurles to Urlingford

15 October: Leaves Urlingford by car for Roscrea via Borris-in-Ossory

18 October: By car to Roscrea

29 October: Walks from Roscrea on the road to Birr

31 October: Birr, Kings County

4 November: Walks from Birr to Ballinasloe, Co. Galway

5 November: Walks from Ballinasloe to Loughrea, Co. Galway

8 November: Walks and takes post car from Loughrea to Galway

11 November: Begins to walk back to Urlingford, stays in Oranmore

12 November: Walks from Oranmore to Loughrea

13 November: Walks from Loughrea to Killimor, Co. Galway

14 November: Walks from Killimor to Banagher

18 November: Walks from Banagher to Birr

19 November: Walks from Birr to Roscrea

1 December: By car from Roscrea to Urlingford, Kilcooley

4 December: By car to Durrow

5 December: By mailcoach to Dublin via Abbeyleix, Maryborough, Stradbally, Athy, Kilcullen, Naas

1845

9 January: Leaves Dublin by coach for Wicklow

14 January: Walks three miles from Wicklow to Wexford coach

27 January: By car to Waterford

28 January: Bianconi car to Clonmel

29 January: Clonmel to Cork via Bianconi car: Cahir, Mitchelstown, Fer-

moy, Rathcormac, Watergrass-Hill
and Glenmire

6 February: Cobh via steam packet,
Ringacoltig

7 February: Cork

8 February: By carriage to Blarney, Dr
Barter's Cold Water Establishment

9 February: Walks to Cobh, ferry to
Ringacoltig

15 February: To Cloyne by ferry and by
foot

16 February: Rockview

17 February: Carrigacrump Quarry

18 February: Steamer to Cobh

19 February: Steamer to Cork

24 February: By coach from Cork to
Bandon

25 February: Bandon

26 February: To Bantry via coach

28 February: Walks to Glengarriff

8 March: Walks to Kenmare, Co. Kerry

10 March: By car to Killarney

11 March: Walks to Ross Island

13 March: Walks to Torc Cascade,
Muckross Abbey, tour of the lakes

18 March: Walks to Killorglin, Bay of
Ross to Mountain Stage

19 March: Walks to Cahirciveen

24 March: Walks to Valentia Island

25 March: Ferry to mainland, begins
walk to Waterville, stays at Ballybrack

26 March: Walks to Derrynane, walks
back to Ballybrack

27 March: Ballinskelligs Bay

28 March: Walks to Killoyra

29 March: Walks on toward Killarney,
stays near Beaufort

30 March: Walks to Killarney

31 March: Walks to Gap of Dunloe,
stays near Hyde Park

1 April: Walks to Dinis Island

2 April: Walks back to Killarney

3 April: By car to Tralee

4 April: Defrauded by car company,
begins to walk to Dingle, picked
up by car after eight miles

7 April: Ventry

8 April: Dingle

12 April: Excursion by car from Dingle
to Dunquin

14 April: By car from Dingle to Tralee,
another car to Tarbert

15 April: Steamer from Tarbert to Limerick

19 April: By car to Ennis, Co. Clare

21 April: By car to Gort, Co. Galway,
walks on to Oranmore

22 April: By ass and cart from Oranmore to Galway

23 April: Walks from Galway to
Oughterard

24 April: Walks from Oughterard to
Recess

25 April: Recess

26 April: Walks to Derrynavglaun

27 April: Walks towards Clifden, stays
near the town

28 April: Arrives in Clifden

1 May: Walks to Roundstone

3 May: Walks back to Clifden

5 May: Climbs Diamond Mountain,
Letterfrack

6 May: Walks to Tully

7 May: Walks back to Clifden

8 May: Walks to Omey Island via
Claddaghduff

9 May: Walks from Omey Island back
to Clifden

10 May: Clifden

15 May: By car from Clifden to
Oughterard

16 May: By car from Clifden to Galway

26 May: By car to Westport, Co. Mayo,
via Tuam

28 May: Climbs Croagh Patrick

2 June: Walks to Newport, Achill Sound

3 June: Achill Sound

4 June: Walks to the Achill Mission at
Dugort

5 June: Walks to Slievemore, Dugort

10 June: Walks back to Achill Sound

13 June: Walks from Achill Sound for
Newport

17 June: Walks from Newport to Westport

18 June: By car to Castlebar, Sligo

19 June: Sligo, Glencar, Carrick-on-
Shannon by boat

20 June: Carrick-on-Shannon to
Dublin

8 August: Belfast and Glasgow via
steamer

PREFACE

A Preface is like a porter at the entrance of a castle or a dinner-party; however necessary his attendance may be, and however dazzling his livery, he can expect but a hasty brush from the passers in; it is the castle they want to see; it is the dinner they have come to eat. Knowing, however, that every public act demands a public explanation, I give my candid reasons for doing so strange a work, and for doing it in so strange a way.[1]

We have had many "Pencillings by the Way," and "Conciliation Halls," and "Killarney Lakes" from the tops of coaches and from smoking dinner tables.[2] But the one day's walk on mountain or bog, one night's lodging where the pig, and the ass, and horned oxen feed,

> "Like Aaron's serpent, swallows all the rest."[3]

"Remember, my children," said my father, "that the Irish are a suffering people; and when they come to your doors, never send them empty away." It was in the garrets and cellars of New York that I first became acquainted with the Irish peasantry, and it was there I saw they were a suffering people. Their patience, their cheerfulness, their flow of blundering, hap-hazard, happy wit, made them to me a distinct people from all I had seen. Often, when seated at my fireside, have I said to those most dear to my heart, "God will one day allow me to breathe the mountain air of the sea-girt coast of Ireland – to sit down in their cabins, and there learn what soil has nurtured, what hardships have disciplined so hardy a race – so patient and so impetuous, so revengeful and so forgiving, so proud and so humble, so obstinate and so docile, so witty and so simple a people."

Those who then laughed at my vagaries, have all gone down to the dust. The world was before me, and all mankind my brethren. "I have made you desolate. I want you for other purposes. Go, work in my vineyard," was the word.[4] I conferred not with flesh and blood. No pope or priest, no minister or prelate augmented my purse, to enable me to spy out the nakedness of the land. I came "a warfare at my own charges." I came to gather no legends of fairies or banshees, to pull down no monarchies, or set up any democracies; but I came to glean after the reapers, to gather up the fragments, to see the poor peasant by way-side and in bog, in the field and by his peat fire, and to read to him the story of Calvary.[5] I came to linger with the women at the foot of the cross, and go with them early to the sepulchre. I have done so; and should the fastidious reader say that this condescending to men of low estate, this eating with publicans and sinners – above all, this lodging in a manger, is quite in bad odour if not in bad taste, he must be told it was because there was no "room for me in the inn," or because my pained feet could go not further.

I had counted the cost. I knew there were professed Christians in the nineteenth century, who would be forgetful to entertain strangers, and would ask, "where hast thou left those few sheep in the wilderness?"[6] I knew there were doorkeepers in the house of God, who would say, "Sit thou here under my footstool," if the "the gold ring and goodly apparel," were wanting; and I knew that *she*, whose delicate foot never treads the threshold of the poor, would scruple the propriety if not the reputation of her who does it.[7] I have not "dipped my pen in gall" towards any of those; I have mentioned no names where they could be readily avoided, and then, in most cases, where gratitude required me to do so.[8]

I ask no reward – I ask no sympathy. This sowing by the side of all waters has been abundantly paid by the "God save ye kindly," and the "Fear not, I am with you."

Reader, I would not be an egotist – I would not boast; but I would speak of that Almighty Arm that sustained me, when, on a penny's worth of bread, I have walked over mountain and bog for twenty and twenty-three miles, resting upon a wall, by the side of a lake, or upon my basket, reading a chapter in the sweet Word of Life to some listening labourer. And when at night-fall, in some humble lodging-house, my potato and salt were taken, my feet bathed, then could I sing of mercy; then could I say, what lack I yet? I never had one fear by night or by day, nor ever cast a longing, lingering look behind, to my once loved home across the ocean.

Should the devout reader be disappointed at the want of gravity in some of the details, he can only be told that the facts are delineated as they occurred; not to make a story or a book, but to present to the reader the rustic as he is – the seemly and the unseemly, the beautiful and the deformed, the consistent and the inconsistent. Whoever mixes awhile with the heterogeneous jumble of Irish sadness and Irish mirth, will find that to be grave at all times,

"Exceeds all power of face."[8]

One great difficulty in the narration has been the pronoun *I*. Many interesting facts have been partially illustrated, and some wholly suppressed, because this officious letter must figure so prominently.

Allow me to say to every Christian and every philanthropist "turn not away from your own flesh."[9] There is a vast amount of talent in its native rubbish in the mountains of Kerry and Connemara, and in the bogs of Connaught. Far too many roses have already wasted their "sweetness on the desert air" – too many a dark-haired Kerry girl has lavished her graces on the mountain goat and sheep she has tended, without once reading the story of the Ruth and Rebecca whom she, in occupation, unknowingly imitates.[10] I do not say, Do the work as I have done, but, do it, and do it better. If my steps will not serve as a pattern, my aberrations may as a warning. Their proprieties and improprieties are before you; and you must show me a "more excellent way," or I shall certainly do the same thing in the same manner, if again honoured with the mission.

It was never my intention to tax the Irish public with another volume, added to the huge pile already written on Ireland. It was my design to go silently through among the poor, and tell the story to my own countrymen; that they might be induced to labour more untiringly and effectually for the destitute portion of this nation, who are daily landing upon their shores. But I heard the sound of an "abundance of rain;" the cloud is spreading over mountain top and lowly glen; they that "for want and famine are desolate," are crying, "give us food to eat, we loathe this light manna;" and from many a pulpit through the length and breadth of the land I hear, "Thrust in the sickle, for the harvest is ripe."[11] The treasury is open and the rich men are casting in their gifts. Accept the mite of the widow; it is small indeed, but it is "all her living," and given heartily and cheerfully.[12]

The reader is assured that nothing has been added to meet the state of the famine of 1846 and 1847. Facts are related as they occurred and were described in 1844 and 1845; and these facts then indicated that an explosion must soon take place, and that Ireland must be turned inside out; so that all the world might see that, deformed as may be her surface, her vitals show a disease hereditary, obstinate, and still more odious, which opiates or ointments cannot cure.

Thanks to the Hibernian Bible Society, which furnished me with the Word of God in English and Irish, through the instrumentality of a friend, who also procured for me tracts and other suitable books for distribution, on my last tour round the coast.[13] It was not till four excursions had been made in the interior, that my name and object were known. They, therefore, are not amenable for any thing I have said or done. I was not a "chosen vessel" of theirs. God reward their bounty, by the finding "after many days," of this bread "cast upon the waters."[14] "Thou knowest not which shall prosper, either *this* or *that*."

Thanks to all those who have spoken kind words to the stranger; and thanks to those who have felt called to give the distant look or the cool rebuke – the former have filled my heart with gratitude, and the latter have made me cling closer to the High Arm that sustained me.

ASENATH NICHOLSON.
Dublin, June 10th, 1847

CHAPTER I

Departure from New York – The Author's Parentage – Fellow Passengers – Death on Board – A good Captain – Death of a Drunkard – Arrival at Liverpool – Voyage to Dublin and Arrival at Kingstown – A Chapter of Accidents – Difficulty of obtaining Lodgings – A Morning Walk – Visit to a Roman Catholic Clergyman – The Linen Hall – The North Union Poor House – Letters of Introduction – A Strange Reception – Asylum for Unmarried Ladies

It was in the spring of 1844, May 16th, that I stood upon the deck of the ship *Brooklyn*, and saw the last spire of New York recede in the distance.[1] It was the home of my childhood – the land where hopes and disappointments had ebbed and flowed; where I had looked out through smiles and tears, till the last earthly tie was severed; and where the last tear was dried on the graves of those most loved.[2] I had no more to shed. It was with a stoical indifference I heard the last farewell, and took the last grasp of the hand of him who asked, "When shall we look for you home?", and then I shut myself into the narrow cabin, which was to be my parlour and bedroom during the voyage, heeding neither wind, or wave, or monster of the deep.[3] It was not the rich, the honoured, or the happy I was hoping to meet; it was not their salutations or presents I was going to seek for. It was the poor and the outcast. I was about to visit those who in dens and caves of the earth, were "forgotten by their neighbors," and who heard no kinder voices than the whistling of the winds, or the screeching of some desolate owl among the mountains and crags where they had made their habitations.

I was alone. Not a soul in the ship but the captain knew my name, or understood my object, and leaving the command of the vessel to him, and the working of the ropes to the sailors, I betook myself to the opening of my parcels, to ascertain what necessary supplies they contained for mind and body in a voyage like this.

> "My boast is not that I deduce my birth,
> From loins enthroned, and rulers of the earth;
> But higher far my proud pretentions rise,
> The child of parents passed into the skies."[4]

My home education was of the most uncompromising kind. My parents were descended from the puritanical stock; they taught me that goodness alone was greatness; that, in order rightly to estimate the worth of a man, his gold watch and equipage, his title and station, must be deducted; that a conformity to the customs of the world, when they clashed with the sound principles of the gospel, or the strictest rules of morality, was not only a sin, but meanness of spirit. My father had read little and thought much; and though somewhat orthodox, yet he cared not whether his neighbour prayed kneeling or standing, if he prayed in the true spirit, or whether the psalm were in a minor or a major key, or performed in common or triple time, if sung, making melody in the heart to God. He hung no Quakers, nor put any men in a corner of the church because they had a coloured skin. He rebuked sin in high places with fearlessness, and forgave all personal injuries before forgiveness was asked.

My mother remembered the poor, and entertained strangers; hated oppression, scorned a mean act, and dealt justly by all.[5] She taught me that in order to be healthy, I must rise early, and if I desired to take an honest breakfast with a proper relish, I must earn before eating it; that to find friends, I must show myself friendly; that to live peaceably, I must allow my neighbours to go out and in, eat, drink, and dress when and how they liked; always avoiding putting my head into a hornet's nest, if I would not be stung. "And when you are sent from home," she emphatically said, "conduct yourself well, and your good name will take care of itself; always remembering that a character which requires lawyers and doctors, ministers and elders to look after it, is not worth a groat." With these principles in my head, if not in my heart, I was sent into the world, to make my way, through good and through evil report, as best I could.

I looked out upon the seas; the vessel was well under weigh, and the dizzy passengers had already begun to exclaim, "O dear! I am dreadfully sick."

My chum now entered; we were shut in – and, like or dislike, there was no alternative; snugly packed as we were, there was no escape, and we immediately set ourselves about, as Eve's daughters are wont to do, ascertaining each other's pedigree, object, and destination. I found her to be an Irish lady, born and bred in the city of Dublin, but she had passed five years in the city of New York, to which she had become greatly attached. She had left her husband and three children to go on business to Ireland, and though she cast many a "longing, lingering look" back to them, yet she never forgot that she must do good unto all when opportunity presented, and she never neglected the performance of that duty, when necessity required it. Her tall and noble figure, her high open forehead, united with an unpretending though dignified manner, and the benevolence of her heart, which beamed in her placid eye, made her to me an object not only of interest, but of warm attachment. Often, when she returned to the berth from some errand of kindness among the sick and distressed, have I said in my heart, "Who would not love such an angel of mercy?" Thus was the beginning of my journey prosperous, and all anxiety for the morrow was banished by the blessings of to-day.

Our cabin companions consisted of the widow of a clergyman, with her son and daughter, who were returning from New York to England, their native country; an Irishman, who had spent the last twenty-five years in America; a naval officer; an editor from the United States (a genuine American); and the young Irish wife of the mate, on a visit to "her people." These, with one exception, gave more cause of praise than blame, and made me quite willing to balance accounts with them all when we parted.

All was quiet after the first wrenchings were past. On the third morning after our departure, the captain came up from the steerage, saying, "We have had a death on board." The wife of a Scotchman occupied the same berth with her son, a boy of thirteen. She went to bed the preceding evening in as good health as when she came on board, and she slept the sleep of death in the night. Her husband and another son of twenty were in a berth above them, and knew nothing of the circumstance till the young boy awoke, and found his mother cold and stiff by his side.

On descending the steerage stairs, I saw the accompaniments of death as they never had been presented to my view before. The rough hands of the sailors were wrapping the slender body in hempen cloth, and fitting iron weights to the feet, to cause it to sink. The father and the eldest son looked silently, if not coldly on; whilst the younger boy, in a flood of grief, was interrupted occasionally by the stern command of his father to "hold his tongue."

The body was placed on deck, and at twelve the captain assembled the crew, read some passages of scripture, appropriate for the burial of the dead, prayed (for he was a man of prayer), and four sailors raised the board containing the body upon the railing of the deck, turning away their faces; one dismal plunge was heard; the parted wave closed again, and all was hushed, save the suppressed sobs of the young son. The captain whispered, "The husband was not kind," and each turned to his monotony again.

The voyage went quietly on. The captain assembled the crew as often as possible, for prayer and praise, and gave good proof that a ship may be a temple of worship, and that sailors may be treated as men, and be men still. There was no scolding, no flogging, and but little swearing, to make us feel as if we were on board a slave-ship or a man-of-war.

We had proceeded some eight days, when the widow's son, who had been in the navy, and had lost his health by his excesses, gave sad proof that

"A soldier's arms,
Through the vanity and brainless rage
Of those that bear them, in whatever cause,
Seem most at variance with all moral good."[6]

He was, at all hours of the night, either at the door of his mother and sister, demanding gin, or roving about the cabin with reddened eyes, declaring that his frenzied brain would make him mad. Sometimes he appeared suddenly in our midst, almost in a state of nudity, on deck, or at table; till, like a maniac as he was, nothing but coercion could restrain him, and he died on a bright Sabbath morning while we were at breakfast; and before the sun had gone down upon the ship, the unfortunate young man was plunged beneath the waves. The mother and sister sat at a distance, while the prayer and burial went on, tearlessly viewing the last office for the dead, when, turning away, a low murmur from the mother was heard, "Ah! I could not save him."

Twenty-one days took us into the Channel, and seven more of calm set our feet upon the dock at Liverpool, at a late hour of the night.[7] The next took us to the custom house, and there, to my happy disappointment, was demanded no duty, the officer kindly telling me that, as my books were for gratuitous distribution in Ireland, he regretted I had not a thousand more, and that he should make no charges. A tea-cup full of oatmeal stirabout and milk, a night's lodging in a dwelling contiguous to the hotel (for the talkative landlady had her house full) made a charge of six English shillings, beside a sixpence each to two servants, neither of whom had I seen till I stood at the door to depart.

At two o'clock I took the packet for Ireland; and when I stood upon the plank which was to conduct me on deck, and looked upon the loved face of her who had been my never-tiring companion on the voyage, I longed that I might meet in a land of strangers a heart like hers.[8] She returned to go to Cork, and we have never met since.

"We shall remember this voyage," was the last sentence from her lips that fell on my ear.

"You have parted with a friend," said a solitary woman, "and are you a stranger?"

This was a welcome sound, and a few moments' conversation told me that the law of kindness had not died on the lips of her who had just left me.

A tempestuous night made the sea-sick inmates of the crowded cabin wish for the day, for there was not a comfort or convenience to be had; and when the bright morning dawned, it brought the unpleasant intelligence that we should not see Dublin till the tide should come in, which would be five in the evening. But we had neared the bay, and were in sight of the enchanting harbour, granite buildings, and green sloping hills of Kingstown.

"I have travelled much," said an intelligent gentleman, "but have never found anything surpassing the beauty of the bay of Dublin and the Cove of Cork." This bay was in my eye; and I was in it. Yes! the sea was behind me, and the fair Emerald Isle, with the motley assemblage of beautiful and painful objects, was before me. I gave myself to rummaging the scanty knowledge I had of Ireland, to ascertain whether I knew anything tolerable of its true condition and character, and what did I know?

I knew that between the parallels of 51 and 55 of north latitude there is a little green spot in the ocean, defended from its surging waves by bold defying rocks; that over this rock are sprinkled mountains, where sparkle the diamond and where sleep the precious stone; glens, where were the rich foliage and the pleasant flower, and where the morning song of the bird is blending with the playful rill; that through its valleys and hillsides were imbedded the gladdening fuel and the rich mine; that over its lawns and wooded parks were skipping the light-footed fawn and bounding deer; that in its fat pastures were grazing the proud steed and the noble ox; that on its heathy mountain slopes the nimble goat and the more timid sheep find their food. I knew that proud castles and monasteries, palaces and towers, tell to the passer-by that here kings and chieftains struggled for dominion and priests and prelates contended for religion; and that the towering steeple, and the more lowly cross, still say that the instinct of worship yet lives – that here the incense of prayer and the song of praise continue to go up. I knew that no venomous serpent is lying in the path of the weary traveller, and that the purest breezes of heaven are wafted from mountain-top to lowly valley, giving health and vigour to the life-blood, and causing the "inhabitants of the rock to sing."

And I had been told, that over this fair landscape hangs a dark curtain of desolation and death; that the harp of Erin lies untouched, save by the finger of sorrow, to tell what music was once in her strings; that the pipe and the dance are only aroused like the last brightening of the flickering lamp, as it ceases for ever; that the tear is on her cheek – she sits desolate, and no good Samaritan passes that way, to pour in the oil and wine of consolation. Lover and friend are put far from her and she is a hissing and bye-word to those who should lift her up; and she has long reaped down the fields of the rich, while she has tasted none of their "pleasant bread."[9] Small as this little fund of knowledge might be, I almost regretted that I had heard the tale of her woes, lest a morbid sympathy should dim the true light, and lead me to stumble, if not wholly to wander from the right path.

A lady from Liverpool, whose sable weeds and care-worn cheeks told that she was a child of sorrow, proposed that, as we were alone, and must pass the day together, we might go on shore, and visit the monument erected to King George.[10] We had read the names of the lords and earls who erected it, examined the prints of the shoes cut in marble at the foot, where his kingship stood when he visited it, and had seated ourselves upon a block of marble, and there concluded to go into the railroad office, purchase tickets for Dublin, and leave our luggage to follow us in the packet. Putting my hand into my pocket to get a shilling for my ticket, I missed my pocket-book; this pocket-book contained all valuables of purse and scrip, and not a farthing had I out of it.[11] My character, as far as letters of introduction might go, had gone to the winds; but as I expected to pay no lodging or travelling fees by it, the money was the great concern. This was a sad landing indeed on a foreign shore, where I had already seen so many asking palms, that I could not hope much for my share. A "horror of darkness" came over me, and while I stood petrified, the good woman set off at full speed towards the block of granite, where we had been sitting. I moped at a distance, muttering, "It will do no good," while all the sage counsels given me in New York, of being among strangers, unprotected, alone, unknown, and uncared for, like spectres stood in array. My kind helper reached the fatal block, but no pocket-book was there. "There, I told you so." "What will you do?" Then for a few moments we mingled our sorrows; she had tasted deeply of worldly afflictions, and could only say, "If you have no money, you have no friends." At that moment an aged pilgrim, in ragged garb, called from a distance, "Have you lost anything?" "Yes, a pocket-book." "What colour?" "Dark red." "I have found one, but have not opened it."

Did not I love the old man? and when I gladly put a bit into his hand, was I not thrice thankful that I had lost it, because it put a piece of bread into the mouth of an honest child of want, and thankful that I had found it for my own benefit; and then the finding it had given so early a proof of Irish honesty; for one of the dreadful predictions of my fate was, that if I was not murdered outright, I should certainly be robbed.

We heard the car, and no time must be lost. On examination, I found that in pursuit of my pocketbook, I had lost my ticket; ran into the office, paid for another, and lost my keys. After considerable bustle I found them, and then commenced regulating government affairs a little, because the railway clerk required a second shilling for a second ticket. "I am obliged to do so, madam – another person might find it, and get the ride; you have found your pocket-book, and should be contented." I saw my mistake, and determined to learn better manners in future.

Dublin was the next encounter, and a lodging-place the first concern. A gentleman in Liverpool had given me the name of a respectable lady, but her rooms were occupied. But learning that I was an American stranger, and recommended by a friend, she managed so as to deposit me comfortably till I could do better. For a moment all was as I wished; the modest unpretending looks of the lady, and the unostentatious appearance of comfort, promised a pleasant resting-place from the storms I had just left.

Not so. "It is the little foxes that spoil the vines."[12] Trifles are the busy ants that are constantly building four molehills of evil and good, showing what and how we are in the true light. They are the pole-star that guides us, and the thermometer by which the daily temperature may be well ascertained.

The brother, who was master of the house, came in to his dinner, and set all adrift. "She must go to a hotel; if she has come to visit Ireland, she will want such attendance as we cannot give." In vain the kind sister expostulated, begging him to read my good letters of introduction. "She must go to a hotel," was the alpha and omega; and when the good woman with a sorrowful face brought the message, my disappointment placed the whole account to the uncompromising disposition of unfeeling old bachelors.

The "attendance I should want" was afterwards ludicrously illustrated, oftentimes, in Connaught and the wild mountains of the coast; when I found myself sitting in company with a ragged family, around a basket of potatoes taking the "Jumper" from my hand.

"What will you do? will you step across the way, where lodgers are accommodated, and take my name?" I did so, and here found single blessedness exemplified in two maiden ladies; and when the stern unyielding negative was given, "Surely," thought I, "Dublin must be the deposit where all haters of matrimony resort, to vent their spleen against "upstart married ladies," and "saucy dirty urchins."

Night was approaching, my luggage a mile and a half from me, and it was Saturday; the kind stranger, who sympathized so deeply at the misfortune of the pocket-book had called to accompany me to the packet, with a care to procure our luggage, but I had no home but the street, and where could I take it?

A servant that moment entered and said, "A house not far distant can give you a room." I went, and was received; the happy kind woman was thus opportunely relieved from the dread of "offending God," by displeasing her brother.

The kind lady procured a car, and accompanied me to the packet, much fearing that I should doubt Irish hospitality, though she had fed me when I first entered the house. She then returned to the door of my new lodgings, to see that all was safe, and bade me a kind good night.

My room was a back parlour on the first floor, rather gloomy; all the arrangements were different from my own home, and it was the first night in Ireland. My head was pillowed, but my brain took liberties which it never has ventured upon since; for when it had thrown off the scum occasioned by the first day's fermentation, the pool became quiescent.

Monday. – The lady who first entertained me went out to show me a little of the city, and Cole River View, where my letter of introduction was to be delivered. This letter of introduction, by the way, was no small item in the account, for I was assured by the Irish gentlewoman in New York who presented it, that it would introduce me to all the Protestants in Dublin of the better class; but as the poor and the peasantry were the objects of my visit to the country, I commenced my acquaintance that morning by saluting as many of these as I could on the way.

The rich scenery, heightened by a pleasant sun, threw around a lustre upon all about me, which kept my imagination awake, diffusing a cheerfulness to the poor labourer, which made his burden more light; for in Ireland it may emphatically be said, "a merry heart doeth good like a medicine" – the merry burst of wit following the hasty brush of the tear from the eye, is always a happy transition, not only to him who sheds that tear, but to the sympathizing looker-on. God, who knew what Ireland would suffer, made it so, and God does all things well.[14]

We reached the tasty cottage to which my letter was directed, but the person who should break the seal was absent, and we were invited to call again.

The cabins were my center of attraction, as I had never before seen a thatched roof, an earthen floor or the manner of cabin housekeeping. I saw new things, and if I found nothing to imitate, I always found something to admire. The first we entered was cleanly; the dishes tastefully arranged upon a white cupboard, and a family of young girls in cleanly garb. And had I visited no other, I might have written a romantic tale on the bright pots and buckets of the Irish peasantry. They were employed in a sail-cloth factory. The next we saw was a pitiful reverse. A slender, discouraged-looking man was sitting on a stool in one corner; a sickly-looking mother, with four ragged children, in another; all waiting the boiling of a pot of potatoes, which certainly fell short of the three pounds and a half allowed to each man in the poorhouse.

"Do your children go to school, sir?"

"No, ma'am; we could not get them clothes to be decent on the street. I work at blaichin', ma'am: I have eight shillings a week, and pay five pounds for the cabin, without a fut of land."[5]

I deducted the five pounds from the twenty pounds sixteen shillings, leaving him fifteen pounds sixteen shillings to feed, clothe, and warm six beings; and in fact I could not find many sovereigns left for their education. This being my first arithmetical calculation on Irish labour and economy, I was at a loss to understand how the thing could be possible; but having since seen many things stranger than these, I am prepared to believe in what once would have appeared a little short of miraculous.

Wednesday. – I was requested to call on Dr. M. Our interview ended in a favourable manner, for though he gave me but two fingers, and a long formal bow, instead of the hearty Irish grasp of the hand, yet he became talkative when I told him my object, and said I had chosen the only way to come at the truth; for Ireland had been wholly misrepresented by writers who had only looked at the surface of things. He took out his map, showed me the best route through the country, gave me some valuable information respecting the condition of the peasantry, and requested me to keep in view the condition of servants, as far as I could do so without prying interference. He recommended me to notice their sleeping apartments, and to see how many I should find wholesome and comfortable for human beings to lodge in through the night.

To my sorrow, in going through the south of Ireland, I found his words verified not only in the case of servants' lodging, but their food; eating their potatoes morning and night, when the master and mistress were abundantly blessed with the good things of this life.

Thursday. – I called on Mr. Fleming, a temperance man who asked me, "Have you really come to see the poor of Ireland, and do you expect or want any great dinners got up for you?"[16] Assuring him that I neither wanted great dinners, nor great people to flatter me, he answered, "Be assured if you have come to see the poor, the rich will have nothing to say to you; and don't be disappointed if they not only treat you with neglect, but say many wrong things about you."

Friday. – Visited the annual exhibition of the arts; and saw some specimens of taste beyond what I had anticipated.[17] The bog oak of Ireland (which is found buried in the earth) when polished, and made into many articles of taste, is a beautiful specimen not only of the skill of the mechanic, but of the richness of this neglected island in its bowels as well as upon its surface. Here were chairs, tables, and small fancy articles of the most exquisite beauty, which were made from this wood. Among its highest ornaments was a standing "Father Mathew administering the pledge to a peasant," both as large as life; the peasant kneeling. The complacent look of the kind apostle of temperance is a happy illustration of the "peace and good will to man," which mark the footsteps of this unassuming man, wherever they can be traced.

Saturday. – Was introduced into the Linen Hall; here is a sad memento of Ireland's blighted prospects of her once proud manufacture of this useful article. The desolated Hall, with its appendages, which once included two acres of ground, now and then in some dusty room shows a sack or two of linen, and in some dark hall a few piles of linsey-woolsey. Here was the son of an old inheritor of some of these rooms, when, in its glory, its coffee room was thronged with men of business, now standing almost alone in its midst, selling linen, to tell the enquirer what it once was.[18]

My next visit was to the poorhouse, for I had heard much of their well-managed laws from all but beggars, who gave them no share in their affections.[19] The house contained one thousand seven hundred persons of all ages, and all who were able were at work or in school. The rooms were well ventilated, and the floors daily washed. The aged appeared as comfortable as care and attention could make them. One old lady was pointed to us who was a hundred and six years old; she could read without glasses, and had the use of all her faculties. The dinner-hour was near; three pounds and a-half of potatoes were poured from a net upon the table for each individual; fingers supplied the place of knives and forks, and the dexterity of a company of urchins, in divesting the potato of its coat, and dabbling it into the salt upon the table, caused me imprudently to say, "I am happy, my lads, to see you so pleasantly employed." 'Silence' was written upon the walls, but this unlucky remark of mine changed the suppressed titter into a laugh, and the unfortunate wights were turned into the yard, in spite of all mediation on my part, as being the aggressor. But the loud laugh and buoyant leap of these boys testified that the loss of a dinner could not bring sadness into the heart of these merry Irish lads.

The most admirable arrangement was shown in the beds, which were made of straw, and emptied every month, and clean straw substituted. The straw taken out is cut up, and flung into a large pit; the suds from the laundry are then conveyed to it by a channel, and it is thus converted into a rich manure. The yearly profit from this plan is from £130 to £140; this is a great economy, beside the advantage of cleanliness to the inmates. This manure is sold for the benefit of the institution, and a multitude of swine are fattened on the offals of the food, and are sold for the same purpose. Twice a week soup is given, and stirabout and buttermilk in the morning; the aged and invalids have bread and tea when required.

Letters of introduction I greatly dislike, for two reasons. They place two parties in a constrained position; the individual who presents the letter feels a kind of dread lest he may be thought a burdensome extra appendage, which, if received, will only be out of complaisance to the friend who sent the letter. The person who receives it may feel that, though he respects the friend that sent it, yet it comes in the very time when it should not, when all was hurry of business; and how can time be lost in showing picture galleries, and making pic-nics? Beside, the mistress may have a bad servant, the house may be in disorder, and one night's lodging would turn a room or two topsy turvy, and often the visitor is politely handed over to some neighbour as a compliment, for a fresh introduction. I have so often been peddled about as a second-hand article in this way, that I have now letters of introduction of years old, which I never have presented, and never shall.

Believing that the actors alone in the following tragedy will be the only persons who will understand who I mean, I shall not spare to tell the whole truth. I had promised to accompany the young ladies home from church, and dine with them, when the letter of introduction was left; I did so, and was introduced to a spot where the style of house and lands showed them to be a vestige of an aristocratic race. The partner had gone down to the dust, leaving a son and three daughters on the paternal estate, with all the insignia of comfort around them. They were of the Established Church, lofty in their views, great haters of the low Irish, and quite careful that the Apostle's injunctions should be religiously observed, where servants are required to "be obedient to their masters."

"I receive you," said the sister to whom the letter was directed, "on the strength of the note you brought; but I must be candid in saying, I am not partial to the Americans, because they keep up no distinction of rank, and eat with their servants."[20]

Dinner was soon brought, when a maiden lady, whose age had been stationary probably for the last twenty years, was introduced. This lady had seen enough of the world to make her vain, possessed enough of its wealth to make her proud, and had religion enough to make her a boasting pharisee. I soon knew I had much to fear and little to gain, for she called for a new bottle of wine to be opened, as the doctor told her she must always use a little at her dinner, or brandy, if she preferred it; for she was bilious. "See, madam," said she to me, "our Saviour made wine, as the marriage could not be celebrated without it; and Paul said to Timothy, 'Use a little wine for your often infirmities.'[21] Do you see, madam, God has made all these things for our comfort" – taking a glass with much relish at the same time. Seeing me decline a plate of flesh, "What! don't you take meat? Have the doctors told you it's bad for you? Why, do you know that meat was given on purpose for the benefit of man?" Here followed an unbroken lecture on the creation, the command given to Adam, to controul the beasts of the field, the fowls of the air, and the fish of the sea, and make them his food. Then the practice of our Saviour. "So you see, madam, I have the Bible at my tongue's end; and here's Miss W—, a good Christian, a church-going woman. Come now, don't go to church to-night. You came from America, and can tell us much about it. This would do us more good than a sermon. Come, come, what do you say to all this?"

Not a word had been uttered to interrupt this pellmell volubility, when the presiding sister said, "Mrs. N. is a disciple of Mr. Graham, and perhaps would give us a little lecture on flesh eating."[22] "O!" cried the antiquated heroine, clapping her hands, "that's it – that's the thing – that's the thing!" Sipping her wine again, "Come," nodding her head, "you may make a convert of me; come, I'm ready. Now begin. Hear, hear!" The uproar became quite theatrical, for all joined in the chorus of "Hear, hear! Begin, begin!" To give a little rebuke, but more to make an honourable escape, I asked, "How do you spend your sabbaths? Perhaps something else would be better." All with one voice cried out, "Give us a lecture – a Bible lecture on flesh eating – now! now! and we will be all attention." The lecture commenced, when soon the whole four pounced upon me, and with one vociferous tumult, crying and clapping their hands, and the chief speaker exclaiming, "Now! now! we have got it – Hear! hear! Why now, you must be a fool, or out of your mind. I thought you were in a decline, you looked so emaciated and so woe-begone."

In self-defence I was obliged to say, "You will excuse me from making any attempts to proceed. I sincerely think the lady who has been speaking must be insane, or half intoxicated." This finished the battle; the ridicule was turned into rage; I left the table followed by the youngest sister, and we both went into the garden. Apologizing for the warmth of the lady she said, "you must know that she is highly respectable." "But lacks good breeding," I continued. "No indeed," rejoined the miss.

The eldest sister made the same apologies in essence, and I remarked, that the conduct I had seen to-day in this house would have disgraced the lowest American table, even where servants might be permitted to take a seat! I then took my bonnet and shawl, made my salaam, and departed.

This, reader, was my first letter of introduction, and it was a letter which, when given me in New York, I was assured was the very one that would introduce me into the first Protestant society in Dublin.

Truly, I never had spent the hours of a sabbath so profanely in my life. I was vexed at myself, and disgusted with the spider-web education of females in the higher walks of life; but I was not discouraged; neither did I rail at all Ireland, or tax her fair daughters with being the most affected, the most impudent, and the most ignorant of all others. I have not found it so, though this specimen in a family of high pretentions was then and still is a problem quite difficult to solve.

On Wednesday morning I walked with a young lady to the Phoenix Park. On our way we met many interesting things, which made me enquire, who shall heal the wounds of bleeding, dying Ireland? So far as taste of man and nature's best skill could make it, every spot is full of interest, but every pleasant object in Ireland is dashed with some dark shade, which defaces, if it does not entirely put out, the beauties of the picture. In my pleasant morning walks in the land of my fathers, I had never been accustomed to meet the pale-faced dejected mother, and the ragged child, begging "a halfpenny for a bit of bread." This morning a modest-looking woman approached with a basket of oranges, and without giving her the pain of a refusal, I said, "I am sorry, ma'am, I have not a penny to buy an orange." I then asked, "Have you a family?"

"Yes, ma'am; and their father's been dead this eight months, and they are all helpless around my feet."

"Have you been to breakfast?"

"No, ma'am, I come out to get a bit, if I could sell a little of these. A morsel will not cross the lips of one of us till it is bought by these."

"How much do you make a day?"

"Sometimes sixpence, but moretimes not so much."

As I passed on, "sometimes sixpence, but moretimes not so much," sounded in my ears; and yet this to Dublin ears would scarcely be called a cry of distress, or the speaker an object of compassion. And often have I been answered, when pleading for the poor, "What's that? They are used to it." "Used to it!" The longer the poor have suffered, and the lower they have fallen, the more haste should be made to rescue them.

As I returned, the novel inscription of "ASYLUM FOR UNMARRIED LADIES," on the plate of a door, attracted my attention; and I begged the privilege of visiting it.[23] I found this was an institution for single females of respectable character, who were advanced in life, whose means were limited. Here they are provided with shelter, fuel, lights, and furniture; twenty-one females, with every comfort that order and cleanliness could bestow, were here. Each manages her own affairs, such as cooking and taking care of her clothes, as she chooses, – as much so as if in her own house; and such as are able are expected to pay 2s. 6d. per week. This makes them feel an independence which persons in all grades are fond of claiming. Pity, great pity, that bachelors are not taxed with all these expenses, for they above all other men demand the most attention from females when age advances. This institution was formed by two or three young females, and much credit do they deserve for their laudable undertaking. May they find as good a shelter if they shall ever need one!

CHAPTER II

Dialogues with the Poor – An English Prophecy – Clontarf Castle – Plan for the Relief of the Destitute – A Dying Saint – Journey to Tullamore – Family Affliction – Visits to the Poor – The Jail – The Poorhouse – Irish Beggars – A Scene on leaving Tullamore – Return to Dublin – Extraordinary Spectacle on the Road – Connaught Labourers – The Two Convicts – A Man's Merit cannot be judged by his Coat – Another Visit to the Dying – A Military Congregation

"Come, ladies, the morning is sunny. You have taken your tea, and a little excursion into the outskirts, where the air is free and balmy, will do you good. A kind look and word to the poor of this world would cost but little, and it might resuscitate some dying hope, and wipe some falling tear from the widow's or orphan's eye." I must go alone and my first letter of introduction meeting such a sad repulse, I fortunately substituted American stranger. It was a day of interest, not because I was in a great city, not because I saw squalid poverty in every street, but because I saw this poverty standing out in a kind of self-possessed freedom, which seemed to say, "Though I am divested of my beauty, though I am shorn of my strength, there is on me a germ of life that shall one day come forth."' Its very antiquity commanded respect. "Do you think," said a grey hair'd old man, "that Ireland will never see it, my children's may; for God is good."

He was leaning upon a wall, covered with rags of various colours, yet cheerful and uncomplaining.

"And what, sure, sent you here?" cried a wretched looking woman, bearing a little mug of beer. "You must be going astray in yer mind to leave so fine a country. The Irish are all kilt, ma'am. They can get no work and no bread."

"But why do you buy this beer if you have no bread?"

"Ah! I've a pain in the liver, and it's for my strength I take it."

"Where do you live?"

"I don't live nowhere; I'm only strugglin' to get my bit;" at the same time sitting upon the ground and saying to herself, "God save her, the cratur, she's goin' astray in her mind."

I went into cabins of filth, and I went into cabins of the greatest cleanliness whose white-washed walls and nicely scoured stools said that "she that looketh well to the ways of her household" lives here. All ages saluted me as the American stranger, and said one, "Ye'r a wonderful body; and did you come alone? Oh! America is a beautiful country, and if I was there I would get the mate." Seeing a repeal button in the cost of a man standing by his car, I enquired, "Do you find employment, sir?"

"But little, ma'am; I suffer much, and get little. O'Connell has worked hard for us, and is now in jail.[2] I'm waitin' here for a job, and the thief of a fellow won't get on to my car with my repeal button in sight. But I will wear it. Oh! the country's dyin'; it's starvin'; it's kilt. And O'Connell won't let us fight, and I 'spose that's the best way."

A cleanly woman, knitting upon a wall, told me she was English; had been in Dublin a year; her health was poor, and she had come out for an airing. "But oh! these miserable beggars. They think they shall get free; but England is so grabbing they never will; and besides, there is an ancient prophecy that England is to fight and conquer the whole world, and give them all the gospel."

"Where did you find this prophecy?"

"They say it's in the Bible."

"To what church do you belong?"

"To the Protestant."

"You should read the Bible for yourself, and see if you can find such a prophecy."

"I've a prayer-book" –

Leaving this learned theologian, I found a woman sitting upon a stone, with a basket of gooseberries by her side, from which she had sold but three halfpence farthing's worth since the preceding morning.

"I have three children to feed," said she, "and God knows how I can do it; when they were babies around my feet, I could feed 'em, and put decent clothes on their bodies; but now I can get no work."

For a halfpenny she poured twice the value into my bag, which I refused; when, with the tear in her eye, she said, "You would give more if you had it, and you speak a kind word to the poor; and what's a handful of gooseberries?" Turning to the old men who were breaking stones, I said to them, "You are aged, and how much do you have for this labour?"

"Sixpence ha'penny a day, ma'am."

"Is that all?"

"Ah! that is better than idleness," said the younger, "and my wife gets a job now and then which helps us a little."

Clontarf Castle was now in sight; at its gate was a surly porter rudely abusing a poor woman for entering its enclosure.[3] The reader may be reminded that a faded dress, tattered shoes, and weather-beaten bonnet have no right through the gate of any gentleman's estate; and looking about upon my own, at the same time using my pass-word, I hoped a more ready entrance would be granted.

"I am sorry, ma'am, I cannot let you in, as you are an American; but none can enter without a pass."

"Your master, sir, has a splendid estate, but I should prefer being a little poorer than the steward of all this."

"Not I: if the rich can't be happy, I don't know who can. Why, this man has his coach-and-four, his horses for hunting, his good dinners and wine, and what has he but comfort?"

"But, sir, a good conscience is better than all this."

"What have we to do with that? We're all born, but we ain't all buried; and what's behind there is nothing to us."

The associations about the castle were such, that my disappointment was considerable, that I would not be admitted. Colman's graphic description of a battle fought there in the year 1014, which was more than awful, had left upon me such an impression, that I wished much to see the spot.[4] A little girl, filthy and ragged, carrying a dirty cloth containing a few raw potatoes, approached with a courtesy, saying, "Lady, I am very hungry; I haven't had one mouthful to eat since yesterday morning."

"Do you tell me the truth?"

"I do, lady."

Her voice faltered, and a gush of tears relieved her.

"I have no father or mother, and live with a grandmother by the bridge. The folks, ma'am, have certainly gone out of this world. They hunt me from their doors, and hav'nt given me one morsel to-day?"

"And have you had no breakfast to-day."

"Not so much as would fill a bird's eye, lady; I tell ye the truth."

She kept close to me, and continued chattering in the most simple manner, and wondering what ailed the world, and what would become of her, saying "O, I'm so hungry!"

In the evening, I sat down "to gather up the fragments" of the day. I had seen painful things, I had seen pleasant things, and though all were common events, yet out of the varied materials, I had put up this little parcel as worthy a second reviewal. "What ought to be done can be done." This ignorance, this hunger, this patient double-distilled misery sit with a bad grace on a benevolent Christian city like Dublin. But you answer, "It was always so, and always will be."

Suppose fifty ladies in the city, who have leisure, should go out at ten in the morning, and mingle promiscuously with the poor upon the street, take their number, ascertain who is worthy, and who is unworthy; who need instruction, and who will receive it; who are idle from necessity, and who from choice; who can do one kind of work, and who another, and who can do nothing at all; who are old, and who are sickly; who can go to a place of worship, and who cannot, &c.[5] By four o'clock in the afternoon each lady could ascertain the true condition of twenty persons at least, making in all a thousand, who might be truly deserving, and who, with a little assistance of work and necessaries, would soon be placed beyond want. But be careful that the payment be a full equivalent. Nothing gives the industrious honest poor man more encouragement than this; it makes him hope; he sees something tangible before him; he sees he may yet have a decent garment and a comfortable meal, independent of his rent; and he feels that he may sleep without the dreadful torment of a debtor's pillow. Let this going out into the "high-ways and hedges" be continued, and how many disconsolate hearts could be lifted up; how many tears would be wiped from the cheek of the orphan, and how many blessings from the lips of those who are ready to perish would be poured forth. This has been done, and can be done again. Dublin stands nobly prominent in her charitable institutions; there are none, save the poor sailor, but have a place in her kind provisions for the destitute; still there is much land to be possessed.

Monday, July 1st. – In company with a young lady, visited the cabin of a poor dying saint. She stood on that narrow neck of land between the two worlds, which to the poor sinner is a fearful position, but to her it was like the last step to land from tempestuous voyage, where she would meet her best kindred. Her earthly friends had forsaken her, because she had left the Romish church, and though griping poverty was pinching her five little ones, and she must leave them to a selfish world, yet she said, "I have not one anxious thought about them. Jesus," she emphatically added, "does all things well; and last night he gave me such a cluster of light, that the whole room was enlightened by his presence; and soon, yes, soon I shall see him as he is." How has Christ honoured poverty, and how he delights to dwell with the poor and contrite!

Tuesday, July 2nd. – Must leave for Tullamore. I had removed my lodgings from the first kind house where I stopped, and had found in the second all that hospitality which is so congenial to a stranger, and was becoming much attached to Dublin; but rest was not my errand to Ireland, and the kind daughters of the family accompanied me at seven in the morning to the fly-boat, where I was packed as tight as live stock could be in any but a slave ship.[6] Here I found a company of would-be intelligent Irish and English aristocrats, who, on "both sides of the house," were professed enemies to the poor Irish, calling them a company of low, vulgar, lazy wretches, who prefer beggary to work, and filth to cleanliness. How much of this may be true I pretend not to decide, but this may be safely hazarded, that it is an established law of our nature to hate those we oppress. The American slaveholder, while he keeps his foot upon the slave, despises him for his degradation, and while he withholds a knowledge of letters, and closes the Bible against him, hates him because he is ignorant and a heathen.[7] In eight hours we reached Tullamore, a distance of fifty miles, and the first novelty was the market-place.[8]

The appearance of the people here was not prepossessing, for there was not one among them decently clad, and every thing indicated that a last effort had been made to set off the merchandise to the best advantage, while the looks of the seller seemed to say, "We have toiled all day, and caught nothing."

A son of the lady to whom I had letters, conducted me to the terrace, and as the letters were from her daughter in America, I expected a cordial reception, and was not disappointed. Tinctured a little with aristocracy, well educated, and disciplined by family disappointments her mind had become chastened, and she appeared as if struggling to support an independence which a heart sinking under silent grief could not long sustain. The children were well trained, and had been educated mostly at home by herself. Her husband was of good family, and had speculated her property away, and as the last resource fled to that "house of refuge," America; and an absence of three years, without sending her any relief, left suspicions on her mind that all was not well. I had seen her daughter in New York, who had followed her father thither, and she begged me to search out the family in Ireland, and do what I could to comfort her mother. My errand was a painful one, – family troubles can seldom be mitigated by foreign legislation; and while this noble-minded afflicted woman made full, meaning, but indirect enquiries, her voice faltered, the tear was in her eye, and for a moment I regretted that I had complied with her daughter's request. Her well-regulated family being assembled around the family altar, she read an appropriate prayer with practical observations, adding suitable ones of her own, which made the devotions pleasant to me, for it savoured of a heart that had been made better by the things it had been called to suffer.

The next morning, the twin daughters of eleven years accompanied me into a lane to see the poor. Here I found these lovely girls had long been acquainted, for they enquired of a poor old man about the growth of a pig, and kindly patted the well known pets of donkeys, goats, and dogs, calling them all by name, while the mistress went into the garden to pluck a bouquet for the fine girls, who, she assured me, were the smartest in the parish.

I had always heard the Irish were celebrated for giving the pig an eminent berth in their cabins, and was a little disappointed to find that though it was really so, yet there was some nicety of arrangement in all this; for in two cabins I found a pig in a corner snugly cribbed, with a lattice-work around him, a bed of clean straw under him, and a pot of food standing near the door of his house, to which he might go out and in at option. And in both these huts, though the floors were nothing but the ground, yet these were well swept; a peat fire was smouldering on clean hearths, and the delf was tastefully arranged upon the rude shelves. An old cobbler sat with his lap-stone, and said he could make one and six and one and tenpence a day, and he took care of the bit of ground at the rere of his cabin for the rent of it. "My wife, praise be to God, is dead, but I can get a comfortable bit for my children." An old blind man of seventy-two, sitting at the door of his cabin thanked God that he had no right to complain, though he had seen better days; for he had "two kind girls, who, when they had done all in and out of the cabin, got little jobs now and then, which kept the bread in all their mouths." On looking into the cabin, nothing could be cleaner. Here, too, the family pig was snoring snugly in his crib in one corner of the room; and here, in all justice, I must say that these pigs were well disciplined for when one of them attempted to thrust his nose into a vessel not belonging to him, he was called a dirty pig, and commanded to go to his own kettle, which he did as tamely as a child or a dog would have done.

Another cabin attracted us by the tidy white aprons upon two little girls who were standing at the door, and their nicely attired mother, with clean cap and handkerchief, who welcomed me heartily to Ireland. On my commending her for her cleanliness, she said, "Plase God, poor folks should be a little tidy who have nothing else to set 'em off. Would ye walk into the garden? Maybe ye'd like a rose or two." We willingly complied, and found an acre of kitchen garden well cultivated, with a few flowers interspersed, which they rented for nine pounds, and sold the avails for the support of the family. She plucked her fairest roses and ripest gooseberries, and bade me God speed, long life, and a safe return to my own country.

I returned from this lane much gratified by the cleanliness, simplicity, and comfort of this humble people; for I had ever associated a mud wall, a thatched roof, and a pig as an inmate, with all that was wretched in the extreme; and I had, so far as this lane could speak, abundant evidence that a very little will make the Irish content, and even happy.

In the afternoon I visited the jail, a building, with its appendages, including an acre and a half of land. It contained eighty-one prisoners; seventeen had been that morning sent to Dublin for transportation.[9] They were all at work; some cracking stones, some making shoes, and others tailoring or weaving. Their food is one pound of stirabout, and milk in the morning, and four pounds of potatoes for dinner. There are two hospitals, one for males and the other for females. The drop where criminals are executed is in front; four had suffered upon it within the last two years.

From the prison I went to the poorhouse, which was conducted on the same principle as that of Dublin; but the funds were so low that but three hundred could be accommodated, and multitudes of the poor were suffering upon the streets.[10] A flourishing school was in operation, the specimens of writing doing honour to the teachers. The children are fed three times a day; they get a noggin of milk at each meal, with porridge in the morning, potatoes at noon, and bread at night.[11]

The next day rain kept me within doors, and I had the painful annoyance of seeing beggars constantly walking back and forwards before the parlour window; nor would they depart, though often told they could have nothing.[12] The sister, who supported the family of her brother-in-law, now returned from Dublin. She was a woman of some worth, and apparently possessing much piety. The poor afflicted wife and mother, as soon as her sister returned, and the excitement abated, became unwell, imputing the cause to her visit at the poorhouse; but sickness of the heart was the mover of it all. In the morning, when I went to bid her adieu, she answered not a word, but looked as if in a state of deep despondency: –

> "When woman droops, she droops in silence;
> The canker grief gnaws stealthily, but sure;
> The pallid cheek, the sunken eye alone
> Give note of death's dire work within."[13]

Report has said something of the class of beggars in Ireland; but her busy tongue, extravagant as she often is, could not exaggerate here. It was scarcely eight o'clock when I reached the coach, but the beggars had assembled before me; for the going out of this vehicle is the hey-day of expectation. To them a foreigner, or a stranger, whom their shrewdness will readily detect, is a kind of common plunder, and escape is a hopeless undertaking. The coach was to leave at half-past eight, and while I stood waiting, I saw some half dozen of men with spades standing in a cluster, and enquired if they had work for the day. "Not a ha'p'orth, but we are hoping to get some." I asked what was the price of labour. "From six to tenpence, and we don't get work half the time at this."[14] "And does this support you?" "O ma'am," said an old man, leaning on his shovel, "we hope to see better days, plase God; it's but a sorry bit this gives us." "Father Mathew has done much for you."[15] "Yes, praise be to God, as early as now in the morning, the people round here, standing as they do now, would be cursin' and fightin'; but now, thank God, there's not a word from their lips."

The chief centre of attraction was now where we stood, as I was a stranger. They attacked me with, "God bless you," "A penny, if you plase, lady," "A ha'penny for a poor woman and child, whose father is dead this twelvemonth," "One ha'p'orth for an old man,"and "The price of bread for a poor boy;" the boy grasping my clothes and holding fast, in spite of my efforts to disengage myself – the cries and importunities redoubling, while, like swarming bees, they sallied out from every quarter, till the crowd was immense. In vain I preached loyalty to the government, temperance, and peace; my voice was lost in the clamour of "Plase, lady, it's the ha'p'orth ye'll give us, thank God." The overseer of the coach, from his window seeing my dilemma, hastened out, and kindly begged me to get upon the coach, where they could not annoy me so seriously. He helped me aloft. Labourers and beggars, some on crutches, some with two legs, and some with one, mostly clad in coats of divers colours, variegated with all shades and hues; boys with a garment suspended from the hips, hanging in strips, making a kind of frill – these all followed in pursuit. By the time I was well adjusted, a sea of upturned faces, some with hats and caps in hand, to catch the falling penny, lavished all sorts of blessings on America and the kind lady who had come to see them, who as yet had not given them a farthing. Waving my hand for a moment, all was silent. I endeavoured to count them; there were about two hundred and twenty, one half at least beggars. The huddling became so confused that I could not proceed, and I resorted to exhortation, telling them to be true to their young queen; that they had a Father Mathew to keep them sober; a never-tiring friend in O'Connell, who *said* he would "rot in prison for them if need be"; and under all these encouragements they must be patient. "That we will, lady, and the blessin' of Almighty God be on ye, and the prayers of the blessed Vargin, if ye'll give us the penny." The scene had now become, to say the least, ludicrous, painful, and unseemly. I had travelled by sea and by land among the savages of my own country, the poor abused slaves on the plantations, the degraded, untutored native Canadians: but this eclipsed the whole. I looked down upon the forbidding mass, and saw every lineament of talent, every praiseworthy and noble quality, every soul-speaking glance of the eye, every beauty of symmetry, that God's image ever possessed, united with every disgusting, pitiable incongruity that imagination could depict. Much did I wish that the good queen would leave her throne for the one on which I was sitting, and see for a few moments her subjects, her loyal Irish subjects as they really are, disgusting to refined eyes as it might be. She must, she would pity, and though her administration had done nothing to produce this state of things, yet her administration should and could produce something better. I begged the coachman to make speed, knowing that a few pennies dropped among them would endanger faces and eyes, if not pull me from the coach; and the promise was given, that when my bag of money should come from America, part of it at least should be poured down upon them. "Faith," cried a poor woman with a dirty urchin hanging to her, "and ye'll be here no more, if the bag's to come with ye." The coachman attached his horses, leaving the whole town with the troop of ragamuffins swinging hats and caps, cheering America and the queen, shouting and calling for a penny till we were out of hearing.

When we had well escaped, "What is this?" I begged the coachman to tell me. "It is the case of all Ireland wherever you travel; a fine country, but cursed with bad laws." "But whence could all these miserable objects that swarmed around the coach proceed?" "From the mountains and places around; they all know the time that the coach goes out, and are always in readiness; they are not all street beggars, only trying their hand at the coaches and canal-boats."

Tullamore is the assize town of the King's county; it is situated nearly in the centre of the Bog of Allen, and the proprietor, the Earl of Charleville, has done much to improve it. Good schools are established, and the poor in the town are more comfortable than in many others in the vicinity. The road lay from Tullamore through a part of King's county and Kildare, to Dublin, a distance of fifty miles; and forty-five of this it was lined on each side with hawthorn and cinnamon-briar hedges. The briar was in full bloom; the air had been purified by the preceding day's rain; and the fragrance of the sweet briar, united with that of the new-mown grass, which lay here and there as we passed, made a day's ride of the pleasantest I ever enjoyed, so far as sweetness of air and beauty of scenery were concerned. But the beggars we had left, and the beggars that met us at every village where the coach stopped, made me dread the appearance of a human creature. We passed the most beautifully culti- vated fields, where not a stone or stump could be seen, and saw gardens joined to the most forbidding-looking hovels, where roses were blooming upon the walls, and even upon many a thatch were waving flowers of var- iegated beauty; so that the unaccustomed stranger must ask, "What means this strange contradiction? How can such taste for farming and gardening be blended with such unseemly rags, such debased minds, and such a lack of self-respect as many of these beings manifest? What must be the state of that people, who can walk and breathe in such a paradise of delights, and not be assimilated in some measure to the more than enchanting prospects around them?"

"Look! look!" said the coachman, "if you'd see a sight." The sight should not be recorded, for the credit of human nature; but how can the evils and deformities of Ireland be known, if they are not exposed? and how can eyes that have always been looking out upon these things, dimmed as they must be by constant use and the fogs of national pride and national self-complacency, see these discrepancies with so clear a vision as the less accustomed and the less interested can see them? But the sight. At our left was an old ragged woman, bending beneath a huge pack, and fastened upon that was a boy of thirteen (as the coachman and a passenger averred, for they both knew him) with legs entirely naked, not only hanging at full length, but dexterously applied to the old woman his mother, when he wished her to hasten her speed, while he held his cap in hand towards the coach for pennies. This was allowed by the mother to excite compassion, as well as to indulge the lad, for the passenger observed that he would not walk. He had once seen the mother put him down, when he leaped upon a stile, and thence to her back giving her a kick, saying, "There now, go on, Miss Lucy Longford."

We next saw a caravan of Connaught labourers, on their way to Eng- land to get work. One horse was drawing nine of these men, with a woman sitting among this score of legs, on the bottom of the cart; and the coachman assured us that the "owner of her" was the one between whose feet she was sitting. He further informed me, that the practice of these people is to go out to gather the English harvest, which arrives before the Irish, and at the same time wife and children go out to beg. The cabin- door is fastened, and they agree to meet there on a certain time, bringing home the avails of the labour, and they go in together at the unfastening of the cabin.[16]

Stopping at a village, a woman presented a basket of oranges, and a troop of beggars fell upon me as suddenly as though dropped from the clouds, demanding the pennies I had received in change for the orange. And so clamorous were they, that I felt myself in danger, and distributed all I had, which did not supply the whole. One was so rude in pulling me, that I should certainly have called for the police, if the coachman had not relieved me by applying his whip, and leaving her behind.

Upon the back seat of the coach were two convicts sentenced to transportation, chained together, with three policemen as a guard. The eldest was a hardened veteran, singing merrily as we proceeded, with roses stuck in his cap. The younger, a youth of about eighteen, was sad, looking as if he was on the verge of bursting into tears. The sight was affecting. Poor boy! he might be fatherless, but have a mother whose heart has doated on him, and who still yearns over him; while, in some unguarded hour, the fatal deed has been done, which severs him not only from her, but from his country for ever; which makes him a disgraced exile, and drives him farther into the thick meshes of sin and temptation.

When we arrived at Dublin, in Barrack-street, where the convicts were to exchange carriages, the host of beggars that surrounded us could only be equalled by the throng at Tullamore; and it is a matter of wonder how, at a moment's warning, such a herd of vagrants can be collected.[17] They are like Pharoah's frogs; they compass the whole length and breadth of the land, and are almost as much to be dreaded as his whole ten plagues; they leave you no room for escape on any hand; dodge where you will, they are on the spot, and the ill-fated stranger needs a fathomless bag, who ventures on a tour among these hunger-armed assailants.[18]

The passenger who accompanied us proved most happily that a man's merit cannot be judged by his coat. His was so much defaced, that when I found him seated near me, I felt a little annoyed. I was afterwards ashamed of myself for this weakness, for I found in the course of conversation, that he was well read in the history of his country, had travelled out of sight of the smoke of his own cabin, loved Ireland, appreciated its virtues, and acknowledged its faults; and though he was no enemy to O'Connell, yet repeal was not his hobby. If their bogs could be drained, their mines explored, their waste land reclaimed, and the labourer well paid for his toil, he would as willingly be under the English crown as that of the Irish. Peace was his motto; "If we cannot have our rights without bloodshed," he added, "let us die oppressed and hated as we are." He alighted from the coach, while the horses were being exchanged, and unasked returned with a list of every place from Tullamore to Dublin, written in a most neat and legible hand. My mistake in this man gave me a valuable hint, which has been of much service in my long tour through the country.

When the evening hour of reflection, in my own room, found me along, I looked back upon the events of the day, and though the reader may see little in it that is interesting, yet to me it was a rich and valuable one. It was the last day of the first excursion I had made in Ireland, and it had given me in brief detail much of its true history. The heart-stricken woman whose house I had left in the morning, the labourers and beggars at the coach, the enchanting scenery and exhilarating air, the old woman and son, the Connaught men, the convicts and passenger, would each make a valuable chapter on the suffering, crime, beauty, deformity, and intelligence of Ireland.

"A might maze, but not without a plan."

The next morning I visited the sick saint, whose animated cheerful countenance told that the peace that passeth all understanding reigned within. To the question, "How became you a Christian?" she answered, "God Almighty made me one; yes, praised be his name, when I was a great sinner, he called me."

"How different," said the young lady, as we passed out, "is Christ's teaching from man's. She makes no mention of prayers, going to church, or reading the scriptures, but simply, 'God Almighty made me a Christian.'"

My young companion then accompanied me to Irish-town, and we heard a sermon from "Go ye into the world, and preach the gospel to every creature."[9] The organ and music were excellent and appropriate, and the Queen's regiment, cap-a-pie in warlike habiliments, with furbished guns and bayonets in their pews, made a most peculiar set-off to the principles of the text, which are "peace and good will to men." But never did a hundred of young soldiers in any house of God do more credit to good air, food, and exercise, than did these. Each had his prayer-book, and read with as much apparent devotion as though the success of a battle depended on it.

CHAPTER III

Visit to the County of Wicklow – A Tremendous Coach-load – Horrors of the
Journey – Safe Arrival and kind Reception – A Happy Family – Shelton Abbey –
Arklow – Beautiful Scenery – Arklow Fishermen – Domestic Turmoil – Rathdrum
– The Vale of Ovoca – Wicklow Gold Mines – A Hungry Man – An Old War Horse
– A Scriptural Answer – Visit to a Rectory

On Wednesday morning, with my good friend at Dorset-street, I found
myself at the coach at half past five. She left me, and an hour too soon
prepared me a little for the day's strange movements which were before
me. The hideous loads of trunks, chests, hampers, sacks, and baskets,
which for an hour were in ominous fixings and re-fixings, gave fearful note
of preparation. "Where shall I sit? – My trunk must be here – My band-
box will be all jammed up – And won't you please make a little room for
my legs?" began half an hour before the horses were brought, while I at a
respectable distance stood with basket in hand, waiting a clearance of the
ladder, that I might ascend. Seeing an opening I improved it, and fixed
myself in mid air with one foot on terra firma, the other seeking rest and
finding none. and now the full tide of battle set in. I had been seated by
the coachman in a few inches of space, just left by an old fat man in
breeches who had moved to have a trunk put up; and when he turned
about for his seat, and found it filled, "You have got my place, ma'am." "Sit
still," jogged another fat Irishman, "make sure of what you've got; and
here sir, you can take it quite aisy on the top." Behind us was a kind of
scaffolding, erected of sufficient width to seat two. Here, after much
grumbling, the old man with his bundle was adjusted, his footstool the
necks of each of us, who in turn handed or whirled his heels to the next,
while the poor man ever and anon was heard to say, in a subdued tone,
"That woman's got my sate." "Be aisy," said my fat neighbour at the left,
when I gave signs of pity for the old man. "He's doin' quite well." And now
the storm was working into a tornado. A modest looking young girl, who
had waited patiently to be seated (for all this time we had not stirred an
inch from the door) asked what she should do. "What shall you do?" said
the boor of a coachman. "Sit where you promised, or don't sit at all, on
the top of the luggage." There was no alternative; what with hoisting

from below, and the old man pulling from above, she was seated upon her perilous throne, while we had a second pair of heels to dispose of, to the no small annoyance of the poor man on my left, who did not like to make the same rude arrangement of them as he made of the old gentleman's.

We had proceeded a few miles, with nineteen upon the top, and one appended to the back, when a loud call from a car arrested us, with, "Can you take a few more passengers?"

"As many as you please," answered the glad driver. The clamour, the entreaties, and threats of the passengers, that it was unlawful to load any vehicle so unreasonably, and that they should make complaint, were all unavailing; the car was emptied of four solid bodies, beside a box or two for each, with baskets and lesser appendages, and all transferred to the coach. The poor affrighted girl over our heads was now ordered to alight, by the profane blustering coachman, and without ceremony was packed among us, though we already had eight where five could only have a tolerable seat. This was truly fearful as well as intolerable; a corner of a trunk was resting on my shoulder, and twenty miles I rode without having the free liberty of my head or full turning of my neck. The beautiful Vale of Ovoca we entered, but my cramped position kept me from one solitary look at it; the ponderous coach was threatening at every jostle to plunge us headlong. The "Plase be so kind as to move an arm or a leg"; and "Do be aisy, my good friends, you put my hat into all manner of shapes," went on, and, taken as a whole, it was the most perilous, the most uncomfortable, laughable, provoking ride that could be imagined.

I was the first passenger called upon by the coachman, when we reached Arklow; and enquiring in surprise what he could mean by asking money for perilling our lives, and then abusing us because we had sense enough to know it, I assured him I never would pay a man for abusing me, as that could always be procured without price. He walked away amid the laughter of the multitude, without soliciting money from any other. Twenty-nine were on and in the coach, and he expected a shilling each from most of them. I was heartily thanked by the good-natured Irishmen, but this was a poor compensation for a forty miles' ride of peril and the loss of my luggage.

My carpet bag was missing; and as the coachman, by way of revenge for the loss of fee, would not look for it, I was left to make my way without it, a mile and a half to the house where my letter was directed. Endeavouring to take a shorter route, I was entangled in hedge-rows and plunged in ditches. Every one of whom I enquired gave me a different direction, while all of them agreed that I was "goin' astray," and some told me I must "be cracked." At length, climbing upon the top of a wall, I found a man digging in a pit, and called out, "Will you tell me the way to Mrs.— and what kind of a woman she is," (for my vexatious ride and my perplexing walk had made me quite suspicious.) His reply was, "Ye must take the lane, and go by the monument; and the woman is not a bad one; she's a snug farmer, and set five barrels of potatoes to the poor in Arklow last winter."¹ This was a cordial for my fears. "And how much do you have a day for labour?" I enquired. "But a sorry bit, ma'am. I stay here all day without my dinner, because my wages won't buy one. Plase God, I hope we shall yet see better days in Ireland."

Following his guidance, I found myself at the gate. An open lane shewed the placid sea, and the far-famed mountains of Wicklow. About the door were roses, a shrubbery, and lilies of the most beautiful kind. I entered so fatigued with the day's excursion, that I cared but little whether smiles or frowns received me. A daughter met me in the hall, and presenting her the letter from a long absent brother, she invited me in. The mother was called, and though she gave me no Irish "thousand welcomes," yet when she saw the letter from her son, and heard the sad tale of my coach ride, the loss of my carpet bag, and my walk through quagmire and ditch to her house, she invited me in to a well furnished table, with every appendage of neatness and order.² The party consisted of the mother, the eldest son, four daughters, a little niece, a young lady and her brother who were lodgers, and two ladies on a visit. The vexations of the day and the embarrassments of a stranger were soon lost in the courtesy and flow of kindness manifested, and I felt as if seated at the dinner table of an intelligent New England family, where familiar friends had assembled. After dinner the mother invited me to the garden, saying, "We have made our arrangements for you to spend a week with us, and if we did not wish it we should not ask it; so, this point is at once settled, and we will show you what we can of our country and people." The kindness of this offer was greatly heightened, when I ascertained that the young gentleman who lodged with them had offered his room for my accommodation, and that he was to share the bed of the son of the mistress.

Reader, do you love domestic life, where plenty, order, and comfort reside? Then come to the garden of Ireland, the county of Wicklow, and I will introduce you to a family where all these rare qualifications may be found. This widow had been the mother of eleven children; one had been drowned, and his monument, with that of his father, was near the dwelling. A son was living in New York, and two in Ireland; four daughters were at home; the youngest had made a choice for herself, and was well settled near the family, in one of the tidy cottages that adorn the parish, where Lord Wicklow has lavished his good taste so profusely. Industry and economy were happily blended in this family; the daughters, unlike many in Ireland, with smaller incomes than they, were not unacquainted with all that appertained to the good management of a house. Their plentiful board was spread with wholesome food of their own preparing, and every apartment of the house testified to their handy work. The morning and evening prayer ascended from the altar here; and though not in accordance with my own habits of extemporaneous prayer, yet never did I assemble for the family devotion, but I felt on retiring that my heart had been warmed and my resolutions strengthened in serving my God. It may with propriety be averred, that when the morning and evening prayers are offered in a family circle, that family is generally the abode of peace and good order.

>"Give me the sweet abode, however humble,
>   Where every child is taught to speak the name
>   Of God with reverence; where, morn and eve,
>   The lowly knee is bent around the hallow'd
>   Shrine of prayer and praise."[3]

The following morning the mother walked with me to Arklow; and there, to my great joy, was my carpet bag left by the coachman on his return. I found that my aged companion had not lived in vain; for beside having, after her husband's death, paid some hundreds of pounds of debts that were in arrears, she reared eleven children in habits of industry, educated them for good society, and gave them all tolerable portions. She has a mind stored with interesting anecdote of the history of her country, especially that part belonging to the days of ninety-eight. The poetry with which all the narrations of the Irish peasantry are mingled, makes an observing listener willing to give them Ossian for their countryman, for they spontaneously breathe out many of his sentences, without ever having known his book or his name.[4]

Shelton Abbey, owned by the Earl of Wicklow, is a spot of much interest, not only for its beauty, but for the happy traits of character united in the earl and his family, who make the lot of the poor peasant tolerable, if not cheerful.[5] Lady Wicklow has established three schools among the cottagers, which she supports; and she visits from house to house, enquires into their wants, and gives them premiums for cleanliness. Slated roofs are substituted for thatch, and on visiting fifteen of these cottages in one day, I saw not a dirty uncomfortable one, and only one where the shrubbery and flowers were not blooming in tasteful profusion about the windows and whitewashed walls. One of the earl's seven daughters, writes religious tales for the cottager's children, and gives them as rewards for industry and cleanliness. The earl supports a school for boys, where they can be kept till the age of fourteen. I visited one of Lady Wicklow's schools, and saw a group of cleanly, well managed children, who are instructed by a maiden lady of good capacity. The children are Roman Catholics and Protestants, and on enquiring into their attainments the answer was, "They are educated according to their rank; they belong to the lower order, and reading, writing, arithmetic, and a little knowledge of the maps is all the education they will ever need." This was a dark spot in the picture, which emphatically said (contrary to the injunction, "occupy till I come"), "Hither shall thou go, and no further." What does this principle say to the wise plan of the Almighty in the distribution of his talents? If the Saviour gave them to the poor, was he wise in doing so? Did he say, when he gave five talents, "I give you these five; but as you belong to the poor of the world, you must hide all but one."[6] What steward over God's poor can give a good account of his stewardship, who has directly or indirectly checked the rising of an intellectual talent, which would be used for the glory of God, or the benefit of man?

Shelton Abbey has the appearance of a castle. It is a granite building, with a belfry for the clock, which makes a tower of no mean pretension. In the interior of the edifice there was no lack of good taste or splendour. The family were in London at the time of my visit; but the servants and gardener, left in charge, showed us the premises. A little spinning wheel, with flax on the distaff, stands in the parlour as an ornament and a pattern of industry. Whether Lady Wicklow has taken "hold of the distaff" with her own hands, and furnished her house with fine linen, was not told us; but she certainly has strong traits of one of Solomon's virtuous women.[7] The pictures were numerous and costly. The enormous representation of a stag-hunt, with dogs holding by the teeth a poor stag in the act of leaping headlong, formed a cruel contrast to the benevolent countenance of the earl hanging near it.

"I would not enter on my list of friends,
The man who needlessly sets foot upon
A worm."[8]

A call at the cottage of the young married sister of the family where I was stopping, gave an additional zest to the beauties of the morning, and the scenery around. She received us with such simple-hearted kindness, and spread such a well-prepared repast in such a little parlour, and in so short a time, while her chattering little girl decked us with the freshest flowers of the cottage, that I almost wished my lot had been cast in the parish of Kilbride, *after* I had received my education. After our palatable lunch, we went from cottage to cottage, our company swelling at every stopping place, welcoming the American stranger; the salutations being often, "Welcome, thrice welcome to our country; a thousand welcomes to Ireland."

The children all joined in the salutations, and we ascended an eminence that overlooked the sea. Need I tell the reader I was proud of the honour of sitting in the midst of that group? Twilight was gathering around us, and the richly cultivated fields, with here and there a costly domain and the thatched cottage of the peasant, were at our right and left; for we had left the ornamented part of the parish. But here the eye was not pained with squalid poverty, and had I not since seen any of the desolations of this ill-fated isle, I must have said, "If this be Ireland who shall weep over her?" I regretted that the fall of night made a separation necessary, for I loved to hear the tiny voices of the children, as they plucked the wild flowers, and filled the lap of the stranger; and when, at a gate, or the door of a cottage, I heard the "God bless ye, lady," I sent up a hearty wish to heaven, that all Ireland's enemies might be touched with feelings like my own.

The next day we visited Arklow, and our only object of curiosity was the decayed castle, of which but one tower is left.[9] This the sergeant of the barracks, who had the care of it, kindly offered to show us. It was built in the year 1200. Now, it plainly tells that the battering ram had not been applied in vain, for it is crumbling to ruin. Our guide conducted us to the top by winding-steps, to look out upon the adjacent country, and see where the great battles had been fought which had deluged that part of the country in blood.

The battle of Arklow, while "seed-time and harvest remain," will live in the memory of all who saw it, or shall read of it.[10] The prospect was both grand and awful; the river Ovoca was at our feet, winding gracefully through the rich vale called by its name. At our right hand lay the sea; at our left, the mountains of Wicklow; behind us the town of Arklow, and near where I stood was once the skull of Hackett, which had been affixed to the top of the castle, in the days of the rebellion. This man had killed many a Protestant, and in return they shot him, took off his head, and placed it upon the top of the castle, where it remained till a few years since, when a wren made her nest in his mouth, and it finally tumbled down, and received a burial in the side of the tower.

When we left the tower, we visited the fishermen's settlement on the sea-shore. This consists of perhaps three hundred huts of a squalid appearance outside; but on entering one of them, we were happily disappointed, for we had a cordial welcome to a neatly whitewashed room; the cupboards in the kitchen and little parlour were neatly arranged, and the bed neatly curtained. This is quite common, even where the pig has a bed on a pile of straw in the corner.

When we were about leaving the settlement, we heard a most fearful noise in a distant cabin, and as we approached, it became more terrific. We hesitated, fearing that the work of death was going on. We ventured at last, and saw a mother in a most violent paroxysm of rage, standing over a girl of eleven years old, with a stick in her hand, threatening that she would kill her, and that instantly, if she did not ask forgiveness; the girl screaming in apparent fright, pleading not to be killed, but refusing to confess. We entreated the mother to desist for a moment, and to allow us to speak. Pale and trembling with rage, she answered, "I will break every bone in her lazy body, ladies; I will kill her now." We entreated that she would allow us to speak to the child, and finally succeeded, the mother meanwhile taking an infant in her lap of eight weeks old, and giving a spontaneous history of her family, interlarding it with principles that would do honour to the most cultivated woman. "I have eleven children, ladies; six younger than the scrawl that has so provoked me, and she hasn't done a ha'p'orth for me to-day. She has been on the street since six o'clock. Laziness! laziness! ladies! Shouldn't she be bate? and when I got her in, and gave her a slap, she gave me impudence, and went into that room, and fastened the door on me, and she wouldn't ask my forgiveness, ladies; and she wouldn't ask God's pardon. I wish I could bate her, and not get into a passion." "You must tell her priest," said one of the young ladies. "And that I will; he'll hear of this. But she's been petted at school, and it won't do to pet such scrawls; and before she will be idle and filthy, I'll kill her. She'd better be dead than lazy and dirty. I sent to Dublin and got a piece of calico, and made them all dacent. I saved a piece to mend 'em with, and you see here's a rent in this child's arm (holding up the arm of a little girl), and that lazy girl won't put on the piece; and she can sew well. I can't have my children ragged. I can't have 'em dirty. It's a sin, ladies. Their father toils, poor man, till dark night, to keep their clothes dacent, and keep 'em in school." Here a shrivelled old woman entered, saying, "And what's all this? This girl is as fine a slip as ye'll find in all Wicklow, – a fine scholar." "You see, ladies," remarked the mother, "how she's petted; that's the trouble. They must be bate."

We then insisted that the child should hear us, telling the old woman that she had been very wicked, and that her mother ought to punish her. "Ah! poor woman, and she's kilt with so many of 'em, – the craturs; and she strives to make 'em dacent, and so does the father; and she'll be a better girl – and won't ye?" Among us all, by exhortations and entreaties, we succeeded in getting a promise from the offender that she would try to do better; that she would go immediately, and mend her sister's elbow; and she voluntarily thanked us kindly for our good advice. The mother also thanked us, and said, "What will I do to keep down my temper? When I see this child in the street in bad company, all goin' to the bad, larnin' nothin' but what the divil tells her, ladies, shouldn't I be mad?"

It was raining, and we could not go out: all was hushed save the pattering of the rain upon the doorsteps, and we sat down in silence, each apparently inclined to meditate on the scene before us. The stillness seemed like the great calm that followed the voice of the Saviour, when the surging wave of the maddened ocean shrunk away, and blended together into a placid molten sea. The paleness of the mother was exchanged for that wholesome ruddiness so prevalent among the cleanly Irish peasantry, contrasting finely with the clean cap that was becomingly adjusted upon her high forehead. The unconscious infant, in a clean pink frock, was sleeping on the lap of the mother, which was covered with a tidy apron. The refractory girl had ceased her sobbing, and showed a face and features of talent and interest. A little girl of six years old was standing at our left, with face, hands and feet clean, her hair well combed, her frock and apron whole and cleanly. A tidy girl of about fourteen was nicely adjusting the dinner dishes upon a white cupboard with the greatest care and stillness. The room into which the young rebel had fastened herself was clean, and for a cabin nicely furnished, as could be seen through the open door. The room in which we were sitting contained a bed in the corner, in a kind of enclosure, with a clean covering, and at a little distance were two barrels, with a pile of straw between them, on which a couple of fat pigs were extended asleep.

The silence was broken by my asking the woman, "Is your daughter industrious?" alluding to the one at work. "God be praised," said the mother, "she never gives me trouble; she's always as you see her – none but the girl who has been so petted." Fearing "the clouds might return after the rain," we gave her the most friendly cautions and wishes, and kindly admonished the penitent girl, who followed us to the door, adding her thanks for our kindness; and we left this fisherman's cabin, hoping that none had been made worse by our visit.

"What good sentiments," remarked one of my companions, "have we heard expressed from that mad woman! how clean her cabin! how nice her children! and what a mother would she have been had she been educated!" We all looked upon the poor woman with feelings of the deepest pity. She possessed every ingredient of mind to have fitted her for the best of mothers, with the highest sense of what her daughter should be, and her own responsibility to make her so; yet as she had never been cultivated herself, and had not the least restraint upon her temper, we had reason to fear that the wayward girl might yet fall a victim to the mother's rage. We had visited the schools in Arklow, and thought of again calling to find the teacher of this child, but did not. In these schools, which are supported by private individuals, Protestants and Papists are taught the scriptures daily; and though they appeared not quite as cleanly as Lady Wicklow's, yet they merited more praise than censure."

A ride on a pleasant day, through a pleasant country, in pleasant company, with a good horse, an easy carriage, and buoyant health, induces the fortunate traveller to note pleasant things in his journal of the country and people, especially if the tea be prepared to his liking, and sent in at precisely the right time. Such was my happy lot when my hostess, her daughter, grand-daughter, and a young man took a seat on a car, and accompanied me through the enchanting Vale of Ovoca to Rathdrum. At Newbridge we met a rustic funeral procession, in all kinds of habiliments, and on all kinds of vehicles appropriate to that class; while the black pall, with knots of white ribbon a few inches apart, from the head to the foot of the coffin, borne on the shoulders of four men, as a substitute for the "sable hearse and nodding plume," told us that the body enclosed there had withered in the morning of life. We had scarcely passed when a gladsome wedding party, on their return from the church, where the vows had been performed, burst suddenly into view, at a short turning of the road, and their every look and action said,

"All men think all men mortal but themselves."[12]

A gentle shower sprinkled us, but gave additional interest to the scenery, as we rode through the shady grounds of the tasteful domains. The grand Castle of Howard was looking out upon our right, as if hanging upon the top of a wooded precipice; the domain of Mr. Parnell, cousin to the Earl of Wicklow, lay in our path.[13] He had visited the United States, and from the city of Washington he had selected a plant of no mean growth, and fixed it in this laughing Eden, which, while the rain-drops were glistening in the sun, now looking out upon the broad-spreading tree and verdant lawn, said, if happiness dwell not here, we must seek the fugitive in other skies where purer spirits dwell.[14]

On alighting from the car, we were received by a most unassuming young woman, a relative of the good lady who introduced us thither, and in the few hours we stopped, we had one of the happiest specimens of conscientious devotedness in a mother to the welfare of her children I had ever seen. She had three, and "How," she asked, "how shall I train them for usefulness in time and a happy immortality?" She was a mother of prayer. "You have a church near by," said I, "and a good pastor I hope, who helps you to guide your little flock."[15] "We have," she answered emphatically, "and it is through his kindness, his faithfulness, and his untiring watchfulness, that I have been most deeply made to feel my responsibility. The church you see here was built by himself, and he labours in it without pay, employing curates as he sees fit, and all the parish are visited by him, the poor as well as the rich. He watches over the children, and they look to him as their father." Happy pastor! good shepherd, that cares for the sheep, and looks well to the lambs of the flock. The memory of such will never perish. It can be said of him, as of Goldsmith's village preacher,

> "Even children followed with endearing wile,
> And pluck'd his gown to share the good man's smile."[16]

The little town of Rathdrum contains about two hundred families, and is fitted up with considerable taste. A poorhouse well filled adorned the outskirts.[17] But the ride home –

> "Now came still evening on, and twilight grey
> Had in her sober livery all things clad."[18]

It was Ireland's summer twilight, lingering long, as though loath to draw the curtain closely about a bright isle in a dark world like this. It was early in July, the rich foliage had attained its maturity, and not a seared leaf was sprinkled on bush or tree, to warn that autumn was near. For the first mile the road was smooth and broad, lined with trees; now and then a white gate with white stone pillars, opening to some neat cottage or domain; the glowing streaks of the setting sun had not left the western sky, and glimmered through the trees; while the air, made fragrant by the gentle shower, diffused through body and mind that calmness which seemed to whisper, "Be silent; it is the Vale of Ovoca you are entering." We descended a declivity, and the vale opened upon us at "the Meeting of the Waters." The tree under which Moore sat when he wrote the sweet poem had been pointed to me in the morning. We now stood near the union of the two streams, where the poet says,

> "There is not in the wide world a valley so sweet,
> As that vale in whose bosom the bright waters meet."[19]

The rich variety of wood; the still, clear, limpid water; the hill and vale, in some parts dark and wild, in others light and soft, ever and anon relieving the eye by some new variety; but above all, the pleasant association that this vale, however dark and deep its recesses, harbours not a venomous serpent or reptile – no, not even the buzz of the mosquito is heard – made it unlike all others. We rode three miles, scarcely uttering a syllable all the while; a holy repose seemed to rest on this hallowed spot, as when it first bloomed under the hand of its Maker, and imagination was prompted to say, as no serpent has ever coiled here, the contaminating touch of sin has not left its impress.

Never did I leave a spot more reluctantly; it was a night scene which never has faded from my eye, and I hope never will.

"O! the last rays of feeling and life must depart,
Ere the bloom of that valley shall fade from my heart."

In the deep silence, the voice of God and the soft whisper of angels seemed to be there. These voices said kindly, "There is mercy yet for poor erring man." It appeared like the bow of the covenant, telling us to look and remember that though this world has been cursed by sin, yet a new heaven and earth are promised, of which this is a shadowy resemblance.

The borders of this valley are interspersed with gentlemen's seats, and here and there dotted with the whitewashed cottages of the peasants; and the rich cluster of foliage upon the hillsides, upon bush and tree, almost persuade you that the dew of Hermon has fallen upon them. Stranger, when you visit Ireland, visit the Vale of Ovoca. If you love God, here you will see him in a picture that must be read; if your stay be limited, waste it not in deciphering a time-defaced stone, telling the bloody deeds of some ancient warrior, or the austerity of some long-lived ascetic, but linger in this spot; stop at the neat little hotel, erected on purpose for the accommodation of the stranger; and morning, noon, and night explore its never-dying beauties of light and shade. Three times did I go through, and when I turned away at last, I felt that

"I could stay there for ever to wander and weep."[20]

The fairy pictures of Ireland had now opened upon me so vividly, that had it not been for the beggars of Tullamore, I must have said, surely this country is quite a monopolist in its pleasant things; but little did my enthusiasm anticipate the check that awaited it.

The next day a ride to Killahester, upon the mountains, five miles distant, took us to the house of my hostess's son. He accompanied us to the Gold Mines, in a deep ravine; these were discovered more than forty years ago, and the government then attempted to work them, but soon abandoned the project.[21] Now any man may search here for gold, where and how he pleases, and we found four men patiently at work at their own risk. They informed us that they often dug for days in succession, and got not a particle of gold; then they find a little, sufficient to encourage them, and they patiently labour on. Enquiring of a lad of twenty, "Suppose you work a month, and find none, what would you then do?" he replied, "O we don't mind that; the good may come at last." Happy for the poor Irish, that their organ of hope is so largely developed, otherwise they would sink under their accumulated burdens. They showed us a specimen of the gold. It was about a guinea's worth, and was quite pure. The lad who produced it said, "We be never disheartened." Well they might take courage, for digging in a rock for gold, with a few grains now and then as a reward, is as good an equivalent as working for sixpence or eightpence a day, and buying their own potatoes. The inhabitants of this mountain are many of them poor, and live in dark mud cabins, with a scanty supply of food. My friend, at whose house I stopped, observed that the labourers who live under the farmers are in a better condition than those who live under the land-owners. The latter allow but tenpence a day, out of which the labourer must find his own food, while a great farmer often gives fifteen pence and part of the food. My friend was one of these great farmers; he had two hundred acres of land, and paid his labourers in that proportion.

Passing a gate, we saw a man at work with a small dog, whose emaciated body and trembling skulking manner induced me to say, "Your dog, sir, looks as if you do not feed him enough." "And that I don't," was the answer. "And why not? you should kill him or feed him better." The master made no answer, but that silent eloquence which speaks louder than words. As we walked away, "Poor man!" said the farmer, "he is much of the time hungry himself; he gets but little work, and I doubt not but he is in want of food this minute." The sad proofs of Ireland's woes were then beginning in the county of Wicklow, and I could not enjoy the palatable meal of bread, cream, and fruit, so much did the desponding man and his famished dog annoy me. The sight was then new to me, to see a man in a season of plenty about his avocations without sufficient food to eat, and a faithful dog, meagre and starving, watching and obeying the will of the master. But these have since ceased to be objects of wonder.

On Saturday I visited the estate of a gentleman who had perched his mansion on the brow of the Vale of Avoca.[22] Here, through porters and dogs guarded the buildings, yet we were admitted into the outer porch of the temple, and had a walk among evergreens and flowers upon the margin of the vale; and we seated ourselves upon a rustic seat, to feast again upon the never fading beauties of the river and vale at our feet. A distant landscape of cultivated country was stretched beyond, and the whole looked more like a fairy land than a real spot of earth, trees, and water. We were disappointed that we were not allowed to enter the premises, and see the greatest curiosity of the whole, a mare of the age of fifty years, who carried her master to the great battles forty-six years before, in the days of the rebellion. She is said to be in good flesh; her head is white with age, her body grey; and the daughters of the man who was once her owner but is now dead, have the beast kept, and well tended on this estate, out of respect to both their father and the animal. The simple-hearted cottagers who accompanied me presented a picture of the patriarchal days and manners, that made me regret that artificial life and

"trade's unfeeling train
Usurped the land and dispossessed the swain."[23]

Calling at the cottage of a peasant, attracted by the beauty of the shrubbery, and to enquire the way to Ballyarthur, "Pardon me," said the woman, and hastening into the cottage, she returned with her bonnet and shawl, and said, "I will go with you, ladies, and show you a near way." She was advanced in life, and something corpulent; and her effort to climb over stiles, and pass hedges and ditches, for the accommodation of strangers, called for an acknowledgement. Her scriptural answer was noticeable, "But we are told, ma'am, that we musn't turn the stranger out of his way."[24] Happy would it be if all who read the scriptures more than this unnoticed woman would practise its precepts as well.

CHAPTER IV

The Church of Kilbride – A Methodist Minister – Methodism in Ireland – Visit
to the Rectory – Teetotalism unfashionable – American Courtesy to Females not
universal in Ireland – The Seven Churches of Glendalough – Foolish Legends connected with this locality – Strange Exhibition of Party Spirit – Return to Dublin –
Lady Harburton's School

On Sabbath heard the rector of Kilbride preach a most searching sermon,
from "Knowing the terrors of the Lord, we persuade men," insisting that
we should always be reminded that God loves justice as well as mercy, and
that he gave an awful proof of this love in the punishment of his Son. The
congregation was small, but quite in accordance with every thing in the
parish, neat and respectable; the music was sweet, and "Old Hundred"
was performed in that soul-stirring, soul-fitting manner which is so peculiar to that tune when well performed. If set tunes are performed in
heaven, "Old Hundred" and "Luther's hymn" must be favourites in that
"great congregation." This rector and his lady were among the first in the
morning at the sabbath-school, which he opened by prayer, this being his
usual custom. When introduced to him as an American, I was happy to
find that his rector-ship had not robbed him of that beautiful urbanity so
characteristic of the native Irish, for he gave me a hearty welcome to Ireland in true Irish mode. "I passed," said he, "three pleasant years in New
York, and left it with great reluctance. I am quite attached to its customs
and people in many respects, especially their hospitality to strangers and
their politeness to females."

Sabbath evening supped at the house of Mr. Burke, a Methodist clergyman. His companion was one of those prudent wives who are from the
Lord. Her children were educated by herself (the proper business of
mothers), and their becoming deportment testified that the pruning-
knife had been applied in season. Mr. Burke told me that the Methodists
now number in Ireland about 29,000 members, and 100 preachers. Certainly these indefatigable labourers have done no small business to make
their way through Popery, Prelacy, Presbyterianism, and Independency.
They are instant in season and out of season. Went to Arklow at seven,
and found a plain chapel, with a plain man in the pulpit, and heard a plain

sermon preached to a plain people, all in accordance, with every nail fitted to its place.

On Monday the family of my hostess were invited to make a social visit at the rector's. His cottage, like those of most of his neighbours, was surrounded by shrubbery, and a little lawn spread out at the front.

"The soil improved around, the mansion nest,
And neither poorly low nor idly great."[3]

It was consistency outside, and within neatness and good order prevailed. The mother of Mrs. D. and Mr. D's sister, together with the usual accompaniments, children to the number of three, composed the family of the rector and his lady. The sister had travelled considerably, was highly intelligent, and the wife and mother would do honour to any exalted station. The evening passed pleasantly and profitably to me, as Mr. D. gave what he thought the true condition of Ireland, and the cause of her sufferings, namely, popish influence and the bad government of England in the beginning, together with absenteeism. In his opinion, if repeal were granted, the extermination of all Protestantism must and would take place.[4]

The reader will not think that the flowers and shrubbery, the politeness and attention of the people of Kilbride, had so won upon me as to dim my vision to all that is unseemly, when I add that in this intelligent, refined, and religious little party, I felt that a wiser and holier Being might say, "I have somewhat against thee." Here was a sudden check upon my happy evening, when, to my surprise, I saw the wine giving its colour in the cup.[5] So long had I been accustomed to view it as an evil and bitter thing, that I thought all Christians felt the same, since the Lord commands us not to "look upon it when it is red," "when it moveth itself aright;" and especially since in America it is generally believed that in Ireland all classes of the people have got rid of the sin of intemperance. I had seen it before on Protestant tables, but did not expect it among the clergy; but I had many things to learn, and this fact was one, that this heaven-inspired movement of temperance in Ireland not only owes its effectual origin to the Papists, but is continued and supported mostly by them.[6] May God in mercy to poor Ireland open the eyes of the officers of the church, and the leading men among the nobility, to act as he would have them act. I looked back on New England twenty-five years ago, and then saw the clergy and nobility demurring whether it was sinful to drink in "moderation."[7] I looked upon them now, and heard them unitedly cry out, "Touch not, taste not, handle not, but shun the appearance of evil," and I looked upon this lovely family down the vista of a few short years, hoping and believing that they too would be emancipated, and walk forth unshackled from tyrant custom and tyrant appetite.

The time of departure arrived, and a second subject was discussed. The rector had said an hour or two before, "You will find that the habits of our country differ widely from yours, in regard to the attention paid to females by the gentlemen. While the gentlemen there are sometimes over attentive, they are here often neglectful, if not uncivil." I regretted to hear this, for though I had come determined to meet all and every thing as unfeelingly as possible, yet my education had taught me to believe that the attentions paid to females should spring from their dependence; and this dependence is generally greater in age than in youth. It is much to be lamented if Irish mothers have not instructed their young sons, that to suffer a female, especially an aged one, to go out at night alone, to climb into a carriage without assistance, or to stand up in church while men are sitting, is unkind, uncourteous, and highly reprehensible.

Pardon this digression. We had on our bonnets and shawls to go out, and the kind rector had his staff and hat in hand to accompany us. "We cannot allow you," said a young lady, "to take all this trouble; we can very well go alone." "No female whom I have invited to my parlour or table shall go out of my house unprotected on a dark evening." "Amen!" responded my heart, for I could not see how any man could do less, and be a man still; but the uneasiness that the ladies manifested, plainly told that they had not been accustomed to such attentions.

"You must see the Seven Churches, before you leave the county of Wicklow," said my good friends.[8] This visit to the Seven Churches is a memorable one, not only on account of the marvels which we saw and heard, but the pleasant and painful associations with which it is connected. The young husband of the daughter of my hostess offered to accompany me to the place, seventeen miles distant, with his wife, and another lady. It was in the midst of haymaking, and he left his business, hired a horse and car, and we started at an early hour on a beautiful sunny morning. We stopped a few moments at the Copper Mines, which were then in operation, and had been for twenty years.[9] They had at that time explored a mile in depth into a mountain of rocks, and found sufficient encouragement to proceed. Eight shillings a week was the labourer's compensation for this arduous toil. Our ride was pleasant, and the country rich for the first part of the way. Within a few miles of the Churches, the mountains become higher, and are covered with heath, giving them a barren and dry appearance. The entrance to this celebrated spot is not through lawns or pleasure grounds, but between a wall of strong mountains on the right and left; and the few cultivated spots looked to the stranger to be scarcely a sufficiency for the poor peasantry, who soon gathered in thick array around us when we arrived, to show us the wonders, or to ask a penny. Old men and maidens, young men and children were on the spot, each with the utmost servility ready to "sarve" us in the best and "chapest" manner. We were obliged to shake them all off except one, who was engaged, and handed over to me, as I was a stranger, and my party had visited it before. The sensible reader shall be troubled with only a very little of the consummate nonsense with which my ears were stuffed during the long six hours we passed among these ruins.[10]

The first object of interest was a round tower, standing alone, one hundred and seven feet in height, and about six and a half in diameter, with windows at some distance from the top, and no door nor entrance whatever except the windows. For what purpose these incomprehensible towers were built every body attempts to tell us, and nobody satisfies the enquirer, even if he satisfy himself. Even my guide told no legend in connection with it. The burying-ground in which we were standing was the next wonder. Its age is traced by the peasantry back to the first peopling of this "land of saints;" some asserting that St. Patrick was the founder, others going farther back; but among the rude, defaced, and dilapidated stones, I did not read one inscription of more than a hundred and fifty years ago; however, I did not read all, and many were written in such hieroglyphics that the Jesuits who wrote them might best decipher them.[11] The graves were pointed out to us where five priests were deposited; and there were deep holes in these graves, whence the consecrated clay had been taken, which we were informed would cure all diseases, however obstinate. One of the company now cried out, "See that child hanging from a high grave-stone – she will be killed if she falls." "Oh, never fear," cried a young woman, "she hangs there every day; she's puttin' purgatory over her, ma'am; she tells her mother she won't live the year, and she does it for penance, lady."[12] "Ah! she's a wonderful child, that" – responded my guide, who now told me that the wonders he was about to relate had been told to him by his grandfather, and might be all believed. An enormous stone cross stands here for the benefit of single persons, who, if they can embrace it backwards, will be certain of a partner within a year.[13] The guide told us he had done so to accommodate gentlemen who had visited there, and as often as he had done it, his wife died, till he had lost five, and was fairly tired out. The cathedral is a coarse stone building, now gone to decay, a monument of what it once was. It must have been very strong, but small and dismal, and of many hundred years standing.

It is unnecessary to describe every object of interest that we saw among the ruined churches, of which enough remains to keep alive the legends of the superstitious, and the curiosity of the stranger.[14] The very name and the romance connected with the mountains, the lakes and St. Kevin's bed, will continue to attract the traveller. The stone where the orphan boy stood daily, and was fed by a deer, which St. Kevin called from the mountains to shed her milk into a hole in the stone for the child, still remains. and you are shown the marks of the child's fingers. The round rock, flat upon the top, under which a fire was made, which St. Kevin ordered to be kept hot to bake the cakes of King O'Toole, is also pointed out. Among the good deeds ascribed to the saint is the building of the churches. Being poor, he had no land to build upon; King O'Toole owned that country, and St. Kevin had fled into a cavern which overlooks the larger lake, to avoid the snares of the beautiful Kathleen. Feeling a most holy desire to establish the worship of God in these mountains, he applied to the king for land. The king had a pet goose, which had stood at this door seven years without either flying or walking; and he told the saint if he would make his goose walk, he would give him as much land as she would fly over. The saint took the goose in his hand, and threw her up in the air, and she flew down the glen upon one side of the lakes, and up the other. Thus the whole glen became the saint's, and next comes the building of the churches. "You must know," said my guide, "that no lark flies over this glen, nor no lamb ever lies down in it." When these churches were building, the labourers complained that they were obliged to work from lark-rising till the lying down of the lamb at night, for a penny a day. St. Kevin told them that the lark should never fly over the glen, nor the lamb lie down on it again, which promise has been kept sacred, and these lines from Moore are repeated with much pathos:

"By that lake, whose gloomy shore
Sky-lark never warbled o'er."[15]

The two lofty mountains which overhang these lakes and glens were once visited by King O'Toole and a Scottish giant, who shook hands across the lake; and the king, after having drunk the health of the giant, handed him the tumbler. All this you must believe if you are not a downright heretic, and this is but a beginning of the marvels. There are a few realities which might be worth the notice of the traveller, if they could be reached beneath the rubbish that covers them.

Seven churches once stood here, whether all built at the same period is not certainly known; if so, the spot must have been thickly peopled; but when these people lived, and how they subsisted in this narrow glen, is a mystery. Two majestic mountains overlook these lakes sleeping at their base, leaving little room for cabins, though a few are sprinkled upon the border of the lakes on one side. By the side of a moss-covered pile of stones, which was one of the churches, was an open grave, said to be King O'Toole's. The head of his coffin, which was stone, lay upon the ground, the grave having been opened to ascertain whether his coffin were there. A stone cross stood upright, bearing marks of ancient workmanship. At the bottom of this monument lay a moss-covered stone, with carvings of serpents and hieroglyphics.

The stranger cannot but pause and reflect, in the midst of these legends and foolish superstitions; there must have been here, in years long gone by, a peculiar people, a people if not literary yet religious, who selected this deep dell for the purpose of adding solitude to their devotions. The remains of seven churches without any vestiges of dwelling-houses, give to the whole a deeper mystery. Though a hot July sun was shining with unusual fervour, a subduing stillness reigned around the lake; and one green spot of trees, wild flowers, and grass, through which ran a clear, soft murmuring stream, added a romantic beauty to the scene. I had stolen a moment from my gabbing interpreter, to enjoy by the side of this stream a little rest and reflection, when a shrill shout, followed by a hideous echo, burst upon my ear. It was the old barefooted Kathleen, who has acted for twenty years as a guide to St. Kevin's bed, and who carries presumptuous visitors on her back up the steep and dangerous cliff, in the face of which is the cave where the saint had lived. Into this cave she assured us she had carried Walter Scott, Thomas Moore, and many other great personages, and it only wanted myself to complete the list. Assuring her that I had not the least ambition to immortalize my name by a ride upon her back, and a tumble into the lake beneath, from which a rescue would be impossible, I left the honour to such as might better deserve it. As she still insisted, and the guide added, "It would be a great loss not to see where the good saint lay," I ventured a little way up the steep, and was glad to find a place for my sliding feet to rest, whilst one of our party, an adventurous young woman, went on. She reached the precipice, and placed her hand on the shelving-stone that covered the cave. The yawning, black, and deep gulf was beneath her, and the slightest jostle might have plunged her headlong. Her husband, seeing her presumption had seated himself at a distance waiting the fearful event in silence; for myself, I turned not a look in that direction, fully expecting to hear a shriek and sudden splash into the lake beneath. In a few minutes she was near us; perspiration, she said, started from every pore, and tears streamed from her eyes, as she found herself actually hanging by the rock over the precipice; and she was glad to be again by the side of her husband.

Kathleen returned, redoubling her assurances of my safety, if I would trust to her "sure fut," but she was forced to content herself with giving specimens of the strength of her lungs, while the mountains returned the screams in faithful echoes. My guide determined not to be outdone, and he screamed out exclamations to the giants and fairies, who all answered by repeating the same distinctly. We saw a line of stones cross a bog of eighty or a hundred yards, arranged in the shape of crosses, where pilgrims in more holy times went over upon their knees doing penance. "You must know, lady, that this was a place of saints," remarked our guide solemnly. Our walk was now interrupted by a line made across our path, of sweet-briar, and held at each end by two little girls. Supposing they were at play, I said, "You are jumping the rope." "No, ma'am, it's a turnpike." "And must we pay toll?" "If you plase, lady." We had three of these turnpikes to pass within a few rods, and toll was required at each. This was a contrivance of their mothers to draw money.

It is difficult, in going through Ireland, to know whether to be disgusted at the whining cant of the beggars to move your pity, or provoked at their deceitful impudent efforts to extort your money. And it must be equally difficult for beggars to demean themselves honourably; if they appear servile and religious, then they are hypocrites; if like men and women transacting other business in life, then they are impudent. It is painful to see the cunning arts of young children, trained from the cradle to beg, when the parents are not honest. But it is well for Ireland that its paupers in general are not a dangerous thieving race; if they were, they are so numerous, that the more favoured classes would never be secure. When we had paid toll at the gates, came the last marvel shown by our guide. It was a bush over a round pool of water, the branches tied thickly with rags, which had been used for washing eruptions upon pilgrims.[16] You are informed that St. Kevin blessed this pool, and it cures all who wash in it. A few more fooleries are practised upon the credulous visitor, and the guide dismisses him as have done his own duty well; the stranger has only to believe. When all was finished, I said, "You do this for money, sir." "I get my bread by it, lady, and yesterday [which was the sabbath] I made eight shillings." "And do you believe one word of all the ridiculous stuff with which you have been cramming us?" "I tell it, lady, as I heard it." "But do you believe it yourself?" He looked confounded, and answered, "No: but I made only one story to fill up the time as we were passing along."

When we returned to the inn, a devout-looking woman met us, and gravely asked, "Have you washed in St. Kevin's pool? Depend upon it, lady, there is the greatest vartue in it; it cures all sorts of evils." I replied by asking her, "And have you ever washed the wicked one himself?" Astonished, she looked at me, "The divil, ma'am, did ye mane? The divil can't come here. This is the place of saints." One of the ladies who accompanied me said, "You have lost your character as a Christian, and they'll want no more of you in this holy place. You have laughed at their money-making lies, and no one ever does that here. They expect you to receive it all in good faith, and to admire when you go away the skilfulness of the guide in entertaining you." A word respecting the innkeeper, a fat good-natured mass, tumbled together in not the most scrupulous manner, but as incredulous respecting the holiness of the spot as his interest would allow him. "I know less of the wonders of the place," he said, "than those that visit here; but as people will come, I will entertain them," which he did in a most comfortable manner, and at a moderate price. As we were going out, he called to me, and gave me a word of advice. "Do you, madam, publish a sketch of these wonders and give new names which nobody can interpret, and your book will circulate well in Ireland. But be sure you express no doubt on the subject yourself."

Our guide was no novice at story-telling, for he told my friend who had accompanied us, that he would visit his neighbourhood, and entertain him any evening with stories, as soon as he could get time to make some good ones; adding, "This is my business, you know, but I will ask you nothing as you brought the lady." He had been twice paid for his bundle of lies to me; my friend feed him in advance, and I paid at the close. This ridiculous farce, practised for a long time, loses little of its interest even in the nineteenth century. And though the invention is attributed to Catholic superstition, yet it meets many a believing heart in Protestantism. The guide called himself a Protestant.

On our return we ascended the serpentine, closely swept road, that conducts the traveller through the woody enclosure to the top of the hill, on which stands the romantic Castle Howard, looking down with her evergreens about her upon the beautiful Vale of Ovoca. Nature and art seem here to have done their utmost to render the spot not only grand but lovely. The lady of the castle was absent on a fashionable tour to England, leaving the house-keeper to show the castle and reap the benefit. The interior is fitted up with all the appendages belonging to high life, dogs, leopards, statues, and ornaments – so varied that nothing seemed left for the mind to supply, but the placing in the library of a few dozen volumes more moral in tendency than the works of Voltaire.

My visit to the county of Wicklow being finished, I am happy to say that both country and people exceeded my sanguine expectations. The natural scenery, the cultivation, but most of all the peasantry, possess a kind of fascination, which every unprejudiced traveller must confess. Many of the peasantry are cleanly, intelligent, and industrious, and an inviting charm hangs about their cottages, which says to the stranger there is peace and comfort within; and when you enter, you feel you are welcome. The Irish greeting cannot be misunderstood; and here the same kindness and the same order prevailed among Catholics as among Protestants. I called one Saturday evening at an humble cottage, where the children, to the number of five, all took their seats unbidden in a corner. Their neatness and good conduct caused me to look about more particularly, and there I saw the signs of a prudent wife and mother. "You see," said the young ladies as we passed out, "the management of this poor woman; she is always clean, always comfortable, and her children always tidy though poor." They had been kept to school, and, by the strictest economy, the family had never been obliged to trouble their neighbours in sickness, ever having needful supplies for such exigencies, though possessing not a farthing but the daily labour of the father. They never partake of tea, coffee, or ardent spirits; or meat, except at Christmas.

I must leave Wicklow with a grateful remembrance of undeserved kindness, for the last words I heard were "My house shall be welcome to you whenever you come this way."

When leaving New York, a friend said to me, "Give us all the information of the country you can; but don't touch politics. That is miserable work for a woman." But I soon found in Ireland, it was a great misfortune that I had not acquainted myself more with at least the technicals of the different parties; many egregious blunders might have been saved, and not a word need have been spoken. "You had better take *the Radical* to Dublin," said a man, "It is not so crowded as *the Conservative* coach."[17] I nodded assent, without knowing the coach virtues of either term, as applicable to anything in my case, or indeed the case of Ireland, as I have since known it. I took *the Radical*, was well seated, well used, and found my journey back quite the reverse of the sad and savage one down. These were O'Connell-days, and this *Radical* was a repeal coach. "What do you think of repeal?" said a well-dressed gentleman; "as I never had the pleasure of seeing an American lady before in Ireland, I should like to know her opinion." "A woman, sir, I am told, should not meddle with politics, but this I will venture to say, that Ireland ought to be redeemed from her bondage, and whether it be done by repeal or some other instrument, let it be done." This man was a Roman Catholic priest; his parish including the fishermen of Arklow, who were all teetotalers, not one having broken his pledge.[18] He was well skilled in the doctrines of his church, but complaisant, and patient under contradiction; and report says he has done much to improve the morals and the condition of his people. When I alighted, I was determined to remember *the Radical* coach, not forgetting the kindness of the driver.

On Monday after my return to Dublin, I visited the schools originally established and supported by Lady Harburton, a lady of great fortune and benevolence.[19] These schools do much honour to the teachers as well as to the founder. The infant school numbers about one hundred and forty, and was conducted like those I had been accustomed to see at home. Here was a school of little boys, instructed in the scriptures and the first rudiments of geography; a privilege which, though they were the children of the poor, was not denied them, as in Lady Wicklow's school. The school of young girls was as good in arrangements as I had ever seen; order, cleanliness, and attention were strikingly manifested. The superintendent was quite intelligent, and thorough to the last degree in all her investigations. The reading, examination in the scriptures, in ancient and modern geography, arithmetic and grammar, showed honourable faithfulness in both teacher and pupil. But I regretted sincerely the severity of the superintendent. A little more tenderness mixed with her rebukes, I could not but think would have accomplished as much good, and left a more favourable impression on the hearts of the pupils. Goldsmith's country schoolmaster did not more richly deserve the character of a petty despot, than did this otherwise excellent teacher, for if of him it might be said,

"Full well the boding tremblers learned to trace
    The day's disaster in his morning face;"
of her it might be added,

"Full well the busy whisper circling round,
    Convey'd the dismal tidings when she frown'd;"
for her frowns were the preludes to heavy blows.[20]

The children of Catholics composed a respectable part of the school; and if this were a fair specimen of schools in Ireland, the children of the country would have no claim to pity on the subject of education.

CHAPTER V

The Second Cabin of a Canal-Boat – Much ado about Sixpence – A Blind Fiddler – A Jaunting Car Jaunt – Arrival at Kilkenny – Cordial Hospitality – Kilkenny Beggars – Journey to Urlingford – A Rural Physician – Ride in a Turf Kish – The Poor Widow's Welcome – A Country Dance – Departure of an Emigrant – Lamentations thereupon – Kind Reception in an intelligent Roman Catholic Family – An Irish Wake – A Faction – Fair at Urlingford – Costume of the Peasantry – Visit to a National School

On the following Thursday I took the fly-boat on my way to Kilkenny. When I went to Tullamore, I took my seat in the first cabin, but being then closely packed with a stiff company, I now preferred to get a comfortable seat, to pay less, and learn more of Irish character by going in the second cabin.' The two last objects were realized, and what was lost in honour was made up in amusement, for Irish wit had here full play. An unfortunate miss from Liverpool, with more tongue than brain, opened the scene by telling the captain that she paid more, by sixpence, for a ride in that dirty ditch, than for crossing the raging billows from England; and besides, a boy in the cabin, bigger than she was, had not paid so much. "But, miss, if you please, it's not by weight but by age we go." "Age! indeed! and who told you that?" A wag from one corner of the boat cried out, "and 'spose, captain, you take a look of the two jaws on the two sides of the tongue." "The divil a bit could ye gain by that," answered an old man, "that long loose tongue of hers would fret out eleven pair of teeth before a hair could turn white on her pate."

The battle now rose high.

"And maybe the girl would stand up and show how long she is; and if but a slip, she must surely have on leggins." The girl was instantly on her feet. "There, do you think I am as big as the boy?" "And that you are," rejoined the captain, "and I think you are married." This she positively denied, and insisted on the sixpence. "Will nothing else do?" said the captain; "I will give you a dinner of beef-steak, and pay all expenses of whatever you may choose." "And though," said another, "you may have had breakfast, you cannot have too much of a good thing; and if you don't choose the steak, you can take the tay and toast." "The sixpence is all I want; the sixpence is my due; and will you, captain, give me the sixpence?"

A fat old woman sat at my side, guarding an enormous wallet that lay at her feet, with two huge bonnets upon her head, which, though by their material, they might have been modelled some ages apart, yet by dint of bending a little here, and widening largely there, they so exactly fitted that they might be said to be of the same ton. This thrifty manager arose in all the majesty of matronly experience, and made her way through masses of legs and mountains of luggage, till she reached the clamorous maiden, who was still standing, and demanded an audience: "And sure the like of ye couldn't be found in a day's walk in Ireland; and can't ye stop your bawlin' about a paltry sixpence? and where's the mother that rair'd such a scrawl? If she's out of the ground, why didn't she keep ye under her eye till ye had sinse?" All to no purpose! she still insisted on the sixpence. "Yer a fool, and ther's no use in talkin'." "And do you think she's the only woman that's a fool?" answered an old man who had been snoring in the corner. An old grey haired blind fiddler now entered the boat. This gave a new and interesting turn to the scene. All eyes were intent, and all ready to sit closer, and huddle away baggage, to make a "dacent sate" for the fiddler. The old woman resumed her position at my side, and the blind man took the fiddle from his green bag, and played a melancholy air of true ancient Irish. He was a good performer, and though he played some lively airs, yet to me he seemed not to be at home, but gave them because he must. That meek subdued look, which always sits on the face of the blind, was emphatically his; old, and trembling with age, he commanded veneration, while his blindness awoke both the pity and benevolence of the passengers. They gladly responded to the call of a youth, who said, "If you plase, old man, hand out your plate; 'tis time for a collection." The fiddler drew from his threadbare vest pocket a little tin plate, which the young man passed about, and a few shillings were put into the hands of the thankful musician, who was then set on shore to make his way to an appointment for the evening. These blind fiddlers are somewhat numerous, especially in the south of Ireland, and are treated with great humanity by all classes.[2]

The Liverpool girl, who seemed a little composed while the fiddler was performing, now reminded us that the predominant wish had not yet died, for she remarked, "The sixpences were so plenty here for the fiddler, I should think you might give me back mine that the captain took from me." We now reached Athy, and happy was I to exchange the tedious maid for a seat on the novel Irish car, with a genteel young lady on one side, going to Kilkenny. The rain commenced, which deprived me of seeing the country as I wished; but troops of ragged urchins, who rushed from the national school, and from every cabin we passed, made up the deficiency. I was sitting alone, and succeeded, unperceived by the driver, in beckoning three of them upon the car. Their ready answers solved all my questions about the country, for what Paddy left out, Micky could supply, and they manifested none of that rudeness which is so often met among city boys. We passed a barren spot of country, but were soon repaid by here and there a rich domain, tenanted by some grasping landlord, who kept the poor about him cringing for a day's work at sixpence or eightpence a day. A Protestant gentleman joined the lady on the other side of the car; he was a talking noviciate, just entered upon his charge. He left in a few miles, and a Roman Catholic clergyman, grave in demeanour, supplied his place. The young lady had the exclusive privilege of both, and my little, civil, and profitable companions left the car at the beautiful town of Castlecomer.[3]

We reached Kilkenny, and the young lady left the car without bidding me a cold good-bye. In a moment she returned with the lady of the house, who in a most pleasant manner said, "Come in, you are an American stranger; come in, and take tea with us, and I will send a servant with you to your lodgings." Joyfully I accepted the offer, and found within a well ordered tastefully arranged house, and the mistress a highly accomplished widow, who had been reared in affluence, educated in the best manner, and was then engaged in teaching. The piano and the harp, the ancient boast of Ireland's better days, were there, and the lady, who had been educated in a convent, knew well how to touch the heart by her melody. Her two little daughters, who were but children, did honour to her who had trained them with a skilful hand. Never had I seen high birth, beauty, and noble intellectual attainments more happily blended with a meek and quiet spirit than in this accomplished woman. Though she was a Roman Catholic, yet the higher class of Protestants were anxious to place their daughters under her care; with this proviso, that a Protestant clergyman should visit there weekly, and give religious instruction; and that each day, when prayers were read in the schoolroom, the Protestant children should retire.

The next day, as I entered the parlour, the young Protestants were passing in, while the Catholics were praying above – a very accommodating arrangement to keep both religions from contamination.

Being obliged to leave that day, I can say little of Kilkenny, only that the streets were narrow, and the beggars as saucy as elsewhere, demanding a penny after a positive refusal.[4] The coachman and waiters were more rapacious than any I had seen; one positively demanded payment for opening the lid of the coach-boot, and dropping in a small carpet bag. Six beggars accosted me at once, passing five other persons who were on the car, till my patience was exchanged for disgust. What a disgraceful state of things, that a body of people should become public nuisances, when there has been no famine nor pestilence in the land, and where the rich soil might well reward the husbandman, if the government were suited to its condition.

We set off for Urlingford with a car so loaded, that none but Irishmen would have suffered the inconvenience patiently. I was going to Urling-ford to visit the parents of nine servant girls who had lived with me in New York, all from one parish, though of different families; and when within five miles of the place, I asked the driver if he knew a widow of the name of —.[5] A commonly dressed man, seated on the luggage above my head, stooped down and whispered, "Are you not Mary H's mistress?" I answered in the affirmative, and he made such an outcry that coachman and passengers entreated to know what could bewitch the man. He alarmed me, he shook me, and called me all manner of good names, regretting that he was a teetotaller, that he could not "trate" me, that the parish had looked for me till their hearts were broke. His volubility never ceased till we reached Johnstown, where the car left us, leaving a walk of more than two miles, to my destination. Here a raspberry cordial was pre-sented to me, and we passed through the little village, followed by men, women, and children, who were all told by my gallant, that I was Mary H's mistress. Each one proffered the hand, saying, "Welcome, welcome to Ire-land." We entered the house of a man calling himself a doctor, who showed us to a beautiful garden, when he whispered in the ear of my friend, that he wished the privilege of removing a wart from my face.[6] I supposed some of his medicinal herbs were to be the medicine. I declined for the present, when he assured me it was by saying a few words over the wart that he could remove it, my guide testifying that he had known many a cure in the same way. I begged the miracle might be deferred till I could again, and he then insisted I should wait and be sent in his car. Assuring him the walk would be pleasant, we passed out, and were invited into a smoky cabin, and I went through the etceteras of an Irish welcome. The doctor's car arrived, and proved to be a dray, with a peat-kish upon it. To me it was a curiosity. I had seen the country-women returning from sell-ing peat, cowering in one of these vehicles, but never expected to be so elevated myself; but elevated I was, sitting upon the bottom, my back to the horse, and my companion in like condition by my side.[7]

And now began my cabin life. I had read with the deepest interest, in the writings of Charlotte Elizabeth, that the peasantry of the county of Kilkenny were unrivalled in kindness; but burning words from graphic pens would faintly delineate what I there experienced from that interesting people.[8]

We reached our destination, and alighting from the kish, I was told, for the honour of the spot, that here, some two hundred years ago, lived a noble lord who had twenty noble sons. With these he daily rode out, with each an attendant, on twenty noble horses, all shod with silver shoes. I was desired to stay outside till the way should be prepared for my reception. In a moment I was ushered in as a "fine gal he had found in Kilkenny." The family were sitting at their supper of potatoes and buttermilk, around a naked deal table, upon which the potatoes were poured. The widow, two grown-up sons, and a grandson, constituted the group; and when I was seated, all for a moment were silent. "This is Mary's mistress," said my companion. Simultaneously every potato was dropped, all rose, and with a kind of unaffected dignity reached me the hand, saying, "Welcome to our cabin!" They then sat down and all was silent again. "We've been long waitin' for ye," said the mother, "and was in dread that ye might be lost; but ye must be wairy and in want of the tay." I assured her that a potato would be a greater relish. "Ye can't ate the potato," said she, the sons joining in the assertion, till by actual experiment. I soon convinced them to the contrary. The reader should be informed that the daughter of this widow had, in three years' service at my house, sent home £40, which had not only kept her mother in tea and bread, but had given them all the "blessed tobacco" beside. "She had been home," the old woman told me, "on a visit, and made such an overturnin' in the cabin that they had like to be destroyed; not a ha'p'orth of a pig, duck, or hen, could take it's bit in the place; not a straw could be left upon the flure in the mornin' and now," she added, "we will all be kilt if ye have not a clane bed and a nice bit to ate." To do her justice, her place was cleanly, although two comely pigs that were fattening for the fair, and a goodly number of turkeys and ducks, took their repast in the cabin on the remains of the supper.

My bedstead was behind the cupboard, in the kitchen, meeting the wall on one side and the cupboard on the other, with a little aperture at the head for an entrance. This was the widow's bed-room, and here, upon a soft feather bed, I was put; but the sheet, – a married daughter had taken her clothes to wash, and she must put me in one she had used herself. She was greatly troubled. Giving her all the comfort in my power on the subject, she bade me good night; and though I would not wish the reader ever to be packed in feathers in such a narrow box in a hot August night, yet I am not unwilling that he should know that my first night in a cabin, with all its concomitants, was a sleepless one, and one which can never be forgotten. The dawning of light found the good woman stealthily peeping around the cupboard, and with a shake of the head, I heard her whisper, "Ah! she didn't lie down in her bed, the cratur." She crept to the hearth, made her peat-fire, swept every vestige of dirt from the earthen floor, and sat down to smoke. Her sons soon joined her, each in his turn taking a "blast at the pipe," and then walked slowly out, "for," said the mother, "she's wairy, and a fut of ye mustn't be movin'." That day was a memorable one. In this parish lived a young married girl who had been a servant in my house in New York, she had returned and was living a mile distant; she had been aroused at midnight by the men who conducted me to the parish, and early the next morning she was at the door. Anne was young, handsome, and tidy, and had been a great favourite in my house. I was a little concealed when she entered, and did not recognise her till she fell on my neck and wept. "Ah! and it's ye that may bawl, when yer two eyes meet the one that took you a slip, and made ye the thriftiest woman for the man that owns ye in all the parish." Anne spoke not, nor could she for some time. "And do I see you? and what can we do for you in this humble place? John is waiting to see you, but would not come with me, till I had seen you first." "Ah! and John's the lad that's caught the clane bird." "What shall we do for you?" was again the question. "You cannot stay in our cabins; they are not fitting; you must come with me; I know best what you want, and will get what you say." The whole parish was now in a stir, work was suspended, and a general levee held. They talked of building bonfires; they talked of uniting and buying a sheep to kill, though not one had eaten a dinner of flesh since Christmas. The grey-headed and the little child were there to welcome me, to thank me for "thinking of the like of such poor bodies," and from some miles around visitors called before the setting of the sun to look at the American stranger, and bid her God speed. "What will she ate, the cratur? it's not the potato that raired her." Two children begged the honour of going seven miles in quest of fruit, and went. Night and rain overtook them, yet they persevered, slept away through the night, and cheerfully returned the next day with two pears and a spoonful of blackberries, which was all they could procure. All went away sorrowful that so "nice a body should be so trated," and all asked me to visit their cabins, "though they were not fittin' for such a lady."

The next morning Anne again called to invite me to her house, and to say she had been sent by a few in the parish, to invite me to attend a field dance which was to be on the next day, and the Sabbath. In surprise I was about to answer, when Anne said, "I knew you would not, and told them so, but they begged I would say that they had no other day, as all were at work, and sure God wouldn't be hard upon 'em, when they had no other time, and could do nothing else for the stranger." I thanked them heartily for their kind feelings, and declined. Judge my confusion, when about sunset on Sabbath evening, just after returning from Johnstown, where I had attended church, the cabin door opened, and a crowd of all ages walked in, decently attired for the day, and without the usual welcomes or any apology, the hero who first introduced me seated himself at my side, took out his flute, wet his fingers, saying, "This is for you, Mrs. N. and what will you have?" A company were arranged for the dance, and so confounded was I that my only answer was, "I cannot tell." He struck up an Irish air, and the dance began. I had nothing to say, taken by surprise as I was; my only strength was to sit still.[9]

This dance finished, the eldest son of my hostess advanced, made a low bow, and invited me to lead the next dance. I looked on his glossy black slippers, his blue stockings snugly fitted up to the knee, his corduroys above them, his blue coat and brass buttons, and had no reason to hope that, at my age of nearly half a century, I could ever expect another like offer. However, I was not urged to accept it. Improper as it might appear, it was done as a civility, which, as a guest in his mother's house and a stranger, he thought, and all thought (as I was afterwards told) he owed me. The cabin was too small to contain the three score and ten who had assembled, and with one simultaneous movement, without speaking, all rushed out, bearing me along, and placed me upon a cart before the door, the player at my right hand. And then a dance began, which, to say nothing of the day, was to me of no ordinary kind. Not a laugh – not a loud word was heard; no affected airs, which the young are prone to assume; but as soberly as though they were in a funeral procession, they danced for an hour, wholly for my amusement, and for my welcome. Then each approached, gave me the hand, bade me God speed, leaped over the stile, and in stillness walked away. It was a true and hearty Irish welcome, in which the aged as well as the young participated. A matron of sixty, of the Protestant faith, was holding by the hand a grandchild of seven years, and standing by the cart where I stood; and she asked when they had retired, if I did not enjoy it? "What are these wonderful people?" was my reply. I had never seen the like.

I visited the dwelling of Anne, and found her with many little comforts not common to her class. "Why do you not wear a bonnet?" I enquired. "I came back," she replied, "from New York to live in a cabin, and I must not put myself above others who associate with me." John was industrious and thrifty, and proud of a visit from the mistress of the girl who had come from the other side of the waters. Twice while in the parish a cleanly-dressed woman called to see me, but did not invite me to her cabin, because, she said, she would be ashamed to do so, though she really wished me to go. I was told of it, and the third time she called, I asked if I might accompany her home. She was delighted, and said, "I was in dread to ask ye, but was ashamed." Her cabin was perfect neatness. At night, under pretence of getting a bucket of water at a distant spring, she walked an Irish mile to buy a penny roll of coarse bread for me – a loaf of bread she had not seen in her cabin that summer. Slipping it into my hand, she said, "Don't let William know it, or I must tell where I got the penny." I called at the humblest place I had ever seen one morning, and found a poor widow and her daughter eating their potatoes. I went out, and soon reached a running stream so deep that I could not cross without wading. While I hesitated what to do, the widow called after me, "Stop, lady, and I'll carry ye on my back, ye'll be destroyed." She had pulled off her shoes and stockings in her hut, and ran after me, and though small in stature, yet she assured me she was "strong, and sure on the fut," – and could carry me safely. I positively refused such a compliment from grey hairs, and with great difficulty turned her back, and went myself in another direction.

A sister of Anne's was about setting off for New York to look for service. Two brothers and two sisters had previously gone there, and succeeded well. She was to go with three others at ten o'clock in the evening, for Dublin. The time arrived, and the whole parish, young men and maidens, aged men and children, had assembled. For an hour previous all was silent. The hour drew near, the girl arose, flung herself upon the neck of a young companion, and gave a most piteous howl. It was reciprocated by the other, who cried, "Aw, Kitty, will ye crass the wide ocean, and will we never again dance in the field? O my darlin, my comrade, and why will ye go? O oh! and what will we do?"[10] Kisses and sobs suppressed further utterance. The aged mother then approached. "O mavourneen, and why do ye break the heart of her who raired ye? Was there no turf in the bog – no pratees in the pit – that ye leave the hairth of yer poor ould mother? O my darlin', my only vourneen, and it's nine of ye I've raired, and as soon as yer heels are out of the ashes, ye run away from me, my darlin'. And what will ye do in the wilds of America?" She clapped her hands, and

cried, "My darlin', my fair-hair'd darlin', and was it for this I raired ye?"
The howling now became louder, one after another arose, and united in
the lamentation. Then a man from the midst cried out, "And be gone
from the house, and stop your bawlin'; ye go to sarve yourselves, and why
do ye bawl about the thing that's yer own choosin'?" He elevated a stick
he had in his hand, and made a signal towards the door. All rushed forth,
following the girls to the car, and the burst was more violent – the welkin
resounded with howlings, while the mother sat down in the corner upon
a bench, clapping her hands, rocking her body, and muttering, "O, aw, my
fair-hair'd little girl, and why did I say ye might go? Ah, fool that I was,
and these ould eyes will never see ye again. Ye'r gone, my girl,
mavourneen, my darlin'."

An invitation had been sent me from Urlingford to visit a family of
respectability, a son of which was in New York. This invitation introduced
me to the families of the gentry, some of whom I found intelligent, and
all hospitable and well bred.[11] In the family of a flourishing shop-keeper I
passed many pleasant and profitable days. The man had thought of many
things besides selling broadcloths and muslins, though he had made quite
a fortune by that. They were Roman Catholics; unwavering in their opinions, but not illiberal to those who differed from them. A bible was in the
house, and presented to me whenever I might wish to use it. I was present more than once when the family were assembled at evening for
prayers, and they kindly said, "We will not ask you into the room, as it
might be unpleasant; we wish every person to enjoy his religion in his own
way."

In this family I attended a wake, the first I had seen in Ireland. An
aged woman, the mother of the shopkeeper, died while I was there; ninety
years had whitened her locks; she had been a useful mother, trained her
children to habits of industry, and lived to see them thriving in business,
and respected in the world. On her tongue had been the law of kindness,
and her hands were always stretched out to the poor and needy. When I
visited the house of her son, feeble as she was, she would leave her chamber, and go into the kitchen to take care that my dinner was suited to my
taste. The workmen in the house were her peculiar care. From many miles
round the rich and the poor assembled. "Never," said one, "when I was a
slip of a boy, did I go on a mornin' to buy the loaf at her shop, but she put
a bit of bread in my hand to ate on my way home." She was laid in an
upper chamber, upon a bed covered with white; she was dressed in a dark
brown frock, with white ruffles at the wrist; a square cloth fringed with
white was on her breast, with the initials of the order of the "Blessed Vir-

gin," to which she belonged. A neat white cap, with black ribbon, and a white handkerchief about her neck finished the dress. Curtains of white, tied with black ribbons, were about her bed; and the usual appendages of candles and consecrated clay were at the foot, with a picture of the Virgin and Child hanging over her head.

The house was large; every room was occupied, and though the attendants were gathering from neighbouring parishes through the night, yet all was stillness. "In former days," whispered an aged matron, "ye would not see it so; before Father Mathew put down the whiskey, it would frighten the life of ye. A bucket of whiskey would be on the flure, with a cup in it, and not a sowl on 'em but would take the sup till their brain would be crack'd, and then the singin', the jumpin', and tearin', till the priest would be called in with his whip, and bate 'em, the divils, till they all was quiet." Here was no liquor, but cordials; a warm supper in the different rooms was prepared, and every new guest was invited to sit down and partake. Here the rich and the poor had "met together" to mingle their tears, and not an untidy garment pained the eye. The hour of burial was six in the morning. At five, a breakfast of steak, ham, and fowl was provided for the nearer friends, and those who were to accompany the corpse seven miles, where it was to be interred. The corpse was then put into a coffin of black, with the consecrated clay about it, and was placed upon the bed; the family came in, and gave her the parting kiss; one servant, who had been a labourer about the premises for years, went to the coffin, looked at her for a moment, kissed her, then covered his face with both hands, and burst into loud weeping. "Well may he cry, poor Pat," said a servant girl, "for many a good bit has he had from her hand; and when I come to the side of her bed a few days ago, she said, 'Do take care of poor Pat, and see that he has enough to eat. I am afraid he will be neglected when I am gone.'" Poor Pat was simple. These testimonials of kindness to the poor are precious mementos of the dead, and will be held in sweet remembrance, while the memory of the oppressor shall rot.

The white linen was taken from about the bed, pinned over the heads of the old women, and tied in the middle of their backs by black ribbon; the coffin was placed upon the body of a carriage, and the two old women were seated upon it. The driver, with a band of white linen about his hat, led on the long procession. It was a Sabbath morning; the sun was rising; I thought of the sepulchre; I thought of the women that were early there; I saw the stone that was rolled away; I looked in; I saw the clean linen in which Joseph had wrapped the body: I knew the Saviour had risen, and I turned away to think of the wake at Kilkenny.

Saturday evening. – After having paid an agreeable visit in the vicinity, I started by moonlight on a car for Urlingford, accompanied by a faithful servant girl, to guide the horse.[12] I sat with my back towards the animal; for this is the way of riding on a "common car." When within a mile of the town, we heard music, and supposed it to be one of the Temperance bands with which the country abounds. But on coming nearer, we saw a motley company of men and women, with spades and baskets, some on foot and some on the cars, following the sound of fife, flute, and drum; and upon enquiry we found it was "the faction."

The custom of the peasantry, in this part at least of the country, has been to assemble in hundreds, and reap down a harvest, or dig a farmer's potatoes, taking their musicians with them, who play through the day to amuse the labourers, and escort them home at night. This they never do but for those whom they respect, and the generous farmer who has fed and paid his labourers well, is sure to meet with a return of this kind. Women will go out and bind sheaves, rake, and toss hay, pick up potatoes, &c.; and the sight to a stranger is not only novel, but pleasing. The ambition manifested to accomplish much, and to do it well, is often beyond that of a paid labourer, and the hilarity over their dinner and supper of potatoes, and butter, and "sup of milk," is to a generous mind a pleasant sight; for, drunk or sober, rich or poor, it is the Irishman's character to remember a kindness, and to do what he can to repay it. We passed this interesting company, listening to their music till it died away in the distance; and though I knew they were going home to lie down in floorless cabins, with no prospect of better days, yet for the moment I saw more to envy than to pity; for these people are so happy with little, and make so much from nothing, that you often find them enjoying when others would be repining.

I had seen a dance, a wake, and a faction, but had never seen a fair; and being invited to occupy a seat in a chamber at Urlingford, which overlooked the field of action, I did so.[13] "You'll not see such fun, ma'am, now," said my companion, "as you would have seen before the days of Father Mathew. Then we had a power of bloody noses, broken bones, and fine work for the police; but ye'll see fine cattle, and fat pigs; and maybe it's the bagpipes ye'd like."

By ten o'clock all was in motion, and fatter cattle, finer pigs, fowls, and butter (none of which could the peasant ever enjoy) never adorned a fair. The first interesting object which closely fixed my attention was a rosy-cheeked, short, plump girl of about twenty, perched upon a stand, crying like an auctioneer, "Come, boys, here's the chance; only a ha'penny!

Come now while it's a goin'; try your luck." What this luck could be I could not make out; the ha'pennies were continually pouring in, but what was the equivalent was not explained till all was over. She had a lottery-bag, containing all sorts of trifles, their names written on tickets, such as pins, needles, combs, tapes, ribbons, thread, &c. The purchaser drew a ticket from the bag, and might find perhaps a great pin, a needle, or a bit of tape; now and then the anxious eyes of the expectant might greet an article of value twice worth of his ha'penny, while many went away with sorrowful hearts. It was said her lottery-bag at night was an exulting remuneration for her day's exertion, the cost of all that it contained in the morning being but very trifling. A ludicrous lesson of unlettered human nature was displayed by a company of tinkers selling asses. To recommend his own, to lower the value of his neighbour's, and to be heard above the rest, is the struggle of every dealer in these commodities. To accomplish these desirable objects, it must not be supposed that the forms of eti-quette would be strictly regarded, and sometimes a box on the ear or the cheek, and a pulling of caps, if not of hair, among the women (for the wives of these operatives are on the spot also), make up a ludicrous vari-ety. The dress and dialect, the development of self, the spontaneous wit, with the humble appearance of the uncomplaining donkey, make the scene to an unaccustomed eye one of amusing interest.

One matron was this day carried from the field by the police. Leaving my eminence, I mingled in the group, hoping to be unobserved; but the good cabin woman, Mary's mother, found me out, and invited me into a house. I soon found Father Mathew was not there, for a young female was dealing out "the good creature" to a happy company; bagpipes were play-ing in the street door, and a jolly group were keeping time overhead by loud stamping. I was invited into a back apartment, where sat a company of men and women at the upper end of the table, with bread, tea, and whiskey before them, and a huge hog, dressed for the market, swinging to and fro over the lower end. "Welcome, welcome to Ireland!" came from every mouth, accompanied by a bowl of tea from a man, and a glass of whiskey from a woman. This finished the Urlingford fair; and turning away, I left the room without either tea or whiskey.

The fair, as a whole, was not censurable; never on any public day in any country had I heard so little profanity and noise, or seen so little disorder and disputing, the tinkers excepted. The peasants, too, were tidily dressed, and with great uniformity; the men in blue coats, corduroy breeches, and blue stockings; whilst a blue petticoat, with a printed dress turned back and pinned behind, coarse shoes, and blue or black stockings (when they have shoes) a blue cloak, with a hood to put over the head, in case of rain, constitute the dress of the women; and thus attired, a Kilkenny peasant seeks no change in storm or sunshine. The habits of cooking and eating have scarcely varied for two centuries; their cabins, their furniture, have undergone little or no change; the thatched roofs, the ground floor, the little window, the stone or mud wall, the peat fire, the clay chimney, the wooden stool, the pot, and the griddle, have probably been the inheritance of many generations. As to cleanliness, their habits are varied, as with all other people; and if few are scrupulously tidy, few are disgustingly filthy. Though every peasant in the Emerald Isle knows that he belongs to the "lower order" (for his teachers and landlords are fond of telling him so), the Kilkenny rustic, by his self-possessed manner in presence of his superior, says, "I also am a man;" and you do not see that cringing servility; you do not hear "yer honour," "yer reverence," "my lord," and "my lady" so frequently as among many of their class in other parts of Ireland. They are not so wretchedly poor as many; for though few can afford the "mate," except at Christmas or Easter, yet most of them can purchase an occasional loaf, and "the sup of tay," and all can, and all do, by "hook or by crook," get the "blessed tobacco." They are fond of dancing, and a child is taught it in his first lessons of walking. The bag-pipes and fiddle are ever at their feasts, especially the latter; and the blind performer always receives a cordial "God bless you." The sweet harp has long since lost her strings, except perhaps in some ancient family, and there it is nursed as some valued plant, and kept as a memento of ancient Tara's halls. The generation that is passing away have but little education; many of them cannot read, but the children are rapidly advancing. The national schools are doing much good. One which I visited in Urlingford gave the best specimen of reading I ever heard in any country.[14] A class of boys read a chapter on the nature of the atmosphere; the teacher then requested them to give a specimen of synonymous reading. This was readily done, by dropping every noun, in the course of the lesson, and giving a corresponding one of the same import. It was so happily executed, that the listener would not imagine but the word was read out of the book. I was handed a book, and was requested to select a chapter where I pleased. I did so, and in no case did a pupil hesitate to read fluently. Their specimens of writing were praiseworthy, and their knowledge of arithmetic in all the schools is beyond what I could expect.

CHAPTER VI

Cabin Life – Urlingford Spa – Rebuff from a Clergyman – New Birmingham Colliery – Village of Grange – The Police – A Good Methodist – Mr. Barker of Kilcooley – Yankee Doodle – Residence in the Neighbourhood – Visit to Thurles – Ancient Abbey of Holy Cross – Journey to Clonmel, Dungarvan, and Cappoquin – Visit to the Trappist Monastery of Mount Mellary

The habits of cabin life and cabin hospitality have so much sameness, that the specimen which follows may answer for the whole.

I had walked much through the day, and about seven in the evening reached the cabin of a woman whose daughter had been a servant in my house in New York. My reception was most cordial. In a corner, where a bed might have stood, was a huge bank of turf, and a pile of straw for the pigs. There was but one room beside, and the family consisted of some five or six individuals. The cabin door being open, the pigs, geese, ducks, hens, and dogs walked in and out at option.

After the usual salutations, the girl was bidden to go out and dig some potatoes; the pot was hung over the fire, the potatoes were boiled, the table was removed into the adjoining room, and a touch from the finger of the matron was the signal for me to follow her into supper. On a naked deal table stood a plate of potatoes and a mug of milk, of which I was invited to partake. The potatoes must be eaten from the hand, without knife, fork, or plate; and the milk taken in sups from the mug. I made no delay, but applied my nails to divesting the potato of its coat, and my hostess urged the frequent use of the milk, saying, "it was provided on purpose for you, and you must take it." It must be remembered that sup of sweet milk among the poor in Ireland, is as much a rarity and a luxury as a slice of plum-pudding in a farm-house in America. I ate plentifully, both from hunger and courtesy, and we then returned to the kitchen.

The good man of the house soon entered, and gave me as hearty a welcome as an Irishman could give; and the neighbouring women and children gathered in, till the pile of turf and every stool was occupied. A cheerful peat fire was burning upon the hearth; the children were snugly cowered in each corner; two large pigs walked in, and adjusted their nest upon the straw; two or three straggling hens were about the room, which the woman caught, and raising the broken lid of a chest in one end of the apartment, she put them in; the dog was bidden to drive out the geese; the door was shut, and the man then turning to me, said, "You see how these pigs know their place, and when it's a little cowld not a ha'p'orth of 'em will stay out of doors; and we always keep a handful of straw in that corner for their bed." The company seemed quite inclined to stay; but the good woman, looking well to my comfort, called me at an early hour to the next room, and pointing to a bed which had been erected for my accommodation, said, "This troop here would be talking all night; ye must be tired, and see what I've got for ye." This was a bed fixed upon chairs, and made so wide that two could occupy it; and she assured me that so glad was she to see me, that she would sleep in a part of it by my side. It was certainly an extra extension of civility to leave the good man, who, by the way, had two daughters and a son of sixteen to sleep under the same covering, and in the same room with us. His bed was made of a bundle or two of straw spread upon rough sticks, and a decent woollen covering put over it. My bed, so far as sheets were concerned, was certainly clean, and in a few moments the kind woman and her husband and children were quietly laid to rest for the night. When all was still, a half hour of profitable reflection prepared me for a sweet night of rest.

In my own native land I had slept under rich canopies, in stately mansions of the rich, in the plain, wholesome dwelling of the thrifty farmer, the log-cabin of the poor, and under tents on the hunting-ground of the Indian, but never had I been placed where poverty, novelty, and kindness were so happily blended. I fell asleep, nor did the barking of a dog, the squealing of a pig, or the breathing of man, woman, or child arouse me, till I heard, at sun-rising, "Well, Maggie, how are ye this mornin'? D'ye know I was lonesome without ye." "God be praised," responded the good woman, "and I hope ye are well, Johnny." I looked into the Castle at Windsor, where Prince Albert, Victoria, and the young princes were reclining, and I very much queried whether their feelings were more kindly or more happy this morning, than were those of these unsophisticated peasants.

Now for the breakfast. The good man and the children had eaten their potatoes before I left the bed-room; and when I went out, "Maggie," said the husband, "will ye do as I desired ye?" "To be sure I will," said Maggie, putting her cloak over her head, and going out. Giving me "God bless ye," and tendering his best thanks, he said, "I must go into town, and leave ye; God speed ye on yer journey, and bless ye, for coming to see the poor."

An hour passed before Maggie returned, for she had ditches to cross and hedges to pass, to get a piece of bread for the "American stranger." The table was spread with bread, butter, a cup of tea, and a sup of milk. The tea and butter I declined (as I do not use these articles), but the bread and sup of milk made me a comfortable breakfast.

When I had finished, and the women and children had called in from abroad, to say good-bye to the "American stranger," my kind hostess said, "I must show ye to the road, which will save ye a good bit; for I love ye as well as I do my own gal that sarved ye." The walk was long and somewhat difficult, but the kindness and cheerfulness of my good guide made it quite tolerable. After setting me in a straight course, she said, "And the good God bless ye, and speed ye on yer return to your own country, and bless ye well, the cratur! for comin' to see us."

Urlingford Spa is supposed to contain mineral qualities of a medicinal nature so efficacious, that for years it has been quite a resort for invalids from various parts of the country.[1] A brother of the good woman with whom I had first lodged, kept a house for the accommodation of visitors, and had invited me to visit them and pass the night. A four miles walk up a tedious hill made the sight of the thatched inn a welcome treat to my eyes.[2] The family consisted of the father and mother, three daughters, and a son or two, who all assured me they were "right glad to see me." But the house was so filled with company, that they had no room to put me in but the kitchen. "What must be done?" was the question. "Where must the cratur be put, and what would she ate?" I assured them that no delicacy or luxury was required, and a piece of bread and a couple of pears made me a comfortable meal; and the old man taking a hint from his spouse that the room was wanted, invited me to visit the Spa. A little stone enclosure, with a gate, secured the well from intruders. The water was running from a little pipe into a reservoir, and here had people of all nations resorted for more than a century; yet no bathing establishment had been provided, nor were any accommodations prepared for the visitor, except what a thatched cabin, with corresponding conveniences, could afford.

A dandy with whip and cap came driving up in a single gig, drawn by a prancing horse. Addressing in Irish the old woman who was attending at the water-pipe, they held a jovial chat. At length, taking out his watch, and saying, "I must be off; it's my dinner hour;" he whirled away: and as he turned to go, a young woman remarked to me, "He's a humorous fellow; he's always the same, as full of fun as ye see him now." I enquired who he was. She replied, "The priest of the parish – a Catholic, to be sure, ma'am."[3] "He seems to be very well fed," I remarked. "And why shouldn't he," was her reply, "when he has a large domain, and every thing in his house – money and attendants in plenty?" The old man now invited me to take a view of the country, from the top of an eminence which overlooked a valley that extended for many miles on either hand, whilst immense ranges of mountains, at a distance, surrounded the whole. The view was beautifully grand; the air was the purest and sweetest imaginable, and the fields of grain in every direction invited the sickle; the hawthorn hedges, cutting in fanciful sections the whole landscape, divided one kind from another in tasteful variety; while the white cattle, which now so much abound in Ireland, and the white thatched cottages of the peasant, were spotting hill and dale. We then descended, and entered the door of the good man, when a sister met us, saying, "I don't know where in the world, ma'am, we can put ye, for the rooms are all full." I felt the repulse keenly; for my long and fatiguing walk, and the lateness of the hour, made it look like an impossibility to proceed any farther. I sat down upon a stone at the gate, not knowing what next to do, when two stout Irishmen, who were lodgers in the house, kindly approached, saying, "Don't sit here, ma'am; walk in; surely there must be some place for a stranger." I refused, saying I could rest where I sat, as the family had informed me there was no room for me in the house. For a time the case looked desperate, for I had been previously told that every cabin was full, and it was quite too late to walk four miles to find a lodging. The old man and his wife now came, and stood in silence leaning upon the wall over the place where I was sitting, seeming to say, "I wish I could find a place for ye; for ye're a stranger."

At length the old man, seconded by his wife, said, "Come in, come in, and sit the kitchen; ye can't stay here; we're sorry we can't do better; we had hoped that some of our lodgers would have gone before ye come, for we wanted ye here." I followed them into their floorless kitchen. Sitting by a comfortable turf fire, I became drowsy; the two kind Irishmen were sitting in the room, and supposing me to be asleep, one said, "Poor thing! she must feel quair in a strange country alone. I wonder how her people would trate a stranger in her situation – would they trate her tenderly?" "Aw! to be sure they would," answered his friend; "the Americans have always showed great love for the Irish." "To be sure they have," answered the woman of the house. Thinking it time to awake, I enquired the time; it was late, and I had not been told that a lodging could be provided; and rising from my chair, I said, "I must seek some place to stop for the night." "And that ye won't," responded the woman, "we will do what we can." And her husband, with much decision, said, "Ye can't and shan't go." The question was thus settled, and a daughter was sent out to get a bed from a neighbour's, which she brought in upon her back, and adjusted upon chairs; and after a repast of some potatoes and salt, without knife or fork, I lay down in the kitchen in a clean bed, and not a being in all Ireland slept more sweetly than I, with my body-guard wrapped in her cloak on the floor at my side.

I arose refreshed, and after taking my breakfast of the same materials as the supper, I said good morning, and resumed my journey. A long walk down the hill led me near the extensive domain of a Protestant clergyman, on whom I had been requested to call, as a frank, intelligent man, who could give me information concerning Protestantism in the part of the country where he was located.[4] I had called the day before, and was told by a man servant that he had gone to Kilkenny with his wife, and would be back in the evening. "Call," said he, "in the morning, and he will be at home." The hall-door was open when I ascended the steps. A well-dressed lady crossed the hall without welcome or nod. I rang the bell, and the same servant appeared, saying, "The master has not returned." I hesitated, having no doubt that the person who crossed the hall was his wife; and descending to the next lower step, I leaned against the railing. The servant walked in, and in a moment the door was shut in a violent manner, and I walked away. He had a rich living, and read his prayers weekly to a flock of perhaps one in one hundred of the population of his parish.

My next visit was to the Colliery at New Birmingham.[5] At an early hour the vehicle was to set off on which I was to have a seat. This was a baker's cart, and I was perched on the top of the box, with no resting place for my feet but the back of the horse, which required some exertion for me to reach, as well as strength of nerve to keep them there. A brother of like occupation with my companion accompanied us, and as the carts passed the cabin, the inmates poured out, not only to see the "American stranger," but to admire the throne on which she was elevated. The merry driver did his duty in pointing out every object of curiosity on the road, as well as procuring me a welcome to Ireland from every man, woman, and child that we met, and an invitation to call on them on my return. One old man crossed a field to see me and invite me to his house, saying, "I have heard of ye, and I give ye a hearty welcome to our poor country." Promising all as I passed that I would call on my return, we moved slowly through the settlement. Reaching the foot of a hill, at the corner of a wall lay a female wrapped in a cloak. Approaching her, I uncovered her face; she looked slily upon me, and drew the cloak over her head, when the driver called out, "She will not speak to ye; she is a silly cratur, who sleeps out of doors, going where she pleases; and when the storm is strong, somebody gets her and locks her in; but she bawls so loud they can't keep her; she's innocent, and has lived so for years."

A few little neat houses now opened upon us in a village called Grainge, and the police (who are met all over this country, giving quite a relief to the eye), came out from the barracks, and gave me a hearty welcome.[6] "And did you come from America to see us – from that fine country? and when do you return? I want to go to that land. I wish I could go with ye." I asked, "Have you business enough to give you exercise?" "No indeed! Father Mathew has so changed every thing, that our profession is entirely needless in some parts of the country." "I wish I was in America, and so do we all," said another.

A company of labourers repairing the road now stopped as I approached. "And how much do you have for this work?" I enquired. "But a little entirely; scarcely enough to give us bread; and when do ye go back? I wish I was there." "And how much do you get a day?" "Eightpence, ma'am; and it's but a little of the time we get that." "And what do you eat?" "Eat! ma'am, we eat potatoes when we can get 'em", and right glad too we are to have 'em." "And have you no bread?" "Bread! ma'am. Faith! that we don't; if we can get a sup of milk once a day, or a little salt, it's all we look for." "And how can you live on such scanty fare?" "We can't die, plase God! and so we must live." "Are ye all teetotallers?" "Indeed we are; and have ye any in America? and are you one, ma'am?"[7] On my answering in the affirmative, and bidding them good morning, they all said, "God speed ye! God bless ye! and I wish I could go with ye."

These poor creatures, wherever I go, are truly objects of great compassion. They are subjected to a virtual slavery, which is but a step in advance of the condition of the American negro.[8]

I could not escape a house or cabin without being accosted, and I walked the distance of three miles up and down a hill with all sorts of company; some coming to meet me, and invite me in to rest, offering me a potato, or some milk; till at length a man was called in from the field by his daughter, to show me the colliers at the mines. The machinery was in operation, and the mines were eighty yards under ground, for the distance of three-quarters of a mile.

My letter of introduction was to Mr. Scanlan, a Local Methodist preacher, who acted as agent among the miners, and also as a kind of missionary. His good wife sent a little daughter to show me to his office. He received me kindly, explained the machinery, etc., and introduced me to the miners, who welcomed me heartily.

This agent was in appearance all that a Christian should be; unassuming, and full of that benevolence which does not exhaust itself by words and tears, but makes sacrifices of individual ease to promote the good of others. He possessed talents which would adorn a higher station than that of weighing coal and inspecting mines; but for a small salary he is spending his time, and truly "condescending to men of low estate," to do what must be done, and what few possessing his abilities would be willing to do. "Tell your mother," he said to his daughter, "that she must not let Mrs. N. leave us to-night." His wife willingly seconded the hospitable invitation, and my stay was protracted to two nights.

This mother acted as school-teacher to her children, who were seven in number, and appeared to be tractable pupils; they were instructed to fear God and keep his commandments, as the whole duty of man. I regretted leaving this family, who had made my stay so pleasant; and leaving them, too, buried in coal-pits, and deprived of the privilege of educating their children, or enjoying life more congenial to minds of their stamp.

I visited the house and pleasure-grounds of an estated gentleman near the mines.[9] The gardener kindly showed me the grounds of his master, presented me with such fruits and vegetables as he thought I liked, and introduced me to the dairy-maids, who showed me the Irish manner of making a kind of cream-cheese. This is done by putting the thick sour cream into a cloth, hanging it up till the thinner part has dropped from it, and then putting it into a hoop like a sieve, and pressing it down tightly. The house was elegant, the ottomans and stools covered with needle-work wrought by the hands of the mother and daughters. The servants spoke kindly of the master and mistress. It is quite pleasing to find, here and there, a landlord who sheds comparative comfort on his domestics and poor tenants, and gives them cause to bless rather than curse him in their hearts. "Here is a dispensary," said the housekeeper, "which the mistress keeps for the poor, and when any of the tenantry are sick, they are supplied with medicine gratis. The master keeps a hundred men and women in his employ, including miners, and pays them punctually the eightpence a day, beside granting them many extras, which greatly lighten the burdens of the poor."

I found but one thing to regret in the good family of the Methodist; two gentlemen called, and the kind woman, according to the usage of the country, presented her whiskey, not because she wished to do so, but because they wanted it. I begged her to renounce this wicked custom, and all who heard me acquiesced in the correctness of my principle, but thought that when taken in moderation the strong drink could do no possible hurt. One of the party was a Roman Catholic. He invited me to his house, and introduced me to his wife, who made me feel quite at home, and her four talented little sons wanted nothing but a little of Solomon's rod to make them an ornament to society.[10] Here I was entertained with Irish legends and tales, which lost none of their interest by the manner in which they were related.

The celebrated estate of Kilcooley has descended by hereditary title from the days of Cromwell, till it is now lodged in the hands of one who shares largely in the affections of all his tenants, especially the poor.[11] The wall surrounding his domain is said to be three miles in extent including a park containing upwards of three hundred deer, and a wild spot for rabbits. A church, and an ancient ivy-covered abbey of the most venerable appearance, adorn a part of it.

But the pleasure of walking over these delightful fields is enhanced by the knowledge that his tenants are made so happy by his kindness. To every widow he gives a pension of £12 a year; and to every person injuring himself in his employment, the same sum yearly, as long as the injury lasts. His mother was all kindness, and her dying injunction to him was, "To be good to the poor." His house has been burned, leaving nothing but the spacious wings uninjured. An elegant library was lost. His mother, whom he ardently loved, was buried in a vault on the premises; and his grief at her death was such that he left the domain for twelve months. He supports a dispensary for the poor, who resort to it twice a week, and receive medicine from a physician who is paid some sixty pounds a year for his attendance. I was introduced to the family of this physician, to see his daughter, who had been a resident in New York some six years, and hoped soon to return thither to her husband and child still living there. As I was seated, a little son of two years old, and born in America, stood near me. I asked his name; "Yankee Doodle, ma'am," was the prompt reply. This unexpected answer brought my country, with every national as well as social feeling to mind, and I clasped the sweet boy in my arms. Let not the reader laugh; he may yet be a stranger in a foreign land. This name the child gave himself, and insists upon retaining it. O! those dear little children! I hear their sweet voices still: "God bless ye, lady, welcome to our country," can never be forgotten. Nothing was neglected that could contribute to my comfort. If I begged them to take less trouble on my account, the daughter replied that she had lived in America, and had been a partaker of the hospitality there exercised towards strangers, and knew well the comforts there enjoyed; and that all which could be done for an American stranger was little enough. At first I supposed this extreme kindness must soon wear out. Not so; for months this house was my home, and the last hour I spent in it was if possible more friendly than the first.

While in this family, I attended the Protestant church on Mr. Barker's domain, and heard the curate read his prayers to a handful of parishioners, mostly youth and children. By the assistance of a rich uncle of his wife's, he can ride to church in a splendid carriage, which makes him tower quite above his little flock. His salary is £75 per annum.

My visit among this hospitable people had been protracted partly by inclination, and partly by unavoidable hindrances, until I had visited every house and cabin in the neighbourhood. I sometimes spent a day in a farm-house, cooking, in the American style, a pudding, cake, or pie, which to these bread-and-butter eaters was a perfect anomaly. My talents, I began to fear, were becoming too popular for my own interest, and at length I made myself ready to depart. "If you can stay," said the kind doctor, "don't leave us; my house shall be your home while you stay in Ireland; but if you must go, God speed you." It was then I felt the worth of kindness. I was going out, scarcely knowing where; unprotected in a strange land; and where should I meet with such kind voices, and such hearty welcomes again? Hardly could my tongue utter one word of gratitude for all the kind offices shown me, and I gathered up my effects and myself upon the car, accompanied by the doctor's kind wife, who was going to convey me ten miles to Thurles, and introduce me to her sister residing there.

The morning was pleasant, and had not my heart been a little sad, it would have been congenial to every feeling of my mind, so naturally fitted for the enjoyment of rich scenery in nature.

Thurles is an ancient town in the county of Tipperary, somewhat neatly built.[12] It contains a good market-house, fine chapel, college for Catholics, nunnery, and charity school, with a Protestant church, and Methodist chapel. My reception here was cordial, and the house quite in American taste. My stay was continued a day or two longer than I at first intended; and as Tuesday was market-day, it presented a favourable opportunity of seeing the peasantry, who appeared more cleanly and comfortable than those of many towns in Ireland, though much like Kilkenny. In company with Mrs. W—, and her sister, Mrs. Burke, I took a ride of three miles to visit Holy Cross.[13] On our way we passed a splendid estate, now owned by a gentleman who came into possession suddenly by the death of the former owner, for whom he acted as agent. Last Christmas they had been walking over the premises in company; on their return, the owner met with a fall, and was carried home to die in a few hours. It was found he had willed his great estate to this agent, who is much elated at his happy exaltation. Holy Cross was the most venerable curiosity I had yet seen in all Ireland. We ascended the winding steps, and looked forth upon the surrounding country, and the view told well for the taste of O'Brien, who reared this vast pile in 1076.[14] The fort containing the chapel is built in the form of a cross; the perpendicular part was that which we ascended. The architecture, the ornamental work, and the roofs of all the rooms displayed skill and taste. The apartments for the monks, the kitchen where their vegetable food was prepared, but still more, the place where repose so many of their dead were objects of deep interest. "Here," said the old woman who interpreted for us, "is the place of saints," pointing to the graves. "Here lie my husband and two children, and many a dark and hungry day have I seen since I laid 'em there." Some of the inscriptions on the monuments were so defaced, that they could not be decyphered, and the gravestones were so huddled upon one another, that it was quite a confused mass. Pieces of skulls and leg-bones lay among the dust which had lately been shovelled up; and as I gathered a handful, and gave them to the old woman, she said, "This cannot be helped. I pick 'em up and hide 'em when I see 'em, and that's all can be done; people will bury here, and it's been buried over for years, because you see, ma'am, it's the place of saints. People are brought many miles to be put here; the priests from all parts have been buried here, and here is the place to wake 'em," showing a place where the coffin, or rather body, was placed in a fixture of curiously wrought stone. The altars, though defaced, were not demolished; the basins cut out of the stones for the holy water were still entire; and though many a deformity had been made by breaking off pieces, as sacred relics, enough remains to show the traveller what was the grandeur of the Romish church in Ireland's early history.

The next evening I accompanied my kind Mrs. W— out of town, and felt, when she gave me her hand, and said, "Please God, I hope to see you again before I die," that I was parting with a real friend. I then returned to her sister's, who did all she could to make me comfortable. She was a Catholic, and her husband endeavoured to induce me to become one also, fearing I should lose my soul out of the true church; but his zeal was tempered with the greatest kindness.

When I was about leaving Thurles, Mrs. B— said, "You should see Mount Mellary before leaving Ireland." Enquiring what it might be, my curiosity was awakened by what I heard, to see it, and I resolved to take a car the next morning, and make my way thither, a distance of more than fifty English miles. I had hoped to stop at the Rock of Cashel, but was obliged for the present to content myself by seeing its lofty pinnacle. Perched upon the top of a rock, it has stood the ravages of centuries, looking out upon the world, and the city beneath its feet, which is now going fast to decay. Cashel looked more deserted this day than usual, as a rich brewer in the city, a brother of Father Mathew had died, and the shops were closed in honour of his funeral.[15]

When travelling by coaches and cars, I had been so much annoyed by the disgusting effluvia of tobacco, that I dreaded a "next stage," the changing of horses being the signal for a fresh lighting up. Seating myself upon the car at Cashel, my hap was to be stowed behind a rustic who had reloaded his pipe, and began puffing till my unlucky head was enveloped in a dense fog, a favourable wind wafting it in that direction. Knowing that the consumers of this commodity are not fastidiously civil, I forbore to complain, until I became sick. At length I ventured to say, "Kind sir, would you do me the favour to turn your face a little? Your tobacco has made me sick." Instantly he took the filthy machine from his mouth, and archly looking at me, "Maybe yer ladyship would take a blast or two at the pipe," resumed his puffing without changing his position. I was cured of asking favours.

Passing on from Cashel, a Roman Catholic priest seated himself upon the car, whom I found polite and intelligent. His first enquiries were concerning American slavery. Its principles and practices he abhorred, and he could not comprehend its existence in a republican government.[16] I blush for my country when, on every car, and at every party and lodging-house, this everlasting blot on America's boasted history is presented to my eyes. Even the illiterate labourer, who is leaning over his spade, and tells me of his eightpence a day, when I in pity exclaim, "How can you live? you could be better fed and paid in America," he often remarks, "Aw, you have slaves in America, and are they better fed and clothed?" My priest took his leave, and his seat was occupied by a deaf old man who was a sorry substitute; but a few hours carried us to Clonmel, a town neat in its appearance, containing about twenty thousand inhabitants, amongst whom are many Quakers.[17] Here some of the "White Quakers," a small body of "Come-outers" from the Quakers, formerly resided, but they have removed to Dublin. These people bitterly denounce others, but take liberties themselves under pretence of walking in the spirit, which by many would be considered quite indecorous. The men wear white hats, coats, and pantaloons of white woollen cloth, and shoes of undressed leather; the women likewise dress in white, to denote purity of life. Seeing a labourer digging a ditch under a wall, I asked him the price of his day's work. "A shilling, ma'am." "This is better than in Tipperary, sir." "But we don't have this but a little part of the year; the Quakers are very hard upon us here, ma'am; giving us work but a little time, and if a poor Irishman is found to be a little comfortable, they say, 'he has been robbing us.' The English, too, are expecting a war, and they want us to enlist, but the divil of an Irishman will they get to fight their battles.[18] O'Connell is not out of prison;" and stopping suddenly, leaning on his spade, "How kind America has been to us; we ought to be friends to her, and the Irish do love her." He grew quite enthusiastic on America's kindness and Britain's tyranny, dropped his spade, climbed the wall where I was standing, and expatiated on Ireland's woes and America's kindness till I was obliged to say "good-bye."

A new car and driver were now provided. These drivers are a terrible annoyance, with their "Rent, ma'am." "Rent! for what?" "For the driver, ma'am." "I will give you an order on Bianconi, sir."[19] I had been told that Bianconi paid his coachmen well, and forbade their annoying the passengers, but afterwards found that they receive from him but tenpence or a shilling a day, out of which they must board themselves. I was sorry I spoke so to the driver, and hope to learn better manners in future. I had now a solitary road to pass, and no fellow passenger but a police officer sitting on the opposite side of the car. Our route lay through defiles in the intricate windings of the Knockmealdown mountains, and had my faith been strong in giants, fairies, and hobgoblins, the dark recesses and caves in these mountains would have afforded ample food for imagination.

The sun came out from the dark pavilion in which he had been hidden through the day, to take a last look upon the eastern crags and lofty mountains he was about leaving. The stillness of death reigned, except when at long intervals the barking of some surly cur told that a miserable hovel was near. Then some barefooted mother, with a troop of besmeared and tattered children, would present us with undeniable proofs of Ireland's woes and degradation. Not a human voice was heard for many a long mile. Reaching across the car, I asked the police officer the name of the county. "I don't know, ma'am," was the reply, though he was then probably within the precincts of his own location, as he soon alighted from the car. The last light of day left us as we emerged from these romantic mountains, and entered the seaport town of Dungarvan. We proceeded onwards, and were joined by a company of pleasant young women, who, finding that I was a stranger, procured for me lodgings when we arrived at the town of Cappoquin. There was a gentleman from Clonmel, who had a son in New York, and who invited me to his house on my return, and the evening passed pleasantly with two or three talkative Irishmen, whose good nature when in exercise is always a compensation for every inconvenience. I was now in the region of romance, on the banks of the Blackwater, and three miles from the famous Mount Mellary. The following morning, in company with two countrywomen, an old lady and her daughter, I attempted to ascend the mountain. A dark deep ravine lies at the foot, the silence of which is broken only by the murmur of a little rill, which stealthily makes its way to the river that runs by the town. We were upon the ridge of the glen, picking blackberries, when a company of men with carts were passing, one called out, "Sure ye'd take a lift up the mountain; the way is long and tedious." A board from the back part of the cart was taken out, and the daughter was helped up with "Mickey," and the mother and myself with "Paddy." The aspiring steeple of the monastery now rose in full view; the cultivated garden, the extended lawns, and fields whose ripened corn had just been gathered by the hand of the reaper, were spread on each hand, and in front of the chapel. We reached the porter's lodge, some roods from the monastery, where we descended from our cars.[20] We saw a monk approaching, in his gown and cowl, and hoped he might be coming to meet us; but he passed in silence, not casting a look upon the prohibited article, *woman*, and entered the lodge. Reaching the monastery, we were met by men and women, some walking, some riding from the gate to depart, and a pleas-ant-looking monk approached, and beckoned us to follow. Giving him my card, he drew on his spectacles, and reading "New York," his countenance lighted up, and he broke silence, "Then you are from New York; and how long? And have ye left friends after ye? And did ye come to see Ireland?" repeating "America," as he led us into the garden, which was beautifully laid out as a place for ornament, and the burying ground. Twelve of their number are sleeping there, with a wooden cross at the head and foot of each. We were next introduced into a long hall, where were wooden pegs upon each side, bearing the robes used for the week day, and over each the name of the owner. A narrow passage led us a few steps lower into the chapel. This is imposing, for, contrary to my expectations, it was more grand than gorgeous. The richness and tasteful finish of the decorations were beautiful. The lofty ceiling, the pillars of imitation marble at each end of the altar, and a large stained-glass window behind it, which threw over the whole a light peculiarly grateful to the eye, had a happy effect. In the rere was the gallery for the choir and organ; the latter was a present from a gentleman in Dublin, who is now one of the brotherhood. It is an instrument of finished workmanship and tone. We were next shown into a long corridor, on the end of which is written "Silence." No monk or visitor is here allowed to speak. We passed three of these long walks in silence, and then the dining-room was opened. Here were tables placed for a family of ninety-seven, with a knife, fork, and spoon to each person, a piece of coarse bread wrapped in a clean cloth, and a tumbler for water by the side. No flesh, fish, eggs, or butter is eaten by the monks; and from September to the twenty-fifth of March, they take but one meal a day, except a collation four ounces of bread in the morning; the other months they take two meals a day. We were next shown the sleeping-room: this is on true philosophical principles – a spacious, clean room well ventilated, without a carpet, with a slight partition between each bed, leaving room for the free ingress of air, and a green worsted curtain before each door, elevated some inches from the floor. The beds are narrow, and made of straw, with a coarse covering. We were next seated in the guest's room, when a monk entered, to whom our guide introduced me as an American, and a friend to the Irish. He warmly welcomed me to the country, and set upon a table bread, butter, and wine. Learning that I took no butter, "What shall we get for you then?" said our guide, "you are worse than ourselves. Why should you live so?" Explaining my reasons, "Very good," was the answer. I assured them that I should make a good dinner on bread and an apple, which the kind lady had given me, and they left the room. The bread was made of what is called in England second flour, the bran taken off, and the corn ground coarsely; it was brown and very sweet, and my companions testified to the good quality of the butter; both were made by the hands of a monk.

When we had been left a suitable time to finish our repast, the guide returned, presenting a book to register our names.[21] We presented him with a piece of money, which we saw written over the door was requested to be given to any in attendance; he said to each of us, "Maybe you cannot consistently spare this; if so, we do not wish it." We assured him we were more than compensated. He then said, "Walk down," and showing us to a little room at the foot of the stairs, without asking us to sit, he introduced me as an American, enquiring, "Did you leave your native land alone to seek out the poor in Ireland?" Then turning to a brother, he said in an under-tone, "This is doing as Christ did. And," said he, addressing himself to me, "what, after all, do you think of Ireland? It is true she is a little island, but she has made a great noise in the world. She is, and has always been, poor in spirit, and struggling with poverty, and Christ has said the kingdom of heaven belongs to such." The being "poor in spirit" did not seem quite to the point, but leaving no time for argument, without apology, one after another presented the hand, saying, "Good morrow," and retired.[22] The guide took us out at the door, thanked us for coming, wished me a safe journey, showed us a shorter route over the mountain, and said, "Farewell."

As we looked back, and saw what a barren waste had been converted into a fruitful field by the hand of untiring industry, I felt an earnest desire to learn the history of this Herculean task; and at evening a member of the family where I lodged, who had been conversant with its history from the beginning, gave me the desired information.

These monks had been united with the brotherhood at La Trappe, in France, but had been banished thence. Those who were Irishmen returned to Ireland, in number about sixty, with but three shillings as all their earthly possessions. Some thirty pounds were collected, and sent to their relief the evening after their landing, and they soon fixed their eyes on this barren spot as the place for a future residence. Lord Kane, the owner of the mountain, offered six hundred acres, for a shilling a year per acre for twenty-one years; then, for half-a-crown an acre for ninety-nine years; and the lease to be renewed at the end of that term.[23] This being settled, the bounds were laid out, and the neighbouring priests invited their people to take spade and mattock, pick and shovel, and assist in making the wall. The day was appointed, the people assembled in crowds, each with his instrument of husbandry, and formed a procession at Cappoquin, with the monks at their head, carrying a cross. A band of music escorted them up the mountain, and the provisions and implements of cookery were carried on carts, the women following to cook the provisions. Thus commenced the wall, and so continued daily, the band going up at night to escort them down, and ascending with them in the morning. The mountain was then a rocky, sterile, unpromising spot, covered with heath, and, to any but the eyes of a monk, wholly impervious to cultivation. They built a temporary shelter when the wall was finished, and remained there, working with their own hands, till a fruitful harvest gladdened their toil, and the "desert rejoiced and blossomed as the rose."

In 1833, the corner-stone of the grand chapel was laid. Thousands from all parts of Ireland collected. The monks, dressed in their robes, performed high mass before a temporary altar, erected under a tent, and a multitude of seventy thousand united in the celebration. A sermon was preached by the bishop, and the corner-stone was laid. Under this stone were placed the different coins, from the sovereign to the farthing. On it was inscribed: –

Aug. 20th, 1838. Pope Pius VII, Sir Richard Kane, Baronet, and Lady Kane, patrons. Right Rev. Dr. Abraham, Roman Catholic Bishop of the Diocese of Waterford, the layer of the foundation-stone. Very Rev. Dr. M.V. Ryan, Prior of Mount Mellary Abbey.

The latter being the first abbot in Ireland since the Reformation. The foundation being laid, the work went on, till what now meets the wondering eye was completed. Not one of Eve's daughters has contaminated its purity, for the work is wholly performed by the monks, and the housekeeping does honour to the establishment; the cleanliness and the arrangements coinciding with those of the Shakers of America.[24]

They retire a quarter before eight, and rise at two, when the bell of the chapel is rung, and they perform private devotion till six; then mass is performed in the chapel, and each goes to his respective labour. Perfect silence is enjoined for certain hours of the day, when they make known their wants by signs. They have a mechanic's shop where tailors, cabinet-makers, saddlers, shoe-makers, carpenters, weavers, etc., perform their work; and likewise a printing-press. All the labour is performed by the monks. They have twenty cows, a good stock of horses, and sheep and fowls of all kinds; and though they eat no flesh themselves, they present it in all its varieties to those who visit them. So economical are they of time, that during meals, one stands in an elevated pulpit, reading and lecturing, that no time may be lost in idle words at table.

The following Sabbath I had appointed to visit and read to an old woman upon the mountain, and we heard a sermon in the chapel. The sight of nearly a hundred monks, dressed in priestly robes, with all the accompaniments of grandeur, cannot fail deeply to impress a credulous people. When the deep-toned organ was swelling upon my ear, when the incense was ascending, and the people bowing to the floor, a kind of awe fell upon me, as I thought of the days of the church's former greatness, and what she is still destined to be and to do. The subject of the sermon was that of the guests at the wedding taking the highest seat, and the preacher expatiated beautifully and scripturally upon the sin of pride, referring to Lucifer, Nebuchadnezzar, Belshazzar, and Herod.[25] He dwelt on the depravity of man, and his liability to fall, saying he had a dead soul in a living body, exhorted them to be faithful in the penance of confession, to ask Jesus to forgive them, and the Blessed Virgin to pray for them. He was in look, manner, and eloquence, one of the most finished specimens of public speakers I had ever heard. His dress was becoming, and his figure beautiful. The simple unostentatious pulpit was a narrow corridor, extending from side to side of the chapel, parallel with the gallery, with a railing upon each side, and not a seat of any kind to rest upon.

My young and intelligent guide, who was a Catholic, turned into a part of the monastery to light his pipe, and left me to make my way down the mountain alone.

CHAPTER VII

The spirit of Caste injurious in Ireland – Journey to Youghal – The Blessed Well of
St. Dagan – Cabin Hospitality – Uncourteous Reception by Sir Richard Musgrave
– Rebuff from a "great, good man"" – Rejoicing at Lismore for O'Connell's Liber-
ation – A Disaster – Brutality of an Inn-keeper's Son – Dungarvan – Two silent
Quakeresses – Thoughts on Irish Hospitality – Unsuccessful Application to Bian-
coni – Strong National Peculiarities of the Irish – Unpopularity of Stepmothers –
St. Patrick's Well – A Poor Old Woman – A Baptist Minister – Happy Molly

Of all the miseries entailed upon poor Ireland, that of "caste" is not the
least, and in some circumstances you may as well be a beggar at once, if
not a drop of high blood can be found in your veins, or if some title be
not appended to your name.

Report had said that England was taking the liberty to break the seals
of letters going from Ireland to America, and to retain such as did not suit
her views of matters relative to the country.[1] I had been in Ireland more
than three months, had paid postage on a package of letters, but had
received no answer, and was in much perplexity on account of it. When
about leaving Cappoquin, I was advised by the good man of the house
where I lodged, to call on Sir Richard Musgrave, who lived on his estate
a mile and a half distant, and would give me information respecting the
transmission of letters; adding, "He is condescending in manner, peculiarly kind of heart, a true friend of Ireland and O'Connell, and delights
in doing good to Catholics, though himself a Protestant."[2] All these qualifications were certainly something, and I reluctantly consented to call at
his house. I found that he was not at his country residence, but was
spending a few weeks on the sea-shore, at Whiting-Bay, eighteen miles
distant.[3] A steamer was about to start for Youghal, down the Blackwater,
and would take me fifteen miles on my way. The morning was a little dull,
but the sun at ten o'clock broke through the clouds, and lighted up such
a landscape as is impossible for me to describe, for Blackwater scenery is
Blackwater scenery, and nothing else.[4] It was not a cloudless state of mind
that caused this bright vision of things, for I was going against my own
inclination; but the reality so broke upon me at every new winding, that,
in spite of myself, I must admire if not enjoy. A preceding rain had given

a lively tint to tree and meadow, and nature appeared as in the freshness of a May morning, though September was well advanced, and the yellow hue, contrasted with the more sombre foliage of tree and hawthorn with which meadow and water were fringed, heightened the beauty of the scene. The cows and sheep were grazing upon hill and dale, and the song of the happy bird lent its notes of harmony. If for a moment the prospect was confined by a short turn in the river, the next a broad vista opened which displayed extended towns, rising cultivated hills, a stately mansion perched upon some shelving rock, and now and then a mutilated castle or abbey. Five ruined castles meet the eye in sailing fifteen miles upon this river, and though they speak loudly of the uncertainty of all human greatness and human hopes, yet they are a kind of pleasing proud memento to the heart of every Irishman, that his now oppressed country had once her men of cultivated tastes as well as of warlike feats.[5] When passing through the vale of Ovoca, I thought that nature could do no more than she had there done; but on the banks of the Blackwater she showed me that a bolder stroke of her pencil had been reserved for this outline. Let the traveller gaze upon the picture, and tell us, if he can, what is wanting.

At last the town of Youghal, with her noble bridge, met the eye.[6] The drawbridge was raised for the steamer to pass, and we saw the houses extended along the sea-shore, on the vicinity of a hill, commanding a noble prospect of the sea. The busy population in pursuit of gain by their bartering and bantering, told us that self here was an important item, though not a beggar put out her hand, invoking "the blessing of the Virgin" for your penny. A ferry-boat put me safely on the other side, leaving me a three miles walk, partly upon the beach, but mostly inland, and thus giving an opportunity of seeing a peasantry who speak English only when compelled by necessity. Making enquiry from cabin to cabin, not one bawled out, "Go along to such a place, and enquire;" but each one left her work, sometimes accompanied by two dogs and thrice the number of pigs, and led me a distance on the way, with a kind "God bless ye," at parting. A troop of boys now came galloping at full speed, intent, one might suppose, on sport or mischief. But each had a book under his arm or in his hand, and I saw they were returning from school, and saluting them kindly, they gathered around me, listened to the story of schools in America, and earnestly asked such questions as to them seemed important. At our parting, each was emulous to direct me my way, lest at the "cross-road" I should mistake. "Now, ma'am, don't you take the left;" "Nor don't ye go straight on," said a second, "but turn to the right," &c. And when, like so many young deer, they bounded away, I blessed God that the dawn

of education was breaking upon Ireland, and that the generation now rising shall feel its genial ray, and by her power have the independence to
assert their country's heaven-born rights.

But the great man was not yet reached, and I was weary with walking.
A little girl, with a heavy burden on her back, said, "And is it Sir Musgrave,
ma'am, ye would see? you should go up that road, ma'am, and the way is
much shorter." That road had long since been passed, but the girl added,
"Ye are on the road to the Blessed Well." "Blessed Well! what is that?" "I
don't know, ma'am, only people goes there to pray." This reconciled me a
little to the mistake of the path; and walking on, a clump of trees was
pointed out as the sacred place. There was something superstitiously
pleasant in the appearance and associations about this well.[7] It was eighteen hundred years ago since Jesus, "weary with his journey, sat down on
the well," and the woman of Samaria came out to draw water.[8] Here was a
spot where thousands had knelt, and drank, and gone away as dark as they
came; ignorantly supposing that some saint had sanctified its waters. As I
was musing, a young damsel like Rebecca old, with a large brown pitcher,
"came hither to draw."[9] She was "fair to look upon." I saluted her, she
answered pleasantly in Irish, and after filling her pitcher walked away.[10]
Never did that living water of which Jesus told the woman of Samaria look
more precious than now; never had I more ardently desired to tell a
benighted traveller "the way, the truth, and the life;" but I could not speak
her language, neither could I, like Jesus, have told her "all that ever she
did."[11] How many of these sincere devotees who come here to drink, have
ever tasted of the well of salvation, God alone must decide.

A large stone, with a wooden cross fixed in it, stands at the head of
this well, and a beautiful tree waves over the whole. St. Dagan, we are
told, blessed this water some hundred years ago; and so efficacious has it
been, that cripples, who came on crutches, have gone away leaping and
praising St. Dagan, and the blind have been made to see. So infatuated
have been its devotees, that the Bishop has thought it expedient to pro-
hibit its resort, as being a place where miracles are no more to be
expected. So unmindful was I of its healing virtues, that I actually turned
away without tasting its waters. Fearing I had gone astray, I made my way
to a cabin door through mud and filth; here a woman pointed me to the
house of the great man, and added, "Maybe ye are wairy, and would like to
sit down a bit." I gladly accepted the invitation, and followed my guide
into the small cabin. Here were two men sitting upon a table in a corner,
an old man smoking, and a wretched-looking woman, who like me was
weary with her journey, and had "turned in hither," and was sitting upon

the ground. In the centre of the room stood the dinner table, with the remains of the potatoes on which the family had been dining. A tub of potato-skins and water stood near the table, from which two huge matronly swine, and eleven young sucklings, were eating their dinner, and I, in return for the civility shown me, could do no less than extol the beauty of the little *bonnels*, and the fine bulk of the mother.[12] The mistress took a wooden bowl, mashed a few fine potatoes into it with her hands, and, adding milk, called a couple of more favoured ones, and fed them from it. Upon a cupboard stood a plate of tempting well-cooked potatoes, and I asked leave to take one. This was the signal for a fresh effusion of kindness, and the good woman left her pets to their own guidance, and selected with her hands one of the finest, divested it of its coat with her nails, and handed it to me. I was caught in my own trap, and was obliged to surrender; and before the first was masticated, a second was in readiness, and so on, till I was positively obliged to refuse the fourth, much to the grief of the good woman, who was "in dread" lest I should go away hungry.

"Sir Richard," said the old man, putting his pipe in his pocket, "will sartainly consider your case. He is a good man, and his wife is a kind woman." And now, with three fine potatoes in my stomach, and thrice the number of blessings on my head, I departed to the "great man's" abode. The sea was dashing against the gravelly beach at the front of the dwelling; an air of comfort was shed around; and when the porter responded to my knock, and had gone to present my card, I looked about the hall, and seeing no false appendages of greatness, and being soon invited into the parlour by the gentleman himself, I felt as much at ease as when eating my potatoes in the cabin. I introduced myself, and the object of my errand, while he peered at me over his spectacles, and seemed to listen with attention. He read my letter of introduction, and returned it without note or comment. I stated the exigencies of my case, as a stranger in a strange land, and asked if he could give any information as to whether the English government had really taken the liberty to open and retain letters. He looked silently upon me, with a gaze which seemed to say, "I wish this insignificant woman could finish her story, and let me return to my lunch." "I may be keeping you from dinner, sir." "I was taking lunch, madam; my dinner hour is five." "Do you know, sir, and will you tell me, whether you think this report true or false?" No answer: he took out his watch; I understood the signal, and rose to depart. "I can give you no advice on this subject." As I was going into the hall he said, "Maybe you would take something to eat." "I am not hungry, sir," replied I. My heart rejected this coldly proffered bread. Then did the cabin woman's potato look doubly valuable, and I blessed God that he had left some poor in the world, that every vestige of humanity and kind feeling might not be swept from the earth. The heart of a stranger was emphatically mine. I had travelled a distance of twenty miles for the privilege of being treated with the coldest indifference by a titled gentleman. Yet I was not sorry. I at least learned something. This man was celebrated for his urbanity of manners and kindness of heart; the well intentioned friends who advised me to apply to him were certain that he would solve my difficulties; and I had gone more in complaisance to their good feelings, than from a favourable opinion of the undertaking on my part. I had visited Ireland to see the poor, to learn its manners and customs, and how they would treat American strangers in any and every condition. I was placed in peculiar circumstances, and a few kind words, if they would not have helped me out of my dilemma, would have cost him but little, and have been grateful to me. But not even a generous look could be gained, and I hoped my friends would see that this boasting of the benevolence of great men is often but boasting, and whoever follows them to get good, will generally find himself in pursuit of an ignis fatuus, which perchance may land him in a quagmire.

The sail back upon the enchanting Blackwater was if possible more pleasant than in the morning. The setting sun cast a mellow light on tower, castle, ivied abbey, and tree; and the vesper song of the bird, seeking its shelter for the night, had a soothing effect upon my mind after my zig-zag pursuit of Irish aristocracy.

To atone for yesterday's adventure, the good people of the lodging-house advised a ramble to Lismore, as castles, bridges, and churches, besides "Lord Devonshire" himself, were all there. A plain-looking man offered his services as my guide, for Lismore was on his route home, and he knew every nook and corner "right well," and would show me all with the greatest pleasure. But we must take a circuitous road, and call on another "great and good man," who could not give an unkind look, for he was "made up of goodness." In vain I pleaded my excuses; my guide was a familiar acquaintance of the gentleman's, and could remove all impediments to an introduction, and I was obliged to yield. We went over gravelled walks, through rich lawns, and sheltered pathways, till behind a high wall we saw the numerous chimneys of this "great and good man." He was a Scotchman and a Presbyterian. A labourer on the top of the wall called out, "The master is at dinner, and cannot be seen." A nurse with a sweet infant in her arms was sitting upon a stile, and half an hour was beguiled in listening to the good qualities of both master and mistress, till the kind girl, eager to acquaint the hospitable woman that an American lady was without, hastened in, and I saw her no more. "The master is coming," said my guide, "and I will go and tell him who you are." He did so, and I was a mile on my way to Lismore, when he overtook me, muttering that the man had returned from giving orders to his men, and they went to the stile, and no American was there. I had stopped a full half hour for the hospitable mistress, who knew I was in waiting, and then went away. Not a cabin in all Ireland would have treated a stranger thus.

But leaving the "good and great man," let us walk to the pleasant town of Lismore.

When my guide had conducted me to the town, and showed me into the celebrated church, which in the days of the never-forgotten Cromwell was defaced, and taken possession of by the Protestants, he abruptly took leave, saying, "I have showed ye all I can."[13] I stood alone in the midst of that venerable pile, looking at its pictures and stained-glass windows, through which the setting sun shed a mellow light, throwing upon its walls a softened sadness, which, as the flickering rays died away, seemed to say, "The glory of Erin is departed."

The town was in high glee, for O'Connell was liberated.[14] One of the newspaper editors who had been imprisoned with him was there, and bonfires blazed in various places, their smoke giving to the tasteful little town the appearance of a reeking furnace. I hastened to the bridge, to look at the castle of the Duke of Devonshire. It is situated upon an elevated site, overlooking the romantic Blackwater.

Three miles and a half were before me, and night was gathering around. So absorbed was I in looking at the never-tiring beauties of the scenery, and so thick were the hedge-rows with tempting blackberries, that by the time the curtain of night had descended I found I had lost my spectacles! This was the ultimatum of all the vexations of yesterday's chase after a "sir," and to-day's hunt after a "great and good man." These spectacles were of superior excellence, were very expensive, and had been selected in New York as peculiarly suited for travelling. They brought every distant mountain and castle in bold relief before my eye, when riding in a car or coach. Now I found it was truly the "little foxes that spoil the vines."[15] I had become so enchanted with the almost supernatural beauties of Ireland, that no troubles could sit long on my heart while looking upon them; but now this consolation was gone. I sat down upon a stone to think what I should do next. I was in a thick wood, three miles from Cappoquin. The evening was still; the noise of joy and gladness fell upon my ear from the town, and I bent my steps towards it. The light from the bonfires and barrels of blazing tar, drawn by noisy boys, was glimmering through the trees. Ireland was rejoicing that O'Connell was free. "It's many a long day that we have been lookin' for that same to do somethin' for us, but not a ha'p'orth of good has come to a cratur of us yet. We're aitin the pratee to-day, and not a divil of us has got off the rag since he begun his discoorse," said a peasant woman near me, not scrupulously tidy in her apron or cap.[16] Making my way through the crowd, I reached the whiskey lodging-house. A hearty greeting from the good-humoured daughter, who was attending at the bar, was sullenly responded to by, "I've lost my spectacles." "And you've seen the good man, and the beautiful church of Lismore." "I've seen no good man." "Oh, the cratur's weary! But the priest'll find the spectacles, for he'll cry 'em from the altar next Sunday." I retired amid the din of rejoicing, and have heard nothing of priest or spectacles since.

Wednesday, September 17th. – I left my lodgings before five in the morning for Kilkenny. It was very cold for the season. I knocked at the door of the hotel, where I was told the preceding day that I must be at that hour, and was answered by a man who had rushed from his bed to the door half clad, with hair erect, demanding in surly tone who was there, and what was wanted. "The car, sir." "The car don't come till half after five." "I'll step in if you please, sir, and wait." "You won't. Do you think I'll sit up for you to come in?" "What shall I do, sir?" "Go back where you came from." "The door is locked, and the servants in bed, and I could not get in." "Then stay out of doors," he shouted, and shut the door rudely upon me.

I did stay out of doors, and it was indeed a cold berth. I was obliged to keep walking, for no smoke yet ascended from cottage or cabin. Upon a distant green hillock a little smoke was slowly winding up: going to it, I found it was a stump smouldering out its last dying embers for the honour of O'Connell. Seating myself beside it upon my carpet bag, and stirring it with my parasol, I begged it to give one cheer more for the long life of him for whom it had been blazing, and the warmth of one who was well nigh freezing. A ragged labourer approached to light his pipe. "And sure what brings ye here so airly, lady?"

"The civility of your innkeeper, sir."

"The innkeeper, ma'am, is a woman of dacent manners, and wouldn't trait ye so; it was the vagabond of a son she keeps about her."

"And what has this decent woman been doing these twenty years, that she has not taught this vagabond son some of her good manners?"

"Faith, that I can't tell, and by your tongue ye must be a stranger in the country."

I had only time to say I was from America, when the horn of the car-man summoned me from the company that had gathered around, one of whom called after me, "And do ye think we will have the repale?"

"I could wish that the next stump by which you light your pipe might be kindled to celebrate the jubilee of your freedom."

It was affecting to see how the hearts of these poor ill-paid labourers were everywhere intent on that one object, repeal. They feel daily more and more the iron hand that crushes them; and were it not that Father Mathew has sobered them, and O'Connell is enjoining "peace, peace," their forbearance would cease.[7]

The sun was now rising in a clear sky. Never had I been so willing to leave a spot in all Ireland, but I grudged them my spectacles. I had scarcely found a comfort in Cappoquin. The father, son, and daughter where I lodged were employed in repairing the house, and selling ardent spirits; and though occasionally a kind wish was bestowed, I was left to carry out this kind wish as well as I could. But this unlucky visit was not a fair specimen of my tour through Ireland; and, even here, another time might have been quite the reverse.

I might call on Sir Richard with a fresher trimming on my bonnet, and receive a kind answer to my enquiries. The door of the estated gentleman might be opened if the hour were more favourable. I might stop at the same house when it was undergoing no repair, when the carpets were laid down (for they told me they had carpets), and I might call at the door of the innkeeper when the young boor had risen from his lair, when his hair was combed and his face shaven, and he might give me a complaisant "walk in," and a seat by the fire till the car should arrive. These evils I determined should not annoy me; but oh, my spectacles! I could not enjoy the scenery without them, and was compelled to see the country through the descriptions of the carman, who was my only fellow-traveller, and somewhat intelligent.

At seven we reached the flourishing sea-port of Dungarvan; flourish-ing it might be, at least, if such a harbour were anywhere but in poor Ire-land. The houses were built with considerable regard to taste, and the population had the appearance of more comfort than in many towns of Ireland; but the same complaint of poor price for labour, and the same enquiry, "Do ye think we shall get the repale?" saluted me from all to whom I spoke.

Here two Quakeresses joined the car, and rode to Clonmel, and cer-tainly they were proofs that woman is sometimes silent, for from nine till three they sat, and scarcely uttered a word. I made a few ineffectual efforts to talk a little about the country, but gave it up as hopeless. The Quakers are a worthy people, but when I hear of the poor labourers reaping down their fields for a shilling a day, I cannot but say, "One thing thou lackest."

The gentleman who had invited me to visit him at Cappoquin was at the car when we arrived there, and showed me into the house, where much apparent kindness was manifested. And here let me remark that the Irish peasantry cannot be surpassed in hospitality; but in proportion as independence and rank are attained, this hospitality does not always meet the stranger with the same warmth and sincerity. It seems to say, "We know that the Irish people are proverbial for their hospitality, and I must keep up the credit of my country; but had you not come to my house, I should not have troubled myself about you." I always managed well for myself in doubtful cases, by saying that I had met with such unbounded kindness among the poor in Ireland, that I could not doubt the national reputation for hospitality was well merited; and when I was invited to partake of it, I would not insult the Irish character by any suspicion of sincerity on their part. I was advised to avail myself of Bianconi's offer to all foreigners, to travel upon his cars free.[18] This Italian, who some twenty years before came into Ireland and went about with a box selling trinkets, had by dint of industry and good management become rich. When he commenced his cars, he travelled for weeks without a passenger; but perseverance conquered, and he now owns thirteen hundred horses, and cars in proportion, and is at the head of Ireland in this department. He was at this time mayor of the town of Clonmel. I felt a delicacy in making my appeal, but yielded to the urgent entreaty of the friend who gave so many assurances of success from this best of men. My sensitiveness on the subject of great and good men had become so acute, that if left to myself I should have preferred staying upon the lower step. The request was made through the clerk of the mayor, my letter of introduction to a friend of Bianconi's being unsealed; the result was a failure, Bianconi refused; and the clerk told me frankly, that if I had come to see the poor of Ireland, I had come on a very foolish errand. He had left me waiting till the car had left, and I had not money to take me to Urlingford unless I went that night.

Unhesitatingly I turned to the gentleman who urged me to this step, and threw myself upon his protection until the next car should start. My stay was continued three days, till I had seen outwardly the most interesting part of Clonmel. Passing one evening through the churchyard, I saw the door of the church open, and was attracted by the voice of a child above; following the sound, it led me to a large upper chamber, where sat a man reading to a tidy-looking woman, amusing herself with a child. This man was sexton of the church, and though a Protestant, did not seem so well suited with all the arrangements of that body as most of them were. The weekly meetings were kept up, he said, but often only three attended.

"And how do your Catholic brethren and you agree?" "Very well," said the woman; "we find them quite obligin', and I must acknowledge they are a more humble people than the Protestants."

This acknowledgment, though a merited one so far as I had seen, I did not expect from that source. I had seen rich Catholics and rich Protestants, and seen them both similarly circumstanced, but acting quite differently when any manifestations of either pride or benevolence were concerned.

The characteristics of an Irishman are so marked, that whether you find him living on a bog or in a domain, in a cabin or in a castle, you know he is an Irishman still. His likes and dislikes, his love and hatred, seem regulated by a national standard. One of their deeply infixed characteristics is hatred to stepmothers.[19] The poor victim might as well enter her name on the black roll, and make a league to become a witch at once, as to undertake this crusade; for indulgent or severe, idle or industrious, amiable or unamiable, she is a stepmother still.

In this family, one of these victims presided, or rather tarried; and the very atmosphere of the house seemed to whisper stepmother, wherever a child appeared. A daughter of seventeen offered to accompany me in the evening to the well of St. Patrick, two miles from town, but this hopeful girl was not out of her bed till eleven in the morning, and when the time arrived she could not accompany me, "she had no leisure but on the Sabbath." The stepmother looked significantly, and I enquired if her daughter had any business which was pressing? "She lies in bed, as you see, taking her breakfast after the family alone, and sits till dinner time; she has nothing to do, but I mustn't – I'm a stepmother," giving another significant look.

I went alone to the St. Patrick's well, and was directed as many different ways as I found Paddys to point me.[20] At length two fine boys left their sport, and conducted me back over a wall, and showed me the winding path through shady trees, down a declivity to the dark solitude where the sacred well was sparkling. Soft and pure was this water, like most which I found throughout Ireland.

Two aqueducts conduct it underground a little distance; it then forms a rill. A stone cross stands near for the benefit of pilgrims, and a decayed church, whose mutilated altar, with its rude inscription, carries you back for centuries, to the time when the Irish Roman Catholic Church was in her glory.

Every thing about this frequented spot is calculated to fill the mind with a chastened if not religious awe. The dark wood behind the old stone church, the rippling of the little brook, the ancient stone cross, the seclusion of the spot chosen for a place of worship, the lateness of the hour, my distance from the land of my fathers, and the thought that this is the green spot in the ocean, where have figured and still live a people unlike all others, filled my mind with painful, pleasant, and romantic ideas. But I must now leave this sacred dell, for though neither snake or lizard could coil about my feet, yet it was sunset; and ascending the serpentine path, I reluctantly left the enchanting spot.

The first object I beheld at the foot of a hill when I had gained the road, was an old woman with a sack of potatoes on her back, suspended by a rope across her forehead. The whiteness of her hair, the deep wrinkles of her face, the sadness of her countenance, and the feebleness with which she tottered when the burden inclined to slide from her back, so affected me, that never had the miseries of Ireland stood before me in so broad an outline as now.

"You are old, madam, to be carrying such a heavy burden up a hill like this."

"Ould and wairy, ma'am, be sure; and it's many a long day the good God has been puttin' this on me. I must keep a little cabin over my head to shelter a sick gal, who has this six years been on my hands, and God Almighty don't bring her yet."

"And have you any more children?"

"I have three abroad, I don't know where. They forget their ould mother, and never write to me. I raired six of them after the father died. Two are married in Ireland, but they keep away; I s'pose they are afeard the sick one would want something if they should come. I kept 'em all to school, till, like the birds, as soon as they could fly, they left the nest."

"And do you have any bread?"

"Not a ha'p'orth, ma'am, but potatoes; sometimes the girl, when she bleeds at the lungs, says she can't swallow 'em; and when I get a ha'p'orth, it's a sup of milk, a candle, and a bit of turf, and not a farthin' can I spare for her. Sometimes she says, 'If I could smell a little tay, how it would revive me,' but I can't, no, I can't git her a drop. I never have begged, ma'am, in all the long days of distress I have ever had." "Well, madam, your days on earth are well nigh finished, and you are nearly home." "Yes, I am near my home, but it's the heart, ma'am, it's the heart, after all; the prayers don't do without the heart. But the mighty God have mercy on a poor cratur like me, it's all I can say." She stopped to adjust her pack, and I saw her no more. The reality of this picture of patient suffering needed no aid of the imagination to make it as perfect a one as I had seen. But in every place I go, woman is made a beast of burden; and where this is allowed, and men are not paid for their toil, no legislation can elevate a people.

I turned aside into a little chapel, and heard a Baptist minister preach a sermon to five auditors, on the righteous dealings of God.²¹ I breakfasted with him in the morning; a loaf of brown bread, butter, tea, and an egg, formed his repast. This simple breakfast, which may everywhere be found on the tables of the gentry, is quite a rebuke on American extravagance. And hard as is the fate of the labouring man, I think he is greatly indebted to the potato for his flow of spirits and health of body.

This clergyman had a church of only twelve, but in a town of Quakers, Roman Catholics, and Protestants of the Established Church, who had occupied the field long before him. Nothing, he said, but love for his people kept him from going to America; adding, "My country cannot long endure the miseries she now suffers; some change must soon take place."

The next day I was to leave for Urlingford, and the lady of the house where I stopped said, "You must see an old woman we have in our cellar; she's the wonder of us all. She sleeps on a handful of straw upon some narrow boards, a few inches from the floor, without pillow, or any covering, but a thin piece of a blanket, and the clothes she wears through the day. She goes to mass at five in the morning, with a saucepan, and fills it with holy water, which she offers to every friend she meets, telling them it will ensure good luck through the day, and then sprinkles it about her room." At this moment, Molly, unobserved, stole softly upon us. When I met her laughing eye, and still more laughing face, I could not refrain from laughing too. Her cheeks were red, as though the bloom of sixteen rested upon them; her hair was white, yet her countenance was full of vivacity. She looked the "American lady" full in the face, and pressing my hand, said, "Welcome, welcome; good luck, good luck to ye, mavourneen. Come into my place, and see how comfortable I am fixed." We followed to Happy Molly's cellar; five or six stone steps led us into a dark enclosure, with a stone floor, which contained all that Happy Molly said she needed.

"Where do you sleep, Molly?" Taking me by the arm, she pointed to the corner, behind the fire-place, "Here! here! and look, here is my blanket" (which was but a thin piece of flannel) "and here, you see, is an old petticoat, which the woman where I stopped pulled out of my box, and tore it in pieces, ma'am, because I couldn't pay two pennies for my rent; and then, ye see, ma'am, I came here, and praise God they be so kind; oh, I couldn't tell ye how kind."

"Where's your pillow, Molly?" "Oh! I want no pillow, ma'am, and I sleep so warm."

"And where are your children, Molly?" "Some of them gone to God, and some of them gone abroad, I don't know where; I never sees them. They forgets their ould mother. I nursed six, and one for a lady in Dublin. I never gave them any milk from the cow."

"Had you a cow, Molly?" "A cow, and four too, and a good husband."

"And you are happy now, Molly?" "And why shouldn't I be? I have good friends, and enough to eat, a comfortable room, and good bed."

"Where do you get your food?" "Oh, up and down, ma'am."

She did not beg, but all who knew her, when they saw her, would ask, "Well, Molly, have you had anything to-day?" If not, a bit was given her. She is very cleanly, and always healthy. When I was leaving, I stepped down to say good-bye. She was sewing on a bench at the foot of the stone steps, and when she found I was going, she seized my hand, and kissed it, saying, "Good luck, good luck, American lady, the good God will let us meet in heaven."

God surely "tempers the winds to the shorn lamb" in Ireland.[22] Such unheard-of sufferings as poor Erin has endured have drawn out all kinds of character, except the very worst.

CHAPTER VIII

Nunnery at Thurles – Monks' School – Dialogues on the Road – Grateful Reflections – Nocturnal Alarm – Affecting Incident – A Gay Consumptive – Parting from True Friends – A Jolly Company – Lamentation on Lying – Walk to Roscrea – A Weariful Woman – A Centenarian – Charity Sermon – A Christian Sister – A Poorhouse – Visit to a Great Brewer – A Funeral – Father Mathew – Remarkable Vivacity of the Irish – Self-denial – Short Commons – A Snug Protestant Farmer's Household – Cool Reception

At eight o'clock in the evening, I was again by the table of Mr. B. in Thurles; and next morning entered a nunnery, and was shown all the apartments, the chapel, and the beautiful garden, which, as one said, "is all the world to us; here we live, and here we are as happy as we can be in this life."' "I hope you will yet be a Catholic," said one kindly to me, as we passed out; "it is the only true church."

They appeared to be well informed on American affairs, and very intelligent. They have a school of girls, many of them Protestants.

"What," I asked, "do you do about their religion?" "Oh, we don't interfere with that."

The monks have a school of boys, who are taught all branches requisite to the duties of life, and at a suitable age are apprenticed to places where they still keep an eye over them.' If any are ungovernable, after the third complaint by the master, the monks take him away, and throw him upon his own resources. If the master is too severe, he is removed to a better one.

The car left me at Thurles, and leaving my carpet bag, I set out to walk to Urlingford, a distance of ten English miles, and it was now two o'clock. It was a profitable walk, and not a lonely one, for these simple hearted people were meeting me at every corner, coming out from their cabins, and walking "a bit" with me; enquiring about America, and telling me of their country. One said, "We have a neighbour here from America." He was called from a field, and introduced; "I have a great partiality for the people in your country," said he, "but I hate their cursed slavery, and left on that account. I lived with a planter who had four hundred slaves, to whom he gave a peck of corn each a week, and worked and whipped them hard. I could not bear it, and left him, and came away." To the honour of the Pope, be it said that he has prohibited slavery in the church.[3] Passing on to a company of men cracking stones, I asked, "How much do you earn in the day?" "Tenpence, and how do you think we can keep the breath a goin' with this, ma'am, and put a rag upon the back? Would you give us a shillin' in your country? If you would ensure me twopence more than I have here, I would start to-morrow. And do ye think we shall get the repale? They won't let us fight, and, by dad, I would fight this minut if they would let me. We are oppressed to death by the English, and we can't live much longer. What do they think in America?"

So anxious are these suffering creatures for the repeal, that they cannot let a stranger who speaks to them pass without asking the question. Such a specimen of self-controul as they manifest, though many of them are keenly alive to their privations, is truly unparalleled in any nation. O'Connell now restrains them by a nod. Will he always be able to do so?[4]

As I left these warm-hearted patriots, an old man told me I had three miles to walk, "and the night will fall on ye, but nobody'll hurt ye here, ma'am." I had gone a little distance, when he called out, "Do ye belong to the army?" A little mortified, I begged he would not think I belonged to that craft.[5] "I hope, sir, you have not a bad opinion of me?" "Oh, God forgive me. Pardon me, lady: I had not such a thought of you, ma'am." I found that the wives of the officers accompanied them, and he thought I might be of the number. I had walked six and a half miles; night had "come on me," but the moon was now and then struggling through the misty clouds, when a man passed me upon a jaunting-car, and asked how far I had to walk. "You had better get up and ride, the way is lonely." Gladly I did so, and found him a plain, common-sense farmer, who, going through all interrogations of America, and talking over the woes of Ireland, ended by asking, "Do you think we shall have the repale?"

I heard a kind welcome most gladly at the house of Mr. C. in Urlingford, and gave him a particular recital of Mount Mellary. Being a Catholic to the bone, he cannot but love such an establishment as this. He has ever treated me with kindness, and placed me under obligations for many little favours, which as a stranger were very grateful to my feelings. The remembrance of these kindnesses are sweet and salutary on a foreign shore, which none but a stranger can fully appreciate. I went next to Dr. White's. Of this family I can never say enough. Never, never can I forget their unparalleled, unceasing good nature, always in exercise; never with any display, but always as though they were obliged to me for accepting it. My food, my lodging, my fire, my walking or riding, must be all for my highest comfort. The kindness of this family was confined to no sect or nation, the rich or the poor. The beggar, too, had a kind welcome.

A few mornings after my return, at the dawning of day, I heard a loud knocking at the door, and supposed some messenger in haste had called for the doctor. This was followed by the most unearthly scream, which was long and repeated. I first tried to collect myself, to ascertain whether I was asleep, in the body or out, for nothing that was human like this had I ever heard; and surely nothing superhuman would make such a shout at a door inhabited by man. I looked out, but durst neither arise or call for help. The family and servants were all above; and when repeated yells had echoed and re-echoed, the servant opened the door, and all was still. I could not see what entered, and waited for an explanation, supposing there must be some out-of-the-way animal appended to the family. In a moment, the servant entered with, "Don't be afeard, ma'am; it's only the beggar woman that sleeps out of doors. She always comes at light to get the potato, and if I am not up, she makes that scream to wake me. She won't hurt ye. She's innocent, and goes away when she gets the potato." This was the beggar I had seen asleep under the wall, when going to the mines. I ventured out, and saw her snugly sitting on the hearth, enlivening the turf under the pot. She was more than good-looking for a woman who must have been forty-five, and seventeen years of which she had buffetted storm and sleet, snow and rain, in open air. She shrank from my rude gaze. I said good morning; she made no answer.

"Why are you sitting here?" I added. "Waiting for the potato, ma'am."

When the potatoes were ready, she selected the quantity and quality she liked, took them in her petticoat, and hurried out.

Her voice was soft, and her manners childlike, wholly at variance with the terrific scream she made at the door. The doctor gave me the history of this strange anomaly. "She was of a good family, married well, and in all Ireland," he added, "there was not a better housekeeper. But her husband died, and by a train of misfortunes, she lost all. Her relations were treacherous, and she was at last ruined. Disappointed, and jealous of the world, she determined to leave its society, and wandered from home, living on the little money she had; washing her clothes in the brooks and springs, as she met them; keeping herself cleanly for years; sleeping in open air, wrapped in her cloak. She appeared sane, but never saluted any one, nor never asked charity, till all she had was gone. Whether she had recourse to that noise as a defence was not known, but it proved a sure one. The police had endeavoured to take her into some shelter from the rain, but every one would take up his 'two heels,' when she set up that scream. No one in the parish ever molested her; every child is afraid of the yell." She had found her way to the doctor's house years before, and he had made her welcome to a breakfast and dinner, and she now calls at the dawn of day. If the servant be not up, she gives the scream, and the door is soon opened. Twelve is her dinner-hour, and the time is always understood. She is losing her care over her clothes and person, though she is quite removed from the appearance of a dirty beggar. She never whines, nor tells you of the Blessed Virgin, or promises prayers; but simply asks, in a pleasant tone, "Will you give me some potatoes?" She never stops to eat them in the house, but gives a short "Thank you," and goes hastily out. This is "the beggar that sleeps out of doors," and the rustics say to all who pass, "Don't ye disturb her; for this same bawl would frighten the life of ye."

The hereditary sufferings which have been transmitted from father to son, through many generations in Ireland, have developed every propensity of the heart in striking characters, and every variation of mind may be seen in one day's walk, by an attentive observer, – from strength to weakness, from love to hatred, and from right to wrong. "Do you wish to see a new object?" said Mrs. W—, "step to the door." Here sat upon the ground a young woman, with a sweet infant in her arms, her person genteel, her features peculiarly symmetrical; a placid blue eye, finely arched eyebrows, and a high smooth forehead, fair skin, and brown hair; a subdued voice, and of the gentlest manners. She approaches softly, often without speaking; and if a piece be offered, she sits down quietly, feeding the infant, which she always calls General, and of which she is peculiarly fond. While eating, she mutters to herself, often using the name of William.

"And who is William?" I asked. "He's my husband, ma'am." "And is he kind to you?" "He is not, ma'am; he bates me." "And for what does he beat you?" "Because I don't bring him home more potatoes, ma'am." This was spoken in the most childlike simplicity, and like one that had been chastised for an alleged fault which had never been committed.

Enquiring who or what she might be, her simple history was, that her husband was a brute, and had so misused her that she had become insane, but perfectly docile. He turned her upon the street daily, to beg her own bread and his food; and when she returned with a scanty supply, he flogged her, while she never resisted, nor upbraided him. As she adjusted her General upon her back, she muttered something about her William, touching the hearts of all with pity, and they could only say, "Poor thing! she is crazed." And no wonder if the greater part of Ireland were crazed.

Not a week since I have landed on these shores, but I have seen sufferers, should their tale be told, which would move the pity of the most unfeeling.

As I was enquiring one day of an old woman the distance to a place, "Ask the lady to walk in, and rest her a bit," said the old man. I walked in, and found a cleanly swept cabin, a bed behind the door, and a little pile of turf and a couple of stools. The old man had his spade in his hand, and when I asked him what he had a day, "Not scarcely enough to give the sup and the bit, ma'am." This emphatically tells the story of the manner of eating among all the peasantry. They take the potato in the hand, bite off a bit, and take a sup of milk from the cup. "Have you children?" "Not one at home. The last that stayed with me was a fine lad of twenty-two. He was ailin' a bit, and went to bed there, and slept well through the night; in the mornin' he asked for cold water. There was none, and I said, 'Wait and I will go to the spring.' 'You can't go now; it's too early,' and turned away his face, and departed. That was the last of my body, God be praised! and now the father and I are alone, and shall soon be with him, for ye see we are old, and toil'd many a wairy day to rair our lads, and now the wide waters or the grave separates us." There was a kind of pathos in the old lady's allusions, which savoured of ancient days, when, as Cambrensis says in the twelfth century, "the Irish always expressed their grief musically."[6]

When I returned to the doctor's, I found among his beneficiaries a pale young girl of nineteen, interesting in her manners, who had come there with threatening symptoms of a decline. She possessed all the Irish vivacity, and though with a severe cough and husky voice, yet she was always in a cheerful mood; and her lively song and merry laugh told you that her heart was buoyant, though pain often held her eyes waking most of the night. Her voice was sweet as the harp, and often when I heard it at a distance, could not persuade myself but it was a flute. She had stored her memory with the songs of her country, and her company was always acceptable among her class on account of this acquirement, as well as the power of mimicry, which she eminently possessed. She would screen herself from sight behind some curtain, and go through a play, performing every part, and sing with the voice of a man or a woman as the case might require. One night she had been amusing us in this way, when she appeared from behind the screen, and a marble-like paleness was over her face. I said to her, "I fear you have injured yourself." She answered not, but sat down, and sang "The Soldier's Grave" in so pathetic a manner, that I wished myself away. They were sounds I had heard in my native country, but never so touching, because the voice that made them was so young, and probably soon would be hushed in death. Even now, while writing, I hear her sweet voice humming a tune in the chamber where she sits alone in the dark. She is of humble birth, and her mother is a widow, and she has had no assistance of education to raise her above the poorest and most ignorant peasant; yet nature has struggled, or rather genius, through many difficulties, and placed her where, even now, she appears to better advantage than many who have been tolerably educated; but the flower is apparently drooping, and must soon fall from the stem. Yet she will laugh and sing on, even when those about her are weeping at her premature decay. Last evening, a dancing-master came in with a little son, each of them having a fiddle; and the music and dancing commenced. Mary (for that is the invalid's name) was asked to dance, and complied; and with much ease and grace performed her part. This no doubt she would not hesitate to do, while her feet could move, did she know there was but a week between her and the grave. From childhood she has been taught to practise it, till it is interwoven in her very nature, and has become part and parcel of herself.

Again I must leave these people and this family, and take a tour to Roscrea; and every thing was done to make the journey comfortable. A car and driver were provided to take me twenty miles, which was the distance, free of expense. "You will come back to us," said the doctor and his wife, "and you shall always find a welcome home, and wish we could do better." "Why is it," I said, as I passed from the sound of these kind voices, "that such favours should be shown to me by these strangers who had never seen me, while many were looking on me with suspicion, and wondering what strange fancy should have brought me here?" They manifested no fear about my heretical Protestantism, though I talked freely, and read the scriptures in their hearing many a time. They conducted me to the Protestant church, showing me the way, and then turned to go to their own. I felt that their liberality in opinion and conduct was quite a rebuke on many, who profess the guidance of the scriptures and the teaching of the Holy Ghost.

A letter of introduction was given me to a sister of Mr. C— of Urlingford, who lived six miles from Roscrea.[7] A ride through a pleasant country, and on a good road, took us at sunset in sight of the spot where the letter was to be presented. The boy had seventeen miles to travel that night, and I sent him back when in sight of the town, and made my way through all sorts of company alone. A fair had been held, and happy was I to ascertain that among all the motley group, not one was staggering, not one was boisterous, or disposed to make disturbance. A "God save ye kindly, lady" from every rustic, with his pipe, and pig and ass he purchased at the fair; and the women with the burden on their backs did the same. Could I fear from such a people as this?

I reached the house of the shopkeeper, and presenting my dread letter, was kindly received, and kindly entertained. The master had grown rich by dint of the best of management; his father, it is said, having given him a barrel of flour, telling him to make his fortune on that, which he did. He was a baker, now a thrifty shopkeeper. But I had a little cause of regret here, for I heard one evening loud talking and singing overhead, and one of the sons apologized by saying a few friends had walked in to spend the evening by themselves. "Will you go up and see them? If you wish to see all Ireland, there is a part of it, and they will be proud to see you." Without getting my answer, he went to the room, and told the company an American lady was wishing to see them. "Welcome, welcome. Bid her speed." I entered, and found six men and two girls, who had been drinking till quite merry.

"What will ye have, lady? We are glad to see an American." "I am a teetotaller, and wish you were all the same." I soon found this was no place for exhortation. They had taken a little beyond the "moderation," and when one cried one thing, and one another, I was quite glad to make my courtesy, after being told by an old man that, beggin' my pardon, he believed I was a nonsensical woman, goin' about the country. They all cried out, "A blackguard, she is a dacent body." And I was glad to make my escape from this hornet's nest; but my lecture to the family, when I went down, was still more unpalatable; for they sold the "good creature" moderately; and "what right had I to trouble myself?" seemed to be the feeling, when I was treated hospitably, though this was not said. Some unpleasant things followed, in which a servant was involved, which I regretted; for though she was blameable, yet she did as most servants do in all Ireland, and did as she was trained; and leaving all personalities out of the question, I would say, that the habit of teaching servants to say the "mistress is out," and telling lies of convenience, leads to most serious consequences.[8] And though this is not confined to Ireland, yet here it has full play; and not among Roman Catholics only – all, all are poisoned, and often have I found myself totally led wrong by some wink or innuendo from the mistress to the servant, and when I have admonished the servant, "What can I do? I must please the mistress, or lose the place." The habit of deceiving, if it can be done adroitly, without detection, and answer the present demand, is not thought sinful by many from whom I should have expected better things. The lower order are always in the fault, when this habit is mentioned; but children and servants are what their mothers and mistresses make them, in most cases.

I was once seated at a dinner-table in a fashionable Protestant family; and the mother, who was a widow, had three young daughters at her side, when she entertained her guests with a recital of a cunning lie, deeply laid, which succeeded happily, in cautioning a young man to do better; and she ended by saying, "Did I not do it admirably? He never detected the lie; and don't you think I am a good manager?" All answered in the affirmative, that it was most excellently done. The daughters joined in the acclamation, and all went off most flatteringly. The servant was in the room when part of this happy lie was related.

Is this a solitary case? I wish it were; but many of the like have I met all over Ireland. I speak not in anger, but in kindness. It is a dangerous evil; an evil which, when diffused through society, is a fatal blot upon the character; and here let me beg you not to deceive yourselves, supposing that it is confined to Protestants or Romans, higher or lower order; it is everywhere.

In the city of New York, some five years ago, the female members of a congregation appointed a meeting to agree that they would employ no more Catholic servants, because they were so intriguing, and their children, who must be in contact with them, were learning to be deceptive and be liars. Thus, these girls must lose their places, because they practised what they had supposed was praiseworthy. When I mingled in society in this country, I could see no difference in any religion or party; I found, to my sorrow, all were implicated, with exception of some few families, and the peasantry of the mountains. "Where is boasting then? it is excluded."

Pardon this digression, and pardon this preaching. It is not my ill-will towards Ireland but my good will; it is not my hatred, but my love that makes me speak thus. I would that she had not a stain upon her garments. I would that all I have said on this point were an error.

"But you would be a very unsafe guest," said a shrewd lady, very much given to this fashionable intrigue, "if you are seeing and exposing these habits." Unsafe indeed! unsafe! I cannot sympathize with such unsafety. I never was afraid any stranger would come in contact with myself and servants, lest they should detect our intrigues. The family where I was stopping had treated me kindly, and had done no uncommon wrong; but I ventured to tell them the wrong, which was certainly taking great liberty as a guest; and I would not place them behind any family of the gentry in activity in business, hospitality to the poor, thrifty management, and respectability, as the world has baptized it.

After this night's encounter I made myself ready to depart, having stayed a day longer than I intended; and I left at an early hour, to walk six miles to Roscrea. My kind friends sent a boy with an ass and car to carry me, which overtook me in sight of the town. I was fatigued; a hill was before me, and a mile to the place. I got upon the car; the obstinate ass absolutely refused to receive and carry the burden. In spite of the beating of the boy, and the kind coaxing of myself, he was as obstinate as an ass still; and I left the wayward brute and boy to manage as they liked, and walked into the romantic town of Roscrea, among ruins of castles, abbeys, etc., some built by the Danes, some in the year 1200, and all going to decay. The people here appeared better dressed; the women wearing bonnets and shoes more generally, and their gowns not pinned up.

Protestants, Catholics, and Methodists, have their churches here, and I was told that tolerable good feeling exists among them all. Being detained by rain in the house where I lodged, I had opportunity to see a little more of domestic life in a Protestant whiskey-house. The old lady had some higher notions of cleanliness than all her Irish neighbours, saying she had caught them by travelling in England. She was lame, and could not walk; but for the poor servant's sake, I could have wished the lameness were in her tongue. This servant she employed for the paltry sum of four shillings a quarter, leaving her to make out the remainder by the low practice of begging from lodgers and guests. Whether this poor girl was at work or at play, doing right or doing wrong, all was the same; she always went out when she should stay in, and stayed in when she should be out. She was young, unused to service, and "tremblingly alive" to please her mistress, but never succeeded. This woman was Solomon's "continual dropping in a very rainy day."' It was a cold wet day; I could not stay in a fireless room, and was obliged to see all that passed. When any one called for a dram, lame as she was, with a soft voice and happy smile, she would hobble to the whiskey room, and fill a glass.

It was a market day, and a goodly company of five came in, and made the cleanly kitchen a depot for their market lumber, much to the annoyance of the old lady; who, though she pleasantly invited them, yet wondered how they dared be so impudent the moment they had gone out. But at evening, when this family came in, and the father asked the mother what she would drink, and what he should get for the children, it was lovely indeed. The mother drew near this gate of death, taking her children, notwithstanding all my entreaties to leave them out of the gulf, and the children all declaring they did not want it. But the father said his children should fare as well as he did, and so all swallowed the liquid fire together.

Finding I was from America, the good man invited me to his house, for he intended selling off, and going there; and the boys said they would have the lumpers boiled at seven o'clock on the following Monday, if I would walk the five miles to enjoy them. This I promised to do if possible, and said good night. "A fine family, that," said my lame hostess; "he is a great farmer, has some hundreds in the bank, and if he goes to America, he don't go empty handed." So much for the salutary effects of the whiskey on the kind heart of the old lady, towards this annoying family.

The next day was the Sabbath, and I enquired for the clean Testament which the good woman had told me, the day previous, had always been kept clean. It was locked in a drawer, and the good man, after considerable fixing, prepared the key, and produced the tidy-kept book. It certainly spoke well for cleanliness, for a leaf had not been ruffled, nor a page sullied by the wicked finger of man or woman. It had been as securely kept as the Roman Catholic man, in a neighbouring parish, told me he kept his – he "tied a string about it." When I had carefully used this treasure, it was locked again, and I saw it nor its precepts any more, till I left the house.

Among the crowds that returned from early mass, was an old woman of one hundred, quite sprightly, and who never fails of being every morning early sitting on the gallery steps; and as passengers go in, they drip a little into her hand. I found many old people in this town, as well as in all towns I had visited in Ireland; and not in any case had I found one who had lost his faculties.

I went to the Protestant church alone, and was twice asked by the sexton if there was no person in the town with whom I was acquainted. "Not one," I answered. "Not any one?" "No, sir, not any one," at the same time telling him where I lodged. "I will put you in his seat then." O! what a thousand pities I had not borrowed a gold ring!

The sermon was a charity one, and the introduction an encomium on the Christianity of the English; her disinterested benevolence, that though she was particular to gather her own brood, yet she was willing that all should have the benefit of her wings; that all denominations, though not of her church, were receiving bountifully of her kindness. Some wicked intruder whispered in my ear, that moment, "Tithes! tithes! take all the poor unbeliever has; but pay me my tithes."[10] He ended this sermon beautifully and scripturally by saying, that nothing at the last day would be accounted as benevolence; but what was attended with self-denial. The landholders, he said, would have a great account to give; for his part, he would rather be a beggar than be rich, and have a heart to join house to house and field to field, instead of giving to the poor, and "dispersing abroad." Excellent theology! If MENE TEKEL be not written on the practice.[11]

When I returned from church, some potatoes were crisping on a nice gridiron for me, which the father had put there. A son of twenty-five was called in to dinner, and told his mother that the old jackass, his father, had taken the best gridiron to crisp my potatoes, and utterly refused taking any dinner on that account. He stayed in the kitchen while I ate my potatoes, with his back towards me. What were the peculiar virtues of this gridiron I did not learn; but, by way of apology, the mother told me that this "old jackass" was a *stepfather*.

Monday morning, rose at five, to meet my engagement with the boys, where the *lumpers* were to be in readiness, and bade my hostess adieu, with her scolded servant and hopeful son, whose every look and action reminded me of Solomon's rod, the nicely kept Testament, and the bar of whiskey, and I said, on going out,

"I would not live always, I ask not to stay,"[12]

if I must stay in a tabernacle like this. The rain poured, and passing a few doors, I was spoken to by a daughter-in-law of my hostess, who invited me to stop a few days; this was an unexpected kindness. She belonged to the society of Christian Brethren, and seemed to understand the gospel principle of treating strangers, better than many who are sitting under the teaching of learned theologians.[13] "I have stayed," she said "in the Protestant church, which had the 'form without the power,' till I could stay no longer." She visited with me in the houses of those of like faith, whom I found very spiritual; but I fear in danger of running into the same error that others in America of their belief have done, viz. that of being so afraid of the law, as having no law at all. Father Mathew, they said, had been a great curse; because all he did was under the law; and they really regretted he had ever been among them; though some families had had more bread, they acknowledged. And I was severely rebuked for wishing to see him; and, as a Christian, I had no right to have anything to do with him.

Had I never seen the hydra-headed monster, bigotry, before, I should have put myself on the defensive; but here, reader, the case is hopeless. With but one eye, one ear, a darkened understanding, boasting heart, and half a dozen tongues, he has so much religion, he has none at all, or nothing that is tangible. He stalks through the earth wielding a rod of iron, and woe to the victim who comes in his way; boasting of being taught of God, he lacks the first principles of religion, viz. charity and humility, without which all is lost. But all such people have a certain race to run, and if the seeds of saving grace are sown in their hearts, this grace will sooner or later break off the fetters. I said no more of Father Mathew, but went to hear him two days in succession.[14]

What a pity, pity, that the reasoning faculties of the Irish as a nation have been left so uncultivated, and that instinct and impulse have so powerful an ascendancy. But above all, what a miserable religion is it that does not humble but exalt the possessor!

Thursday. – Walked away from the town, and unexpectedly made my way to the poorhouse – every thing in order, every thing in keeping – a healthy spot, and good fires enlivening the hearths of the old people, which appeared more like luxury than poverty.[15] But the constant complaint of all in these houses, when they can be heard by strangers, is the "thinness of the stirabout, and the want of the tay and tobacco." An old female confined to her bed looked entreatingly upon me, to whom I said, "You are nearly home, ma'am." "O!" she answered, "I have offended God, and what shall I do?" She appeared in great agony of feeling, knew she must soon die, and afraid of the judgment, I pointed her to the blood that cleanseth from all sin. Instantly a woman came behind me, and readily called out, pulling me at the same time, "Come out of this place," hurrying me on. As soon as we were out of the room, she begged a few pennies, changing her disgusting tone to one of softness and supplication. "Shame!" said I, "that you should rudely draw me away from that pitiful old woman, to beg." Knowing that the inmates are not allowed to ask charity, as they are constantly living upon it, I declined, and asked her how she should dare to take such liberties. This custom of begging is so prevalent, that I can find neither nook nor shade where to be safe, except in the middle of a sermon; they will follow you to the church door, and be on the spot when you come out.

Friday. – I went to see a ruined antiquity, two miles from the town, and the walk to it was more like Elysian fields than that of commonplace earth and water.[16] Here were the seats of the wealthiest landlords, fitted up in the most elegant style, and the miserable cabins of the poor full of woe. Here was one of the most extensive distilleries still in operation in all Ireland, and Father Mathew has a large field yet to occupy.

Calling in at the house of an Englishman, who was an extensive brewer, I found him in his parlour, with a well-dressed sister from London, and was introduced to them as an American lady. "I never saw but one American lady," said the sister, "and she was very wealthy; but the most ignorant, unlearned creature that I ever saw that was well dressed." "Alas for my ignorant countrywoman!" I sighed, "and will you tell me what part of America was her residence?" "Halifax," was the reply. Her brother seemed mortified, and a silence ensued, when it was broken by my saying, that sorry was I to say, that all the British colonies were in a pitiful state as far as education was concerned, and that whoever visits them in the Canadas, will find that but few comparatively are educated of the native inhabitants. She was silenced, and should have blushed at her own ignorance of the geography of the country; for she actually thought Halifax belonged somewhere in the United States. I am truly disgusted at so much national pride as is everywhere met with in travelling, and when I feel any for my own, it is only in self-defence. The conceited boasting of those who have never read anything but a prayerbook, and never travelled beyond the smoke of their own chimney, is truly annoying.

Saturday evening a funeral passed, and I joined the procession, and followed it into the chapel yard. The corpse was carried around the chapel, and then brought back to the corner where the grave was prepared. A gilded coffin, with a lid put over like a band-box, was a novelty quite unlike the snug mahogany one, screwed closely down, with a plain plate upon the top, which I had been accustomed to see. I expected and even hoped to hear the Irish howl; for when the corpse was let into the grave, the poor old widowed mother, who had crept a mile from the poor-house on her staff, to see him buried, fell down upon her face, and gave the most piteous cry.[18] Another old woman rushed towards her, calling out, "Stop, ye are goin' to do what nobody does now. Get up and stop the bawlin'." She was pulled up, and by force dragged away to a seat, and told peremptorily by a man to stop her crying. "Ye can't bring him back, and what's all this bawlin' about what ye can't do?"

"That is the very reason, sir," I said, "why she weeps; because she cannot bring him back; let her give vent a few moments to her grief, and she will be relieved."

Turning to her, I asked, "Is this your only son?" "One little boy I have with me in the poor-house, ma'am. It is hard for mothers to see their children die."

She was calm in a moment, and sat pale and silent till all was over. The daughter, of about eighteen, took the sheets with which the coffin was carried, into her chequered apron, and a spade which had covered with earth the coffin of her brother, and after all kneeling down upon the ground to pray for the soul of the departed a few moments, they went silently away.

Poor simple unheeded rustics! No "sable hearse or nodding plume" has honoured your procession; no gilded mourning coach has brought the crippled grey-hair'd mother to see this son of her love put in his narrow house; no richly attired friends stood by when the tumbling clods were rolling upon his coffin, to support her, and shed their crocodile tears at the loss of so goodly a child. No! she had the fearful sin of being poor; this alone must shut her out from sympathy, must not even let her weep. The sister, too, was implicated; this blot of blots, this foul disgrace of poverty was found on her. The homely apron which she toil'd to purchase must wrap the shroud, and her coarse laborious hands must lift the spade which covered the bosom of her brother.

At eight o'clock the next morning, Father Mathew gave a stirring scriptural discourse on the importance of temperance, proving from scripture, as well as from facts, the sin of using ardent spirits.[19] The concourse was immense, so that they "trode one upon another." At twelve o'clock he gave another address. His simple, unaffected manner carries that evidence of sincerity and integrity with it, that no one can doubt but he who loves to doubt. His unabating zeal is beyond all praise; yet at this late hour do I hear his name traduced by his countrymen, who are ascribing his object to a political one. Yet among all his traducers not one can be found who is an abstainer, whether he took the pledge from him or from some other one; and I should not hesitate to say that in all Ireland he has no enemies among the teetotallers; few among the drunkards; but many, many, among the moderate drinkers.

Monday morning he was again at the chapel, with hundreds of children urging their way, who

"Pluck'd his gown to share the good man's smile."[20]

It was a lovely sight; angels could not weep at this – not a child was frowned upon, though the crowd was pressing, so that with difficulty he made his way. Some of the little ones he took in his arms; on all heads he put his hand, within his reach. I ascended the gallery, and enjoyed an undisturbed view. A large circle was formed; in the enclosure of this circle were the children, kneeling down, clasping their hands, and lisping the pledge. Those who could not speak were carried in the arms of their mothers, and they, kneeling, repeated the pledge for them. Many a little one, when rising from its knees, did he raise in his arms, kiss and bless it, then send it out from the ring. Three hundred that day took a pledge to abstain from the use of tobacco in all forms. This dirty article he ridiculed, and begged of mothers to abstain from the shameful practice.

Among all the motley group, not one child was heard to cry throughout the day, and they might continually be seen crawling on all fours, pushing their heads through the mass, to take the pledge, or make their way out from the circle. One little child of but two years and three months, when she took it, pushed her blue bonnet through the crowd, sprang to her feet, murmured in a sweet tone, "Fadder Matty," running about the chapel, nor could she be stopped. She was caught up, but would not be hushed, and when her name was asked, it was "Fadder Matty," till, by this continual chatter, she so attracted the attention of all, that she was carried from the chapel, and the song was heard till it died in the distance.

A few moments before four, the assembly broke up, and mothers and children ran after the good man, the mothers crying, "The baby, plase, wants the pledge." The pledge was given to many a baby in the chapel yard, and on the street, till the coach, which was about starting, shut the kind-hearted man from their sight.

I succeeded to reach him through the crowd a letter of introduction, and only had time to say, "I hope to see you in Cork." This was a day of great triumph to Father Mathew. "My hope, my strong hope," he said, "is in the children; they never break the pledge; and if the rising generation can be saved, the great work will be accomplished."

I had heard much of this man in my own country, but here I saw him, and must acknowledge he is the only person of whom I had heard much praise, who ever met the expectation given. He more than met it; he passed it by. He was farther removed from all that could render him sus-pected than I had supposed, and I was convinced that acquaintance must remove all honest distrust.

Had the object of my visit to Ireland been to have rummaged castles and abbeys, old graveyards and bridges, for antiquities to spread before the public, the public (to say the least) must have said, "We have caught nothing." Many and most of these things I did visit, but they left no other impression than to convince me that a powerful, religious, and intelligent people must have inhabited this island; and they urged me on to penetrate into bog and glen, mountain and cave, to see the remains of this people, to ascertain what vestiges are left of the high-toned greatness, the mag-nanimity of soul, the sweet breathing of poetry, and the overflowing ten-derness of heart, which must once have pervaded this isle. I must not anticipate; but here will say, that if you will follow my zig-zag path through bog and heathy mountain, I will show you in these fastnesses, and among these rocks, a people on whom the finger of God has left an impress that cannot be misunderstood. If you get weary, we will sit down by some sparkling rivulet, and lave us in the purest and sweetest water that ever flowed, but the water of life proceeding from the throne of God. If you get hungry, some mountain Rebecca shall say, "Come in, ye stranger, and take a morsel, and we will set ye on yer way." Though not a torn leaf of the written volume of the word of God could be found, yet there emphatically this word is written, believed and practised.

Before leaving Roscrea, we will ascend to the top of the castle, and see the town. This ancient building is now used as a barrack.²¹ Dr. Downer, who politely showed it me, was well acquainted with its history, and observed, "You see what remains of its former greatness, and what a lesson it gives of the frailty of human grandeur."²² Cromwell had been here; and though it is said the memory of the wicked shall rot, yet his is still flourishing in the hearts of all Ireland.²³

At night had full proof of Irish merriment, illustrated by half a dozen young men from the country, who had come into town to assist a man in digging his potatoes. Finding they had nowhere to lie down after the fatigue of the day, they ate their potatoes, "and rose up to play." The dancing and singing were so boisterous, that they shook the cabin, and reached the ears of most of the neighbourhood, who supposed they must be intoxicated. But all were teetotallers, and had not taken a drop; yet they never relaxed during the night, and the morning found them still in the same heart, though they had worked hard the preceding day, eaten nothing but potatoes, nor slept any through the night. An Irishman, to whom the circumstance was related, answered, "The Irishman's merriment begins at his christening, and ends only when he has been well waked." It is even so. The poor Connaughtman, when at work for a rich landlord for fourpence a day, will eat his potato, sleep in a barn, he will sing and dance as merrily as the rich hunter about the lakes of Killarney.

A little incident occurred one morning, which egotism and boasting would forbid noticing, if both duty and inclination did not call for an acknowledgment of God's never ceasing care over his creatures, especially to me in a land of strangers. A genteel tidy woman came into the house every morning, to assist for an hour or two, and get her breakfast. This woman was sitting by the fire, when a son of the landlady took up a pennyworth of bread which the poor woman had just bought, with a penny she had borrowed from his mother. He said, "Is this yours, Peggy?" "No matter, Mickey, you are quite welcome; take it – take it." This was all she had for a breakfast for a daughter, who had walked thirteen miles the evening before from a place of service, to see the mother. I had gone to my room, and she entered. Seeing me, as she thought, a little sober: "And, ma'am, I fear ye are fretted. Don't fret; the Lord is good. It was never so dark with me as this minute. My little slip of a gal is come, and I have no breakfast for her, and it's hard, ma'am, to have a child come to ye, and not have a bit to give her to ate; and I have taken off my petticoat, and pinned a piece of flannel about me, and the good God have mercy on me, I don't know what to do," importuning me at the same time not to fret, the Lord would certainly take care of me. "But I have sixpence beside to pay for my rent, and the good God send it to me, or I shall lose my little cabin tomorrow." When her face was turned about, the sixpence was put into her hand; in an ecstacy of joy, she fell upon her knees before the donor. This woman had been the wife of an officer, and had seen something of fashionable life, but had not lost that native heart-feeling which the uneducated Irish so eminently possess. In her concern for me, she forgot the application of exhortation to herself; though she was fretting, she seemed not to know it. These Irish are a great anomaly to all but the Almighty: reader, remember the sixpence.

I was about departing for Galway, in hopes of finding some money in the post office, which was to be sent there from Urlingford. This money was to come from America to Urlingford; I had but five shillings before the sixpence was paid, and the distance to Galway was more than seventy miles. On this four and sixpence I must sleep, and eat, and ride, unless I should walk. Should I not meet my money at Galway, I must walk back, making one hundred and fifty miles or more.

It was October 29th, when I resolved on leaving Roscrea, and walk to the Protestant friend, five miles on my way, where the boys were to have the lumpers prepared some mornings before. The road was very muddy; the good woman who was so obliged by the sixpence would go with me to carry my basket. Rain soon began to pour, and we returned. Sitting down, meditating what next could be done, John Talbot, a Quaker, entered, saying he had engaged a passage on a car of a friend, who would carry me to the spot where I wished to call. What could be brighter? The rain ceased, and I got upon the car with the Quaker and his lady, and quite soon enough reached the Protestant family, for the company of these friends was agreeable and instructive.[24]

It was now nearly three o'clock, and making my way to the cabin, through a muddy lane, I met sights untold; but I will tell you what I can. There were two pigs, two dogs, two cats, and two batches of chickens just introduced upon the theatre of action, which were enclosed in a niche in the wall, and a huge pile of potatoes just poured upon the table for the workmen and children. A hole in the mud floor for the pigs and poultry to take their "bit," wooden stools and chairs to sit down upon, and a pot not inferior in size to any farmer's in Ireland. This was my friend's kitchen, and these were the appurtenances, and this was the nice family whose money was in the bank, whose children were trained by a superior teacher, and whose virtues wanted no finish but teetotalism. I thought I saw a sly look from the Quaker, and a meaning reciprocation from the spouse, when I was extolling the farmer on the car.

When my thoughts were a little collected, I said, "Well, my boys, the lumpers I see are ready." "They are for the workmen; father and mother are gone to Birr, and won't be home till nine o'clock." Birr was the place I had hoped to see before I slept; but it was now three o'clock, the road quite muddy, and the lumpers were not for me, and the father and mother gone. I resolved to test more fully the kindness of the Quaker, and entered his gate. "Thee had better stop, and rest thee till to-morrow; and then see thy friends." It was most thankfully accepted. It would be useless to say that neatness and comfort abode here; the good housewife made her own bread, and baked it as bread should be baked. They were Quakers, and that one word in every nation comprises all this. A supper of comfort, with fresh apples upon the table – the first I had seen on a table in Ireland – a cheerful fire, and clean bed, made me almost forget that a wide ocean separated me from the privileges of home. But another day was in prospect; this day arrived, and taking my breakfast at seven, I hastened away, about nine, again to the thrifty farmer's.

The night's rest had made no improvement in the cabin; the keepers of it had returned, but so refined had they become, that the master, who was standing bolt upright, as if to guard the hole of the floor where the pigs breakfasted (for he was near it), told me as soon as I said "Good morning" that the "mistress was out;" and so she was, for I saw her slide into a little room back of the outer door, as I entered. A short good morning ended the call. These things are not written to ridicule what could not be avoided, nor to expose faults which are and should be kept hidden; but they are written because they might be avoided, and should be censured; they are nuisances which no family, having the light of revelation and the benefits of decent society, should present to the world. They are a libel on the character of Him who is purity itself, and who abhors all that is filthy. Poor human nature!

CHAPTER IX

Birr – A Miserable Protestant Lodging-house – Rich Distiller's Family ruined by
Intemperance – A Wealthy Eccentric – Lord Rosse's Telescope, and Lord Rosse –
A Baptist Minister – Courtesy of the Children of the Irish Peasantry – Another
Unfortunate Letter of Introduction – Walk from Ballinasloe to Loughrea – Miser-
able Condition of the Poor – A returned Emigrant – Fellow Travellers – An Inter-
esting Trio – Reading the Bible – A Scripture Discussion – A Connaught Catholic's
Experience of Church-going – Market-day in Loughrea – A Shebeen House – A
Pig's Honesty – Remorseless Staring – More Bible Reading – Scarcity of Female
Beauty in Galway – Staring in Galway beyond Description – Ancient Burial-ground
– Visit to a Presbyterian Minister who had just married a Rich Wife – Labourers
standing in the Market-place – Miserable Lodgings – Walk to Oranmore – The
name of "American Stranger" a Key to the People's Hearts – A Connemara Girl

My walk of five miles was not tedious; the air was wholesome, the lark was
singing, the road smooth, and the scenery pleasant. The town of Birr was
the residence of Lord Rosse and his telescope, and here I had hoped to
have a feast of some other worlds of light but this, on which I had so long
figured to so little advantage.' It rained as I entered the town, and turning into a neat little cottage, found a kind welcome by the cleanly master
and mistress, who are Roman Catholics, and was invited to eat, and they
directed me to a Protestant lodging-house. I say *Protestant*, because the
Catholics knowing me to be one, generally selected this sort, supposing I
should be better pleased. They told me the people were kind and
respectable; this was true, but the rooms were dark and without floors,
and two enormous hogs which were snoring in an adjoining closet were
called out to take their supper in the kitchen, which made the sum total
a sad picture.* I was kindly urged to take supper, and sat down with them,
took an apple, and passed a solitary evening. Not that I was sorry for my
undertaking, but the lack of all social comfort, where comfort should be
expected. When I went into my bed-room I felt like bursting into tears;
every thing looked so forbidding, and so unlike cleanliness about the bed.
Clean sheets were begged, and clean sheets were granted; yet it was a

* A cabin-keeper near Roscrea, who kept her pigs in the room, told me "An' troth,
ma'am, I'd take him into my bed wid me, if he'd thrive any better." Her bed was curtained and her cabin was clean.

doleful night, and in the morning, after taking some potatoes, and asking for my bill, fourpence was the answer. Cheap indeed! I paid her more.

The morning was dark; the rain poured fast. At six, a hearse passed, bearing the corpse of the son of a distiller, who fell from his horse, and was killed, when intoxicated. The keeper of the lodgings remarked, that he had seen the father, and twelve sons grown to manhood, in church together. Seven of these sons have died by intemperance. Are whiskey-making, whiskey-selling, and whiskey-drinking attended with a blessing?

I set off in the heavy rain to find the house or castle of a rich man, who was considered a great eccentric. He was owner of three domains, but had divested them of all their frippery, had put on a frieze-coat and brogues, and literally condescended to men of low estate in dress and equipage. He had taken many orphans into his house, and provided them food and clothing. When I reached his dwelling, my clothes were profusely drenched. Mr. S— was not at home.² I asked the housekeeper if I might step in till the rain should abate, and dry my clothes. She allowed me to do so; and I followed her through a long gangway of desolated halls, to a kitchen, and found a company about to dine in the same way and on the same materials as the cabin do. The rain continued, and an invitation to stop over night was not needed a second time. A fire was made in a parlour, where no carpets or supernumeraries met the eye. Tea, bread, and butter were offered, and the housekeeper made every thing pleasant. She had embraced the principles of her master, who had taken her, when but two years old, begging her from a widowed mother, who was embarking for England. He had been a father, indeed, she said, and the care of the house was entrusted to her.

When I was comfortably prepared in my lodging-room, with a fire and clean bed, and contrasted it with the preceding night, in what extremes do I find myself, from cabin to castle, tossed like a "rolling thing before a whirlwind," yet never destroyed. I slept in peace, and thanked God that in Ireland one rich godly man could be found, who called all mankind his brethren.

In the morning, I took my breakfast, was kindly invited to come when Mr. S. should be at home, and went out, and called at the lodge-house, where was a godly-woman, poor in this world, but rich in faith. A pleasant hour was passed with her, for with such, lessons are to be learned which the rich cannot teach. The rain had deluged the country the preceding night; and many a poor cabin was swept away with the miserable furniture, and the affrighted inmates had fled, with their children in their arms, naked as they were, from their beds of straw.

The lawn containing the telescope of Lord Rosse was open, and passing the gate, the old lady who presided in the lodge asked me to go through the grounds, which were free to all. Much did I regret that clouds obscured the sky the whole time I was in Birr, so that not one gaze could I have through that magnificent instrument. The pipe is fifty-two feet in length, and six and a half in diameter. The earl is mentioned as a man of great philanthropy, and much beloved by the gentry and poor.[3]

Sabbath. – Heard the Baptist minister preach to an audience of five, and he likewise broke bread to three. He observed, when he went out, that he felt it his duty to kept the light a burning, the more so, as there were but a few tapers kindled in the island. In the intermission, heard a sermon in the neat Methodist chapel, and that day and evening heard four good sermons.[4] At the house of Mr. W. heard a Roman Catholic, who had been converted from Popery, relate his exercises of mind. A few others had renounced the doctrines, and united with Protestant churches. The priest at whose chapel he attended had left also, and become a Presbyterian preacher.[5] It was remarked by a Presbyterian clergyman, that when any become converts from that church, they are the most spiritual Christians of all others, and we must take great strides to keep up with them.

November 4th. – Early on foot. I commenced a walk to Ballinasloe. The sun rose most beautifully; such a morning my eyes had not greeted for months; nothing was wanting to make sky, cloud, air, and earth most charming, but the curse of poverty removed from this beautiful island, or the curse of oppression, rather. The poor labourers were going to their work, smoking or singing, their tattered garments but an apology for clothing. As I passed the wretched cabins, now and then the happy voice of some child singing a merry song greeted my ear, and on the muddy path before me I heard a little girl of eight years old, who was seated on a car, driving an ass, humming a monotonous tune, and going to her, said, "Good morning, little girl." "Good morrow kindly." "Will you let me put my basket on your car?" "I will, ma'am."

The manner which the children of the peasantry answer any question is quite pleasant. They never say "yes," or "no;" but "I have not, ma'am," "I will, ma'am," "I do, ma'am," or "I do not, ma'am," &c.[6]

"Where have you been, little girl?" I enquired. "To carry my father to town, ma'am."

It was early; she had been more than a mile, and was returning, singing, to her breakfast of potatoes, which she said she had not yet taken, clothed in miserable habiliments, and as happy as the child of a king. Getting a very pretty "Thank ye, ma'am" for an apple, I gave my interesting companion good morning, who said, "I must turn up the lane, ma'am." I looked after this self-possessed child, bare-headed, bare-footed, seated on a car, guiding an ass, at that early hour, going out without breakfast, and surely she lacked nothing but to be the daughter of Lord Rosse to enable her to measure the distance of the planets at the age of sixteen. But hush! "She must be kept in her rank."

I met many interesting characters through the morning; and whether labourer or beggar, most of them were smoking, and one of them in a fretful mood. I talked a little with all, and scarcely spoke to one who did not drop something in my ear worth recalling. It is noticeable in all the peasantry of Ireland, that whether the idea be new or old which they advance, it will be given in such a novel dress, and in so unexpected a manner, that something new, and often something beautiful, will be suggested to the mind.[7]

At the foot of a hill, two miles from the town, I sat down upon a stone, opposite a company of men and one woman, digging potatoes. "She seems to be a lady," said one, peeping through the hedge to see me. The woman left her spade, and did the same. I was about to enter into conversation, when a young man with his wife going on a car to the town, invited me to get up, and ride. A long hill was before me, and the ride was acceptable. I resolved to avail myself of every invitation to ride on any vehicle, however humble; for two reasons – to rest me, and to learn more of the people than I could by walking alone. To be a peasant myself, was the only way of getting at facts which I was seeking.

Now for the reception. Dr. White, in his good nature, had urged a letter upon me to a family whom he had befriended, and of whom he had the highest regard. He had not seen them for some years; "And will you," he said, "do me the favour to give them this letter yourself?" I could not refuse him, though, when he added they had become quite prosperous, and were very much afflicted when he first became acquainted with them, I well knew what to expect, if they were like most upstarts in life. But go I must, and go I did, and here is the result.

My first depot was into a whiskey-room, and a chill came over me. By this they had grown rich. A brother of the family had spent some years in America, and was much attached to it, but unfortunately this brother was absent. Another was behind the counter, busy in measuring whiskey, and in every nation where property is acquired by this degrading practice, the finer sensibilities of the heart are all blasted, and no age or station commands either attention or respect, that does not administer to the interests of the traffic dealer. Long I waited before the customers were served.

Then seeing a little pause, I presented the letter. It was read, but "Who is this Doctor White? Did he ever live in Thurles? I think I have heard of him, but don't know him. My brother, who has been to America, would be happy indeed to see you, but he is gone to Dublin; he would render you any service. My sister too is gone, and the family are quite deserted."

I then asked the privilege of writing a note to the doctor, which was readily granted; while I was doing so, in an adjoining room, a young woman entered, and passed through without speaking. The brother then came in, and begged me to step into the next door and write, as the room I was then in was not his. When I entered the door, the young woman who had previously passed through, was standing in the room, with the letter from Doctor W. in her hand, whom the young man introduced as his sister. I saw the manoeuvring; but took all in sober earnest. The sister was so delighted to do something for Doctor W.; he had served them years ago, and she should never forget his goodness. "Do walk up stairs, and tell us what we can do for you? You must have some dinner, and I will give you some chop till dinner is ready." Finding I did not take flesh, she was flung into great distress, "What should she do to make me comfortable?" Some cheese and milk were brought, and she talked religiously on self-denial, was much given to despondency, loved retirement, suddenly begged pardon, but she had an engagement, and would leave me unmolested to finish my lunch and my letter.

The brother soon entered, asking for his sister; but she would soon be in, and he regretted much that he was so busy, that he could not go about the town with me. The blarney was under full sail, and who does not like blarney? So I finished my letter, walked into and through the pretty town, visited the lunatic asylum, a noble building, with many hundreds of lunatics.[8] I returned to the house at sunset; all was solitude, as if the finger of death were in the dwelling. The servant who opened the door spoke not, and I went up stairs to get my basket and parasol. The parlour door was locked. I sat down on a little couch near by, when the servant came softly, well schooled in duplicity, and in a soft tone said, "My mistress told me to say we have no beds for you; your basket is in the hall; she has gone out to spend the night." "Where is my parasol?" "O you can't have that; it is locked in the parlour. You can call and get it to-morrow." I did call on the morrow, and left a note for the sentimental young lady, which I hoped might do her good in her solitude.

In a neat little cottage I found the cleanest accommodations. They were a snug little room on the first floor, with a nicely curtained bed, a turf fire, two candles, and some crisped potatoes, and all for the bill of fourpence. I was certainly the gainer, even had I wished to have stopped with the doctor's friend; and had I been kindly received, I should not have enjoyed such secluded comforts as were mine in that silent retreat. When I was in quiet possession of all these enjoyments, I sent up a prayer that I might be cured, effectually cured, of putting myself in the power of the proud, the ignorant, yes, the ungodly world to abuse me, – to trifle with every feeling of my heart, which naturally inclines me to be credulous.

Why am I not content with the resources God has supplied me, without running to silly worms for aid which I can do without? Why not turn to the God that is within me, and there seek that honour which comes from above? Give me truth, justice, and integrity for my letters of introduction, and I will ask no more.* Two young men in the house divided the thirty miles to Galway into three parts, giving me stopping places each day, to see the country; and early in the morning, in a pleasant if not happy mood, I was on my way, refreshed with rest, determined that no treatment in Ireland should make me unhappy.

Walking a few miles, it began to rain. Turning to a miserable cabin without a window, or a chimney, the smoke issuing from the door, I found a widow preparing a basket of potatoes for her ducks. "Maybe ye'd take a potato, ma'am," taking a couple, and peeling them with her fingers. I took them, and they made me a comfortable repast. At two o'clock I entered a second cabin; a poor widow woman was carding wool, sitting literally in the mud. These huts are always muddy, where the thatch is poor and the rain can penetrate. Five children were about her, waiting for the potatoes which had not yet been put over. They had come in from their work hungry, and the sum total was a pitiful sight. Asking her if she tilled any land, she answered, "I pay rent for five acres, but the children cannot till it. I am waitin' till they are rair'd, hoping I can then raise somethin', and if I give it up, I cannot get it again." Poor as she was, she had paid a pound an acre on this land, by going out with her children and working in the fields, at threepence and sixpence a day.** The reader must know, that in many parts of the south and west, when it is neither seed time or harvest, many a man works for sixpence, fourpence, and often in the winter for threepence a day.

*If the professed Christian, with the Bible in his hand, do not know his duty towards the stranger, then let him "tie a string" around that Bible, and go into some mountain cabin where the Bible has never been, and there take a lesson.
**Does this look like idleness? Many a poor widow have I seen, with some little son or daughter, spreading her manure by moonlight, over her scanty patch of ground; or before the rising of the sun, going out with her wisp about her forehead, and basket to her back, to gather her turf or potatoes.

She begged me to wait for some potatoes, but I could not. Passing on, I found a man and his wife winnowing oats by the wayside, and sitting down upon a pile of straw, told them my pedigree; and so interested did they become, that I was urged to go in and take some potatoes, which they said were already boiled. I went in, and the sight of the hovel was frightful even to me. How can man, who is made in the image of God, sit here, eat here, and sleep here? was my honest and silent enquiry. A sickly dirty child of two years old, that could neither stand nor talk, was sitting upon a dirty pillow, and two or three more in rags about the hearth. From this abode a daughter of eighteen was preparing to go to America, to get her pound and a half a month for service.[9] In this cabin she had been born, in this had she acquired all the knowledge of domestic duties she possessed, and from this cabin she was about to be transported into that depot for all and for every thing that by "hook or by crook" can float across the waters.

A letter of introduction, reader, was wanted by the mother, and of recommendation too! What could I do? I had eaten of their potatoes, and money they would not take; "But if ye'd spake a good word for my daughter, it's all I would want, and she's as strong a gal as ye'd meet in a day's walk." The good sense of the mother at last hit upon a proper expedient; she saw her mistake, and only requested that I should write my name for the girl, and when she went to New York, she would take it and show it to me, should she find me there. I wrote a few lines, much to their gratification, which the mother and daughter read with ease. This little attention they greatly appreciated, and we parted mutually honoured by exchange of favours.

I had left the cabin when the mother called after me, "Will ye call, lady, upon Mrs. L—. She lives on the hill; she is rich, and could do anything for ye that ye might be wantin'. She's a good and kind lady to the poor." Assuring her I had not come to visit the rich, and that I had enjoyed a good dinner in her cabin, she then pointed me to a family who had spent some years in America, and returned with a handsome fortune. I went to the house; the mistress was gone, but going to the barn, I found the man busied at work, who appeared quite Americanized. He told me much of New York, for he had left it since I had. He was whole and tidy, and made quite a contrast to the tattered one working with him. "You must go in, and take some dinner with us," he said. "I have had some potatoes, sir, and do not need any."

"Potatoes!" he answered, disdainfully. "You can't eat potatoes. I know what you have in America, and how you all live." For a half hour I felt transported to New York, forgetting that I had ten miles to walk, with a basket on my arm, in Ireland, alone. This man ten years before went to New York, with his newly married wife, not worth a pound; both went out to service, and both laid by money, and have now returned with a pretty fortune, "to lay their bones," as he said, "on the old soil."

"This goin' to America," said the labouring man, "makes the Irish, when they come home, quite altered entirely."

I felt like leaving home when I left the yard, but in a few minutes walk a new companion accosted me. A traveller with a stick and bundle in his hand saluted me with, "A fine day, ma'am, for walkin', beggin' your pardon; and how far may ye be travellin'?" "To the next town, sir." "And that's the way I'm a goin'; and as ye seem to be a stranger (English, I 'spose) if I can sarve ye any way, shall I take yer basket? Ye seem to be light on the fut, but the way is long before ye." "It may trouble you, sir, as you have a bundle."

"Not at all at all, ma'am. I wish 'twas twice as heavy. I always love to mind strangers, and ye'll see all the Irish so entirely. I'm a gardener, and goin' to Galway to be a steward, and do ye go to Galway, ma'am? I'll carry your basket entirely, ma'am, and get ye a good lodgin' place, sich a nice body as ye seem to be must feel quare among strangers; but ye've nothin' to fear in Ireland. Ye may travel all night, and nobody'll touch ye, ma'am." I did not believe it then, as I do now, for I had not travelled by night alone, as I have since.

His volubility never ceased, till a beggar woman, with an enormous sack of potatoes under a ragged cloak, joined us, and we formed a trio of no common interest. She was a woman of more than sixty, yet the bloom had not left her cheeks, and when I said, "You look young and strong." "I am aged, ma'am, and my breath is getting cowld," was the answer. Pity, I thought, that such a breath as yours had not been drawn in some more fortunate isle, where

"Beauty's gems and woman's worth are better known."

She would and did keep our company, though twice she stopped to rest. A well-dressed woman joined us, with her shoes and stockings in her hand; her feet, like mine, were crippled, and we entered the large town of Loughrea as night was falling. Here the beggar and tidy woman left us, and through the narrow muddy streets we wended our way, to the extremity of the town, which is a mile and a half in extent, if my guide and weary feet may be believed.

My never-tiring companion conducted me into an apartment, which looked more like the end of all human hopes than an abode for the living and breathing; and had I been in any other country but Ireland, I should have shrunk back, fearing I had entered a den of robbers. The grand-mother, man and wife, a joyous host of ruddy, truly dirty urchins, with pigs, and stools, filled the muddy cabin almost to suffocation.

"And can ye give this lady here a clane bed, and it's she that can tell ye she's from New York, and a stranger; and I wouldn't leave her in any dirty hovel we'd chance to find."

The potatoes were now emptied from the pot; I asked for one, always finding this was the best and surest avenue to their hearts. One was immediately undressed, and put upon the coals. The old grandmother said, "Our beds are all in one room, and maybe the lady, bein' a stranger, she wouldn't like to sleep with so many; and while she's aitin' the pratee, I'll go and seek a lodgin'."

This was kind, and quite in keeping with all my feelings. "And be sure," called out my companion, "you get the clane room and bed."

She returned with good tidings, and I was introduced to my new lodg-ings, a little different from the one I had left, but not in the best keeping; but I was in Connaught, and Connaughtmen were there. In the evening I observed the mistress in a separate apartment reading, and asked what she had that seemed so to interest her. "A good book," was the answer. Knowing they were Roman Catholics, I did not think it was a bible; and when she put it into my hand saying, "Have you read this?" pointing to the miracle of the loaves and fishes, I was happily disappointed. "Will you read it?" she asked. I did so, and much more besides, while the men who were sitting by seemed deeply interested; and one poor Connaughtman, on whom nature had not lavished all her gifts, and education had not given one specimen of her handywork, was in gaping astonishment, and wondered why he had not heard the like afore. "By dad," said he to the landlord, "and why didn't we never hear the like from the praist?" The landlord being one step in advance in intelligence, and a little piqued for the reputation of the priest, silenced him by saying, "But sure we have, and a great dale more." Some five or six chapters had been read, when the Connaughtman suddenly enquired, "And do ye go to church, ma'am? I was never in one but once," he continued, "and the divil take me if I ever get cotcht there again. Oh, musha, had ye been lookin' at me there." "What was the trouble, sir?"

"The life was scar'd out o' me, ma'am, and the heart lept up to the mouth." "And tell us what so frighted you?"

"Why, ma'am, I had heard of the old English church in Galway, that it had images and sich like, to be seen, and I was goin' by to mass, and see the door open, and thought it might be no harum to peep in a little. A soldier was at the door, with a soord, and a divil of a leg had he under him but critches, and when I had but just got behind a post, peepin' at a picture in a dark corner, a man in block bobb'd up before me, his tail scrapin' the ground behind him, musha me! I can't tell how long. I thought it was sartinly the Old Nick, and I run here, and I run there, but for the life o' me I darrint run back, for the soldier with the soord was at the door, and he would strike me, and I could hear the black man draggin' his long tail after him. I sees the back door open, and made out into the churchyard, for d' ye see, I'd ruther be with the dead than with the livin', and I skulked among the stones till I found a place to dodge out, and right glad was I to get off with the life in me, and by dad, ye don't find me in a church again."[10]

This simple-minded man told this story in all sincerity, nor could he be persuaded but that the sexton, with his black gown, was the Old Nick sent to frighten him for entering the church.

November 7th. – A market day in Connaught, and a great curiosity indeed to a stranger; because not only are all sorts of men, women, and children congregated of the lower caste, but there all sorts of people bring all sorts of creatures and things with them, in all sorts of conveyances.

I had an opportunity of seeing this peculiar class of people in a true light as they are at home, for where buying and selling are concerned, you see the man in his real character. "It is nought, it is nought," says the buyer, while the seller protests it's the finest and choicest in the kingdom; and report has said that a Connaughtman loves money. This being a public house where I was lodging, it was common plunder for all. Sacks and bags, geese, turkeys, pigs, asses, horses, and cows were all brought in, and lodged in the kitchen, or carried into the yard, while the owner went out to make fresh purchases. The landlord was a teetotaller, but the good woman, more bent on gain, was selling her whiskey without a licence, and many a glass on that rainy market day not only replenished both the tea-canister and snuff-box of the seller, but gave a new and a happy zest to the wits of the buyer. One woman had purchased a pig, and fearing, as she expressed it, the pig was not honest, she was unwilling to pay her money till she had kept it a week, to prove its soundness. The man wanted his money, and the woman would not give it, unless some one would come forward, and testify to the honesty of the pig. She appealed to the man of the house; he was incorrigible. She insisted, she urged, that he should be bail. "That I won't do, ma'am, I'll not be bail for the honesty of the pig."

"Well, then, the man should let me have it upon trial, and I'm as honest a woman as there is in all Galway, and that I can show any day." The clamour grew louder; the man was forced to beg pardon for some rude words he had used, and the woman, after telling him his pardon was granted, left seven shillings till the honesty of the pig should be proved, and took her pig, and departed. It was said that this was all intrigue on her part, to have the use of her money as long as she could.

Though not a simpleton did I see among the throng, yet there was the least semblance of refinement in look or manner that I had ever seen in any place whatever. Not one did I see that day which could tempt a desire for further acquaintance. But the ultimatum of all, the "head and front of the offending," was the staring. Their incoherent gibbering never stopped, except when they suspended all to stare at me. I can bear a common gaze with common patience, and am ready to acknowledge that it is natural, and that it is proper to desire to look at a foreigner when he passes, and to gratify that desire should not be censured. But here my case was dreadful, if not awful. I could not get out; the house was thronged. One would be pressing his way through the room to the stable, with a horse, and pause to take a survey from head to foot. Another would be tying up a bag, and suddenly stop, and look me full in the face. A third would let her burden from her back, minutely examine me, then turn to the master or mistress, and in Irish make her comments. In short, if I never was noticed before, this day I was a distinguished personage. Scarcely a word of English was spoken through the day, and therefore I could gather but little, only through my eyes, except by the woman and her honest pig." She performed in plain English.

When night arrived, all dispersed. My Connaughtman, who had entertained me the evening previous, again called to beg me when I should be in Galway, to go in and see that dreadful church where he had been so frightened; "and should ye see the man in black, then ye'll pity me." He insisted, too, that I should take him home with me as a servant. "And do ye think, Micky, the gentlewoman would have ye walkin' by the side of her?" said the landlord.

"Oh, no," said Micky, "I would walk behind her, if I could only see her country." However remote I might find the peasantry from society, however ignorant of books, however cunning, or however simple, they all knew something of America, and all were hoping some day or other to see it." Their questions would often be intelligent on the geography of the country, and often they would make serious blunders, yet all would be correct in some particulars.*

*It is not to introduce America in every page that mention is so often made of it, but to show the peasantry.

The noise of the scripture-reading the preceding evening had gone far and wide, and many called in to ask the mistress if the kind lady would read again. This was unexpected, but gladly did I comply. The poor simple men often exclaimed, "Why did we never hear this?" Paddy, the master of the house, could read well, and was somewhat skilled in debate, and the Virgin Mary was introduced. I asked him if he believed the Testament I had in my hand to be true? He said, "Yes, every word of it." "The last chapter in that book says, 'whosoever adds to it, God shall add all the plagues, etc.' Now in all that book not an indirect mention is made of any adoration that must be made to the Virgin."[13] The wife instantly exclaimed, "Now, Pat, what have you to say? You're sack'd, you're sack'd, and I'm glad of it." When any one entered to stop a little, she would repeat it, saying, "Aw! you could not answer that, my lad." Though she was still in the church, yet she had read and thought for herself; and could multitudes of these people be taken by the hand, and led out from the machinery with which they are surrounded, they would drink in with eagerness the Gospel of life. I related to them stories from the Bible which they had never heard; yet the story of Calvary was well understood, and they made a better application of the scriptures they did know, than do many who read them daily.

Friday. – Early I prepared for a walk of eighteen miles to Galway. The road was muddy, and there was quite an appearance of rain. The kind people did all they could do for my comfort, and asked me twopence a night for my lodging. This was the stated price to all. I was soon joined by a man and his wife, with a car, riding alternately, which made the journey slow, and they kindly relieved me of my basket; and I walked nine miles with tolerable ease. I was resting upon a stone when the post-car arrived, and offered to take me to Galway for a shilling.[14] I paid it, light as was my purse, and reached the town at two o'clock, with half a crown.

This ancient sea-port is celebrated in history for many a wonderful tale. It is not an inviting city for a stranger, on a muddy day; the suburbs are wretched in the extreme, and not in all Ireland, Bantry excepted, can there be found more that is forbidding to the eyes of strangers. The fish-women, which are abundant there, are coarse and ugly in their looks, and none in all Connaught could exceed them in staring; and follow me they would, from street to street, from shop to shop.[15]

I found a comfortable lodging-house in some respects, and in some it was uncomfortable; but knowing that slender purses must not put on airs, I went to the post office to ascertain whether a letter were in waiting, but found none. Sixpence a night for lodging was the price, and find my own potatoes. I had five sixpences, and with these I must make my way back to Kilkenny. I had no fear, for I knew all would be right, and so I perambulated the town, and saw what I could see, enjoyed what I could enjoy, and then went home for the night.

The next morning I walked to the docks, and would not forget to say, that in Galway I never went alone. A man or two, and perhaps half a dozen women, would be in comfortable staring distance; and this morning, dreading the repetition of the yesterday's annoyance, I went early, but a Connaughtman was on the spot, with pipe and dog; nor did he leave me, nor did he speak to me, nor did he cease staring at me, when the position was a favourable one. The docks have been built at immense expense, and the unfortunate man who pledged himself to do the work died with grief at his misfortunes.[16] A few solitary masts were bowing gently to the breeze, only mementos of Ireland's dearth of commerce. This ancient harbour has been the depot of many a bloody vessel, laden with instruments of death and carnage, to lay waste the fair isle; and many a startling legend is now related of deeds of darkness and of murder, which have ever blotted the fame of this bright gem of the sea.

Overlooking the harbour is the oldest burying-ground in Galway, and it is literally crammed with the dead.[17] Throughout Ireland, in every large town, there seems to be some pre-eminent burying-place, which has peculiar virtues, on account of some holy man or men having honoured it by their bones; and there, while living, the eye is directed as the most desirable bed in which to sleep when dead. The opening through a tumbling wall was free, and thither I repaired, with the Connaughtman and dog in pursuit.

"What walls can guard me, or what shades can hide?"

I was really afflicted; I had chosen this early hour, before seven, that I might unmolested enjoy in that harbour and churchyard a little reflection, where staring eyes would not settle on my face, or smoke of tobacco penetrate my nose. And like the poor affrighted man in the church, I "ran here, and I ran there," and dodged behind the tomb-stones, but could not escape; he was there, bending over the top, in full gaze upon me; and could I have spoken Irish, and told who I was, and what was my errand, as I had often done, there might have been some hope in my case. I left the spot in vexation and despair, and he left it too.

I would not join in all the ridicule and censure which the world has ever been ready to heap on suffering Connaught. There is good sense, there is wit, there is benevolence, and there is intelligence too. Even in many a smoky hut have I sat down, and been profited as well as amused, by the knowledge they had acquired, and their manner of communicating it. They are an inquisitive people. They desire to come at the whys and the wherefores; and if defeated in one way, they will resort to another. I was the strangest anomaly that had ever visited them, and as I could not speak Irish, what could not be gained by talking must be made out in gaping. Let this serve as an apology, though it did not lessen my indescribable vexation. I was in torment "for a' that."

On my return, the market people were assembling, and my way was so hedged up, that in the fruitless effort to make a passage out in the right direction, I became so confused that all points of the compass were alike; and my only concern was not to lose the little sense remaining in me. Not a creature would budge, for they had me in close keeping, and no time should be lost in making out "the cratur." At length I was free, and begged of a woman, at the door of her house, to place me in a right direction. She kindly did so, and I returned and seated myself over the turf fire in the corner, to fix on some other peregrination; and resolved to make a call on the Presbyterian clergyman located there, having been told by the gentleman of the house where I lodged, that he was approachable, and knew much of the country.[18]

I had no letter of introduction, and felt much more independent on that account. Knowing that from humble poverty he had become somewhat affluent by marriage, and lived in aristocratic style. I knew with such that the forms of etiquette must be most strictly regarded, and was careful that strings and pins should all be in their proper place. The walk was a long one, the road muddy, and the gibbering of all who pretended to direct me in the right course so confused me, that I was in danger of a return of the morning's mood; but finally the lodge belonging to the clergyman introduced me to a fine gravel walk leading to the mansion, and I was soon knocking at his ministerial door. A young interesting girl opened it. I handed her my card, requesting it might be given to Mr. F. She did so, and soon returned with the card and Mr. F's answer, "Mr.— says he has nothing to give to-day."* Disgust and indignation struggled a moment, and elevating my voice, so that he might hear, I said, "Say to Mr. F. I did not come to ask charity, but a few questions, which to me were important." "Tell the woman she may come in," was the prompt reply. The woman did go in, and found the man of the pulpit sitting near a table, with a newspaper as large as a small pocket-handkerchief in his hand, a dandy watch-chain hanging in dandy manner about his neck, slippers on

---

* Whether the beggars in Galway carried cards, when they solicited alms, I did not learn.

his feet, and dress in like accordance.

His wife was much older than her spouse, and what she lacked in youth and beauty was imperfectly made up in frippery. Her dress was a crimson-coloured satin; a gold watch was glistening at her side, and pink ribbons were about her cap, neck, and arms; but to her credit be it said, she was sewing. The fact is worth naming, because it was the first time I had seen in the country a fashionable lady with plain sewing in her hands. As I looked upon the inmates of this well-trimmed parlour, and upon the lord especially that adorned it, I said, "Can this be a messenger from God, to announce to a lost world the gospel of truth?

"Lay not careless hands on skulls that cannot

Teach and will not learn."[19]

After adjusting himself in speaking attitude, he condescended to say, "I will answer any question respecting the state of the churches you may ask." He spoke of the poor as being in a deplorable state, and the wife said my object was certainly a laudable one, and she presumed I found the people kind. "So much so," was my answer, "that I had sometimes thought it would be best to keep them so; for when a few hundreds were added, I had seen them almost entirely divested of humanity, if not of common civility." My good parson found a loop-hole, for he said, "Ah, you don't know the poor as well as I do; they are cunning and all the kindness they show is to get favours." "Not so had I found it;" I could say, "that when they saw me weary, and I told them my journey must be hastened because my money was well nigh spent, then was the time when they doubled their entreaties to detain me, without charges." A few months before this, in the cabins of the poor, this man could be found reading to them, and kindly administering to their wants. He was then poor, and employed as a Bible-reader, "And now," said the wife of a curate, "he can only afford pennies, where he could give shillings at that time." It was getting late; I talked of muddy streets, of rain, the difficulty of the way, the many hours I had been out – all to no purpose; his pantry would not unlock, nor did a "cup of cold water" greet my lips. I left wiser than when I went, and the next day heard a sermon from this same man on Christian benevolence, expatiating on its importance, and its benefits to the soul. His congregation was small, and part of them were soldiers in military dress, with the weapons of death standing by their side. Certainly the Christian church has got a very supple kind of religion, if these warlike principles can find a shelter in it.

On my return to my lodgings, I saw a company of men assembled in a square, and supposed something new had gathered them; but drawing nearer, found it was a collection of poor countrymen from distant parts, who had come hoping on the morrow to find a little work. Each man had his spade, and all were standing in a waiting posture, in silence, hungry and weary; for many, I was told, had walked fifteen or twenty miles without eating, nor did they expect to eat that day. Sixpence a day was all they could get, and they could not afford food on the Sabbath, when they could not work. Their dress and their desponding looks told too well the tale of their sufferings. When I had passed them, looking about, one was near me, walking slowly, picking a few shreds carelessly in his fingers, his countenance such a finished picture of despair, as said, "It is done; I can do no more." I three times halted, and paused to speak to him, but could not give utterance; as soon as I met his countenance, hunger, wife, children, and despair were so visible, that I turned away, and could only say, "Good God! have mercy on poor Ireland."

When I reached my lodgings, the landlord remarked, that every week the poor creatures are coming in from the country, and often they stay two days without eating, watching and hoping a chance may come; and sleep where they can; and then most of them go away, without getting any work. "Go to now, ye rich men, weep and howl."[20]

My lodgings should not pass entirely unnoticed. In all lodging-houses I had found that a single room was an extra privilege scarcely to be expected; and often the man, woman, and children would be fixed in the same apartment, with one or two transient lodgers, as the case might be. This is not so in hotels. In this house, the apartments looked tidy; and I was shown to a chamber where were two curtained beds; one of these I was to occupy. Before retiring, the woman said, "I shall sleep down stairs, the child is sick, and nobody will be in your room but John." "Who is John?" I asked. "My old man," was the reply. "Your old man! Be assured, madam, I shall be your company down here then." "That you don't; you shall have a good bed, and room where you can rest." The matter was settled by telling her in plain English I would not go into the chamber. As a penance, I was put into a confined room, with her mother and sick boy across the foot of my bed, bolstered and tucked against the wall, so that there was no danger of falling out or off. The poor old mother was dying with the asthma, keeping up almost a continued cough, and could not lie down; and when she was not coughing, her unearthly breathing so frighted me, fearing she was in death-agonies, I kept calling, "Woman, woman!" (for I did not know her name.) When she was coughing, she could not sleep; and when she slept, I could not wake her. Nothing but the cough could do it. Thus two doleful nights I kept my eyes waking, not conscious that I slept at all; the third night I slept a little from downright necessity. But complaining was out of the question; there was an empty bed, and the wife seemed glad to punish me for casting contempt on as good and as quiet a man as there was in all Galway.

Monday, at two o'clock, finding my letters had not arrived, and that three nights had made quite an inroad into my half-crown, I saw that a walk to Urlingford was the only alternative. The kind woman urged me to stay another night, and when I told her my money was nearly spent, she invited me to stop free from charge; I did not, and the mud and clay made me almost regret that I had refused.

A young student from Dublin, who was lodging in the same house, accompanied me two miles out of the dreadful suburbs of that city, which for filth and wretchedness exceeded all I had seen. I could do no more than look in, for an attempt to wade through would be next to perilous. When the young man returned me my basket, and said, "You will reach Oranmore by dark, if you hasten (a distance of about two miles and a half), and possibly I may see you in Dublin," I had no alternative but to nerve myself for what was before me. Oranmore I had never seen; I might not reach it till dark; and then a lodging! This was the most to be dreaded of all. On I went, sometimes leaving a shoe in the clay, and never finding a dry spot for my feet, till at sunset the little town was reached. Two applications for lodgings were refused, both full; the third one received me. But when I asked, "Will you give me a clean bed?" "I had rather have two men than one woman," was the answer; "two men will sleep together, and make no fuss; but women are always finding fault."

"True," I said, "we always find it so in New York."

"New York! have you lived in New York? I too was there six years, and wish I was back again; but my husband was homesick, and would not stay." Every thing was now reversed; she thanked God for bringing me, telling me I might stay in welcome as long as I would. She took me into a snug room, and said, "See! I keep my beds as they do in New York, make them up nicely, and leave off the sheets till a lodger comes, and then give him coarse or fine, flannel or linen, as he may choose, and you may have which you like." This was turning the picture indeed. Pat came in, and made me as welcome; and we talked of New York to our hearts' content. "I was a fool," said Pat, "that I came away."

She lived with a clergyman's family though she was married before leaving Ireland, and Pat was employed elsewhere. They had not been idle nor improvident, but saved considerable, and returned to spend it in their own country. They kept a shop and lodgers, and had many little comforts which are not common in Ireland. This was truly a pleasant evening to me, and the next day rain kept me there, much apparently to the gratification of the kind creature. I told her what a fearful purse I carried; "And I'd not empty it of a farthing, if you had a million."

Reader, wonder not that I love the peasantry of Ireland. Imagine yourself in my real condition and state of mind when I entered that house, and then meet the same kind, unmerited, unexpected reception from those for whom you had done nothing, and feel yourself changed into a friend, instead of a stranger and a lodger. We talked and read till a late hour, and then I slept undisturbed.

The reader may be told, if he never heard it whispered, that the Irish as a people have a quantum of leisure on their hands. The cabin housewife has done her morning's toil, when the potato is eaten and the pigs and fowl have been fed; no making of bread, no scouring of brass and silver, no scrubbing of floors or cleaning of paint, makes her toil heavy; and in a few weeks' travel I found that, when I stopped in a village for the night, and wished to make the most of my visit, nothing was necessary but to call at some cabin, tell them I was an American, and had come to see the poor, and ask them to direct me to a good lodging-house. This was electricity itself; all and every thing that could be done would be, and by the time the lodging-house was found, the fame had reached through the little hamlet, and a levee was on the spot in a few minutes. So in Oranmore; but the good woman of the house, putting on some of her American notions of propriety, insisted that I should not be "gaped to death," and often told them in sober earnest, that they must keep away, unless they had some business to the shop. All was unavailing. Night and day they were squatting about me, admiring my comely dress and comely hair, telling me that my face was young, and many a good day was before me yet; and seldom did they leave, till they made me both young and beautiful, with the best of all appendages added, a heavy purse of money. Here I talked and here I listened, here I read and they listened, and the little village of Oranmore will always be held in pleasant remembrance.

But, kind readers, no bliss is perfect, and here in this happy group was one which, when I looked and while I write, was and is an object of painful, pitiful, and ludicrous contemplation. It was a mountain Connemara girl. I found that the district of Connemara, through all Ireland, was considered as a distinct item altogether. This people are pointed out to strangers as the Americans would point you to the wildest tribes of their Indians. Here is one before us, and though faintly described, yet what is drawn is as near the thing itself as my skill at pencilling can make it. She was in this lodging house to take the charge of a sick boy who had come there for a season. She was dressed in red flannel, the costume of all the mountain peasantry of that country, and this colour, they tell you, is chosen to keep away the fairies. Leaving the dress, we will look at the person. She was tall, thick-set, had broad shoulders, high cheek bones, small eyes, and near together; black coarse hair, cut square upon a low forehead, and body and limbs of huge dimensions. Two broadly-spread feet, which had never been cramped by cloth or leather, told you that they had braved every hardship incident to feet in any clime or nation. These pedestals were surmounted by two pillars, which wanted neither strength or size; and when she moved, it was always with a grace peculiar to herself, and when she sat down, it was always upon the floor. This flannel dress was cut after the same model of all her countrywomen's, being a jacket pinned closely about her; a petticoat so long by some twelve inches as modern custom sanctions; and beside it had undergone great changes since it left the loom, for wear and tear had fringed and frilled it, and though it legally belonged to the jacket, yet its binding was reaching up two inches below it. Thus, cap-a-pie, dress and symmetry, she made out such a figure as the tenderest heart might encounter without fear of being broken.

She had another qualification, viz. that of singing; this was always performed in Irish, and with tones and gestures which made every auditor feel to the bottom of his soul. I had often heard her, and one day had a curiosity to look into the kitchen where she was at work, to see her unperceived when singing; and imprudently laughed, not in ridicule, but because it was wholly unavoidable; she heard, and would never sing again. No apologies on my part, and no entreaties of the mistress could ever prevail."

"She dispraises me," was the answer. She would never eat, but sitting upon the floor, with both elbows upon her knees, and the potato between both hands taking the "bit," without putting the potato down, gnawing it until all was finished; then she would take the "sup," and raise another potato to her lips, and go on.

I could never look on this strange excrescence without wonder, and asking on what commission could she have been sent into a world like this. But I should do great injustice, yes, I should sin, should I leave the picture here. I should be holding up to ridicule a being of God, who may have more favour in his eyes than the writer; and though this is not a caricature but a true picture, yet there is another side to it, and I would be guilty, like Ananias, of keeping back a part of the price, should I not show it."

Ireland, above all nations of the earth, has suffered most in her character by the ignorant and too often malicious injustice of writers, who were either awed by the opinion of others, or incapable of discrimination themselves. They have caught her fairy tales, they have gathered up her blunders, they have poetically told of her "gems of the mountains and pearls of the ocean," they have laughed at her tatters; but who has lifted these tatters, and shown to the world that under them is buried every noble principle that could elevate a people? Yes, the poor cringing labourer, touching his hat to the haughty lord, who never looked manfully in the face of him he served, has a soul burning within him capable of all that is praiseworthy, of all that is godlike. And would justice be allowed to lift her voice in his behalf, that soul would look out, and speak, "I, too, am a man." Yes, the poor Irishman has a mind that can and that does think; but, like the American slave, he is told by all the world, " You do the working, and I'll do the thinking."

I must return to my Connemara woman, and say she possessed the greatest kindness of heart, and felt the least attention given to her as the highest favour. She was unobtrusive, and shrank from the least rebuke in look or word, though without the least appearance of anger. She would watch to do some little favour to the mistress or to me, and do it in the most quiet and unassuming manner. When I left, and offered her my hand, she hesitated, looked at the mistress, then at me, and from a kind of wild smile she settled into a seriousness that seemed to say, that she thought herself an outcast, unworthy of the notice of any. Her every look and action indicated that she felt she was an exile from all the world, and must ever remain so. She was faithful and trustworthy to the last degree, and had she been born on any mountain but a Connemara one, she might have escaped the imputation of being the ugliest and most awkward woman in Ireland.

CHAPTER X

Walk to Loughrea – Thoughts of Home – A New Day – A Fellow Traveller – Cabin
Theology – Such a Bed! – Eyre-Court – Hearty Welcome in Banagher – An Anxious Mother – A Noble-Hearted Daughter – Incursion of a Troop of Connaughtmen into an Inn, and how they behaved themselves – Visit to Mr. S. – Rejection –
Christian Kindness of Poor Mary and her Brother

The time to go arrived, and at ten o'clock the sun looked out, and I
promised my urgent friend, should the clayey road be impassable, I would
return and spend another night; and though for four Irish miles I was literally sticking in clay, I kept on, hoping the road would improve, and stopping when I could walk no longer, and feeling I must not and could not
go back; and at last a man with a team overtook me, saying, "God save ye
kindly, lady, and the mountain is a long one, and will ye put the basket on
the load?" He kept my company for some miles, and then stopped to feed
his horses, and gave me my basket; which, to my weary feet, already blistered, seemed to be almost an insupportable clog, and much more so, as
night was gathering, the mountains were wild and barren, the cabins, like
angels' visits,

"Few and far between."'

And five miles long and dreary I walked, and met not a living moving
being, nor could I find a stone or stick where I could sit down, and stand
still or walk on I must. I wished to reach Loughrea if possible, and hurried on till my strength gave way; a welcome stone by the side of a wall
met my eye; I sat down, leaning my back against the wall, and looked
across the Atlantic. I there saw cheerful fires lighted; I saw friends gathered around them; I heard them say, "I wish I could see what Mrs. N. is
doing to-night. By this time she believes we told her the truth, when we
advised her to stay at home, and keep out of difficulties which she must
unavoidably meet in a land of ignorant, reckless strangers. Pity she could
not find Irish enough in New York to keep her busy, without going to that
land of darkness. Well! she always would have her own way, and she must
abide the consequence." I saw too my own once happy parlour lighted,
and the books gathered for the evening: and did I wish to draw around
the table, and participate in the enjoyment? I did not. No, I did not.

Should I sleep the sleep of death, with my head pillowed against this wall, no matter. Let the passer-by inscribe my epitaph upon this stone, *fanatic*, what then? It shall only be a memento that one in a foreign land loved and pitied Ireland, and did what she could to seek out its condition.[2]

It was now dark. A heavy fog and mist were gathering fast, and I could scarcely discern the earth from the sky. A man passed. "Will you tell me, sir, how far it is to Loughrea?" "Two miles and a half." "Then I must stop by this wall for the night. I cannot go further." "Not a word of lyin'," was my only consolation from the man, and he passed on. I arose, and made an effort to walk. Another man passed. The same interrogation was now answered by, "A mile and a quarter." This was gaining rapidly without walking a yard, and passing on a little, I made the same enquiry, and was answered, "A short mile, ma'am." I was confused, and knew not whom to believe; but was so willing to be deceived, that by limping and halting, wading, and enquiring of all I met, I at last reached the twinkling lights of the suburbs of the town.

The kind voice of the woman where I lodged on the journey down, was music to my ear, and Pat was called to participate in the joy. "And what shall we do for ye, the cratur!" A long box was in the room. I flung myself upon it, and for an hour, amidst the repeated questions, "What shall we do, and what can ye ate? Ye'r destroyed, and the heart's gone out o' ye," I kept my position, really fearing it was over with me, and my walking was ended. I had walked eighteen Irish miles, in clay, and over tedious mountains, since ten o'clock. My situation was not the most flattering. I was among a people, though kind, who could not appreciate the object of my visit to Ireland. They were poor, and needed every penny which belonged to them. I was a stranger, and had been accustomed to better accommodations than they could afford, had been disappointed in getting my money, and could not reward them for extra attentions. The lumbago, which for many months had made me a cripple in New York, now threatened a visit, and the sum total was not the most pleasant. Did I despond? No! my philosophy and my religion (if I had any) came to my aid; and the question, "Of what use is your religion, if it will not sustain you in time of need?" brought me to my feet. In the passing of this hour on the box, I was not alone. The intelligence had reached many a cabin, that the "plain-discoorsed and the beautiful reader" had returned, and they hastened to bid her welcome. Seeing me in this dilemma, the rejoicing was turned to mourning, and the "cup of tay, the cup of tay, was all that could refresh her, the cratur." I took a cup of cocoa, bathed my feet, and reluctantly said good night, being too much fatigued to read to them. But

I gave them my hand, and from my heart did I pray that God would emancipate poor neglected Connaught.

My bed-room and appurtenances were not in the most tempting fix. A dirty chaff bed, with a pile of potatoes at the head of it, and the servant across the foot, said, "Here you are." I passively committed myself to the care of Him whose aid I certainly needed, and whose watchfulness, I felt, had ever been my only support.

I slept, awoke, and was greatly refreshed; and though I had taken but a few ounces of food since nine the previous day, I felt not the want of any. The weather had changed a little for the better, and at eleven o'clock I took my last shilling, paid my fare, and with blessing upon blessing on my head from the family and cabiners, I left the muddy, miserable-looking town of Loughrea, escorted by no insignificant number to set me right.

> "Rare are solitary woes; they love a train,
> They tread each other's heels."[3]

The pleasant change now turned to a heavy cold mist, and a strong wind was blowing full in my face. The road was a complete bed of clay, but how could I go back, and how could I stay there? The way was quite lonely. Now and then a solitary cabin, with its duckpond and manure-heap in front, hung out the sad insignias of desolation and filth within. I sat down upon a stone – yes, a stone. Ah! how many times have I in Ireland realized the literal import of "The shadow of a great rock in a weary land." My basket was heavy to my weary feet, when suddenly stood before me a clean barefooted woman, with neither bonnet, shawl, nor cloak, saying, "God save ye kindly, lady; ye look wairy. Shall I take your basket a bit?"

O that sweet voice! I shall never forget it. Sorrow had mellowed it, for she had passed lately under the merciless hand of oppression. "And how far may ye be walkin'? I am on this way a bit, and will lighten the burden of your feet a little. I'm sorry to see so dacent a body walkin'. The likes of me are us'd to it." I felt interested to know her history, and enquired if she had a family. "No, thanks be to God, they're all dead but one little gal, and if Almighty God will spare her to me, it's all I'll ask of him" "Have you a house?" "No, praise God, when my husband died, the landlord hunted me from the cabin the night he was put in the ground." "And where did you find a shelter?" "Praise God, a poor widow, seeing my distress, took me in, and I get my bit as I can. The child is sick, and I've been to Loughrea this mornin' for a little medicine, and a morsel didn't cross my lips since yesterday." We were then seven miles from Loughrea, making fourteen that this barefooted, cloakless woman had walked, and it was now nearly three o'clock.[4]

Two miles we walked and talked together, and many a judicious hint did I gather, many a little unmeaning disclosure of the sufferings of the poor by the oppression of their masters, and many a fulfilment of the promise of God to the widow, in the unexpected helps she received when desponding. We reached the muddy lane that led to the cabin, she returned me the basket, and for the first time since in Ireland I felt a rising murmur that I could not wipe the tear from the eye of the widow, by giving this one what would have been a little token of my kind feelings, and made her at least a comfortable breakfast. "I would not take it from a lone stranger like you," was the answer, when I told her my condition. How many hearts like these are aching in Ireland, and how unheeded do their sorrows fall on the public ear!

Alone I hurried on over the solitary way, the most desolate of any I had travelled. There seemed to be nothing on which man or beast could comfortably subsist, and no shop, where a mouthful of bread could be procured, greeted my eye. I had taken but a half-penny roll in the morning, and began to desire a little food. Night came on, and unexpectedly I found myself in a muddy little village, and enquired for lodgings; was refused at first by two, and almost despaired; but a little girl introduced me to a house, which, if it had no comforts, had yet some novelties, and I had an interesting evening with the most ignorant people I had met, yet not deficient in Irish cleverness. The woman said she had no place but one, and that was filled with oats, which had not been threshed, but two very genteel ladies lodged there the preceding night. Oats are certainly clean dirt, and if genteel ladies had slept there, I assured the good woman I would not be squeamish, if she would give me a clean bed. But, kind readers, your eyes never saw that bed! Now all preliminaries were settled, and my "dacent clothes and proper discoorse" told that I had been well bred and born, and must have "a great dale of money in my purse." I then had just ninepence, and was fifty miles from my place of destination.[5]

The potatoes were boiling, and when poured upon the table, the mistress selected three of the finest and fairest, and flung them into my lap. This was the thing needed, for I had concluded to go to bed supperless, as I could do better without eating than sleeping. A neighbouring woman was called in, and when she found that I was "so high born, that my accent was so plain, and that I could discoorse so beautifully," she was delighted. Pausing a moment she abruptly said, "And do ye give in to the Blessed Vairgin?"

"Aw!" said the other, "what's the use in talkin'? you can't confete with her." [I leave the reader, if he have an Irish dictionary, to interpret the technicals of the language.][6] Answering her, that I believed the Virgin was a good woman, and that she is now in heaven, but the Bible had never told me to worship her. "The Bible, the Bible! the Church says so, and that's enough."

"But God says, 'whoever adds to that book, he will add unto him all the plagues written therein,'" &c.

"There! there! I told ye so – I told ye, ye couldn't confete with her." Pat now entered, and hearing of my heresy, "Ye're wrong – ye're wrong." "There now, ye've got your match in Pat," answered the exulting wife. Pat told me that, "Whatever I might plase to ask of the blessed Vairgin, if I asked in sincerity, I should be sure to have it, for she had more power in heaven than every saint there."

I begged the talented Pat, if he had nothing to do but ask any favour and it would be granted, to apply immediately, and have her remove them out of their poverty and filth, and give them their rights as a nation.

"There – there, Pat, ye may stop your discoorse. There now, ye can't confete with her, and I told ye so in the beginnin'."

"And did ye say ye don't drink the tay? Ye're the first dacent woman that's born and bred among dacent people that don't do that."*

"Aw!" answered the visiting woman, "there's no use in talkin'. She hasn't got sinse; that I see afore, poor thing! She'd never left so fine a country to be walkin' in this, if she'd the right sinse. Aw! she's crack'd."

I certainly admired the result of the kind woman's observation, and told her hundreds in Ireland, of better learning than she, had thought the same. "Give her the bed, the thing!" she said to the mistress as she went out; "she's wairy."

Now what could have been better? These ignorant, knowing people, when they had come to the conclusion of my lack of sense, or aberration of mind, took no advantage, but used more lenity; for though I had spoken lightly, as they thought, of the Blessed Virgin, and dishonoured their holy faith, yet they imputed this to "a lack of sinse," of which my rejection of the tay and laivin' my fine country were abundant proofs.

The room was now shown me. The pile of straw, which reached nearly to the upper floor, so filled the passage to the bed, that I made my way with some difficulty, and the first fair and full glance of the bedding, by the light of a candle, so filled my eyes, that I extinguished the light instantly. I knew a second look would keep me out of it, and rest I much needed.

*Tea-drinking is a mania in Ireland. This woman boiled some in a pint cup, and supped it with her potato without milk or sugar.

And here I gave some proof of the truth of the woman's assertion, that I "had not the sinse," for why did I not lie down upon the clean straw? I spread a pocket-handkerchief upon the bolster, and managed as well as I could to forget where I was, and what might be about me.

The morning dawned; I heard a great pushing at a back-door, which led from my room to the yard.

"The door wide open flew."

In walked a majestic pig, weighing three hundred, and moving towards my bed, elevated his nose, and gave me a hearty salute. I said "Good morning, sir," and he turned to the oaten straw and made himself busy, till the mistress entered, and I asked her if she would do me the favour to lead out my companion. She heeded it not, but walked away. In a few moments she returned, and a little more entreatingly I said, "Madam, will you be so good as to take out this pig?" She was angry at my repeated solicitations, but finally took away the domestic with her into the kitchen, with a mutter, "What harrum?" and violently shut the door. Seven times was the door from the kitchen opened, admitting to my apartment either the master or mistress, before I had an opportunity of making my toilette.

The room had neither window nor crack, but my sense of feeling had become so acute, that I managed very well without seeing, and made my ingress to the kitchen, and asked for my bill. Twopence for three potatoes and a night's lodging. I paid it cheerfully, which left me sevenpence; and bidding good morning to the mistress, who manifested quite a shyness, I hurried out, for she evidently thought me "wild," and wished me away.

After walking four miles on a tolerable road, I bought a halfpenny roll, and hurried on quite happily with sixpence and a halfpenny, which would buy me another roll on the morrow for my breakfast. This was not the most sumptuous fare, but it was so sweetened with the pure breath of heaven that was fanning my lungs, the sun shone so pleasantly, the lark sang so sweetly, and the poor peasants spoke so kindly, that I actually felt that I should never be happier this side the gates of the heavenly city. I could not think of a single thing needed but what was in my possession. I was not hungry, I was not naked, I did not wish a carriage; and I felt that all earth, air, and skies were mine. I had suffered hardships that few in my condition could have endured; but I was receiving the legacy that was left me eighteen hundred years ago, that, through much tribulation, all who will follow Christ must enter the kingdom.[7] I was happy, I knew in whom I trusted, and heartily did I say, "What lack I yet?"

I reached a beautiful little place called Eyrecourt, toasted my piece of bread, and went on at two o'clock to walk five miles to Banagher.[8] The road was quite muddy, and my feet were now blistered. I was obliged to wear coarse shoes, and my feet, never having been accustomed to them, were tender. Darkness overtook me, and the way became quite difficult. I enquired of all I met the distance to the bridge, and the distance to the town; and the way lengthened in proportion as I passed on, till I found myself upon the bridge; and meeting a woman, she led me to a lodging-house, which she assured me was as "clane and dacent as I could find in a day's walk."

This lodging-house in Banagher has associations which will live in grateful remembrance while memory lasts. Did they say, when I entered wet and weary (for I had walked for hours in a heavy rain), did they say, "Who is this strange woman, at this late hour asking for lodgings; she must be mad?" but "Come in, come in, ye're wet and wairy. How far have ye walked in the stawrm? Come into the kitchen and dry yer clothes, and ye must be a stranger, and we'll get ye the cup of tay; ye must be hungry." All this was said and more, before I had told them who I was, and what brought me there. When this was known, if possible the kindness was redoubled. I told them I had but sixpence-halfpenny in my purse, and could only get a night's lodging and two or three potatoes. "And that you will get; and a week's lodgin' in welcome. Not a ha'p'orth of them two crippled feet shall go out of my house till they're hailed," answered the man. The servant was called to fetch water to bathe my feet, "And we'll do what we can for ye, the cratur!"[9] And faithfully did they perform their promise; they were kind to a fault. They were Catholics, but they listened to the Word of Life with the most profound attention, and without any opposition. They told their neighbours they fully believed I was inspired of God to come to Ireland, and do them good. What was this good? Certainly not money, and this they well knew.

They gathered about me in the evening in crowds; and when I had read two hours, such a breathless silence was in the room, that I looked about to ascertain whether all who were behind me had not left it, when I saw the place was filled to crowding, sitting upon the floor; and so quietly had they entered that I knew it not. Till one o'clock I read, a peasant woman, sitting at my feet, holding a candle; and when I said, "You must be tired," "And that I ain't, the long night wouldn't tire me, to be listenin' to ye."

"Ain't she a Protestant?" an old man whispered. "She's a Christian sent here to discoorse us, and do ye think the like of her would crass the ocean to see the poor, and discoorse 'em as she does, if God hadn't sent her?" The old man seemed satisfied, and the point was settled by "Aw! there's no use in tawkin', the like of her couldn't be found in all Ireland." This last was said audibly, while I was turning the leaves of my book for a new chapter.

Among this group was a peculiarly interesting woman of forty-five, who had been the mother of twelve children. Six of them, she said, had "gone innocently to heaven." She was endowed with good talents, had been well bred, and was quite engaging in her manner. But the desire she manifested for her children, their education, and their eternal good, almost exceeded belief. She raised her hands, her full grey eyes glistening with tears, and said, "Can you, will you tell me how I can get to your country, where I can place my children under a good and virtuous influence, and where they will be taught the way to heaven as they should be? We are here in darkness, darkness! Our clergy are good for nothing; they go to the altar, and say mass, but they preach no sermons. They give no other instructions, and who is any better? We have schools, where they learn more that is bad than is good. I go to bed at night, and I pray, pray. I wake up, and do the same, and here I am. Will you talk to my husband, and tell him what privileges you have in America. I can do nothing with him; he does not feel the accountability of training the children, as I do, and could I persuade him to go from this dreadful place, I would work night and day, not for myself, but for my children." I heard her through, and said, "You say you are all in darkness, and I say to you, Christ and his word can give you light. Believe me, you must read the Bible; your children must read the Bible; or they never can reach those high attainments which you so greatly desire. There is a science in that Book of books that can be found nowhere else, and this science cannot be taught except by the Holy Spirit." "Is it so?" she eagerly said. "Have you a bible?" I enquired. "No; we have never had one." The mistress then remarked, "There are but two Catholic families in all Banagher that have a bible." "Well you may be in darkness, if you have not the chart that God has given to guide you to heaven." The company now dispersed, when she entreated again. "Do say what you can to my husband. He may listen to you." "That woman," said one, when she had gone, "has always been goin' on in this way. Her children, she says, are goin' wrong, and her husband cares nothin' about it."

A little clean curly-headed girl called the next day, the youngest of this doating, anxious mother, and led me round the corner to show me her home.

"Welcome," said the mother; "you find me in this dirty cabin, where the pig and the shoemaker's bench are always with me. I live in wretchedness: I was not so rair'd. But my husband will have it so; he is a passionate man; but it was a runaway match; and though he often beats me, yet I am fond of him still. Forgive me for making so free with a stranger, but these dear, dear children; my heart is burning up; it is scalded for them, and I cannot get rid of it. We are not poor, though we live here in this humble cabin with pigs. I can spin, weave, and make all kinds of cloth." She then went up a ladder, and brought down two nice specimens of worsted and flannel cloths, which she had manufactured. "And could any such work as this do any good in America for my children? I believe," she added." "Almighty God has put this in my heart, and what shall I do at the day of judgment when I meet my children?" I listened to this woman with the full conviction that the Spirit of God had enlightened her, and would yet bring her further out of darkness into his marvellous light.

I went to church, and found a small congregation; but so engrossed was my mind with the sermon I had heard from the woman, that I was but little improved by what I heard there.

The evening introduced me to a family, where I was invited by the father to see a daughter of seventeen years of age, who had three weeks before had a leg amputated. She was sitting upon the bed, and looked to me uncommonly interesting. She was handsome, becomingly dressed, and received me with a dignified cheerfulness that would have suited maturer age and higher education. She was mistress of the tidy cabin; her mother was dead, and she was the eldest of a pretty group of cleanly dressed children, who looked to her as their guide. When I spoke of her misfortune, she cheerfully answered, "I must submit to what the Almighty puts on me."[10] I went away, and was told more fully the cause of this sad misfortune, of which no mention was made by the family.

The father had a mill of some kind, and was in the habit of taking his dinner in it. This daughter had prepared it, and carried it to the mill; but it was later than the usual hour. The father was angry at the delay, and lifted his hand to strike the faithful child. She, to avoid the blow, stepped aside; her dress caught in the wheel, and her leg was torn nearly off. This family discipline needs no comment. The cheerful girl, it is said, has never been heard to reproach the father.

When I returned from this cabin, a new era opened. A company of Connaughtmen, in rags and dirt, returning from their potato digging in the county of Kilkenny, had turned in hither for the night. They wanted a pot of potatoes; they wanted them cheap, and they wanted them in "good speed." All this could not be accomplished without some bustle, and the good man offered the potatoes for twopence half-penny a stone. That, they in plain language declared, they would not pay. This took some time to settle, and ended by their going out and purchasing the article elsewhere. This adjusted, then came the lodging. They must be up at two, to pursue their journey; they must lodge in one room; and this room must be the one occupied by me, as no other was of sufficient length and breadth. I cheerfully relinquished all claim, as I was but a guest, and the floor was spread with et ceteras for the lodgers to lie down. The clamour and clatter which commenced and continued were somewhat peculiar to themselves. I had quietly put my Polka coat upon a chair in the kitchen for a pillow, and with a second chair managed to make myself a bed; and as this bed, like the other, was gratis, I had no right to complain. The peat fire was dimly burning at twelve o'clock, when the master came in, and hearing the tumultuous jabbering, and feeling the house to be shaking to the centre, he ran up stairs, telling them to be off, every blackguard of 'em, as it was two o'clock, and not a minute more should they stop in his house, disgracin' the divil himself. They declared they had paid for lodging till two o'clock, and they had not slept a ha'p'orth. He drove them up, and they tumbled down stairs to the kitchen. I had placed myself in an upright position, and was in a corner. They, as if by consent, all stopped short in a semicircle about me, and in perfect silence surveyed me attentively, and my condition for a few moments was not an enviable one.

There were nine of these nondescripts, not one of them with a whole garment or a clean face, standing in array. The room was nearly dark, and the master not in it. I seriously thought of my sixpence-halfpenny, but before having time to offer it, the good man of the house entered, and poured them out of the house at once. They had the kindness to give the man a timely caution when they were on his steps, for they told him seriously that the stranger in his house was a man in disguise, and that he had come to do some great mischief in the country, and they had not a ha'p'orth of a doubt but that he had hapes of sovereigns. He added, "Some of the blackguards would not hesitate to take your life, should they meet you alone."

These men certainly are distinct in their appearance from the provinces of Ulster, Munster, or Leinster. Yet I should not feel authorized to say that they are more malicious or dangerous than their neighbours. They are more coarse in appearance and manners; but they do not lack either shrewdness or hospitality. In justice I must say, I have experienced more real kindness from these people, than from many of more refined education and fashionable appendages.

Reader, if you are prone to be incredulous; if you are but a nominal Christian, if you know not how to believe in God without doubting; if you cannot trust him with your body as well as your soul; if you are not wiling to deny yourself, and never have done it, and if you do not believe in "particular providences," in particular exigencies, you may as well lay down this book, – at least pass over a few succeeding days, for they will appear like fairy tales, and the teller of them as a silly if not wicked impostor.

Monday. – These Banagher friends wished me "God speed," without taking a farthing, and told me their house should be welcome as long as I would stay. The time had come; new things were before me, and these new things I must meet.

In a few hours I found myself in Birr, dining with Mr. Walsh, and he insisted that I should go that evening to visit the good Mr. S. at whose castle I was so kindly entertained by his housekeeper, and should find him there, as he had just left Birr, with a lady in his carriage for his home. "In him," he added, "you will see the Christian in a new and striking light. Go, I beg you; it will refresh you on your journey, and you will have it to say, when you return to your country, that in Ireland you found one rich man who lived wholly to God, and to serve his fellow-creatures." I went. At the lodge I was told he had left for Rathmore, where he had another castle, and, added the good woman, "It is but five miles. The road is good, you are quick on the fut, and it would be well nigh worth a voyage across the Atlantic, to hear the lady who is in his house discoorse on the subject of religion."

It was now sunset, and clouds were gathering. I hesitated, "Go, in the name of the Lord, and he will receive you kindly," and setting me on the path, she bid me "God speed." Darkness, rain, and tempest soon overtook me; the way was quite dreary, and I much feared I should lose my path, and I felt that the errand was quite an uncertain one. It was a sad night; a small parasol was a miserable defence against the furious wind and pelting rain; and yet I felt more composed and less shrinking than I do now, while writing it. I had not the least anxiety. I neither knew nor cared what was before me. I saw a faint light in a cabin window, some perches from the road, and felt my way to it, and enquired the distance to the castle. "A short half mile; but ye'll be destroyed in the staurm. Ye had better stop a bit." Telling them I must go on, they stood in the cabin door till I had reached the path, and as well as I could, I made my way forward.

The darkness was so total, that a beast could not be distinguished from a man on the path, and in a few moments I heard walking behind me. I turned about, but could not tell what it was. "The staurm is heavy and the night dark on ye, and I'll show ye to the castle." This was a young man from the cabin I had just left. I thanked him sincerely, and said, "It is a great blessing to have so good a landlord as Mr. S., one who gives so much to the poor." "A divil of a ha'p'orth will he give, only to sich as are of his religion." "I have heard he often puts his hand into his pocket, and hands a poor man a pound he may meet on the way." "And I hope ye'll meet the pounds when ye get into the castle, but we'll turn into a cabin here, to a man who keeps the gate, and he'll go with us."

We turned into this cabin, and here found William and Mary, a brother and sister advanced in life, who, as Mary said, had been "bred, born, and raired on the ground, and knew the father and mother of this good man; and he will like to discoorse with sich a nice body as ye are, a fine biddable woman; and if ye love the poor, he'll be glad to see ye; and ye should stop with me through the rain to-night, but he'll give ye the cup of tay and the fine bed; and ye shall have my cloak, and I'll go with ye and see ye snug in." While this long preface was going on, the young wag who accompanied me gave signs of unbelief, which Mary rebuked by, "And, Pat, it ain't you that have sairved him, as we have." She got her best cloak, and fastened it about my neck, for my clothes were dripping with wet, and we all went out for the castle gate, but William, who stopped to keep the cabin.

The bell was not answered till the ringing had been long and loud; at last we were admitted into the kitchen. There was an interesting sight, – a company of fifty-two were sitting down to a supper of potatoes and buttermilk, mostly orphans. A few aged people were among them. They had just arisen from prayer. I saw, through the door, a table with bibles, and was informed his custom was to pray before supper with the family.

Mary made known to the housemaid what a biddable, nice body she had brought to the master, and begged her to go and give information. The girl hesitated. Mary spoke again; at last the messenger went in, when a fine maiden lady of fifty majestically approached, "What is your name?" Telling her, she answered, "You can't see Mr. S." "Did I understand you?" I asked. "Mr. S. can't see you." This was the good woman who was "worth a voyage acrass the Atlantic to listen to her discoorse." The good Mary was aroused, and rising up, she said with much decision, "It seems that Mr. S. is not at home. Come, ye shan't stay out in the staurm; my poor cabin can give ye a shelter;" and taking me by the arm, she drew me towards the door. The maiden lady whispered in her ear that she must have a cloak, seeing that I had hers on my shoulders. Mary supposed she was to be presented with some cake and tay for the stranger and refused the cloak in contempt.

The rain was pouring, the wind was blowing, and I was wet and weary, but not in the least disheartened. Pat had no sooner reached the street, than a whole edition of Irishman's honour, benevolence, sense of propriety, wit, and anathemas on the lord and lady of the castle was commenced. "And there's the puttin' the hand in the pocket, and takin' out a pound for the poor person, turnin' a dacent body into the black stawrm; and there was the blackguard of the near hypocrite, sittin' by the table, where he'd just been praichin', and sayin' his prayers. 'Tis true he feeds the hungry childer, you see, but a divil of a bit would a scrawl on 'em have, if they should be in a chapel, mindin' their own prayers. And do ye mind that scrawl of a puffed-up bladder, that come swellin' out to ye? She'd had her lesson; she wasn't bid to ask ye to stop from the stawrm, and have a warm sup, and rest yer wairy bones in a good bed."

Had I been disposed to have censured the lord or lady of the castle, Pat's graphic description of their religion and conduct left nothing unsaid, and I was silent.

We entered the cabin of Mary; the brother was lying down, and the fire was dim upon the hearth. Pat gave the turf a little stir. "And see here, Will, see what I've brought ye." Will started from his bed. "And here's the wet and wairy stranger. I've brought her back to ye; the good saint of yer master wouldn't left a whole bone in her body." "Now ye don't say, Pat, he was goin' to bate her." "Be aisy, Pat," said Mary, "the divil is always standin' up in yer throat; let me spake." Turning to me, she said, "Now ye will forgive Mr. S., won't ye? He's a good man."

"But didn't he show the fondness so hard for the stranger, that the heart would been broke in her, if I hadn't got her away." "Now," said Will, "tell me the story."

Mary began, and but for Pat, would have told a plain and true one, but he was so constantly interfering, that she succeeded but badly, and turning to me she said, "And yer of his religion, ain't ye?" Telling her I did not belong to his society, "Aw! and why didn't ye tell me. I shouldn't a' took ye there. I should known he wouldn't bid ye welcome." "Aw! that's a purty faith," said Pat; "that's the religion he carries under that vagabond of a frieze coat; that's the lesson he's larn't out of that blessed book that he's taichin' the scrawls he's feedin' and braikin' the heart about; he'd better take up his owld brogues, and carry his two heels back to the church he left, then to be denyin' the religion he was raired in, and be walkin' the earth such a hypocrite."*

Poor Mary was completely outdone, and could only say to me, "But ye

*Mr. S. formerly belonged to the Episcopal Church.

will forgive him, won't ye?"

Will made another effort, and said, "Aw! Pat, ye'r too hard on him. Wasn't we raired on this ground, and didn't my father sarve his father? And he's not turn'd us from his gate, though we don't go to his church, nor rehairse his prayers." "And well he needn't turn ye out; he knows better than that. Wasn't yer father as good a dog as ever watched the gate of a castle, and didn't he train ye, his curs, to bark for the son as well as himself for the father? And what does he do for ye? The cabin and the potato ye have; but where's the tay and the bread? Ye haven't a bit for the stranger."

I looked upon this wag of nineteen, and said, "Is this the growth of Ireland's bogs and ditches? Are such, the plants of a nature's gardens, left unheeded and trampled under foot, crushed in the budding by the careless passenger? Ah! little do the proud, titled, and estated ones of Erin know the power of mind which is embodied under the ragged garments, their ill-paid labour compels the toiling ones to wear. Little do they know that while they look with contempt, or make themselves merry at the expense of their unlettered blunders, that these 'things of nought' are scanning their every action, are reading them through, and could they write a book, would tell them true tales of their character, which they never themselves understood, and which would make their ears tingle."

Pat said, "Good night, with good luck to ye, stranger, and maybe ye'll have the pound note in the mornin'." "Aw! that Pat!" said Mary, "there's no use in tawkin'."

Mary now had enough to do to make the stranger comfortable; a pile of dry turf was added, lighting up a white-washed cabin, and white scoured stools, table, and cupboard, which amply compensated for every other inconvenience. She had nothing but the potato and turnip, and "Sure ye can't ate that." "Put on the pot," said Will, "it's better than nothin' to her cowld and wet stomach." Now could I bring the reader into this cabin, and spread out the whole as it was pictured to me, I would say I am paid and more than paid for my visit to Ireland.

When the potatoes and turnips were boiled, they were mashed together, some milk and salt added, put upon a glistening plate, a clean bright cloth spread upon the deal table, and Mary sat down groaning at the "strangeness of the master, and the miserable supper of the biddable woman," and starting as if from profound meditation, "What are we after awl? God save us awl, the best of us, we poor miserable bodies; we think we're somethin' when we're nothin'; when sick, we think if God will let us live, we'll do better; he gives us another start, and we go on the same gait, and so till the breath grows cowld in the body. I can give ye a clane bed, and lay ye warm in it."

"And where will you sleep Mary? Do not let me turn you from your bed." "And that ye won't. I'll find the comfortable place for my bones." I was led to the bed-room, and in this floorless cabin what did I there see? A nice bedstead, a clean covering, two soft flannel blankets, and linen sheets, white and glossy with starch, and curtains about the bed as white as could make them. The feathers were stirred in a narrow compass to make the bed softer, so that but one could have room in it, and in this I was put; then a clean flannel was heated by the fire, and put about my shoulders, another about my feet, "to take the cowld and pain out of my wairy bones."

When Mary had finished putting the covering snugly about me, she placed the curtains closely around the bed, and softly went to the kitchen hearth. The door she left open, and I could see what passed there. She crept to a stool, and kneeling down, she prayed. Yes, unlettered as she was, I believe she prayed, and I believe God heard that prayer. She arose, and leaning her face upon her hands, she sat, gently swinging her body, now and then looking towards my bed, and waited till she thought me to be asleep. Then putting her cloak about her, she crept stealthily into my room, and peeped through the curtain. Seeing my eyes closed, she carefully put the drapery together, and crawled behind me upon the naked bed frame; for she had put the bed all under me; and in a few moments this unsophisticated, practical, humble Christian was asleep. She did not intend I should know she was there, and why? Lest I should think she had made sacrifices for me. Was this doing her good works to be seen of men? Did I sleep? Not much. Gratitude to the kind Mary, and more than all, gratitude to God, that he had brought me to see, in this day's and night's adventure, the practical import of the parable of the good Samaritan, kept me waking."

When the day dawned, Mary softly stole to the kitchen, and made her turf fire; swept and dusted the floor and furniture, and while her potatoes were boiling sat down to meditate, with her face leaning on her hands. William arose and whispered to Mary, and went out softly, shutting the door.

I went out, and the kind Mary feared greatly that I had not slept, and that my breakfast would not sairve me. "And will ye," she said emphatically, "will ye, from the heart, forgive Mr. S.? He'll be sorry when he thinks on't, that he sent a lone body out in the stawrm." Assuring her I would from the heart forgive him; "And will ye forget it?" That I could not promise; the lesson was too good a one to be forgotten; "But, Mary, I will make the best possible use of it." The breakfast was soon ready; a hand-ful of meal put into the mashed potatoes, made into a griddle cake, with a "sup" of milk, was all that kind-hearted Mary could offer. And when this was taken, I prepared to depart. "How can I let ye go, and not have the Master hear ye discoorse, yer so knowledgeable a body?"

I was fastening my cape about my shoulders, when she approached, took hold of it as if to assist me, and looking me full and steadily in the face, said, "Mind, when ye go to heaven, and I come to the gate, tell yer Lord to let Mary Aigin in; 'for when the rich master turned me out in the stawrm, she took me into her cabin, and sheltered me from the tempest, and gev me a clane bed for the night.' And will ye forgive the master before the night comes on ye? Aw! ye must forgive, and the Lord forgive him for his strangeness to the dacent woman that had been rair'd to good things." She went with me, and set me on my way, and ardently did I desire that I might meet poor Mary, where the rich and the poor shall be rewarded according as their work shall be; and when she turned from me, I prayed that I might be so honoured as to have a seat at her feet in heaven. For I could have no doubt but that spirit of forgiveness, and that meekness which she manifested, must have emanated from the sanctify-ing influences of the Holy Spirit.

I would not have offered any reward, had it been in my power; for I had before learned that reward offered, for food or lodging given to a stranger, was always rejected, on the sacred principle that it was given for God's sake. This offering of Mary's was the widow's mite indeed. "It was all her living." It was given with sacrifice. She gave up her choicest com-fort, her nice, her comfortable bed, and she relinquished this comfort without so much as naming it.

The rich master was feeding the poor without any sacrifice; he needed it not, and beside he was gratifying that strong – that blinding propensity so inherent in man, of winning to his favourite party antagonist practices, if not antagonist principles, bringing them to say, "You was right, and I was wrong." Oh, what a blessed lesson had been before me in the short space of eighteen hours! It whispered in my ear, never to take a man's reli-gion, whether in a tartan or a frieze coat, in silver slippers or in brogues, till I should follow him home.

I was afterwards told, that the causes of my rejection at the castle were, going to hear hireling Protestants preach, and Father Mathew give the pledge.

CHAPTER XI

Novel Interior of a Cabin – No Lodging-place – Dreary walk through mud and rain
to Roscrea – What to do for a bed? – A profitable Sixpence – Start joyfully, with
fine weather, and threepence in my purse – A Lift from a "friend" – Money-letter
at Urlingford – Reflections – Honesty and kindness of the poor Irish Peasantry –
Parting from cordial friends – Garrulous fellow-traveller – Perilous position –
Return to Dublin, and kind reception – Puzzling Voyage of Discovery

The morning was cloudy, and rain began soon to fall. I was five miles from
Roscrea, and it being but about ten in the morning, thought best to go
into a shelter till the rain might subside. A little cabin, with the tempting
flower pot standing in the window, saying, "Here are order and content
within," induced me to call. It was built of rough stone, and was not
white-washed; but when I entered, the scene was changed. Such a room
in cabin or cottage never had met my eyes. The room was small, and in
the midst of it stood a centre-table of the highest polish. On it were gilt-
edged books, shells, flower-baskets, specimens of Ireland's diamonds and
gems; and under it were all the iron and tin utensils used for cooking, glistening like so many mirrors. There was no floor but the ground, but a nice
straw mat was at the door, a hearth-rug of no mean quality, a number of
covered stools for the feet, a nice looking-glass and table, and a bed of the
best appearance, with fringed curtains surrounding it. Two well-dressed
ladies were sitting in the room, with a beautiful little lapdog on a soft mat
at their feet. As I first entered, I thought of a room of fairies, and hesitated, to see whether the beautiful images made on my mind by Mary's
neat cabin had not swelled to this fine picture. "Walk in," said one of the
ladies, "and take a seat from the rain."

They were sisters; one was married to a police officer, and told me she
had not, in her life, been six miles from that cabin where she was sitting.[1]
How and where she acquired this taste, and where she had been taught
such a finish of housekeeping, so distinct from all her neighbours, is difficult to understand. They sat till five o'clock without eating, though they
gave me a biscuit, and they sat without working. The rain continued, but
the young ladies told me that they had an engagement that evening, to
attend a christening, and must be out. There was a lodging-house near,

and the unmarried sister offered to accompany me, adding, "The woman is quite odd, and may tell you she can't lodge you, when she can." We went. A positive denial was the result. I begged her to give me a shelter from the pitiless storm, giving her my usual pass-word, "American stranger," telling her that the Irish were so hospitable, and if she would visit my country I would do her all the good I could. All this cringing and coaxing was unavailing. "I have told ye I wouldn't lodge ye, and that's enough." There was an inviting bright fire upon the hearth. I begged her to let me lie down upon the chairs, and stop till the rain should cease, and I would go out at any hour. "I shall not keep you, and that's enough." I next went to an English family; they refused because they had just moved in. It was night, and very dark, and the rain and storm increased. I set my face towards Roscrea, and was struggling with wind and rain, when I saw the smoke of a cabin coming out the door, which a woman had opened, with a pot of potatoes she was carrying in. I enquired the distance to Roscrea. "You arn't a-goin' there to-night; turn into the house a bit; a smoky shelter is better than a stawrm. And why did ye not stop in the lodgin'-house back?" Telling her I was refused; "and did she think she never might be wawkin', and want a lodgin' place? Ah, she's a blackguard; she stands there sellin' whiskey from mornin' to night, to the vagabonds about the place."

This cabin had not one redeeming quality. Two pigs lay in one corner upon a pile of straw; three dirty children were on the hearth; a miserable bed, one chair, a stool or two, and an old tottering table, made the sum total of this domicile. And in addition to the smoke from the turf on the hearth, a copious volume was poured in from an adjoining room, from over a partition which extended mid-way up. What could I do here? Breathing was quite difficult; and, in or out, my case was no promising one. The poor man came in from his work, and sat down by a little low table, and held his arms around the edge, while the good woman poured the potatoes upon it. He picked out a large one, which he said weighed a pound, and, taking off the coat with his nails, presented it to me. I toasted it upon the coals, ate a part of it, and went to the door; and seeing that the rain had not abated, and that I must go, committed myself to him "who rides upon the stormy sky," and went out. "If I had a place, you should not go," the poor man said, as he saw me going.

My lot for the next two hours was not a pleasant one. The road was dreadfully clayey and hilly. I waded through darkness, mud, and storm; sometimes in the ditch; and but once met a human being, whom I found to be an old man, who pitifully exclaimed, "Ye'r lost! ye'r destroyed! and ye've two miles under yer fut to the town." These two miles were replete with realities – no imagination here. I reached Roscrea about ten, and every thing in town was still, but the loud pouring of the rain. I was bewildered, and knew not a single street, till I saw by a lamp a girl; and enquiring for the market, found the old stopping place of the kind woman who had invited me to stay, when passing through. And the first salutation when she saw me enter, was, "I have no place to put you here – I am obliged to sleep on the boards myself."

My clothes were dripping with wet; it was past ten; and the rain was tremendous. "I believe that I am not to have a lodging in Ireland to night," was my answer. "I will go with you to Mrs. T's." She went, I was refused, and the friend left me, and returned to her house. Mrs. T. said she had taken two more than her usual number, and every bed was filled.

Now, kind friends, if you have followed me through rain and storm to Roscrea, remember the sixpence given to the poor woman when I passed through the town, and mark its progress. I stood, not knowing what to do. In a hotel I could not get a bed, for want of money.² A voice from a dark corner called out, "Ain't ye the American lady that went through here a few weeks since?" I answered that I was. "I've heard of you, and you shall have a bed if I sit up. You kept a cabin over a poor woman's head, and God won't let you stay all night in the stawrm." The mistress was in bed; this woman went to her, told her who I was, and extolled my excellencies so vividly, that the mistress said, "I have a bed in the garret where the servant sleeps, but there is nothing but a ladder that leads to it. I could give her clean sheets, and a chaff bed, but am ashamed to offer such a place." I heard it, and said, "A ladder is no objection; give me clean sheets, and all will be well." The mistress arose, made me a cup of coffee, and brought bread and butter, and put me in a situation to dry my clothes. I ate some bread, and took "a sup" of milk, ascended the ladder, and never slept sweeter. "Cast thy bread upon the waters, and after many days thou shalt find it."³ I had found my bread in the place where I left it, and at the very time I most needed it. But for that trifling sixpence, I should probably have stayed under some hedge that night, or been walking upon the street on my way to Urlingford.

At five in the morning I was down stairs, called for my bill, and was told it was threepence; nothing of the supper, and half price for climbing a ladder. I had now threepence, and but twenty-six miles before me. I went forth, the clouds were swept from the sky, the stars were looking out; it was December, and the day was just dawning; the grass was green, made young and fresh by the rain, and the morning bird had begun his song. I should be ungrateful to say that I was not happy. I was more than happy, I was joyful, and commenced singing. I was standing upon a green bank, admiring the scenery, when the thought occurred to take out my purse, look at my threepence, and realize, if possible, my true condition. A stranger in a foreign land; a female, alone, walking with but threepence in my possession. I did so, and the sight of the pennies, rude and ungraceful as it might be, caused me to laugh. "What lack I yet?" was my prompt reply, and then was I happy that I had been compelled to test my sincerity in visiting Ireland, and my firm unwavering belief in the promises and care of God. I had but just returned my purse to the bag, when I heard a carriage, and a call, "Stop, and take a ride to the next town. Here is the American lady that stopped at my house." This was the Quaker at whose place I stopped on my route to Galway. This ride carried me six miles from Roscrea, to the place where I had stayed at the shopkeeper's, when on my way.[4] I was met and welcomed at the car by a son of the family, with, "We're glad to see you; Uncle has a letter for you at Urlingford, with money in it from America; but he found the seal broken at the office, and thought it might be unsafe to send it on to Galway."

A breakfast was prepared. I passed the day in making repairs in garments sadly racked by storms and trials before unknown, and the next morning the boy and car were sent to carry me to Urlingford. My money was in waiting, my friends were as kind as when I left, and I sat down to rest and reflect.

I looked back upon the strange journey with peculiar feelings. Through storm and sunshine, by night and by day, without harm or fear of harm, had I wandered. I looked down upon the shoes which a lady presented me in New York, and could say with the children of Israel, "My shoes waxed not old on my feet," though they let in the water; but they made a decent appearance outside, which among the peasantry is a matter of great moment.[5] Filthy as they may be called in Connaught, yet a clean collar and cuffs would immediately be noticed, and mentioned as a proof that I was a "proper person." And I was more careful to be in tidiness when among the poorest peasantry, than when among the gentry; the latter could make suitable allowances for all defects, and the former thought it, from its rarity, an attainment of great merit.

The protecting kindness of God must be recorded in particular, as I never had been in the habit of being out alone after nightfall in city or country, and should have shrunk from it as improper, if not dangerous. Here, the peace of mind, the unwavering trust which I ever felt in the arm that sustained me, kept me not only from fear, but kept me joyful. Yes, I was joyful, though a stranger, alone, upon desert mountains, and in deep glens, without money, and often without food, – sometimes sleeping upon naked chairs, sometimes upon a pile of straw, and sometimes not at all. Yet my strength never failed; no pain of the head or sickness of the stomach, no cold or fever ever assailed me. Yes, I can say, that I then knew and felt, that the bank of heaven was full, that it could never fail, that the banker knew every deposit, and knew when and how to give out as the depositor needed; and that he would withhold "no more than was meet," and no longer than was necessary.

"Do not, I beg you," said a kind clergyman, who is mentioned in this journal, "ever suffer yourself to be out after dark alone in Ireland. It is presumptuous, it is dangerous." This was his last injunction, and twice has he written me the same caution. I thanked him kindly, but could not understand his fears. I had but one feeling, and that was trust; and when night unavoidably overtook me, whether upon a mountain or in a city, what was that to me? I loved to hear a footstep in my path, for I knew it would be accompanied with a "God save ye kindly;" and that salutation ever has sounded to me, when alone, like the voice of Him who said, "My peace I give unto you." And often have I answered the kind peasant by saying, "The Lord does save me kindly." These were halcyon days, days of my best and richest, days when I turned to the God that was within me, and laid hold of his strength.

Another most important object was attained by my travelling as I did. The Irish, their enemies would have it, are murderers; they will kill a person for a few shillings. I was days and weeks in the wildest parts, certainly much better attired than they were, often with a small locket about my neck, which they supposed was a watch. They knew I had crossed the Atlantic, they knew I was alone, and they did not suppose, till I told them, but that I had money in abundance; and for the most of the time I was wholly in their power. Why did they not use this power? Why, on some lone mountain, three and five miles from any cabin, did they not leave my bones to bleach there? Or why did not some dark glen cover the stranger for ever from the ken of man? I learned too, the true nature of their hospitality, and proved to a demonstration that it was not feigned; for invariably when I told them I could not reward them for their potato or lodgings, "And didn't ye crass the ocean to see the poor? Ye may stay as long as ye will."

Facts might be multiplied of unparalleled kindness from the poor; but I must prepare for other scenes. My body and mind were both strengthened by rest and kindness at the doctor's, where I had been most of the time since my return; and at Dublin I must depart. And so urged was I to spend the Christmas there, that I felt obliged to say I should not, for *could not* answered no purpose. "If you will leave us, the blessing of God go with you," was the reply; and man, horse, and car, cake and cheese, were ready. I felt that morning that the air of Kilcooley and Kilkenny was wafting fresh kindness, that the birds sang it, and the dogs barked it; and when the doctor, his wife and daughter, with the little Yankee Doodle, accompanied me to the gate, I begged that not one of them should speak. I looked a long farewell. A wave from the hand of the doctor, a tear in the eye of his companion, were the last I saw; and a "God bless you," from the little Yankee was the last I heard. I hurried the driver to take me away. Why should I linger? This was not my rest. I should not find the like in many families; it could not be expected, and it would have paralysed those strenuous efforts which must be made in accomplishing what was before me.

Thirteen miles brought me to the pleasant town of Durrow, where I stopped for the night, to take passage in the morning for Dublin.[6] Here I found an afflicted woman, whose husband had seven years before gone to New York, and she had not once heard from him. The sight of an American opened anew the channels of grief, which had already done a serious work. Kindness was here lavished without weight or measure, and when I called for my bill in the morning, "We cannot ask you anything, for you have had nothing," alluding to a straw bed which had been prepared by my request. I paid them more than the ordinary price, for they had done more than is customary to be done for lodgers.

At five, while the waning moon and twinkling stars were still looking out upon the beautiful landscape beneath them, I was upon the car, with a talkative young coachman, and rode five miles, passing the domains of the rich, whose high walls and widespreading lawns made a striking contrast with the thatched hovels and muddy door-yards of the wretched poor around them. Never had I rode in Ireland when the stillness, the scenery, and the hour of the morning all so happily combined to make the heart rejoice as now. But the one dreadful, ever-living truth, like a spectre haunts the traveller at every step; that Ireland's poor, above all others, are the most miserable, the most forgotten, and the most patient of all beings. I heed not who says the picture is too highly drawn. Let them see this picture as I have seen it, let them walk it, let them eat it, let them sleep it, as I have done. Let them look at these disgusting rags, with eyes not dimmed by constant use, and hearts not seared by love of avarice. Let them look on Ireland as though she were some distant isle, ruled by some pagan lord. Would they not say, blot her from the earth, sink her in the sea, scatter her to the winds, or make her more comely in the eyes of men?

I could not but say, while passing these forbidding cabins, "Sleep on, for when you awake it must only be to fresh misery; it must only be to idleness or unrequited toil. You are now free from the voice of the imperious landlord; you do not now see the squalid, half naked child asking for the potato; and you do not see the light of that sun, which only shines to you to light up your degradation."

We now reached the handsome town of Abbeyleix, as the caravan was about leaving for Dublin. A garrulous old Protestant of more than eighty, who said he built the second house in Abbeyleix 48 years before, the daughter and granddaughter of the old gentleman, an elderly Catholic man, a young Irish girl, and a live turkey made up the passengers, including myself.[7] When I had answered the knowing old gentleman all questions about America, from the sitting of Congress to the cultivation if pigs, geese, and turkeys, he told me in turn the wonders of his nation, some of which were quite incredible, if not ridiculous. His daughter, who was a married woman, and well dressed, seemed to enjoy the unceasing volubility of her father; and when I remonstrated, she added, "O! he must be gratified," and I then said I must leave the caravan. He was well dressed, had read much, and apparently belonged to the higher class of society, so called. What surely am I to next meet in travelling through Ireland? All sorts of characters, in all sorts of condition, were meeting me at almost every turn.

The conversation now turned upon the subject of giving the Bible to the common people; the Catholic urging that when they could not read it, what possible good could it do? And that it was so little valued by them, whenever they had any of it, they used it for wrapping-paper, and often for lighting their pipes. The debate was ended by passengers crowding in, so that the ride was quite uncomfortable. I had previously asked the privilege of riding outside, to escape the old man, but was denied, because the coachman said it was quite unsafe. The door now opened, and the coachman invited me to take a seat upon the top, promising to make me as comfortable as possible. I would not refuse, because I had asked the favour; and though the eminence looked perilous, it must be tried. There were no seats upon the top, and I was fixed upon the edge, my feet hanging down, with a heavy coarse sack flung across them to keep them warm, which I was obliged to hold in one hand, and with the other to grasp a wire, to secure me from falling from this dizzy height. This position I found so uneasy, I was obliged to draw my feet up on the top of the caravan, and in this cramped condition rode fifteen miles to Dublin. Here, in my old lodgings, I found additional welcome, for it was followed by an invitation to make the house my home, free from charges.[8] My trunks had been well minded, and the kindness here seemed but the other extremity of the chain, beginning at Doctor White's.

I visited many of the public places in Dublin; and in my perambulations alone about the city, noticed quite a difference in the kindness and civility of the lower class, especially about the docks, to that of the same class in the interior. An enquiry concerning a street would always be answered with civility, but if any misunderstanding or confusion be manifested, a second enquiry is often followed by rudeness. This is generally the character of all seaports, in every country.

The sixth of December, at eight in the morning, I took a piece of bread, and went out upon the circular-road that surrounds the city.[9] Soon finding myself in a labyrinth, where water, bridges, mud, and cabmen were in a confused mass, and not knowing how to get out, I enquired the way. A wag called out, "Follow your nose, woman." This answer would not have been given by a Connaughtman, or a mountain peasant; but knowing he was an Irishman, I received it in good part, and answered that I had followed it till it had brought me into the ditch, and I found it was not a good guide, and I now wished some instruction from more experienced ones. With one consent, every man left his cab, eager to direct me the shortest way, each having the best knowledge; till the confusion, and the kindness, I was directed all points of the compass but the right one, and I hardly knew whether to stand still, move forward, or go back. I went from them, and enquired of two labouring men, who told me I was wrong; a third insisted, "She is right;" following the direction of the two first, a woman of whom I enquired told me I was certainly wrong, and led me on about docks and walls, till, tired with the chase, I told her this could not be the way. In anger she turned away, declaring she would say no more. Another met me, said I had been led astray, pitied me much, took me about a circuitous wall, showed me the ships and houses as kind of landmarks, adding, "You must go to the quay, cross the river, and you will be on the circular road." By this time I was so crazed, that all roads were alike, and in despair took the track around the wall again, and stumbled upon the woman who had left me in anger. "Here comes this woman again," she said angrily to another. "Yes," I answered, "here she comes again, and is half crazed." "I knew that afore." By this time I was quite a penitent, and begged her to tell me once more, and I would follow her direction. She did so. It was a long way, but it led me to the ferry. I crossed, and reached the spot on the circular-road from which I started at two o'clock, having taken the whole circuit, a distance of twelve to me weary miles, and so confused that I cannot now remember one perch of the way.

CHAPTER XII

Start for another Tour – How to carry a heavy Load with little trouble – A formidable Animal in the Caravan – Wicklow – Visit to a Poor Cabin – Half-a-crown earned in Three Months – Attentive Auditory – Wretched condition of a Sick Woman – The bright Old Man of the Mountain – Sabbath Hymn, and the Company collected thereby – The Scholar with his Iliad – Visit to Wicklow Lighthouses – Wexford – Infant School – A tolerant Catholic

Jan. 9, 1845. – A pleasant stay of four weeks in Dublin made a journey around the coast, which I had resolved to take, look a little formidable, as it was in the depth of winter; but the work was before me, and difficulties must be surmounted.

I had become sufficiently acquainted with the peasantry of Ireland, to know how to gain access; and had resolved that this access should be made an avenue if possible to do them good. They were not in general so ignorant nor so bigoted as I had supposed, many of the children had access to some kind of instruction in most parishes I visited. I found that money, as a reward for any little favour (except among the guides), was refused, and I resolved to give them books, as well as to read among them as I had previously done. The preface of this work informs the reader how these books were furnished. A good selection of tracts on practical piety, school books, and English and Irish Testaments made up the catalogue.

I will mention the manner of carrying these books, because it proved to me so convenient; and if any other persons should ever climb the mountains and penetrate the glens as I did, they may find it expedient also. I carried no trunk, but a basket; had two pockets in which the tracts were put; and upon a strong cord fastened two bags, into which I put the Testaments, and appended this cord about me, under a Polka coat.[1] When on a coach or car, these did not incommode me; and when I stopped at a town, to visit upon the adjacent mountains, I took from a bag what was required, put them in my basket, and went out, always minding to carry a Testament in my hand, which every peasant walking with me would ask me to read.

Thus equipped, like Abraham, I "went out, not knowing whither I went."[2] The family where I stopped had anticipated my wants, and furnished me with such little et ceteras as to a traveller are very grateful, and the two mindful sisters accompanied me to the caravan, which at half past three was to go out for Wicklow. I was cheerful; I was happy; till one of the ladies called out, "Look! there is a Connaughtman." At the entrance into the caravan sat a man with blue stockings to the knee, corduroys above, grey coat, and a pipe in his mouth. This to me was the "avalanche" more formidable than beds of straw, potatoes without salt, nights of wanderings on bleak mountains in rain and storm. Not because he was a Connaughtman – not because he was poor – not because he was ignorant; but because I hated to my very heart the stench of tobacco, and the wholesale, never-dying staring which penetrated every fibre of my frame, and set every nerve ajar. Laugh who may, I could not help it.

As I approached the vehicle, the kind man moved, allowing me to sit near the door. A countryman and countrywoman were in the caravan; the former soon fell a-snoring; and a ride of twenty-two miles in "darkness visible" brought us to Wicklow. The man awoke, and offered to find me a "proper lodgin'-house," and in my hurry to escape the Connaughtman, I left my parasol, and lost a guide book which I never found. The man found me a comfortable lodging-place, bade me "God speed," and departed.

The next morning, though it rained and the wind was violent, I walked upon the sea-shore, and seeing a miserable hut, made my way to it – a dark, cheerless abode. A man and sickly old wife were sitting by a pot of potatoes, which was kept boiling by means of dry fern, which the man was constantly applying to keep up the blaze. Three children of their own, and a nurse child, were in the room; the latter hiding herself because she was nearly naked. "She is ashamed, ma'am," said an elder girl; "she's not a ha'p'orth to cover her, and we can do nothing but give her the potato." The father said he had earned but half a crown in three months, had nothing to do from morning to night but sit, as I saw him. His wife was evidently in a decline, and when I spoke to her of another and better world, where the inhabitants should no more say, "I am sick," she turned aside with a look of disapprobation; and the husband, by way of apology, told the daughters to bring their premium bibles they had got in Sabbath school. "We are Protestants, ma'am, and the children go to Sunday school; but it's many a day since the wife and I could get a dacent suit for the Sabbath." "Your pastor visits you?" I said. "Not a ha'p'orth do his feet ever crass the threshold of a poor man's cabin like mine, ma'am." I could only pity, and left them as hopeless as when I found them.

In the evening, the woman of the house asked, "Have you anything nice to read, ma'am?" Telling her I had, she prepared to listen, when a fish-woman entered wet with rain, and seating herself by the fire, commenced a stream of talk, sense and nonsense, Irish wit and Irish vulgarity, so compounded and so overwhelming, that I was about leaving the room, when a man of the house whispered, "She has lost her mind, ma'am. Two years ago she had two sons, fine young men as ye'd find in a day's walk, and they were drowned in the say, and she never had her mind since." I took my books, when she enquired, "Are ye going to read, ma'am?" "If you wish, I will, if you can be quiet." "Be sure I will," and seating herself at my feet upon the floor, she listened with the deepest interest. She sat for more than two hours, nor could she be persuaded to sit anywhere else; and when I read some of the last words of the Saviour, in the book of John, she clasped her hands with wonder and joy, asking, "Was that for poor sinners like me?" She seemed clothed and in her right mind, and I could think of nothing but the calm that followed when the Saviour rebuked the wind and the sea.[3] My auditory had increased to a goodly number, and when I finished, they enquired, "And could ye sell a few of these books?" Telling them they were not to sell, but to be given; "And maybe ye'd give us a little one," meaning the tracts, which they had seen, and "Our children shall read 'em, lady," said one. With all the simplicity of children, they talked of all the good things they had heard me read. "And it's many a long day since we've seen the likes of ye, and heard the nice things ye have said to us." Thanking, blessing, and bidding me God speed, they went out.

Saturday morning. – The woman had the Evangelists and the book of Acts, of the Douay translation, reading them most attentively, exclaiming, "God be merciful to me, a sinner!" This book she kept under her counter, and every moment, when at leisure, she was reading; nor was this a transient fit, for when I commenced reading a chapter in John, she went before me, repeating it verbatim as she had learned it before, till nearly the whole chapter was rehearsed.

A ramble in the afternoon gave me a beautiful prospect of the sea and town. Meeting a peasant, and enquiring the way, "And ye're a stranger, and have ye seen the light-house a mile and a half from this? They will be well worth a walk to them," he said. I determined to go, but turning into a cabin, a sight was there presented which diverted me from every thing beside. On a pile of straw, placed upon a bedstead in the corner, lay an emaciated woman without a sheet or bedspread of any kind, but an old cloak which but partly covered her; and shivering with cold, sitting in the ashes, were three small children; and in another corner, a pile of straw upon the floor, where they slept. The woman made incoherent answers at first, but soon was collected, and apologized for her seeming rudeness, by saying she was ashamed she had answered a lady so; and I soon saw she was of no mean extract. She informed me her husband had been three months in the hospital; that her bed and bed-clothes had been pawned for food; that she could now relish nothing but rice and bread, and these she could not procure. "The doctor used to be kind," said the mother. Taking the eldest daughter, I went in pursuit of him: the doctor had forgotten them, and could say no more than that she must go to the infirmary, or lie as she was. I went to my lodgings; the woman had nothing to spare; directed me to a hospitable Catholic lady, who never refused. She was ill; could not be seen. I went away disheartened, and was passing among the crowd, when the servant called after me, "Mrs. D. says she will see you." Hearing that I was an American, she hoped to hear of friends there, and when I returned was received with much affability; and telling the sad tale of the dying woman, she pitied, gave a few pence, enjoining me not to mention the donor, adding, "You know if we mention our alms-giving, it will do the giver no good at last." A little covering was purchased at a pawnbroker's, some bread and rice added, and carried to the wretched cabin. Stepping in a few doors from this abode, and begging a female to look in, and see that the poor woman should not die so neglected, "We are all starved, and perishing with want, lady," was the reply, "and cannot mind our neighbours." I went to my lodgings, and passed the evening, reading to attentive auditors to a late hour.

Sabbath morning. – The sun arose pleasantly – a welcome sight, as my eyes had scarcely seen a cloudless sky in seven months. Taking a few tracts, I went out to ascend the wild mountains, which lay back from the town, and whose heathy sides I was told were sprinkled with smoky cabins. Climbing rocks, crossing hedges and ditches, I at last saw a cabin on the brow of a hill, and entered its humble door. An old man was shaving; wiping his razor, "God save ye kindly, lady; and sure ye must have gone astray, to be so airly out on this wild mountain; ye must be a stranger; and have ye no comrade to be with ye?"

His tall stooping figure, his noble bald forehead, the sprinkling grey locks upon the back and sides of his head, the lustre of his eye, and the smoothness of his placid face made him an object of deep interest at first sight; but when he told me he had breathed the air of seventy-five winters on these mountains, without a "ha'p'orth of sickness, or a pill from the doctor," and could read my books with a naked eye, I was almost incredulous. "If ye have a Douay Testament, I will try my hand at one, lady; but will not touch any other." Promising to return with one, if I had any, he accompanied me a good distance up the mountain, and making a low bow, which would have done honour to a Parisian, he bade a good morning, adding, "Ye must be in haste, ma'am, if ye would be in time for chapel." The light-house soon met my eye, standing upon a craggy rock – the old one, which had been struck by lightning, all shattered and useless, waiting at a respectful distance.[4] But the bold, the awful grandeur of this place – how can I describe it, that the reader may understand me? The gate was fast closed that led to the neat white dwelling-houses upon the brow of the rock, and making a circuitous route, I descended into a glen, then up a wild craggy steep, by the help of both feet and hands, and found myself upon the top of an awfully grand rock, partly covered with grass and firs, overlooking the then placid waves that lay at the foot. The sun was shining, and, though January 12th, birds were singing, and green spots of grass were here and there scattered among the ploughed fields at a distance. Far at my back were extensive cultivated lands upon the mountains, which, by their natural unevenness, still retained their wildness; and at my right was stretched the fine strand of Wicklow. Not a human being was near, but God had left an impress there which could not be misunderstood. I sat down, and looked into the abyss, eddying, deep, and dark, in a niche between two rocks at my left. The sea was spread out at an interminable distance to the eye, sparkling in the sunbeam, and bearing a solitary sail floating at ease. Taking off my bonnet, I paused to wonder and adore. It was the resurrection morning. I saw no sepulchre here hewn out of the rock, but caves were scattered on right and left, where ancient chieftains had made their abode. I commenced singing my favourite hymn,

"Majestic sweetness sits enthroned;"[5]

and when finished, looked about, and saw the shadows of eight boys who were standing upon the rock behind me. They were at a distance, beyond the rock, had heard the singing, and leaping up the sides, stood in breathless silence, nor did one of them stir till I kindly saluted them, when a laughing face of ten years said, "And ye sung well, and didn't we hear it?" The people at the light-house had heard, and came running upon the brow of the rock, on the other hand of me, not knowing what strange sounds could be floating upon the air so early.

I turned and looked upon the group of wild mountain boys, buoyant and light-footed as the hare they were pursuing, as they stood, undaunted though not impudent, before me; and said, "What was Ireland once, and what is she now!" In spite of oppression, her children, free as the mountain air, eat their potato, hunt their rabbit and deer, leap upon the rocks, laugh and sing, dance upon the green, and tell you tales of ancient Irish days, and throw out their light sallies of wit, which seem like an inexhaustible fountain, bubbling spontaneously at every breath.

"And are you going to church or chapel, my boys?" "All Protestants," cried one. "That we ain't," answered a second; "some are Romans, and some Protestants."

"We are after hunting a hare, ma'am."

"And what will yo do if you take one? – divide it among you?"

"The dogs kills it, ma'am; and the one that picks it up first gits it; but if two gits hold at once, they fights till one bates the other, and then he carries it off; so that's the way, ma'am."

"But," said the laughing one, "will ye take me with ye to America?"

"And what could I do with you? I am not going yet."

"O take me along, and when ye eat, give me something – that's all, ma'am, I'd want; and so I'd always be about ye; d'ye see, ma'am?"

"And couldn't ye get through the gate? Come, and we'll open it for ye."

They did so, and a light-keeper's wife, young and pleasant, with a neat shoe and open thin stocking, with prayer-book in hand, going to church met me.[6]

"You have not seen the light-house under the rock, ma'am, which is the greatest curiosity in all this country." Of this I had heard nothing before. "You should return and see it when the lamps are lighted."

It was not church-time. I returned to town, in company with the young woman and laughing boy, who kept near us down the mountain, a distance of two miles; then leaping over a wall, he left us for chapel. Returning to my lodgings, the woman had locked the door of my room, and gone to mass, and I was compelled to wait the return of the light-house keeper in the kitchen, till both church and mass were ended. Twilight was gathering, and the young stranger had not called as she promised, and taking a few tracts and a Douay translation for the old man, I ascended the mountain, and entering the cabin, was cordially welcomed. The gift was gratefully received, and the daughter of the old man accompanied me on, till reaching a gate we met a young man well dressed, with Homer's *Iliad* in his hand, who politely showed us through the gate to the rock, where in the morning I had lost two tortoise-shell combs, when singing to the boys. The mountain linguist found them, and then read aloud the tract, "The worth of a dollar." He was a good reader, and when I offered the tract as a donation, he answered, "I thank you, ma'am; I have a good library at home, and you had better present it to some one who has no books." I was now forced to resort to the strange fact, that has often been related of Ireland, that among her wildest mountains and glens shepherd boys are found reading and talking Latin.[7]

Darkness was gathering, and showing me through the gate, my learned linguist and cabin-girl bade me a good night, and returned to their smoky abodes in the mountain; and a short walk led me to the light-house, and an apology from the young mother, that she was a stranger in town, and could not find my lodgings, corrected all suspicions.

"Will you see the light-house under the rock?" I followed the wary steps of my courteous pioneer and her two little ones, till she led me to the top of the awful precipice. A high wall was on the right, and stone stairs made the descent safe, and the wall partly kept from the view the awful abyss at our feet; when we had descended thirty or more steps, the wall turned and passed before us, and peeping over, the top of the light-house in the deep below met our eyes, as if actually coming out of the gulf beneath, and casting its glaring light upon the dark waters around. A kind of horror mixed with admiration came over me; the first impression being, that this was a picture of the abode of the lost; but looking up over the top of the rock, I saw the crescent moon looking down with such complacency, that I knew the despairing were not there. I gazed in silence, for I had nothing to say.

At the bottom of this frightful precipice, a tabular rock juts into the sea, on which the light-house stands. Sufficiently broad is this rock for the neat little dwelling-house of the keeper, sheltered from the wild winds, which are often blowing furiously over the precipice above. When I had wondered and wondered again, I was introduced into the cottage of the keeper, who kindly showed me into the light-house, and explained the principle on which it is built. Government has mercifully provided this guide, at the bottom of this dangerous precipice. While the one from the top tells the mariner, at a great distance, that difficulties are near, the one at the bottom kindly shows him how to avoid them. Four paid keepers are here, two Catholics and two Protestants, with salaries that give them a genteel support, accompanied with but a little labour. Mr. Page took me a winding path up the rock, avoiding the steps, and I tarried with the young guide, meeting again the laughing boy, who had followed me in the morning; and who fixed himself behind my chair, pulling my dress at every pause, and whispering, "Won't ye sing, ma'am, and take me along with ye when ye go?" I actually sang in self-defence, for he would not take a denial; and at every close he laughed outright by way of chorus. "Pat," said the young housekeeper, "keep your laughing till the lady is done." Pat heeded not, but laughed on at every pause, turning my grave psalmody into the highest merriment.

The scene now changed; clouds suddenly covered the heavens, and furious winds howled dismally through the night. "You see," said the keeper, "the necessity and mercy of these lights. Storms like these are often howling, and they come so suddenly, that vessels would be in continual danger without them."

The next day I dined on kale and excellent potatoes at the house of a Roman Catholic, who was one of the four keeping the light-houses, and father to the merry Pat, whom they had excluded from my presence, because "he is bold, ma'am; he is a bold boy." The lateness of the hour urged my departure from this hospitable place, and peeping into the barn where the banished Pat was busied, I told him he must sober his face, for I was going to leave him. And the question, "Why don't you take me along? and ye ain't going without me?" made me hurry, lest he should be in pursuit. I was left at the gate by the husband of my young Protestant guide, with a "God bless ye," to combat with furious winds and pelting rain. Hurrying to the cabin of the graceful old man, he said, "And I'll show ye to the gate, for the night'll be heavy on ye, and the road'll be muddy under your fut." The road was indeed muddy, and cracked stones had been put on for a mile, which made the walking almost intolerable. It was a long, dreary, bewildering walk, and a "Welcome, welcome!" at the door of my lodging, "ye'r destroyed," was a gladsome salute to my ears.

The town of Wicklow, with its narrow unpaved streets, presented few enticements to a stranger; but her glens, her richly cultivated fields, bordering on the sweet Vale of Avoca I had traversed before, were pleasant mementoes; and now the wild mountains, with my graceful old man, light-houses, and the laughing boy, were increasing the load of pleasant and painful remembrances, which, in spite of all stoicism, did force a womanish tear from my eye.[8]

January 14th. – Arose early to depart, and felt a regret at leaving so kind a home and so interesting a woman. In search of knowledge she was hungering and thirsting, at times insensible to anything else; dropping her Douay gospels when a customer entered, with her handkerchief wrapped about it, and catching it up the moment her shop was vacated. I left a small Bible on the counter one morning, to go out and spend the day, and the next morning I heard her telling the story of Joseph to a servant with the most minute correctness. "Pray," said she, "that I may not lose my soul," as she grasped my hand for the last time. I had a three miles' walk before I could reach the coach in anticipation, with a boy to carry my bag, and should have mentioned that the hostess would take nothing for my food, and but little for my lodging. I reached the stopping place of the coach in good time to give a temperance lecture to a company of travellers, who were taking their punch; at first they made light of it, but soon became sobered when I cited them to the judgment, where we must all appear. And here allow me to say to Bible-readers, that never in all my tour did I fail of a patient hearing among the most incorrigible or trifling, whenever I solemnly cited them to a day of final retribution. They seem to have a most solemn awe of a judgment to come, and the obligation they are under to a Saviour for his death and sufferings. I had a great and attentive audience, with a multitude of "God bless and speed ye on your way; for sure ye're a wonderful body, and the like of ye never was seen." A good seat on the coach, and a pleasant ride through Rathdrum, Arklow, Gorey, and Enniscorthy to Wexford, made me forget I was a passing stranger in a strange land. At Gorey, an intelligent Irishman got upon the coach; he was full of talk and pleasantness, gave me much information of the places we passed, offered to find me a good lodging house, and show me the town of Wexford the next day.

It was dark when the coachman blew his horn at the town, and my talkative companion, after repeated efforts to procure private lodgings, sent me with the coachman to the office, with the promise to send a man and find a lodging, which was done by placing me in a hotel. This was unpleasant; for a solitary female feels herself more in a crowd, and cannot mingle with the inmates at all, to get or give information; but here I was kindly treated, had a parlour and bed-room entirely to myself, a kind servant to do all, stayed twenty-four hours, had two meals of potatoes, milk, and salt, and the whole for a shilling. It was a well ordered house, conducted by two young sisters, orphans, who were left in charge of this by their father; and to the stranger I would say, call at the Farmer's Hotel at Wexford, for comfort and respectability.

In the afternoon looked into a poor cabin. The woman received me kindly, but seemed depressed with poverty, said her husband had had no work for weeks. She had two children in an infant school, one seven and the other five; and though the eldest had been there years, and the youngest months, yet neither of the two could read.* Curiosity led me to this infant school; found them eating dinner, with each a huge potato in the left hand, and a tin cup of soup, out of which they were supping from the right. This was an additional proof of the habit I had often noticed in the Irish in America, that they always prefer eating the potato from the

---

* Through all Ireland I had noticed that few good readers could be found, either among children or adults; but the writing in general was good.

hand as bread, to using a knife and fork. This was a Protestant parochial school; but more Catholics in attendance than Protestants; and the teacher observed that the Bible was daily read; "and I find the children of the Catholics much more ready in the scriptures than the Protestants, and make me much less trouble in getting their lessons. I cannot account for the fact but so it is." The circumstance is easily explained. The scripture which is expounded to them by their spiritual guides, is impressed as being of the most awful importance, and its consequences of the most weighty import; and when they get access to this testimony of God, they are prepared to treat it as such. The Protestant child relishes it no better than a stale piece of bread and butter, which he is often forced to eat as a punishment, when his stomach is already satiated. An intelligent gentleman from Dublin remarked, he was whipped through the Bible by a Protestant uncle when a child, and had hated it ever since.

Returning to the kind woman, she went in pursuit of lodgings, and enquiring at five, the sixth took me in for sixpence a night. The woman was poor, her house was tidy, and I stopped with her, found she managed discreetly with her little all, and was extremely anxious about her young children, that they might be well educated. "I send them," said she, "to a Protestant school, because it is the best one.⁹ God be praised, my parents never larnt me to read, and my children shall not be bred in such ignorance." Darkness was over her mind, but it was darkness that was *felt*. I read to her a tract, and some of the most touching passages of Christ's life, which filled her with admiration; thinking me a Catholic, she added, "Ye know none can be saved out of our church, but yet I have lived with so many good Protestants that I could not see why they are not as good Christians as we, and why can they not be saved if they do right?" Telling her all that fear God and work righteousness will be saved, and that I had determined to take Christ for example, and his word for a guide, and obey neither priest nor minister no farther than they obeyed God, "Ye are right, ye are right," was the answer. She was in her own way truly religious, and watchful over her temper, and a better pattern than many who are much in advance in a knowledge of the world and books. Her husband is a drunkard, had gone to Dublin in pursuit of work, spent his money, and was torturing her with entreaties for more. Father Mathew has much to do yet to redeem Ireland from the curse of whiskey, for in high life it retains a deadly grasp.

CHAPTER XIII

Public Buildings in Wexford – Unexpected Delay – American Family – A Rare
Lady – Appreciation of Teachers – Doctors differ – Delightful Family – Overload-
ing of Vehicles – Waterford – Clonmel – Car Travelling and Companions on the
Road – Lodgings in Cork

Thursday, January 16th. – Another bright morning dawned, and I improved
it by walking to the chapel, a fine one with a friars' convent and library
attached to it.[1] At a little distance is the nunnery.[2] Over the town on the
hill stands the college, a splendid establishment; the chapel has the most
splendid stained window I had seen in all Ireland, and while admiring it,
a devotee arose from his knees, accosted me civilly, and insisted I should
go through the college, and then entered warmly into the merits of the
church.[3] Priests and students passed us, while, as each drew near, the
ardour of the good man increased. Both logic and argument would here
have been useless, and when the strength of feeling had subsided, for the
want of opposition, he pointed me to the grand pile, containing college,
chapel, the house of the priests, and a large house for the Sisters of Mercy
which stands back of the college. Seventy students are here, preparing for
the priesthood under the instruction of priests.

A holy well is on the wayside between the college and town, but the
virtues of these wells are somewhat on the wane; the priests are not
encouraging a resort to them, and but now and then a solitary devotee is
seen kneeling beside their sacred waters.[4]

From the college I went to the jail, and found my complaisant coach
passenger giving orders to his men, who were building a large addition to
the prison.[5] He showed me the cells of debtors and criminals which are
exceedingly clean and well ventilated; the pavements about the doors and
yards were tastefully laid out in flowers made of small stones, and at one
door was the Irish harp and "Erin go bragh." Finding a school here, where
the young found guilty of petty theft are instructed, I gave each of them
tracts, and some portions of scripture, and distributed them throughout
the cells. The prisoners are all at work or at school when not sick; a novel
sight to see shops in a common jail, and all kinds of trade going on, and a
regular routine of education. I was introduced into a room called "Master

Debtors," such as pay their own board, or rather such as find themselves. Two women were here in a pleasant room; one, the widow of a British officer, had accompanied her husband to the West Indies, was intelligent, and seemed quite astonished at seeing me, supposing that I had come as an inmate. My laughing guide enjoyed it much, claiming the honour of bailiff. The bedsteads were all of iron, with comfortable coverings, a shower-bath, and a good pump of water near by. The women and girls, which were put in for petty theft, were sewing and knitting in a pleasant room. Their thieving was mostly for taking potatoes, driven by hunger to desperation, or some trifling article to exchange for food. Yet on the whole the place looked little like a house of punishment, and doubtless most of them were in a better condition than when at home.

From the jail, I went to the poorhouse alone.[6] This stands upon a hill on the west side of the town, in a healthy romantic spot. The paved walks, with pebbles put in like those at the jail, first attracted attention. A middle-aged woman at the entrance begged for a "ha'penny to buy snuff." Telling her if she had food for her mouth, her nose would do quite well without feeding, and that I should do very wrong to give it to her for that purpose, she went away amazed. The matron approaching, I enquired if I could be shown the rooms. "Do you wish to be taken in?" she asked. "Not exactly then," I answered, "though I might wish to soon. I have come from America to see the country, its institutions, manners, and customs." She apologized, and took me into the hall, where the children were being seated at dinner. Three pounds of potatoes and a pint of buttermilk to each, "Enough," I said to the keeper, "to well nigh cram them to death." The commissioners were entering to inspect the rooms. I was admitted among them, and shown the apartments. Seventy were on the sick list, many with eruptions occasioned by cleansing the skin, and giving clean food;* the old women all begging for a "ha'penny to buy snuff," till it was truly disgusting. Tobacco in Ireland is one of its greatest curses; it is a mania infecting all classes, from the lord to the beggar; and thousands are now strolling the streets in hunger, when they might be made comfortable in a poorhouse, because they are forbidden to use this nasty weed.

I offered some tracts to a company of boys who were making shoes, when an overseer interfered, "We take no tracts here, madam. Your books may be good, and your tracts good; but we have a valuable library and good schools. Here, sir," turning to the teacher, "take this lady along, and

---

* This is well known to physiologists, that cleansing the skin, and using coarse bread will throw off all impurities of the blood, and when these impurities appear upon the surface it is a favourable symptom.

show her the books." After showing me the library, specimens of books, &c. I was politely handed out, and departed, feeling that an embargo had been laid on my enquiries and investigations, which I had met nowhere else in Ireland.[7]

Friday. – A tremendous rain kept me in, writing to American friends, and on Saturday went to the steam packet office, to secure a passage for Waterford. The packet had not arrived; I felt a little disappointed, and hardly knew where to direct my steps. My lodgings were gloomy, and my work in Wexford was done, and a longer stay would be but a punishment and loss of time. "It may be for something that I am detained, which will cause me to be thankful," I doubtingly said, when crossing the threshold of the infant school I had previously visited. "You had better visit the parochial school," said the teacher. I went because I had nothing else to do, and found a school of boys supported by the Protestant church.[8] The rector and curate came in to catechize them; the rector was thorough in his investigations, and faithful in imbuing their young minds in the holy principles of the Christian belief, as inculcated in the English church. Learning that I was an American, he said, "You should visit a family of Americans here; the mother has lately come from there." This was a fresh impetus, and without preface or apology, I turned my steps towards the "Hermitage," the place where lived the American lady. The mud was intolerable, and standing nearly over the tops of my boots in it, I demurred whether to proceed, when my country prevailed, and I made an onward effort. A peasant with a cart, wife, child, and other etceteras, now called out, "Maybe you'd get up on the cart a bit," and gladly I accepted, and was carried to a better road, and soon found the gate, which opened upon an extended lawn, presenting a wholesome and somewhat tasty house, a little, as I would have it, in American style.

My sanguine expectations were a little repulsed, at the distant reception with which my warm salute was returned by the widow and her daughter. They could not trust their eyes, ears, or my testimony, that a journey from New York could bring a solitary female to visit Ireland. A meek, unassuming woman entered the parlour, attired so unostentatiously, that I supposed her some kind of necessary appendage to the family. "Did you come to see the poor of Ireland? I love the name of those that love my Master." Supposing she was one of the poor, I spoke kindly, and she gave me her hand and went out. "Lady Nevin," said the widow, when she was out, "lives in the Hermitage, and is a pattern of goodness to us all. She said truly, when she told you she loved those who loved her Master, for she is continually visiting the poor, administering to their wants, and talking to them of the Love of Christ." A strange lady surely! such an one I had not met in Ireland, and when afterwards I visited the Hermitage and saw her meek, unassuming manner, her simplicity of dress, and the arrangement of her house, and heard her kind words of the poor about her, my heart said, Would that all the titled ones of Ireland had been with Christ, and learned of Him like this disciple! Then would this poverty-stricken isle sing for joy and gladness.[9]

The American family had been introduced to Ireland by the estated gentleman, whose parentage was somewhat pretending, but who, by a natural defect of the lip, could not speak clearly, which doubtless had served to keep in subjection that pride which is too much the offspring of high birth, and caused his good sense, clear judgment, benevolence, conscience, and firmness to have full scope, and made him the Protestant gentleman, if not the Protestant Christian. His wife was a genuine New Englander, trained in the land of "steady habits," (the state of Connecticut) and could not, would not like Ireland. Her husband had visited New York, and persuaded her to leave her country for himself and estate, and the mother, a widow, having no other child, had followed her. An adopted son, on whom they placed their affections, was the only little one that adorned their hearth.

I was detained another week by the packet, and visited the scattered cabins in the neighbourhood, and heard an unanimous chorus of prayers and blessings bestowed on their kind benefactors, particularly the good Lady Nevin. The little adopted favourite led me one morning to his school; over hedges and ditches, through bog and field, we made our way, to shorten the route, and reached at last the stop where the

"Village Master taught his little school."[10]

He was a Catholic, and under a threadbare coat, he carried a warm heart, and his head was not void of good common sense, clear discernment, and close thinking. "I despise the principle," said he, "of censuring a man because he does not attend the same church or chapel with myself. Let me see him love his country, and do by his neighbour as a Christian, let me see him love mercy and practise justice, and it is enough."

The little boy of my friends was the only Protestant child in his school, and when I invited the teacher to call upon us, his answer was not only indicative of high and noble sentiment, but a stinging rebuke on American practices in this country. "I thank you madam, for your politeness, but I never put it in the power of aristocracy to treat me with contempt. Should I visit your friends, my dinner would be laid in the kitchen with the servants, and my society be the gardener and groom." I was not prepared to believe him, and on my return mentioned it to the mistress, who replied, "It would be so; my husband would not allow me to act otherwise, and I have never invited him to the house for the same reasons. I am much pleased with the instruction he has given our son, and should be gratified in showing him respect, but the laws of society in which we move forbid it."

I begged her, as an American, to show her husband a "more excellent way," if possible. I pointed her to the country she so much loved, where teachers are ranked in the highest grades of society, and to whom the child is ever pointed as a stimulus to exertion, knowing that as the teacher is prized, so will be the instructions he gives, for it is an established law, that the stream never rises above the fountain, and this accounts in part why the common people of Ireland are so content without education, and why so few among them, who are in a way of instruction, arise to eminence. A teacher whose salary compels him to wear a ragged coat, is a sorry profession hung out for the child to acquire, and a daily spectacle of indifference if not disrespect. A twenty-pound salary, coarse boots, rusty hat, and a potato eaten from hand in the kitchen!

Again went to town to secure a passage, and found three intelligent young ladies, who were sisters, employed in acts of mercy for the poor, and who assured me that though reduced in circumstances, they should never be lowered in society, because descended from "high blood." "I acknowledge no high blood but the blood of Christ," was my answer. While stopping with these sisters, a summons arrived from no mean quarter, requesting urgently my appearance at the house of a high Protestant lady, full of zeal for the church and compassion for the poor. I went with a budget of sorrowfuls, to lay down at her feet, gathered from her suffering nation, but no sooner was I admitted, but the "tout ensemble" of the lady told me I had brought my parcel to the wrong shop.

"Madam, you are an American, I hear, and I have sent for you to learn from your own lips what brought you to this country."

"To learn the true condition of the poor Irish at home, and ascertain why so many moneyless, half-clad, illiterate emigrants are daily landed on our shores."

Inadvertently using the word *oppression*, I feared a retreat would be my only security.

"*Oppression!* So you have come to Ireland to stir the muddy waters, have you?"

"To look at them as they are, madam."

"Oppression! The Irish are not oppressed but by their nasty religion."

"But does their religion compel them to work for six or eight pence a day, and eat their potatoes on the side of a ditch? Does it compel them to reclaim a bog, for which they are paying twice the value, without the encouragement of a lease for their improvements? And does it compel them to pay a tenth for the support of a religion which they neither believe nor hear?"

The tempest was not at its height, and I only succeeded in adding, that had I dropped from the moon upon this island, without any previous knowledge, whether men or angels inhabited it, and surveyed these beautiful domains sprinkled over its surface, and seen the walking rags that by hedge and by ditch, in bog and in field, are covering the length and breadth of the land, I must have known that these fields had been "reaped down for nought."

A cessation of arms for a moment ensued to admit a visitor, who by her low courtly bow and long train told us she had *dabbled* if not *dashed* in high life. Seating herself in a corner, she listened with intense interest while the good lady resumed the subject, and remarked, that the poor in Wexford are both comfortable and happy. The stranger arose, and, with another low bow, said, "I must go, madam; the poor in Wexford are in a most suffering state; I have been this morning into the fishermen's cabins; the fishery has all failed, and they sit desolate and idle, without food or fuel."

This was an unexpected indisputable letting down of the whole argument, and at this loop-hole I made my escape, without an invitation either to stop longer, or call again.

Returning at night through mud and tempest, I found a quite different commodity in the person of a Mrs. P—, whose two young daughters are the "polished stones," which might adorn any palace where grace and virtue reside.

"You find poor Ireland," she said, "in deep affliction; and can you see any way to better her condition?" An invitation to her house was accepted, and I then found that the love of kindness was not only upon her lips, but in her heart; her house and family were so well regulated, that I could see no cause for improvement, and I feared my stay would be made quite too pleasant. The lawn before the door, with its pile of wild rocks – the bird that tamely sat upon the window-seat each morning for its crumbs – the sheep and the goat that licked the hand of the sweet girl that caressed them – the pony that lapped the cheek, and the spaniel that lay at the feet of these children of kindness, added to the cheerful comfort of the well-paid, well-fed, faithful domestics, made this house to me a little Bethel. One Sabbath was spent in it, and it was one of profitable quiet rest; the domestics and children the day previous had anticipated its approach, and, by long habit, had made all things ready.*

The mother, daughters, and myself rode upon a car to church, through the deer park and well laid out lands of a lord, who is not an absentee, but stays at home, making his tenants comfortable. A sick curate gave us a sickly sermon; his stinted salary gave no spur to rhetorical flourishes or well-turned periods, and his sunken cheek and husky voice warned of hasty dismission to another, more permanent parish. On our way home, a mile distant from each other, we passed two fools, who lived upon the street, and were better clad than their more sensible neighbours of the labouring class, strong and hearty, good-natured, and always welcome to the inhabitants, for their innocent mirth and ready wit, which would have made them well qualified for king's fools.

At evening I must say adieu to this pleasant widow and lovely family, and return to town to my old lodgings. My American friend arrived with a huge piece of plum-cake, of my own baking at her house, and being laden with kind wishes, a boy, cart, and ass were equipped *cap-a-pie* to conduct me thither; but not without "casting many a longing look behind" did I leave this spot, going out I scarcely knew whither.

The next day was spent with the three sisters, who prepared me coarse bread and cocoa for my journey on the morrow, which saw me depart, packed upon a car, with a sailor on one side and a quiet josy on the other, who kept his *terra firma* without any variation, occasionally saying, "I'm afraid ye're crush'd, ma'am," and this continued for thirty-three miles to the old town of Waterford. The unmerciful loading of cars and coaches in Ireland, the whipping and driving to "keep up to time," has no parallel in any country I have travelled. A lame and worn-down horse is often loaded with six and seven passengers, and all necessary baggage, often with a galled back, and then beaten till I have, when expostulation was unavailing, jumped from a car, ready to resolve I never would ride a mile upon any vehicle drawn by a horse, while in the country. It is true, merciful men have enacted merciful laws against cruelty in the country, and these laws are sometimes enforced; yet still, could the dumb ass "rebuke the madness" of these Irishmen as often as he is unmercifully beaten, Ireland would have talking asses, added to her incongruities, in every part of the island.

My stay in Waterford was short. A walk through and over the town

---

* I have mingled in families of all classes, in different countries, and have never found one of good order, refined manners, and strict morality that did not regard the Sabbath.

gave me a view of its buildings, and entrance into the cabins a sight of its misery. One poor Englishwoman told me she was a Protestant, but appeared to know no more the meaning of the word, or the way of life and salvation, than did the seat on which she was sitting. And lamentable as it is, the lower class of Protestants, wherever I have met them in Ireland, are more ignorant of their religion than the same class among the Catholics. Their teachers do not pay the attention to the poor of the flock, as the ever-watchful Catholics do; and the prayer-book, mumbled over at church, is the only pilot many among them think necessary to take them safely into port.

I saw nothing here of particular note, but the quay, which is convenient and handsome, and an old round tower for the transient confinement of unruly persons bearing date 1003 marked upon its dingy front.[12] The house where I lodged could boast little else but filth, and the people who resorted to it vulgarity, and at three in the afternoon again took a car for Clonmel. I had now again reached the depot of Bianconi's monopoly, and found sound and lame horses, double and single cars, with aprons "tattered and torn," and dilapidated seats, defaced by long friction, still adding to his purse, while his coachmen, thrown upon the public with tenpence and a shilling a day, if not asking for rent, are "looking daggers" at every passenger who ventures to leave without a shilling; yet Bianconi is a "noble man."[13] "All men will speak well of thee, when thou doest, well for thyself."

I was tremendously crowded, but said not a word, for I had found that silence in all troublesome cases was the best defence and only remedy. A stopping place packed another talkative, would-be-learned Irishman at my right; and as the stars looked out upon us, he turned to a neighbour, and talked scientifically of the planet Jupiter, and his moons, ventured a little upon the ring of Saturn, and ended with an ardent wish to see Lord Rosse's telescope. So sorry was I when the lecture ended, that had it not been presuming for a woman to know that the moon is not a pot of curds and cream, I should have proposed a question or two, to have kept alive the conversation.

A night in Clonmel was spent, a good portion of it in seeking a lodging-place, my kind friend O'Connolly accompanying me, and at last a tolerable one was found for sixpence, and early on the morrow, I took a Bianconi for Cork.[14] A long ride of fifty miles in a snowy wintry day, on an open car, with the wind blowing full in my face, and my seat the next one to the horses, made me more than willing to reach the city. About midday passengers were exchanged, and a young Englishman, a young boarding-school miss from Dublin, and a spruce Dublinite, fresh from the army, with two dogs, a big and little one, were seated upon the car, the larger one, dog-like, sitting upon the seat, the small one upon his master's lap. We had proceeded but a few miles, when a huge Goliath, with brandy-blotched face, and beef-eating front, made application for a seat, and the senior dog was transferred to a box over my head. The restless animal, tied to the box, had no certain resting place but on my shoulders or bon-net, and at every jostle of the car, his talons took a fresh grip of the foun-dation beneath him. Twenty miles, in this deplorable plight, brought us at nine o'clock to Cork.

Enquiring of the coachman for a lodging-house, he said he could pro-cure a clean one, and sent his son as a guide, who led me through a dark alley into a house, whose very threshold was most frightful, and the room itself more so; and shrinking back, and saying, "I think I will not stop," the coachman peremptorily said, "show her a room." Giving a hasty peep into the bed-room, he added, "You can give this lady a clean bed," and then hurried down stairs, leaving me standing like a petrified statue, to take my own time and my own way. Looking in, if my astonished eyes needed anything to make out the picture, here were the materials. But what is the use of conferring with "flesh and blood," when there is no alternative? My fate was irrevocably fixed for the night, and demurring would neither change the place nor remove the pain, and collecting myself, I enquired if I could have a few potatoes. They were boiled, and put upon a dish with a cup of salt; and disrobing them of their coat with my fingers, my supper was soon made. And here, by way of admonition and comfort, allow me to say to all whom it may concern, whenever your adventurous lot, like mine, may be cast in the mountains of Ireland, where bread is scarce, and flesh none, the inside of a potato is the safest and surest defence against not only the inroads of hunger, but other doubtful etceteras, which (begging pardon) a filthy cabin and exceptionable cabin-keeper might present.

The family consisted of husband and wife, grandmother, and five intelligent interesting children, which would have adorned a better nurs-ery. They gathered about me, to see and read the books; and the eldest, a lad of fourteen, took a small Testament, and read to the parents the four first chapters of Matthew, for they could not read. The dread of an ingress to the bed-room kept me conjuring new schemes to divert the children till a late hour, but it must be encountered. The coachman was obeyed, for I had clean blankets to my bed, though some bushels of potatoes were under the foot of it. By pulling away a dirty cloth, which served for a pane of glass, and removing an unmentionable or two, in a half hour my olfactory nerves had no cause for complaint, and never had I slept sweeter in cabin or hotel.

In the morning, eating a couple of potatoes, through snow and sleet, I made my way to the house of a Baptist minister, passed the day; and here, though a table was spread with knives, forks, and plates, potatoes and salt was my hap alone, for bread at a dinner is not the accompaniment where potatoes and flesh are provided.[15] The father returned at evening and accompanied me to his vestry, to attend a prayer-meeting and recommended a lodging-place, which was a happy contrast to the last night's encounter, and where I found the missionaries Jassom, Howe, and the widow of the unfortunate man that was accidently shot at Otaheite.[16] Mrs. Fisher, the lady who kept the house, entered most deeply into my undertakings, and ceased not to do what she could, during my pleasant stay in Cork. Her feelings for the stranger did not die in empty words; she *acted*.[17]

CHAPTER XIV

Reception from Father Mathew – The Aged Nun – Temperance Tea Party – Danger of becoming a Public Character – One Source of the Reverence paid to the Priest – Ursuline Convent and its Elegancies – Sail to Cove – Beautiful Bay – Search for Dr. Power – The Begging Whine – Trip to Blarney – Racy Old Priest – "The Blackguard Salt Herring" – Wonders of Blarney – Dr. Barter's Hydropathic Establishment – Our Jolly Priest is no Teetotaller – Walk to Cove – Pleasant Little Maidens – Delightful time passed in Dr. Power's Family

Saturday, Feb. 1st. – Called at Father Mathew's. His house is quite plain; the hall-door is fastened open from six in the morning, till the same time in the evening, saying to the citizen and stranger, "Ye are welcome."¹ The carpet of the hall is loose straw, and a woman sits at the entrance to receive and point the visitor to the room on the right, where the "rich and poor meet together," to take the pledge, or spend a leisure half hour, to watch the movements, and listen to the salutary cautions and word of kindness from the lips of this devoted man. My letter of introduction had been given him some months before, in a crowd, when he had only opportunity to say, "I will see you in Cork."²

"Why did you not come to me when you first came to the country; you knew I would have taken care of you?" was the greeting he gave, when I entered.

The room is entirely devoid of ornaments, except the papers pasted upon the wall, as cautions to the intemperate. Benches are arranged about the room for those in waiting, on one of which, in an obscure corner, I took my seat, and saw the lame and deformed, the clean and the filthy, the well-clad and the tattered, kneel and take the pledge, and enter their names in a book, which the clerk who registers them said counted five millions and four thousand. To the meanest beggar he speaks as kindly as to the titled gentleman, and to the suffering I often saw him slip a little change, bidding them depart, and not disgrace him by breaking the pledge.

He invited me to dinner at five o'clock, and his dining-room wore the same unassuming appearance, as does every thing about him – no carpet, no sofa, and not an appendage but what was absolutely necessary. His table is arranged in the most finished order, and the cooking, which is done by a man, is of the best kind. He seldom dines alone.

The next morning, at eight, he invited me to the chapel, to see an aged nun renew her vow, who had fifty years been teaching the poor, and had never been out of that convent.³ She approached the grating which separated the room from the chapel, with her black robe and veil upon her head, while the meek man congratulated her on her long faithfulness in labouring for the poor, and pointed her to the reward in heaven which he trusted was in store for her, gave her the thanks of the convent, and pronounced his benediction. He spoke of crowning her, a ceremony usual on such occasions, but she refused the honour. She then renewed her vow in an audible but softened manner, promised to be faithful unto death, &c. The ceremonies closed, I then accompanied Father Mathew to the convent, where I had been invited to breakfast with him. The breakfast was the first I had seen in American style in Ireland, and though their beefsteak, coffee, and other etceteras I declined, yet good cream, the best of bread, and jam made a palatable repast. The nuns sat by the table, but did not eat, and were surprised and distressed at my abstinence. I was here introduced to the nun who had renewed her vow; and when she told me she was eighty-four, and not a furrow had old Time made in her plump placid face, I was compelled to take her word for it, for there was no other testimony. Father Mathew sent his man to show me the way to the Independent church, telling him to go in, and introduced me to the sexton.⁴

The next evening a temperance meeting was held in a neatly decorated room prepared by the poor fishwomen, who were teetotallers. "You must go," said Father Mathew, "as you wish to see the poor. These women, five years ago, were the greatest nuisances in Cork; but they took the pledge, and not one has broken it."

I went. The rich, too, were there; they had been invited because it was the poor who had made the feast.

The room was crowded; tea was prepared, and the meeting was opened by three cheers for the Queen; and I could not mention the unexpected kind feeling bestowed thus publicly on me, were it not a duty which I owe to a class of people whom I had ever been taught felt nothing but bitterness, and acted nothing but persecution to their opponents. But justice, not sectarianism, must be my motto; character, and not popularity, must be my watchword.* I was a Protestant, and they knew it.

---

* As the Roman Catholics in America are mostly from Ireland, it is a desirable object to ascertain what this religion has done for them at home, and what character they manifest where it has been most cultured.

Father Mathew arose, and introduced me to the audience, telling them my object in Ireland was to visit the poor, and learn their true condition; adding a sketch of my manner of travelling and living, which I had never told him.

When the cheering and welcomes had subsided, Father Mathew, in a low voice, said, "You must speak to this people, you can do them good; get up without delay, and tell them what you came for." My eyes affected my heart; I had never before seen such a respectable-looking company of the poor assembled in Ireland, and accompanied, too, with the rich and the noble, taking their tea together. I briefly stated my motives in visiting Ireland, congratulated them on the progress of the temperance cause, and sat down.

An old grey-haired priest arose, and said, "I have read of prophets, I have read of apostles, I have read of martyrs, but among them all, I never read nor heard that ever a woman left her country alone, to search out a poor people – to suffer privation with them – to learn their true condition. What shall we do for her, and how shall we express our gratitude?"

This was reciprocated through the room, and when the meeting ended, not one of that great multitude would leave the house till each had given the hand to say, "Welcome, welcome to our country."

The next day, this old priest called at my lodgings. I was out, but he left a pressing invitation that I should visit his parish – said he was a poor man, and could give me nothing; but would show me his people and the country, and that he would happily do. He found me at Father Mathew's, and redoubled his invitations. The same evening a temperance meeting was held at the Rock. The promise was made that I should not be invited to speak; that supper and music would occupy the time, and no speech-making. Not so; Father Mathew again said, "Do what you can for this people. Say what you feel, and say it as you please."

The notices made of me in their papers, brought me before the public so prominently, that I begged them to desist. I had wished to go through Ireland as unobservedly as possible, asking no honorary attentions.[5]

The city of Cork, as a whole, has much that is interesting. The houses upon the hillside that overlook the main city, the Dyke with rows of trees for a mile and more, and the country-seats sprinkled in vale and on mountain, show the observer that taste, as well as wealth, has had something to do in the management.

Upon Wellington-bridge I met an Irishman, who said, "I have just got out of a bad scrape – have been to the churchyard with a hearse; the horses took fright, and I was drunk, and was very near being killed." "Come with me to Father Mathew, and take the pledge." "I could not keep it," he replied, "and it would do no good." He had made his wife take it, but as for him there could be no hope. A priest then passed, when he touched his hat in a respectful manner. "What honour you pay to these men. I see no touch of the hat when others pass." "Not to the man," said he, "but to what he may have about him. He may have been to visit some dying person, and have some of the broken body of the Saviour around his person." The expression was to me so novel, that I said no more.

Took dinner at Father Mathew's, and met an intelligent priest. A brother and young son of the apostle of Temperance were present.[6] The order of the table, the nicely prepared vegetables and fruit, the social enlightened cheerfulness, with neither porter or wine as a stimulus, certainly would have honoured a Protestant clergyman's table, and made me ardently desire that they might "go and do likewise."

Wednesday. – Visited the celebrated Ursuline convent at Black Rock. A note of introduction from Father Mathew, with the young twin sisters of the family who had once hospitably lodged me, for guides, made the walk pleasant; and the reception was cordial at the convent.[7] We found a spacious building on a rising ground, commanding a view of the Lee, and a company of healthy cheerful-looking nuns, affable and intelligent, teaching a school of young ladies, and poor children. Pianos were in every room, and in some we found two; every thing bore the appearance of comfort and good order, with much taste and style. A little, well selected museum, added much to the interest of the establishment; and a more thorough education is here obtained, than in any other school. A nun played upon an organ with good taste; and a look into the chapel of the convent, richly fitted up, finished the views of this inside world, which, observed a nun, "As this is all the world to us, why should we not gather as much of its beauties as possible around us?" The extensive walks, shaded with trees, and well laid out garden, must compensate considerably for all without. A dinner of pea-soup and toasted bread was to me a rich treat, but the twin sisters were forbidden by their church to partake, as it was Ash Wednesday, and a rigid fast was imposed. The poor girls fretted and murmured the long walk home, hoping such penances would be "few and far between." In vain I preached cheerful submission as a test of obedience – that no bowing to church or priest – no long fasts or long prayers, would be available, if performed by compulsion, or to merit a reward. They did not understand my farfetched dogmas, and would not be persuaded, but that a day of suffering like that must meet an ample reward. The dinner-hour brought me to Father Mathew's table, where three kinds of fish, with puddings, jellies, and fruits, were substitutes for pig, beef, and poultry, which Lent forbids. The fastings of both Romans and Protestants are often more ludicrous than grave; for while the poor culprit takes a light breakfast for conscience' sake, he trebles his supper for his stomach's sake, determining that the "sun shall not go down" till he is paid his wages.

Thursday. – Took a lunch with a lady who had expressed a desire to see me; and this desire resulted in happy consequences to me, ever after while in Cork.[8] After a pleasant interview, she made an appointment to visit Blarney on Saturday. I went out, took the steam packet for Cove. The prospect up the river was beautiful, giving the view of Black Rock, and the convent, Monkton, and its tasteful cottages and pleasure grounds. Stepping ashore, I made my way alone up the hill, to the highest look-out upon the beautiful bay of Cove, and realized all that had been told me in America by every visitor as well as by Irishmen, "that the Cove of Cork is not surpassed in beauty by any bay on our globe." Its islands and extensive reach, with its green shores, even in winter, looked like blooming lawns and summer shades, inviting the saunterer to bowers of repose; and to every lover of scenery allow me to say, "Visit the Cove of Cork, should you ever take the tour of Ireland."

Upon the top of the hill are springs of clear water, which send forth rivulets down its side, ever fresh and never failing, furnishing the dwellers on the sloping hill a supply the whole year. Enquiring of a woman, raising a bucket of water from one of these sparkling rivulets, if she could direct me to a lodging-house, one standing near responded, "You can give her one, and as clane a bed as in all Cove;" and I had no cause to regret meeting these cottagers. The room was clean, the bed wholesome and the charge moderate; and at five I made my entrance into the town over a wall, down a precipice, partly by stairs, to a range of cabins sheltered under the hill, and jutting into a narrow path that bordered on the sea. Seeing a woman at her door, I asked, "Can you tell me where Doctor Power lives?" Her answer was a piteous whine, that her husband had not been able to airn a sixpence for weeks, and begged me to go in and see "the poor cratur." All this without a word of Doctor Power. When the question was repeated, and the answer, "Will ye walk in and spake to the man?" which savoured so much of an attack upon my scanty purse; that, saying I was in haste, and must find Doctor Power, I turned away. "And y'ill meet him a bit under yer fut," she called out in a healthy creditable tone. A seven month's travelling in Ireland had taught me a little discrimination. Begging, here, is so common and so respectable among the poor, that many resort to intrigues and petty ingenuities when they meet a stranger; which is a kind of dishonesty not only to the stranger, but to the thousands who, by the last extremity, are driven to this method to escape starvation.

The next cabin with open door, I put in my head, and saw the mother with five children sitting upright in bed, all putting on their "apology" for clothes; and certainly no small nest was ever fuller. The good matron told me where I should find the house in question. I lingered long enough to learn that the father of this "joyous genealogy" had arisen an hour before out of the same bed, and gone to his work. Ye downy-bed sleepers, what say ye to this? What say you to these your own countrymen? And "who maketh thee to differ?" and "what hast thous that thou didst not receive?"

Enclosed among trees at the margin of the water, was the festooned cottage of Dr. Power, adorned with walks and shrubbery; and at the door stood the titled gentleman and his lady, about to enter their carriage for an excursion to Cork.[9] A letter of introduction from a brother of his in New York gave me a welcome reception, and stepping into their carriage, I went with them to Cork, promising a return in a few days.

Mrs. P. is a genuine American, a daughter of the well known Judge Livingston of New York, amiable and courteous to all. I was proud to find in one of my own country so much kindness, so much affability in rank so high. The doctor was an Irishman by birth, but had spent much of his early life in America, and imbued so much of republicanism, that respectability in coarse boots and jacket, received as hearty a grasp of the hand as when dressed in morocco or broadcloth.

At five, again seated at the hospitable board of Father Mathew, where I was daily invited to dine while in Cork. New guests were present each day, always accompanied by his brother, who was an overseer of the workhouse.[10] He was a promoter of morality and good order, and sympathized deeply in all the movements of temperance.

Saturday, February 8th. – The kind Mrs. Danker called in her carriage, accompanied by a young lady and the only son of Mrs. D., a boy of seven, with a basket of eatables, and I joined them on the promised tour to the far-famed Blarney. Our first depot, after a seven miles' ride, was to the door of Father—, his name quite out of mind by looking at the man himself – a genuine Irish priest of the olden coin.[11] He met us at the door with a three-cornered hat upon the top of his crown at a respectful distance from his ears, and so pliable at the corners, that it seemed bending to hear whatever the divine might wish to communicate. He carried a red full face, jolly countenance, with bone and muscle, aspiring to the weight of two hundred. He gave us a true Irish welcome, and ushered us into the kitchen till a fire would be made in his bed-room, which served, too, for drawing-room and parlour. "I'm allowed no wife and brats to privilege me with the comforts of a separate parlour; and a poor parish priest must take his herring as he can get it. But this forty days Lent! My heart is scalt and my tongue parched with this blackguard salt herring, and not a divil of a fresh bit of beef are we allowed; and so you see I can set you no dinner but a bit of bread and cheese, and a fish." Assuring him we had plenty in our basket, he presented a bottle of wine with a volley of anathemas on tobacco, declaring that "no man that used it was fit for the divil."

The old priest was a great antiquarian, could tell us all that had transpired in Ireland since the year 1, in natural or political history, the nature of all sorts of minerals and vegetables, and assured us that no man living knew these things so well. And besides, he had the best disciplined parish in all Ireland – the best fed and the most honest people in all the world. I was informed by others that this was all true.

"If ye'll take no dinner, though I hate Blarney, yet, for the sake of this American, I'll go and show ye, and walk with her while the ladies ride." For a mile my wondering ears were crammed with tales of ancient chieftains in Ireland's days of glory, till my ohs and ahs of wonder growing fainter, he ordered me into the coach to leave him to take a shorter route across the meadow; and soon the fat priest, triangular hat, and dog, were lessening in the distance. But when we overtook him, and he found that his company were not allowed to take their carriage through the gate, his indignation was roused, that menials dependent on him should dare to use him thus.

Now came Blarney, the celebrated Blarney, where many a name is carved; where lords and ladies, peasants and beggars, have strolled and sat. Here was the seat pointed to me, where Mrs. Hall, the writer on Ireland, rested; and the old priest suggested the inspiration I might receive by sitting there on the same stone, by the same stone summer-house. The whole is a romantic spot; a hermit's cell of stone, where he slept – his kitchen, where he cooked, and the grave where he is buried, were all shown us. The rocking stone on which Prince Desmond was crowned, some centuries gone by; ancient trees, seats of moss-covered stone of the richest green, running water, laurels and ivies, green lawns spread out, made it a place of the most pleasing interest. It belongs to the family of Jeffreys. Lady Jeffrey has improved it much." She passed us while we were admiring, and told our guide to show us all that it contained. The grand castle containing the Blarney stone is a great curiosity, standing as it does on an awfully high rock, overlooking the river far below it, deep, and winding its way among trees and thick grass. To me it was frightful to look out from a loop-hole, and see the river below; and to climb to the top to kiss the Blarney stone, stretching my neck out of the window over the dizzy steep, would have been madness, though I was told many a silly boy and girl had done it.

When we had admired – for this was all we could do, as the entrance to the inmost apartments was closed – we walked to the lake, and sat down to calm our excitement by its placid waters, while the little son of my friend was in playful glee sporting around us.

We must and did leave, our priest hurrying home to arrange matters for our reception, while we went to the cold-water establishment kept by Mr. Barter.[13] To describe the apparatus would be impossible. In a circular, well-finished, thatched cottage, are the different douche and shower baths, warm and cold, prepared with the best finish. All manner of pouring and showering, plungings and washings, have here appropriate fixtures. His spacious well-ventilated house for the reception of invalids, does credit to the owner, who told us that one hundred and sixty patients had made the experiment, and every one had been cured, and none but obstinate cases had applied. They are allowed no ardent spirits, tea, or coffee; and flesh meat but once a day. The Doctor appeared to understand his business well, and is apparently a worthy philanthropist. With regret I left this place, wishing for a longer and better acquaintance with the principles of this institution; but night was gathering, and the patience of the old priest would be exhausted. We found him standing by the window of his bed-room where he said he had stood two hours, till his "heart was scalded," watching our return. And more than all, he had invited one of his curates and the doctor to dine with us, on his fish dinner. They had disappointed him, and every thing was wrong. Three women of the peasantry were sitting upon the bed, by the side of a table, regaling themselves with bread, cheese, and whiskey, which the good Father assured us "they liked right well."

We would not take dinner, and hot water was ordered for whiskey punch, and wine brought on. Now the battle commenced; the jolly priest touched his three-cornered hat, at the same moment drinking my health most heartily, while I in surly contempt turned aside, without nodding to the salute. "Ah! she's disgusted, I know. Well, ma'am, if you'll appoint a day, I will make a party in my barn as big as I did for Mrs. Hall – one hundred and sixty – and you shall see my fine parish. But this fish, ma'am, that we are forced to eat through Lent, this fish, ladies! Why, I kept Lent once, and ate nothing but salt herring, till I was scalt entirely – I was a lump of salt, ladies" – then swallowing a glass of hot punch, "I am sorry you don't know what's good, ladies." This toasting and drinking were kept up till lateness and darkness both urged a departure. We were accompanied to the door by the loquacious priest, and a glass of hot punch for the coach-man, who, in answer to my remonstrances, answered with an, "Aw, and I shall drive ye the better for wawrmin' my stomach a little." What can be said to coachmen, and labouring men, that will be available, when the "good creature" is presented by the holy hands of the priest or clergyman? We had safe ride home, though the rain was severe, and the night dark, the road muddy, and the driver's noddle steeped in hot punch. The point was settled on going home, that the day had been a more than interesting one; and if the "well-disciplined parish" of this jolly priest bore any resem-blance to the training they had been under, a dinner at the barn would have been one of no ordinary relish.*

The next day heard a prosing, commonplace discourse from the Bap-tist minister where I dined on the potato and salt, in which he said he had no sympathy for a religion that comes out in a certain colour or cut of the dress, or particular kinds of meat and drink. This sentence was so entirely a digression from text or sermon, that I pocketed the rebuke for not par-taking of the swine's flesh at his table, and "hoped to learn better manners as I get along." After service, taking a bundle of tracts, I walked to Cove. On my way, two little cleanly-dressed girls were before me, reading a col-lection of scripture admonitions from Father Mathew; approaching them, I asked, "What are you reading, little girls?"

"Something, ma'am, that Father Mathew wrote." They had come out of chapel, where they had obtained this document from their priest. They were but children of ten and eleven, and the girl who was reading was no novice in the art. I presented each of them with a little book, and thank-ing me, delighted, they ran on to a company of girls before them, but soon returned, saying, "Here are more little girls who can read, and haven't you a book for them? Maybe you couldn't spare 'em, but they would be very glad of one." Her interesting manner so won upon me, that she might have drained my basket, had not an older one in the party checked her importunity. My company was now quite numerous, for men, women, and

---

* I would not be unmindful of the kindness shown me by this humorous priest, neither would I make or strive to make myself witty at his expense; but I visited Ireland to see people and priest as they are, and here was too good a subject to be thrown away. It was true Irish coin, and I valued it not the less for appearing in its native dress.

children were following in my train. I gave them each a book, and walked on to the next village. All who accompanied me disappeared among the cottages, saying, "God speed ye," and left me alone. In a moment the two whom I first accosted, came out, and said, "We are goin' on a message to the bridge, and will be with you a bit." The bridge was passed, it was getting dark, and I said, "You had better return, your parents may chide you." "No," said the youngest of but nine years old, "ye are lonely and the night'll be on ye, and we'll go with ye to the town. We'd as lieve go with a stranger as with one of our own." The artless simplicity with which she said this, and the expression of kindness which lighted up her countenance when she spoke, strongly inclined me to take her in my arms, and snatch her away from a land where the poor must be kept in their rank because they are poor.

The instinct of kindness which is so strong in the children of the peasantry, is remarkable throughout the country, and offers to the observing stranger a redeeming substitute for all other privations. My little companions took me in sight of the town, and pointing forward, "and ye'll find the ferry on a bit," said "God speed ye," and scampered away, with my heart in galloping speed after them.

The ferriage was a penny, which was given on entering the boat. Stepping ashore, I was accosted with, "Fourpence, ma'am; fourpence is the ferriage you must pay me." "You did not know sir, a yankee knows full well when the fair is paid." "You're a thief," said a countryman, "let the woman pass on," and the crowd gave way to allow me to go through. This was taking the advantage of the lone stranger, and quite the other side of the glowing picture presented by the little girls.

A half mile took me to the desired heaven of Doctor Power's, and I felt as if I were by an American fireside where peace and good order prevailed. Here I passed a week, where every thing was done for my comfort. The children were a source of diversion and interest, being talented, intelligent, and kind-hearted. Under the superintendence of a judicious mother, a kind father, a sensible experienced grandmother, and good governess, they must improve. A dancing, drawing, and music master weekly attended, dancing in Ireland being considered a necessary part of eduction, even by many of the church. None of the higher class ever omit it, and the lower so manage, that at an early age the peasantry spend much time in dancing to the bagpipe, or the discordant vocal performance of some rustic. "It's all the sport the like of us have," said one who invited me to a field dance. Old and young, priest and people, participate, approve, or disapprove as the case may be.

My stay in this family was protracted, from a reluctance to leave a society which had become doubly endearing from what I had and must again encounter in my tour through Ireland. For, though I had been treated very kindly in good families, yet I had found few where the household management had been so home-like; where a genteel lady would go into her kitchen, and prepare with her own hands the nice dish for her guests; where labourer and animal shared in that kindness, which, though easy to bestow, yet is seldom manifested where wealth and fashion predominate.

CHAPTER XV

Cloyne – Difference between Upstarts and the really Wellbred – Practical Proofs
of the same – Wonderful Natural Caves – City Jail of Cork – Humane Governor –
Prison Discipline – Taking leave of a good man – Character of Father Mathew –
No Monopoly in Orthodoxy – A Night in Bandon – A Peasant Family employed,
a rare sight in Ireland – Arrival at the miserable town of Bantry

Saturday, February 15th. – Mrs. P, her mother, and two children accompanied me in their carriage four miles to the ferry, leaving me three miles to walk to Cloyne.[1] I had letters of introduction from the governess to a couple of families in high life; the first, born in obscurity, the second of princely descent. "You will see," said my friend, "in these two families the extremes of silly pride and genuine unostentatious nobleness of character – where if worldly distinctions claim any share in merit, they are the legitimate owners of a great share." A hurried walk, in somewhat an uneven and uninviting scenery, brought me at last to Cloyne. Making my way by enquiry, the house was pointed out, and a stupid servant took my letter, saying, "The young ladies are out," but soon returned from the kitchen saying they had gone to meeting. She had left the note with a brother of the young ladies, who had broken the seal, and after a half hour of most tedious suspense, I regained the note, and went away to a neighbouring house. I was soon called for by the sisters, who invited me in, and the first question after being seated was, "Is this the way the Americans dress? Indeed I thought they dressed very tawdry." "This is the dress which Americans would wear when travelling, madam." The character of Americans now went through a fiery ordeal. A gentleman had lately returned from New York, who testified he had seen Irish servants at balls, among the highest classes; and had at parties seen pies with crusts an inch thick, and so tough he could not bite them. So much for American dress, American republicanism, and American cookery, as a preface.

As Cloyne could boast of some antiquities, I was conducted to see the most remarkable, and the church built in 600 by the Catholics first claimed our attention. This church is now fitted up for Protestants, and retains as much of its ancient appearance as possible, claiming to be one of the noblest works of antiquity.[2] The hieroglyphics on the stones under which the dead are deposited, and many remains of ancient workmanship, tell emphatically for the taste of the ancients, as well as the passing away of all that is earthly. The chapel where service is performed contains the bishop's throne, which by some amalgamation has been doomed to be the seat where all bishops, either Protestant, or Catholic, must be ordained. Tablets, ancient and modern, are upon the walls of the aisle and church; the aisle is the width of the church, and longer than the chapel itself, and seems to be waste entirely. Next to the bishop's throne, my young heiresses told me was their pew, claiming to hold the highest rank in the church![3]

We next prepared for an ascent into the tower, which is the most complete of any in Ireland, built by nobody knows whom, nobody knows when, and nobody knows for what purpose.[4] It is now used for hanging a bell, to call people to church. We ascended a flight of seven steps to the height of 102 feet, and had a most commanding view of town and adjacent country; but so perpendicular were the stairs, that I was tolerably crippled for two days following. It was night when we reached the domicile of these newly estated misses, who did all that was rational to make me comfortable, so far as eating and sleeping were concerned, minding to entertain me with the out of the way vulgarities of New York, its commonplace magistrates, its little respect to rank and fortune; assuring me that their authority was good, emanating from an assistant editor of Gordon Bennett.[5] But Sabbath morning was the test of the civility of these religious housekeepers, for they assured me that they were communicants in the church. As the bell was ringing, the eldest observed, "You will stay at home with me to-day, I am not going to church."

"Why stay at home? You say your minister is a good preacher, and why should I not go to hear him?"

"O, the people stare so much at strangers."

"What, in the old refined town of Cloyne, and where the people, you say, are quite religious! Surely they do not go to worship God, if they are so proverbial for staring at strangers that they must be kept away!" I waited with bonnet and coat on, till the bell ceased, and then enquired, "Have the sisters gone?"

"O yes, they would not stay till the services commenced, because people stare so."

"I will make my way alone," was my answer; and the polite sexton, willing to show a stranger all due respect, escorted me through the church, and showed me into the honourable pew next to the throne, where the two young prudes were seated, with prayer-book in hand, so intent on their devotions that they heeded me not, till I called at the foot of the stairs leading to their chamber to say "Good-bye." The two elder sisters had prepared me a good dinner, and received me on my return with much cordiality; and as my visit was now terminated, the eldest sister said, "You must not walk to Mrs. Fitzgerald's.⁶ We have a good jaunting-car, and will send our man to convey you thither." But listen, reader! The jaunting-car proved to be a cart, with a bunch of oaten straw for a seat, and when all was equipped, the elder sister said, "We wish you to tell Mrs. Fitzgerald that you rode on our jaunting-car to the lodge; and be sure you get off at the lodge, and she will not see you!"

This was too much, and indignantly I said, "I won't, I will not lie for any one;" ashamed at the silly pride, but more at the impiety of the eldest, who acted as mistress of the family, and who ten minutes before, while at my dinner, had been telling me of her late conversion to the love of the Christian religion.

This was a fair specimen of many such, started by accident into an estate. These daughters had lately become heiresses to an inheritance by the death of a grandfather, who having no lawful heir, left his patrimony to their father, his illegitimate son. The daughters, wishing to get into society to which by birthright they were not entitled, endeavoured "by hook and by crook" to make up for all deficiencies of high blood, which in Ireland is the ultimation of all silly aspirants to nobility. It is not her strong forte, but her weak side, her silly, her effectual drawback to real excellence, especially in woman. The Irish women, were it not for this discrepancy, would stand out as a model of all that is dignified in their sex; for, wherever can be found the legitimate possessors of princely birth and education, there is found a dignity, blended with the most refined affability, which makes the meanest dependent feel she is in presence of a protector.

Saying a long and lasting adieu, not forgetting the absconded prudes who had kept themselves secluded from sight since their return from church, I ascended the cart, which would have been declined had not rain and stiffness occasioned by climbing the tower, made it imprudent to undertake a two miles' walk. The driver, true to his trust, dropped me at a respectful distance from the lodge, in sight of the mansion, which was on the top of a hill in a placed called "Rock View." Here was a genuine noble family, of the true Irish race, of olden blood, wealthy, unsophisticated, unassuming, and condescending. The mother, a widow, with eleven children, all whom she had well educated, and elevated to respectability in different stations in life, was in the midst of her household, as the centre of attraction to which they were all drawn. With courtesy they received me as the bearer of an introductory note from a friend, and as a stranger. The accomplished sons and daughters of this family, alluded not to any higher lineage of their own than the meanest peasant. Their religion was Roman Catholic, but had I not seen a crucifix in the daughters' bed-room, I should not have known it.

Monday. – I visited the great rock, from which the place receives its name, and which contains a valuable marble quarry.[7] The labourers, some years since had, in excavating the rock, found caves of immense extent, which are objects of peculiar interest. One into which I was shown had a narrow entrance, widening as you advance, and in somewhat a zig-zag direction until it brings you into rooms ornamented as if done by a chisel, these ornaments many of them hanging from the ceiling. Here are seats like small benches; an altar which had been much defaced by the ruthless hands of visitors carrying away pieces of the candlestick, &c. These chambers of imagery had been explored to the distance, some said, of a quarter of a mile, by the aid of a lantern, and no end yet found.

The cave, from continued rain, was covered with three feet of transparent water, which had percolated through the stones, and I could only set my foot upon the rough side, and put in my head, and sing, which produced a long and sonorous echo, so that it could be heard at a great distance. These caves altogether are a wonderful and beautiful curiosity, and have given rise to a multitude of legends by the superstitious, and are still considered as sacred, because they have been the habitation of chieftains and fugitives from justice, or saints to do penance. The top and sides of the cave in many places, appeared as if icicles had been formed and congealed upon the rock, lying in parallel lines, and shining like polished ivory. Nature certainly must have been sitting alone and undisturbed for centuries, to have cut and carved such a spacious hall.

But caves, Rock View, and the kind-hearted Fitzgeralds must be left; and I returned to the house to prepare for a final departure. But rain prevented, and another pleasant evening was passed with this hospitable family. Early in the morning my breakfast was prepared, a respectable carriage made ready, and I was sent to the steamer, with my passage paid to Cove. This excursion was not a lost one. The two families where I stopped were stereotyped editions of every family I had then, or have since seen, in like conditions throughout the country; and so marked are these characteristics, that an observer need seldom mistake, without once enquiring the pedigree.

I must again leave; the constant adieus had become quite painful, and

I knew when I should leave the family of Dr. Power, that privations and fatigues must attend me. My stay here had been the rest which was needed. No bustle of parties, but a quiet calm sitting-down in the midst of a well-regulated family, where peace, comfort and intelligence resided; where walking, reading, thinking, talking, eating and sleeping, had their appropriate places. The kindness of the people of Cork will be had in everlasting remembrance; it will not wear out, but grow brighter by use. I said "Good morning," and went out for ever from the beautiful Cove of Cork; leaving behind many a grateful remembrance, which none but a stranger can fully understand.

Thursday. – Mrs. Danker treated me with a visit to the city and county jails, which were so entirely novel and intricate in their windings, that I could not describe them to a stranger.[8] Perfect order and cleanliness prevail. From ten to five a school is kept open for men and boys, whether criminals or debtors; and from twelve to two for women. In the county jail we found but one chapel for Catholics and Protestants, where all assemble and hear a Protestant sermon. In the city jail is a chapel for each. The exterior of the city jail is beautiful, built of stone tastefully arranged. The panes of the windows were small, and concealed the dismal appearance of the iron grates within. The governor was a man of sense and feeling, and said he often felt it his duty to mitigate the punishment of prisoners, when he found good conduct, and granted them what little indulgences were in his power.[9] When he first took charge of the institution, he found many boys in a room, quite happy with their lot; but putting them in separate cells soon sobered them, and had the most salutary effect; for the Irish, he observed, have a great fondness for society, and a superstitious horror of ghosts and fairies. The number of boys, he added, had quite diminished since he made this regulation; but he remarked that solitary confinement for adults, was a dangerous and in many cases a fatal punishment; the mind of very few, if any, could bear it with safety. They had sent him one, he said, to be confined in a solitary cell for a fortnight, prohibiting any one to speak to him in the time. He stayed a week, but so injured was his intellect, that he had no doubt another week would have made him an idiot. Where they are ignorant and untutored, they had the most dismal forebodings and dread, the mind having nothing on which to feed, but what was of the most gloomy if not of the most frightful kind. A celebrated and experienced English judge has declared, that he should never sentence any to solitary confinement.

The prisoners in this prison, when not at study, are at work at various mechanical trades; the women washing, spinning, and sewing. They have gardens and beautiful walks, where they are allowed at stated times to go and recreate themselves. The ridiculous treadmill, too, is a part of the punishment, where three hours a day they must step to no available purpose. When man takes punishment into his own hand, he has so little of the wisdom of God in the distribution, in the quantity as well as the quality, that he makes serious and irreparable mistakes. The barbarous relic of a treadmill is a standing testimony, that Christian nations who practise it need to learn the first principles of civilization.

Friday. – A day's ramble through mud and rain made me but little wiser, and no better, and stopping at Father Mathew's I dined with him for the last time. He expected to leave town the next day, and I to do the same, never to return. I felt at leaving this good man, that I was leaving one whose like I should not meet in any other place. "I hope to meet you again," was the simple farewell, with a "God bless you."[10] The remembrance of his unabating kindness can never die, and the least I can do is to leave one page in my journal as a just memorial of his worth.*

Father Mathew, taken in the aggregate, is a character which must put the finger of silence on the lip of even bigotry itself. If any one finds fault, it must be because his unceasing unostentatious acts of goodness rebuke his own sluggishness. He unites the meekness of a Moses with the unyielding firmness of a Paul; and while he reasons with severity on temperance, and a "judgment to come," before a worldly-minded Felix, he dashes in kind sprinklings of mercy to the repenting prodigal who says, "Father, I have sinned."[11] While he shows "mercy with cheerfulness," he forbears not the deserved caution or rebuke, where the recipient may have caused his own sufferings by imprudence. While the rich guest at his table feels a subdued respect, the poor feels he is in presence of one by whom he is remembered with that condescending kindness, which narrows the awful gulf too often fixed between the rich and the poor. While universal praises are falling on his ear, and the multitude are saying, "It is the voice of a God and not of a man," like the angel before whom John was about to fall and worship, he says, "See thou do it not."[12]

Like the eagle, the nearer he approximates to the sun, the clearer his vision, and the less the squibbings of the marksman affect him – so, as this heaven-born towering mind goes from glory to glory in his lofty moral flight, the adulations and censures of men die on his ear like the echo of the mountain sportsman, or the distant murmur of the waterfall. When he speaks in a crowd, it is not that the eloquence of his tongue, or the

*In my remarks on this man I have consulted no taste, no opinion, and no religion but my own; and if any think me a heretic, I can only say, "What I have written, I have written."

happy figure or turn of a period may be admired; and when the loud cheerings drown his voice, the lighting up of his countenance is not that of inflated vanity, but a grateful manifestation of approbation that his brethren can appreciate the worth of that cause which lies so near his heart. Though cradled in the lap of affluence, he is as unostentatious of pedigree as the shepherd boy, who claims no descent beyond the thatched cabin that gave him birth. Though the weight of an intemperate world is rolled upon him, yet he forgets not the wants of the humblest menials, nor suffers the smallest favour to go unrequited. Consistency is the sheet anchor which keeps all steady. His house, though the resort of the great and noble, has no tawdry display of finery, nor rich gildings, serving only as useless ornaments of family greatness. His religion is truly catholic, dealing no anathemas to the dissenting who may differ from his creed in belief or practice; and his whole life, though one of daily self-denial, is an even tenor of chastened patience and cheerfulness. He has wiped more tears from the face of woman, than any other being on the globe, but the Lord Jesus; and thousands of lisping infants will bless the providence that gave them an existence in the same age with Father Mathew. May God give him length of days, and a crown of glory in heaven, which shall shine as the stars for ever and ever!

Going from Father Mathew, I met a kind lady at whose house I had spent a night, and accepted an invitation to turn into a chapel, and hear a sermon by an old priest who was a great favourite of hers. The subject was the suffering of Christ, and the text, "My God, my God, why hast thou forsaken me?" In discussing it he said, the necessity of Christ's suffering consisted in the entire inability of a self-destroyed finite being repairing an infinite loss, and making any atonement which could satisfy Divine Justice. That a sinful being could not do a meritorious act. That all he could now do, he owed to God before he fell, and that all and the only hope of the sinner was not the cross, and warned all to flee to the stronghold while they were "prisoners of hope." In conclusion, he said he had in a long life attended many death-beds, and the lamentations of the sinner were not so much that he had been an immoral man, as that he had neglected the "great salvation;" that he put off the great work of repentance till to-morrow, when salvation is offered only to-day. I was not prepared to hear so orthodox a sermon in Lent, and when I went home mentioned it to the Protestant lady where I lodged, who informed me that this old man was second to none but Father Mathew in alms-deeds, and was considered a faithful preacher, even by those who had no fellowship with the Romish Church.[13]

Saturday, 22nd. – I made preparation for leaving Cork, but the kind Mrs. Fisher persuaded me to stop till Monday, and refused any compensation for the long time I had been with her. What shall I say of the kindness manifested to me in Cork? This city had not lost its civilization by being civilized. In all other large towns in Ireland I had noticed, the more wealth and show, the less kindness and urbanity of manners. Cork is ranked as high or higher in literature than any city in Ireland, and its management is quite under the jurisdiction of the Roman Catholics.[14]

Monday, 24th. – Go I must. Mrs. Danker called, and said, "If possible I will see you at the coach." When I arrived, she was in waiting, with two or three other ladies, and when I was snugly seated in the carriage, she again gave me her hand, putting into mine a pound note. The coachman gave me no time to thank her, and thus was an additional debt of gratitude incurred, which I shall never pay. A supply of oranges had been purchased by the ladies, and I was pursued by a lad throwing them into the coach for many yards after we had entered the main street, to the no small amusement of the lookers on.

Bandon was my place of destination, at least for a night, about twenty miles from Cork; and with a note from Mrs. Danker to a friend, who would show me to a lodging place, I alighted from the coach. The dwelling was found, but I was admitted no further than the hall. The letter was read, and I was pointed to a house over the way – the lady had no room; to another – no room; to a third – no room. I returned, and stood upon the steps of the door – no invitation to walk in. The young lady insisted that I should go to a public house. In the meantime she sent a boy to three supposable cases: all refused. It was now ten o'clock. The servant accompanied me to a distant hotel, where I was received, and left my muff in pledge while I returned to the coach office for my luggage. The keeper of the coach-house inn kindly returned with me, and we were met at the door by a young lady, saying, "Your room is taken, and we cannot accommodate you."

I seriously feared my complaisant guide would take a freak, when he found that I had utterly been refused by so many, and leave me to make my way as best I could. But he invited me to his well-regulated house, and I stopped the next day and night on account of rain; and for my vexatious reception in the town, he said I should pay nothing in Bandon. This is a handsome town of about twelve thousand inhabitants; formerly Protestants, but now mostly Catholics. It was once famed for the weaving of corduroy and tickens, but all have gone down, leaving the town like many of its sisters in Ireland, sitting idle without employment.

The inn-keeper was an Englishman, and showed his attachment to Ireland by having resided in it twenty-five years, and marrying three Irish ladies since living in the country, beside having one buried in England. The English, though not the greatest admirers of Ireland, as a whole, yet seem to have no objection to the Irish ladies for wives; and in this they certainly show good taste.

Wednesday morning. – The town was all in mourning for the sudden death of Father M'Sweeney, who was a favourite among Protestants as well as among Romanists.[15] Shops were closed, and business suspended in all parts of the town, and the mourners went about the streets. In groups might be seen the inhabitants, talking of his worth, and saying "the like of him was not in all Bandon," and "the loss of him will never be made up." A Protestant observed, he was a "good adviser to his parish, and a peace-maker in the town, and his memory will long be cherished by us all."

Taking a walk far out of town, I went into a miserable cabin, where two old women and their two daughters were at their wheels, and a third old woman carding. This was an unusual sight, for seldom had I seen, in Ireland, a whole family employed among the peasantry. Ages of poverty have taken every thing out of their hands, but preparing and eating the potato; and they sit listlessly upon a stool, lie upon their straw, or saunter upon the street, because no one hires them.

These simple-hearted women had never seen an American before, and all work was suspended to give me a thorough greeting, and to examine every part of my clothing; and when I took the cards from the old woman's hands, and they saw I actually knew how to use them, "Aw, God bless the cratur, and she ain't above her business." Seeing about my neck a golden locket, which I told them was a memento of the kindness of Father Mathew, the old woman clasped it in her hands most affectionately, with blessings upon my head and on that of the "apostle," whose pledge she had taken, and all her family with her. In every cabin the name of Father Mathew is like music, and in the greater part of Ireland he lives in the heart of both lord and peasant. "Blessing, blessing on your head, the cratur," as I left, was poured upon me, till I was well out upon the street, "ye're a right wonderful woman, and that ye are."

At half past two a farewell to the kind Englishman's wife and children was given, and I was whirled out of Bandon, amid the din of saucy idlers, waiting about the coach, and one bawled out, "Mistress, a sixpence, and ye owe me sixpence." When I was seated on the coach, he had handed me my basket, which was standing near by, and for this he demanded a fee. I had paid a porter for *his* services, and this was wholly an uncalled-for supernumerary. The never-ceasing annoyances of these appendages to coaches and cars, make travelling one of the greatest evils encountered in going through the country. You are teazed till you allow them to do what you do not wish to have done, and then abused if you do not reward them.

My company was not the most intelligent, but civil; even declined smoking for my accommodation, which was a mortal sacrifice to an Irish-man; and had I not been an American, I fear I should have been puffed most thoroughly. A talkative old man said he was about sailing for Amer-ica with four sons, who were determined to go, and he should take the old woman along with them, though she was "ould;" but he would not have her fretting herself after him, and "so, lady, we will go together." He offered to find me a "dacent lodging," but left me when we reached Bantry, to make it out at my leisure. I went into the miserable coach-office, and saw poverty and desolation pourtrayed in every part of the dwelling where the family resided. The children were interesting, could read, and giving them some little books, I begged the good mother to direct me into some comfortable place, as the night was dark, and I was a stranger. She sent an intelligent boy, who soon found a genteel house, kept by three sisters and a brother, as a shop and lodging-house. The nicely fitted parlour and bed-room were inviting retreats, and here may I date the commencement of all that was marvellous – all that was roman-tic – all that was painfully exciting, and all that was wholly indescribable in my tour through Ireland, and I would say –

"If you have tears, prepare to shed them now."[16]

Come, sit down with me, and weep over the sad desolations of your stricken country; and while you weep, reflect, when a righteous God shall make inquisition for blood, if you have said, "Be ye warmed and be ye filled," while the garment was in your wardrobe, the bread upon your table, and the word of life upon your shelf – what shall shelter your head from the avenger of the poor?[17]

CHAPTER XVI

Exploration in Bantry – Poverty, Wretchedness, and Filth of the Dwellings – Grand Poorhouse standing unoccupied – Wigwam Row – My attendant, John – Employment a Novelty – Beautiful Bay of Bantry – Glengariff – Bad choice of a Lodging-house – A motley Audience – No Refuge from the Staring – Morning Levee – Lord Bantry's Cottage – Hospitality at the Gatehouse – Call at my ill-chosen Lodgings

When about leaving Cork for Killarney I intended taking the shortest and cheapest route; but Father Mathew said, "If you wish to seek out the poor, go to Bantry, there you will see misery in all and in every form." I took his advice, went to Bantry, and there found a wild, dirty sea-port, with cabins built upon the rocks and hills, having the most antiquated and forlorn appearance of any town I had seen; the people going about not with sackcloth upon their heads, for this they could not purchase, but in rags and tatters such as no country but Ireland could hang out.

The night was dark and rainy when I reached the town, and a comfortable parlour and cheerful fire hid from my eyes the appalling desolation that brooded without. The morning opened my eyes, to look out upon sights which, as I write, flit before me like haggard spectres. I dressed, went forth, and made my way upon the rocks, found upon the sides of them some deplorable cabins, where smoke was issuing from the doors, and looking into one, the sight was appalling. Like an African kraal, the door was so low as to admit only a child of ten or twelve, and at the entrance a woman put out her head, with a dirty cloth about it; a stout pig was taking its breakfast within, and a lesser one stood waiting at a distance. The woman crouched over the busy swine with her feet in mud, and asked what I wanted?

In truth, for a moment I wanted time to collect myself before I knew what I wanted; at last I told her my errand was to see how they do in Ireland, among the poor. "An' faith, you see enough on'em here." Looking in, I saw a pile of dirty broken straw, which served for a bed for both family and pigs, not a chair, table, or pane of glass, and no spot to sit except upon the straw in one corner, without sitting in mud and manure. On the whole, it was the most revolting picture my eyes ever beheld, and I prayed that they might never behold the like again. Leaving this abode, I ascended the rock a little higher, and entered a second. On the left hand of the door was a bank on which lay a young man upon straw; and upon a couple of stools sat the master and mistress, waiting the cooking of a pot of potatoes for breakfast. "Is any one sick?" "No, no, idle, idle," answered the mother; "nothin' to do, and so he lies in bed. The old man here has not airn'd but a shillin' since St. John's."' "And how, do tell me, do you live?' "We gets our potato when we can, ma'am; and that's all, ye see." "So you live, because you can't die." "Just so, lady; because the Almighty God don't see fit to take us away, an' we must be content with what he sends us; but sure, may we ask, what brought ye here among these wild rocks?" "To see the poor of Ireland; and I hope to go through the country, and see them all." "And ye'll have a long purse when ye return." Supposing she alluded to money, I told her, "Not a pound perhaps." "But ye'll have the whole chart of Ireland, ma'am."

I looked at this woman, and at the appurtenances that surrounded her. "The whole chart of Ireland," from lips that could neither read English nor Irish! She had a noble forehead, an intelligent eye, and a good share of common sense, she had breathed the air of this wild mountainous coast all her sad pilgrimage, and scarcely, she said, had a "dacent garment covered her, or a wholesome male of mate crassed her lips, save at Christmas, since the day she left the parents that raired her." Telling them I wished some one to carry my carpet bag to Glengariff, the old man said he had a son as honest as any lad in Bantry, and he should take it for a shilling; the bargain was quickly concluded. A lofty well-finished poorhouse was back of these abodes of misery, and the old lady leaving her potatoes, showed me up the slippery path-way to the gate.' She had said there was no fire but in the kitchen and the school-mistress's room, I replied that this was not the case in any other poorhouse I had visited, and I should like to see it for myself. When we reached the gate it was closed, and no admittance; the keeper was not there, and not a person in it, and never had been, though all things had been ready for a year; the farmers stood out, and would not pay the taxes. The old lady was right respecting the farmers and their taxes, but was quite confused about the fires and fire-places. The poorhouse was certainly the most respectable looking of any building in Bantry; and it is much to be regretted, that the money laid out to build, and pay a keeper for sitting alone in the mansion, had not been expended in giving work to the starving poor, who might then have had no occasion for any house but a comfortable cottage.'

I waded about the town an hour more to find, if possible, something more tolerable; but disheartened I returned to my lodgings, which were the only oasis in this woe-begone place. The next day found matters no better, and after again wading through a few streets, I returned disgusted at the nausea, which was sickening in the extreme. I left an Irish Testament where the man of the family could read Irish well, and where no Bible had ever been. The peasants in this part of the country are not so afraid of the scriptures if they speak Irish, because they attach a kind of sanctity to this language.[4]

The next morning looked a little propitious, and I hurried to Wigwam Row, to apprise the boy that he must take his potatoes, and be ready for the journey.*

This Wigwam Row is entitled to a little explanation. It consists of a row of cabins, built literally upon a rock, upon the sloping side of a hill, where not a vestige of grass can grow, the rock being a continued flat piece like slate. The favoured ones who dwell there pay no rent, having been allowed in the season of the cholera to go up and build these miserable huts, as the air upon the hill was more healthy. And there, like moss, to the rocks have they clung, getting their job when and where they can, to give them their potatoes once in a day, which is the most any of them aspire to in the shortest winter days.

I found them still in their nest, and after much beating and battering at the crazy door, the old man peeped out calling, "Who's there? and won't it do as well for me to go?" "I have no choice," replied I. "And will ye get breakfast on the way?" This was a modest hint that I should give him breakfast, though it had been adjusted that he should take his before we left. "I shall return and take mine, and you must take yours at home in the mean time." I said this to keep him to his bargain, intending to give him some when he should call. "In an hour," said the old man, "I will be with ye." The hour had not expired when the old man was at the door, with, "We had better take the airly part of the day." He had not stopped for his potato, and more than probably he had none, and must get the shilling before the potatoes could come. Dividing the breakfast with the old man, I hurried through mine, and the wallet with all appurtenances was swung upon a stick, and snugly adjusted upon the back of my fellow pedestrian. The modest sisters wished all prosperity, giving a smile as they saw us go out. Men, women, and children had watched the movements of

* I could not but say when standing on this spot, "How long, O Lord, how long" can such dreadful sufferings – such odious filth be allowed upon a world like this! Sure some volcano, some hailstone, or some fire, some overflowing flood, some miasma, or some earthquake, must obliterate them from sight, and "that right early."[5]

John, and met us upon the walk as an escort. "John, which way? and what now? sure and ye ain't goin' to lave us?" John was a man of some independence, and a little tact withal; and he managed to let them know by a slight toss of the head, and a significant look, that he was about business which interested the parties concerned, and should give account of none of his matters. Ludicrous as the scene might be, and playful as seemed their jokes, yet the real truth was affecting – John was about to earn a few pence, and the favour was a great and enviable one. They had looked and sauntered about the miserable town for days and weeks for such a boon, in vain, and now the lucky John had drawn the prize!

We soon left sight of Bantry, for mud retarded not my progress, and we hurried on to the no small amazement of all we met, who in multitudes were going to town for market. But the Bay of Bantry – the bay of all bays – stretched out on our left with its islands, and the rugged rocks on our right, so attracted my notice, that what with gaping on either hand, and looking now and then how to avoid the mud, my gallant John would be far before me. He would often sit down upon a wall, till I was within speaking distance, then giving the wallet a further hitch upon his shoulder, would rise and hasten on, thus not leaving me a moment for rest. At last I contrived to lighten my burden, by taking my huge black muff, which was quite the gaze of men and women, as well as the fright of all the children in mountain and glen, and drawing it up closely at one end, so that the Irish Testaments that were in it could ride safely, I called to the old man, and begged him to allow me to fasten the muff to his wallet, as the day was getting warm, and it quite impeded my travelling. Hanging at one end, and being large and made of the fur of the black bear of the American forest, it made John an object of still greater interest to the wondering peasantry, who all seemed to be quite acquainted with him. He was born on one of the islands of the bay, and had lived all his days within the sound of its waters. "And what is this, John? and what sort may the cratur be that's hanging at your back?"

I now succeeded in keeping pace with my guide for a time, and by dint of management kept John in tolerable mood. He would now and then mutter out that the place was a "divil of a starved one, that not a ha'p'orth could be got if the heart was broke." Taking the hint, I presented him with a piece of bread from my muff, which appeased for a little his clamour, and we pursued our journey amicably together. But no happiness is unalloyed. On a sudden, a terrible crash, was heard, and lo! the handle of the basket had given way. Out tumbled books, Wicklow pebbles, &c. and a complete overturning of all the contents of the wallet took place. With strings and pins, matters were again adjusted in a tolerably good way; but John, in fastening all together, had the shrewdness so to manage that the muff was again turned over to me. Drawing near the town, a cabin of tolerable appearance met our eyes, and the tidiness of the abode was now held out to me as a bait. "She can give as clane a bed as any woman in the kingdom." I heeded not, till the hotel of Glengariff burst upon our view. Here the praises were redoubled – "Ye'd find every convanience, and as chape as any lodgin'-house in all the country." I had, before leaving Bantry, been told there was a private lodging that would serve me better than the hotel, and I determined if possible to spend the Sabbath there. It was a sad mistake. John was the better judge, and should have been obeyed.

The lodging-house at length appeared, and before a filthy door were horses, men, and asses in thick array. John with his wallet squeezed through, and I followed before the passage was closed. "This is the way, ma'am," leading me up to a dark whiskey deposit, entered by a hole a few feet high. In this place stood a dirty woman pouring muddy coffee into bowls, and sending it to a mass of ragged countrymen, who were drinking it without milk. She was occasionally interrupted by a call for hot punch; "Going, going," was the answer, and going they were in very deed. This lodging was the height and depth of all that I had seen in depravity. "Can I have some boiling water?" "When the men are sarved, ma'am." John had seated himself upon a bench, quietly smoking, past all hurry, though in the greatest haste for the last three hours. Saying to him, as he was in fear of night, he had better take a loaf of bread and not wait for the kettle. "Aw, I'll wait for the kettle, plaise God." The kettle came, a bowl of cocoa and a loaf of bread were soon dispatched. "Take care of yourself and your thing, ma'am, or ye'll not have a ha'p'orth belonging to ye," he whispered as he went out.

When John was sitting upon the wall, eating a piece of bread, by the way, I asked, "Do you expect to go to heaven?" "No, ma'am, I shall never go to heaven. The poor, ma'am, are great sinners, and must not expect to go there." "The poor will certainly go to heaven, if they repent." He still insisted, "The poor are very wicked, and must not expect to go there. No, no, ma'am, I shall not get there." As he was departing, I said, "John, I shall see you no more, and I beg you to go to Christ, and be saved." He paused, resting on his stick; then giving me a piercing glance of desponding bitterness, he shook his head, and answered emphatically, "That can never be for me." What had so firmly fixed this opinion, I could not nor can I imagine, for it seems to be the prevailing consolatory belief of the peasantry in Ireland, that the poor are in a much better way for heaven than the rich, and they bear their poverty often with great patience, because they shall soon be better situated. Not so with John. His mind had been differently trained, and though he seemed fixed in his belief, he made it a duty to submit to his fate. I felt regret at parting with this ignorant old man, for though not skilled in books, he was a shrewd child of nature, and had been for half a day a more amusing and profitable companion, than a college dandy, "fresh from the mint," could have been.

I stepped back into the room, and for a few moments gave the gaping multitude full scope for curiosity. They stood before me, they sat down by my side, they minutely examined my dress, they asked all sorts of questions concerning America – "An' may be ye didn't know Mick Flanagan, or Pat Dogherty. An', by dad, she's a dacent body, and she never come the long way without a good bit in her purse," &c. When the wonder began to flag, I put my luggage into the care of the hostess, and went out to wander in the glen, and by chance came upon an old bridge, quite decayed, which is said to have been constructed by Cromwell to march his army over, when he wasted Ireland. The arches are still standing, and a footpath is over them, which has been crossed by every tourist in the glen for a century or more. The name of Cromwell by every peasant of Ireland is of hated memory, and scarcely a decayed castle, bridge, or abbey, but what the stranger is told, "This is the doin' of the blackguard Cromwell."[6] Finding a cabin, which from its size and appendages bore some signs of comfort, I ventured in, hoping something a little tolerable might meet my eyes. But "four-footed beasts," if not "creeping things," were here stalled and fed, and the people were of the same kin with the house I had left. I made my way upon the top of the rocks overlooking Bantry Bay, with a troop of ragged urchins in pursuit, and a young spruce dandy, who told me all he knew of the marvellous, till the dusk of evening warned me back to my luggage and lodging. I recoiled at going in.

Ascending a rock overlooking the road, I had a view of things if not unutterable, yet quite inconceivable. Beneath me were a group darkening the street and air, of all ages, from "the man of grey hairs" to the nursling at the mother's breast. Not an individual, man, woman, or child, had on a whole garment, and many of them like "Joseph's coat," were variegated with "many colours;" patches of all shades, with thread of all hues, adorned the limbs of these congregated rustics, who had heard of my arrival, and had come out to see the "wonderful body" that had left her "country and kin to say the poor Irish." Looking down upon them my "eyes affected my heart." They were God's creatures, made in his image, and bound to the same tribunal with me; thrown into different circumstances, they had developed different traits, and many among them might have occupied better upon the little that had been given, than the more elevated aristocrat who looked down upon them with contempt. They looked up, some leaning upon their spades, some crouching under heavy burdens, and all silent as if waiting the opening of some oracle. Singing a hymn, in which all instinctively joined, if not devoutly; I said a few kind words on the subject of temperance, and the regret I felt that I should find this glen given to the immorality of drinking, when a great part of Ireland had become so sober. They murmured a response – "By dad, she's right," and slowly walked on, while I descended to enter the lodging. I felt myself in a peculiar predicament, no escaping from this forbidding stopping place, and these forbidding people; it was a place and company quite different from any I had seen even in Connaught. I was pursued into the lodging-house, and went through a second and more fiery ordeal of staring. They came nearer, urged me to "smoke a blast," or to "take a drap" (notwithstanding my lecture), talked of my coat and bonnet; some bracing themselves against the wall, some sitting close by my side, and others squatting upon the ground at my feet. Fortunately for me, the organ of fear is not so largely developed as in some of more flexible texture, and my greatest suffering arose from pity and disgust. "Can you give me a few potatoes?" Four were brought in a saucer, and some dirty salt, pulverized with a knife, and likewise put in a saucer. The company were all in attendance till the supper was ended. Hoping to thin the group in some way, I asked for water to bathe my feet. A little was brought in a pot, and placed before me. "I cannot use it here." "Put it in the room," was the command.

"The room!" Reader, suppose you look in. This room was up a broken, stair-case, leading from the kitchen. A dilapidated door with a broken latch, like an inn among the far western wilds of America; a floor of loose boards, gaping wide between joints into the kitchen below; and all sorts of lumber, from the three-legged chair, broken chest, and crazy table, to the plough-share, with the worn-out gear of the ass, and basket for peat and manure. The bed and etceteras are unmentionables, and in this varied profusion I was to spend the night. As my door was past all fastening, a company at whiskey and cards, in a chamber "near a kin," at every pause in the whiskey or play, would in turn push my door a little wider, and look in. This continued till one o'clock, when I, still sitting, knew by the "God bless you's," and "ye'll be late for the night," that the company were retiring, and placed myself in a position to sleep, had sleep been in attendance. But sleep or no sleep, the Sabbath dawned pleasantly on this wicked den, and I hoped to be first in the kitchen; but to my chagrin a goodly number were in waiting, and in ten minutes from my landing at the bottom of the stairs not less than a score had arranged themselves, making sure of a suitable place to stand or sit, where the most favourable gape could be secured. Nor had one wasted a precious moment too long at the toilet. Some stood with hair erect, some with an apology for a shirt, and some with remnants of coats; some with waistbands sufficiently strong to hold both hands and despairing legs, hanging with a deadly grasp by a tatter here and there; some with dresses turned over their heads, and some pinned about their waists; some with cloaks, and some with caps, and all with naked feet. They had all got most quietly fixed, when I gathered up my effects, put them in charge of the girl, and hurried into the glen, stopping neither to warn or rebuke. – A morning long to be remembered.

Being told there was no church held in the place, and that Lord Bantry was a Protestant, lord or no lord, I determined to venture to his house, and if possible spend the day with him. "He's a convairsable body, and he'll make ye right welcome," said one that I passed on the way. At the gatehouse, the cleanly woman met me at the door, and kindly invited me in to take breakfast. This unexpected courtesy was more to me than she imagined or I could express, for I had expected to spend the day fasting, probably among the rocks in the glen, unless by good fortune the "convairsable" lord should be pacific. The neat little cottage, and cleanly-spread table, were such a contrast to the den I had just left, that I felt that "mercy had not clean gone for ever," and I was still within the reach of something human. Breakfast being ended, a little girl was sent with me to the top of a high rock, in view of the cottage called Lord Bantry's "look-out," from which the wonders of the glen are seen to good advantage. Descending the rock, the little Mary returned to prepare for chapel, and I ventured to the cottage of Lord Bantry.[7] It had a picturesque thatched roof in part, and was situated in a lawn free from rocks, sufficient to distinguish it as the abode of the "lord of the soil."

This valley of romantic wildness cannot be described. To attempt a description of Glengariff would be a waste of words. Writers of different nations have told of its eagles' nests; its huge rocks, flung together in all shapes, overgrown with moss and ivy; its lakes, rivers, and streamlets, its deep ravines and lofty mountains. And yet Glengariff can never be understood but by actual observation; by walking or riding, by every mode that ever man invented, with spy-glass and telescope has it been explored, and yet beauties and wonders remain untold.

I sent my card in to the noble lord; and he returned it by the hunched-back girl in attendance, who civilly said his lordship was quite ill, was sorry he could not see me, but would send a boy to show me the curiosities of the glen. This was not the most desirable nor the most profitable way to spend the Sabbath, but stay in the whiskey-house I had left I would not, and from the gate where I breakfasted the family had gone to mass, and locked the cottage. I followed the boy, who took me an intricate path, and stationed me before the game-keeper's lodge, and seated me upon a stone. The game-keeper's wife invited me into a neat little parlour, and showed me every thing of interest about the mountain. She was English, and quite unreconciled to stop in Ireland. She was getting a Sabbath dinner, and showed me her bee-hives; and here I tried the strength of her hospitality. Having been told that the English in Ireland were not so courteous to strangers as the Irish, I made a trial by saying, I had been told in New York that Ireland abounded in honey, but I had not had the good fortune to meet any, and I was quite fond of it. She made no reply, nor offered me either milk, bread, or honey. I have since met with many English who were exceedingly hospitable, and hope I may have no just cause of complaint against my ancestors, with whom I am happy to claim affinity. When I reached the lodge, the hospitality was repeated by the generous offer of a room and board without any charges. What could be kinder, and what could be cheaper?

"The house where you stayed last night is not fit for any human creature, and you cannot be in a worse condition in any spot in the glen." "Blessed are the merciful." This family were English, had lived in Ireland twenty-five years, and had become so identified in every way with the country, that they preferred it to their own; and no stranger could suppose by their phraseology or warmth of heart, but that they were of the genuine stock of Irish. They were Roman Catholics.

Two days rain kept me in the house, only giving opportunity for a call at the Saturday night's lodging place to take my luggage. The man and his wife were taking breakfast at eleven o'clock. He was a pledge breaker, and she a professed teetotaller, only taking her hot punch when going to bed, and he a besotted drunkard. When I told them why I left the house, and represented to her the disgrace and sin of her employment, she left her bowl of tea, and went away. He hastily arose, and took down a large Douay Bible from a dirty shelf, over the kegs of whiskey, and only wanted time to "discoorse me," to show both his knowledge of scripture, and the lawfulness of his employment. "Deacon Giles' distillery" could not have shown greater zeal. This wicked house had been, I was told, the ruin of the glen. It had been five years before baptized by Father Mathew, but he then gave pledges for a stated period, when requested, and when the time had expired, many rushed headlong into the fatal vortex. "They are too much for me," said the poor priest, "since that publican's house has been opened."

CHAPTER XVII

Rambles in Glengariff – Household Manure – Kind Little Guide – A Gallant Offer – Splendid Interior of the Slated House – A Rare and Lofty Larder – Perilous Transit – Wild Natives – Dwelling of the Three Sisters – Spiritual Fallow Ground – Man sometimes behind the Lower Animals – The Author delivers a Short Sermon – Good-bye to Glengariff and the Hospitable Family of the Gatekeeper – Lakes and Mountains – Publican versus Priest – Ride among Turf Baskets – Early Matrimony

Hearing there was a Protestant school in a distant part of the glen, with the guidance of the little "sure futted" niece of my benefactress, I made my way thither. On our route we passed a couple of rocks, celebrated for having been the abode of a family of seven for three years and a half. Lord Bantry at last built them a cabin, and turned them into it. This novel habitation is composed of two rocks, meeting overhead, like the roof of a house, and so wide at bottom that there was room for a bedstead. A fire was built by the side of the rock inside – "As all the world might see," the smoke issuing from the apertures at either end, according to the whim of the wind. The upper end of the rocks are so snugly joined, that they could be closed with leaves and brush, as the occupants might choose. It seemed impossible that the room could contain seven living moving beings, with "all appurtenances to boot;" but so it did. The good woman was often heard singing at her wheel in front of her house, where she sat spinning by the side of a clear stream, under branches of evergreens, while her five ruddy children were playing around her. Many a passer-by, on his way through the glen, turned in "to see this great sight," and left a little in charity, which kept these happy tenants more than content; for it is said they were quite unwilling to leave when the man-built cabin was in readiness.

Our path was over rocks, through mud and bogs, till we reached the abode of the Protestant teacher, who was sick, consequently her school was suspended. She had two infants, the youngest two days old, and was living in the house of her husband's mother. Though they could boast of Protestant rearing in the town of Bandon and were comfortable in land and cattle, yet the cabin was a genuine dirty one, bearing the same marks of degradation as their less enlightened neighbours. The teacher showed some specimens of needlework, which were quite creditable, and conversed with a share of good sense; but the impress of the virtuous woman, "who looketh well to the ways of her household," was not there.¹ She had five pounds a year for teaching, three of which were paid by a Protestant society, the other two by the parents of the children.² It certainly told much for her philanthropy, to go upon this desolate mountain, and "do what she could" for the benefit of the wild mountaineers, for such a scanty remuneration.

A bowl of stirabout, glowing in melted butter, was presented by the mother, but I was not competent to the undertaking.³ With much difficulty I persuaded her to allow me to take my own way, for I had long since been so divested of sectarianism, that Protestant filth was no more palatable than Roman Catholic. I here speak plainly, because neither the scantiness of their means or cabin made such intolerable housekeeping necessary. We then visited a national school, and here was a picture deserving a glen. A female teacher first saluted us, with a company of girls before her, plying the needle. "I taiches sowin,' ma'am, and they gets along finely," presenting shirts they were making. "But do you give no other lessons?" "I doesn't, ma'am; they can go to the master if they wishes to larn raidin', but they says they bee's too old."⁴

The master was busy at his desk, his cap put on with quite an air of dandyism, and the sly urchins were cutting and carving for themselves. At last the stripling approached, welcomed me very civilly, and added, "I am quite ill, am but young, and have much to learn before I can expect a great salary." This was good sense. His salary did not exceed ten pounds. In short, the school as a whole, was such a place as every child should shun. A boisterous altercation took place between the master and mistress about the key of the closet, she insisting she would carry it home, as she should be first in the morning, and want the work; he protesting for that very reason he would not allow it, because he had articles that were valuable to him, and they should not be disturbed. She threatened to acquaint the priest. "The sooner the better, and ye'll find ye're talking to a man of sense." The children of the master, and girls of the mistress, manifested, by the lighting up of the countenance, that each was ready to fight for his or her own general; and we left, never learning how the battle was decided.

Thursday. – Going out to call at the hotel, I turned into a bye-path, and seeing a row of cabins, went to one, supposing I could take a nearer route than the public road, by enquiring the way.⁵ Putting in my head, I saw misery doubly distilled. I at first was met by two yearling calves, and there being no window in the cabin, I could not well see into the interior, and concluded that it was nothing less or more than a cowhouse. But perseverance showed me it was the abode of six full-grown mortals, master, mistress, and four daughters, sitting upon stools before a peat fire. On the left was a pile of manure, which the cow and calves had been providing from the preceding November. This manure each morning is pressed down, and a little dry straw or leaves put over, thus forming a solid mass, which being kept warm both by pressure and a fire, the owners affirm, makes it much richer. On the right was a board extending from the corner of the fire-place, of sufficient length for a bed; and over this board, upon the ground, was straw spread for the whole family's sleeping-place. The furniture was a pot to boil potatoes, an old basket, a few stools, and an old cupboard with plates, and –

"Broken tea-cups, wisely kept for show."

To my first enquiry, "Can you tell me the way to the hotel?" I received no answer, all looking with amazement at the first and only bonnet that had ever looked in, and said good morning to them. Again I asked the way; the old man rose and said, "Come and I'll show ye," and led me to a path among the rocks. "An' may be ye're a stranger, an' I'll not put ye out of the way." Here was old patriarchal law, though I was told they could neither read nor write. This hotel, which the natives say is "dacent and proper," is quite commodious, and, being the only one in the glen, commands all the visitors from various parts of the world. My Saturday night's entertainment was a just rebuke for turning a deaf ear to the counsel of my friend John, when he said, "Ye couldn't do better, ye'll find every convainience."

On my return, the kind little Mary, with clean apron and nicely combed hair, was ready to accompany me up the glen to the "Eagle's Nest;" and no nest was ever more famed in history, as the reader shall presently hear. On our way to this place we had a river to cross without a bridge, and the late rains had so swollen it, that the stepping-stones were covered. Mary waded the stream, and I made my way over rocks, bogs, and hillocks, till despairing of success; a ragged peasant, driving a horse with two baskets of lime across his back, called out to Mary, in Irish, "I'll go and lift her across." He was old, and I did not think it safe; and beside, the kindness was too great. He rolled up his pantaloons, waded the river, and proffered his services in Irish. I declined; when he found a place where, taking me by the hand, he helped me, at considerable peril, over the slimy rocks; and, ascending the precipitous bank, he braced his feet, pulled me up the steep, and set me on terra firma. He could not understand English, nor I Irish; but he understood the meaning of a few pennies put into his hand, and seemed quite satisfied.

In half an hour we reached the slated house under the mountain; and, as a slated house is considered a step in advance towards gentility, and the tenant of this had leased the whole "Eagle's Nest," and all were sub-tenants under him, he deserves a conspicuous place in the history of this glen. The entrance of the house was blockaded by an old worn-out horse, with two baskets of lime on his back, which the mother and two daughters were striving in vain to let down. The maidens stepped aside, and we crawled under the straw bridle of the horse, and entered a room, which could boast the same lineage as the one I had visited in the morning, only the manure was not so evenly patted down, but was in isolated hillocks about the room, and the calf and pig were leisurely walking between them. The conveniences were all near the fire, but the old lady made a breakage of sufficient width to place a stool, and a piece of turf to elevate my feet from the ashes. Here I was seated, with all the family around me upon the hearth, except a boy, whose gaping curiosity could not draw him from a ladder on which he was swinging in one corner of the cabin.

"Do you read Irish?" I asked the woman. With a pause of astonishment she looked upon me, then upon her girls, and, with a child-like laugh, said, "I read! The like of me read! Not a ha'p'orth of Irish or English." The daughters were in like condition, and as much diverted at my strange question as the mother. Speaking of the goodness and mercy of God, they sobered at once; and after talking a few moments, we left without presenting any books, as they could not read.

We tried another cabin; in like condition, only darker, and the roof thatched. Then attempted a third, but here the pile of manure was so elevated, and the smoke and darkness of the cabin such, that both Mary and prudence urged a retreat. The children from the thickly clustered cabins crowded forth, and one bawled out, "A penny for a crass, ma'am." This means, translated, a ribbon crossed upon the arm, to be worn on St. Patrick's day, which was near at hand.[6] Never, never, had pictures like these met my eyes. I was nearly struck mute. Human nature had never before shown me what she could do when allowed to have her own way. Yet these people can say the Lord's prayer, go to chapel, wear a decent cap and cloak, and are not so poor but that all have cattle, and some money in reserve. The kind Lord Bantry, it is said, gives every rational indulgence, and seldom sends any empty away in distress; but he never enters their cabins to rebuke their filth, or offer them premiums for any improvements they might make, as some have done with good success.

The "Eagle's Nest" was the last wonder, deriving its name from an eagle having made its nest in a fissure of the rock towards the top of the mountain.[7] And you are told that a man named Sullivan supported a family of six, as he testified, by going to the nest daily, and taking the flesh of lambs, hares, and deer, which were left for the young ones. This tremendous mountain has a hideous, grand, and awful appearance, looking down upon these wretched abodes that are smoking beneath.

But the getting home was the next question. Determining to cross the river when anything like probability appeared, I saw something tolerable, though my watchful guide said we should "be destroyed" getting through the bog and rushes on the other side. So engrossed were my thoughts on what I had seen at the Eagle's Nest, that I heeded neither the admonitions of the careful child nor the peril that lay in my path. I stepped upon the rocks, not once looking or thinking what might impede me on the other side, telling the girl to go on before me. She insisted, "Ye'd be lost, ye cannot get up the bank," but after much hesitation she reluctantly obeyed. I soon found myself in a perilous situation; the rocks slippery and far asunder, the water deep and turbid, and my Indian rubber shoes were the most unpromising part of my security, as I could neither take them off, nor maintain my position, but with a great effort. I saw my folly, and commended the wisdom of the child, whom I directed to take a horizontal direction up the bank, and with a kind of vacant anxiety bordering on petrifaction, I watched till her well-guided feet stood on the steep bank over my head. What could I do? To retrace my steps or stay where I was, looked alike impossible, and to try to ascend the bank would be almost madness. There was no alternative but onward. I clasped a bunch of hanging twigs, they loosened the earth, and I felt myself sliding. The presence of mind of the guardian angel Mary saved me; she caught the twigs, and with an almost supernatural grasp she said, "Take hold of the top, lady, and I will hold fast at the bottom so that you can't pull them up." It was done, I was on the bank, and not till I looked down the precipitous steep did I realize the presumptuous step I had taken. But my stupidity was God's instrument to save me; my mind was so absorbed on what I had seen, that it was deadened to every thing beside, and fear or concern was not awakened. The watchful child, as though my life had been entrusted to her care, guided my way with the discretion of an experienced general.

We made a safe journey home. The strange things I had seen, and the difficulties I had surmounted, were sufficient for meditation; but above all how to approach Lord Bantry, and entreat him to do as others had done, visit the cabins and work some change for the better – was a weighty incubus which I could not shake off. As I passed his cottage, a message was sent out inviting me in; but the lateness of the hour, and the plight of my feet, together with the state of my mind, urged me on, lest as a whole he might mistake my drabbled dress, twisted awry bonnet, and absence of mind for "a loss of the sinse," and I hurried home.

The next morning, a little more restored, I called at his door, but the butler informed me he could see no one, as he had a bleeding at the nose; so he escaped what he ought to have heard years before. I took another day's ramble up to the head of the glen, a distance of nearly three miles, and never was a glen to me like this. From the top of a rock sometimes a shout burst upon my ear, then some wild mountain girl would cross my path, then a peasant or two, with braided straw saddles and baskets across the woe-begone donkey, with a salute of "God save ye kindly, lady" – then some way-worn old woman, with a rope about her forehead, supporting a ponderous sack of potatoes or turf upon her back, would greet me. Meeting a path leading from the main road, I followed it, and seeing a broken cart, supposed that human beings must be among these rocks, and upon my left I saw an aperture into what I thought might be a cave or mountain den, and approaching, found a pig nestled in some straw, and a voice from within called out, "Maybe ye'd like to come in and take a hait by the fire."

Had this invitation proceeded from a sepulchre, it could not have been much more surprising – and not half so unnatural for the abode of the dead as the living. I stooped down and walked over the obstinate pig – stumbled in, and here saw patient misery in somewhat a new habiliment.

Against a huge rock – for there was no chimney – there burned a few little twigs of wood. Three sisters – the eldest seventeen, the second twelve, and the third two, all nestled in straw, for there were not stools enough for each; and neither bed nor table encumbered the room.

"Where do you sleep?" I asked.

"Poor folks must do as they can, ma'am – we lie here," pointing to a pile of straw on the left. The little child now asked for a potato. "I have none for you." Not a particle of food did this destitute abode contain; and giving the child a couple of hard biscuits, she gnawed them greedily – for the first time probably having had a piece of bread in her life.

"How do you live?"

"As we can, ma'am." I then spoke of Jesus Christ. "I don't understand ye," said she. "Do you not know whom I mean by Jesus Christ?" I asked.

She could not comprehend me, and the second sister said, "We don't go to church or chapel, ma'am." I enquired how long they had lived there.

"One year, ma'am." They had no father, and the mother had gone from home, begging, I supposed. I knew not what to say to them, nor what to do for them; they were perishing for "lack of knowledge," and the beasts of the desert had more comfortable dwellings than they.*

This day finished my tour in the glen, and it had been the most peculiar of any I had had in Ireland. I had learned to a demonstration, that man left to instinct alone, will not make himself as comfortable as the beasts of the field, or birds of the air – they will construct their habitations and nests when wanted, with perfect system and even with mechanical taste – while man, with no stimulus to activity but barely the food that sustains him, will lie down in stupid content, in the most filthy, disorderly habitation, and even make a merit of doing so. Here were literally exemplified the words of Job, when he said of the poor – "They embraced the rock for a shelter." "For want and famine they were desolate."[8] "To dwell in the cliffs of the valleys, in caves of the earth, and in the rocks – among the bushes they brayed, under the nettles they were gathered together."

Often have I seen the poor famished women gathering nettles to boil, because they had no other food.[9] And here I would add, if any one thinks that man has anything to boast since the fall, let him explore the mountains, the glens, the caves, and even the towns of Ireland: and, lest he should find a loop-hole for his pride, let him go to the places where the Bible is known, and if the grace of God have not changed the heart, he will find the same degradation in morals as in those places where it has not been read.

Saturday morning, March 7th. – Had made all ready for leaving the Glen. My obligations to the family where I stopped were of no ordinary kind.

"I was a stranger, and they took me in."[10] I had enjoyed religious intercourse by conversation, by reading the scriptures, and by prayer, in a more familiar way than in any family I had visited; and though this glen, in point of filth and whiskey-drinking, stands pre-eminent, yet they suffered the plainest rebuke without a retort. They received tracts, and thanked me after reading them, for giving them such kind advice; and the priest, who lived some miles from the glen, sent a message by his clerk, thanking me for the advice I had given, and the tracts I had distributed.[11] And though I would not intersperse my journal with preaching a long sermon in every chapter, yet here it would be timely to say, that a right spirit and a right manner have much to do in the success of introducing any princi-

* This is not mentioned as a specimen of the ignorance of the peasantry as a whole, for in no place did they appear dark on the subject of Christ's death and sufferings.

ples clashing with long cherished ones of our opponents.

Should a sanctimonious monk, full of zeal for his church, with crucifix and rosary in his hand, come into our houses and tell us we are all going to perdition, because we did not say his prayers, and embrace his faith, and insist that we should assemble our household to hear the truth from his lips, should we do it? Should he rail on our clergy, and denounce our Sabbath schools, think you he would get a patient hearing?

Let us reverse this picture – let us allow our brethren of the human family the same prepossessions, however absurd they may be, till, by a course of Christian charity, we show them that the religion we profess is indeed what we call it, a religion of love, and calculated to do the most permanent good.

Should any one visit Glengariff – if it be Glengariff still – and from cabin to cabin commence an attack upon popery, and priests, images, and the "Blessed Virgin," he might be grateful if he escaped unhurt; but let him go with a heart warm with a Saviour's love – let him tell them of this love – let him tell them if they do not repent, they will all likewise perish – let him rebuke them sharply for all their profanity, Sabbath-breaking, drunkenness, &c. – and let him pointedly tell them that all this wickedness comes from hatred to God, from wicked hearts of unbelief, and they will respond – "An' you're the one that knows it" – they will gather around him, they will ask him to read, they will enquire for his books, and sometimes they have asked such to pray for them. One said to another, "Ain't she a Protestant?" "I don't care what she is," was the spirited reply, "nothing but love to God could bring her across the ocean to see such a poor people as we, and stop in our cabins to discoorse us, and give us good books. She's been well rair'd, the cratur, and that she has."

But we must not stop in this glen. The morning had opened, the sun looked out upon a clear sky, and the boy who was to accompany me had eaten his potatoes, and was ready at an early hour. "You shall give us nothing but your prayers, and you shall have ours; and if ye wouldn't think it too much to leave the little book to Mary, she loves it so well, I will cover it with linen, and she shall read it twice a day, we should be more than paid."

This little Mary had entwined herself around my heart by so many acts of kindness, as well as her good sense and integrity, that when she took the little book, and said, "I thank you kindly," I felt like snatching her from the Glen, and fixing her in a soil where she should no longer "blush unseen."

Master and Mistress, Mary, and the little affectionate dog Vixen, stood out upon the clean pathway and lawn before the cottage – a moment's pause – "and we'll never forget ye," was the last sound that fell upon my ear; for, as I proffered my hand, and saw the tear glistening in the kind eye of little Mary, I hastened away without speaking.

I looked back, the sun was shining upon this little group; the holly, the arbutus, and the laurel – my favourite shrubs of the Glen – were quivering in its rays at their side. I was going forth upon wild, heathy mountains, and should see the little company no more, "till the heavens be rolled, together as a scroll."[12] They had been more than kind, and how had I repaid them? Had I done what I could to scatter light in their path? Are they no worse for my coming among them? was my heart-felt enquiry. Have the evening prayers which they nightly asked me to put up in their family, and the reading of the sweet words of eternal life, which for the last ten days had been heard in their dwelling – had these entered into the ears of the Lord of Sabaoth, and would they return with a blessing upon their heads?

The little Vixen watched the return of the family into the cottage, and leaped after me, keeping the opposite side of the stream till he had entered the thickest of the wood, and then attempted crossing it, nor could we urge him back; and not till the little Mary appeared and turned him away would he leave us, and we soon lost sight of them for ever.

Our path lay over brambles amid rivulets and walls, up one of the tallest mountains in the glen, where many a traveller has ascended to take one of the most picturesque views in all Glengariff.[13]

It was a long and difficult ascent, but courage kept me steady, and when compelled to sit down upon a crag or hillock, the smoke of a cabin by the side of some rock or hill, the shouting of children, the towering mountains stretched beyond the glen, and sleeping lakes that lay at our feet, made such a picture that I forgot my weariness, and the long Irish miles I had yet to walk. I was told that there are in this glen, and upon the mountains, three hundred and sixty-five lakes. This I am not prepared to prove or dispute, yet, judging from what I met, I think it may not be improbable. The hill was ascended, we reached the newly walled road made upon the top of a narrow ridge of mountain, with a glen on each hand at our feet, a precipitous steep of many yards leading to these ravines, which in most places made a dizzy and fearful sight to the traveller. At length the tunnel, hewn through a rock like the arch of a bridge, met our eyes. Here was the wonder of wonders. For the distance of eighty perches a hole is cut sufficiently wide and high for coaches to pass, and the only light admitted is from the entrance at each end, and one little aperture in the top.[14] The water was percolating through the rock, and darkness made it a prison not the most inviting for a long tarry. Giving full scope to my voice in singing, the echo was tremendous. The grandeur that burst upon the view when we emerged, was, if possible, greater than when we entered it,[15] nor did it cease till we had walked two miles. We then came in sight of a tolerable-looking house at a distance, and found it belonged to the priest of the glen. I was fatigued, and willing to avail myself of the acquaintance I had with him through his clerk, whom he requested to thank me for my labours in the glen, we went in. The priest had gone, but the kind housekeeper, so far as words could speak kindness, manifested the most ardent desire to make me comfortable, but could give me no refreshment, as they lived far from any town, and their bread was all brought from Bantry. "But ye'll meet him on the way, and ye'll know him by the sing of the white horse which he rides." The boy, like my old man, began to talk of the lateness of the hour, and we hurried away. Within three miles of Kenmare we saw the sign of the "white horse," and without preface or apology, I introduced myself. He thanked me kindly for lecturing his people at the glen, and said he had got discouraged. Five years before, the good Father Mathew had made them all temperate, but that publican's house had upset the whole work. I begged him to visit their cabins, and lecture them on their filth. – "I have done so, but they heeded nothing I could say." He lived seven miles from them, had another parish in charge, and he knew not how to remedy these evils; "but to-morrow I have been thinking of making a trial from the altar, and I would take the liberty of using your name." Poor man! if indeed he felt the necessity of using me as a scare-crow, certainly I should not object, but I doubted the efficacy of the remedy.

While talking with the priest, who directed me to the best lodgings in town in his name, a ragged young man, with a cart and high railing about it, filled with turf baskets, drawn by a miserable-looking pony, passed us.[16] This was the time for the onset. My boy had been complaining much that the "night would be heavy on him," and he contrived to make a happy disposal of me for his own benefit. This was done by taking down the railings and fixing the baskets in a kind of circle, so that by sitting on one that was inverted with my feet in the space, I could be snugly poised. When I reached the cart the driver said, "Ye had a wairy walk, and maybe ye'd be kind enough to sit on my humble cart, and ride to town; we've fixed a sait here, will ye get up?"

This was too plain to be misunderstood, and too polite to be rejected: the boy responded, "And maybe he'd be willin' to carry the luggage too."

"That indeed," said the accommodating man. "Then ye'll not want me, and I can go back." This was done, and well done on their part, and they assisted in adjusting me and my luggage. The boy was paid and turned about, and I, with a new companion, and in somewhat a new mode of travelling, was under favourable auspices for reaching the town. My young driver talked fluently of America, and said he should go there but for the little gal he had married, who would be lonesome without him.

"The little gal you have married! you are not yet twenty!"

"That I ain't, and the gal is but thirteen or fourteen."

"Nonsense, nonsense. What can you do with a wife?"

"And maybe I don't know; why, work, and take care of her."

"And how much do you have a day?"

"Sometimes the sixpence, and when I gits a job with the pony, it's a shilling or fifteen pence."

"And with this you expect to support a wife?"

"With the turn that she can git now and then from a lady."

He was a sharp-nosed stinted boy, not in appearance more than sixteen, yet he had as high hopes of aggrandizement as though a candidate for parliament. Enviable content! happy misery!

CHAPTER XVIII

Accident at Kenmare – Arrival at Killarney – Dread of Heretical Books – Turk
Waterfall – Funeral Wail – America's good fame – Lions of the Lakes – "Sweet Innisfallen" – White-robed Procession – A Third Funeral – Dry Bones – Battle of the
Ghosts – "Pair of Slippers" – Test of Orthodoxy – Staring! Staring! – Another Hospitable Gatehouse – Lord Kenmare's Park – Calm Sabbath Morn – The Little Peti-
tioner for the "Word of God" – A Door of Access

It was certainly an object of no small interest at Kenmare, that such a
"dacent body" was not in a coach, and the fat contented old lady, to whom
the priest directed me, knocked the ashes from her pipe, saying, "And it's
you that's the lady." The village assembled in the evening and listened to
reading till a late hour, ever finding it a better way before distributing
tracts to read something interesting, which always awakened a curiosity
to become better acquainted with them. Sabbath morning, going out to
an ivy-covered decayed castle near by, and attempting to climb a wall, my
cape blew over my face, my foot slipped, and I fell upon the pavement,
and so great was the jar, that for a moment I supposed my fate was sealed,
and that in Ireland, and in that unpromising-looking town,[1] I must endure
probably months of suffering with a disease of the spine, as I had done in
New York.[2] A company were passing to mass, and two old men helped me
a little upright, and placed me against the wall, leaving me to my meditations, which were not the most flattering. I looked about upon the desolate town, and recoiled at the thought of being left in it, and made an
effort to arise; with considerable suffering I reached my lodging, and in a
little time quite regained my former position. Heard a dull sermon with
dull ears.

This town has nothing interesting but a suspension bridge, with two
richly ornamented pillars, and a handsome pier.[3] The next morning,
though urged to stay, I bade adieu, started for the fairy land of Killarney,
and rode through a wild tract of twenty miles, till the "Upper Lakes" of
the far-famed Killarney met my sight.[4] Nothing here appeared peculiarly
striking; the day was chill, the company dull, and I was making up my
mind, that if I had visited this spot for novelty or beauty, I might better
have stayed in Glengariff. I stepped in to enquire for lodgings, and was

quite happy when safely out upon the street; and enquiring for Mrs. Casey, to whom I had been recommended at Cork, I found a comfortable home during my stay in that place.[5]

Ross Island was the first in the morning to which I resorted; and, reaching the gate of a beautiful thatched cottage, saw the proprietor in the garden, who invited me through the gate, and accompanied me about the several walks.[6] Though in the month of March, it was blooming with greens and flowers. The different openings upon the lakes were made with a most happy skill, and the parts which were left wild were selected with judgment. The gardeners of Ireland display much taste in adjusting their rough stones, their rustic seats and summer-houses; and in fitting up a pleasure-ground, they seem to possess a correct judgment in knowing what to cultivate, and what to leave wild. This spot possesses beauties which to an admirer of nature cannot fail to please.

At ten I returned, the hour that the labourers breakfast; and the family finished at eleven, so late are the Irish about rising in the morning, that the best part of the day is often lost. I sauntered through the town, and here Glengariff scenes were acted over by a mob of boys, women, and girls with cloaks over head, some in pursuit, and others running before, and then stopping to have a full gaze. So much had I heard of the beauties of Killarney, that I was quite disappointed in the refinement of the people. A boy accompanied me to the Victoria hotel, situated on the bank of the lower lake, a mile from town.[7] In summer this is well filled with company from various parts of the world to visit these enchanting lakes. I was quite annoyed by a boy asking for books. I gave him a copy of the Douay gospels, and he went away pleased; in an hour he was running after me, crying, "This is a Protestant book, and I won't have it."[8] Telling him what it was, and asking why he was so afraid of it, he answered, "I rather have my own religion, and should not like to take a Protestant book;" he took it a second time, and at evening came running, and rudely thrust it into my hand, saying, "I know this is a Protestant book, and I will not have it." The boy seemed grieved, that, as he supposed, I had deceived him. He had carried the book to his mother, and she had told him it was one of the Protestant tracts that had been distributed there to injure Romanism. A little girl of twelve stood listening, and said, "Madam, will you let me have the book? You shouldn't be giving your books to every scrawl in the street." Fearing, notwithstanding her judicious caution, she might be a "scrawl," I declined, telling her to go home and think of it, and if she continued to want one, to call at my lodgings Sabbath evening at six o'clock, and she should have one. "'Tis the Word of God I want, ma'am."

March 13th. – I took a walk of four miles to the celebrated Turk mountain to see the cascade, and when I had reached the foot of it, I sat down upon a seat to meditate undisturbed on this beautiful sight.[9] Four white sheets of water have for ages been coursing down a rock of eighty feet in height, wearing channels of considerable depth, and on their way have received some small rivulets issuing from the sides of the mountain, pouring together into one basin at the bottom. The mountains on either hand are lofty, wild, and precipitous. I attempted to make my way over the slippery stones to reach the basin, but found it too hazardous, being out of the hearing of any human being, and should I tumble into the stream, or break a bone, my fate would be irrecoverable.

An hour was gone, and admiration, if possible, was increasing; but looking to my left, I saw a path leading up the mountain, and followed it. In a few yards it opened a small view of the lakes, and as you ascend the view widens and widens, till you see spread out before the lawns, the middle and lower lakes, with their beautiful islands, and the grand Kerry mountains stretching out beyond. Seats at proper distances are arranged, where the traveller may rest, and feast his eyes on the beauties beneath his feet. But when the top is reached, the awful precipice overhanging the cascade, would endanger the life of any one to overlook, were there not a railing erected for the safety of the visitor. Here I sat, and thanked God that he had given me eyes to see, and a mind to enjoy, a scene like this. More than three thousand miles from my native country, on the top of this awfully wild mountain, where many a stranger's foot had trod, I was enjoying a good reward for all my labour. The sun was shining upon the unruffled lakes, the birds were hopping from bough to bough, mingling their songs with the untiring cascade, the partridge fluttered in the brake at a distance, but I knew no venomous serpent was there. I was unwilling to leave the spot, and had not the promise of returning to witness a funeral at two o'clock urged me away, my stay might have been protracted till sunset. I lingered and looked, and like Eve when leaving paradise, said –

"And must I leave thee!"

I returned not till I had explored the end of the woodman's path, over a bridge that crossed the chasm beyond, and then took a last look of this coy maiden, standing once more at her feet. Though she cannot boast the awful grandeur of the bold Niagara of my native country, yet she has beauties which can never cease to please. She has an unassuming modesty which compels you to admire, because she seems not to covet your admiration. She is so concealed that the eye never meets her till close upon the white folds of her drapery, and when, but a few paces from her feet, I turned to take another look, I could not see even "the hem of her garment."

On returning to the gate, it was locked; the woman who had kept it had given me the key; I had carelessly left it in the door, without locking it, and she had fastened the gate and taken the key. I could neither make myself heard, nor climb the wall; a sad dilemma! A return to the cascade seemed to be the only alternative; but following the wall, an end was happily found, and the road soon gained. Stopping at a neat little lodge, bread and honey were brought to me in such a simple patriarchal manner, that the days of Rebecca and Ruth were before me.[10]

The loud "wail" for the dead soon sounded from the mountain. "She's a proper woman," said one, "and her six children are all very sorry for her, the cratur." I went on to the gate till the multitudinous procession arrived, bearing the coffin on a couple of sheets, twisted so that four men could take hold one at each end, and carry it along. Women were not only howling, but tears were fast streaming from many an eye. When they reached the abbey, the grave was not dug, and here was a new and louder wail struck up. While the grave was digging, eight women knelt down by the coffin, and putting their hands upon it, and beating with force, set up a most terrific lamentation. The pounding upon the coffin, the howling, and the shovelling of earth from the grave made together sounds and sights strange, if not unseemly.[11] The body was to be deposited where a brother and a sister had been buried, and when they reached the first coffin, took it out, and found the second rotten, they took up the mouldered pieces and flung them away.[12] The bones of the legs and arms, with the skull, were put together, and laid by the side of the coffins; the new coffin was put down, and the old one, which was the last of the two former, was placed upon it.

When all was finished, they knelt down to offer up a prayer for the dead, which was done in silence, and they walked away with much decency.

Muckross Abbey is of itself enough for a book; but as so much has been said of it to the purpose, and as minute descriptions of castles or abbeys is not the object of this journal, the reader will find elsewhere what could not have room in a work like this.[13]

On my way to the cascade, I stopped at the gate of the lodge on the borders of the lake, and the keeper said I could not be allowed to enter on any conditions. "I am a stranger from New York," said I. "Come in, come in" was the response. She conducted me through, and pointed me to the best views upon the lake; and seeing a pier built out to an island, I followed, and found a delightfully fitted up spot with caverns, sitting-rooms, rustic seats, and walks. There was once an old castle built upon this rock, and caves were made by the wearing of the water in the rock on which the castle stood.[14] Going to the dwelling upon the shore, men-servants and maid-servants came out to salute me, yet none asked me in, though welcome was given me to visit all the domain without any restriction. But America is all the theme by the labouring class of Ireland; glad was I, that, notwithstanding her abominable slavery, yet here is a little green spot, where I could rest and look my enemies in the face undaunted.[15] The free states of my own country have ever been an asylum to the foreigner, and the reward of his labour has been given him. The ragged labourer has soon exchanged his tatters for decent apparel, the bare feet of the cabin girl have been covered, and the basket has been taken from the back of the peasant woman. I would acknowledge with gratitude that, throughout the length and breadth of Ireland, the poor have required no letter of introduction but the name of America. It has opened the gate of many a porter's lodge; it has shown me into many a prohibited pleasure-ground, and given me many a potato or cup of milk in the cabin, when the aristocrat would have looked with suspicion on the letter of introduction from the best authority.

One of the servants was fitting for a voyage to Boston, and asked what she should most need to recommend her. I answered, cleanliness; that want of this could not be supplied by any qualification, however good in New England.

Thursday. – Two boatmen, for five shillings, took me upon the lakes, and showed the various curiosities. We saw Goat Island, where were two cottages, one of great beauty, but found no inmates – the island called O'Donohue's Library, having stones so arranged about the edge that they have the appearance of books lying slantingly upon each other – a circular pond, now called "Father Mathew's Coffee Basin," once the resort of punch-drinkers, and called the "Devil's Punch Bowl" – and another pond, which was the favourite resort of Sir Walter Scott, and called by him the "Meeting of the Waters."[16] This pond is surrounded by beautiful shrubbery, into which the lake empties itself by four different ways, a nook peculiarly fitted for the play of an imagination like his. The Eagle's Nest came next, a lofty mountain much like the one in Glengariff, but no frightful inhabitants there.[17] Here the proud eagle uncontrolled soars fearless of the marksman's arrow, as lord of both sky and mountain; here, too, are cradled the young eaglets till fitted for flight; and the boatman showed me a cavity in the rock where a nest has yearly been made; the nest was once robbed, and two of the young eagles are now kept for pets in Killarney. An adventurous man, with a pistol and hook in his hands, was fastened by a rope round his body and legs, the rope was carried to the top of the rock and there made secure; when he had reached the nest, he grappled the hook, secured the young, fired his pistol and was let down.

We sailed back from the foot of the mountain, and viewed the shores from the middle lake. Here the water has worn the rocks till it has formed beautiful caverns, called wine cellars. In some places pillars are left, which look as if hewn by a chisel.[18]

The famous Innisfallen was not the least of the beauties of these lakes, sung by poets and admired by all – a green spot where stands a castle, or rather the remains of one, but no cottage.[19] The island was beautifully green, and sheep were feeding upon it. The Bed of Honour, about which so many ludicrous stories are told, is in quite a perilous place for a retreat of safety, a point of the rock juts into the lake, in the side of which is a little shelf, where it is said two runaway lovers hid from the wrath of a father and affianced husband who followed.[20] The fugitives went out to meet them, and the lover left the matter to the honour of the betrothed one, who, notwithstanding the partiality which the maiden had evinced for another, bore her away, and made her his unwilling bride. The story answers well for the purses of the guides, who are sure to add every variety that can give zest to the tale.

But Innisfallen has beauties which can scarcely be exaggerated, and if art has any part in rendering landscape lovely, a cottage here would be at least a pleasant variety. The lady who owns it has proceeded so far towards a commencement as to send a huge pile of lime to the spot, and a few stones, but the selfish thought that she had no children to enjoy it, and that she would not build it for the benefit of strangers, prevailed, and the rubbish remains as a memento of the lady's love for posterity.

On our return we had a view of the ivy-covered castle on Ross Island.[21] The side fronting the lake was completely overrun with ivy, except a few little white spots, which at a distance had the appearance of patches put on. The place, the plan, and finish of this castle, are a worthy comment on the taste of the ancients, and the former prosperity of Ireland. The boatmen obeyed to the letter the command given when setting out, not to give one fairy tale.[22] Consequently my eyes were not diverted, nor my imagination stretched, to make out beauties and wonders which were not exactly before me. The realities of Killarney lakes are enough without any varnishing. As a whole, a fairy land in reality, I had read much of it; but when I saw it, I determined to mock no reader with a description, as I had been, but invite all who may choose to have a spare shilling, to give it to a common-sense boatman on the lakes of Killarney.

Friday early, I heard the tolling of a bell, and was told it was the convent bell, tolling the funeral of a nun, the matron of the institution.[23] I passed by the crowded gate, and though the keeper was preventing the entrance of the crowd, finding that I was an American stranger, the porter said, "Welcome, welcome," and opened the gate. This was a favourable moment; the crowd, without preface or apology, rushed in, and pressed me by force into the convent yard. The procession was conducted by priests in white robes, followed by twelve girls in white; then the nuns in white robes, with black veils, and all bearing lighted candles; the priests reading prayers in Latin, intelligible to all but the listeners. They entered the high walled enclosure where the nuns are interred, and chanted a plaintive funeral song while the corpse was being buried.

A gentlemen approached, asking, "Have you seen the interment?," adding, "had I seen you before, you should have been admitted, as you are a stranger."

I next walked through the gate leading to Lord Kenmare's domain, a happy appendage to the lakes, ornamented with walks and seats, and two rustic thatched cottages, made of small round sticks of wood with the bark on, and put together like patch-work, in diamonds, wheels, and stars; the floors are laid in small pebbles, in wheels, and the whole together is in perfect taste.[24] The sun was shining upon the sloping green lawn, and the lakes below were sparkling in its light. I was just seated in one of the cottages, gathering around me the dancing fairies of the imagination, when a wail for the dead fell on my ear. Surely this morning thus far was devoted to the ghosts of the departed. I hastened from the enchanted seat, and found that the procession was moving to the burying-place upon the hill, the oldest in all Killarney.[25] The undying propensity of all ages to look, and if possible to accompany a funeral procession, led me on, and I waded through, and climbed over walls, to follow the dead, but did not succeed in time, the death-cry having ceased before I could reach them.[26]

A youth tending cattle upon the hill showed me into the burying-ground and old church, said to be 1,150 years old. An old tower, and the Bishop's chair, being no more than the remains of an old tower, in shape in its ruins like a large chair, stand at a distance.[27] But the sight of sights is the pile of dry bones in one corner of the churchyard, and scattered all through it, as well as around it. Skulls with open jaws and teeth, and all the bones of the body, are here in thick profusion under the open sky. It is said that the burying-ground is as old as the church, and the peasantry of Ireland retain a strong propensity to bury their dead with their ances-tors, consequently this is the spot where Killarney dead must lie, though the bones of kings and nobles are rooted out, and scattered to bleach in the winds and sun of heaven, to make room for them. While standing with the mountain herder, a man, whose cabin "joined hard" to the bury-ing-ground, accosted us. I asked if it was not unpleasant to live near so many dead bodies and dried bones. "Not at all; it's the livin', ma'am, that do the hurt," adding a story which requires both Irish cleverness and Irish brogue to be well understood.

A young mountain lad had been to a fair, and took too much whiskey; on his return up the mountain, his path lay across this burying-ground. As he passed a tomb-stone, a couple of goats were pushing with their horns, and "rattling them like sticks." This terrified fellow ran home as fast as his staggering would enable him, and fell shaking upon the floor, and it was not for hours that he could understandingly tell the astonished family what had caused the fright. At last he informed them, "that all the ghosts that had been buried for the last forty years had come out of their graves, and were killin' each other, for he saw them fightin' and heard the bones rattle, and they were all in their windin' sheets around the ground." "For a twelve month," said the narrator, "Paddy could hear nothing else when he went to town, but the 'rattlin' of dead bones killin' each other'."[28]

This burial place, like most others in Ireland, is situated in a pleasant spot, and it would seem that the ancients had a regard for good air, exten-sive view, and a noble church for the comfort of their dead. The country here slopes down to the lakes. The Kerry mountains rise in the most var-ied shapes, and topped with snow, glistening in the sun; while many a green field with cattle and sheep spreads out at their feet, making together so picturesque a view, that I sat down upon a wall, with my cabin man and mountain lad at my feet, for two hours; and they in turn did what they could to amuse and instruct me.

On my way down the mountain, seeing a most miserable cabin, ven-tured through the door, and found it was the home of the mountain boy I had left.[29] He certainly made a happy change when he left the dirty, smokey hovel, where men, women, pigs and cattle, geese, and turkeys, all had one common lodgment, if not one common bed. The old man, the boy's father, said "He had lived there sixty years, was now in a decline and ould, and hoped, through attention to the duties of the church, to get to heaven at last." He was pointed to the "Lamb of God, who takes away the sin of the world;" but he could not understand how he could be saved out of his church, nor how he could be lost if he obeyed its mandates.[30] Now for civility and hospitality. The old man said "An' yer feet are destroyed with the mud, and wouldn't ye have a pair of slippers, and rest yer feet, and stop and take a fresh egg?" Have a pair of slippers! In a hovel like this! All the curiosities of the churchyard now vanished. The egg I did not dispute, for a goose was quietly seated on a nest in the corner, and a hen had just left hers under the cupboard, and was cackling about the room. The mother put a basket of potatoes into a tub, and washed them with her feet, and suspended them over the fire to boil for supper. Every thing was in train for a repast, but making my exit as civilly as I could, after heartily thanking them (for their hospitality could not be disputed), my lodgings were reached, with an escort which had increased from cabin to cabin, and from passengers on the way; some asking for books, some enquiring about America, and one among the better learned asked what I thought of the 'Blessed Virgin'? "This will cut the garment," reported the woman. "As ye think of the mother, so ye'd love the Son, and if yer tracts say nothin' of her, we would not read 'em." I found in this town more suspicion that my books were dangerous, than in any other. The just reason was, that a well-meaning person, with more zeal than knowledge, had scattered through it tracts, treating entirely on controversial points between Romanism and Protestantism; which so aroused the bishop, that he had issued an edict that no book, or tract, should be received from a Protestant, unless its contents were first ascertained to be of the genuine kind.[31] Happily for me, mine were unexceptionable, and when they found that neither my books nor myself were designed to proselyte them to a party, but lead them to Christ, they rejoiced exceedingly, and received the books with great cordiality during my whole stay in the place.

Saturday. – Hesitated how to pass the day; my dread of going out upon the street was greater in Killarney than in any other town; though it is a place where strangers constantly resort, it would seem that I was a more interesting spectacle than any whatever. My coat was made of good cloth and in the newest fashion, my bonnet was the same, but my muff was black and large, and thinking that the coat might be a little novel to the peasantry, and the muff a fright, I resolved that morning to avoid all occasion of offence. The post office was the place of destination, and putting on a cloak, which the peasantry wear both in winter and summer, and leaving the muff behind, I went out quite early, hoping to escape unmolested. Not so; my fate was fixed. Men, boys, women, and girls, were on the spot, who all regulated their movements in unison with mine. If I hastened my pace, they did the same; if I walked slowly, they did so too; and if I stopped, this was still more favourable for the gaping. It was market-day, and a fresh recruit was on the field; some dropped their sacks and hurried on, lest I might be too quick for them; others, with baskets and buckets on their heads, managed so adroitly as to draw up to the spot in good time, near where they supposed I was going. Reaching the post office, I paused and seriously asked a countryman, who was leisurely surveying me from head to foot, "How do you like my looks? Don't you think me a queer looking woman?"

"By dad, ye're a dacent lookin' body," said he.

I dropped in my letter, and with a hurried step walked away, when a huckster woman bawled out, "She's a beautiful wawlker, God bless her."

What could I do, what should I do, with this indescribable annoyance of being followed through the town, over hedges, and even into burying-grounds, to be gaped at? The misery was enhanced by knowing that this proceeded from no ill motive whatever, for they would have protected me at the risk of their own safety, and I hated myself that my sensibilities were such, that I could not be more patient under the unavoidable ordeal.

We will now, reader, escape the market-women and visit Lord Kenmare's deer park.[32] At the gate a more than ordinary looking woman met me, and in a pleasant manner invited me into her cottage. It was cleanly, and she was tidily dressed, and had no occasion to say she had been "better rair'd." She was religious, and when she learned my object to Ireland, in admiration she exclaimed, "Blessed Jesus, make me thankful, and bless and protect her! The people in Kerry, ma'am, are very dark; some of them are married, and can't say the Lord's prayer. I bless God that he sent you to Ireland. And what can I do for you? I have nothing to give a stranger, a lady like you. I am sitting desolate and alone in my cabin. My husband is dead, my children are gone, and I keep this little cottage at the gate for my bit of bread."

I read a tract to her called the "Worth of a Dollar," and presented it to her.[33] She clasped it, raising her hands and eyes, saying, "Is this a present for me? I was going to ask where one could be bought, and now you have given it to me. I have a friend who loves the world too much, and this is the book I'll give him to read. I've often told him he'd lose his soul if he didn't let go of the world." She was not ignorant of the Word of God, and repeated some scripture, though she had no Bible. I presented her with the Douay gospels, and read some portions to her, when with emphasis she exclaimed, "It is good, but where is the 'Blessed Virgin?' Didn't she bring forth the blessed Saviour, and didn't she wrap him in swaddling clothes in a manger, and didn't the breath of oxen warm his blessed body?" The expression was new, simple, and touching.

She showed me the best walk through the park to find the glen behind it, and heaped renewed blessings on my head, for leaving her the books. Walking a little distance, some labouring men saw me, and informing them I was an American, and asking the way to the glen, one dropped his spade, and, in spite of remonstrance, would show me to the gate, lest I should "go astray." The law of kindness is most indelibly written on these poor peasants' hearts. If they meet a stranger, and need require, they will give to the utmost, they will do to the utmost, and not let him know they have made any sacrifice.

Glens had been my peculiarly pleasant walks in Ireland, but here I was in a way to get too much. I followed a clear stream for a mile or more, and saw no outlet. Darkness was gathering, and my prospects were not the brightest; at length a bridge led me across the stream, though the glen, to a deep ditch, on the top of which was a fence made of poles. Down the ascent of the ditch on the other side was a crazy ladder made of sticks, and to reach this I must climb and cross the fence. The risk looked dubious, and I walked away, ascended the hill, but could find no outlet; returned, and resolved to make the effort, much fearing the second part to be the fall made a few days before. Throwing my muff and parasol before me, I made the leap, and happily succeeded. A long walk was before me, and –

"Wide o'er the scene her tints grey evening flings,"[34]

but one happy reflection was, that I should escape the staring in town by the darkness. And so it proved.

Sabbath morning early, taking my Bible and a few tracts, visited Ross Island. Entered a cottage in a wild part of it, gave the son and daughter each a small book, when the mother in kindness asked me to walk in a see a child who was sick with the small-pox.[35] I assured her I had no desire to become acquainted with the small-pox in this way. "The disease is in Killarney entirely." Leaving the door, I seated myself on a rustic seat by the side of the lake, and enjoyed a Sabbath hour, with the Word of God and the book of nature before me, opened to as bright a page as the volume could produce. For Killarney is not evanescent in her friendship, pleasant and cordial to-day, as is often said of the nation, and to-morrow unkind and forbidding. These lakes and this scenery never can tire; a spot where "Nature wears her sweetest smile."

But I must leave this temple of God, this open air adoration, and take my reader to a little church, to hear a short discourse, from "Enter in the strait gate."[36] The little company that attended was not the best comment on the success of gospel truth, though the worshippers appeared devout.

At six o'clock, taking as usual tracts and books, I went to the gate-house of Lord Kenmare. Here was a family of children, who had been well educated for the peasantry, and giving a book to one, it was read audibly, and received that hearty response that every subject treating on benevolence ever does among the poor of Ireland. Charity is the alpha and omega, the sum total of all that makes the man or woman, with these people. Without it your religion, whether Roman or Protestant, is but as a sounding brass or a tinkling cymbal.[37] And a distinguishing feature which cannot be too much admired, is, that when they give, they give unsparingly from their pittance, and when they receive, they do it with as much thankfulness, when the smallest trifle is offered, as when the donation is quite bountiful. When the child was reading the story the potatoes were preparing, the milk and eggs put on, and I was invited to "the egg and sup of milk, ma'am, but you couldn't take the potato." I had taken supper, but never declined a potato, and always took it in my hand, which to them was as sure a test of good-will and sincerity on my part, as are the grip and well-known pass-word to the initiated brother mason.

As I went out, four little girls were at the gate, where they had been waiting an hour to ask for books. "It's the Word of God I want," said one, "which you promised me last Friday. I went to your place at six, as you told me, and they sent me to the gate, and I have been waiting an hour, ma'am. And have you got the Word of God for me now? it's what I want."

"I am not certain but you will destroy it if I give you one."

"Destroy the Word of God! Who would dare do that?"

A woman now interfered, "And what's this you're saying? If you touch one of her books, I'll tell the bishop." The bishop's house was at our left, but a few yards distant. "He has told us we must not touch a Protestant book." "I don't care if you do tell the bishop. If I can get the Word of God, I'll read it." This was plain English, and then turning to me, "I know, lady, you'll give it to me. You said you would." "But," continued the woman, "they are the same books that the Protestant man had, to put down the church, and speak against our religion." Turning to the woman, and telling her I had no books but what the bishop would approve, and that they were Irish and Douay Testaments, &c. she begged pardon, and walked on, the little girl exulting, said, "There, I knew the lady was right."

When we reached the lodging-house, the testaments and books were presented; but no urging would the girl be persuaded to take any books but the scriptures, though she was told they contained beautiful stories, and were handsomely covered. "It's the Word of God I want, and nothing else," was the only answer, though the three others were better pleased with a coloured tract than with any other book.

The next day was devoted by the citizens of Killarney to St. Patrick. At twelve the temperance band awakened me, by playing very sweetly the air of St. Patrick's Day, reminding me of New York, when the Irish emigrants there celebrate the day, rekindle old associations of their beloved Emerald Isle, sing the songs of their native land, and live over again the by-gone days of the country so dear to them. Early the chapel bells called to mass, and from every mountain and glen the people poured in, with the green shamrock in their hats, the children with some kind of ribbon upon the left arm, which they called the "crass."[38] Sabbath was called Palm Sunday, when a sprig of palm was carried to chapel to be blessed, and worn home in the hat; this was changed by some on Monday for the shamrock. The multitude huddled to mass three times a day, and passed the afternoon and evening looking upon each other, but not in quarrelling or drinking. To avoid the staring without, and the thronged house within, I again visited the park, and under a shady oak should have enjoyed a sweet sleep, with my muff for a pillow, had not the gate-woman found and invited me in. Another treat of reading she enjoyed, but declined taking any books, lest the bishop should punish her. Reading to these people what they can understand, and what they should practise, is the best mode of access, and the surest way to do good. Having few or no books of their own, and many not being able to read at all, a story of practical piety, a clear and pungent explanation of the most essential doctrines connected with the life and atonement of Christ, are listened to with the deepest interest. And not infrequently will the sower find, if he watch the growth, that the seed has sprung up, promising a fruitful harvest.[39]

CHAPTER XIX

Fellow Travellers on the Kerry Mountains – Bay of Ross by Moonlight – "Fine Stage-house" – Loss of Appetite – Feet bathing Extraordinary – Kerry Trick – Glorious Morning on the Mountains, in spite of Hunger and Weariness – Cabin Courtesy – Woman a Beast of Burden – Lodging-house at Cahirciveen – A Saucepan an Unattainable Luxury – Religion and Filth – Guests to the Fair – Curly-headed Biddy –Battle of the Sticks – Sabbath Services – Protestant Whiskey-selling – Improved Quarters

Tuesday, March 18th. – I concluded to go west, and visit Cahirciveen, a distance of thirty miles; to walk the first ten, and wait for the car till next morning at the town of Killorglin. I soon had company, and a call for books from every peasant who passed, having a basket on my arm, and some tracts upon the outside. "An' maybe you've somethin' that's nice," said one; giving him a tract, he read with much attention, "an' sure you don't give these? There's not many the like of ye. Ye must be from England." "From America," I said. "From America! and what brought ye here among the poor?" When the object was explained, "Then ye must be wawkin' for the good of your soul." This I often found the most difficult part of the story to be understood. If penance were not the object, what could induce me to put so much trouble on myself?

A kind parting left me with a countryman, who was going to the same town with a load of flour, and as heavily as his cart was burdened, he insisted on my taking a seat. "The wawkin' 'ill be heavy on ye." I declined, but put my basket on his cart, and he carried it till we reached the miserable dirty town of Killorglin. This shrewd Kerryman displayed much of that common sense, observation, and inquisitiveness, so peculiar in the peasantry of all Ireland, but especially in the Kerryites. We reached the filthy town, and finding no better stopping-place than a public house, where a woman was dealing out the "good creature," and so forbidding were her looks and every thing in keeping that, though rain began to fall, I resolved to go on eight miles further, where the teamster was going that night, rather than wait for the car next morning. I was now getting into the heart and essence of Kerry, the land of O'Connell, the country noted for the inquisitive disposition and cunning of the peasantry. And though it would be absurd to suppose that a county line could designate the character and habits of a people, yet throughout all Ireland there is one grand feature telling you who is Irish, and definite minor ones telling the stranger there are different children belonging to this common stock, who speak different languages, and wear different costumes. The Kerryites are said to have a mixture of the Spanish, who many years ago found their way among these mountains, and the Kerry women have black or dark hair, and in general are quite handsome.

I had not walked far before I "cast longing lingering looks behind." My feet were blistered, the road stony, and the rain threatening. Often I sat down upon a stone by the wayside, feeling quite unable to proceed. I could get nothing to eat, and my breakfast had been a light one, and my condition was not the most desirable.

Night came on. My companion had met with a fellow-traveller of the same craft, taking a load of flour to the town, and each man lit his pipe, and jabbered in Irish to my full content; having me sometimes in sight, and sometimes out of sight, sometimes far in the rear, sometimes in speaking distance, when my companion would call, "And sure ye ain't wairy; and when we've crassed the stones a bit, ye'll have a lift on the cart," or, "it's a fine stage-house ye'll see as there is in all the three kingdoms." The name of a stage-house, to an American ear, is associated with all that is comfort; and hearing it was an Englishman that kept it, I was buoyed up with the hope that I should meet with a clean lodging, for never did a weary traveller deserve them more.

The clouds had dispersed, and the young moon was looking from as pure a sky as was ever spread out over this misty isle of the sea. The Bay of Ross, with all its witchery, arose in view. A little mountain girl had met me from a foot-path that led among the rocks, and as we suddenly made a turn, which opened the bay unexpectedly, "And ye'll have as fine a bay, ma'am, in yer eye as in all the kingdom," fell on my ear. I stopped suddenly, and on either hand

> "Bold and craggy rose each mountain form,
> To brave the heavens, the lightning, and the storm."

The girl seeing my admiration, triumphantly added, "And did ye see the like in all your travels, ma'am? I must leave ye, lady, for my way lies up the mountain a bit, and ye'll not be lonely, for the moon looks bright, and the road is now aisy to the fut. Good night, and God speed ye on yer journey, and return ye safe to yer own country."

Through all this I had stood on the margin of that bay, looking up the heathy crags, then upon the placid sea, that was here and there reflecting the rays of the moon, then deep shaded by some cliff that looked down upon it, sheltering some fisherman's mud-wall hut at its foot. I uttered not a word, till the "good night"of the Kerry-girl awaked me from the reverie. Her light foot stole quickly away, and I was standing alone, for my carmen were jabbering far out of sight. Taking my cruel boots from my blistered feet, I hurried on, till the voice of one of my fellow-travellers bawled out "And sure ye ain't a-gazin' at these black mountains, it's the pratee and the night's sleep I am thinkin' on." Again I sat down upon a stone, put on my boots, and, determining to make "virtue of necessity," endeavoured, as I followed the cart, to forget my pains by singing. This, to my wonder, drew upon the hillsides and path, groups of all ages, where I had scarcely noticed a cabin, giving me a moonlight view of moun-taineers and fishermen, who followed me with good wishes, and com-forted my spirits by telling me of the "short bit" that was "under my fut," and the "dacent people" I should find at the lodging. My Kerry guide had intentionally passed the stage-house, and stopping to rest his horse at the top of a hill, pointed around, saying, "At your left a short bit and ye'll see the lodgin'."

Here I pause, for we were in view of this "dacent lodgin'," and a little time is requisite to gird ourselves for the coming conflict.

Supposing I was approaching the "tidy stage-house," my steps were accelerated, and looking on my left saw a thatched house of considerable dimensions, and a pile of well packed manure at the door.³ Here stood two goats and a ram, each with a stout pair of horns, and the ram was using his with much dexterity against a spirited girl, who was pulling and beat-ing the "bold blackguard," to get him aside, that the "lady might come in." I stood at a respectful distance till the battle was decided in favour of the girl and myself, and looking in, saw a cow fastened at the entrance, stand-ing upon straw and filth, and her young calf to the right, near the fire. The smoke was making its way as well as it could through the door, eight beings in the shape of men were lolling upon a settee and benches, with one stretched at full length upon a table, his head hanging off at one end, and the mother, three daughters, the two teamsters, and myself, with geese, and hens at roost, made up the group in the room and about the fireside of this "stage-house." The whole together was so complete an overthrow of all my expectations of an Englishman's lodgings, that what with my miserable feet, empty stomach, and prospects for the night, I was quite indignant, and pettishly demanded of the consequential land-lord why he lived with his cattle in the house, when I saw he had a barn near.

"The cow has a new calf, ma'am, and she is warmer in the house."

My senior comrade now ordered a pot of potatoes which were soon in preparation, carried to an adjoining room, and a splinter of dry bog-wood put into a crack over the table as a torch to guide the way to the mouth. I was invited to walk in, but though I had not taken any food but a piece of bread early in the morning at Killarney, and had walked twenty-five miles over the roughest path I had ever trod in Ireland upon the strength of that, yet the sight within the walls of that cabin hushed the clamour of my stomach, and I left my fellow travellers to sup alone. The master of the house entertained me with a historical account of Dublin, which he once visited, assuring me it was twenty miles across, containing sixteen hundred public houses of entertainment, and the laws very strict. No persons meeting on the walks were allowed to shake hands; if they did so, they were immediately put in prison; he had seen it done repeatedly. This bundle of lies was well received by the auditors, as this man was quite an oracle of the mountains; and modestly telling him that his statements were all untrue, we turned to another subject.

My feet needing bathing, the pot which had been used for the boiling of the potatoes was presented, and in presence of the ten male eye-witnesses gathered about, the girl who fought the battle with the ram washed my feet in spite of all remonstrance, the father and mother urging my consent as being a duty to a "wairy stranger." While this was in progress, the father whispered a second daughter to "put on the feather bed for the lady," and in a half hour my bed-room was in readiness, with another splinter of bog-wood put into a crack to light me on the way thither. This bed-room contained three beds for father and mother, three daughters, and myself. I was allowed to retire first, the same attendant standing by in real primitive fashion, to help me to undress. The washing of the feet of strangers and guests is, in these mountains and glens of Ireland, a literal and beautiful illustration of our Saviour's example, "So ought ye to wash one another's feet."[4] They will not allow you to perform this office yourself, without an absolute refusal; and then, with apparent disappointment, they stand aloof, as if deprived of a most desired favour. The custom of an attendant to help the stranger undress, is mentioned by Henderson in his visit to Iceland, where the mother or eldest daughter claims the honour; and though the unaccustomed stranger may at first feel it an intrusion, yet the fastidiousness is soon relieved by the simple unstudied manner in which it is done.[5]

In half an hour all were snoring around me, and soon my troubles found a quietus, which lasted till five, when my Kerryite stood at the bed-side with a bog-wood torch. "And maybe ye wouldn't like to go on so airly?" Saying "Yes." "An' in the name of God we'll go on." I hurried up, and lo! he was gone, and I have not seen him since! This I was told was genuine Kerry roguery, done for the sole purpose of enjoying to himself the gratification of my surprise and bustling to hurry on, and join his company.

I paid a shilling for this rare treat, and hurried to catch the first gleamings of light upon these towering heath-topped mountains. The sea again broke upon my view, the road was made upon a mountain so steep, that a stone wall was necessary to keep the traveller safe, and the look down into the sea in many places was truly terrific.[6] A solitary star was here and there still twinkling in the west, a mountain-top behind me was white with snow, and as the morning advanced, the rays of the sun shot athwart it, and rested upon the smooth surface of the sea, leaving a heavy shadow from the mountain beneath, giving a picture of light and shade which the painter could alone delineate. The varied colour of the purple, grey, and brown of the mountain, the wildness, the song of the morning bird, the "Alps on Alps" rising to view, the cascades of the most sparkling crystal gurgling from their sides, transported me beyond loneliness, hunger, or pain of blistered feet, and at short intervals I was fixed to the spot as when looking on the moonlight view the preceding night. I occasionally mixed my rude voice with the song of the bird and music of the mountain waterfall, and with a heart full of thanksgiving, did I bless the God of love, that he had made this isle of the sea. Persecuted and hated as it is, it has riches of scenery, riches of minerals, and riches of mind, which all others might covet.

For hours the scenery, though continually varying, lost none of its interest, and I had walked five miles of Irish measure of such painful enjoyment, before the clamours of hunger told me that I had taken no bread since seven on the preceding morning, and here no bread could be found. Not a cabin had greeted my eye, save a little clump of mud-wall or rough stone huts, where bread would have been as strange a guest as a plum pudding in the kraal of a Hottentot. Excitement, which had thus far been a kind vehicle, now gave way, and weariness, pain, and hunger, demanded their rights. Seeing a little girl dip her bucket in a clear mountain stream, I saluted her. "And ye look wairy, lady, wouldn't ye walk in and rest ye a little by the fire?" Gladly I followed into the lowly, but clean cabin, and was offered the only seat in the room, and that was made of braided straw in the shape of a cushion. They tried in every possible way to comfort me, offering to bathe my feet. Telling them a piece of bread was what I wanted to buy, the girl, the only one that could speak English in the family, told me I could not get any for some miles. "But wouldn't ye stop and have a potato? they will boil in a little bit." I cheerfully consented, and that cabin will ever be associated with the deepest and kindliest recollections. Two girls, a son of twenty, and the father and mother, made up this family. While the potatoes were boiling I read the Testament, the girl interpreting to the mother, who in tears of gratitude was expressing her admiration both at the reading, and at the goodness of God, who had suffered a saint going on pilgrimage, as she thought, to enter her humble cabin. "She's crying, ma'am, because she can't do as much for her soul as you." Here, as in many parts of the country, it was difficult to make them believe that I was not some holy St. Bridget going on penance.[7]

The old man was in bed, had been a cripple for years with the rheumatism; he had listened to the reading, for he would occasionally clasp his hands, and respond in Irish. He crawled out, and drew on his rightful rags, knelt down and said his prayers, and by a smile, nod of the head, and hearty grasp of the hand, gave me a kindly welcome to his cabin. The potatoes were boiled, and poured into a basket; a board was then put upon the top of the pot for a table and the potatoes poured upon it, and the family drew around giving me a commodious place. We had comfortably adjusted ourselves, when the delighted old man took an egg from a hen who was sitting near, and, reaching it to me, made signs that I must have it boiled. His countenance changed into regret when I declined, and I was sorry that my appetite should then refuse so cheerfully an offered boon. But toasting some potatoes on the coals, and eating them without any condiment, for they had not even salt, I made a good and palatable breakfast. I gave some books to the children who came in, and offered the woman a little money for her hospitality; she thrust it back, giving a frown of half anger, and half grief, and the daughter said, "She gave ye the potatoes in the name of God, and d'ye think we'd take money for it?" I put it in the old man's hand, who told the daughter, "I will take it for God's sake, but not for the potato." Here I found another proof of the custom among all the peasantry, to refuse money for hospitality shown to a stranger; and I gave books, which were never refused, when presented as tokens of good will.[8]

I arose to depart with quite different feelings than those at the house where I slept, for though in the most abject poverty, they seemed cultivated, and full of the "milk of human kindness." Though their feet had never trod upon a parlour carpet, nor the delicacies of a sumptuous table ever crossed their lips, and though I might have been the only female with both bonnet and shoes that ever sat down in their cabin, yet their manners savoured more of genuine politeness than did many of the inmates of lordly houses in cities, boasting of the greatest refinement. When the poor old man extended his trembling hand, and the daughter, who was speaker for them all, pressed me to call on my return, I felt like parting with friends, and said, "I dread to go alone." The daughter interpreted to the mother, who said, "She won't go alone, God will go with her." The expression coming at such a time and from such a person, was a word in season, and as valuable to me as though it had been dropped from the lips of a divine.

I went out with blessing upon blessing on my head, and a dreadful day it was. My lameness became so intolerable, that at short intervals I was obliged to sit down, and when this did not refresh me, I lay down upon a bank of earth overgrown with grass, with my basket under my head, feeling that I could go no further. Again rising and reaching a spring of fresh water, I washed my face, but this did not ease my pained feet. Again I lay down upon the wall, with my parasol over my face, when I heard footsteps, and a female voice saying, "She's a stranger, and wairied out; maybe she's sick." "Rouse her," said the man. I lifted my head, and saw a man and woman, with a little boy, standing beside me. They too had travelled many a long and weary mile, and found this little orphan boy, who had lost father and mother, and was travelling to a distant county where he was born, hoping to find a home. "God help all travellers," said the woman, "I knew you was a foreigner by your dress and by your tongue." They bestowed much pity, and left me; again I made an effort; a girl came out of a cabin. "O, ye're kilt, ye can't reach the town, ye'd better stop, it's a long and wairy road." The next I met were two young women. Enquiring the distance, one said, "There is no place you can stop but in some poor cabin. I could give you a clane bed, and fresh egg, but no mate, for it's Lent, ma'am, and we ain't allowed to ate it. Ye're lost, ye're destroyed, and ye can't get to town; it's a long mile to it now, ma'am."

"She might stop till her feet should be hailed," said the other, "the cratur."

Thanking them from my inmost heart, I thought it best to proceed. The car was now coming, and with joy I hailed it. "No room" was the answer, and onward was the only alternative. Reaching the bottom of a steep hill, two girls were resting by a wall, one with a little bundle, the other with a basket of turf; to me it looked sufficiently weighty to make a donkey stagger. "And do you, my girl, carry this on your back?" "I does, ma'am; but ye are wairy, ma'am, and have ye long to walk?" The girl with the small bundle took up my basket, and the other adjusted the turf upon her head; this was done by a rope of straw put into one side of the basket, and fastened across the forehead; a cloth is doubled and put over the forehead first, that the rope need not fret it.⁹ When I looked at this rosy faced girl of seventeen, and saw the symmetry of her features, the brilliancy of her eye and beauty of her teeth, what a pity and what a sin, I thought, to take such a finished piece of God's workmanship, and convert it to a beast of burden! Weary and crippled as I was my real condition called for fresh gratitude, that I was not born in oppressed Ireland, where woman can never be woman if not born to an earthly inheritance.¹⁰

Asking the girl if she was not tired of my basket, "O no, ma'am, I wish it was greater, if it would lighten your fut." We sat down upon a bank, and taking the books from my basket, I presented each of them with portions of the scripture. Offering the girl who had carried them a tract, telling her it contained an interesting story, "I will take the Word of God," was the answer. This "Word of God" at the south seems to possess peculiar value in the minds of many of the peasantry, in spite of all training, and often have they not only astonished, but instructed me, by the appropriate applications they have made of this Word.

"Can you show me to a neat lodging in Cahirciveen, where they do not sell whiskey?" The girl with the turf said, "Show her to Mickey M'Gloukin.¹¹ I have been thinking of that, and she has rooms, and can give her a clane bed, an' is a nice approachable woman." This all looked inviting; but, following the girl to the door, I was met by the same dark and dirty room, the same crowd of starers, with pipes and attendant appurtenances. Flinging myself upon the first stool, and asking for lodging, she answered, "An' I wish I could give ye a room, but the house is all in disawrdher, tairin' it up." "But can you give me a clean bed?" "That I can." "And a room where I can be alone, away from gapers who are ready to swallow me up wherever I go?" "I can give ye a room to yourself, ma'am."

So fatigued and faint was I, that the two goats and ram could have had no terrors, and a comfortable room and chair been before me, rather than striving to walk further.

"Can I get any food in town?" "You can; put on the kittle, Biddy, to make some tay, and take off the pot of potatoes." "Keep on the pot of potatoes, I will eat some of them, I take no tea." "Aw, and where's the like of ye?" I sent out and procured some cocoa, but nothing in the house could be found that could prepare the article. Every thing was named belonging to pot, kettle, iron, copper, or tin; but the two-pail-full pot for potatoes, and the tay kettle for tay, were the only vessels. "Run out, Biddy, and ask Kate for her tin cup." The cup was procured, with the injunction "not to put it over the fire." "And how am I to boil the cocoa if the cup must not go to the fire?" "An that you can't. Never mind, she hasn't the sinse."

My table was in a room where the kind woman was obliged to throw down straw, to keep my feet from the mud while eating. This woman was very religious; mass and the rosary were all her theme. It was the last week in Lent, or rather "Passion Week," and "Passion Week" it was indeed to this devoted woman. She talked of Holy Jesus, the Blessed Virgin, incessantly, when she was not scolding her servants and children to make them more devout. When a few moments could be spared, she would throw her cloak over her head, run to chapel, return, and drop upon her knees in any part of the house, bidding all to be quiet till her prayers were finished. Taking occasion once to say to her, that Christ commanded us to pray in secret, she looked with astonishment as though all was upset; and in a half hour she was dragging her little girl of six into a retired place to say her prayers, adding, "It will do you no good if you say 'em here."[12] She wept much when I read some tracts, and regretted deeply that she could not read the scriptures; "An' ye're the one that can read the 'Word of God.'" She was a strange compound of good and evil, and more to be pitied than derided. She seemed to hunger for what she could not obtain, and had ears to hear, but who should teach her? "She has done what she could" in her own way, and could heaven be attained by jumps and snatches, and "Passion Week" continue during her earthly pilgrimage, this woman would certainly be entitled to a prominent seat among the guests. My bed was a good one and a clean one, in this she said truly; but the giving a room to myself was a little slip of the tongue, for it contained a bed for herself, husband, and two children, beside another in waiting the first night, but the second a goodly host of Kerrymen were on the spot. A few moments before one, I was awakened by the clatter of three pairs of heavy shoes, and loud talking, and heard the woman say, "You can two of you go into the next room." "No, we'll all quat here," was the reply. They did "quat here" at the foot of my bed, and jabbered awhile in Irish, and then were snoring in full chorus through the night.

It would be no more than rendering what is just and equal to say, that I was neither lonesome nor afraid of robbers, and I really believe that the Irish peasantry are as free from coveting "other men's gold, or silver, or apparel" as is possible for a people to be, wretched and poor as they are. They will ask for the penny with a very good grace, and load you with blessings when you bestow it, but they neither upbraid when refused, nor seem envious at the purse or equipage of any neighbour, however heavy or splendid they may be. "We must be content with what the Almighty God sends us," or, "must not fly in the face of God Almighty," seems not only a current phraseology in their mouth, but a fixed principle of the heart.

On Saturday a fair was to be held; my feet had improved a little, and I should have left, but rain came on, and I stayed indoors.[13] Friday night the gathering from the country commenced, and seven new lodgers required some little change, and I was removed into the gangway at the head of the stairs, where all must pass on the way to bed. When each had gone to his lair, I went to mine, and when each had risen and clattered through, I did the same, and there was no nook in which I could ensconce myself but the kitchen. Here had gathered the whole fraternity, beside many of the sisterhood from without, some sitting on stools, some on chairs, others standing in waiting posture, some squatting near me, and looking me sharply in the face. The question, impious as it was, did certainly arise, whether these creatures had immortal souls, and could be made society for angels? Yes, through the blood of the Lamb they could, but if nothing unclean can enter heaven, they must not yet be quite ready.[14]

They were waiting for breakfast, and as all could not afford "bread and tay," the great pot of potatoes was in constant requisition, one "squad" waiting on their haunches for the first to be served. One of a little more energy than the rest was hurrying the boiling by thrusting in his cane, with which he had walked through the mud, and from the bottom turning up a prize, squeezing it, and if not fit for mastication putting it back. No sooner was one batch done, than another supplied its place over the fire until the whole were served.,

Curly-headed Biddy had dodged into a corner among the forest of legs, where she sat busily fixing her hair, when the mother bade her instantly go away and say her prayers. Biddy heeded it not; "Go away, and say your prayers, I tell you, and say them in private, too." Biddy would not leave the warm spot till pulled out, and in a few moments she was in the gangway where I lodged, in the middle of the floor upon her knees, her fists together, and mumbling her prayers as devoutly as a mad child could do.

It was now eleven, and when the third or fourth pot-full was poured out, the woman asked me if I would take a couple of potatoes. I told her they had been boiled in dirty water, and beside every man who had a cane had washed it in the pot, so I must be excused. And here followed a profound lecture on the filth of the country, telling her that if the people had no other sins attached to them but this, it would be sufficient to keep them out of heaven. "To be sure it will; sloth and filth are two deadly sins. God save the poor Irish!" This was said with much feeling, and cruel as might appear so severe rebuke on so humble a penitent, I enforced it with double severity by adding that the county of Kerry was the most hopeless of all places I had seen and I could devise no better way of cleansing them than by hunting them out with dog and gun, and burning their cabins after them. She bore this with apparent resignation, not seeming to feel herself in the least implicated.

But the fair. This like all other fairs was managed by buying and selling to the best advantage, for the Kerryites are characterized by their tact in bargaining, as well as in all other movements. The men were certainly better clad than any I had seen at previous fairs, and what met my warmest approbation was, the corduroys were not numerous; substantial blue cloth pantaloons adorned the legs of most of the Kerryites. A stripling clerk of the parish priest's entered, and requested to examine my books, as their care over the flock required that they should be particular that nothing should interfere with their religion.[15] "We wish to know whether your Irish testaments are the true translation, by a bishop of our own church." Showing him one, he could not satisfy his mind without taking it away for a close examination. "We have had some trouble in this part of the country, by men professing to be teachers, and sowing errors among the people. And are you, ma'am, sent out by any religious sect?" Answering him that I was sent by none but by the Lord Jesus Christ, and, as far as I was capable, his doctrine and his alone was what I inculcated, and what I should inculcate, and these doctrines I found contained in that book he held in his hand – he walked away with the Testament to decide on its merits, promising to see me again, but never did.

"A fight! a fight!" was now the cry.

"Up flew the windows all."*[16]

Sticks were flourishing in the air, and to appearance they were fighting each other instead of the persons. One old woman rushed into the crowd to rescue her Paddy, and she was dragged along regardless of age or sex, her cloak was torn from her, her cap set awry (bonnet she had none), and while one pulled one way, another seized the other side, till the sight from the ludicrous became painful, lest she should be "pulled in pieces." The priest was called, but they heeded not the threats of denunciations

* They certainly had windows in Cahirciveen, and whole panes of glass, which needed only a little cleaning to give comfortable light within.

from the altar, which he assured them they should have on the morrow. Sacrifices were more to them than altars or peace-offerings, and he was obliged to leave them as he found them, to rattle their sticks, as they did till midnight, though it was next day reported that no dead or wounded were carried from the field that night.

In the evening a tidy well-dressed young woman came in, whose dialect and manner were so much like the Americans, that I asked if she had not been there. She answered that she had resided in New York ten years, and returned to take charge of a sickly mother. I had noticed throughout all Ireland when a servant girl returns from America that a great change is evident in dress, manner, and language. She ceases to become a beast of burden, and the basket on her back, which she then throws off, she will never lift again. She confines her services more to the inside of the cabin, and this undergoes a manifest change for the better.[17]

Sabbath. – The rain was copious, but I made my way to a Protestant church, and heard a good sermon on the resurrection.[18] The speaker had but few to listen to his graphic description of the rolling away of the stone from the door of the sepulchre, yet some of the bonnetless women who were seated in the corner of the church reminded me of the lingering Marys, who watched at the cross, and followed the sacred body of their Saviour, and beheld where they laid him.[18] When the services closed, I enquired of a gentleman if he could direct me to a comfortable lodging-house. He was the parochial school-teacher, and quite a favourite in the parish, and he sent me with a girl whose parents were Protestants and sold whiskey; a house not a whit before the one I had left, either in cleanliness or morality. It is a stubborn fact that where this traffic in ardent spirits is carried on, there is confusion and every evil work.

I took some potatoes and bread with them, while they dined on roast veal, pork, and cabbage, the good woman saying it was Easter Sunday, and the family expected something new. It was evident here that the reading of the scriptures was not so much needed, as the right practising of their principles. When the teacher called to invite me with him to tea, I waited not for a second invitation, and when I had reached his house, my lady sent word that she could not lodge me, though she had promised to do so. The schoolmaster, who seemed to hold the keys of the Protestant part of the parish, kept me quiet till half-past ten, by assuring me he could fix me in comfortable lodgings at almost any hour. We went to the house of a Methodist, but they were in bed; went away, and demurred awhile.[19] "We must return," said my persevering gallant, "and knock them up." It was done, and the servant gave me a tidy bed in a tidy room and long life to the good people of the house, whose kind salute in the morning emphatically impressed me with the force of the sweet passage, "I was a stranger and ye took me in."[20] I was urged to take breakfast, and no charges but that of being "faithful unto death."

CHAPTER XX

An Americanized Irishman – Armed Defence – Modern Mermaids – Island of Valentia – Employment and a good Landlord – Conversable Coast Guard – A Child's Mute Appeal – Poverty and Low Rents – Ridiculous old Custom – Derrynane – O'Connell's Library – Cold Comfort – Hospitable Port in the Storm – Lighthearted Burdenbearers – Kerry Dancing and Kerry Kindness

Monday. – My walk this morning was intended to be to the island of Valentia, and fortunately a man called who was going to the place; he had been in America, and, as he said, "Come back because he was a fool," and was now so poor he could not return. He had lived in Vermont, and found them "so hospitable, so nate, and so well-fed, that he could never be content in Ireland again, feedin' on the potato;" neither could he again ever endure the "boorish manners of the blackguard Irish among the black mountains. Don't they kill you, followin' you about, and starin' at you?" As he spoke, out poured from a smoky cabin seven ill-looking lads and lasses, with most of them an arm over the eyes, the better to take observation. But the poor things had but just prepared to take a sure aim, when my care-taking guide pounced upon them with his uplifted stick, threatening unsparing vengeance if every "dirty scrawl" didn't that instant go into the house. They fled like frighted sheep over a wall, and never looked back upon us till secured in the door of the cabin, where, joined by the mother, they could take a survey in spite of threats and sticks. "And you're the mother that rair'd the blackguards, and your smoky cap tells that you're fitted to the work." A couple of girls had kept behind us for some distance, either from modesty or fear of my guide, who flourished his stick at all who passed, if he or she had the audacity to venture the most sideway glance at my ladyship. Hearing their footsteps, he suddenly turned, and, "Where are ye goin'? Go a-head, and not have the boldness to be paradin' along behind the lady, and many's the long day that ye'll ever see her like again." The poor girls had committed no misdemeanour, and passed on abashed, not knowing what the choice thing could be that had dropped among them, requiring such watchful protection.

In vain I begged him to spare the well-intentioned women and children, and let them gratify a curiosity natural to all. "It isn't me, they'll humbug; they'd stare the life out of ye, before ye'd reach the say." As we approached the shore, my guide pointed to a wretched cabin, saying, "There lives a proud mother, who rair'd a gal of her own sort, who was employed gathering the seaweed from the rocks all her days. She went to New York, and I called upon her there, and because my broadcloth wasn't so fine as the gentlemen about her, she refused to see me, and went into a chamber to shun me. Ah, and wasn't she sure I should tell of her kin that belonged to her, and the smoky hut where she gathered up her heels!"

The employment of females here, though I had seen a little of it before, was of that degrading kind, that I felt like revolting from the sight. Men and women go out in boats, to gather seaweed that adheres to the rocks, which is used for manure. They take a long pole with hooks upon the end, wade in, standing often to the armpits in water, and scrape the weed from the rocks, put it in the boats, and the men take it ashore; the women remaining in the sea often through the day. At night they take a basket-full upon their backs, and bend to their wretched cabins, to boil their potatoes, and lie down upon the straw; and in the morning awake to the same hopes, and go to the same employment. Woman is here worse than a beast of burden, because she is often made to do what the beast never does.*[1]

We crossed in a ferry-boat to the rock-bound island of Valentia, where the white billow was dashing in playful wantonness against every bold rock, which like well-built battlements, guarded the coast. By the skill of my guide a lodging-place was provided, though at first refused. The woman was followed into the kitchen, where my qualifications were so pourtrayed, that they won at last upon the young bride, who consented. This neat little spot looked like a haven of rest, compared with the town I had left. The cottages were tasteful, the yards cleanly, and the little village was quite a manufacturing one. A slate quarry, of great extent upon the coast and upon the mountain, was in excavation; two hundred men, and sometimes more, here found employment for a shilling a day, and this has been in operation for nearly thirty years. An English nobleman, much beloved by the islanders, owns the quarry, stays continually upon the

* "Eight months in the year we drag at this, praise God," said a poor woman. I looked back to the garden of Eden and was it for this that a help-mate was made for man? Is this the being that is destined to mould the minds of his children, to look well to the ways of his household, and make him "known as he sitteth at the gate among the elders?" Surely Ireland's Bible teachers must have added their own theology to that of Henry, Clarke, and Scott, to have produced such a version as this for the station of woman.

island, and spends his money there; his wife likewise is a pattern of good-ness.[2] His house stands upon the sea coast, with no wall but the surges of the ocean, which gives a happy relief to eye and mind while passing along this precipitous shore.

The light-house is an object of great interest, being built upon a rock, which was once Cromwell's fort; one of his cannons now stands upon the wall, fixed there as a memento of his heroic deeds.[3] The family keeping the house are from Dublin, and quite accomplished. I went out and seated myself upon a rock, overlooking the sea, watching the poor women gathering the seaweed, and the dashing of the surges at my feet, till a sprinkling of rain, and the lateness of night, warned me of my distance from home. I thought of the poor exile of Erin, and wondered not that

"In dreams he revisits the sea-beaten shore,"[4]

of his own beautiful isle, where the finger of the Almighty has pencilled so many sublimities as well as beauties. When I reached my lodgings I was as completely drenched as the poor women with their seaweed, and had quite spoiled a valuable coat and velvet bonnet.

The house was tolerable, but the charge so high that I went away quite dissatisfied, and gave them a cold parting; disgusted that any of the Irish should take advantage of Americans, who have so many of the destitute of that nation upon their shores. Going out to look at the slate-cutting machinery, the whole island seemed to be on the spot. One bawled out, "Here is a man who has been a long time in your country." The man responded, "How do you like Ireland? I hope they trate ye well. They ought, Americans are so kind to the Irish there. They are the kindest craturs in the world, ma'am, in Vermont." I found in myself that love of country and pride of heart, which I had endeavoured to suppress, when he said that he had been in the town of my birth, and was treated with the greatest hospitality.[5] The machinery for sawing, cutting, and polishing slate, is quite a curiosity, mostly performed by steam; and is a work of great utility, much to the credit of the proprietor. The island itself is on the whole a well regulated and cleanly place. The little church on the hill tells the traveller, that, though the worshippers are few, yet the assem-bling of those few together is not forgotten. The Catholics have a chapel on the other side of the island.[6]

My American friend was all attention, conducted me to the boat, and left me in the protection of a Kerryite, who was to accompany me on my way to Waterville. I took out a portion of the Douay Testament, which he read aloud as he walked, making comments which would have done credit to any who had been taught the scriptures, like Timothy, from a child.[7]

The Word of God to the peasantry of Ireland is a treat which they greatly enjoy, especially among the mountains. As I parted with my companion, he kindly offered to send his boy and donkey to carry me a few miles, if I would call at his cabin. I declined, for the purpose of seeing both the country and people, and giving him the scriptures he held in his hand, I said adieu, not without hoping that the ten miles' walk we had performed together, would be blessed by the Saviour to the good of this unsophisticated peasant. What an honour to be counted worthy to meet these poor of this world on their own level, and tell in their listening ears the story of Calvary. How many opportunities of doing good when walking by the way, as well as when sitting in the house!

I now reached, as the sun was setting, the neat little well-known cottage by the sea-side, called the "Sportsman's Hotel."[8] I called for lodgings; at first was refused, because they were building an addition to the house, and had no place to put a "dacent body;" but telling them that I was an American, and easily packed away, I was immediately made welcome and comfortable. In the morning, offering to pay my bill, the woman declined any compensation, and sent me on to the "kind-hearted O'Connell's," where she had seven years resided, and whose family she knew would treat me with the utmost civility, adding, "I was told never to let a stranger pass the threshold without placing food before him."[9] Leaving the little town, the crowd was so great, that I enquired where could so many lodge as met me at the doors. One gentleman in good costume came out, invited me in, whispered to his wife, and she put down a couple of eggs, and I was urged to breakfast. Telling them I had just breakfasted, "Can I do anything for you? You shall be welcome to anything we have, if you will eat or drink."

"I do not dispute an Irishman's sincerity when he offers kindness, especially if he is not an 'upstart' in life." "I am not Irish but English; have been in America when a boy, and well remember their kindness."

In fact the kindness of my country appeared in quite a flattering aspect; and though as an individual, while there, I had not experienced an overcoming weight of the commodity, I was now in the way of getting it through another fortunate channel.

Saying good morning to police men, labouring men, women, and children, and passing on, a resolute man interrupted me by "Let me enquire are you a foreigner? I am likewise a stranger here, a coast-guard; and did you ever see or hear anything like Kerry? The people jabbering like blackbirds, and these wild rocks and mountains, the most frightful, ma'am. I'm from the north; and where are you going?" "To O'Connell's sir." "And there you'll find the hospitality; but be sure you take the new road, it's the smoothest under foot. And I wish I was going too; but I'm stationed here, and so I can't go with you; stationed here to guard the coast against smugglers, do ye understand?"[10] There was something peculiar in this man's appearance; he seemed to have caught the wildness of the scenery around him, or his occupation had given him that watchful restlessness that made me feel uneasy in his presence, and I was relieved when he said, "I must not walk any further with you, ma'am."

I was just settling into a quiescent state, when from behind me one called out, running at full speed, "Pardon me, lady, you are from New York; you never heard of a dress-maker by the name of Roan, a daughter of mine who has not written me in nearly two years, and isn't it in Greenwich street she stops?"

"I do not, sir, recollect having the honour of her acquaintance." "I'm quite sorry, ma'am, that business takes me out of town; I would take my carriage, and carry you to Derrynane. That's the place! And ye'll not return to-day, nor to-morrow. Keep the new road, ma'am, and the Almighty God go with you."

Again was I left to myself, and the strange view around me; not knowing how to choose, which most to admire, or which to enjoy, so divided was my mind between mountain wildness, roaring dashing waves, green sea and rocky island, wild mountaineers leaping from rock to rock, or climbing up the wall made for the protection of the passenger upon the precipitous steep, and the amazed children who followed me in companies. Hearing the quick patting of feet behind me, I turned, and a little girl of about six years looked me in the face, saluting me in Irish, and anxious to be understood. Six others were in pursuit, leading each other, and jabbering in rotation. I saluted them, and the youngest screeched in fright, turning and giving side-glances. A little coaxing at length consoled her, and though she appeared to feel safe in my sight, yet had I dropped from the clouds in their midst, they could not have been more at a loss to know what the being could be. A length, all but the first who saluted me, turned up a stony ascent, and were soon out of sight in the mountain passes – as pretty a group of faces as town or city ever could produce. The little companies who stayed behind, kept close to my side, looking me smilingly in the face. I gave her a penny; but this was not the thing desired, for she indifferently took it, looked at me, then up the mountain, settling her countenance into a look of disappointment. Then starting as from a reverie, as if some happy thought had directed her what next expedient to try; but seeing me at a loss to get her meaning, in apparent despair she turned through a niche in the wall, down a steep descent, to a cabin near the sea. I have ever regretted that I did not follow this sweet child, for she was clean, and her tiny white feet would have adorned the drawing-room of any lord in Kerry. I might have ascertained whether it was the instinct of hospitality, so strongly implanted in the Irish heart, or whether some case of suffering which she wished me to relieve, was the cause of her great earnestness. I looked after her, as her stealthy foot made its way cautiously down the rocks; and as I saw the last waving of her dark hair upon the breeze, I asked, why has a wise God left so much of his finished handy work to dwell in dens and caves of the earth, where hares and rabbits, owls and magpies, are the only companions to recipro-cate their worth?"

Seeing a hole in the wall, and a hut upon the other side, I crept through, and found a widow sitting in a corner, with a pig on the skirt of her dress, asleep, and three little children beside. Seeing no bed, table, or cupboard, but a niche in the wall, in which were a couple of plates, I asked her where she slept. "Here, ma'am," pointing to a pile of straw by her side. She said she had a bed, but no place to put it. "I wish I had something to give you to eat, but I have not a bit of bread, nor a potato." "I wish I had something to give *you*," I answered, "for I see no way how you can live."

This was a fair specimen of all the mountaineers around the residence of O'Connell. But when I enquired the price of ground, and found they were giving but a shilling an acre, for the same kind of mountain land I had seen elsewhere rented for twenty and twenty-four shillings, and no ejectments allowed, I wondered not so much that they were loud in their praises of him, and that I heard the voice of singing and laughter, from cabin and rock, from potato-ridge and bog, wherever a peasant was using his spade or hunting the hare." From the top of the mountain here may be seen the celebrated light-house, on what is called the Skellig-rock; a dangerous place to approach, and where the adventurer must sometimes pass a week before he finds it safe to leave. This is the place to which the people of Kerry and Cork, on Shrove-tide eve, amuse themselves by hunt-ing out the old maids and widows, putting them into carts, on asses, and all kind of ludicrous vehicles, to send them to Skellig-rocks. The streets of Cork were alive with this class of people, pursuing such as they deemed worthy a residence there, and often is the joke carried so far, that some are conveyed miles out of town, and set down, and left to make their way back as they can."

When I reached the summit of the mountain, and the sea with its wild shore, islands, and dashing waves broke upon my view, I knew the abode of the wonderful man O'Connell was near, and I paused to take a full view of the wildness around. Here then did the keen, deep-meaning, and nondescript eye of this never-tiring agitator seek out an abode; here were the principles, the agitations, of the ever-stirring mind nurtured and fed; and as here wave after wave dashes against the rock, so has agitation after agitation dashed with impetuosity against the Gibraltar of England, as yet impregnable. But hush! a woman must walk softly on political pavements.[13] A circuitous well-made road winds down the mountain, and you see not the indescribable mansion that is embosomed in rock and tree, till within a few paces of the spot.[14] Here no walls or surly porter, demanding a pass, hedge up the entrance; but a path like that to a New England farmhouse, leads you on, and you may take your choice of entrance into the heterogeneous abode, by kitchen, chapel, or hall; choosing the latter, I rang the bell.[15] An old man answered saying, "I am only a stranger, and will enquire if you can have admittance." A waiter came next, and ushered me into the parlour, saying, all were from home, but Maurice O'Connell and the house-keeper.[16] The countenance of the latter was to me better fitted to drive away the enemy than to invite the friend; and the sequel proved more than I dreaded, when I met her cold penurious look and manner. She showed me into the library, which presented a tolerable assortment of Encyclopaedias, lives of saints, Waverly Novels, law books, &c. The drawing-room contained all that is needed for ornament or use. The portrait of O'Connell, engraved to the life, taken while in the penitentiary, and one taken some years before, are not the least objects of interest in the room. The portraits of his wife, daughters, granddaughters, and sons, form the most important ornaments in the house. Among the family group, are a brother and sister, the sister in the act of swinging, sitting in a rope; the little brother with a roguish smile, holding the rope, and a little dog looking on, enjoying the sport. It is the happiest touch of nature, in portrait paint, I ever saw.[17] A chapel, not finished, is attached to one end of the house. A tablet giving its history and the name of the founder, is being in readiness, as a fixture for future ages. A well-fed priest was walking about, ready at any notice to perform any religious duty, within the pale of his conscience, for the good of the family.[18]

The walks, the beach, and the foaming sea, the tower upon an eminence – the all-manner of shaped angles and triangles, added and superadded to the main body of the house – the place where it stands, and the person who designed it – all taken into consideration, make it a house and spot quite different from all others. I lingered, and looked, and left it as I found it, and can no more describe it than before I saw it.

A lunch was before me at my return into the house; the long table was in the dining-room, around which are seated, when O'Connell is at home, a goodly number of his children; and sometimes thirty-six grandchildren have been seated together there, with priest and guests, partaking the bounties of this hospitable board.

While enjoying my bread and cheese, the threatening clouds began to drop rain: it was now twenty minutes past four. I had a wild mountainous walk of five miles before me, and the wind was howling tremendously among the bleak mountains. I said to the housekeeper, "I dread the walk, my feet are blistered, and should the storm increase upon the mountain, as there is no place to lodge, what shall I do?" "It will be bad for you," was the reply of this fixture in female form, as she showed me out of the house. I said, "Should you ever visit New York, I will do as much for you, if you will call on me." My fate was now fixed; I was out and the door was shut, and never did the bolting of the prison gate of a condemned culprit, grate more harshly upon the ear, as the turnkey "shut him in," than did the closing of this door of the "Agitator," when its last echo died on my ear. It was then the "Repeal" of this union of wind and rain was the pitiful cry of my heart. The rain and wind were in my face, and the wild mountain before me. When I could face the storm no longer, I turned my back, and endeavoured to walk in that way. A poor woman and her basket were sheltered under the wall, and she cried out, "And why, ma'am, are ye out in this stawrm? and sure why didn't ye lodge at Derrynane?" "Because they did not ask me," I replied. "And sure they wouldn't turn a stranger out on the wild mountains in such a stawrm as this?" "And sure they did," was all I could say.

I went on as I could, till the mountain was ascended; then the wind was at my back, and I soon had trouble to keep upon my feet; and for some perches there was actual danger of being dashed against the rock on one side, or thrown over the wall into the sea, upon the other. Two men upon a horse were blown aside from the path, and I in the same direction. One hat fell from a rider's head, and was blown a good distance, when my parasol held it fast, till a footman could carry it to the owner; and we were all going zig-zag as best we could, till the repeated gusts had spent their fury. I was once forced against a rock, and saved myself from being lost by clinging to a shelving part of it, till the gust passed over. It was a sad night – one which cannot soon be forgotten, and while my despairing grasp held me to the slippery crag, my soliloquy was, "And is it from the house of Daniel O'Connell that a female stranger has been driven this perilous night? Is it from the house which, above all others, I had been told in my own country, was the welcome resort and tarrying place for every stranger of every clime, that I had been virtually turned out to perish, if not saved by little else than a miracle?" True Daniel O'Connell was not at home (happy thought!), but where was the "generous Maurice?" He was sitting at home by a comfortable dinner, and might not have been told that a stranger had been there. Though I dealt out no anathemas, yet I did say, that the unfeeling instrument of my suffering, his housekeeper, was a bad representative of a house like his – that the hospitable abode of such a man, should have a sentinel at its post that had a common share of common hospitality. Fool that I was, that I did not ask her, as I thought, to let me pass the night in the tower, rather than risk my life on this bleak mountain! Again I ventured on amid pelting rain and furious blasts, till night overtook me, and a company of mountian peasantry met me. "And where have ye been, this bleak evening – not to Derrynane?" "Yes, to Derrynane." "But I'm sorry I didn't know it. I live a mile from the Abbey, and would have made ye quite comfortable in my cabin; and why didn't ye stay? I've been lookin' for ye. I wanted to talk of New York." It was not New York that was in my thoughts. I cared not a whit whether they were burning or freezing; it was the bleak rugged mountain – the mad, foaming sea, the whirlwind, and the storm that I was combating; and above, and beyond all, it was the "It will be bad for you," of the penurious voice of the housekeeper at the door of O'Connell, that was ringing in my ears. At ten I reached the hospitable dwelling of Jerry Quirks. "Welcome, welcome to my house, and stay as long as ye will, without any charges." Never was a salute more timely; never did a salute sound more sweetly.[19]

Next morning the tempest was still high, and venturing upon the strand, I there saw, as at Valentia, crowds of females busied; and speaking to one, she replied, "These stawrmy nights ma'am, blow good luck to the poor; they wash up the say-weed, and that's why ye see so many now at work."

The company increased, till I counted more than sixty; and busy, merry work was made of it; running with heavy loads upon their heads, dripping with wet, exultingly throwing them down, and bounding away in glee. Truly, "A merry heart doeth good like a medicine."[20] "And are you not cold?" "O no, ma'am, the salt say keeps us warm, the salt say, ma'am, never lets us take cold." "And how many days must you work in this way, before you get a supply?" "Aw, sometimes not fawrty, but scores of days." "And all you have for your labour is the potato?" "That's all, ma'am, that's all; and it's many of us that can't get the sup of milk with 'em, no, nor the salt; but we can't help it, we must be content with what the good God sends us."

She hitched her basket over her shoulder, and in company with one older than herself, skipped upon the sand made wet with rain, and turning suddenly about, gave me a pretty specimen of Kerry dancing as practised by the peasantry. "The sand is too wet, ma'am, to dance right well on," and again shouldering her basket, with a "God speed ye on yer journey," leaped away.

I looked after them among the rocks, more with admiration for the moment, than with pity; for what hearts, amid splendour and ease, lighter than these? And what heads and stomachs, faring sumptuously every day, freer from aches than theirs, with the potato and sup of milk? This woman, who danced before me, was more than fifty, and I do not believe that the daughter of Herodias herself, was more graceful in her movements, more beautiful in complexion or symmetry, than was this "dark-haired" matron of the mountains of Kerry."

Wandering among the cabins, I found nothing new but the same questions of "What brought ye the long way?" and the same gush of kindness from a poor cabin woman, who followed me out with such warm wishes, that it was affecting – "What can I give the lone stranger, who has come the long way to see us? I've not a ha'p'orth; and could ye eat the egg? Maybe ye hav'n't had the breakfast? I wished I had a penny to give ye." Assuring her that I needed no breakfast, and that it was but few pennies that I required, thanking her again and heard in the distance, "Aw, she's light on the fut, the cratur."

On my return to my room, I found a work called "Rambles in the South of Ireland," by an English lady, prettily and candidly written; free from that sarcasm on Irish character and Irish manners so calculated to throw contempt on the nation, which such works are, and which is quite too prevalent among writers who visit the country to write a book." Some hap-hazard expression, made to give the sentence a lively turn or happy ending, may fix a libel on a people, which will be read and believed by many generations.

CHAPTER XXI

Rough Road – A kind Offer declined – Lonely and Late – The Funeral Lament –
Maurice Raheley's Lodging House – Perfumed Bedchamber

The time of my departure drew nigh, though the wind had not abated,
nor the sea become quiescent; yet the sun found a narrow loop-hole to
look down a few moments, and say, "Make your farewell in haste, if you
would have my company through the lone mountain before you." It was
three o'clock, and a walk of eleven Irish miles, covered with broken stone,
fresh from the hammer, was before me. Killoyra was my destination, and
Maurice Raheley's house, which I was assured was "nate and tidy." The
hospitable inn-keeper would take no pay for lodging or board. Blessed
inn! O, if the world, for every ten miles were filled with the like, then
might travellers eat, drink, smoke, and sleep, without this melting away of
gold and silver.

A little mountain girl, from a rocky foot-path leading from the ascent,
accosted me. "And sure ye hav'n't far to walk alone?" Answering her, "To
the foot of the mountain." "To the fut of the mountain! and the night 'ill
be on ye; but I'm in the way with ye a good bit." She was a pleasant companion for two miles, when a comely well dressed young man, on a good
horse, accosted me, wondering at seeing me on foot. "The wild scenery of
these mountains," I answered, "was one great inducement, and to shorten
my route, another." "And wouldn't ye get up, and let me give ye a lift of a
couple of miles?" I looked at the lively steed, the sprightliness of the
young man, and had I been in my teens, might have been strongly
prompted to accept the offer. But as my appearance to the complaisant
gallant was nothing favourable, I declined, and he walked his horse to
keep me company, giving me intelligent answers to my enquiries of the
state of the country, presenting the same dark picture of its hapless condition as others had done, till a different road turned him away; and when
I saw the grey courser galloping off, and heard the last sound of his hoofs
upon the path, I paused – all was solitude.

The sun had sunk behind a black mountain, twilight was letting down
her soft curtain upon the heathy landscape, and not the buzz of an insect
fell upon my ear. Not the smoke of a cabin curled in the air, and neither

man nor beast met my admiring eye. Nature seemed here to say, "Walk softly, and let me enjoy my solitude alone." From a far distant mountain, a mournful sound fell on my ear. It was the wail for the dead. It swelled in heavy tones, and then died away, as they who chanted it descended a valley; thus alternately rising and falling, for five long miles, did this lamentation float on the air. The solitude, the lateness of the hour, my distance from the land of my fathers, among so primitive a people, whose Bible customs have been retained since the mourning for Jacob in the "threshing floor of Atad," made this lamentation a pleasant mournful accompaniment over the barren waste I was walking.[1] The rustics afterwards told me it was a lone old woman who had died in her cabin on the mountain, and she must be brought "to lie with her kin in the valley."[2]

The shadows of night were now heavy on the outstretched bog before me; a woman and young lad came out of a cabin, and the youth said, "This is a lonely road for a lady to walk, and where can ye be goin?" "To Maurice Raheley's" – "Maurice Raheley's! and the night is now nearly on ye, and ye've a long two miles under yer fut; we'll be on the way a half mile on." They gave me directions in the kindest manner and turned away. The night "was on me;" the road, long and dreary, was before me, covered with coarse gravel, without the smoke of a cabin or the sight of sheep, cow, or ass, to tell me that I was not alone in the world. The stillness of death reigned; for in Ireland the night knows not the howl of the beast of prey, and it was not the season for the chirping cricket; and not a sound for more than a weary mile once broke upon my ear. The barking of a dog from a far distant mountain, suddenly told me that I was in the precincts of man's abode. "Welcome, dog," I said; "however coarse and ugly you may be, you have the voice of a dog, and could I reach you, I would pat you on the head, I would give you a piece of bread from my bag;" but, alas! I had but a scanty crust. The Irish peasant dogs, like their masters, are patient and kind; many a one has met me at the door of a cabin, and instead of barking as a surly dog would, by the wagging of his tail and inviting look of the eye, said, "Walk in, walk in, stranger; my master will make ye welcome to our fire and our potato."

If ever a being wanted to see Maurice Raheley, I was that being. At last I descried a human form approaching. "God save ye kindly, lady; and what misfortune has brought ye among these lone mountains to night? I'm sorry for ye; for, if I can see rightly, ye're no common body. And where's the comrade that should be wid ye?" Telling him who I was, and what was my object, he added, "And ye'll soon be at Maurice Raheley's lodgin', God speed ye." I hurried on with fresh vigour, and at last, on a hill, the slated roof of the long desired dwelling appeared. Meeting a man a few paces from the door, I said, "Is this the lodging-house, sir?" "This is no lodging-house, but he'll keep ye, as ye're alone and a stranger." My heart, which had been beating high with expectation, began to flag a little; but wading through the usual preface to almost every cabin in Ireland (a manure heap) I met at the crossing of the threshold, cows, calves, sheep, and lambs, occupying half of the room, which was made up with a host of children, and I asked, "Are these all your family, madam?" "Some of 'em are man-sarvants and maid-sarvants, ma'am," was the reply.

"Do you take lodgers here?"

"We don't, ma'am."

"But why have I been told this by so many of whom I have enquired?"

"I know not, unless to lead you astray, ma'am."

"And what am I to do? There is no house where I can go."

"We'll not send ye out to-night, as ye're a stranger."

Soon I heard the sound of a pot behind me; the good housewife was pouring in potatoes. "And they're for you, ma'am," said the old grandfather. A bowl of milk, saucer of butter, and cup of salt, were soon before me, by the side of a bountiful plate of potatoes; and while I was taking, with a high relish, my potatoes and salt alone, a son of the family read aloud a tract which I gave him.

In the midst of this stable the mother brought out two clean linen sheets, and aired them, lit up a fire, and soon I was invited "down" through the lodging-place of the cattle, into a bed-room without a floor, with a proud pile of more than fifty bushels of potatoes, fresh from the pit, which the mother said was but a bit for all the family. The smell of these, with that issuing from under the door where the cattle lay, and the smoke from the newly made turf fire, made my condition not only unpleasant, but so suffocating, that I feared at times serious results. Glad was I when the faithful cock in the next room announced the day. I arose, and asking for my bill, was answered, "Nothing." I gave him the usual price, and English sixpence, and went out.

CHAPTER XXII*

Sunrise on the Kerry Mountains – Novel Duet – Mountain Air or City Smoke? –
Irish Roads – A Teetotaller in Bad Company – Awful Night – Sabbath of rest at
Killarney – Gap of Dunloe – Guide Persecution – The "Crazy Woman" – Where
to spend the Night – Bright Wood Fire – Recollections of Childhood – Dinis
Island – Debt of Gratitude

The morning was beautiful, the light and shade upon the picturesque
mountain which I must cross were of a new and varied kind. To give an
idea of them I can only say, cross the Kerry mountains in a clear morning
before sunrise, and if there is a soul within you capable of being roused,
that soul will be stirred. I soon found myself in something like a vast
amphitheatre, with mountains piled on mountains, "Alps on Alps;" covered with heath, without a tree, the sun-rays streaming athwart from
behind me to the top of the mountains before, leaving me in a dusky
pleasant solitude which was entirely new.' I walked two miles, and passed
one cabin by the road-side, and a few scattered ones at a distance upon
the sloping hill. The enchantment increased, and the breezes of heaven
that morning wafted a new and exhilarating fragrance. I sat down to enjoy
it upon a moss-hillock, and commenced singing, for the Kerry mountains
are the best conductors of sound of any I have ever met; they in some
places not only give echoes, but thrills, as the ever-busy wind penetrates
the circles and caves. I had sung but a passage, when, from over a wide
stretched valley, a mountain boy, with a herd of cattle, struck up a lively
piper's song, so clear and shrill that I gladly exchanged my psalmody for
morning notes like these. It was to me a hymn of praise; it said that God
had compensated in part for all the deficiencies of food, raiment, society,
&c. by the almost holy inspiration of the mountain air, which, in spite of
all painful drawbacks, will impart a spontaneous cheerfulness, keeping
pure that life-blood which spreads vigour and health unsought by medicine. I listened till a pause ensued, and again commenced; instantly he
responded, and though the distance was a mile at least, yet alternately we

* The original edition of *Ireland's Welcome* did not include a chapter heading for Chapter XXII, jumping straight from XXI to XXIII; however running-heads in that edition
suggest that a chapter XXII was intended to begin here.—*Ed.*

kept up the song till his was lost in the distance. Seeing a sparkling rivulet leaping down the mountain before me, I ascended to its side, stopped, uncovered my head and hands, laved and revelled in almost unearthly delights. The wide circular valley at my feet, the Kerry mountains, with their blossoming heath and playful streams, were made on purpose for me, surely, that morning, for they were just to my liking; and the sun and heavens, too, shed a light which said, "Look! for you never again will see this same morning on this same Kerry mountain."

A little girl, at a distance upon a rock, was gazing in astonishment, wondering at seeing a moving being with a bonnet upon her head on this mountain. Still further on had a man ascended the point of a hill, and stood in silence. A pony slowly approached, looked, and turned away. There was not a cabin in sight, nor the smoke of one; but somewhere lived men, women, and children in these defiles. The road was a new one, lately cut through this mountain; no carriage had padded it, and mine was certainly the first American foot that had ever trod this bold, defying height; and in my pride I looked down upon cities, with all their little fripperies, with a kind of contempt.[2] Ah, who would have your smoke, your brinks, and your marbles, huddled into confined streets and stenchy alleys, when the unadulterated air of heaven might be yours, where God has thrown together, in awful grandeur, piles on piles, and scattered the rising springs, and sent down the laughing rivulet, and wound the serpentine brook and river in every varied profusion? Romantic as I was, the spot was more so; and as I sat upon a rock, eating a deliciously sweet and dry crust, with my bonnet and parasol by my side on this fairy spot, had youth and beauty been mine, the pencil of a tourist might have made out a mountain landscape of no small interest.

I must proceed; the crust was finished, the mountain top ascended. I looked back, and could my voice have reached across the Atlantic, I would have shouted to them, "Come and see my enviable site." I was not willing to turn away from this enchanting eminence, but through the cleft upon the other side, scenes as beautiful caught my eyes. A wide extent of valley was spread out, interspersed with bog, heath, and grass, with the prepared ridge for the potato; far beyond were mountains, grand and high, lifting their proud summits; now and then a pleasant little lake was sparkling in the sun-beam. The smoke of cabins and large flocks of noble-looking sheep, were scattered here and there. Some straggling children among the rocks saw me, and looking up, paused a moment, ran towards a cabin, and climbed upon a pile of stones. I shouted and shouted to them, but could get no answer, they seemed riveted to the spot, unlike all upon these mountains, who at first sight would generally run at full speed, sometimes screeching with fear, then ascend some eminence, and when I had well passed, burst out into a wild boisterous laugh, saying in effect, "She's gone, she's gone, and the danger is over." It was only in the wildest mountains that the children were timid, and this I was informed was occasioned by never having seen a woman with a bonnet upon her head; they supposed the bonnet was a part of the strange being.[3]

As I descended the hill upon the other side, new scenes awaited me. The treat I had just been enjoying was too rich for constant food. The road now became almost intolerable, gravel stones had been flung on for ten miles, or more, without being trodden down; my feet soon were blistered, and walking was grievous. Bridges over small streams were not made, and I must cross upon slippery stones, or wade. I cannot speak ill of the roads of Ireland, for in most parts they are not only good, but faultless, and this would frequently have induced me to walk, had I no other cause. Often, when my indignation against the rags of Ireland would swell across the channel to the house of parliament, "Ah, but see what beautifully enticing roads have they made, for the bare feet of the beggars to walk," would be the soothing reply. But the road I was on had not been finished for the traveller. Never before could I realize the import of doing penance by walking with pebbles in the shoes; the tops of my boots were loose, and every few moments I must stop, and pour out the gravel-stones collected in them. Besides, I had turned from the route intended in the morning, which was to Killorglin, for the purpose of going through the Gap of Dunloe, and was told when it was too late that it would lengthen my route six miles.[4]

Night was coming on, and a lodging-house was the thing really needed. One was pointed to me, which when reached was nothing but a stable, and used for cattle as well as people. They answered, "Never mind him, we don't take lodgers." Hobbling along, I became an object of great wonder. The country was now thickly sprinkled with cabins, and all the moving beings which they contained turned out, to salute, to gape, or to follow me. My suffering became so acute, that I felt like fainting; and stepping to a door, I asked if lodgings could be found in the vicinity. "Not any this side of Killarney," was the answer. "I cannot reach it then, and must stop by the wayside." I had walked more than twenty miles, ten of which had been on round or sharp pebbles for a carpet; sometimes getting upon a cart, and carrying my boots in my hand for a little mitigation. I had eaten nothing but the happy dry crust on the enchanted morning, and the aggregate was a considerable burden to think of supporting four miles longer. The bare-footed woman of whom I enquired said, "If I had a bed, you should not go any further, but come in, and sit down, and rest ye a bit." This I did not refuse, and followed her into the lodge, sat down upon a bench, and there remained. She kindly offered to do the best she could, which was to put some straw upon the floor, and place me on it. This was a rich prospect. The potatoes were in readiness, and when engaged in eating them, the husband entered, intoxicated, wild, and noisy. Never were a morning and evening at greater extremes than this, in my state of feeling.

I could not get away: the scene was terrific. Three men entered, two to drink with the master, and the third, a teetotaller, to keep the whole sober. Till one o'clock they stayed, sending out a girl for fresh supplies, and no entreaties could get the man of the house to bed. I begged the sober man to find me some retreat, but he could not, and at two they all departed, leaving three females to contend as we could with the infuriate wretch, who had undressed himself and promised to lie down, before the sober man left him. As soon as the men had passed the gate, he seized the tongs, grasped the throat of his wife, and told me if I spoke or attempted to stir, he would throw me into the river, which was deep, and passing under the window of the lodge.[5] The affrighted woman struggled and screamed, and I succeeded by stealth in getting the tongs, and carrying them out, together with the spade. It rained, and I stopped out, till the violence within was so frightful that I feared murder would be the result, and ventured in. A calm followed, and he approached the bed of his three affrighted children, bade them a long farewell, and went out into the rain, after putting on his clothes.

The straw was spread upon the floor for my bed, and without any covering I placed myself on it. The cock at the door soon told me it was day, and though the rain was still pouring I said good morning to the suffering woman, and went out. My feet were so blistered, the road was so clayey, and the rain poured so profusely, that the four miles to Killarney were long and sad ones.

Every thing was done by the good Mrs. C. at the lodging-house, to make me forget the sorrows of the last twenty-four hours; and a Sabbath of quiet so refreshed me, that on Monday I ventured upon new perils.[6] I had found in all my tedious walks that a night's rest restored me to vigour, so that I was prepared for a fresh undertaking every morning, even when chairs, or a pile of straw might be the bed. Not so with a ride upon a coach. It was almost impossible to secure a seat; and when, by the crowding and jolting of a day's jaunt, I became fatigued, this fatigue made a visit often of many days.

The Gap of Dunloe has had so many visitors and so many historians – has given so many echoes, and paid so many guides – that what remains for me is to say that I walked five miles to reach it, and found an old man at the entrance, busied in his field, who insisted on leaving all to accompany me. I told him I preferred the walk alone, that a guide would confuse me. They always hurried on, disgusting me with all sorts of fairy stories, diverting my mind from every thing useful, and leaving it in a labyrinth more bewildering than the voice of nature with the eyes for handmaids[7] "But ye're a stranger, and I would take no pay; ye cannot go alone," &c. I escaped, and entered the wonders. The little lake, the craggy mountain on the right, and the purple one of the left, first opened to view; the richness and beauty of the latter scarcely can have a rival, and most of the peaks on both sides are enveloped in clouds,

"And mid-way leave the storm."[8]

A rugged foot-path led me on till I reached a cabin, and a young man was ready as a guide. I told him I could make no possible use of one. "But he can show you the shortest route." This was true Kerry cunning; I answered him that it was impossible to stray from the path, as there was but one, and that could not be left without climbing precipitous rocks. He turned away, and in an under-tone said, "Ah, she understands." Passing out, I met two gentlemen with a guide, who had a half hour before burst a good rifle when making echoes. When they had passed I sat down upon a rock, to make echoes for myself by singing a hymn, and these two gentlemen concealed themselves to listen, returned to Killarney, and reported that they had enjoyed the sweetest echoes imaginable in the gap, from a crazy woman, who passed them alone, and sang two sweet hymns, while they were secluded within hearing. The novelty of seeing a woman without a guide led them to suppose I must be crazy. I soon met another, then three more, all insisting I must have a guide; and in no way could I escape but by insisting that I should not accept of one.

At last this pile of rocks on rocks, mountains on mountains, was passed, and I stood upon the top, looking upon the other side, where the mountain scenery, like all other Kerry beauties and sublimities, must be seen to be understood. I had read something of them before seeing them, but had no just conception of the reality. Enjoying the treat in silent admiration, I heard the sound of footsteps, and looking about, was saluted, "Sure ye're a wonderful wawker; I have followed ye a mile and a half through the Gap, and couldn't overtake ye. And why should ye be alone? Sure the like of ye never was known; an' where may ye be from?" "From

New York." "From New Yawrk! an' what's the raison that ye're here alone? and have ye no comrade?" "Not a comrade in the world, sir, nor kindred who care for me." "An' ye're come to this poor country! An' ye must have a dale of money." Had I been afraid of robbery, I should have shown him my purse; but looking at him as a whole, I feared no evil. He was old, carrying a staff from necessity, and so dirtily dressed, that if he had no living things about him, it must be because they had left to find a richer, cleaner pasture.

The path wound around the mountain to a deep valley at the head of the lake, and through what was once the tasteful domain of Lord Brandon, now grown over with weeds and thistles, and looking more suitable for the abode of the screeching owl and dancing satyr than the pleasure-grounds of a lord. A slovenly farmer had rented it, and left every where the impress of sloth and bad taste. His wife, when we entered the cottage, was sitting upon her haunches on a settee, with her heels drawn under her, in the commendable occupation of knitting. Her children and domicile appeared as if "the virtuous woman, who looketh well to the ways of her household," had not passed that way.[9] The tower and garden, like Solomon's field of the slothful, were grown over with nettles, and the stone wall thereof was broken down.[10] And had the surly owner, who once expended thirty thousand pounds to make this a spot of proud wonder to strangers, been allowed again to walk over these grounds, if his penurious heart still retains any earthly relish, he would have dealt out anathemas against the miscreants, who had so effectually defaced all that was once beautiful in the eye of the visitor.

I bade good evening to the housewife, who never left her post, and the bold officious guide followed me out to ask a penny for tobacco. So annoyed had I been with his company, that I begged him to return when on the mountain; he would not, and I resolved that I would furnish him no means for smoking, as a compensation for such intrusion. I now hoped that I might be suffered to make my way alone, to what place I knew not, for here the road terminated. Hyde Park cottage was what, when I left Killarney, I hoped to see, but at this place was told that it now existed only in name.[11] All I could do was to go on, and make a path for myself through mire and bog, till I plunged into a thick wood. It was sunset, and began to rain. To go back through the gap was impossible; and before me was a dark wood, without a path, and full of pits of water. I looked about for some rock under which I could creep and stop for the night; a comfortable one soon met my sight. To stay under the rock would ensure me a shelter, no venomous serpent was there, rain could not reach me, and I felt not the least timidity. Had a father or brother been with me, and I had looked to him for protection, I should have felt some repugnance; but the Protector, who was constantly about my path, I knew never "slumbers or sleeps," and feeling not the least hesitation, I was about stooping to make my ingress: but when I heard the barking of a dog, and the sound of an axe, I demurred.[12]

The rain would make the difficulty of getting through the swamp greater, and I waded on. A cottage appeared, but they did not take lodgers. This was the third night in four that I had been deceived in respect to lodging-houses, and began seriously to think that Kerry archness had been gratifying its cunning on me. The astonished family could give me no "tay, nor no bread, but," said the master, "the night and the rain are heavy on ye, and the walk is seven long miles to Killarney; ye would be destroyed, an' we'll give ye a bed." The cottage had a stone floor; a bright wood fire was blazing, the floor and hearth were nicely swept, and no astral lamp shone brighter than did that pleasant fire.[13] The sweet days of childhood, when the green mountains and valleys of Vermont were my home, when brothers and sisters had assembled around the glad fireside, rose in review.

"I thought of the days of other years, and my soul was sad."[14]

Never in Ireland had an evening of such welcome sadness been mine. A pot of black minion potatoes were prepared for me, while the family waited to boil those of an inferior quality for themselves. This was genuine cabin hospitality. They had a few choice potatoes reserved for planting, and some of these must be provided, because the stranger must not have an inferior article. We talked of Dunloe, of Killarney, and of Hyde Park, the owners of which had all gone down to the dust. "But," said the man, "had you seen the rector of Hyde Park, he was the one that the people loved; he was so kind to the poor and sick, not a ha'p'orth of a cabin in all the parish but his fut was in; and though he was a Protestant, yet he sarved the Catholics with as many a good turn as he did his own; and when he died, wasn't there the lamentation! His people, ye must know, won't have the Irish cry when their dead is buried, but not a dry cheek was there that day; and when they brought out the body for the hairse, not a ha'p'orth of the Catholics would let 'em do it, but said they would carry it on their shoulders, and so they did. Aw, the like o' him warn't in all the country."[15]

A chaff bed with clean sheets was placed upon chairs by that pleasant fire, and an invigorating sleep prepared me for a fresh walk in the morning. I succeeded in leaving a few pennies when I went away, but regretted that I did, for the woman accompanied me out, saying "An' sure d'ye think we've no heart for the stranger? An' wouldn't ye do the like for me in yer country?" She conducted me into a wood, where a beautiful cascade foaming down a precipice met my eye.

My seven miles' morning walk was but just commenced, when a rosy faced girl of fourteen, with her apron across her arm, containing a few groceries, saluted me. "Good morrow kindly, ma'am, and ye've not been to Dinis Island; it's but a mile down the walk under yer fut, and the road to Killarney is a long five miles.[16] Will ye turn in, and I will show ye to the cottage?" I had met this pretty Kerry girl before, near the same place, who had urged me to see this island, and her sweet face and kind manner now prevailed. She had walked nine miles that morning, and her pretty foot was not soiled, nor, as she told me, was her leg weary, though she was much concerned for mine. A winding path through a beautiful wood took us to Dinis cottage, where the family were breakfasting on bread and tea – the bread of the woman's own making, which was not only a rarity, but a delicious treat.[17] They had lived some time in North America, consequently treated me kindly. The children had clean faces, well-combed hair, tidy apparel, and the cottage bore the marks of the industrious housekeeper. They were Protestants. The mother was teaching her children, as they had no school on the island. But sorry am I to say, that in no family had I heard so much profanity, both from mother and children. I would not expose it; but no one could stay in the house many hours and not hear it, and such sins should be rebuked before all.

A day and night passed here gave me a good acquaintance with the scenery of these lakes, which convinced me that, to admire Killarney beauties, they must not too hastily be hurried over. The little bare-footed girl was always with me when she could get an opportunity, and had been quite a guide to strangers on that island, and was very intelligent. But Killarney and its beauties must be left, and I bade Dinis Island a long adieu; I returned, and prepared for leaving Killarney, and have much kindness to record as exercised towards me in the inn where I lodged by mother and daughters. They were well paid for what they did, but it was done with so becoming a grace and such good will, that it made me feel an obligation which is a privilege to acknowledge. When I was out all night at Hyde Park, they, knowing what the walk must be even with company, were much concerned; and when night came on, sent about the town to make enquiries. Had I been a member of the family, they could not have done more. The gentlemen's telling them they had met a "crazy woman" in the gap, was all the information they could get of me until the next day.

CHAPTER XXIII

Tralee – Public-house honesty – A "Gentleman" – Mr. Walpole's Honourable Dealings – Christianity at Dingle – "They always Stand" – One Bright Spot – The Converts – Education of the Lower Order – Nancy Brown's Parlour – Coquetry and Gallantry – Peasant Girl's Poetry – Learned Priest – Sybil Head – "Look! Look!"– Fearless children – Disappointment and Vexation – Candid Hotel-keeper – Banks of the Shannon

Thursday. – At four o'clock, I took the car for Tralee. The ride was through a somewhat dreary part of the country, with little that was interesting; but the adventures at Tralee were comical, if not tragical.

Arriving at the town, a bevy of applicants from Walpole's hotel poured upon me, to take me to his inn, and to Dingle on his car the next day. I told them I did not choose an inn, but private lodgings. This did not shake them off, till, jumping from the car, I begged some one to show me suitable lodgings. One was pointed out to me across the way, I escaped into the house, and the troop in pursuit. I had but just seated myself in a chamber, when a civil young man stepped after me, and enquired if I wished a conveyance to Dingle. Saying that I did, he then said, "to-morrow at eleven I will give you a seat on my car for three shillings." The distance to Dingle was little more than thirty miles. I made the engagement, gave him my luggage, and as he passed out he said, "You won't disappoint me, I hope." "Certainly not," was the answer. When he had gone, I found that his was an opposition car, that Mr. Walpole had occupied the road for years, had made money by it, and charged more for the fare'. More of this to-morrow.

The house I was in was a whiskey den, and leaving my gloves and pocket handkerchief upon a table in my room, I stepped down, and told the woman who was selling the baneful commodity that though I had asked for lodgings in her house, yet I could not stay to leave one shilling in a place devoted to such evil work, and begged her to think seriously of the degrading wicked business she was in, and abandon it for one that was more honest. She was angry, and talked as a woman would talk in such an employment; and while I was standing there, my gloves and handkerchief were taken. I mentioned it to the woman, who refused making enquiry. I told her this was proof positive of what had so offended her, that the employment was dishonest, and those who were engaged in it were not to be trusted in matters where self-interest was concerned.

The young man was at the door with whom I was to go to Dingle, and went with me to another lodging-house, where, though no whiskey was sold, yet the sad effects were manifested about three o'clock in the morning, by a loud thundering at the door, demanding entrance in a most outrageous manner. The good woman arose, put her head out of the window and enquired who was there, and what was wanting. "A gentleman was there, and wanted his hat," was the answer, and that he would have, if not peaceably, by violence. The mistress told him his hat was not there; he told her it was. She answered that he had not been in the house, but he assured her he would be in, and commenced another battering with fists and boots, till the distracted woman in self-defence went down and opened the door. The "gentleman" searched for his hat, but no hat was there, and he walked quietly away.

I passed a miserable night, took a miserable breakfast, in a miserable dirty room, and went out. Before eleven, which was the carman's appointed hour, I returned to my lodgings to be in readiness when two young lads entered, asking if I had any trunks, and said the car was ready. I told them my luggage was in the care of the carman, and he had said he should go at eleven, and it was not the hour. "The car is ready, and you must hurry to the post office and pay fare." I did so, and as I handed the money into the hand of the clerk, the man who had engaged to take me to Dingle, stepped near, and said, "You have paid into the wrong office." The fraud was evident. They had watched where I changed my lodgings, when I left the night preceding, and had sent these lads to secure my money before the time that I was to go out. I turned to the clerk, telling him I had been deceived, had made a previous engagement with the young man, and he now had my luggage. He refused, declaring he would pay no money back, that the car was ready, I might take it or leave it at my option; my money was in his hands, and there it should be, but he would condescend to take me to Dingle for the three shillings. A crowd assembled. A policeman said, "We can do nothing for you, but you should consult – Esq." He was a peace-maker in the town, and would persuade Walpole to do right.[2]

The peace-maker appeared; the portly Mr. Walpole appeared also. "What do you want, – Esq.?" "To enquire into the affair concerning this stranger." "There is a car ready, she has paid her money to me, and she may go or stay; her money she shall not have." I pleaded a stranger's claim, a female and unprotected. I appealed to an Irishman's honour to an American, on whose shores so many of his countrymen had found a welcome home. He sullenly refused; the magistrate told him it was kidnapping, and begged him to return the money. The great and the small were there, and the good feeling of the police, and indeed all but the man himself, deserve my acknowledgment. One whispered in my ear, "He is not an Irishman, but a Scotch Presbyterian."³ I turned to Walpole, and told him I was happy to learn that he was not an Irishman, and now better understood my true condition. The young man generously offered to give me my baggage or carry me for nothing, as I had once paid. I told him I would not ride with a man who would defraud a stranger, neither would I take his car without paying, but would walk to Dingle if he would carry my luggage. I went on, the policeman begging me to ride, and the poor following and saying, "Ye'd be destroyed, and he's a rich old blackguard. The young man that has the car is as fine a lad as ye'll find in the country." One poor woman, with an infant in her arms, went out of town more than a mile, barefooted and bareheaded, though the sun was scorching; nor could I prevail on her to return. "Ye're a lone stranger, and that blackguard of a Scotchman to trate ye so." When she saw me well out of town, she returned, and I walked eight miles in torment with blistered feet, which had not been healed since my Killarney expedition. The carman then overtook me, with five on his car, and prevailed on me to be the sixth. We arrived at Dingle at nine o'clock, and I stayed at the house of his sister where he lodged, and found the same accommodations, the same food, and the same kindness as in all houses among the poor.

In the morning I arose in the celebrated town of Dingle, a "city on a hill."⁴ Distant as it is from all the world beside, yet it has for the last few years said to all who would hear, "Turn aside, and look at me." Its bay is full of interest, and its people more so; and as the people were my object, I must talk of them. A Catholic woman of much good nature and some intelligence called early, and offered to accompany me to see the town. Her first depot unasked was to the house of a priest; considerable time was taken to get an introduction to his presence, and when we did, his every look and taciturnity seemed to say, "What brought you here?" He was the first I had met who showed reserve, but Dingle had been struggling with party creeds, and as the "soupers," as the Protestant converts are called, were getting quite numerous, the priest had all his sensibilities awake to keep the prowler from making further inroads into his fold.⁵ A newcomer from a foreign country might be the very "wolf in sheep's clothing" to beguile more of the faithful, and, as I was afterwards informed, he therefore kept more caution.[6] So I was sent empty away.

Having an invitation from the wife of a Protestant clergyman, sent by the gardener, I made my way up the hill, in company with a tidy-looking Catholic girl to lead me to the door. Supposing myself invited, I made no hesitation in saying to the servant (who was a long time answering the knock) that I was the person Mrs. G. had invited, giving my name.[7] Mrs. G. was engaged. "Will you give my name?" I asked. She hesitated; went again, and returned with, "She is very busy." What could this trifling mean? Had the gardener deceived me? Is this the house of a missionary? When will the nonsense of a silly world lose its hold of the professed Christian church? I went away disgusted, and was descending the hill when a message was sent, "Will you come back?" I answered, it was of no consequence. "The mistress sent me to ask you." I returned, met the lady in the hall, to whom I said, "Is this Mrs. G. and was a message sent to me by the gardener?" "Walk in," was the answer. "It is of no consequence," I said. "Walk in." I followed into the parlour and was immediately asked my message to Ireland. It was told, and likewise that I had called on the Catholic priest. Surprised, she suddenly answered, "And what did you call on him for? I will never go near any of them. They are a persecuting people." "I thought they were the subjects we were to strive to benefit, and how can we do them good by keeping aloof?" "When they come to us, we always receive them kindly, but we do not proselyte. Though we are accused of going after them, we do not; neither do we bribe them, as it is said of us, by feeding them and promising high wages. There is a man," pointing to one in the field, "who works faithfully here through the week for eightpence a day. Do you call that bribing him? He is glad to have it." "I call that oppression," was my answer. "Well, he is glad to do it."

Again she interrogated, "Do you make a practice of going among the Catholics?" "I make a practice of going among all the poor without distinction, but am sorry to say that 'my own' often reject me, and I should more than once have been without a shelter, if the Catholics had not received me, when the Protestants would not."

I gained but little information, though the missionary himself and his friend Mr. C. were present; the latter I had been told was a spiritual Christian, and I hoped from him to learn the true state of things. They all acted as if dinner were cooling, and the sooner this jesuitical spy shall have done the better. The poor woman who accompanied me stood in the hall during the hour that I stopped, and I begged the mistress to give her a seat or send her away. "No matter, they always stand," was the answer.

I went away without declining dinner, for no invitation was given; and will not be so independent as to say that I was not disappointed. I was grieved; not for the personal treatment, but grieved that so noble so apostolic a work was in the hands of those whose hospitality, whose humility, whose courteousness to strangers, and whose self-denial, were so far behind the principles they professed to inculcate. I went to the house with no prejudice, hoping to hear a true statement of the good work going on; and the poor waiting Catholic woman, who was not a "souper," was telling me on the way that she knew I should be treated kindly, and when we turned from the door, she said, "I was sorry she kept ye so long, and didn't ask ye to take a comfortable bit."

My acquaintance in life had ever been much among the clergy, and though I had long since known they were not exempt from the frailties of human nature, and that Christ's example was always the safest to follow, yet I had never seen them so little given to hospitality, so uncourteous to strangers, and so outwardly conformed to the maxims of the world, as some I had met in Ireland; and yet I heard many edifying sermons from them.

My prospects brightened a little when I was in the evening introduced into a Methodist family.[8] Every Christian kindness was here shown that could be, and I was conducted to a comfortable room and told by the "prudent wife" that here was the Christian pilgrim's room, always kept to entertain strangers. "Here," she added, "you may find a welcome home while in Dingle." Her husband was a coast-guard, a noble Irishman of whom his country might be proud. Three daughters and a son composed this happy family. It was a family well ordered, and one of happy Christian love. Here I stayed, and here I loved to stay; here the morning and evening prayer ascended from hearts kindled by Christian union. Sabbath morning I walked two miles to a poor dwelling, in company with Mrs. J. and her daughter, to meet with an humble few in a little class meeting, and to hear from these poor cabiners, in this remote part of the earth, that same dialect which is spoken wherever the story of Calvary has been told. It was pleasant, it was good to be there. However many times in Ireland have I blessed God that he sent the ever-stirring, warm-hearted Methodists into that island. Their zeal has a redeeming quality in it that few others manifest; it never goes out; the bush, though burning, is never consumed.[9]

Attended church and met the converts, and whether they had changed the Latin version for the English, in changing their prayer books, and knew not the difference, I know not, but only a few among them could read. I visited the converts, and talked with them on their great change, and found them as I found their Papist neighbours, in all respects but one. They invariably answered me, when I enquired concerning the great change which had taken place in their minds, "We do not worship images."[10] But what the new birth implied, or any work of conviction and operation of the Holy Spirit on their hearts, they could tell nothing, for they seemed to know nothing. But here I would be understood. I did not talk with all the converts of Dingle, and would not presume to say but that God has done a great work there; if he has, man cannot overthrow it; if he has not, man cannot support even what they seem to have. But this is certain, they have the unadulterated Word of God; and if they cannot read it, they hear it, and some seed may be sown on good ground, and bear fruit. I visited the Protestant and national school in Dingle; the infant school was under good regulations; the national school in so boisterous a state, that, with knocking and calling, we could not be heard, and were obliged to go aloft into the second room, and there things seemed but a little improved.[11] We had some specimens of grammar and geography from the noisy urchins, which would puzzle the most learned of any language to define, and we went out with a rabble of boys in pursuit, calling out, "American! American!" till we reached our homes.

Our next excursion was to Ventry. Here is a colony of the new converts, with a clergyman at their head, who was once a Catholic priest.[12] A pretty little village, and every thing about it more inviting than otherwise. We visited the Protestant school, and here found a young lady teaching a class of promising young misses; but when we enquired if they were studying geography, as we saw maps hanging in the lower end of the room the answer surprised my Protestant friend, Mr. J—. "The maps are for the boys; these are the daughters of the lower order, and we do not advance them." "But have they not talents to be cultivated? and is not this a professedly Christian school, instituted by missionaries?" "It is," she answered; "but I must do as I am bidden. They are poor, and must be educated according to their station."[13] Again I enforced the obligation imposed on us by Christ, to "occupy till he come." She did not understand me; and though she belonged to the Protestant Church, I could not see that her dark understanding had ever been enlightened by the Spirit of God, or that she was any more capable of teaching spiritual things than the Catholics about her whom she viewed as being so dark. We visited a few converts in the cabins, and I was afterwards cautioned not to go there again, as the clergymen had given them notice that they must not receive me into their houses.*

The next day we visited a school of the nuns. Here were more than three hundred of the poor, taught in the most thorough manner. Their lessons in grammar, geography, and history would do honour to any school, and their needle-work was of the highest order. The teacher observed, "Though they are the children of the poor, we do not know what station God may call them to fill. We advance them as far as possible while they are with us. The Protestants," she added, "do not teach the poor anything but reading, writing, and arithmetic."[14]

"What a rebuke," said my friend, "is this on the practice of Bible Christians! Here is a nun spending her whole life in teaching the poor, without any compensation, and saying, 'We don't know what station God may want them to fill, and we advance them as far as we can.'" Three nuns were giving their whole time in this school.

The bay and mountains about Dingle are objects of considerable interest. Connor Hill, upon which a road is made through a rock which hangs frightfully over the head of the traveller, and the steep descent to a lake, are grand objects. The government has certainly given incontestable proof that rocks, mountains, and water are no effectual impediments to making good roads in Ireland. Why can it not surmount the rocky difficulties of the people, cut them through, give them a tolerable place among the children of men, and enable them to walk forth over these roads, not as beasts of burden, clothed in rags, but like men made in God's image, enjoying the blessings which are made for all, and should be possessed by all?

We attempted to ascend Connor Hill by a circular route, but the higher we ascended, the more the distance seemed to increase, and we sat down under a passing cloud, which so enveloped us, that, though in the morning, it appeared quite like gathering evening, and the cold was very severe. I was glad to get away, for a pressure upon the chest made me feel a difficulty in breathing. We returned home, and passed an immense pile of stones, which had been gathered by passing travellers, who always added one to the heap, in commemoration of a young man who died on that spot when going out for America. Silly as was the superstition, I added one to the mountain.[15]

We visited "Nancy Brown's Parlour." This is a rock projecting into the sea, with a seat upon it like a settee; a romantic spot. At the left is a deep dark cavern of water, running under the precipice, which fills the mind with wonder and sublimity. The morning was propitious, and below us

---

* This did not offend me, neither do I blame him. I mention it only as one manifestation of the watchful jealousy maintained by different parties to keep both their creed and character from contamination.

upon the strand might be seen women, some with jugs, and some with seaweed, children picking shells, and not the least interesting were the busy sea-gulls, hopping from rock to rock, or alighting upon the water, in pairs. One couple, who had stood upon a craggy rock talking in the most affable manner, amused us by a piece of gallantry, as we supposed of the gentleman, which would do honour to any man living in like circumstances. They had sat talking for some time, when a surging wave dashed over them and concealed them from our sight; they appeared again as the wave retired, in the same position, when the adventurous Miss gracefully sailed away, and seated herself upon a rock in the water at a distance, looking back to the mate she had left, who for a time sat unmoved as if saying, "You have rudely left me, and I will not follow you." But in a little time he was at her side, and they commenced a close chat, and then they both gracefully sailed back to the rock they had left. We could not tell whether he was gently chiding her for leaving him, to venture farther into the deep, or whether he was congratulating her on her dexterity in keeping her footing, when the foaming wave dashed so furiously over her white wing. It was a pretty sight.

When returning, we met a peasant girl, with her dress turned over her head, who in the most earnest manner spoke in Irish, and beckoned us to go farther. We declined, and she changed her laughing look for one of pitiful endearing disappointment, which prevailed with me, and I said, "We will go." She exultingly bounded away, leading us forward, looking back to encourage us, for the way was precipitous and somewhat difficult, till she placed us upon an awfully grand precipice. Here she stopped, and, in the most animated manner, pointed us down, then to a mountain across the channel, then to the golden stripes of the sun upon the water, then to the sea-gulls, then to the eastern sky, which was extremely beautiful; and when she saw we understood and were pleased, she was delighted. Had she been a well-educated girl, she could not have displayed more taste for the sublime and beautiful. She was pretty in look and graceful in manner, and when we parted, and saw her entering the mud-wall cabin, a companion of pigs with no employment but feeding them and milking a goat, or gathering turf from some bog, we said, what a pity that such an intellect should be lost, and who must account for all this waste? What a pity that government or aristocratic pride should place barriers to the improvement of the talented poor. In no civilized nation, probably, is there more waste of mind than in Ireland. Should any dispute this, let him visit the county of Kerry. The wild children there among the mountains, who spend their time in herding cattle often show the quickest perception of all that is lovely in nature, and will answer your questions with a clearness that would do honour to a refined people.

Saturday, April 12. – Made an excursion which will long be remembered, in company with Mrs. S. (the woman who first introduced me to the priest, and to the family who so kindly entertained me) and the two Miss Jacksons, and little Thomas the brother. We were supplied with a basket of bread and meat for dinner, and bound for Dunquin. The kind loquacious Mrs. S. had a favourite priest to whom she wished to introduce me on the way. An old church, and some Ogham stones which had long puzzled antiquarians, must first be seen, and then we were ushered in to see the priest. He was sitting by his fire, reading a newspaper, surrounded with Latin authors of various descriptions, and piles on piles of the most antiquated looking books in Hebrew, Greek and Latin. He received us with the greatest kindness, and the most simple urbanity of manners, and never in Ireland had I spent an hour where so much real knowledge had fallen on my ear. He was truly a learned antiquary; retired in that desolate part of the earth, buried in his musty books, he had gathered rich materials for thinking and conversation.[16] He showed us printed volumes of more than two hundred years old, one a geography, one a dictionary, and a few histories. He urged us to stay and take some refreshment. He was old and infirm, but insisted on accompanying us to the gate, upon the top of the pillars of which were two cannon balls, which Cromwell had left in besieging the place. I felt regret at leaving this complaisant old man, for he united the benevolent gentleman with the learned linguist and antiquary. I have since been told he is much esteemed by all classes.

We proceeded across a strand, where the sand was so mellow that our poor horse could scarcely proceed, and, to make up the dreadfuls, one of our traces broke. Happily a rope was found, or we might have been left to wade through the sand and wet, but we dragged through half a mile, and found ourselves on firm footing. Our next object was a tower near the top of Sybil Head, and after sitting down upon the beach and taking a hearty lunch, the young ladies and I proceeded.[17] The way was tedious, and the wind strong, but after much toiling and resting we reached the edifice.

The tower was erected for a telegraph, and was going to decay. Supposing this was the only object of curiosity, I felt a little disappointed. Leaving the young ladies in the tower, I ascended the mountain, which appeared at the top a sharp ridge like the roof of a house. I was just about taking the last step to gain the height, and then call out that I was on the loftiest peak of Sybil Head, when a little unobserved shepherd-girl called out, "Ye'll be destroyed! Look, look!" I looked, and started back with horror. A precipice overlooking the sea many hundred feet below, presented itself, a wall secured a little part, and then a shelving rock, bending over the waves, which were dashing and roaring with awful grandeur. I heard the roaring, but supposed it was the sea we had left at the foot of the mountain, and but for the little shepherd-girl should doubtless have stepped over into the awful abyss. Children, it seemed, were peculiarly my guardian angels in Ireland; three times they have saved me from immediate destruction by their care and kindness. The rocks upon a part of this ridge are like an inclined plane put there by the Great Architect, and form a good security to the cautious. My young companions placed themselves in a condition to look over, lying down, while I held their feet; one hasty peep was all I ventured, it was enough. A young lad and two girls were tending cattle on this awful brow, sheep were grazing upon the brink, and little girls spent the live-long day sporting near its very edge, as unconscious of danger as the bird that flies over them.

O those sweet shepherd children! Every where on the coast I found them, and every where I found them kind and simple-hearted, knowing nothing of the contaminating influences of cities, and gentle as the sheep they are tending. Often have I seen them sitting on the brow of some hill, or on a rock, their silken hair waving in the breeze, their feet naked, a stick in one hand, and sometimes a leaf of a book in the other, and I blessed the Father of all mercies that he had left in one island of the sea a people who still retain the simple life and simple manners of patriarchal days. From the sheep-fold was the sweet psalmist of Israel taken to be king, and in that humble employment was his heart moulded to all those soft touches, which so move the soul in his psalms.[18]

When I looked on these Kerry girls, I thought, shall I pity such loveliness? Shall I wish to tear you away to pent-up cities, to cramp your minds to fashion's moulds, when here Nature in all her forms and freaks, both beautiful and sublime, is before you? The mountain breeze is ever fanning their dark hair, they know nothing, they heed nothing of the vain show of the world, but are content, when at night they have herded their flock, to lie down in their cabin till the early dawn shall again summon them to the mountains. We asked one of these little girls, who was sitting upon the very edge of the precipice, if she had no fear. "Not any, miss," was the answer. I was glad to leave it, yet I could not but look upon what we had left as the most awfully grand spot I had ever visited.

When we reached our car, our company was patiently waiting, but to my awful disappointment told me there was not time to visit Dunquin, and Mrs. S., who seemed to be the heroine in all this day's manoeuvring, told me she had never heard of it before. I have found some fault with others in this work, and have recorded some of their misdoings, and am not so vain as to suppose I have passed through the length and breadth of Ireland, and not done some things and said some things out of time and season. Now here I made a little mistake, and am happy to acknowledge it as publicly as I mention the mistakes of others. This woman had a kind heart, and had manifested as much of it towards me as a poor woman could do; she had taken much pleasant trouble to arrange affairs for this trip, she had waited patiently upon the beach while we were exploring wonders above her, and when we came down, was in readiness to go home. When I mentioned Dunquin, her surprise appeared to me like real intrigue. I thought she could not but know that it was the object of my journey, and I told her so in language which she understood and felt. I hate deceit, and thought here was full proof. The time, too, I could not think was so far spent; but here she was in the right, and had I taken my own course, and persuaded the driver to take us the perilous route, which was nine miles, it would have been a frightful expedition indeed. But we were saved in spite of my determination to the contrary.

So much for disappointment, and hatred of deceit, and so much for not feasting my eyes on Dunquin, which had been a most ardent desire of my heart.[19] But Dingle must be left. My stay had been a long one, and notwithstanding that all the good people there did not understand what kind of religion one must possess, to be concerned about any party but one's own, and that self-denial is neither to be required nor expected 1800 years after the pattern was set in the church – that the world is constantly improving, and the church must keep pace with it or lose her respectability – yet there were a few that received Christ's legacy with all its tribulations. With these few I had passed profitable hours, and from these few I regretted to part. But the morning came, when the car must go out to Tralee. Mrs. Jackson was early preparing me refreshments for my journey, and by the middle of the day I was in Tralee, and stayed long enough to write a note to my friend Mr. Walpole, which I presume was not so palatable as another three shillings would have been. My next car that day took me to Tarbert; stayed at a hotel; the price was exorbitant, and when I expressed my surprise to the woman, saying no other hotel in Ireland was so high, her answer was certainly a candid honest one, "I intend to make all I can out of every one that comes here, and if I can make a shilling out of you, I will."

A walk around the bay gave a beautiful view of this ancient place. The promontory on which the light-house stands, with a few tasty buildings, was a fairy spot. I was shown the remains of all forts, which a gentleman standing by said were built by the Danes, who once figured here to great advantage, till driven out by the spirited Irish. Sending my baggage to the steam-boat, I walked three miles on the borders of the Shannon, to see the beauties of the country, and the Knight of Kerry's demesne, which like all the demesnes in Ireland is more proud than humble.[20]

CHAPTER XXIV

Sail up the Shannon to Limerick – Poorhouse Stirabout – Sleepless Night at Ennis
– Town without Bread – Grievous Ignorance – True Delivery of my one-armed
Charioteer – Basket of Bones – My Carpet-bag ransacked – Learned Schoolmaster
– Exchange of Compliments – Red Petticoats – Old Pedlar and his daughter –
Temple of Nature – The back of the Barracks – Marble Quarry – Completely
Watersoaked – Connemara Hospitality – Bundles of Straw – Sabbath in the Moun-
tain Cabin

I took my seat in the steam packet as a deck passenger, which in Ireland
is synonymous with a corner in a Christian church in America for
coloured people.[1] Here I found a multitude of well-dressed and ill-
dressed, informed and uninformed, many of them going to take passage
for America. The sail on this noble river, the Mississippi of Ireland, was
pleasant, and the city of Limerick one of business and beauty. I found a
neat inviting lodging-house, kept by a well-bred woman from Dublin; and
so pleasant was my stay here, I regretted leaving the city. The town did
not appear so poverty-stricken as many; the people looked intelligent, and
the activity reminded me a little of busy New York. I perambulated the
town, and enquired of cobblers and tinkers what was this, and what was
that. One explained to me all the wonders he knew of the ancient cathedral, where hung on one end the cannon-balls which were taken from it
in Cromwell's wars.[2] It is now used for a military school, and a Protestant
place of worship. The city is three miles in circumference; and but one
gate, called the Water Gate of St. John's Castle, is now standing of the seventeen which were there in 1760.[3] I found a labouring man near the poorhouse, who told me there were 1,700 inmates, and "I don't know what to
say of the stirabout there they give 'em."[4] "And what, sir, is the matter
with the stirabout?" "Why, by dad, ma'am, 'twould give a man waik
quawrters to ait it. They say it runs like wawter." This I found was the universal cry of all the beggars throughout Ireland, when told to go to the
poor-house, "The stirabout is so waik, that 'twould take the life of ye." My
stay in Limerick was too short, though I saw the whole town and its outward curiosities. The people was what I wanted to see. At three I took a
car for Ennis, an ancient town going to decay.[5] Clare Castle, standing a lit-

tle distance from the town, now the abode of soldiers, makes a pretty appearance at the bridge upon the bank of the river. Here too are the remains of a Franciscan monastery, and you are told of a great battle fought here in 1298.[6]

The coachman said he would take me to suitable lodgings, and these lodgings were his own house. His wife told me I must sleep with her if I stopped. It was dark, and I was shown into a chamber where were three beds, and finding a child in the filthy one prepared for me, I wrapped my cloak about me and lay across the foot. At two o'clock the family came into the chamber, and were soon snoring about me, while I kept vigil through the whole night.

Sabbath. – Mr. Murphy preached a most solemn sermon on the judgment, and pointedly applied it to all classes, especially the rich, who bring up their children for this world. The building had once the finest gothic aisles that ever adorned a church in Ireland.[7] Went again in the evening, and heard a second sermon from the same man, and wandered about the town till darkness warned me to return. But the lodging! I had not slept a moment in Ennis, and I enquired if my room was the same? "Where you slept last night," was the answer. Determining that my bed should be changed, even if it were for the worse, I went out, and from house to house made diligent search. The army was going through the town, and lodging-places were taken up. A woman interested herself, and after many fruitless applications she hit upon an expedient. "Good luck to ye, I have it! a genteel woman lodgin' with me will give ye a part of her bed, and she's a lady that wouldn't disgrace any body in the kingdom. Here, miss, I've brought a fine lady from America, who wants a lodgin', and sure ye wouldn't refuse her half of yer bed. She's alone, a stranger, and ye know it isn't for the money I would take her." The miss gave a sideways glance. "And 'tisn't every stranger I'd be takin' into my bed; and how came ye without a lodgin' so late at night?" This was all sterling sense, and telling her how I came in this plight, she changed her tune, and bade me welcome. But I made only a sorry change with regard to comfort, though not so many chums in my room. Paid threepence for my lodging, and took the car for Gort, and reached it at ten o'clock.

Here I went from street to street, and almost from door to door, to find a roll of bread and a cup of cocoa. There seemed to be nothing to eat, and twice when I asked for bread, the answer was, "The people of Gort don't eat, ma'am; we have no bread." I knew not what to say, or what to do; at last I found a few small loaves, and took a penny's worth, and left the town to walk to Oranmore, a distance of fourteen miles. Gort is a neat little town, pleasantly situated, but the answer to the question, "How are you getting along in Gort?" was, "The same as everywhere. Badly entirely, ma'am; Gort is a poor little town: the poor gets no labour, thank God."[8]

The day was unusually warm for April, the sun scorching, and my feet sore: I often found occasion to call at a cabin to rest. One woman was standing at a corner, waiting my approach, and called out, "Good morrow, ma'am; ye look wairy, come in and rest ye a bit." The simple manners of these unsophisticated peasantry are so much like the patriarchs of old, that in spite of their untidiness, they cannot but be interesting to every lover of antiquity. "An' would ye take a sup of milk?" Telling her I never used it, "What can I get ye? I have no bread." I thanked her, and could only satisfy her by saying that I had just been eating some. She then sat down to admire my "comely dress;" a little boy came in, and she asked him who I was. "A lady, ma'am." "See how quick he answers; he knows ye are a lady, because ye're clane and proper." The ignorance of this woman was painful, she seemed to know nothing beyond her own cabin. Seeing that she wanted a pin, I have her a couple of rows; the paper was red, and she admired it with great wonder. A son of twenty came in, and she immediately presented the paper to him. They both held it up and endeavoured to look through it, and both seemed delighted at the novel sight. I was really unhappy at seeing these innocent kind-hearted creatures of want, dying for lack of knowledge. Yes, dead as to anything appertaining to this life, for they had no comforts for the body, and they lived neglected, and apparently knew little else but what instinct dictated. Passing on, I reached the hospitable house of Oranmore, where I stopped in November, and was received with the kindest greetings, and kept without expense.[9] The Connemara girl had long been gone, but no other changes had taken place.

A night's rest refreshed all but my feet, and I attempted a walk to Galway, as I had sent on my carpet bag, and felt a little uneasy. The distance was but four and a half miles, but my feet soon became so painful, that it seemed quite impossible to proceed. An old woman saluted me, "An' ye'll be kilt with walkin', an' wouldn't ye ride for sixpence? I know a poor man who keeps a little ass, that would gladly take ye for that." She took me to a hovel, and called out, "Here, John, wouldn't ye take a lady to Galway for sixpence?" "And that I would," said John, jumping out of bed. It was eight o'clock; the children were preparing for school, and though ragged they were not dirty. There were five of them, all with black hair and eyes, and the mother was a comely well-bred woman. The man had but one arm, and no means of support but by his cart and ass. In a few moments all was ready. I insisted that he should stop and eat his potato, though I saw none preparing. I found afterwards he had none, and no prospect of any till the sixpence should be earned. It was a touching case of uncomplaining want. When we were going away, the woman said, "Maybe the lady hasn't got the change now." Taking the hint that she wanted the sixpence, I said, "Yes." But the poor man's sensitiveness was awakened, and he hurried me away with, "Never mind – never mind," which made me anxious to hear his history. He had been a herder, with twenty-five pounds a year, and brought a swelling on his arm by lifting, which after twelve months of suffering ended in amputation. He lost his employment, and could do nothing but drive about that little ass and cart. "A kind gentlewoman, ma'am, was all my hope for many a year, who called on me to go on an errand to fetch a bucket of water, and never give me less than a shillin'; and many a sorry day since I knew not where to git the potato. But God is good."

We were now joined by a woman who had walked from Gort to Oranmore the evening previous after four o'clock, and was now, with a burden on her back, going to Galway. She said she was forty-seven, the mother of nineteen children, and but three of them alive; the youngest that died was two years old. Gay and cheerful, "light of foot," she was quite an interesting object. We were soon joined by an old woman, who was sitting upon a wall, with a basket upon her back, which caused my coachman to quicken his speed, declaring, "the same that she carried in her basket was enough to give us all the plague, and I'll not be her company," whipping the poor ass, while the old woman was determined not to be outdone – the American lady she must see. The first good woman was quite annoyed, and begged her to keep a little off. "What," I enquired, "are the contents of the basket?" "A dead horse's bones, which she's a goin' to sell, ma'am." This was to me a new, degrading, and humiliating mode of earning bread, which I never could have thought woman would be compelled to undertake. Three well-dressed young ladies mingled in the group, for they had a curiosity to get a glimpse of the American, and accosted me quite pleasantly, not in the least regarding what company was about them. But the man, by jerks and blows, succeeded in leaving the bones in the rear before we reached town.

What subjects for contemplation has this morning presented! The humble clean family; the uncomplaining children going out to school without any breakfast; the suffering man still retaining a sense of honour in refusing the money, and a sense of propriety in escaping from the woman and basket; the sad state to which a country must be reduced, when the cheapest article of food could not be purchased by the poor in a season of plenty, sufficient to make them comfortable; and where woman is made to be anything but what God ordained or fitted her to be, the dishonour instead of the "glory of man."

I gave the poor man a few pennies more than the sixpence, and this so affected him, that I was glad when he bade "God speed," and hastened to buy his potatoes. Was it ever so with any people? And will God always see the poor man's want, and not relieve him. If the cries of Ireland do not reach his ears, their patience surely must, and he will come in judgment or mercy to their aid.

I called at my old lodgings, was welcomed, and learned that the asthmatic mother had gone down to the grave, and that comfortable lodgings could be given without taking a room with "John." I first hastened to the car-office to make arrangements for Clifden, and there found my carpet bag upon the floor in the corner broken open, and the articles lying in fragments about it.[10] I enquired the cause of the agent, who insolently answered, "Your things are all there. An officer's wife said she had examined them, and found the value was not much, and she had left them as she found them; but I must have an additional shilling for my trouble, or the luggage shall not leave the office." I asked him whether as a stranger I had merited such treatment. He cared nothing, he said, for strangers, nor anything for Americans. Offering him a sovereign to change, "he should change it when he knew the weight, but should not trust to my honesty." The sovereign was weighed, and proved to be more than weight. He took the shilling, and asked my name to enter on the book. I declined, and told him I should have no more to do with Bianconi's cars. That I had paid him considerable, and this was not the first time that I had been treated rudely and unkindly by his agents.

"I am quite sorry, ma'am. I should be glad of your money, and you will wear yourself out by walking." Telling him that would be my misfortune, I passed out, found the one-armed man, and agreed with him to take me fourteen miles for two shillings. His price was a shilling a day, and he could perform this journey in a day. He went home, and I to my lodgings, and early in the morning was prepared for the ride, but no man appeared. I took my parasol, leaving my luggage, and went on, hoping the old man might soon follow. The wife of a poor curate soon joined me, with two fine boys, a book and a rattan, going on a two miles' excursion for exercise and air, and gave me as much talk as I could reasonably ask concerning religious societies in Galway.[11] She deplored greatly the delusions of Romanism, but the divisions among Protestants she thought were more to be regretted than all. Her husband, she said, was a spiritual indefatigable labourer in the cause of Christ, and had lost a promised promotion from the bishop, because he had sought to obey a higher Master than an earthly one.

My next call was to the house of a very civil shoe-maker, whose wife showed me every attention, and conducted me into the National school, where I heard better specimens than usual of reading and grammar, and what is quite noticeable in all schools, a knowledge of arithmetic beyond the years of children in other countries.[12] My best wishes for the success of public schools in Ireland, for the more I see of them, the more do I expect that great good will be the result. I passed two other schools that day, but was not in time for either.

The last four miles of my journey I had the company of a police officer.[13] I have invariably found these men civil and sober, and a great blessing to Ireland as she now is.

My place of stopping was Outerard. A clean house and hospitable woman gave me a pleasant evening. The town is a tidy one in outward looks, and is somewhat celebrated for having a mineral well, and a salmon-leap in the river. A bathing-house is made in a rock of curious construction, and a cottage of such beautiful finish that it is an ornament to the town, and a standing monument of the correct taste of the doctor who designed it. The family refused any compensation, sending me away with the kindest wishes, and I turned into a house where were huddled a group of boys and girls. Certainly if there is any skill in packing lumber, they had acquired it, and any merit in a desire for instruction, they deserve it.

When I entered, the "master skilled to rule" was standing one foot upon a chair, his elbow resting upon his knee, spectacles across his nose, a pen in his hand, which he was mending, ever and anon flourishing it, as he vehemently expatiated on some clause in the lesson he was explaining.[14] He bowed long and low to me, and then spoke in Latin to a boy who answered in the same language. Then turning to a bevy in a dark corner, who were urging their rights by hunches and threats, he told them that the wandering Arab in the great desert of Sahara, or the Siberian at the frozen regions of the north, could as well understand the meaning of civility as they; and should he enjoin taciturnity (though that was too refined a word for such boors as he had before him) they would as readily obey him.

"I have done much, honoured lady, for these lads before you, and to say the truth they are the first fellows in the kingdom. Come here; let's hear you conjugate this verb." Before the boy had half run through, "There, lady, what do you think of my manner of teaching?" "It cannot be disputed, sir." "I ought to be promoted for what I have done. Go on, honey, and tell the whys and wherefores. And so you see, lady, no stone's unturned." I assured him I had seen nothing like it in all Ireland. "Hear, hear, my good fellows! Here's a lady of the first order speaking, and mark what she says. I knew when she entered, by her looks and language, she was a lady of the highest order. Now mark!"

"Full well they laughed, and counterfeited glee."[15]

Hear, hear! I made a speech somewhat in keeping with the place and persons, and had I never before felt my own greatness, now was the favourable moment. A long and low bow, ended by two or three short ones and a hearty good-bye on my part, finished the morning comedy.

My journey lay through a wild mountainous country, and the red petticoats scattered here and there upon hill and lake side gave a romantic touch to the strange scenery for many a mile.[16] A walk of six miles called for rest and a little soap for my blistered feet, and turning into a cabin upon the top of a hill, I heard reading as I entered the door. The woman of the house was sitting with an infant on her lap, reading to a friend who had entered, and I soon perceived she had a cultivated mind, though her lot was cast in that desert. She was a Protestant, and said, "You have no idea of the dreadful condition we are in upon these mountains. No school, and scarcely a book, and seven miles from any church."[17] I promised, if I passed that way on my return, to spend a night with her, and bring her some books. I now felt the want of my luggage. An old man and his daughter entered with each a heavy burden, which they tried to lighten at every cabin upon the mountains. They were dealers in dry goods. "I hope," said the intelligent woman, "you will keep the company of these worthy people across the mountain." I had not walked far when a cough behind caused me to turn about, and the girl said, "Ye are quick on the fut, and I feared we should not gain upon ye." The father soon joined us, and after a "God save ye kindly, we're all travellers together," he added, "I rair'd the little gal yonder, and a blackguard of a fellow kept his eye on her for a twelvemonth, till by her consent and mine he married her, stopped with her one month, took the few pounds she had gained by dailin', and went away, the villain, and set up the business, and has never put the two eyes on her sence."

We were all fatigued, our feet blistered, and we sat down upon a bank of one of the beautiful lakes which are dotting this wild mountain scenery for many a mile. Having my Testament in my hand, "Ye have a nice little book," said the old man. "Shall I read a little?" I asked. "Plaise God, ye will," was the answer. I opened at the 14th of John, and read.[18] "Where," said the daughter, "did you get that beautiful book?" "It sounds," said the father, "like our Catholic raidin', and what the priest has told us from the altar." They had heard portions of the scripture, but did not know that this was the Word of God till I told them. The daughter took it in her hand, turned over the leaves, read a few portions intelligibly, and asked, "Where could I get one? Would you sell me this?" I promised one from my basket, should it reach Clifden while she was there. The old man clasped his hands, raised his eyes, blessed the good God that he had met such a lady, and such blessed words which "melt the heart." It was a pleasant hour. We needed no cushioned desk nor fringed drapery, to adorn our pulpit. We wanted no lighted gas to enable us to read our prayers from gilt-edged books. The chandelier of day was hanging out in heaven's high dome, and the pure waters of the lake were sparkling in its beams. Our temple was a lofty one, and as we sat together within its broad portals, we read the sweet and condescending words, "let your heart not be troubled." "In my father's house are many mansions." "Yes," ejaculated the old man, "blessed be his holy name, there are many mansions." I then felt that God was truly a Spirit, and could be worshipped on the mountain top or lowly valley, and needed no temple made with hands.

"Must we go," I asked, as the book was closed, "and leave this heavenly place?" "Plaise God, we must," the old man answered. Our walk was ten miles upon the top of a mountain spotted with lakes.[19] The old man became fatigued, and they stopped as the sun was setting, at a miserable looking lodging-house for the night, leaving a three miles' walk for me alone, with weary feet, before I could find "a dacent house for a body like me." The daughter, to encourage me, told me one of the "good lies" which so much abound, that it was "but a short mile under yer fut." Darkness soon came over me, and no smoke of a cabin cheered my eye. I sat down upon a little hillock, and again looked over the scenes I had passed, and thanked God that I was in Ireland, and that I had met the old man on the mountain, and hoped he would rest his weary old limbs, though I might not find a shelter. I heard a footstep, and as it approached, enquired if the lodging-house of the mountain was near. "A perch or two under yer fut, and ye are in it." I went on; as I reached the door I heard laughing, music, and dancing. It was a barrack; and a piper, with more whiskey than good sense in his brain, was blowing with all his might for the bare-footed girls and merry lads, who were in the highest glee.[20] "Is this a lodging-house?" I enquired. "Go back, and you will find it." I stumbled my way back of the barracks, and opened a door, and a tidy looking woman received me very coldly by saying, "We never turn people out of doors. But why are you here so late? Why didn't you stop back? Are you travelling alone?" By this time my patience was departing, and I answered, "Do you keep lodgers? and can you keep me?" "We never turns folks out of doors." "I do not suppose you turn people out of doors, if you put out a sign to ask them in." The master heard this, stepped into the room, and quite in Irish mood bade me welcome, though he was an Englishman. "Sit down, and make yourself as comfortable as you can. We will do as well as we can for you." A clean bed was provided; two others, well filled, were my companions, but never was rest more refreshing. The next day was rainy, and I employed by time reading, writing, and listening to the music of two fiddlers, who told me they were employed by gentlemen to amuse them at their houses. So fond are the Irish of music, that, in some form or other, they must and will have it. A piper entered on a wooden leg, and called for a glass of whiskey, which the daughter gave him, and feeling a little jealous lest the fiddlers might be thought more than rivals, he gave such proofs of dexterity as put all to silence. "We live so remote," said the man, "that these little droppings now and then on a rainy day make the time pass very pleasantly. In fact, I don't know how we should get along without them. It's nature, you see," holding a granddaughter of eight months old upon the floor to see her dance. "You see, ma'am, they'll dance before they can walk."

The next morning the inn-keeper took me to see a marble quarry in the mountains, which he had explored; the rain beat us cruelly, but we proceeded.[21] The slabs were beautifully variegated with green, brown, and black. This quarry was opened, and then stopped, the owner not accepting the offer of seven pounds a ton by Government. The quarry is immense, and thousands of men might find employment if they would be allowed to work. These mountains abound in the richest minerals. This man has spent much time in exploring and analysing their properties, and has found copper and some other ore. Yet rich as Ireland is in all that might make her a bright gem indeed among all the nations, her Government gives her arts and manufactures but little encouragement.[22]

The sun looked out long enough for me to put all in readiness for departure, and when I had proceeded about a mile, the wind increased almost to a tornado, and the rain seemed to have cleared out all her pipes, and was pouring forth torrents fresh and clean. I was now in a woeful plight – my parasol, which had withstood many a buffeting, soon turned inside out, and became a wreck. No cabin was near till I was drenched. At last a miserable one met my eye, and going in, I was welcomed by two young women, and a young man, who was a traveller too, and enquired,

"Where did ye come from, that ye are out in this stawrm?" Telling him, and that it was fine when I left, he said, "Aw, he's a blackguard and a rascal to let ye from this door to-day. He knew it would be stawrmy, an' he's a honey tongue, but his wife is a sour heifer; and wasn't ye a-payin' the blackguard, that he was so willin' to let ye come?" "I was paying them full price for all I had." "They are divils then, and the divil'll have 'em, and that's the end on't." I heard of Connemara – that it had been a custom from time immemorial, that if a stranger is not welcomed into a cabin at night-fall, or leaves it in a storm, the cabin holder is immediately called upon to enquire into the reason; and if it appears that it is inhospitality, that family is set up as a mark of contempt to its neighbours.[22]

The storm was increasing, and I could not stop, for the mud cabin was nearly as wet as the road; the poor woman said, "If ye could stay, ye should not go out." After walking a few yards, the wind was more violent and the rain heavier. I turned my back, and strove to ascend a hill in that way. In despair I stood; when looking to my left I saw at a distance a cabin, and a little girl standing in the door. She was gazing at me, as I supposed, from idle curiosity, and, as the last alternative, I hesitatingly turned towards the dreary abode. "Welcome, welcome, stranger, from the stawrm; ye're destroyed. I told the little gal to open the door and stand in it, that ye mightn't think we was shuttin' ye out in the stawrm; we've got a good fire and plenty of turf; and though the cabin is small, and not fittin' for sich a lady as ye, I'll make it better than the mad stawrm without; and I'll soon heave over a pot of potatoes, and get ye a sup of milk, and I wish my wife was here. I'm but a stranger; but here sence Monday." All this passed before I had time to tell my country, pedigree, or business to Ireland. But when he heard all that, he was more anxious still to heap me with kindness. A huge pile of blazing turf soon dried my clothes, and I was sitting "high and dry" by the side of the heels of a stage horse, who was taking his lunch from a pile of straw at the foot of a bed. In an hour the potatoes were ready, and the kind little girl brought me a broken soup-plate with two eggs on it, and a "sup of milk." The eggs I gave to a coachman who dropped in to exchange horses, and took some salt and my tea-spoon, which I carried in my pocket; and upon a stool by the side of the pot, on which a basket was placed containing the lumpers, I ate my supper with the family and coachman, not only with a cheerful, but a grateful heart.

Night came, but what was to be my lodging? The bed in the room was nothing but a pile of straw, with a dirty blanket and heavy woollen quilt over it; but the horse, to my great delight, was removed by the coachman, leaving two good bundles of clean straw untouched. The father went out;

a little son fell asleep, and I persuaded him to go to bed, the girl saying, "He mustn't lie there; father told us that we are to sit by the fire, and ye are to lie in the bed." I refused, telling her I should not do it; but when the father came in, he told the son in anger, "he'd break every bone in his body if he didn't go out of that." I at last prevailed on the father to allow him to remain, and told him I had an excellent bed in my eye. "An' sure it isn't the bundle of straw; not a ha'p'orth of yer wet and wairy bones shall lie there to-night." I insisted that I greatly preferred it as a luxury, and finally took one bundle, removed the band, made a little opening, and placed it before the fire, put a second one at the bottom of the door, as the breach was large and the wind piercing; and then with some loose handfuls stopped the crevices above and around, till all was quite snug. Then wrapping my coat closely about me, I lay down in as comfortable a nest, and slept as sweetly, as I ever had in America or Ireland.

The fire died upon the hearth, and the cold awakened me. The day was the Sabbath; the storm had not in the least abated. I had my Testament, and spent the morning reading the crucifixion and resurrection of the Saviour to the family. The father assured me that "he had never heard a ha'p'orth of it read before; we are as ignorant, good lady, as the goats upon the mountain. God help us!" A woman entered with a red petticoat turned over her head, and the man told her in Irish who I was, and that I had come to see the poor. She reached her hand, and said in Irish, "Then she is my sister." The little girl explained, "She is a very religious body, and means you are her sister if you are religious." She was a mountain Connemara girl, but not a facsimile of the one I met in Oranmore. She gave a hearty shake of the hand as she went out, telling the man she must come and see me again. The man said, "If ye could spake in Irish, ye could do good to these craturs, for they are as stupid as the marble-stone."

One told me that they wore red petticoats to keep off the fairies; "and this," he added, "they fully believe."[25] While he was deploring their ignorance, his little son told him he had dreamed a bad dream. "Bless yourself, then, nine times, in the names of the Father, Son, and Holy Ghost, when ye are goin' to sleep, and ye won't drame at all."[26] "Do you believe this?" I asked. "I do, ma'am; the priest told me so, and the priest must know." "The priest, sir, insulted you if he told you so; it is all nonsense, and you should not listen to it." He shook his head at my incredulity, but said no more.

The rain ceased, and I must go to the next lodging-house, about two miles. Asking the man if he could change half-a-crown, "For what?" as I hesitated, "I will not change a half-crown, nor a shilling, nor a sixpence;

nor a ha'p'orth shall the childer take, for that blackguard bed ye laid yer wairy bones upon. If I had a half-crown, I would give it to let ye ride to Clifden." This was true Connemara hospitality, and I went out without leaving a farthing, where I had had value received, and should have felt it a great privilege to give them a little.

I reached the lodging-house, and saw the good woman and all about her in unusual trim for the people in that mountain, and felt much cheered at so neat and comfortable-looking a place. "But we cannot entertain ye, because a daughter is to be married this evening." I then was more anxious to stop, for among all the varieties I had seen, I never had been present at an Irish wedding. I went to a second, was denied; to a third, the answer here was, "She could not accommodate so dacent a body." Decent or not decent, I told her I must stay. The rain was beginning, and I could not reach Clifden that night, neither was I willing to be out so long on the Sabbath. At last she consented, and gave me a good fire, a piece of bread, and a plate of well cooked potatoes, which were always given without charge in every lodging-house where I stopped. The room where I lodged had potatoes cut for planting, which was the creditable reason why a "dacent body" should not be put in it.

CHAPTER XXV

Clifden – Clifden Castle – Irish Holidays – Walk to Roundstone – Hardships of
Irish Tenants – Three Guides pointing three different ways – Potatoes a Curse
upon Ireland – A Rough and Weary road – Absence of Trees – An Aged Pilgrim –
Good Wishes – A Timely Supply – Judicious Advice – A Kind Curate – A Connemara School – Ascent of the Diamond Mountain, and Adventure by the Way –
Tully – No Bread to be had in the Town – The Isle of Omey, and the Natives
thereof – Change for the better in Connemara – Return to Clifden

Monday morning, walked in the rain to Clifden. Was directed to a lodging place, and found an intelligent Protestant woman, who immediately
brought me tea and toast, as she saw me wet and fatigued. The romantic
town of Clifden presented a novel appearance, built as it is upon a hill in
part. The picturesque church stands on an eminence, looking trim and
independent above its neighbours.[1]

Visited the Protestant school, taught by a male and female teacher.
The children are mostly Roman Catholics, and are partly clothed by the
society, and are advanced to grammar and geography.[2] Next I went to the
national school, a great building gone to decay, the school kept by a widow
for the paltry compensation of ten pounds a year.[3] The boys had all with-
drawn, and no interest whatever was taken in the school. Bishop M'Hale
had prohibited the reading of those portions of scripture appertaining to
the lessons; and the teacher, though a Catholic, talked seriously of leaving
the school on account of it. She is an intelligent woman, and at the time
of her marriage had possessed a property of twelve thousand pounds,
which her good husband had the art of spending in a few years. He is now
dead, and she sits in a dilapidated school-room fifty-two weeks every year
for a salary of ten pounds.

I left the school, and ascended a difficult mountain to take a full survey of the town.[4] It was a most picturesque view. Mountains of rocks on
every hand, and the sea behind a little declivity; the scattered buildings
here and there among the wildness of the rocks about the village, make
one feel transported back to days of chivalry, when all the superstitious
legends were in full vogue, when fairies were plying their skill, and knights
and chieftains were the men of renown.

April 30th. – I walked forth after a shower, scarcely knowing or caring whither. I followed a neat romantic path till a splendid stone gateway met my eye, and, quite contrary to monarchical etiquette, the entrance was open and free.[5] I received a hearty welcome from the good-natured keeper of the lodge, and an invitation to walk in and take a cup potato, "the best in all the world," she said. "Ye are welcome to go all over the grounds, no walls or gates preventing. And if the owner was at home, he would take ye through the castle." Her husband led me to the path, and left me to wander in the pleasure-grounds where I pleased. A romantic pile of moss-covered rocks was the first object of curiosity. The roof was broken through, and water trickled from the rocks down to a channel under the stone floor, which bears it silently away under ground. Recesses in the interior made this structure a still greater wonder, and seeing two labouring men, I enquired what it could be. "A grotto, ma'am. An' ye're a stranger from England, I s'pose." "No, sir, from America." "From America! America! welcome, thrice welcome. An' I see ye have the green badge of Ireland," alluding to my green coat, "and do ye know the shamrock?" picking a sprig, and handing it to me; "Ye are Ireland's friend, I know, and do ye think we shall ever get any good? America is doing' much for us, and' we'll neer fight for England." The chief speaker was white-headed; yet he expected to live to see Ireland have her rights. As they said, "God speed ye," I looked after these old men, and surely, I thought, it is true –

"Hope springs eternal in the human breast.
Ireland 'never is, but always to be blest.'"[6]

Following the winding path, I soon found the castle, proud in height and architecture, embosomed in wood, without gate or wall. After surveying it on every side, I was more satisfied with all its plan than any I had seen; for while it looked up in independent grandeur, it seemed to look down with a bland smile, and say to the humblest visitor, "I hope you are pleased." Going on through the wood, I entered a garden such as few domains could boast; tastefully laid out on mountain side and valley, without any enclosure, and gradually losing itself in woods among rivulets and cascades. The apple and lilac were in bloom, in the midst of these varied delights. Now appeared a fairy castle, a house with variegated pillars and open door, made of shells of the most delicate shades, arranged in stars and circles of beautiful workmanship. These showed exquisite taste in the designer, and must have been done with great cost and care. I found that a labouring peasant was the architect of this wonderful fabric, but he was kept most religiously in his rank, labouring for eightpence a day.

Not a spot in all Ireland had been to my liking so much as this, because it breathed such a republican air of liberty. Not a placard said, "No trespass;" no surly porter followed to say, "My master allows no one about the place without a written pass." But here the visitor may sit, stand, or stroll, fanned by the breezes of summer with the sweet scent of every flower, and feel that all was made for his enjoyment. Leaving the enchantment, I went to the rocky shore (for the ocean is dashing its waves in front of these delights), gathered a few shells, and returned by the sea-side, passing a monastery of monks where eighty boys are instructed, and where five monks now reside.[7] Its style and comfort are not like Mount Mellary.

Thursday, May Day. – Here the ancient custom of dressing poles with flowers, and placing them before the doors of the rich, is kept up.[8] Horses and carriages are ornamented with them, and the children of the peasantry call at the doors of the gentry to receive presents.* The holidays of the Irish peasantry present to the stranger the character and condition of this people in the broadest outlines. You see how the liberty, which on such an occasion is allowed the greatest latitude that it ever can take, is chastened by a cringing servility, which says, "I am your humble slave." You see the effort at tidiness and show, which give you the extent of the scanty wardrobe acquired by the ill-paid labour of the master. You see the quick perception of generosity and meanness, as the gift is put in the scale with the donor's wealth and station. You see the full mark of enjoyment, which the Irish heart is capable of reaching above all others, both in sunshine and storm; and you see that God has stamped his image as legibly, as nobly, yes, as invitingly, on the peasant as on the lord.

I determined, if possible, to see Roundstone that day, a walk of ten miles. Walked a few miles, when a little boy of ten years old came up with a staff, and was a pleasant companion, telling me many wonders of the wild barren country. Passing a pile of stones, he paused, and I walked on a few paces; he seemed fixed to the spot. I said, "It is a wild place, boy." "A dreadful place it has been, ma'am, for robbers.[9] There is one buried under that pile of stones there, who lived about here, and stayed on that island in the lake you see back there; it was long they watched him, and at last one night they killed him, and put him under that pile of stones." I enquired after reaching the town, and was told that the story was true; that before Father Mathew had been there, Connemara was infested by robbers.[10]

---

* I was told at Glengariff that the old lord furnishes his pocket with shillings to meet the little girls at the door on May morning, who first present him with an egg, a shamrock, or a bunch of wild flowers.

I asked the boy to read; he did so intelligibly, and answered every question from the second of Matthew, respecting the birth of the Saviour, correctly. "And what," I asked, "is to become of this world?" "The great Judge will come and burn it up," was the answer. He was ready in the scriptures, though he had been trained in the Catholic church.

Two miles from the town a decently clad farmer accosted me. He had been to attend a lawsuit, a case of ejectment. "I have worked," he said, "on a farm since a boy; my father died, and left it to me, three years ago. I had made a comfortable house for myself and family, and been preparing manure all winter to put in a greater crop of potatoes and corn. The agent came round, saw the improvements, and told me I should not sow any seed, but must quit the premises." And he was actually ejected, notwithstanding the encouragement he had had from the landlord to make improvements. From twenty to twenty-four shillings an acre were tenants giving on this rocky spot, which in many places could not be ploughed. "I must take my little all," added the man, "and leave my father's bones, and seek a home in America." Hard is the lot of the poor man in Ireland. If he is industrious, his industry will not secure him a home and its comforts; these he must lose so soon as this home is above the abode of the ox or the ass.

"Why don't you," said I to a widow who had an acre of ground, "make things about your cabin look a little more tidy? You have a pretty patch of land, well kept, and might look very comfortable." "But, lady, I have but one little slip of a boy of fifteen years of age, and he toils the long day to rair a bit of vegetable to carry to market, and he helped me to put up this little cabin, and if I make it look nice outside, the agent will put a pound more rent on me, or turn me out and my little things; and I couldn't pay the pound." These are facts all over Ireland. If the poor tenant improves the premises, he must be turned out or pay more. If he does not improve it, he is a lazy dirty Irishman, and must be put out for that.

I reached Roundstone, and was kindly received by a Christian Protestant woman who had invited me there before in Clifden.[11] Met an intelligent police officer and his sister; and in the morning visited the school, taught by a Roman Catholic, and supported by the Home Mission.[12] It is in its infancy, its funds low, and the children supplied themselves with what books they had, which were few and defaced. I sat in the schoolroom till eleven, waiting for the scholars to assemble, and with much urging succeeded in hearing two girls attempt to read. The teacher is a learned man, but the appearance of his person told that a schoolmaster's salary in Ireland is a poor inducement to plod through the declensions and conjugations of a Latin grammar. The whole together was not attracting. The Testament is kept in school, and the teacher observed, "It is read by all who wish to read it, and the others omit it."

Mr. Crotty, the Presbyterian clergyman who employs the teacher, says he can do no better in the present state of things.[13] Poverty sits brooding on every thing here. A Church of England curate, a Presbyterian clergyman, and Romish priest divide the town among them, leaving a scanty pittance to each of the labourers. Mr. Crotty was once a Romish priest, and is now a thorough adherent to those principles he once denied. He certainly has done honour to the change he has made, if the voice of his neighbours weigh anything; for the Catholics all spoke kindly of him as a peace-maker, wishing to do good to all, and "given to hospitality."

Roundstone, which might as well be called Allstone, stands upon a pleasant bay, and has a strand about two miles distant, of two miles in length, and in some places of nearly half a mile in width, of the finest white sand, and the most beautiful shells in the whole island. Here I spent some hours alone, amid the drifting of the sand, gathering shells, and endangering my eyes; almost threatened with a burial in the vast heaps that are piled nearly mountain high; my feet sinking deeply at every step. An ancient burying ground is back of the strand, and many of the dead bodies have been washed out, and have been found among the sand.[14] The poor peasants, men, women, and children, were gathering seaweed, loading their horses, asses, and backs with it, to manure the wretched little patches of potatoes sown among the rocks. They walked home with me to town, some of them with loads upon their backs which to me looked frightful.[15] "This," said a fair young girl, who had rested her basket a moment upon the wall, "this is what the good God puts on us many a long day, and we musn't complain." I must acknowledge I cannot comprehend how such unnecessary, unheard of, degrading suffering can be made to sit on young hearts like this so uncomplainingly. Working a whole life for a potato! yes, a potato! "We have them for a rarity," said a young Irishman as he rose from his supper, "we have the lumpers three hundred and sixty-five days in a year." "A great blessing," I answered. "The greatest curse that ever was sent on Ireland; and I never sit down, see, use or eat one, but I wish every divil of 'em was out of the island. The blackguard of a Raleigh who brought 'em here, entailed a curse upon the labourer that has broke his heart. Because the landholder sees we can live and work hard on 'em, he grinds us down in our wages, and then despises us because we are ignorant and ragged."[16]

This is a pithy truth, one which I had never seen in so vivid a light as now.

Saturday. – I left the kind Mrs. Moran, where I had stopped, and directed my footsteps to Clifden. The police officers, at my egress, detained me some time at the door of the barracks, with multiplied enquiries about America, and kind wishes for myself.[17] As I proceeded, the wind became so strong in my face that walking was almost impossible. I was soon joined by a woman going to Clifden with a heavy burden on her back. "And why did ye lave Roundstone? The people were all waitin' to see ye on Sunday, and the hotel keeper's wife was to keep ye a few days, for she has been in America, and she'd like to discoorse ye, and she knew ye'd no good place to lodge." With her heavy burden she was soon out of sight, for she must be in Clifden for market. I sat down; the gusts were so violent in my face, that I could scarcely make my way. A man with a loaded team met me, and said, "Ye cannot walk with this storm in yer face; go into the half-way house, and wait till I come back, and I will give ye a ride into Clifden."[18] He had five miles to go, and unload his team, and five miles more to return to the spot. I went into the half-way house, but was glad to get again upon the street, and buffet the storm.[19] I had travelled fifty miles in this part of the country, and never seen a tree or shrub, unless what was planted by the hand of man as an ornament, and this only once. Yet we are told that all these mountains and valleys were once covered with trees; that the bog-oak found so far beneath the surface is one proof, and the turf another.

I soon saw an old man leaning upon a staff, approaching, as I supposed, to beg. "An' ye're an American, an' I've been hurryin' home to see ye; an' ye're alone, and a stranger, and my heart wawrms towards the stranger. I've a daughter in America, an' I didn't hear from her these three years, an' I'd go there to-morrow if I had the manes, if I knew I should die in a week. This is a dreadful place, ma'am. They are all haythens. They buried a parish priest, and dragged him off in a common cart; they did indeed, ma'am, as soon as ye can." The old man's eloquence increased as he proceeded. "I'm from Kilkenny, and the people there are civilized. Oh, must my ould bones be buried here!" I had the Testament open in my hand, and went to a wall, and sat down. He tottered towards me, and I said, "If you will stop, I will read some of Christ's words to you. You are old, and if you love Christ, you will soon be where he is." "Ah, I am a sinner, lady, a great sinner, an ould sinner. But do ye tell me ye arn't lonely on these wild mountains?" "I am not alone; Christ is with me, and I hear him say, 'Let not your heart be troubled.'" "And d'ye say that Christ is with ye! Oh, if I could say that! Oh, if my ould heart could feel that!" I read the 14th of John in his wondering ears, while he, at every sentence which struck him, would lift his withered hands, exclaiming, "And is this Jesus? Did he say this to sinners?" I read, and talked, and read again. The winds had hushed, and the sun shone out, and told me I must hasten; I looked in the old man's face, the tear was trembling in his dim eye; I turned away. "I have kept ye too long, ma'am; pardon me, but my heart wawrms towards the stranger." He tottered away, and I heard him praying the good God to bless the lone stranger. Never can I forget that old man of the mountain.

Within two miles of Clifden I entered a miserable hut, and found a company of women sitting on the floor. The woman of the cabin said, "Are ye a widow?" Answering in the affirmative, "An' I'm the same, and but one cratur in the world that belongs to me, and she's dark, ma'am.[20] I put her in bed a sound child, an' she was dark in the mornin.' She's gone to the next town. She fiddles, but her fiddle is poor, and I can't reach money to buy her a new one." I went out, she followed, pitying and wishing she could do something for me. Looking me earnestly in the face, "Would ye know me, ma'am, if ye should see me again? I shall want to see ye, and know how ye do." She turned away, then called again, "God speed ye, and give ye long life, and may I see ye again." Hoping to hear no more tales of sorrow till I should reach Clifden, I hurried on, but was soon accosted by "God save ye kindly, an have ye travelled much since I met ye?" I looked up, and recognized the old man with his pack, to whom I read the scriptures on the banks of the lake. I recollected my promise to give him some books, but had none with me, and could only say again, "Be ye warmed and be ye filled."[21] He bade all manner of good wishes, and hoped I should meet his daughter in town.

I hastened to the post office with anxiety, and found a letter enclosing two pounds ten, with a bundle of bibles and tracts from the same kind clergyman who had been the instrument, at my first setting out of, getting the bibles from the Hibernian Society.[22] I wept tears of gratitude, that I, a stranger in a strange land, should be so carefully remembered.[23] I went to the coach-office, for though the carriage was paid in Dublin, yet eighteen pence more was demanded, or the books could not be given. This was another trick played upon me by Bianconi's agents; I paid it, resolving never to have any more to do with his agents or cars. I have observed throughout Ireland two classes of men with a superabundant capital of insolence – post-masters, and the agents of coaches and canal-boats. Civility seems to be lost on them, more than on any others I met in the country. This I attributed to two causes; the hurry and perplexity of their business, and the pride of being so exalted above the spade, in a country where stations beyond the peasant's lot are so enviable.

I was now almost happy. I had the prospect of doing a little good, where so much good was needed. The daughter of the old man I met upon the lakes called, and modestly reminded me of the promise to give her the Word of God. She had not forgotten what we read together, and said she had thought much of it since. I gave her one, offering her some tracts, but she, too, wanted nothing but the Word of God. A young Roman Catholic lady was lodging in the house, and she possessed good sense and a tolerable education. She examined the bundle of tracts, and found some on controversial subjects. She begged me not to offer these. "You have," said she, "done good here, by showing to the people that you did not come to quarrel with them about their religion, but to do them good, by giving such books as they might read; but if you circulate these, it will be said you are like all others, and the good you have done will be lost." This was sterling advice, and I followed it. She took a Testament, and it was her constant companion. I have found her reading in bed, and by the wayside.

Sabbath. – Went into the Sabbath-school, and found the old curate and his young wife, with each a scholar teaching.[24] He gave us a cool rational sermon. This curate and his wife were very kind; and the little attentions they showed me left pleasant mementoes on my mind. They invited me to tea, and asked me to play on the piano; they afterwards left the town, not expecting to return till I should be gone, and sent me the key of the piano, as I must, they said, be lonely and I might have access to it at any hour in the day.* A Bible-reader was sick in the house where I lodged, and very poor; but rich in faith. He had laboured long and faithfully in a retired part of this desolate region, slept upon a ground floor, and at last sank under the accumulated weight of his burdens. From him I learned much of the poverty of the country, and much did he lament the want of vital piety in the hearts of those who professed Christ. "I am sick," he said, "of nominal Christianity."

Monday morning. – My heart was light and buoyant, and the young Catholic lady set off with me to Diamond Mountain, a walk of ten miles, where we had been invited by two police-men the Saturday previous.[25] We filled a basket with books, and were early on our way. The walk was romantic, diversified with lofty mountains, transparent lakes, and every variety of man, woman, and child, that poverty could present. Women with all kinds of burdens, doing all manner of work; some shovelling sea-

* This little act of kindness said more for their true Christian hospitality towards a stranger, than money would have done.

gravel into baskets, lifting it upon their backs, and throwing it upon the potato-ridges. "This is hard work," I observed, "for women." "This is our lot," answered one, "and we must do it; but if we had money to go to your country we wouldn't be here." One shrewd woman said, "I wish there would be war; then we'd have both work and money. Anything for a change. Here we toil like dogs and beasts, and live because the Almighty God don't call us." This woman was daily employed at this heavy work, for fivepence a day, leaving her husband and ten children at home, a mile from her place of labour. We passed her cabin, and found her husband doing a little job at coopering. Miserable, miserable huts, and ragged children, so darkened the pleasant scenery of mountain, lake, and river, that my morning buoyancy began to flag a little.

On a rocky promontory of steep ascent sat a Connemara woman, with a red flannel jacket and petticoat, looking out, and a ragged girl standing near. I ran up the rock, sat down at a little distance, and commenced singing. She sat mute, looking into the sea, as if petrified; and though a boat was cheering, and crying "Long life to you," she remained unmoved, and when I proffered my hand, and spoke kindly, she looked steadily, but made no attempt at speaking. We passed down and left her, nor did she move till we had gone from her sight. We next called at a cabin, where a number of children had collected, to whom we gave books. Finding they attended a school near, we entered the school-room, and may I never see the like again.[26] In one corner was a pile of potatoes, kept from rolling down by stones, on which the ragged barefooted children were seated. In another corner was a pile of cart-wheels, which were used for the same purpose; and in the middle of the room was a circular hole made in the ground, for the turf fire. Not a window, chair, or bench could be seen. The pupils, with scarcely a book, looked more like children who had sheltered themselves there in a fright, to escape the fury of a mad animal, or the tomahawk of some yelling savage, than those who had assembled for the benefit of the light of science. This was a Connemara school, and it was all they could do. I had seen sprinkled all over Ireland, schools in miserable cabins, where were huddled from forty to seventy in a dark room without a chimney; but they had benches to sit upon, and their school-room was upon the wayside, while this one was in a wet back-yard. Those parents who are able, pay a penny a week; those who are not, pay nothing; while the wealthiest among them pay half a crown a quarter. I saw many schools of this kind, where the child takes a piece of turf under his arm, and goes two miles, and sometimes three, without breakfast. In many parts of the south, and among the mountains, they could eat but

once in the day from Christmas to the next harvest, and this meal is generally from two till three o'clock.

We now proceeded to the police-station. Here the wife of the
sergeant treated us politely, and placed a dinner of meat, bread, and potatoes before us; and the sergeant then sent two of his men to show us Diamond Mountain, so called from having upon the top a transparent stone
which resembles a diamond, and is used in breast-pins and bracelets.[27] We
waded through bog till the ascent became difficult, and the rain poured
down without mercy. We crawled under a shelving rock, but the furious
wind sent the drops to seek us out, and we again attempted the ascent. To
me it was quite difficult, and a little dangerous, my Indian-rubber shoes
slipping, and compelling me to crawl, and support myself by holding to
the heath. Here I lost a second pair of silver-mounted spectacles, which I
used entirely for reading, and which had served me years for that purpose.
I looked back to Lismore, renewed the lament there made at the loss of
my favourites, and felt that spectacle-troubles were peculiarly my lot.

The mountain was a mile high; one of the men had gained an eminence above us, and commenced rolling tremendous stones down the
precipice, which bounding from hillock to hillock, from rock to rock,
made a most frightful appearance as they tore their way, splitting and
thundering till the mountain trembled as by a slight earthquake. To finish
the drama, he crept upon the highest peak of the rock, where was poised
a stone of tons weight. He gave a desperate push, and dislodged it. I saw
the first movement of his body and fell upon my face, supposing man and
rock were tumbling together. The young woman had succeeded in reaching a shelving part of the cliff, and was holding by some twigs. I ventured,
as the thundering a little ceased, to peep up, and saw her standing like a
petrified monument, her white naked feet looking like marble. When the
rock had shattered in fragments, all was still, and the police-man called
out, "I am here." I looked, there he sat upon the frightful pinnacle, happy,
as he afterwards acknowledged, that he did not pay for his presumption
by going headlong.

The steep upon which the young woman stood was nearly perpendicular; she had contrived to accomplish the ascent by disrobing her feet,
and insisted that I should do the same, and follow her. "Here," she said,
"you can see all the world, and all the sea, and here, too, is a cave." I crept
up with my Indian-rubbers upon my feet, but so steep and so slippery was
it, that I could retain my position only by holding fast to the heath. Here
was a cave like a room, with a stone in the middle for a seat, and the roof
of square stones as if laid by the hand of man. It seemed impossible that

this could be the work of nature, yet what monk or chieftain could carry up his food and his water, and subsist upon the mountain? It was a proud height. A mile were we sitting, or rather hanging, above the level where we commenced, and the sea and earth seemed spread beneath us. The presumptuous man kept his position, looking at the crumbling fragments, and said he well nigh lost his balance, and was shocked at his own bold exploit. We could not reach the diamonds. The rain was pouring, and how to descend was the question. The bare-footed girl could keep her hold, while my slippery rubbers exposed me at every step to a long slide which might be fatal. But by sitting down and sliding where walking was impossible, I succeeded in reaching a cabin near the bottom, in time to secure a couple of roasted potatoes, which the adventurous policeman and girl had prepared from a heap in the corner, where was a fire, and a little girl only to keep it.

We reached the barracks, leaving the diamonds to sparkle at a distance, as all diamonds generally do. But a kind lady gave me some fine specimens which were gathered from the rock, and nothing now remained but to compose my mind with the loss of the spectacles, and a breast-pin of Killarney curiosity in addition.

A good fire and pot of potatoes dried our clothes and filled our mouths; and now for the lodging. The policeman had promised to secure this, but deferred it till night, when we had no time for choosing. And if the compassionate reader had been touched by our mountain adventure, let his sympathies follow us to the lobby at least of our resting-place.

As the policeman led us to the door, "You will as usual," he said, "find cattle in the room, but you will have a clean bed." Ah, the poor hapless girl and myself tested that bed! We entered the house, two cows were lying and chewing their cud, and a horse caparisoned with a straw saddle taking his supper. The mistress was sitting on a stone projecting from the chimney, her head up the pipe of it, smoking. She could lodge us "right well," and we were shown into the room, our feet sticking upon the floor, which when damp is like pitch and tar. We instantly committed ourselves to our fate. The father and mother soon joined us, and men, women, and boys were in an almost open loft over our heads.

Daylight did certainly dawn; we rose in good time, paid our bill, and said good morning to the mistress, leaving her in the same spot where we found her, and at the same employment, with her cows and horse by her side.

Tully was the next destined post, without breakfast. Wind and rain confronted us at every step; we called at the cabins when we could not help it, and certainly they were among the miserable. It was twelve when we reached Tully. I had gone supperless to bed, had passed a sleepless night, and walked through mud and rain till twelve, and now felt the need of food. To our sad disappointment, not a loaf of bread was in the town, and the good Methodist lady where we stopped said there had been none for six weeks![28] Can you believe, who may read this, that in 1845, when there had been no failure of crops, an assize town with tasty-looking houses lived six weeks on nothing but potatoes! An old man kept a shop with a little flour, but so rare was the call for it that he was out of town most of the time, leaving his door locked. He returned that day, so that by two o'clock my hunger was a little calmed by a soda cake. We then visited the National school, taught by the son of the woman where we stopped, and found it under good regulations. The teacher had a salary of twelve pounds a year.

We walked out of town; stopped at a cabin where a Catholic old man, who had been a sailor, kept us too long; for so powerful was the effluvia from various kinds of filth of cabin and cattle, that the girl, though used to such places, became nauseated, turned pale, and was faint. We gladly got out into the fresh air, but the girl was quite ill for an hour. We sought a decent house, found a decent bed, and paid a decent price, and took a breakfast of potatoes with the good Methodist woman. Walked back, and took a second tour on Diamond Mountain for the spectacles, all unavailing, and we returned to Clifden, certainly wiser than we were three days before, and I was certainly poorer.[29] The next morning for Omey.

At an early hour I set off from Clifden (the capital) to visit this island, the distance of seven miles. Reaching a village of the most ancient kind, such as houses of stone, constructed like a loose stone wall, without gable ends – some with tops like a bee-hive, or inverted basket – some with holes for smoke to ascend, and some with no way for its escape but through the door; I selected one of the largest dimensions, knowing that there would be a full turn-out from every cabin and potato-field in sight and hearing.[30] I was not disappointed. As if by magic, in a few moments every neighbouring cabin was vacated, the hillside and bog had not a foot to tread them – every spade was dropped, and in a few moments the ground of the cabin was literally packed with men, women, and children, in rags and tatters – some with hair erect, and some with caps, and some with hats, but more with none. In one solid mass they all sat down upon their haunches, and began their welcomes to Ireland, and their wonder that so "goodly of body should leave so fine a country to see such a poor people;" my polka coat, my velvet bonnet, and all that outwardly appertained to me passed in review. Taking out a tract, I read a little, while they wondered at my "plain spache," and thanked God that they had seen such a devotee, going, as they supposed, on penance. "And sure ye must be hungry – and such a dacent body wouldn't ait a potato." Assuring them I was not hungry, they all rose and joined in one universal valedictory of, "God bless ye, and speed ye on yer journey." One woman followed me out, and begged me to turn into her cabin and take an egg; I told her that I was greatly obliged that she should show me so much kindness, but I must hasten to secure a walk across the strand before the tide should set in.[31]

I crossed the strand, and reached an island a mile in diameter, of one rude pile of stone, with a little patch now and then of green, without a road, the foot-paths being so obscured by sand blown in from the beach, that guess-work was my only guide. Here were huts, some of stone, and some of mud; and here, too, were habitations dug in the sand, as rabbits burrow, and whole families live therein; an aperture to crawl in admits the inmates, serving as door, window, and chimney; on the ground straw is spread, which serves for table, bed, and chair. At each end of this island live the owners, called "lords."[32]

The miseries of that island must be seen to be believed. I went into a hut, and found a family about drawing their stools around a basket of potatoes. They received me with much urbanity, made sensible enquiries of my country, and spoke of the good she had done to poor Ireland. Seeing that their dinner was cooling, I said, "Your potatoes look quite tempting, sir; may I take one?" "Take one!" said the delighted wife, "would ye ate one?" The man added, "I was ashamed, ma'am, to be seen aitin' 'em while you was in. This is a dry bit, without milk or butter, ma'am, and yer country never ait like this." "Can you read?" I asked. "I could once, ma'am, but my eyes are growin' dim." I handed him a tract, and he read tolerably; went out, and called his son to choose one from my bundle for himself, as I had given him the privilege. They had selected the finest potatoes for me, and toasted them upon the coals. They had two guests beside; a beggar, and a friend of their own, and all had a scanty dinner but myself. The guests would not eat till I was well supplied, and the poor man did not make a comfortable meal, and this was the only meal for the day.

The son was sent to show me the path to Lady M—, and, wading ankle-deep in sand, I made my way to it, and found an entrance into the kitchen.[33] The lady had gone to Clifden, and the floorless room was a deposit for calves, pigs, hens, and ducks. Two servants were sitting on the hearth, and handing one a tract, which had a red cover, the scene that followed I better *felt* than my tongue or pen can describe. The girl went out, and in a few minutes the dilapidated door, with a tremendous noise, was burst open, pouring in a host of men, boys, and girls, who were employed planting potatoes; and they with consent pounced upon me, demanding books, and they must be *red* ones. Begging them to be quiet, and I would make an equal distribution (having about fifty with me) – they would hear to none of this, but rummaged my basket, demanding an entrance into my pocket, all clamouring at once, some in Irish, and others in broken English, while the servant girl stood aghast. A man more manageable than the rest, who had entered before the mob, and had been reading a tract, declared to them that the books were "dacent," and that they were blackguards; and after I had given the only one in my possession, he succeeded by physical force to drag them out of the house – such as were dragable, while the others took their own time and own way. I made off, with an apology from the servant, that she could give me nothing to eat, as all was "locked up."

My next depot was to be at the extremity of the island, where lived the other "lady."[34] She, too, was out; but I was admitted into the kitchen, and had a quiet survey of what was passing there. Here I counted sixty-three living and moving beings, quadruped and biped, besides such as walked erect – a kennel of dogs, three coops for hens, chickens and ducks, a calf or two, a pen of young pigs, a fold of sheep and lambs, and an able-bodied goat – these all walked and talked each his own language, with no pugnacious symptoms; and if the "lion and lamb did not lie down together," the goat and lamb did.

But the "lady" – she entered with a goodly-looking daughter of fifteen, both attired in long linen coats, with respectable tails reaching nearly to the ground, worn by the father and brother. They passed through in dignified silence, and in a moment the lady returned saying, "Come down to the parlour." I went down to the parlour, and here was a ground floor, a dirty-looking bed, a few wooden-bottom chairs, and a table by the wall, with one leaf turned up, and a platter of potatoes and a cup of milk. "Will you take some dinner?" I did not decline, for I was hungry, and a long walk before me, and the tide not yet out, and the sun was set. The lady was young-looking and handsome, and the mother of sixteen hopefuls, was rich, and rode out to Clifden, giving great dinners in the city, and on the island assimilating herself to the society around her.

Eight o'clock, the tide was said to be out, and I had a strand of a mile to cross, and six miles to Clifden then before me. A boy was sent to show me the shortest course, and when I had nearly reached the strand, a girl called out, "The mistress says maybe you'll come back, and stop all night." A strange oversight, my pride answered, that this invitation was not given before. I thanked the child and went on, quite to my disadvantage. Midway the strand the sea was quite deep: I waded in and stood demurring; the night was dark, and to find a passage out seemed impossible. I turned back, and made my way to the "lady's;" she then made a shrewd investigation of the cause of my visit. Looking at her altogether, her savage living, her ragged dress, and pretence to high rank, I was disgusted to find myself at the option of such an "out of the way affair," and I told her plainly I came to Ireland because I had a *right* to come; that they were daily sending loads of beggared and abused emigrants to us, and I had come to see how and what they could be at home; and making the application to her own kitchen, she understood me when I said, "I have seen, and am satisfied." She was rebuked, and treated me with uncommon attention through the evening. She gave me a clean bed, in a floorless room, a cup of milk by my side to drink in the night, and in the morning presented me with a dish of potatoes, and I was sorry she had no bread; declining the potatoes, I walked the seven miles without eating, and was much enriched by what I had seen.

My way home was intricate. I found myself entangled in rocks, after crossing the strand, and was a full hour climbing and creeping to get out. I at last found the road, and the village where I stopped the preceding day, and had another meeting. One woman among them had been bred in Galway, and invited me into her cabin, which though dark was cleanly, and remarked that Connemara had greatly improved in the last twenty years. That then their time was spent in the most degrading vicious manner that could be imagined; the can of whiskey was carried from cabin to cabin, and whole days and nights spent in glee and drunkenness; and their persons, their cabins, and their beds so filthy that they were intolerable to all but themselves. I assured her the latter was now the case throughout Ireland, so far as I had travelled; and were it not that they were God's creatures, made in his image; and bound to his tribunal, I would say of many of them, "He that is filthy let him be filthy still," before I would risk my eyes, my nose, or my garments within galloping distance of their multitudinous disgusting unmentionables. "No hope," she sighed, "for poor Ireland!" Glad was I to see Clifden, having eaten scarcely three ounces of food since I left it.

CHAPTER XXVI

Misfortunes in Clifden – Reverse of Fortune – An Aged Pilgrim – Eager Listeners – Visit to a Dying Man – Glorious Sunset – An officious Policeman – Lady Clare – Arrival in Galway – Obtrusiveness of the Women – A Sermon on Baptism – Journey to Westport – Introduction to Mr. Pounden –A devoted Presbyterian Minister – Sketch of a Christian Missionary, such as Ireland needs – Croagh Patrick – Hazardous Ascent of the Mountain – Grand Prospect from the Summit – Return to Westport – Doubts Removed – Filial Affection – A Poor Protestant

Saturday morning. – While across the street speaking to a blind man, my purse was robbed of three half-crowns and a few pennies, by a little servant girl, who had seen me take out some, and run out in haste, leaving my purse and bag upon my bed. Clifden was an unfortunate spot for me. A pair of new gloves had been taken the day previous, my spectacles and breast-pin lost, and now my money. Went out and visited schools, found one in miserable plight, crowded, dirty, and noisy, and the teacher in keeping with the whole.' A second was a well ordered one, the teacher a man of sense as well as learning. A family who opened a boarding school, invited me to pass a few days in their house, and I found them with the remains of a ruined fortune, struggling to educate their own children by teaching others. A class of people quite plentiful throughout Ireland are those who once were in higher life, and are now struggling to keep their hold of the crazy boat. But those are generally found to be the better sort of society; having been schooled in affliction, they have felt the uncertainty of all earthly calculations, and by intercourse with the enlightened class of the community, they have acquired knowledge and habits which make them interesting, and often useful acquaintances. Their pride at the same time has been so wounded, that, if not humbled effectually, they are more condescending and more communicative to such as are below them.

In the family where I lodged resided the mother of the mistress of the house, and she was a character worthy of a place in a better journal than mine. She had seen more than four-score years, yet her intellect was clear, and though infirm, not peevish; cleanly and attractive in her person. By her bed-side I passed many a pleasant hour, reading to her attentive mind the Word of God. One evening after reading, she added, "What blessed words! what blessed words! and may I ask you what you think of the Virgin?" I told her, and added, as I have ever done, the reason why I do not worship her; "because God had not enjoined it;" and then read the 18th and 19th verses of the last chapter of Revelations.[2] She exclaimed, "O my God! what have I done if this be true? what have I done? God have mercy on me." She continued this for some time, she wept, and prayed that God might forgive her; and during my stay, whenever she heard my footsteps in an adjoining room, she would enquire if I were coming in, and if I would read, still continuing the lamentation about the Blessed Virgin. "What shall I do! what shall I do!" she often asked, and was as often told to go to Jesus; and I believe she did go.

Sabbath. – I spent five hours reading by the side of her bed, and was surrounded with a roomful of the most attentive hearers, in great admiration – so much so, it was often difficult to proceed. I read a tract on the operation of the Holy Spirit upon the heart, and an aged man sitting by exclaimed, "Blessed Jesus, who ever haird the like! I'm an ould man, and never before knew rightly what was the meaning of the Holy Ghost. Did ye ever?" he said to the listeners. "No, no," was the united answer. The chapel bell was sounding every hour, when one said, "We hav'n't been to mass this mornin'." "And, hav'n't we haird more than we should there? The like of this raidin' we shouldn't hear in many a day's walk." I was obliged to close. Five hours of constant reading and talking affected my voice, and I could only commend them to God, and say adieu for ever. As they lingered, blessing and thanking me, one said, "Aw, no mass was ever like this, I could be listenin' till the mornin'." These people are asking to be fed, and their ears are open to instruction; but the little facility of reading which the adults possess puts it out of their power to attain much information, and their extreme poverty prevents their giving an advanced education to their children.

Thursday, May 15th. – Prepared to depart, gave all the farewells to the family, and while the trembling hand of the old lady to whom I had read so much pressed mine, her still more trembling voice said, "The Almighty God be with ye, and I do believe we shall meet in heaven." I felt grateful to God that I had met this old pilgrim, and cheered her a little on her passage to the grave. She knew, she felt, that she was on the confines of the eternal world, and her only desire was that Christ would be glorified in her, and fit her to depart in peace. Mrs. M, her daughter, and the young woman who accompanied me to Tully, went out with me a mile on my way, and we called at a cabin to see a sick woman, who the day previous was present at the long reading. I was now obliged to say adieu to my companions, and Clifden for ever. It was painful to leave the interesting girl, who had seen better days in the life-time of her father, and is now destitute of those means of acquiring that instruction which she is so anxious to obtain.

Galway was my destination, and I ascended a car of the common kind, in company with a young married woman, and Wm. Keane, the good man who had offered me a ride from Roundstone at the half-way house. He had a noble heart, and some refinement of manner. I begged to stop at the cabin of the kind man who gave me a lodging on the bundle of straw. Mr. K. went to the door, and called him. He crept out, tottering to the road, a handkerchief about his head; his pale face, his bright eye, and husky voice telling that consumption was consuming his vitals. "I can get no good here, ma'am, and plaise God I shall go back to Tralee if the good God don't take me away." I presented him a Testament, telling him it was the good book I read to him when there. "An' God bless ye, and warn't ye a blessin' to me when in my cabin, and I can do nothing to pay ye." I gave the children some books, and as he turned away, he spoke in a low tone to Mr. K., "Take care of that woman; she's a blessin' to Ireland. She was a blessin' to me; and God I know will bless her." This was too much, when I had been so hospitably sheltered from the storm at his expense. It was I who had received the blessing, and as I saw him slowly creep to his cabin, and knew that he must soon stand disembodied before his Judge, I prayed that the good seed sown in his heart might spring up to eternal life.

We called at Mr. Steely's, where I stayed on my way to Clifden; stopped long enough to roast me a couple of potatoes, and distribute a few tracts. Then passed the pleasant lakes where I read to the old man and his daughter. It was a sunny day, and the mountain and lake scenery was exceedingly beautiful. We reached the Protestant family where I had promised to leave some books, and was entreated to spend a night with them, but could not. "She is the loveliest woman," said Mr. Keane, when we had gone out, "that ever lived on these wild mountains. She's a Christian." He was a Catholic, yet her godly example convinced him that she was a follower of Christ.

It was now about sun-setting, and the ride to Outerard was more than interesting. Such a sun-setting and such a twilight by sea or by land I never beheld. When the sun sank behind the mountain, he left a scollopped edge of gold, leaving the lofty peaks below tinted with the richest blue. The sky, the lakes, and the curling smoke from the cabins upon the sides of the mountains, where the poor peasants had built their evening fires to boil their potatoes – the rustics returning from labour, or from the market at Outerard – the crescent moon looking out as if modestly waiting to do what she could when the sun should retire, made a scene of the liveliest and loveliest interest.

I almost regretted reaching the town of Outerard, but here found pleasant accommodation, and in the morning passed out to walk through the town while the car was getting ready. A policeman stepped up, "Are ye Lady Clare, ma'am?"³ "I am not Lady Clare, sir, but Mrs. N. from New York." "From New York! and what brought you here?" "To see you, sir, and the rest of the good people of Ireland." "To see me, ah! and you know it's my duty to enquire of every suspicious person that comes along what their business is." "Indeed, sir! every suspicious person! And is it your duty to ask every person who passes peaceably through your country what his business is, and to give an account of himself?" "It is, ma'am." "Then you have duties which no other policeman understands, for I have travelled a great part of Ireland, and the police-officers have treated me with the greatest kindness." He turned away, went to the sergeant, and asked if he should arrest me. The officer told him no, to be off about his business; and the woman who accompanied me lectured him so severely for "tratin' a dacent body so," telling him he was "a saucy red-head," that he walked away, silenced, if not ashamed.

This Lady Clare I was told, some twelve years ago, was a gentleman in disguise, who went about the country, inducing the labouring people to swear they would not work for less than a stipulated sum, much greater than present wages, with sundry advantages beside. And if the landlord refused compliance, they would turn out in the night, and dig up his meadows, so that he would be compelled to till them. This game it was said was not in operation in Clare, and the newly initiated policeman, hearing I had come to visit the poor, determined to show his loyalty to government by bringing the lady before it in due season.

We reached Galway, and I felt more inclined to be home-sick than in any place I had before been. I took a different lodging from my old one, but found no improvement; and was terribly annoyed by the Galway women following me from street to street, from alley to alley, fixing their full unblinking eyes upon me. Their ugly teeth, their red petticoats, and repulsive manners made them second to none, even the Connaught corduroys, in all that was to be dreaded.

Sabbath Day. – I went in search of a Methodist chapel; a young man generously offered to show the way, and I found myself seated in a gallery in a Catholic one.⁴ It was late, and the sermon on baptism had commenced. A good exhortation was given to parents to train their children faithfully in the fear of God. The sermon was closed by particular directions how to baptize effectually, should any layman be called, on a special emergency, to perform the rite. We were told emphatically to remark, that in pronouncing the name of the Trinity, if each distinct person in the Godhead were not spoken or named with great slowness and distinctness, the baptism would be good for nothing. This was repeated, that each might be enlightened, and all faithfully enjoined not to forget it. At evening I visited the Protestant Sabbath-school, and listened to a lady explaining the lessons to her pupils, who showed much knowledge of the scriptures, and appeared to be deeply impressed with their value herself.[5]

Monday, May 27th. – I took the car to Westport, a distance of fifty miles. Stopped while the horses were changing, and asked for a penny's worth of bread and a potato.[6] The bread was brought, but was quite sour; they had no potatoes. Asked for a little milk, a girl went to the cow, and with unwashed hands milked a few spoonfuls into a tea-cup, and presented it fresh from the mint. I refused the filthy-looking beverage, took a halfpenny's worth of the sour bread, and asked for my bill. "Sixpence," was the answer. A York shilling for a cent's worth of bread! "A good profit," I said. They paid back threepence. I found in most hotels in Galway and Kerry, what I had not met so much elsewhere, a disposition to take the most they could get, however extravagant the sum.

A few hours brought us to Westport. The coachman provided me a wholesome lodging-place. The next day being sunny, I enjoyed a treat, walking alone over the shady grounds of Lord Sligo, by the side of pleasant water, with all the etceteras of a gentleman's demesne who lived for pleasure. He had died a few months before, leaving his great estate to a son who follows his steps.[7] – "Whatsoever a man soweth that shall he also reap."[8] A monument erected by the citizens to his agent, in honour of his benevolence, is a pleasing testimonial of gratitude, and says that there is a capability in the Irish heart, even among the most degraded and poor, to reciprocate kindness, and a quick perception of justice when exercised toward them.[9] On my return, called into a Protestant school, conducted like all parochial schools in the country, and by the teacher was introduced to Mr. Pounden, the rich rector, whose estate and splendour, I was informed, were not much inferior to those of Lord Sligo.[10] From him I ascertained that considerable had been done for schools, and the spreading of the scriptures among the poor; and I was told by others that he is a man of benevolence, improving the condition of many around him. My next call was to the house of a Scotch Presbyterian, named Smith. I mention his name because I delight to dwell upon it; the remembrance of those "mercy-drops" in the desert, where I was often very hungry and thirsty, is pleasant to the soul." His wife, who is of a good family in England, received and welcomed me with all that Christian courtesy that made me feel myself at home among kind friends. Something was immediately brought me to eat, and presented in that manner and abundance that said, "You will oblige me greatly by partaking unsparingly." Reader, did you ever eat a slice of the "bread of covetousness?" I assure you I have, and it is bitter, sour, indigestible, and quite unfit for a healthy stomach. This was not such bread.

This family's benevolence was on the lips of all the poor in the vicinity; though with a stinted salary, that salary is divided among the children of want, till, as I was informed, oftentimes a scanty supply is left for their own necessities. Would to God, Ireland could boast many more such among the full-fed, over-paid clergy of the country. Here I found a devoted, active, efficient Bible-reader, with a salary of thirty pounds a year, who goes from house to house among all classes, and explains the Word of God to those who have not access to it. He met in most cases with a kind reception, and why? Because he went with the love of God in his heart, and talked of this love; held up Christ and him crucified, which is all the sinner needs. If love will not melt the flinty heart, will bitterness do it? I truly believe that the Word of God would not only have been received with willingness, but sought after by the greater part of the peasantry of Ireland, had it been presented with no sectarian denunciations, and had all the teachers, like this one, been humble, self-denying, and kindly. It is a most important item in the qualification of teachers, that they understand human nature in its various developments. It is not enough that they can pronounce well, elevate and depress the voice according to the rules of punctuation, expatiate on the eloquence of St. Paul, or the sin of Ananias." They should know well not only the broad avenues to the heart, but the narrow streets; yes, and every repulsive forbidding alley. They should know, too, the time of day when these paths can most prudently and easily be trodden. There is not a heart but has its waxings and wanings; there is not a temperament but has its ebbings and flowings; and, like the skillful mariner, they should know where to cast anchor, and when to trim the sails. They should know when in deep water, and when near shoals and quicksands. In travelling the entire coast of Ireland, I needed not to see a Bible-reader, to know his abilities or faithfulness. The Irish peasantry have an uncommonly just conception of propriety and impropriety, right and wrong, benevolence and covetousness. A dabster at his trade, or a filthy-lucre labourer is quickly discerned. "Lay not careless hands," &c.[13]

I was now in the vicinity of the celebrated mountain, where we are told St. Patrick stood, when he banished the venomous serpents from the island.[14] Its lofty sharp peak, at a distance, towering to the skies, looked as if it could scarcely afford breadth for more than one foot at a time. But here we are told the holy saint stood, and here we are shown the prints of his knees where he prayed. Here, too, is an altar for worship, and here the inhabitants of the adjacent parishes assemble yearly, at an early hour, on the last Friday in July, to perform what they call stations.[15] Multitudes are seen climbing the difficult and dangerous ascent, from the town of Westport, to mingle with fellow pilgrims from other parts; to go nine times around a pile of stones, call their sins to remembrance, ask forgiveness, and promise better lives in future.[16] A sprightly young girl I had met on the path offered to accompany me at an early hour to the mountain. I called at her door and knocked; the girl was asleep, and I passed on. A country school-master soon accosted me, and learning who I was, walked a mile with me, to give a history of his school and country. Like most country school-teachers, he had become acquainted with the hearths of all the domiciles in his parish; and to appearance he could rival Goldsmith's controversialist: –

"For e'en though vanquished, he could argue still."[17]

He told me it would be presumptuous to attempt the ascent of the mountain alone, and begged me not to think of it. "You will be lost, and never find your way; and should any accident befall you, no one could know it, and you would perish alone." This was all good sense, and I was more than mad that I did not heed it. Reaching the foot of the mountain, a cabin woman met me, and offered her bright lad as a guide, for any trifle that the lady might plase to give. I offered as a trial twopence halfpenny, for I did not intend taking a guide if possible to avoid it. "Oh, he shall not go for that; but as you are a lone solitary cratur, he shall go cheaper than he ever did, and that's for a sixpence." I happily got rid of the annoyance in this way, and heard, after passing the door, "She'll be destroyed." I went on, and enquired of another the best path. A man answered, "And do ye think ye could reach the top alone? no mortal bein' could do it. But one man ever did it, and then declared he wouldn't do the like again for all the parish. But I have as sprightly a little gal as is in all the country, who will show ye every inch." I made the same offer as to the woman, and received the same answer, and I found him willing to run the risk of having me killed, which he assured me must be the case, rather than lend me a guide for a trifle. I mention these two cases, as the only ones I now recollect in all Ireland, who refused me a favour for a small equivalent.

It was now two o'clock: three Irish miles from the main road, was the top of the mountain said to be.[18] I looked up, the sun was shining, the air was breezy, my strength and spirits were good, and why should I hesitate, when I had so many times in Ireland done more out-of-the-way "impossibilities?" I went on, but soon was lost in miry bog, and intricate windings of deceitful paths, for two hours.[19] At last I lost a beautiful Testament, which had been my companion for many a mile; and when looking for that, a man called out, "Ye arn't thinkin' ye can go up the mountain to-night? Darkness'll be once before ye reach the top, and ye'll perish there. Go home, and some long day bring a friend with ye. Ye're out of the path; the fowls might pick yer bones upon this mountain, and not a ha'p'orth be haird about it." This looked a little discouraging, and I sat down to consider. I looked up at the dizzy height above, then at the sun; thought what a prospect I should have at the top, of the beautiful islands, the sea, and the lakes under my feet; and I made the fruitless effort to find the path. It was a fearful undertaking, and I record it not as a proof of valour or wisdom; it was the height of folly, if not recklessness. By crawling and pulling, a little was gained, till ahead I saw a white track, taking a circuitous route around a smaller mountain, which was to lead to the great one in view. I reached it and sat down; the prospect here was beautiful, was grand. I solaced my eyes, and endeavoured to make up my mind that this would answer without proceeding. But this could not satisfy me. I was in Ireland, on the side of one of its loftiest and most celebrated mountains, and though a dangerous ascent, yet younger and older feet had reached the top, and what others had done I could do. But I was alone, and the hour was late. What if some joint should be dislocated, or I should stumble and go headlong? I might suffer days, and die at last unheeded. "I will go a few yards more and then stop." The few yards were attained. I sat down and said, "Am I tempting my Maker?" A little refreshed, and another point was gained, till a dizzy and almost perpendicular steep, with white round stones for a path – which had been washed by water till a channel was formed, in which lay these stones – was my only road. I made a desperate effort, crawling and holding by the heath where I could, till, almost exhausted, I ventured to look again, and saw a large loose pile of stones upon the top, and knew they must be the stations around which the devotees performed their penances. Another effort, and my feet stood upon the grand pinnacle.

The first sight was so picturesque and dazzling, I supposed my eyes were deceiving me, that the almost supernatural exertion had dimmed the true vision, and false images were flitting before them. Not so. A true map of the most beautiful varied finish was beneath me. Hundreds, yes, thousands of feet below me, were spread out lakes and islands in the ocean.[20] Fifty islands I counted upon my right hand, bordered with various colours; some fringed with sand, some with gravel, some with grass reaching to the water's edge. On the left was the bold island of Clare, looking like some proud king over all the rest. The sun was shining in full splendour, giving to all the appearance of a fairy land. The top of the mountain is oblong, and so narrow, that, had the wind been violent, I should have feared that I could not retain my footing, for the descent on every hand was almost perpendicular.

Here is an ancient pile of stones, and a kind of altar, on which the prints of St. Patrick's knees are shown, which he wore in the stone by constant kneeling.[21] Here, by some mystical virtue or power, he banished all the serpents; and whether, like the devils which entered into the herd of swine, these serpents had the privilege of entering into some other animals, or into men, certain it is, that they do not show themselves in any tangible shape in Ireland.[22] The sun was declining. I sang, and called to the inhabitants below; but they neither answered nor heard me. The descent was now the difficulty. There was another and safer path upon the other side, but this I did not know, and the frightful road was undertaken.[23] One misstep of my slippery Indian rubbers, one rolling of a stone upon which I was obliged to step, would have plunged me headlong. I felt my dependence, yet my nerve was steady. I trembled not, nor was I fearful; yet I felt that the cautions given by the schoolmaster and others near the mountain were no fictions. The sun had not two hours to shine upon the pinnacle, and I on its slippery side, nearly three miles from the abode of men. God's mercy never to me was more conspicuous than when I found myself unhurt at the bottom, for this mercy was shown me in my greatest presumption. I was not going here to see the poor, to instruct the ignorant, or to do good to any child of want. I went to gratify a desire to see the marvellous, and in the face and eyes of all kind caution to the contrary. I pray God I may never be so presumptuous again. When I reached the cabin where the boy was refused, I told the mother that had she sent him, I should have paid him well; but when I found her great concern for my safety was only to make a shilling, I would give him nothing. She immediately brought forth a plate of potatoes and a fish in return for my lecture, without a reproachful word, put them upon a chair before me, and

I ate a potato and went home to Westport, fatigued, yet happy that I had seen what I had, and had accomplished a feat which I was told neither man nor woman could accomplish alone.

The next day a fair was held in Westport.[24] Nothing new or interesting marked the occasion. The people in and about the town are a tolerably tidy-looking peasantry, and though they could not wholly refrain from staring at me, yet I was not in that imminent danger of being swallowed alive, that seemed to threaten me in Galway. Another pleasant call at Mr. Smith's made the day pass profitably. He invited me into his place of worship, which was near his house, and while there I had occasion to speak of a clergyman in Dublin, who was a friend of Mr. Smith, and from whom I had received a letter. I read the letter to him; he seemed pleased, as if a doubt had been loosened but not removed respecting my good character and intentions. Pausing a moment, he said, "And is that letter from my friend? Let me see the handwriting." He took a letter from the same clergyman out of his pocket-book, compared the writing, and seeing there was actually no forgery, he was apparently much gratified.

I was more pleased with the good man now than before; for though he had not intimated by a word that he was jealous of my real character, nor did I let him know that I understood his doubts about the letter, yet I now saw he had been vacillating; and notwithstanding, had he known me to be a saint, he could not have treated me more kindly in word and action than he had done. Though his Scotch caution whispered that he must be upon the watch-tower against deceivers, yet he was "careful to entertain strangers" until he proved that they were impostors.

The next morning I had hoped to visit the island of Clare, a distance of fourteen miles, but was disappointed in getting a boat, and turned my steps through a beautiful wood on Lord Sligo's estate. Half a mile took me to a house, out of which came a mother, two daughters, and a grand-daughter of six years old. This child's mother was in America, and had been gone nearly four years; but so indelibly fixed was the mother in the mind of the child that every woman that is a stranger she hopes may be the one she ardently desires to see. When she found I was from America, it was affecting to see the imploring look she cast upon me. The mother bade her daughter to accompany me through the wood, telling the grand-daughter to go into the house. The child obeyed, but we soon heard her in pursuit. She plucked the bluebell and primrose, and presented them to me; broke great boughs from the hawthorn, and filled my hands; looking with such a winning confidence into my face, that I wished her away. She followed me to the cabin where I stopped, and for three hours sat near me; her aunt could not persuade her to return, neither could I, but by giving her a book; and then she lingered and looked after me till she could see me no more. I found myself surrounded by a group of listeners, all Protestants. One aged man, who had renounced Popery, entered, and the meekness of his appearance distinguished him from the ordinary Christian. He was truly "meek and lowly." I presented him an Irish Testament, which he could read well, and he received it with the greatest gratitude. Reader, he was a beggar, going from cabin to cabin to ask his potato; one of the members of Christ's body, and a member of a rich Protestant church! Here was Christ presenting himself; and they all recognized him as a rare example; yet they sent him, poorly clad, hungry, and wary, from door to door – asking for what? A potato! Look at this, ye proud professed disciples of the Lord Jesus, and say, "What will ye do in the end thereof?"

I found these cabiners warm-hearted, and a tidy industrious people. The poor widow where I first stopped supported a family by weaving, working from sun to sun for tenpence a day at the loom.[25] I was escorted through the neighbourhood, invited to stay all night, and in the evening read to both Catholics and Protestants. The hearing of the ear is certainly given in these places, if not the understanding of the heart. I blessed God, after I passed away, that I had fresh proof that all was not lost that was done for these poor people.

CHAPTER XXVII

Sunday Sermons – Newport – A Relic of Better Days – Arrival at Achill Sound, and
Kind Reception from Mr. Savage and his Family – Visit to the Colony – Mr. Nan-
gle's Protestant Missionary Settlement – Molly Vesey's Lodgings – Visit to the
Schools at the Colony – Walk to the Keem Mountains – A Centenarian – The
Amethyst Quarries – The Author's Acknowledgments and Censures Explained –
Mr. Nangle's Weekday Lecture – Interview with Mr. and Mrs. Nangle – Doctrinal
Conversion is not all that is due to the Convert from Popery – A Reformed Roman
Catholic Priest – Renewed Hospitality at the Sound – Another Short Visit to the
Colony – Newport – Intemperance not banished from the County of Mayo –
Westport – Castlebar – Sligo – A Beautiful Glen – Hospitality in Death – Pic-
turesque Scenery of the County of Sligo – Return to Dublin – the Mendicity Asso-
ciation

Sabbath. – I heard Mr. Smith preach a solemn discourse from Peter, "Seeing that all these things must be dissolved," &c.[1] He invited me to his
house, and gave another proof that he obeyed the Apostle's injunction,
"Given to hospitality." Heard a fluent Derbyite give a discourse from,
"Behold the Lamb of God."[2] These people preach Christ in a clear and
convincing manner, and show that they have been taught of him.

I now prepared to visit Achill, which had from my first visit to Ireland
been the spot I most ardently desired to see.[3] I had heard that it was a little oasis, where the wilderness had been converted into a fruitful field. I
walked six miles to Newport, and called on the Bible-reader of the Independent church, and by his hospitable wife was made most welcome.[4] A
breakfast was soon before me, and an invitation to stop; but as her husband was absent, I engaged on my return to call and spend a night with
them, hoping to hear more particulars about his mission. I passed on,
overtook a poor man walking slowly with a pack upon his back, and said
to him, "We are walking the same way, and you look in ill health." He was
cleanly dressed, and his whole appearance said he had seen better days. "I
am palsied, ma'am, on one side, and can move but slowly." His history was,
that he had been a police-officer, had been struck with the palsy, and was
dumb for three months. He went to Scotland, England, and France to be
cured, spent all he had, became a beggar, and finally by teaching had been

able to purchase a few goods, which he was trying to sell about the country. He was a Roman Catholic, and said he always kept a bible till he was palsied; it was then lost, and he had not been able to buy one since. He added, "I am a sinner, and fear I shall never be saved." "Go to Jesus," was my reply. His ready answer was, "But I must go in faith, and how shall I get that faith? I must go, nothing doubting, for 'He that doubteth is like a wave of the sea.'"' This was sound doctrine, and I sent up a hearty petition that God would put suitable words into my mouth, to speak in season to that enquiring soul. I endeavoured to do so, he thanked me, and gave an interesting recital of the exercises of his mind during his sickness, and since he was able to move again upon the face of the earth. I presented him a Testament. He took it, much gratified, and promised to read it daily; he had already been enlightened by the Holy Spirit into many of its truths, and could teach many who had read it much more. He walked so slowly that I bade him good morning, and passed on to stop at a house and rest a little. While there, he went by, and we fell in company again, and soon overtook a tidily dressed woman, who was his wife. Again we talked on the same good subject, but the mind of his wife was still in darkness.

They left me at a poor town, I supposed for ever, and I reached the Sound at eight o'clock. It was a desired haven for my weary feet, and yet I dreaded to enter it. I looked about on the wild shore, to ascertain where I should find shelter if not received at the hotel. I saw nothing, and made an ingress in the only door I saw, which took me to the kitchen, and asked a little girl if I could have entertainment. She could not tell, but would ask the mistress. The mistress in a moment was before me; and when I saw her uncommonly tall figure, I shrank; but when her kindly soothing voice said, "You are fatigued, and you had better walk down to the room," I felt it was the voice of a friend.⁶ In this room were no pigs, hens, calves, or goats. It was a well-ordered inviting place; an air of comfort, health, and peace said, here is the mother whose daughters shall "arise up and call her blessed." Every question was put to ascertain my wants; they enquired not the strange object of my journey, nor my pedigree, but, "What can we do to make you most comfortable?" O, these are mercy-drops to a lone stranger, far, far from home. These are kindnesses which Christ will remember when he shall say, "I was a stranger, and ye took me in."

A fine little ruddy boy of twelve months was laughing in a sister's lap, and saying, by the clapping of his tiny hands and sparkling of his eyes, "Welcome, welcome, stranger." This boy was the twenty-first child of that mother, all in the dust but four; three lovely daughters moved in that house like young blossoms of future promise. Gladly would I have stayed for weeks; but when two nights and a day had refreshed my weary limbs, and healed a little my irritated feet, I looked across the Sound, and made preparations for leaving their comfortable carpets, cheerful fires, and wholesome beds, and felt that I was leaving home. "Go," said Mrs. Savage, "and stay a week upon the island. Visit the schools, and the cabins, and the curiosities of the island, and you will be well paid."

I had heard much of the indefatigable Mr. Nangle, and wished to hear from his own lips the success of his mission, his sacrifices, and future prospects.[7] I had heard that a fault-finding tourist had been that way, and carried out some evil reports; and I had heard that persecutors had risen up around him, and he sought redress by the arm of the law.[8] Though that law gave him the victory, yet some few lips that had read the gospel whispered that "carnal weapons" were never fitted for the missionary of the cross. I had heard that the benevolent Dr. Adams had left all, and devoted himself unpaid to that arduous work, and that the faithful humble curate was a meek pattern of humility to all around him. On him I was requested to call, and was offered a note to him from Westport for that purpose.[9] These different items made up the sum total of information I had gathered about Achill, and, putting all into the account, my impressions were more favourable than otherwise.

At an early hour I crossed the Sound, intending to walk till the public car should overtake me.[10] I entered the colony without the car, and enquired for Mr. Lowe, the curate.[11] He was not at home. The man of whom I enquired invited me into his house, and told his wife to put on the tea-kettle. Telling her I did not use tea, she presented me with good domestic bread, milk, and potatoes. When the dinner was finished, I was shewn into the dining-hall, where dinner for the orphans was preparing. Nearly one hundred, I was told, were here fed, clothed, and taught to read and work.[12] It was neat and inviting, and the food wholesome and abundant. I certainly was more than pleased. I was grateful that my eyes had seen, and I could testify for myself, that here was a group of children from Ireland's poor that needed no pity. The neat white cabins, and the colony as a whole, looked to me attracting; a barren soil had been converted into a fruitful field by the hand of industry. It was now nearly sunset, and lodging must be found. The hotel was not quite in readiness, and no private lodgings I was told were in the colony, and I was directed to a hill out of the colony, to a "respectable tidy house kept by Molly Vesey."

I walked and waded through deep sand till the hill was ascended, and the huts, of rough stone, flung together without mortar, without gables and circular at the top, made one of the most forbidding looking spots that I had ever seen.[13] Winding among the huddled kraals, to ascertain whether it was possible that a being who had breathed a civilized air could tarry there for a night, I at last was directed to Molly Vesey's. As I looked in, "And is this in truth the tidy lodging-house, where the good people of the colony directed a stranger to lodge? Is this the domicile where the thrifty manager has gathered two hundred pounds, and put it in safe keeping for posterity?" A cow was in the kitchen; a man not of the "finest and fairest" was smoking in a corner; a two pail-full pot was boiling a supper of lumpers, but Molly was not in. I sat down, and she soon entered, and making my wants known, I was invited "to walk down." Hope revived – something better might be in reserve. My fate was fixed. I turned my eyes upon the frightful bed on which I was to be laid, and said, must I drink this bitter cup? A pile of stools, barrels, and such like etceteras, with a long table, made up the furniture, and in the midst of this I was seated. I was for a few moments in a profound reverie. And is this the outer porch of the superb temple I had come to visit? Surely the architect must have a few mouldings and rimmings yet to put on before the fabric will be quite finished. My meditations were soon broken by Molly's entering with a feather bed, and placing it upon a bench; the long table was drawn into a central part of the room, a chair put at one end, a half barrel across it serving two purposes – to lengthen the table, and elevate my head. Seeing what was in reserve, I asked, "What are you doing?" "Making you a nice bed, ma'am." "Why not put me upon the bedstead?" "A stranger sleeps there." "A stranger! Who is this stranger?" "A nice man, ma'am." This was the man who was smoking in the corner when I entered. "And you mean, madam, to put a man into this room to-night?" "What harrum, what harrum?" My indignation was aroused, not did it settle entirely on the head of Molly. In the mouth of two or three witnesses was it established at the colony, that Molly Vesey was not only a respectable woman, but kept a respectable tidy house; and yet that same Molly sold whiskey, and by this got her wealth. Is this then the standard of morality, propriety, and tidiness elevated by the colonists for strangers to gather about? Do you ask the names of these witnesses? I do not know, or gladly would I put them upon this paper. "You may, please, carry your bed away, good woman. I shall not sleep upon it." A whisper was given to the girl, and then, turning to me, "You shall sleep on the bedstead." I was the loser on the score of cleanliness. Had I slept upon the barrel, I might have had a clean cover for my pillow; but I had the room, with all its indescribables, to my own independent self, and in the morning awoke to a brighter view of what appertained to this "tidy lodging-place." A plate of potatoes was offered, which I declined, paid for my accommodations, and was about to depart, when a loquacious teacher gave me a few new ideas and proofs of the merits of the Romish church; he certainly knew something of the history of both the Romish and Protestant churches. After an hour's listening, my escape was effected, through sand and difficulties, to the neat little colony.

Meeting the good Dr. Adams near his own door, I enquired if they had no better accommodations in the colony than those which had been served up to me the preceding night; that I regretted that they had no more *self-respect* than to send a stranger there, even if they had no Bible knowledge of the claims of a stranger. I then asked if I could buy a piece of bread in the place, and was answered "Not any." To do justice to the doctor, he said to the friend at whose house I dined the preceding day, that a comfortable place should have been provided for me to lodge; and I should not have been shocked at his Christian benevolence had he given me a breakfast at his own table. A third, who was standing by, said, "Mrs. Barrett has occasionally sold it;" and the other then kindly invited me to his house for a breakfast; but as there was a little probability of getting bread at Mrs. Barrett's, and the kind man had given me a dinner the day before, I declined, went to Mrs. Barrett's, and not only bought a roll and got a breakfast at two o'clock, but was offered a decent bed in a snug little room without charges, and their kindness never abated while I was in Achill. After breakfast I visited the infant-school. The children, who were orphans, were tolerable in appearance, though the dresses of some needed a little repairing; and their inattention to their lessons was in agreement with the management of the teacher, who certainly did not take her diploma in the University at Glengariff, where the schooldame said, "I teaches sewing, ma'am, and they gets along finely," for there she would have been instructed to offer strangers a seat, and to treat them with a little civility. I next visited the female-school, taught by a young lady from Dublin; the room was cleanly, the scholars the same, and the writing, which was all I saw, commendably done, and the teacher somewhat civil. I then entered the school for boys; they were reading a chapter in Acts, and the teacher requested me to examine them. I did so; they answered well, and evinced good training, and the teacher showed that he was not afraid to be decently courteous. I now felt myself rising a little in the scale of respectability by these three steps of regular advance, and returned quite satisfied with my afternoon's visit. Mr. Barrett requested me to give him any letters of introduction I might have, as he wished to show them to Mr. Nangle. I had one from a Protestant clergyman in New York to a gentleman of respectability in England, a friend of Mr. Nangle's.[14] I had a second from good authority, who was an editor of a Christian paper, and a small religious manuscript, which I though of getting printed: these I sent, accompanied by a note, that I would call when I returned from an excursion to the other side of the island in a day or two.[15]

A labouring man belonging to the colony called in the evening, and learning that I wished to visit the Keem mountains, offered to send his daughter as a guide, adding, "You are not to pay her. I know what it is to be a stranger; you have come a great distance to see our country, and we should be more than brutes not to treat you well." This was a mollifying ointment indeed; and the next morning the cleanly little miss was at the door; we had not proceeded far, when the father joined us, saying, "I was afraid my little gal wouldn't rightly understand your accent, and wouldn't well show you what you want to see, and I thought I had better follow you."

Here was an industrious tradesman, having half-a-crown a day for labour, leaving this, and saying at the onset he would not take a farthing. He took me through an ancient village, built after the manner of the huts where I lodged above the colony, with no roads but foot-paths; and the village being large, we were long making our way through.[16] As we entered, a ragged man was sitting on the top of his hut, with a company of as ragged children, sunning themselves; and seeing a stranger, he rose, and saluted the man in Irish, asking who I was, and what was my country. When he was told, he cried out, "Welcome, welcome to Ireland, twice welcome." His children then all echoed the same. I turned over the wall, and gave them my hand, and as well as I could returned them my thanks. Never could be seen a more miserable group, and never was more kind-heartedness shown. As we passed on, the whole hamlet was in motion; those not in the way managed to put themselves there. The kind salutations, the desire to know every thing about America, and the fear that I was hungry, almost overpowered me. One old woman, who with her fingers told me she was three score and fifteen, whose teeth were all sound, and her cheeks yet red, approached, put her hand upon my stomach, made a sorrowing face, and said in Irish, "She is hungry; the stranger is hungry." We were so delayed that we feared we should be limited in time, and we hurried on a couple of miles to another village of the same description, though not so much inhabited, being used by the inhabitants of the first as a kind of country-seat, common-stock for all who assemble their cattle and sheep, to drive them upon the mountain for pasturage, to fat-ten them at a favourable season of the year.[17] There were but a few now in it; but walking by a number of deserted huts, we came to one where sat an old woman and her two married daughters, by the sunny side of the hut. Asking the old lady her age, she put up her fingers, and counted five score; she asked for a penny, then prayed for me in Irish, and I asked her if she wished to live any longer? "As long as God wishes me," was the answer. "Do you expect to go to heaven?" "By God's grace I do." What could be more consistent, if she understood the import. Keem was now near. This mountain descends many hundred feet, nearly perpendicular, to the sea, through which is made a road about midway, and the pedestrian may look up to the top of the dizzy height, or down in the yawning abyss, as his nerves may best serve him.

Government has here made a good road, for the sole purpose of giving strangers, as well as countrymen, the privilege of walking through, and looking upon this grand height, and visiting the diamond quarry of amethysts, which have been turned to very profitable account by many foreign travellers.[18] I gathered a few, and while standing there, a native from a village of the same description of that just passed, offered a splendid specimen of the stone for a few shillings, which I foolishly refused, not then knowing its value. I shall not soil Mrs. Hall's pretty sketch of this mountain and sea view by attempting a description, but refer the reader to the description itself, and return back to the town, as a four-mile walk is before us. On our return we met the old woman of five score, with a load of turf upon her back, which would have done credit to the strength of a woman of sixty. The villagers greeted us heartily, and were anxious to make more enquiries when we passed, and much concerned lest I should be angry. As we approached the colony, we called at the house of an old Bible-reader, who had been converted from Catholicism more than twenty years ago, and said he had been reading the scriptures to these mountaineers ever since, and so they were without excuse if they did not know the way of life and salvation. We passed out, and the man who accompanied me disappeared without giving any intimation, to avoid, as I have ever thought, the offer of any reward from me. Such noble disinterested kindness cannot be forgotten. Should the reader be led to think that too much severity is manifested towards such as have been unkind, let him read the multiplied acknowledgements of favours, and then taking into account, that but a small part of the out-of-the-way, uncalled-for rudeness and unkindness which I have received has been recorded, he may be disposed to give credit for my lenity. Again, those which are recorded have been divested in most cases of their roughest and rudest deformities.

The next afternoon the weekly lecture at the church in the colony was to be held, and I enquired if any one would allow me to accompany him or her to the place of worship. The answer was, "You need no one; go in, and there is a woman there who will show you a seat." Mr. Barrett accompanied me in sight of the place; told me that the females living near his house, with whom I had often conversed, had gone in, and he and his family could not attend that afternoon. This was all legible hand-writing, easily to be read. I went, saw no seat, and stood till every person except the speaker probably might have testified to the colour of my hair and eyes, before I was shown a seat. At last a female handed me a stool, or small bench, and I took a seat, not far distant from the feet of the preacher. The meeting was not in the main body of the church, but in a school-room. The room was cleanly, the people attentive, the sermon not faulty, and the females dressed tidily. Mr. Nangle must have been apprised of the object of my visit, as I had sent to him either by note or by a member of his church, that I wished from his own lips to get a sketch at least of the success of his mission, for the sole benefit of the American press, as it would be an object of great interest to us. When the amen was pronounced, being so near him, the assembly not large, and the room not a public one, I could not but reasonably expect, without requiring any marked attentions, that he would give me a nod in passing, if not stop to speak. He turned quickly about, addressed a lady of the congregation, and I waited perhaps with too much perseverance, hoping I might yet speak to him; till so many had retired that I withdrew, without a word being spoken by an individual, but not without a most faithful staring, till I was well from the door.

Saturday was the appointed day for me to call on Mr. Nangle for my letters, and I went with strong hopes that I should through them get access to him, and acquire the desired information. I went to the door; Mrs. N. refused to see me, unless I had a special message. I sent word that I had called for papers which Mr. Nangle had of mine. "Mr. Nangle is in the post office, and you can go there, the mistress says." I went to the post office. Mr. Nangle said, "In three quarters of an hour I will see you at my house." Before I reached his door, the nurse with an infant in her arms met me, and kindly said, "Step into the next shop, and when Mr. Nangle comes, I will let you know."* To that nurse I am for ever obliged. I had no sooner entered, than a company were gathered about me, and

* This nurse afterwards apologized for this, by saying that she did it to save me the pain of the abuse which she feared I might receive in the house.

without preface or apology, commenced talking of the merits of Ireland, its wealth, especially at Achill, and how much Americans are indebted to the Irish; that though Ireland had the appearance of poverty, yet she was quite comfortable and independent, and that she had carried much money to America.

I had only time to answer that it was a great pity some of it had not circulated among us, either for their benefit or ours, for we certainly had many of them to support. The nurse now entered, saying, "Mr. Nangle has returned," and she led me to the hall. As I passed the window, two or three young misses, the daughters of Mr. Nangle, were looking through it, laughing in a low, vulgar manner; and I was afterwards informed that the governess, who had more good breeding than influence, rebuked them for their rudeness, but to no purpose. The nurse left me seated in the hall, and Mr. Nangle showed me to the parlour, and handed me my letters without adding a word. I asked some questions about the colony. In a few words he told me its prosperity, and ended by saying it exceeded all expectation.

Having seen a number of the converts who had families, and could not read, I enquired of Mr. N. if they had Sabbath-schools for adults? "Not to teach them to read, but to *read* to them, and instruct them in the scriptures." "Are they not anxious to read the Word of God for themselves?" I asked. He gave me to understand that it would be a difficult task. I then for encouragement referred him to a New York adult school of Irish, where many of the ages of forty-five, fifty, and even sixty, had been taught to read. I was afterwards told that this was considered an officious dictation, as though he was incapable of managing his own affairs.

A female now entered, whose silent, fixed stare and appearance altogether led me to suppose that she was some upper servant in the house; but when she seated herself opposite to me at the table, in presence of Mr. Nangle, her eyes still fastened on me, I knew that no servant would do this in a parlour in presence of her master, and ventured to break the silence by asking, "Is this Mrs. Nangle?" I certainly feared that an indignity had been offered Mr. Nangle by this question, but the answer, with its rude accompaniment, told me who she was, and my own insignificance in her presence. "What brought you here?" "Did you mean, madam, what brought me to Ireland, or what brought me to Achill?" "What brought you to Achill?" "I came to see the colony, and to hear from the founders of it, its progress and true condition, that I might tell to my own country what good work was going on in this remote island of the ocean." "Let me tell you that you came on very improper business." Mr. Nangle now walked silently out. Knowing that a "soft answer turneth away wrath," and that the Irish heart settles into kindness when its first effervescence has been flung off, I waited a little, and asked, "Is not the colony free of access to all strangers?"[19] "Not without letters, madam."

"I have letters in my hand which Mr. Nangle has had; will you read them?" "I can read them if you want me to do so." "I do not, madam, for my own sake. I have not the least anxiety to change your opinion concerning myself." "Do you not think the Virgin Mary can do more for you than any body else?" The question, with the tantalizing manner in which it was put, was so disgusting, that I hesitated whether to answer. I had never before been treated by any female with such vulgarity and so little courtesy. I answered that the Virgin Mary could do no more than she could, if she had the spirit of Christ. The question was repeated, and the only answer I gave was, "If you wish to read my letters, here they are." She read one from a Protestant clergyman; handed it back, saying, "This I suppose is from a Jesuit." Taking the second, she read it, and pushed it across the table without speaking. After a short pause, she added, "You say you come to get information of the colony, and I should say you come to ask charity." "What occasion have I given for this supposition? Have I asked charity; does my apparel appear improper, or like a beggar?" "Your dress looks well enough." I arose, and said, "Mrs. Nangle, if these letters be true, I would ask you, as you profess to be a Christian, should you like to be treated as you have treated me in your parlour this morning, or have your children treated thus?" "I hope my children will never go about the world carrying such letters as these."

I went out. The nurse was waiting at the door, and asked, "How were you treated? Ah! she has a stony heart, and I feared she would abuse you. Smiles are put on, good dinners got up, a fine story told of the colony when the quality come, while the poor servants are stinted and miserably paid."[20] Though I could have no doubt but a woman so unlady-like and unChristian in her conduct as she had been that day, might be guilty of all this, I answered only by saying, "If you are not treated well, why not go away?" "Because I can get no money to take me home."

I reached Mr. Barrett's, and paused upon the steps, and though I could not see the whole colony, yet enough was in sight to show what the hand of industry had done, and I could not be so unjust as not to acknowledge heartily that much has been done, and well done, to make a barren waste a fruitful field. The neat white cottages and the pleasant road made a striking contrast with the hurdles about Molly Vesey's, and the paths around her domicile; but I do not speak sarcastically, when I say that the

manners of the people in the shop where I waited, and in the parlour of
Mr. Nangle, were not in so good keeping with *Christian* refinement as
were those in the cabin of Molly. Pity, pity that Bible Christianity should
ever have a counterfeit! That Christianity, which possesses such a life-giv-
ing power, which is pure, peaceable, long-suffering, condescending, disinterested, forgiving, given to hospitality, self-denying, kind, and courteous
to strangers, how is it perverted by ambitious, proud worldlings in every
generation! I had looked in the cabins of many of the converts in Dingle
and Achill, and though their feet were washed cleaner, their stools
scoured whiter, and their hearths swept better than in many of the mountain cabins, yet their eightpence a day will never put shoes upon their
feet, convert their stools into chairs, or give them any better broom than
the mountain heath for sweeping their cabins. It will never give them the
palatable, well-spread board around which their masters sit, and which
they have earned for them by their scantily-paid toil. These converts,
turned from worshipping images to the living and true God, as they are
told, holding a Protestant prayer-book in their hands which they cannot
read, can no more be sure that this religion, inculcated by proxy, emanates
from the pure scriptures, than did the prayer-book which they held in
their hands when standing before a Popish altar. They must be in the
same predicament with that of a woman in America, who had been a
slave. At the age of forty she gained her freedom, went into a free state,
and in a sabbath-school there learned to read the word of God. One day
she carried her Testament to the superintendent, asking him to show her
the chapter beginning with, "Servants, be obedient to your masters." She
soon returned, and in the simplicity of her heart asked if all Testaments
are alike. She was told they were. "But one verse, the last in the chapter,"
she added, "is not in my Testament. My master was a pious man, and
every sabbath he assembled the slaves and read this chapter to us, and the
last verse was, *And let the disobedient servant be whipped till his back is sore!*"

But I have stood too long on the steps of Mr. Barrett's door. A
reformed Roman Catholic priest, attached to the colony, heard that I had
visited Mrs. Nangle, and called to enquire. Knowing that we cannot
"unknow our knowledge," and that if he had been a Jesuit, he could not
forget the skill, I was guarded.[21] His well managed questions were tolerably evaded, till he asked, "How did Mrs. Nangle treat you, and how did
you like her?" "She treated me, I believe, just as she *felt*, and I ought to be
thankful that towards *me* she was no hypocrite." His answer was, "There
is a great deal of religion in the world, but a very little piety; and after all,
probably the Mahometans are the true church."

I had thought of hearing Mr. Nangle preach the next day, but at that moment the kind Mrs. Savage and her daughter rode up, and invited me to take a seat on her car, and accompany her home. This was a treat. Her well ordered house, her unaffected politeness, proceeding from genuine benevolence of heart, made me lose the feelings of a stranger by her comfortable fire-side and table. With feelings of deep gratitude do I record the kindness of Mr. Barrett, his wife, and children. They had not taken their principles or practices of theology in the colony. They had, I trust, learned them in the school of Christ, before they attached themselves to Achill. On the car was a Christian gentleman from Castlebar, a man of intelligence and kind feeling, who was spending a few days at the house of Mr. Savage. He was acquainted with the colony, and bade me feel no regret at the treatment I had received.

Sabbath morning, a company of children assembled from the mountains, at Mr. Savage's house, where a piece of bread was given them, and then a young daughter of the family took them into a shop, and instructed them in reading and saying lessons in the Bible. It was a pretty sight to see so many children from the bogs and mountains, listening to the voice of instruction from one that was but a child herself. My stay on this wild beach was a pleasant one; not an item was wanting to make the guest feel like a member of the family.

On Tuesday morning I returned to the colony, to get a few articles I had left, and to take a letter to the office I had written to Mrs. Nangle, the true copy of which is now in my hands, and should this be thought too severe, that may appear in a second edition." On my way to the colony, I met a stranger returning from Achill who lived in the country. He had some years since become a convert to the Bible, by reading and meditating upon it, and in a few sentences he manifested such a knowledge of his own heart, of the character of God and of the scriptures, as I had not seen in any person, whether learned or unlearned. He was taught of God, emphatically. How different are such from man-made Christians! A girl accompanied me a mile, who talked intelligibly on the scriptures. A Baptist man, she said, had some years before given her a bible, and she was well acquainted with it. She was a Catholic, but said she intended to join the colonists, for the sake of getting better schooling, and being more cleanly: I advised her to do so. I stopped but a few minutes in the colony, and saw none of my old friends but the family where I had lodged. Walking back, a little shower sprinkled the earth, and a beautiful rainbow appeared. A peasant stopped to admire, and pointing to it said, "A sign! a sign!" He could speak but a little English, and supposing he meant the promise that the world should not be drowned, I spoke of the flood; but he had never heard of it, and gave a vacant stare, then said, "Rain, rain!" He was old, had always lived on that island, and never knew that God had drowned the world.*

The following Friday I left, with regret and gratitude, the hospitable family at the Sound, and took a car for Westport. Stopped at Newport, at the house of Mr. Gibbon, the itinerant and Bible-reader, and passed the time pleasantly till Tuesday with his family and the kind Christian widow Arthur, who kept the post office.[23] A kind of romantic charm seems flung about Newport. Sir Richard O'Donel and his lady have established schools on liberal principles. The lady herself teaches two or three days in a week, and Sir Richard has an admirably well fitted school-room, where he teaches a Sabbath-school himself.[24] The effects of a fair on Monday night showed that Ireland is not emancipated from the effects of whiskey. Rioting and fighting lasted through the night, and in the morning many an inebriate was staggering home to his family. I walked to Westport with the peasantry, and at six in the morning was on a car for Castlebar. Called a few moments on a Baptist minister there, who presented me with a bundle of tracts, which were quite too sectarian to suit my purposes in visiting Ireland.

I stopped at a hotel in Sligo, stayed twenty-four hours, and saw almost the whole town. Took a morning walk three miles from my lodgings to the most beautiful glen I had met, in some particulars.[25] The peasants were so desirous to talk with me on America, that I was three hours going three miles. An avenue, entered by a gate, leads to the cottage, where lives Mr. Nicholson, the proprietor; supposing it might be the breakfast hour, I sat down on a rustic seat, with the sea at my left and the glen at my right; and hearing the sound of a hammer, I entered the glen, and was accosted by a company of labourers breaking stones. "Good morrow kindly, and ye're takin' the pleasantest walk in all Ireland. There's not sich a glen in all the kingdom; and sure ye didn't come alone. Well! no harm 'ill befall ye here, and the master has all free to every one here." "You've a good master, I hope; one who pays you well." "And that he does." "What does he give?" "Eightpence a day." "And you eat your own potatoes?" "Yes, we aits our own potato, when we git enough of that same." I find in all Ireland the labouring classes, when I first speak to them, are ever praising their master. Just as in America, although the slaves may be often

---

* Before leaving the Sound, the palsied man and his wife called to go to the island. "God bless you. The Testament you gave me has been a blessing to my soul." "And that it should," his wife remarked, "for he sits up in his bed to read to me every night."

under the lash or in the stocks, yet to a stranger they durst not speak out, lest some "bird of the air should tell the matter;" so the peasantry of Ireland are in such suffering, that lest they should lose the sixpence or eightpence they occasionally get while employed, they will make an imperious landlord an angel to a stranger.

"Will ye walk through the glen, ma'am?" A road of comfortable width, richly bordered with wild flowers for three-quarters of a mile from the cottage, opens to the eye a rare treat of wonder. A wall of stone rising above the head, upon each side, as smooth as if sawed, and appearing as if once united, overhung with rich foliage, especially the ivy, which in rich fantastical festoons is hanging and twining in every part; and upon one side a part of the wall seems set aside for more favoured ornament, having a curtain of ivy, knotted at top in the centre, as if over a window, then running on either hand a distance of three yards, it falls gracefully down upon the wall, gradually coming to a point as if trimmed with shears. Between these graceful hangings the wall is entirely smooth, and water is continually percolating down its surface, giving a monotonous murmur in the stillness of the glen.[26] As I gazed, supposing the skill of the gardener had arranged this unparalleled ivy curtain, and clustered these knots upon the top, which were three in number, a peasant approached, "Good morrow kindly, ma'am; and did ye come far in the glen?" I answered, "I am fixed to this spot. The gardener must possess exquisite skill to have fitted upon a wall such drapery as this!" "The hand of the mighty God, ma'am. Nothin' else that planted it there – no gardener has ever touched a ha'p'orth, ma'am, not a ha'p'orth." "And what a mighty God must the maker of all this be! What will become of you and me, sir, when these rocks shall be melted, and these mountains around us flee away?" "Ah! that's true for ye, ma'am, I've often haird this world's to be burnt some day or other. That's true, God help us." I was left alone, fixed in admiration for a time; then walked on till a gate and wall told me the glen was terminated. Returned, and took a second view of the enchanted spot.

Reaching the cottage, I was met and welcomed by a man grown grey, and a cripple. But a young wife, just out of her teens, pleasantly invited me into her fairy parlour and ante-room, and then said, "You will have some breakfast – the long walk must have given you an appetite." Brown bread and milk were placed before me, and while partaking it, she told me that three weeks ago she had buried the best of fathers, at the advanced age of ninety; but his intellectual faculties brightened as his body decayed, especially his religious views; that his hospitality, for which he had ever been celebrated, was manifested at the last dying moment. A friend had entered to see him die. He beckoned his daughter to the bed, and enquired, "What is preparing for dinner? This kind friend has come in to see me die, and something nice must be placed before him." These were his last words. His mantle had fallen upon his daughter. The law of kindness was on her tongue. On my way to town, the peasants so detained me by enquiring about America, and what I thought of Ireland, that I had to make much haste on reaching the hotel, to be in time for the boat at three.

I regretted leaving Sligo so soon. Such ready access to all classes was not usual, and I should have been much gratified by availing myself profitably of it. The beautiful and novel Bay of Sligo made me forget all else. Nothing but the Blackwater could equal it, and that could not boast such picturesque mountains. Here are mountains of rock, standing out in circular shape, with the appearance of pillars, as if hewn by an architect; others, like a box, with a cover shut over it, and the edges of this cover plaited. This singular appearance of rock and mountain continued for several miles; while the little islands in the river, the green meadows, and tasteful demesnes upon the border, made an indescribable treat as the sun was setting.

We reached the termination of the route at nine o'clock, and found an expensive lodging-house, as it was crowded on account of the assizes.[27] My next day's ride on the top of a coach was eighty-one miles to Dublin, some part of it romantic. The sea-coast was rocky and wild, and presented little that was inviting for the abode of man. The road took us through a part of Leitrim, Westmeath, and Longford.[28] At the latter place, while waiting for a change of horses, the beggars seemed to have rallied all their forces, followed by the rags and tatters of the town, who surrounded the coach to hear from America. I supposed the coachman had informed some labourers who were in a group, that he had an American on his coach, or they would not have known. I answered the beggars, that I had nothing but books to give. A truce for a moment succeeded, when a clamour for books was set up, similar to the one on the island of Omey. Giving them some tracts, all commenced reading, when one cried out that they said nothing of the Blessed Virgin, and immediately one was torn in small pieces, and thrown upon my lap. The crowd had become quite numerous, and the clamour boisterous. Two or three more tracts were torn, and thrown into the air or upon the coach. Asking if they thought the Virgin was looking upon them, "Yes, yes," was echoed and re-echoed. "How do you think she is pleased with the disrespect you have paid her Son? Those books, which you have torn, are His words, and you have despised them, and torn them in pieces." All for a minute were silent; every laugh was changed into a look of sorrow. "In truth," said one, "we have done wrong; we did not know it; and ye are right, ma'am, and we are sorry." A few words were said on their lost condition if out of Christ, and they listened with most respectful silence, and walked quietly away.

The long ride to Dublin terminated at eight o'clock, and though I knew it was not my own fire-side that I was approaching, yet the same kind greeting and welcome at the home I had left, made me feel that though in a land of strangers, I was not in a family that could not reciprocate my wants, if not my feelings, and do all in their power to make me comfortable. I spent a few pleasant weeks in Dublin, visiting public institutions. The Academy of Painters was a place of interest, because so many proofs are there given that Ireland spares no expense in perpetuating the virtues and talents of her sons.[29] With my first and constant friend Miss H. I went to the Mendicity; and to a tourist this institution is one of no small interest.[30] Paupers assemble here in the morning, and stay till six at night, and get two meals for picking oakum. The breakfast is stirabout; the dinner, potatoes and some kind of herbage pounded together, well peppered, put into barrels, shovelled out into black tins, and set out upon the floor.* Here they sit upon the dirty boards, and eat, some with spoons and some with their fingers. It was a most disgusting sight. The crowd was immense. Never had I seen so much filth embodied in one mass, with so many ugly, forlorn, and loathsome faces. They seemed to be the "odds and ends" of the workmanship of ages, flung together into this pile, as offal that had been picked and culled, torn and shaken, till all that could be used had been worked up. We turned from the forbidding sight into the school-room, where the children of these woebegone parents were assembled for instruction; and here a war was in progress, between the mistress and a woman who had entered demanding the services of a scholar. The mistress refused, and the fight became so serious that I begged the overseer to take the case in hand. He declined, and the battle ended in favour of the mistress. This Mendicity does this: it keeps many from actual starvation, and is a tolerable quietus to the penurious, who would rather see a fellow-being metamorphosed into a brute, than lighten their purses.

Who could look on a sight like this without asking, what political economy could produce such a picture of God's best and noblest workmanship? What fountain but the stagnant Lake of Sodom could send

* I did not then see any tables, though they have them now.

forth streams like these?[31] Where is the somebody that has done all this, and what is his name and genealogy? Bring him out, if he can be traced, in the face of the congregation – yes, in the face of high heaven. Let him be examined before the judges, and if he cannot answer for this his strange work, send him away; let him hide his face for ever from the face of man. If it be voluntary idleness, pay the culprit no premium for sloth and filth. "He that will not work shall not eat," should be the stereotyped motto while seed-time and harvest remain. But if his idleness be, because no man hath hired him; if his rags be the remuneration for days of faithful toil; if there be a watchman on Judah's towers, a nobleman, a husbandman, a shopkeeper, who has defrauded this poor man of his wages, who has kept back part of the price that he should give, let him see to it, and let him see to it in season; for God, be assured, is a correct accountant.[32] Not a figure will be added or subtracted wrong. Not an injured poor man will cry to him for redress, but that cry will be heard. Not a forbidding mendicant, who here has his food flung out to him as though he were a dog or an ass, but has his cause registered in the high court of heaven, and the immaculate Lamb of God is his pleader. And that Pleader never practised, and never acknowledged any benevolence but a self-denying one, and paid no honour to any station but honest poverty. "He took on him the form of a servant." Was this, I ask, disgracing poverty?

CHAPTER XXVIII

Mr. Nangle's Notice, in the *Achill Herald*, of the Author's Visit to the Settlement – Remarks upon this Document and the motives which probably dictated it – Concluding Observations relative to the objects of the Writer's Tour in Ireland, and the Reception she met with from various Classes of the Community

It was in the month of July, 1845, about six weeks after my return from Achill, that I was presented, in the Tract Depository, Sackville-street, Dublin, with an article to read in the *Achill Herald*, which I take leave to insert in this volume as one which should be preserved.' Any document that is worth reading once is worth reading twice. As this was written by a valued man, and inserted in a valuable paper, and as newspapers are liable to be mislaid and torn, I call it again from its repose of two years, that the thousands of subscribers who read the *Achill Herald* may, if they will condescend to do so, have their minds refreshed by what was once thought a matter of deep interest to the religious community: –

"During the last month, this settlement was visited by a female who is travelling through the country. (We have traced her from Dingle to this place.) She lodges with the peasantry, and alleges that her object is to become acquainted with Irish character; she states that she has come from America for this purpose. She produced a letter purporting to be addressed by a correspondent in America to a respectable person in Birmingham;* but in answer to a communication addressed by the writer to that individual, he stated that he has no acquaintance with her, either personally or by letter."

"This stranger is evidently a person of some talent and education; and although the singular course which she pursues is utterly at variance with the modesty and retiredness to which the Bible gives a prominent place in its delineation of a virtuous female, she professes to have no ordinary regard for that Holy Book. It appears to us that the principal object of this woman's mission is to create a spirit of dis-

* The individual here referred to is Mr. Joseph Sturge of Birmingham, who had not seen the letter referred to by Mr. Nangle at the time of my visit to Achill. He has since not only acknowledged the receipt of this letter, but has very kindly entrusted me with money for the relief of the Irish poor.

content among the lower orders, and to dispose them to regard their superiors as so many unfeeling oppressors. There is nothing in her conduct or conversation to justify the supposition of insanity, and we strongly suspect she is the emissary of some democratic and revolutionary society."

In publishing this document, the writer acted as his views of worldly policy suggested, in the circumstances in which he was placed by his conduct towards me. A stranger came from a far country to visit the colony, and came with the best intentions. These intentions had been made known to Mr. Nangle in a suitable manner; but the stranger was sent out to lodge in a most improper place, and this place was recommended by his people. In his own parlour, into which he had invited this visitor, he allowed her to be treated, I will not merely say *uncivilly*, but *degradingly* and *wickedly*. I subsequently wrote to Mrs. Nangle, speaking plainly, unsparingly, and conscientiously, on the responsibilities of her station, informing her that my visit to the colony would make an interesting page in my published journal. What could Mr. Nangle do under these circumstances, but acknowledge the error of his conduct towards me, or else advertise the public in season to beware of this scrutinizing democrat, whose virtues, according to Solomon's ideas, are much to be doubted. I make no apology to Mr. Nangle, I make none to the public, for visiting Achill, and visiting it as I did. I had a national right, a civil and religious one to do so, either with or without letters, as long as my conduct was proper. This city set upon a hill, by the bounty of the religious world and the labours of those who inhabit it, says to all the world, "Come and see our zeal for the Lord."[2] And if there be not some Sanctum Sanctorum for the priests alone to enter, some Holy Inquisition where heretics are to be tried and condemned, then who can be justly prohibited from going about its walls, and telling the towers of this Zion?[3] Who shall be advertised as the "emissary of some revolutionary or democratic society," for looking at its battlements, enquiring after it prosperity, and reporting the strength of its bulwarks?

In conclusion I would say, that though IRELAND'S WELCOME has some dark shades, yet these only serve to give light and life to the picture. Had my reception among the higher and middle ranks been as Christian-like and as civil as among the poor, it would have been one monotonous tissue, which might have spread a false covering before my eyes, so that her true character would have been hidden. Had all men spoken well of me, had all treated me kindly, the woe of Christ must have been mine, and I might have been an idler in my Master's vineyard.[4] They have done me good; and to all who have so little understood the true principles of gospel self-denial and gospel kindness towards the poor, as to censure the course I have taken, they should be pitied, they should be prayed for, they should be forgiven, and be assured that by me they are forgiven. And happy should I be to testify my forgiveness in my own country, and by own fireside, and at my own table, should these comforts ever again be mine. America, faulty as she may be, will extend the cordial hand to the Irish stranger; and if he be poor, she will give him bread and clothing; she will pay him for his toil, and will allow him to stand erect, and call himself a man. I speak of Free America. With the oppressors of the South I have no sympathy. I have often been tauntingly asked, "Why do you not labour for the slaves in your own country?" I answer, "I have done so, and it was a strong inducement to bring me to Ireland.⁵ I saw that most of your nation who land upon our shores are not only destitute, but ignorant of letters, and crouching and servile till they get power, and in all these lineaments bear a good comparison with our slaves." And I could not but ask, What but oppression could produce this similitude? And painful as is the fact, yet it must be told of the Irish in America, too many, quite too many strengthen the hands of the avaricious oppressor, and help him to bind the chains tighter about the poor black man; and I came to entreat you to show your people a better way. I came to beg you to help us knock off our fetters, by sending a more enlightened and free people among us, who cannot be bribed by flattery or money.

But who shall teach them these noble lessons? For while I have seen the same jealousy, the same jesuitical caution, and a greater unkindness in many cases exercised towards me by masters in Ireland, than by slaveholders in the American Slave states, how can I hope better things till better principles get possession of the heart? Let not these remarks be misunderstood; let them not be misconstrued; I speak not of all Ireland. There are noble hearts in the Emerald Isle, who do not practise oppression; but I speak to the guilty, and let them hear. No others will be disconcerted at what I say. I fear not the innocent. I fear not the guilty. The innocent would not hurt me, and the guilty cannot. I was a friend to Ireland before I left home. I have remained her friend here, and shall return, if possible, still more so. Yes, though much of the painful toil might have been spared, and my means of doing good been greatly enlarged, had those who had it in their power received and treated me more kindly; yet it has not loosened one cord that tied my heart to the suffering poor, it has not induced me to shun one neglected alley, where lay on their cold pile of straw the starving and the dying. No, it has stimulated me more to stir up my country to come to your aid, and I will do it so long as my pen can move and my country has a loaf to spare.[6] If any one think me too severe in any of these pages, let him reverse the picture; let him suppose that America for the last fifty years had been pouring in her destitute ragged paupers upon you, by wholesale and retail. Suppose you had welcomed these paupers, had given them labour and bread till they could walk upon the earth as men and women. And suppose, at the end of fifty years, an Irishwoman should be disposed (however strange the whim) to visit that country, to see what these Americans were at home, to learn their manners and habits there, in order to better understand them here, and do them good; should you not expect that the law of civility, the law of Christianity, and the law of equity at least should induce them not only to receive her cordially, but to do all in their power to facilitate such rational designs?

I ask no answer. I put the question not to anger you, not to complain, but to convince you that such were the most honourable, the most Christian-like way to act; and should the like again happen, the Bible mode will be the best to adopt, to "be careful to entertain strangers," till you know they are impostors; and suspect not their letters as forged ones, till some marks of forgery can be detected.[7] What would have become of your poor countrymen, think you, in America, had they been treated thus? I am glad I came; I am glad to be here in your dreadful famine; I am glad to be honoured with doing a little for the wretched among you. Would to God I could do more. Three years almost I have gone over, and looked at your pretty island, and with all my privations, my toil, and cold repulses, I have been paid, doubly repaid; and from my heart can I say, were it not for the suffering my eyes have seen, I should place these years among the happiest of my life. I love you all, and would do you all good, were it in my power. To the Roman Catholics, both duty and inclination require that I should acknowledge a deep debt of gratitude. They have opened the doors of convents, of schools, of mansions, and cabins, without demanding letters, or distrusting those that were presented. They have sheltered me from storm and tempest; they have warmed and fed me without fee or reward, when my Protestant brethren and sisters frowned me away. God will remember this, and I will remember it.

Should I ever reach home, I hope to give a fuller detail of my tour, which embraced all but the county of Cavan. I have made no mention of the north of Ireland, for want of room, but cannot close without saying that in Belfast I spent a few pleasant weeks.[8] The Protestants there made me feel as if I were by a New England fireside, where I was neither wor-

shiped as a goddess or made a second-hand article, though I might perform some domestic service appropriate to woman. Their religion
appeared, in many cases, like that of the heart, and their labours through
the past winter of famine, and which have not yet relaxed, testify that
their faith has produced good works.[9]

I have spoken plainly, that I might render unto Caesar the things that
are Caesar's; and as I visited Ireland to see it as it is, so I report it as I
found it.[10] I have stayed to witness that which, though so heart-rending
and painful, has given me but the proof of what common observation told
me in the beginning – that there must needs be an explosion of some kind
or other. But awful as it is, it has shewn Ireland who are her worthy ones
within her, and who are her friends abroad, and it will shew her greater
things than these.

May God bring her from her seven-times-heated furnace, purified and
unhurt, and place her sons and daughters among the brightest of the stars
that shall shine for ever in the kingdom of heaven, is the sincere desire of
the writer.[11]

NOTES

Introduction [vii–xix]

1. Seán O'Faoláin, *King of the Beggars* 49–50.
2. For a fuller account of Nicholson's life before she travelled to Ireland, see my Introduction to *Annals of the Famine in Ireland*.
3. Séamus O'Maolchathaigh, *An Gleann agus a Raibh Ann* 166.
4. Fitz McCarthy 63.

Preface [1–2]

1. Nicholson wrote *Ireland's Welcome to the Stranger; or, An Excursion through Ireland in 1844 and 1845*, for the purpose of investigating the condition of the poor to raise awareness and relief for the famine-stricken Irish. She had arrived back in Dublin in December 1846, where she spent the winter of 1846–7 running her own soup kitchen in the city. She finished *Ireland's Welcome to the Stranger* in Richard Davis Webb's home on 10 June 1847. Shortly after, she left for County Mayo, one of the most destitute areas of the west, where she spent the following winter.
2. Nicholson pokes fun at the number of accounts of Ireland that were written by travellers who kept their distance from the Irish people.
3. The line from Exodus 7:12, 'For they cast down every man his rod, and they became serpents, but Aaron's rod swallowed up their rods', suggests a combination of human choice and God's enabling.
4. Nicholson may have thought about her work in the 'vineyard' in terms of 1 Timothy 5:5, 'Now that she is a widow indeed, and desolate, trusteth in God, and continueth in supplications and prayers night and day'.
5. Nicholson paraphrases the Book of Ruth 2:3, 'And she went, and came, and gleaned in the field after the reapers'.
6. 1 Samuel 17:28: 'Why camest thou sown hither? and with whom hast thou left those few sheep in the wilderness?' David heard about the reward for killing Goliath; he left his sheep and took up the challenge.
7. Psalm 84:10: 'I had rather be a door-keeper in the house of my God, than to dwell in the tents of wickedness'. Nicholson also quotes James 2:2–3 to show that class has no place in her understanding of Christianity: 'For if there come unto your assembly a man with a gold ring, in goodly apparel, and there come in also a poor man in vile raiment. And ye have respect to him that weareth the gay clothing, and say unto him, "Sit thou here in a good place"; and say to the poor, "Stand thou there, or sit here under my footstool"'. She also alludes to Shakespeare's *Twelfth Night* III, ii, l. 52, 'Let there be gall enough in thy ink'.
8. Nicholson quotes from lines 37–8 of Alexander Pope's 'Being the Prologue to the Satires': 'To laugh were want of goodness and of grace, And to be grave exceeds all power of face'. Seán O'Faoláin admired Nicholson's account because it was not

one of 'unrelieved misery'.

9. Nicholson alludes to Isaiah 58:7, 'Is it not to share thy bread with the hungry, and that thou bringest to thine house the poor who are cast out; When thou seest the naked, that thou cover him, and that thou hide not thyself from thine own flesh?'

10. 'Sweetness on the desert air' may refer to Isaiah 35:1, 'The wilderness and the solitary place shall be glad for them; and the desert shall rejoice, and blossom as the rose'. The Kerry girls unknowingly imitate Ruth and Rebecca's models of domestic love and loyalty.

11. Exodus 11:6, 'There is nothing at all, besides this manna, before our eyes', suggests people tire of the same food. In fact, Nicholson used the quote in the context of the Irish Famine. Nicholson turns to the Book of Joel, which describes the devastation of the land by locusts. Her quote from Joel 3:13, 'Thrust in the sickle, for the harvest is ripe', suggests she thinks that a time of reckoning has come.

12. Mark 12: 41–43. One of Nicholson favourite models is the widow whose contribution of two mites, 'all her living', represents true generosity. Nicholson herself identified with the widow.

13. According to the *Hibernian Society Annual Report*, 1842–49, Nicholson received a grant of twelve testaments in 1845 and one bible and fourteen testaments in 1846.

14. In the Acts of the Apostles 9:15, the Lord calls Paul his 'chosen vessel' to preach before Gentiles, kings and the Children of Israel. Nicholson says she was not the 'chosen vessel' of the Hibernian Bible Society; she was on her own mission. The lines from Ecclesiastes 11:1 promise a return for those tracts and testaments which were 'cast ... upon the waters'.

Chapter I

1. The *Brooklyn* was a stern-wheel paddle ship that made the New York–Liverpool run in three weeks. The ship offered cabin as well as steerage accommodation; Nicholson travelled in cabin class. There is a painting of the ship in the Brooklyn Historical Society. The ship left from Whitehall Slip in the East River not far from where Nicholson ran her temperance boarding-houses between 1835 and 1842. The New York skyline that she watched recede as the *Brooklyn* set sail would have included the spires of Trinity and St Paul's churches.

2. Nicholson's parents were dead; her husband Norman Nicholson probably died in 1841, for she is listed in *The New York Directory* as a widow in 1842. Her brother David lived on in Chelsea, Vermont, until 1851, but she does not mention him.

3. The 'him' was probably one of her friends in the abolitionist movement: William Goodell, Simeon Jocelyn, Joshua Leavitt, Arthur or Lewis Tappan.

4. Nicholson adapts lines from William Cowper's poem 'On the Receipt of My Mother's Picture out of Norfolk', lines 108–11:

> My boast is not, that I deduce my birth
> From loins enthroned and rulers of the earth
> But higher far my proud pretentions rise –
> The son of parents passed into the skies.

5. Nicholson alludes to Hebrews 13:1–2, 'Be not forgetful to entertain strangers for thereby some have entertained angels unaware'. See also the Gospel of St Matthew 25:35.

6. A pacifist, Nicholson later joined the American delegation to the International Peace Society meeting in Frankfurt in 1850.

7. The *Brooklyn* arrived in the English Channel on 5 June after a twenty-one-day journey. The seven additional days to Liverpool meant they arrived the night of 12 June.

8. In *A Handbook for Travellers in Ireland*, James Fraser lists two packet sailings a day from Liverpool to Kingstown. These would have been been the Admiralty's mail packets carrying mail and passengers between England and Ireland. The voyage generally took twelve hours, so Nicholson's travel time from 2 pm on 14 June till the following evening would have been unusually long.

9. These lines appear to be a pastische of Thomas Moore. Nicholson describes Ireland with the traditional female iconography of the *aisling* poem.

10. An obelisk was erected on the sea front at Kingstown to mark the embarkation of George IV from Ireland in 1821. The town's name was changed from Dunleary (Dún Laoghaire) to Kingstown to mark the occasion.

11. Nicholson's lost pocket-book was the first in a series of lost or misplaced possessions: tickets, keys, carpet-bag, two tortoise-shell combs and two pairs of spectacles.

12. Nicholson describes a spoiler with words from the Song of Solomon 2:15, 'The little foxes, that spoil the vines'.

13. There is no place called Cole River View listed in the Dublin directories of the time. There are a Colepark Avenue, Drive, Green and Road in Ballyfermot.

14. Nicholson quotes Proverbs 17:22.

15. While the bleaching worker's eight shillings per week could not cover the expense of school clothing for his children, it was still much more than the eightpence a day labourers earned.

16. The 1844 *Dublin Post Office Annual Directory and Calendar* identifies a C. Fleming who ran the Old England Temperance Hotel and Travellers' Home at 6 North Wall. The Quaker Richard Davis Webb, who became Nicholson's closest friend in Ireland, was the treasurer of the Irish Temperance Union in 1844.

17. The annual exhibition of the arts was organized by the Royal Hibernian Academy, which was located at 23 Lower Abbey Street. Nicholson would have remarked about the life-size, bog oak sculpture of Father Theobald Mathew administering the temperance pledge. A temperance crusader and friend to the poor, he became a close friend of Nicholson's.

18. The 'son of the old inheritor' was no doubt James H. Webb, a linen draper with premises at 10–12 Cornmarket. He was Richard Davis Webb's brother. Their father James Webb started a linen drapery business in Dublin. Nicholson stayed at James H. Webb's house in Monkstown when she returned to Dublin in December 1846.

19. Nicholson probably visited the North Dublin Union Workhouse on Brunswick Street. The Chairman of the North Dublin Union was John Barlow; the chaplains were the Rev L.G. McDonnell and Father P. Murphy. The matrons were

the Misses Catherine Esmonde and Maria Esmonde.

20. Catherine Beecher's handbook on domestic service recommended that servants not eat with the family because the dinner table was one place that the family could gather in privacy.

21. Timothy's stomach and the Marriage Feast of Cana were two biblical rejoiners to Nicholson when she challenged clergy about drinking. 1 Timothy 4:1–5 criticizes false asceticism. See also *Annals* 90, and *Loose Papers* 55.

22. As a disciple of Sylvester Graham, Nicholson was a vegetarian who ate no butter and who believed that the healthiest bread was made from coarse flour. The Grahamites, who avoided caffeine as well as alcohol, would have been accustomed to being regarded as eccentrics or cranks.

23. Nicholson probably visited St Joseph's Asylum for Aged and Virtuous Single Females at 7 Portland Row, Summer Hill (*Thom's* 328).

Chapter II

1. These lines are similar to those of 2 Kings 19:26 and Isaiah 37:27, which describe the people shorn of strength and damaged and confused. Nicholson saw beyond the poverty to the independence of spirit.

2. Daniel O'Connell was imprisoned in Richmond Gaol in June 1844 on charges of conspiracy and sedition.

3. Clontarf Castle, now a hotel, was a small nineteenth-century castle built for C.V. Vernon near the site of the ancient Vernon castle (Fraser 666). Fraser identifies the architect as Morrison but does not say whether it was Sir Richard Morrison (1767–1849) or William Vitruvius Morrison (1794–1838). While Nicholson did not visit Clontarf Castle, she later stayed at Vernon's hunting-lodge, Croy Lodge, in Ballycroy, Co. Mayo, in February 1848. W.H. Maxwell described Croy Lodge in his collection of sketches called *Wild Sports of the West* (1832).

4. Nicholson had gone out to see the site of the Battle of Clontarf.

5. In *Annals of the Famine*, Nicholson wrote approvingly of the work of the Belfast Ladies' Association for the Relief of Irish Destitution, which was founded in 1847. She regretted that Dublin women did not work together actively to help the poor.

6. Nicholson travelled the fifty-seven miles along the Grand Canal on a fly-boat, an iron boat drawn by two or three horses, that could travel nine English miles per hour. Since the Irish midlands are flat, the fly-boats did not have to go through locks. The first cabin fare from Dublin to Tullamore was seven shillings and sixpence (Fraser 676).

7. Nicholson frequently compared the condition of the poor Irish with those of American slaves and Native Americans.

8. There were markets in Tullamore on Tuesdays and Saturdays at the market house built by Lord Charlesville. It is likely that Nicholson was in Tullamore on 10 July, the date of one of the three annual fairs held in the town.

9. The Tullamore gaol, now a factory, stands at the western end of town next to the classically designed court-house. Lewis described it as a 'castellated building on the radiating principle' (II, 652).

10. The Tullamore Workhouse opened on 9 June 1842; it had a capacity for 700 inmates (John O'Connor 263). Fraser says the workhouse was a 'conspicuous object

in the vicinity' (378).

11. The other schools in Tullamore included one for boys and one for girls sponsored by the Earl and Countess of Charlesville. Others were funded by the Board of National Education and by the London Irish Baptist Society. There were also private boarding-schools operated by John Fitzgerald and Catherine Locke (*Slater's* 1846, 92).

12. Nicholson describes instances of the the poor gathered and staring through the windows of houses she visited during the Famine in *Annals* 63, 85, 90.

13. Nicholson's Irish friends in America provided her with introductions to their families and friends. She was asked to help the Tullamore family.

14. Nicholson was concerned about the want of employment in Ireland. She questioned people she met about work opportunities and described labourers looking for work at wages of between sixpence and ten pence per day.

15. Nicholson took every opportunity to promote the work of her friend Father Mathew, who began his temperance crusade on 10 April 1838. He was encouraged by the Quaker Cork baker William Martin, who has been called 'the Grandfather of Teetotal Cause' (Harrison, *Cork* 54).

16. Seasonal harvest workers were a feature of the Irish countryside. Since most travellers visited Ireland during the summer months, they were likely to meet labourers and begging women and children on the road. The better-informed observer like Nicholson knew that chronic unemployment caused this phenomenon.

17. Transportation as a way of disposing of Irish undesirables started with Oliver Cromwell, who dispatched several thousand to penal servitude in the West Indies. By Nicholson's time, convicts were transported to Australia and Van Diemen's Land (Tasmania). Transportation was abolished in 1868 (Connolly 549). The Grand Canal packets terminated near Ringsend. There is not a Barrack Street, but there is a Barrack Lane on the current Ordnance Survey (14th edition) map of Dublin. Barrack Lane is near Beggar's Bush Barracks.

18. All references to frogs in the Old Testament concern the second plague in Exodus. Frogs were associated with the Egyptian goddess Heqt, who was believed to assist women in childbirth.

19. The text was from Mark 16:15. Nicholson's companion may have been Elizabeth Horner, who lived at 7 Dorset Street with her brother Francis Horner, a linen draper.

Chapter III

1. The pyramid-shaped monument which stands in Kilbride parish marks the burial place of the Howard family. See the engraving and description of the Howard mausoleum in Craig and Craig (84–5). Ralph Howard, Viscount Wicklow, erected the marker in 1785.

2. Nicholson's Arklow widow may be Margaret Sherwood. There are monuments to 'John Sherwood of Kilbride who departed this life January 9, 1825, aged 48 years' and to 'Joseph, son of the above who died 21 August 1822 age 16 years' erected by Margaret Sherwood in Kilbride graveyard.

3. These lines might be from a children's prayer. A poem by the Cumberland

Presbyterian minister Robert Donnell (1784–1855) includes the phrases 'a sweet sleep' and 'the abode of the little child'. At the time of his death, Donnell was the oldest Vice-President of the American Tract Society and a strong temperance worker.

4. It is not clear whether Nicholson means that the stories of '98 have an heroic quality to them similar to the stories told about Ossian or that stories of other times were grafted onto local '98 tradition.

5. The Tudor-style Shelton Abbey, owned by the Earl of Wicklow, is now a prison for boys. The Abbey was designed by the Morrisons.

6. The Earl of Wicklow and Cecil, Countess of Wicklow, established schools for their tenantry. Lady Catherine Howard (1831–82) was a Catholic convert who wrote religious verse. It is not clear whether she was the author of the religious tales for cottage children that Nicholson mentions (O'Donoghue 205).

7. Nicholson's discussion of the abilities of poor children alludes to Luke 11:33 and 16, the parables of the talents and stewardship.

8. Nicholson writes disapprovingly of hunting in *Annals* 69, 110, 121–3, 152.

9. Arklow Castle was destroyed by Oliver Cromwell's forces in 1649. Lewis reported in 1837 that there were two barracks on the site that housed companies of infantry (Lewis I, 61).

10. During the 1798 Rising, the Wexford rebels moving on Dublin were stopped at Arklow, where a battle was fought on 9 June 1798.

11. There was an infants' school in Arklow that was supported by voluntary contributions (Lewis I, 61).

12. 'All men think all men mortal but themselves' is a line from Edward Young's 'Night I', *Night Thoughts*, l. 424.

13. Castle Howard was the home of Sir Ralph Howard, Bart. The domain of Mr Parnell was Avondale, the home of John Parnell in 1844. Its most famous occupant, Charles Stewart Parnell, was born in Avondale in 1846.

14. The Forest Park booklet *Avondale* identifies three species of North American trees: Western Red Cedar, the giant Sequoia and the Redwood (27–8).

15. W.S. Guinness was the Church of Ireland pastor in Rathdrum in 1845 (*Thom's* 313).

16. Nicholson quotes from Oliver Goldsmith's 'The Deserted Village' stanza 12, ll. 8–9.

17. The Rathdrum Union Workhouse was opened on 8 March 1842. Nicholson suggests that it was nearly filled to its capacity of 600 inmates by 1844 (John O'Connor 263).

18. 'Now came still evening on, and twilight grey/Had in her sober livery all things clad' are lines from Milton's *Paradise Lost IV*, l. 598.

19. Nicholson quotes the first stanza of Thomas Moore's 'The Meeting of the Waters' from *Irish Melodies* (1808–34).

20. 'I could stay there forever to wander and weep': unidentified.

21. Wicklow gold was mined in the Croghan Kinshela mountains (Lewis I, 60).

22. The gentleman who perched his mansion on the brow of the Vale of Avoca was probably a Mr Bayly whose Ballyarthur estate commanded a magnificent view of the Avoca valley (Fraser 78).

23. The lines are from Oliver Goldsmith's 'The Deserted Village', ll. 63–4.

24. Nicholson frequently refers to Matthew 25:35, 'I was a stranger and ye took me in'.

Chapter IV

1. The Rector of Kilbride was Rev W. Daly. A tablet created for the Kilbride centenary that names all of the rectors lists Daly as serving from 1838–1873. The corner-stone for the present Kilbride Church was laid by Cecil Frances, Countess of Wicklow, in 1834.

2. The text for Daly's sermon, 'For the arrows of the Almighty are within me, the poison whereof drinketh up my spirit: the terrors of God do set themselves in array against me', comes from the Book of Job 6:4. The hymn 'Old Hundred', based on Psalm 100, is set to a tune also called 'Old Hundred' by Louis Bourgeois (c. 1510–61). The Martin Luther hymn was probably the 1529 'A Mighty Fortress is our God'.

3. These lines have not been identified, but they reflect Nicholson's beliefs about the modest way that she believed clergy should live among their neighbours.

4. Daly's belief that Repeal would lead to the extermination of Protestants was probably based on the sectarian incidents connected with the 1798 Rebellion.

5. Nicholson, always critical of those who used alcohol, was scandalized by wine-drinking Protestant clergy. See *Annals* 88, 90, 173, 186, 188.

6. Father Theobald Mathew founded the Total Abstinence Society in 1838; however, his was not the first temperance effort in Ireland. Three men – Rev Nicholas Dunscombe, Quaker William Martin and Richard Dowden – introduced temperance activities to Cork earlier in the 1830s.

7. The first American temperance organizations were designed to promote moderation. Lyman Beecher's *Six Sermons of Intemperance* (1826) challenged the idea that moderate drinking was harmless (Nissenbaum 71). At the same time, he did not call for total abstinence. In 1830, Sylvester Graham began lecturing on temperance in Philadelphia for the Society for Discouraging the Use of Ardent Spirits; his arguments were made on physiological principles. Those principles led to a wider Grahamite programme of diet and other health reforms. At the end of his life, in failing health, Graham turned to alcohol and meat (Nissenbaum 15).

8. In his charts of destinations and mileage, Fraser refers to Glendalough as the Seven Churches of Glendalough (88, 101–3).

9. The German traveller J.G. Kohl visited copper mines near Rathdrum during his 1842 tour of Ireland. He reported that the mines were worked by Cornish men called Williams who also had mining interests in America. Kohl reported that some 2,000 people were working in Avonmore and Avoca (252).

10. Fraser too disapproved of the yarns told by Glendalough guides. He wrote that he tried 'to avoid all those wild flights of fancy mixed up with the silly colloquy and ridiculous legends' (100). On the other hand, Kohl enjoyed George Irwin, his 'intelligent and entertaining guide', who claimed to have shown Maria Edgeworth, Sir Walter Scott, the young Victoria and her mother the Duchess of Kent the sights of Glendalough (242).

11. Nicholson's hieroglyphics were possibly the formulaic Irish inscriptions ask-

ing for prayers for individuals.

12. Samuel and Anna Hall, who visited Glendalough in 1841, also saw Kathleen hanging from the cliff; it was part of the entertainment for tourists. The nineteenth-century Kathleen added a penitential dimension to her performance that reflected Glendalough's tradition as a site for pilgrims (II 232-3). There were riotous 'patterns' there on 3 June (St Kevin's feast) until Cardinal Cullen suppressed the custom in 1862 (Killanin 293).

13. Kevin's Cross is a twelfth-century granite cross about ten feet high. Nicholson may be referring to the custom of wrapping one's arms around the cross for good luck.

14. Like other tourists, Nicholson includes the traditions of St Kevin's bed, the cave above the lake and the legend of the persistent Kathleen in her account of visiting the Seven Churches. Surprisingly, she does not mention Father Mathew's two visits to preach at Glendalough.

15. 'By that lake, whose gloomy shore / Sky-lark never warbled o'er' are the first two lines of Thomas Moore's song by that title, the poet's version of the Kevin/Kathleen legend. In more recent years, Brendan Behan and the Dubliners have sung versions of 'In Glendalough there lived an old Saint'.

16. St Kevin's Well is located near the bridge over the Glendasen River.

17. Nicholson's disclaimers about women and politics are not coyness. She supported the wing of the American Anti-Slavery Society which rejected the participation of women as equals in the movement.

18. James Redmond was parish priest of Arklow in 1844 (Thom's 346).

19. Here again Nicholson judges schools partly on the basis of whether children's education was limited by their class. Nicholson protests the behaviour of a tyrannical teacher.

20. Substituting 'she' for 'he', Nicholson uses lines from Oliver Goldsmith's 'The Deserted Village', stanza 12, ll. 7, 8, 11 and 12, to describe the stern schoolmistress.

Chapter V

1. Nicholson travelled the fifty-four and a half miles from Dublin to Athy for three shillings, fourpence. First class passage was five shillings (Fraser 676).

2. William Carleton describes the numerous blind fiddlers in his sketch 'Mickey M'Rorey, The Irish Fiddler', *Tales and Sketches Illustrating the Character, Usages, Traditions, Sports and Pastimes of the Irish Peasantry*: 'In Ireland it is impossible, on looking through all classes of society, to find any individual so perfectly free from care, or in stronger words, so completely happy, as the fiddler, especially if he be blind, which he generally is' (4). The best known of the nineteenth-century smallpox-blinded fiddlers was the poet Antoine Raiftearaí (Anthony Raftery, 1779–1835).

3. Castlecomer was laid out on the model of the Italian town of Alsinore by Sir Christopher Wandsford in the mid-seventeenth century after Brennan land fell to him (Healy 411). The town suffered damage later in the century and in 1798 (Kilannin 152).

4. Like all the tourists of the time, Nicholson frequently comments about the ubiquitous Irish beggars. Her remark about beggars without famine was prophetic.

5. Nicholson's Urlingford servant girls probably came from the parish of Johnstown, which was known as Fertagh (Fertagh na gCaorach, The Graves of the Sheep) until it was united with Galmoy in 1861 (Dowling 7). That she walked two miles from Johnstown toward Urlingford suggests that her destination was the townland of Mountfinn.

6. The local doctor in Johnstown was John Joseph Delany. His dispensary was at White Gate (*Thom's* 154). Lady Wilde lists a number of traditional ways to remove warts, including, 'Tie up some pebbles in a bag with a piece of silver money and throw it in the road. Whoever finds the bag and keeps the money, to him the warts will go and leave you forever' (Wilde 24). A version of that cure circulated in upstate New York through the 1950s. The writer credits a cure to rubbing a penny on the wart and leaving it on a piano for someone else to find.

7. A kish, also called a creel, is a basket woven of hazel or sally rods. Estyn Evans describes a horse-drawn, wheel-less sidecar of two shafts with a cross-piece that carried a large creel or kish, which was used to transport turf down a steep mountainside. He also describes a wheel-car having a box body or wickerwork creel attached for transport of goods. Covered with straw matting, it became a seat. Passengers sat back to back on each side (173). The Halls have descriptions and engravings of three different kinds of cars including the outside jaunting-car (63–6).

8. Charlotte Elizabeth was Charlotte Browne Tonna's (1790–1846) pseudonym. She wrote a number of pamphlets for the Dublin Tract Society, some thirty novels including Irish historical novels *The Rockite* (1832) and *Derry: A Tale of the Revolution* (1839), and Orange songs (Brown 99–100). Her *Letters from Ireland MDCC-CXXXVII* were written 'to remove an unfounded apprehension, or an unjust suspicion, as to this lovely country and its interesting inhabitants' (iv). She tells readers, 'Yet one thing that is always striking in Ireland – the courteous kindess of all classes when they see it will not be coldly repelled' (77). Her views on the kindness of Kilkenny peasantry were formed during the period when she lived in that county with her first husband, a Captain Phelan (Welch 565).

9. Nicholson's description of her dance welcome reflects not only the hospitality of the people but also the popularity of dancing as a form of entertainment in the countryside. See the mention of crossroads dancing in *Johnstown, Galmoy and Urlingford Parishes* (Dowling 35).

10. Nicholson offers an early description of an American wake complete with the *caoine*-like lament for the emigrant. There is a similar farewell to departing Blasket girls in Maurice O'Sullivan's *Twenty Years A-Growing.*

11. The family Nicholson meant could have been the Nevilles of Marymount or the Helys of Violet Hill.

12. Lewis says Urlingford was the centre of fabric manufacturing and there was an extensive retail trade with the district (II, 670).

13. Nicholson's room overlooked the Urlingford fair ground which was along Lumper Lane. The fair on 15 August coincided with the Feast of the Assumption. The Blessed Virgin Mary is the patron of Urlingford parish. The holy well (Lady's Well) is beside Togher Road on the way to Gortnahoe (Dowling 28).

14. There were two national schools in Urlingford in 1837 – one supported by the

Earl of Kilkenny and one by a Mr Fitzpatrick for 70 boys and 70 girls – and a private school (Lewis II, 671). The old site of the Urlingford National School was on Main Street at the site of the present Texaco station.

Chapter VI

1. Nicholson walked up Spahill to take the waters at Ballyspellin, a well-known mineral spa. Lewis describes the waters as curing obstructions and dropsies (II, 31). Thomas Sheridan praised the waters with the verse:

> All you who would refine your blood
> As fair as famed Llewellin
> By waters clear come every year
> To drink at Ballyspellan.

Jonathan Swift answered Sheridan with a 15-stanza ballad including these lines:

> Dare you dispute
> You saucy brute
> And think there's no refilling
> You scurvy lays
> And senseless praise
> You give to Ballyspellan
>   (Dowling 15)

2. George Delany was listed as proprietor of Ballyspellin House (*Thom's* 234).

3. The parish priest of Urlingford in 1844–5 was Edward Kealy, who served from 1843 to 1880 (Dowling 34)

4. In addition to Charles Hely's Violet Hill, there were two other local villas: Ellenville and Melrose (Fraser 220).

5. Sir Vere Hunt, Bart, named Colliery New Birmingham for its situation next to the coal mines of Killenaule (Lewis I, 208).

6. Nicholson is probably describing Grangehill, Co. Tipperary, which is located in Kilcooly parish and Urlingford Poor Law Union.

7. The Temperance Reports in the State Paper Office, Dublin, refer to the reduced drinking in the southern counties (Kerrigan 86). See also Kerrigan's chapter 'Drinking and Crime' (86–106).

8. Nicholson reported not only workers' wages but the availabilty of work. Nicholson was not the only traveller who compared the condition of Irish labourers with those of slaves in the ante-bellum American south. Kohl pointed out that the Irish tenant was free; 'he can go away whenever he chooses. He has almost all the conveniences of slavery (he is entirely dependent on his master; the lash is only wanting – a fact which must be thankfully acknowledged) without enjoying the advantages resulting from the sympathy and kind foresight of his master' (21). Frederick Douglass addressed that comparison in *My Bondage and my Freedom*, saying, "The Irish man is poor, but he is not a slave. He may be in rags, but he is not a slave. He is still the master of his body ..." (433).

9. The estate Nicholson visited could have been Mr Langley's Colebrooke or Fergus Langley's Lichfen (Fraser 282).

10. Nicholson refers to 2 Samuel 7:14–15, 'I will be his father, and he shall be my son. If he commit iniquity, I will chasten him with the rod of men, and with the

the stripes of the children of men. But my mercy shall not depart away from him
...'

11. Sir William Barker's 1600-acre estate was located near the ruins of Kilcooly Abbey, a late-twelfth-century Cistercian abbey. The Barkers brought in a colony of Palatines from Limerick around 1780 (Lewis II, 71). W.B. and Lady Harriet Barker supported one of the local schools. The Barkers' mansion was burned in 1842 (Fraser 221).

12. Nicholson's list of sights in Thurles sounds like the list in Fraser (273). Lewis described the market house as a 'neat' building in the western part of Main Street (II, 623). The 'fine chapel', built on the site of the fifteenth-century Franciscan friary by the O'Meaghers, was replaced by the Cathedral of the Assumption, which was built by J.J. McCarthy after Nicholson's visit. St Patrick's College was founded in 1836. Both the Presentation and the Ursuline orders had convents in Thurles and both orders offered free schooling to poor girls. St Mary's (Church of Ireland) is east of the cathedral.

13. Mrs W is likely to have been Mrs James Walsh (*Slater's* 1846, 316).

14. King Donal Mór O'Brien endowed a Cistercian monastery on the site of an earlier foundation in 1180. Nicholson was often scandalized by the condition of Irish graveyards: shallow graves and bones of those interred earlier tossed around casually.

15. On 8 September 1844 Father Mathew got word that his youngest brother, Thomas of Castle Lake, near Cashel, had had a stroke. He died the next morning (Augustine 350). Father Mathew spoke of his brewer brother in Cashel in a speech in late 1842 (Augustine 261).

16. Nicholson was an ardent abolitionist. It is likely that the American Anti-Slavery Society was launched from her boarding-house in 1833.

17. The White Quakers were an austere movement led by the charismatic Joshua Jacobs. There were White Quaker meeting-houses in Clonmel, Waterford, Mountmellick and Dublin (Wigham 81).

18. It is not clear what war the old man thought the English were expecting. The revolutions of 1848 were years away and England's Victorian wars – Crimea (1854–56) and the Indian Mutiny (1857–58) – were a decade later.

19. Charles Bianconi (1786–1875), the Italian-born founder of Ireland's first public road transportation system, was Nicholson's *bête noire*. While he was a lifelong friend of Father Mathew, Nicholson believed Bianconi exploited his drivers and defrauded the public by adding on hidden charges.

20. In 1998, Fr Vincent of Mount Melleray said that the Porter's Lodge, where Nicholson was received, is the present reception building. He praised the accuracy of Nicholson's account; however, he said there could hardly have been corn sheaves because there was little tillage. The old church has been replaced, but part of the chapel wall has been preserved. Jones, the organ benefactor, joined the community, left because of poor health, and then gave the organ to Melleray. The Rgt Rev Dom Ryan was Abbot of Mount Melleray in 1844.

21. There is no record of the guest book that Nicholson mentions.

22. Nicholson may have objected to Ireland being described as 'poor in spirit' (Matthew 5:3–11) because it suggests an acceptance of oppression.

23. Henry D. Inglis visited the Abbey in 1834. According to Inglis, Sir Richard Kane, Bart, the largest land-owner of the district, granted the monks some 570 acres of moor and bogland rent-free, on a lease of 100 years (96). Sir Richard lived along the Blackwater; his Cappoquin House overlooked the town (Fraser 232).

24. The old farm buildings that Nicholson likened to the Shakers' were being restored in 1998.

25. Jesus's parable of humility is from Luke 14:8. 'When thou are bidden of any man to a wedding, sit not down in the highest room, lest a more honourable man than thou be bidden of him'. The Lucifer reference is to Isaiah 14:12, 'How art thou fallen from heaven, O Lucifer, son of the morning!' In the Book of Daniel (3:1–7), Nebuchadnezzar set up a golden image; however, Shadrach, Meshach and Abednego refused to worship the image and submitted to a fiery furnace. When they emerged safely from their ordeal, Nebuchadnezzer recognized the intensity of their faith and the power of their God. The book of Daniel also describes Belshazzar, son of Nebuchadnezzar, taking golden vessels that had been removed from the temple and using them at a feast. The words 'Mene, Mene, Tekel' (numbered, weighed, divided) appeared on the wall. That night Belshazzar was killed. The second chapter of Matthew describes the massacre of the innocents ordered by Herod.

Chapter VII

1. If the English were concerned about Irish political views in the summer of 1844, it probably had to do with the state trial against Daniel O'Connell and his associates on charges of conspiracy. The trial resulted in O'Connell's sentence of a year's imprisonment.

2. Sir Richard Musgrave lived near Lismore at Tourin, a home built partly in an ancient ruined castle. An Irish Member of Parliament, he was considered a liberal Protestant land-owner. While he was curt with Nicholson, she would have approved of some of his views. In 1836, he supported Sharman Crawford's unsuccesful efforts to abolish tithes, and he supported measures to provide assistance to the able-bodied poor including a relief bill of his own that did not pass (Macintyre 194, 210–11). Musgrave maintained two public schools in Lismore (Lewis I, 184). Musgrave's father Sir Richard (1757–1818) wrote *Memoirs of the Different Rebellions in Ireland* (1801), a fiercely loyalist account of the 1798 Rising.

3. Whiting Bay is a small bay between Ardmore Head and the Blackwater. Fraser describes several bathing lodges along its shore (244).

4. When Inglis visited the area in 1834, he compared the Blackwater from Cappoquin to Youghal with the descent of the renowned continental rivers: the Danube, Rhine and Rhone (99).

5. One of the ruined castles was part of Musgrave's Tourin. Inglis and Fraser mention imposing homes along the Blackwater: Sir William Homan's Dromroe, Villier Stuart's Drumanna, Mr Usher's Campire, John Kelly's Strancally, Ballinatray and Mr Ronan's estate (Inglis 99, Fraser 232–3).

6. Lewis describes the 'noble bridge' as a 'light and elegant' forty-foot drawbridge built of fir. It was erected in 1830 by Gerry Nimmo according to as design by Alexander Nimmo (II 726).

7. Nicholson is describing St Declan's Well, not St Dagan's Well. Located near Dysert Church at Ardmore Head, it was the site of a popular local pattern held on 24 July each year. Nicholson mentions the bishop's opposition to the tradition that the well could produce miracles. The site has three stone crucifixes, a stone chair and a tank used for ritual bathing by pilgrims (Killanin 68).

8. In John 4:9, Jesus asks a woman of Samaria for a drink of water. As they talk, he reveals that he is the Messiah (25–26).

9. In Genesis 24:15–67, Rebecca, the daughter of Bethuel, gives water to Abraham's servant and follows him to Abraham to become the wife of Isaac and the mother of Jacob and Esau.

10. Nicholson was in an area which has remained Irish-speaking, the Ring, County Waterford Gaeltacht.

11. Nicholson refers to John 14:6, 'I am the way, the truth and the life'.

12. Bonnels: Nicholson's transliteration of the Irish *bainbh*, piglets.

13. The celebrated church was the monastery of St Cárthach (d. 637/8), the most important monastery in Munster in the twelfth century. The Lismore diocese merged with Waterford but had its own cathedral until the Reformation (Duignan 356). Cromwell levelled the cathedral because it was a Catholic garrison. The present church preserves some fragments of the Romanesque church; the stained glass Nicholson admired was by George McAllister of Dublin (Duignan 356).

14. While O'Connell had been sentenced to one year in prison, on 4 September 1844, the House of Lords reversed the judgment (Trench 291). O'Connell was released on the 6th and returned to Dublin in triumph. The countryside celebrated with bonfires. The newspaper editor imprisoned with O'Connell may have been Sir Charles Gavan Duffy (1816–1903), a founder of *The Nation* (1842) and a Young Irelander. He emigrated to Australia in 1855, becoming Prime Minister of Victoria in 1871.

15. Nicholson liked to quote 'the little foxes' to describe a spoiler.

16. See a similar sentiment in W.B. Yeats's two-line poem 'Parnell'.

17. In his 8 June 1843 speech in Kilkenny that was carried in the 10 June issue of *The Nation*, O'Connell said: 'It is the Temperance that will give us the Repeal. Temperance will give it to us; for now I can trust in every one of you; as I am not afraid that any drunkard will, in his haughtiness, refuse to obey my commands. I defy your enemies. Yes, the moral miracle of temperance has rendered the cause of Ireland irresistable. Those who have overcome their vice can not be conquered by any enemy' (McCaffrey 22).

18. The *Dublin Penny Journal* article, 'Individual Exertions: Mr. Bianconi' (8 September 1832), describes Charles Bianconi directing his drivers 'to pick up, free of charge, all pedestrians who cannot pay for a whirl and who seem to be travelling with pain to themselves'.

19. Nicholson may be speaking about stepmothers from her own experience. There is no record that Nicholson had children of her own, but it appears that Norman Nicholson had children.

20. The way to the Well of St Patrick was equally confusing in June 1998, and directions from Clonmel were equally varied. The altar has three stone panels: a central crucifixion with a figure of an angel on the left and the Virgin and child on

the right. A sign instructs pilgrims to say the rosary while visiting 'this healing well'. The place continues to have the atmosphere Nicholson described in 1844. The site was restored in 1969 with donations from Americans: Mayor Sam Yorty of Los Angeles, Armand Hammer and the Irish Israel Society of Southern California.

21. The site of the Baptist church was the corner of Morton and Short Streets. In 1998, two elderly local residents remembered the church as a one-storey building where services were held until World War II.

22. When Nicholson says that God 'tempers the winds to the shorn lamb' she suggests that God gives an extra measure of character to the Irish poor.

Chapter VIII

1. Mr B may have been Richard Burke, a flour dealer located on the New Road, Thurles.

2. Both the Ursulines and the Presentations had convents in Thurles in 1844. The monks' school was probably St Patrick's College, which was later the site of the Synod of Thurles in 1850.

3. Pope Gregory XVI prohibited slavery in 1838.

4. Nicholson's remark was prophetic. O'Connell's constitutional Repeal movement would be replaced by Young Irelanders' physical force movement. Their brief, unsuccessful rising in 1848 resulted in transportation for its leaders. Nicholson understood the frustration that led them to rebellion (*Annals* 14, 119).

5. Nicholson thinks the old man believes that she is a camp follower.

6. The Welsh-born Anglo-Norman Giraldus Cambrensis (?1146–1220?), wrote admiringly of Irish musicians in his *Topographia Hibernica* (1188).

7. Mr C's sister who lives six miles from Roscrea may have lived in Borris-in-Ossory.

8. Nicholson criticized the expectation that servants would lie for their mistresses.

9. Nicholson may have been thinking of the lines from Proverbs 27:15, 'A continual dropping in a very rainy day and a contentious woman are alike'.

10. Nicholson opposed tithes. See *Annals* 28, 184.

11. Nicholson quotes Daniel 5:25–8, 'numbered, weighed and divided', meaning that one were weighed and found wanting.

12. Nicholson's reference to Solomon's Rod was her biblical text for the old adage, 'Spare the rod and spoil the child'. The source of the lines 'I would not live always, I ask not to stay' has not been identified.

13. The Christian Brethren were founded in Ireland by J.N. Darby, who had been an Anglican priest in Plymouth. Puritanical, pietistic and millenarian, the Brethren were committed to spreading the gospel through their churches, which were local and autonomous.

14. Father Mathew visited Roscrea twice in 1840 where there was an established temperance society; however, in 1843, the Ribbonmen (an agrarian secret society) tried to get locals to break their pledge (Kerrigan 61, 104). That may have prompted Fr Mathew's return to Roscrea in the autumn of 1844.

15. The Roscrea Workhouse, designed for 700 inmates, admitted its first inmate

on 7 May 1842 (John O'Connor 263). George O'Malley was the Master and Alice O'Malley was the Matron (*Slater's* 1846, 308).

16. Nicholson is probably talking about Inchnameo Abbey, a Romanesque church associated with St Cainneach. The 'seats of wealthy landlords' would have included Leap Castle, an O'Carroll castle that belonged to the Carrolls of Carrollton, Maryland. In 1844 the castle was owned by Derby Horatio D'Esterra. It was burned in 1922 (Killanin 416).

17. The village of Cloughjordan, two miles west of Roscrea, had a distillery in 1844 (Fraser 266).

18. While Nicholson was often scandalized by the blend of pagan and Christian elements in some of the Irish Catholic religious practices – patterns, pilgrimages to holy wells and funeral customs – she made it her business to witness those events. The Irish howl was the *caoine*, the traditional death cry uttered by the female relatives of the deceased. Nicholson not only admitted that she hoped for a 'howl' but she also defended an old lady's right to howl as an outlet for her grief. The Halls describe the *caoine* with drawings and with a transcription of a *caoine* (I, 225–9).

19. Father Mathew preached on temperance at 8:00 Sunday morning. The text of the Irish Total Abstinence Society Pledge was, 'I promise with the Divine assistance to abstain from all intoxicating liquors and to prevent as much as possible by advice and example, intemperance in others'.

20. Nicholson describes Father Mathew with Oliver Goldsmith's lines about the exemplary village preacher in 'The Deserted Village'.

21. The ancient building was the house of the Damer family which was turned into a barracks for seven officers and 106 of the rank and file (Lewis II, 527).

22. Nicholson's guide was probably William Henry Downer, who was listed in *Slater's* (306) as an 'Apothecary and Manufacturing Chemist' with premises on Main Street in Roscrea.

23. Folklore about Oliver Cromwell survives today, reflecting the deep impression that the horrors of his 1649 campaign in Ireland left in the Irish folk memory (Ó hOgáin 129).

24. Nicholson's rescuer John Talbot was known for his kindness. When he died in 1853, the *British Friend* reported: 'All of the shops in Roscrea were kept partially closed until after his funeral. He was a liberal subscriber to the local charities and emphatically a man of universal love and peace. He was universally courteous to rich and poor and always discouraged drinks. He was anxious by example and precept for the extension of peace toward all. Above all he trusted humbly in the mercy of God through our Lord and Saviour Jesus Christ' (Harrison 96).

Chapter IX

1. In the nineteenth century, Birr was called Parsonstown after the Parsons family. Sir Lawrence Parsons was granted the town of Birr in 1620.

2. The identity of the eccentric Mr S remains a mystery. There was a Thomas Coghlan or 'The Maw' (Mac) living on the road from Birr to Banagher, who was characterized as 'gallant, eccentric and hospitable in the extreme', but he died about 1790 (Hall II, 189–90). Nicholson's description of herself as 'rolling things

before a whirlwind' is from Isaiah 17:13; however, in her case, she is not driven as dust before a storm, but she is carried along under some divine protection.

3. William Parsons, the 3rd Earl of Rosse (1800–67), constructed the giant telescope, a simpler version of the Herschel telescope, that attracted astronomers from all over the world.

4. Nicholson may refer to its neat classical façade, described by Lewis as a handsome building 'with well-executed pediment of hewn stone' (Lewis I, 457). It is at the corner of Emmet Street and The Green.

5. Nicholson describes a Birr parish priest, Rev W. Crotty, who had differences with the Bishop of Killaloe. When the bishop suspended Crotty, he broke with the Catholic Church, and, with a Mr Carlisle, who had been a Commissioner of Education, he started a church whose doctrine was that 'nothing is to be feared but Popery' (Augustine 541). Several parishioners followed him. The Sisters of Mercy were brought to Birr to help counter Crotty (Augustine 539).

6. Nicholson's remark that the children she met on the road in the west of Ireland never said 'yes' or 'no', but 'I have not, ma'am', or 'I will, ma'am' reflects the influence of the Irish language on English as it was spoken in the west of Ireland, and indeed is often spoken today. There is no word for 'yes' or 'no' in the Irish language. One answers in the affirmative or the negative with the appropriate verb.

7. Nicholson's observation about the memorable speech of the country people was shared by other travellers of the time. Some observers resorted to descriptions that contemporary readers associate with stage Irishmen. While Nicholson's accounts of conversations with country people are rendered in authentic speech, they avoid negative stereotypes.

8. Inglis wrote approvingly of Ballinasloe when he visited in 1834 and referred to the 'fostering hand' of Lord Clancarty, an improving and resident landlord (208–11). While Nicholson says she saw hundreds of inmates at the lunatic asylum, it was built for a capacity of only 150 when it was opened in 1833 (Lewis I, 110).

9. Nicholson's conversations with those intending to emigrate and those who returned from America offer some insights into emigration from Ireland to North America before the Great Famine. Kerby Miller estimates that between 80,000 and 1,000,000 Irish emigrated between 1815 and 1844 (193). *Thom's* 1844 lists the rate of exchange as $1=4s 1 1/2 d.

10. The story of the man who thought that the sexton of the Protestant church in Galway was the devil reflects the figure of the devil in Irish legend, where he appears in human form with a grotesque feature like a cloven hoof or a tail. While the devil is defeated in most stories, he is still to be feared (O'Sullivan 21).

11. Nicholson's story of the woman and the honest pig she met at the Loughrea market may reflect the custom of not giving anything away until the sale is made. It also demonstrates the value of the pig to the rural household.

12. Some of the knowledge of America in rural Ireland came from returned Irish, letters home and advertisements of work for labourers (Miller 203).

13. Nicholson would have recognized Mary as the mother of Jesus, but she would have regarded the Roman Catholic beliefs about her that made her an object of veneration – her immaculate conception, her assumption into heaven and her intercessionary powers – as idolatry.

14. Nicholson arrived in Galway with a half-crown. Fraser estimated that the cost of a bed and three meals a day at an Irish country inn would be about six shillings a day. The cost in larger towns or in Killarney would go up to eight shillings and sixpence (vii). The Halls also estimated that a day's expenses in Killarney for the 'moderate' traveller would be 'something less than about seven shillings a day' exclusive of sightseeing expenses (II, 183).

15. Women fishmongers outnumbered men; by 1851, there were seven women to one man (Langan-Egan 19). While other travellers seem not to have been bothered, Nicholson frequently complains of people staring at her. It may have been that she was a woman travelling alone by foot through regions where visitors seldom appeared.

16. The Galway fishing industry before the Famine was extensive but underdeveloped (O'Tuathaigh 140). O'Tuathaigh also notes that by 1830, the port of Galway was a centre of emigrant traffic (140).

17. Nearly a century later when Augusta, Lady Gregory wanted to be buried beside her sister Arabella in that cemetery, she was wedged between Arabella and her husband. She described the cemetery as, 'a beautiful burying-place, lying high, the sun shining on it, on the silver sea' (Kohlfeldt 304).

18. Mr F. was Joseph Fisher, a Presbyterian cleric in Galway (*Thom's* 1844, 276).

19. Nicholson used the lines, 'Lay not careless hands on skulls that cannot teach and will not learn' to describe the lack of charity demonstrated by Rev Fisher.

20. Nicholson quotes from Luke 6:24-6, 'But woe unto you that are rich, for you have received your consolation. Woe unto you that are full, for you shall hunger. Woe unto you that laugh now, for you shall mourn and weep', to express her compassion for the unemployed labourers.

21. Nicholson is probably describing the Connemara girl's *sean-nós* singing.

22. Ananias and his wife Sapphira fall dead shortly after falsely claiming that they have given the entire proceedings of a sale of their possession to the community (Acts 5:1-11).

Chapter X

1. It appears that Nicholson's experience with the hospitality of Irish country people caused her to think of rural cabins as 'guardian angels'.

2. It was eighteen Irish miles from Galway to Loughrea on the main roads of the day. The first four miles would have taken Nicholson to Oranmore. She stops along the road to Craughwell to imagine life back in New York.

3. The lines are from Edward Young's 'Night III', *Night Thoughts*, l. 63.

4. The woman Nicholson met could have been a tenant on the Clanrickarde estate, which featured in later evictions during the winter of 1885–6, evictions that were cited in Charles Stewart Parnell's Plan of Campaign.

5. The 'muddy little village' may have been Killimor, which is about ten miles south-east of Loughrea on the road to Eyre Court.

6. Nicholson may have heard the Irish word *confach*, which can mean sharp as in *labhairt go confach le duine* (to speak sharply with someone).

7. Nicholson refers to the kingdom of God (Mark 1:14) or the kingdom of heaven (Matthew 18:3).

8. Eyre Court was the seat of John Eyre in 1844, an estate settled by Cromwellians. Charles Lever's Charles O'Malley was based on the eighteenth-century owner George Eyre (Killanin 277).

9. Nicholson recognizes the biblical parallel (John 13:14) to the Irish rural custom of bathing the feet of weary walkers.

10. The cheerful miller's daughter alludes to James 4:7, 'Submit yourself therefore to God. Resist the devil and he will flee from you.'

11. Nicholson uses two favourite parables about charity to describe Mary Aigin (Eagan): the good Samaritan (Luke 10:33–7) and the widow's mite (Mark 12:41–3).

Chapter XI

1. The village of Brosna, five miles from Roscrea, is in the parish of Shinrone. The police-officer in Shinrone in 1844 was James Butler.

2. Fraser lists two hotels and two inns in Roscrea: the Victoria and the White Hart, and Smallman's and Brown's.

3. Mrs T's threepence charge is very modest compared with the two shillings and sixpence for tea and a bed that Fraser tells travellers to expect to be charged in Irish country inns (vii). Nicholson quotes from Ecclesiastes 11:1, 'Cast thy bread upon the water: for thou shalt find it after many days'.

4. Nicholson likely stopped in Borris-in-Ossory.

5. 'My shoes waxed not old on my feet' alludes to Joshua 9:13, 'and these our garments and our shoes are become old by reason of the very long journey'.

6. *Thom's* lists the stops on the Durrow–Dublin mail route as: Abbeyleix–Maryborough–Stradbally–Athy–Kilcullen–Naas–Dublin.

7. Abbeyleix was founded on the site of a monastery dating to about 600. Fraser reported that the town had a 'straggling' appearance by 1844 (218). The De Vescis were considered responsible resident landlords. The old gentleman Nicholson met would have built his house sometime after 1756, when the previous Lord De Vesci razed the original village and rebuilt it on a more advantageous site (Lewis I, 4).

8. Nicholson was back at her old lodgings on 5 December 1844. She gives 45 Hardwicke Street as a return address in the summer of 1847; she may have stayed there during her earlier visits to Dublin.

9. Nicholson set off along the North Circular Road, the northern ring road around Dublin.

Chapter XII

1. A polka coat or polka jacket, a new fashion of the day, was a tight-fitting women's jacket.

2. Nicholson may refer to lines from Genesis 12:1–2, 'Now the Lord had said unto Abraham, Get thee out of thy country, and from thy kindred, and from thy father's house, unto a land I will show thee: And I will make thee a great nation', to describe her mission to read the Bible to the Irish poor.

3. Nicholson comforts the distraught woman with words from John 6:17–21 describing Jesus walking on the water and telling his apostles not to be afraid.

4. There were two fixed lights on Wicklow Head. *Thom's* described the Wicklow Head Light as a First Class light which beamed every two minutes (32).

5. Nicholson's favourite hymn was Samuel Stennett's 'Majestic Sweetness Sits Enthroned'.

6. Nicholson meets Mrs Baldwin, wife of Henry Baldwin, the lighthouse keeper for Gorey District, Wicklow Station.

7. The intelligent mountain boy carrying *The Iliad* has his literary counterparts in William Carleton's Latin-speaking schoolboys in 'Denis O'Shaughnessy Going to Maynooth', and 'The Hedge School'. Brian Friel used a classical hedge-school as the setting for his play *Translations* (1980).

8. Nicholas Furlong described the narrow, unpaved streets of Wicklow in the nineteenth century and said it was a town with few enticements (Furlong 170).

9. The school was probably St Patrick's, which was the Erasmus Smith School in Wicklow.

Chapter XIII

1. The Franciscan church in Wexford town was built in 1690 on an old medieval site. It was the only Catholic church in Wexford during penal times. The church was renovated about 1790 and again in 1857 (Conlan 105).

2. The nunnery housed the Presentation Sisters. James Keating (1783–1849), ordained 1808, was Bishop of Ferns when Nicholson visited Wexford. Active and zealous, Keating built the first gothic church in the United Kingdom; he also built two schools for poor children and a convent for the Presentation nuns. There is a monument to Keating in Enniscorthy (Hore 331).

3. The chapel windows Nicholson admired were dedicated to Sts Bridget and John. The Franciscans opened a secondary school in the early 1800s; it was replaced by the present St Peter's College, which stands on Summer Hill. It is the diocesan school for Ferns. The library has a valuable collection of theological works. The friary included the residence of the provincial and a novitiate (Conlan 106).

4. Nicholson disapproved of holy wells and other folk religious customs, liking to note with approval that such practices were discontinued. See *Annals* 137, 222.

5. The governor of the Wexford Gaol in 1845 was Mr Lemuel Gladwin (*Thom's* 1845, 280). Rev Richard Waddy Elgee was the Inspector and Chaplain (*Thom's* 1845, 281).

6. The Wexford poor-house was opened in 1842 with accommodation for 600 inmates. Fraser described it as a handsome building which occupied a conspicuous site near the north entrance of town (121).

7. Always scrupulous about her books and bibles, Nicholson offered tracts to the poor-house library. This was Nicholson's first meeting with resistance to her mission. She would later meet similar suspicion in areas such as the Diocese of Tuam where there was active proselytism of Roman Catholics.

8. In addition to coastal steamers, there were two steamers that went between Waterford and Liverpool (Fraser 121). Nicholson probably refers to the Erasmus Smith funds that supported St Patrick's school as well as the national school.

9. Neither local Wexford directories nor the list of Irish peers identifies a Lady Nevin of the Hermitage.

10. 'Village Master taught his little school' is line 198 from Oliver Goldsmith's 'The Deserted Village'.

11. Nicholson again notices the way that class influences and controls social interaction in Ireland. In some circles, even a schoolmaster would be considered a servant.

12. The old stone round tower built by the Vikings in 1003 is now a city museum.

13. Cummins Hotel, Waterford, was Bianconi's most important regional office. One of M.A. Hayes's aquatints shows the arrival of a Bianconi car in Waterford.

14 The Clonmel–Cork Bianconi car passed through Cahir, Mitchelstown, Fermoy, Rathcormac, Watergrass-hill and Glenmire. Horses were probably exchanged at Mitchelstown.

15. Dr George N. Watson of Marlboro Street was the Baptist of Cork in 1844. Baptist services were held at noon and at 6:30 in the evening on Sundays; there were prayer meetings at 8 on Wednesday nights (Aldwell 104). The Mrs Fisher recommended by Dr Watson was probably the Mrs Fisher at 40 Terrace. See *Annals* 228.

16. The Irish Evangelical Society founded in 1842 supported thirty-five itinerant preachers and scripture-readers who could minister in Irish as well as English (*Thom's* 309–10). There was also an older organization called Scripture Readers for Ireland (1822) which employed "pious men of humble rank" to read the Bible to the poor. Hamilton Verschoyle was its Director.

17. Mrs Fisher may have been Mrs Ellen Fisher, who owned a hotel and livery stable at 1 Caroline Street (Aldwell 174).

Chapter XIV

1. There is a description of Father Mathew's house at 10 Cove Street, Cork, in Augustine (105).

2. Nicholson heard Father Mathew preach in Roscrea. Nicholson and Mathew would have had a number of mutual friends in the temperance movement.

3. Nicholson describes the Jubilee of Mother Clare Callaghan of the South Presentation convent on Douglas Streeet. While Nicholson reports the Jubilee as happening on the 2nd, the convent records indicate that the ceremony was celebrated on 8 February 1845.

4. On Sunday, 2 February 1845, Nicholson attended services at the Independent Church on George's Street, where Alexander King was minister. Services were held on Sundays at 12 and at 6:30; prayer services were conducted on Tuesday evenings at 7.

5. Nicholson reports that her name appeared in the Cork papers during the first week of February 1845. There is no mention of Nicholson in the *Cork Examiner* on 31 January or 2,5, or 7 February, nor is there mention of her in *The Cork Commercial Courier* or *The Southern Reporter* during that time.

6. The 4 February 1845 dinner would have included Father Mathew's brother Charles and one of his two sons. Shrove Tuesday fell on 4 February in 1845.

7. The young twin sisters who accompanied Nicholson to the Ursuline convent on Ash Wednesday (5 February 1845), may have been daughters of the family who entertained Nicholson in Tullamore.

8. Nicholson's friend Mrs D. may have been the wife of Paul Danckert, an accountant, who lived at 107 Lower Road (Aldwell 1).

9. Mrs Power was the daughter of Judge Livingston of New York. The *Cork Post Office General Directory* (1844) mentions a Dr Power (313).

10. Nicholson suggests Charles Mathew was the overseer of Cork Workhouse.

11. The antiquarian priest was Rev Matthew Horgan, the priest who hosted a party in a barn for the Halls (Hall I, 54).

12. Lady Jefferyes laid out a landscape garden known as The Rock Close (Lincoln 90).

13. Barter's Cold Water Establishment, also called St Ann's Hydropathic Studio, founded by Richard Barter (1820–70), opened in 1842. Nicholson returned to Barter's in 1848 (*Annals* 166–7). There is a bust of Dr Barter in the Crawford Municipal Art Gallery in Cork. See the photographs in Lincoln 88, 89.

Chapter XV

1. Nicholson and her party went to Cloyne via East Ferry.

2. The church built in 600 was the monastery of St Colmán mac Lénéne.

3. The young 'heiress' was one of the daughters of Henry Allen of Cloyne House, the former bishop's palace. The house and the demesne land were leased to an H. Allen in 1836 (Fraser 247).

4. The 100-foot Cloyne round tower, the most complete in Ireland, was struck by lightning in 1748–9 while George Berkeley was the Bishop of Cloyne. When Nicholson visited Cloyne, the Dean of Cloyne was the Very Rev Thomas John Burgh.

5. Nicholson refers to James Gordon Bennett, the New York journalist whose *Herald* featured crime and gossip. Bennett was feared and disliked, but everyone read the *Herald*. While Nicholson thought about Bennett in Cloyne, there was a closer Bennett. The Rev. J Bennett was the Chancellor of the Cathedral.

6. Thomas Fitzgerald owned Rockview.

7. Colonel Hooden's Carrigacrump quarry produced a stone that was 'similar to Italian dove-coloured marble' (Lewis I, 381).

8. There is a photograph of the Cork County Gaol in Lincoln which shows the radial plan of the building designed by the Pain brothers. The building is now part of the National University of Ireland, Cork; only the portico has been preserved (Lincoln 75). The Halls also praised the management of the gaols (I, 20).

9. John Murphy, Esq, was the governor of the gaol; the deputy was Mr John Grace, and the inspector was E.R. Townsend, MD (*Thom's* 1845).

10. When Nicholson left Cork on Friday, 21 February 1845, she thought she would never return. In fact, she revisited Cork during the Famine (*Annals* 146–70). She left Cork for the last time in September 1848.

11. The Acts of the Apostles 24 describes the trial of Paul before Felix on the charges of sedition, disturbing the peace and committing offences against the Temple. Felix, who had taken Drusilla from her husband Asisus, was shaken by Paul's preaching about righteousness and judgment. The story of the Prodigal Son is from Luke 15:11–32. Nicolson quotes verse 21: 'I have sinned'.

12. Nicholson admires Father Mathew's humility. Her reference to John and the angel is an allusion to Revelations 22:8-9. When John kneels at the feet of the angel, the angel tells him that he must worship God alone.

13. Nicholson may have called the sermon based on Matthew 27:46 'orthodox' because she hadn't expected a Roman Catholic priest to share her views about the urgency of salvation.

14. Nicholson spoke again about the high standards of education and the excellent libraries of Cork when she visited the city in 1848 (*Annals* 148–9).

15. Fr Daniel M'Sweeney was the parish priest of Bandon, Co Cork (*Thom's* 1844, 261).

16. The lines are from *Julius Caesar* III, ii, 124.

17. Nicholson uses these lines from the Epistle of James 2:16 again in Chapter 25.

Chapter XVI

1. The Irish celebrated the feast of St John the Baptist on the night of 23 June with communal midsummer fires. The evening started with a prayer to St John; then the dancing and singing began. Jack B. Yeats has a drawing in *Life in the West of Ireland* of little boys throwing paraffin-soaked sods in the air on St John's Eve. Since Nicholson was in Bantry at the end of February 1845, the old man had not had a day of work in eight months.

2. The Bantry Workhouse did not admit the first of its 800 inmates until 24 April 1845 (John O'Connor 259).

3. In *Annals* (108–11) Nicholson develops her criticism of the government's Poor Law policy, which favoured workhouses (130 in Nicholson's time, 163 by 1853) over other kinds of relief.

4. While Nicholson believed she had a better chance leaving Irish-language tracts and bibles with Irish-speakers, people resisted them, because organizations such as the Irish Evangelical Society (1842) used the Irish language for proselytism.

5. When Nicholson says of the suffering poor, 'How long, O Lord, how long', she paraphrases Isaiah 6:11, 'Then said I, Lord, how long?'

6. Nicholson knew the connection between the Glengariff bridge and Cromwell. The Halls included an engraving of the three-arched stone bridge with the story that Cromwell ordered the local people to build a bridge by the time he returned or he would hang a man for every hour it was delayed (Hall, I, 154). There was also a diamond-shaped, four-bastion Cromwellian fort at Newtown, a half-mile from Bantry. One of Cromwell's generals (Ireton) built the fort during the Parliamentary War (Lewis I, 165). The fort is on the map of Newtown in *Wild Gardens* (Everett 111).

7. Lord Bantry's thatched cottage was a hunting lodge for the White family before the first Earl made it his permanent residence. Richard White was created the first Lord Bantry in appreciation of his resistance to Wolfe Tone's abortive landing in Bantry Bay in 1796. His son Richard, Viscount Berehaven, settled in Bantry House in 1842 while the first Earl retired to Glengariff Lodge. Lewis describes it as 'situated in the bosom of the glen, enclosed by the lofty mountains and rugged cliffs' (I, 165). There are sketches of Glengariff Lodge by the second Earl of Bantry and by Augusta, Lady Dunraven in *Wild Gardens* (Everett 141–2). While Everett does not mention Nicholson by name, he cites her account mentioning Lord Bantry's hunchback servant girl. Everett mentions other visitors: Prince Puckler-Muskau, Lady Chatterton, W.M. Thackeray and the Halls. Lord

Bantry was a genial host; however, visitors left discreet contributions, for his income was modest after he had made over his estate to the second Earl in 1835 (Everett 145).

Chapter XVII

1. Nicholson may have visited Mrs White's school in Glengariff (Everett 123). The Halls described a family of five living in a hole in the rocks during the summer and working or begging in a neighbouring town during the winter (Hall I, 140). While Nicholson herself was walking around Ireland on her own mission, she always wrote with approval about women who attended to their household duties. She frequently quoted such passages as Paul's Letter to Titus 11:4–5 and Timothy 11:1–10 in support of 'virtuous women'.

2. Lewis described five public schools and nine private schools in Glengariff which educated some 1000 students. Two schools, one for boys and one for girls, were supported by Lord Bantry (II, 165).

3. Nicholson had a horror of butter. Alfred Webb (1834–1908) wrote in his journal: 'Butter was her peculiar aversion. She told a story of her or some friend examining the intestines of some deceased patient and finding them choked with butter' (126).

4. While Nicholson believed that girls should learn sewing, it was not to be at the expense of other subjects. When the girls said "they bees too old", they were translating into English the Irish present-habitual tense.

5. Fraser mentions just a solitary inn in Glengariff (323). Sharing the house with a cow was an old practice that survived through the nineteenth century. People believed that the cow kept the house warm and that she yielded more milk. There was also an old belief that fire protected the cow from evil spirits, and the household fire provided that safeguard (Evans 43).

6. Nicholson encounters the custom again in Killarney on St Patrick's Day 1845.

7. The Halls include a version of how Gorrane MacSwiney sustained the family of his O'Sullivan foster brother with the flesh of eaglets (I, 155).

8. Nicholson paraphrases Job 24:8, 'They are wet with the showers of the mountains and embrace the rock for want of shelter'.

9. Nettles are rich in iron and vitamins. They were a food source during the Great Famine, and they continue to be used in soups and tonics.

10. Friday was March 7th. Nicholson paraphrases Matthew 25:35, 'I was a stranger and ye took me in'.

11. In his 10 November 1845 letter to *The Times* from Kenmare, T.C. Foster identified the parish priest as the Rev J. Sullivan.

12. Nicholson quotes lines about the day of judgment from Isaiah 34:4, 'the heavens be rolled together as a scroll'.

13. The pass on the old Bantry–Kenmare Road is one of the most picturesque spots in Ireland. The road through the pass was built by Alexander Nimmo.

14. The 200-yard tunnel gave access to Killarney. *The Tourist's Illustrated Hand Book for Ireland* (1853) provides an illustration of the tunnel drawn by Mahony (121).

15. Nicholson would have seen the Magillicuddy Reeks as she emerged from the tunnel.

16. The priest of the glen was the Rev Dennis Mahony (Foster 393). The best lodging in Kenmare probably would have been Mr McCarthy's Lansdowne Arms.

Chapter XVIII

1. Nicholson may have been climbing a wall on the way to see Dunkerron Castle or the old keep of the O'Sullivan Mór. Cromwell's Fort is near the bridge.

2. Nicholson suffered from inflammatory lumbago or myofascitis during her time in Ireland and into her later life. While this episode was precipitated by her fall, classic myofascitis is characterized by its sudden onset without a history of injury or stress.

3. Fraser describes the new road from Kenmare to Glengariff passing over the the estuary of the Ruaghty river on a suspension bridge partly financed by the Marquis of Lansdowne (333).

4. Nicholson says she rode from Kenmare to Killarney through wild track that brought her to the Upper Lake. When the Halls travelled on the new road to Killarney in 1842, they said it was one of the best in the kingdom (II, 179).

5. Staying at Mrs Casey's home was not only pleasant for Nicholson, it was much cheaper than the seven shillings a day that was required even for moderate accommodations (Hall II, 183). Mrs Fisher may have recommended Mrs Casey.

6. Nicholson reached Ross Island over a narrow bridge from the shore of the Lower Lake. The island was part of Lord Kenmare's demesne.

7. The Halls said a Mr Finn owned the Victoria Hotel on the banks of Lower Lake and the Kenmare Arms in Killarney (II, 183).

8. While Nicholson was very careful to give Roman Catholics the Douay Bible, which was the first Bible in English to be translated from the Latin Vulgate, many associated bibles of any kind with Protestant proselytizers.

9. The Torc cascade is sixty feet not eighty feet, but it is one of the highest waterfalls in Ireland. Steps lead to the overlook that Nicholson describes. Nicholson saw Niagara Falls during the early 1830s.

10. Nicholson compares her hostess to the virtuous women of the Old Testament.

11. The Halls' visit to Muckross Abbey prompted a long discussion about funeral customs. Nicholson follows their example with a description of keening women.

12. The Halls too were scandalized by the condition of the Muckross graveyard. They described it as being in a 'very revolting state', saying that it was 'often necessary to remove the remains of one inmate before room can be found for another' (I, 220–1).

13. Muckross Abbey, the burial-place of the MacCarthys, the Macgillycuddys, the O'Donoghues and the O'Sullivans, was a Franciscan friary founded in 1448.

14. The old castle was Ross Island Castle.

15. While Irish labourers yearned to go to America, many found themselves in what economists call a "poverty trap". Because of their poverty, they could not respond to opportunties, such as emigration, that would have improved their lives (O'Gráda 77–8).

16. Nicholson describes the Killarney tourist sights pointed out by boatmen and guides. Other writers of the time provide the legends associated with the sites.

The Halls include the O'Donoghue legend (II, 191); Croker's O'Sullivan Punch Bowl narrative links the Mangerton lake with a Finn McCool story (35–7).

17. Nicholson refers to the story of Sullivan of Glengariff, who supported his family of six by stealing the eagle's prey from its nest. Lewis describes the Eagle's Nest as a pyramid-shaped rock that rises from the water where an eagle was frequently seen (II, 130).

18. The pillar-like rock formations are thought to resemble books, so they are called O'Donoghue's Library (Croker 31).

19. The best-known celebration of Innisfallen is Thomas Moore's poem that begins, 'Sweet Innisfallen, Fare Thee Well'.

20. The 'ludicrous stories' were probably versions of the story of Diarmuid and Gráinne. O'Cahill says the landmark was made to reinforce that tradition (50).

21. The Castle was an O'Donoghue stronghold. Tradition says that it was the last castle surrendered to the Cromwellians. There is a local legend that describes a sighting of O'Donoghue on the first morning in May.

22. Not only did Nicholson and the Halls complain about boatmen's tales, twentieth-century travellers like Robert Lloyd Praeger (*The Way That I Went* 1937) and Frank O'Connor (*Leinster, Munster and Connaught* 1950) warned their readers about garrulous boatmen.

23. Nicholson probably visited the Presentation convent located at the end of New Street across from Lord Kenmare's demesne. The convent was the oldest in the Killarney district. As a friend of Father Mathew's, she would have been especially welcome.

24. Lord Kenmare's Kenmare House had a distant view of the lower lake.

25. The oldest burying-place in all Killarney would have been the graveyard of the seventh-century Church of Agadoe.

26. Nicholson not only observed the Irish custom of showing respect for the deceased by walking a few steps with a funeral procession, she never missed an opportunity to join the mourners.

27. Thomas Crofton Croker described the burial-ground of Agadoe in his *Killarney Legends*: 'The remains of the church stand at the back of the burial-ground, which is covered with house-like tombs: behind that the church, close to a gateway, is the base of one of those round towers, whose use and origin have served to amuse and puzzle the antiquary; and in an adjoining field, to the west of the burial-ground, are the remains of a circular fortalice, commonly called the Bishop's Chair' (99–100).

28. Croker offered another legend of the unquiet dead, a ghost legend about Agadoe (101–9).

29. The Halls also told a clever-Kerry-schoolboy story (II, 185).

30. John 1:29, 'Behold the Lamb of God which taketh away the sin of the world'. The text was incorporated into the liturgy of the Roman Catholic Mass, 'Lamb of God, who takest away the sins of the world, have mercy on us'.

31. The Bishop of Kerry, Most Rev Dr Egan, was dealing with a colony of proselytes trying to convert Roman Catholics in Dingle. He would have been concerned about attempts to make further inroads into his diocese.

32. Lewis described the Deer Park as a beautiful and romantic glen through

which the Dinagh flows crossed by a foot-bridge (II, 127).

33. The American Tract Society's 'Worth of a Dollar' urged readers to abandon their worldy ambitions and turn to the kingdom of heaven. The tract would have complemented Nicholson's readings from Matthew 18:3 and Mark 1:14.

34. The source of this line has not been identified; however, variations of the line appear in texts identified by members of the British Women Romantic Poets Project (University of California, Davis).

35. In his article 'Health and Medicine in Galway', James P. Murray notes that there are remarkably few references to smallpox in Galway though the disease was quite common until the middle of the nineteenth century. Murray speculates that the 'silence of the records' may be due to the fact that smallpox marred its victims but did not take their lives (153).

36. Nicholson quotes Matthew 7:14, 'Strait is the gate, and narrow is the way which leadeth unto life and few there be that find it'.

37. Nicholson refers to St Paul's First Corinthian Letter on love.

38. Nicholson had met children calling "penny for the crass" in Glengariff. By Nicholson's time, the Irish in New York had established St Patrick's Day as a way to express Irish pride and solidarity.

39. Nicholson alludes to the parable of the mustard seed in Matthew 13:31–2.

Chapter XIX

1. Mary Burke of Mountain Stage says the old butter road to Cork would have gone directly from Glenbeigh to Mountain Stage and not have passed through Rossbeigh. The old road now forms part of the Kerry Way walking trail.

2. Nicholson must have been on Rossbeigh Hill, where one can see a wide sweep of sandy beach with 'bold and craggy' peaks on either side.

3. Riordan's Shop at Mountain Stage is the site of the old stage house.

4. Nicholson links the country custom of washing the feet of strangers with John 13:14, 'If I then, *your* Lord and Master, have washed your feet, ye also ought to wash one another's feet'.

5. Ebenezer Henderson lived in Iceland in 1814 and 1815. His *Iceland, or the journal of a residence in that island during the years 1814 and 1815* may have been a model for *Ireland's Welcome to the Stranger*.

6. The view from the present road down to Dingle Bay is equally heady.

7. Nicholson recognized that country people might have explained her presence among them by turning to the tradition of saints' legends, generally medieval in origin, that describe their associations with local parishes. Such associations would include local legends, patterns and holy wells.

8. The woman who refused money for hospitality demonstrates the mores of the Irish countryside.

9. Danaher described women carrying burdens on their heads as late as the first decades of the twentieth century (105).

10. Nicholson shared the evangelical ideology that regarded the home as a woman's sphere; however, she was highly critical of the household work that required women's strenuous physical labour.

11. Nicholson travelled to Cahirciveen by the road along Castlemain Bay.

12. Matthew 6:5–6 is Nicholson's response to the behaviour of her Cahirciveen landlady. 'And when thou prayest, thou shalt not be as the hypocrites are: for they love to pray standing in the synagogues and in the corner of the streets, that they may be seen of men. But thou, when thou prayest, enter into thy closet, and when thou hast shut thy door, pray to thy Father which seeth in secret and shall reward thee openly.'

13. Holy Saturday was on 22 March in 1845; *Thom's* only lists fairs on 1 September and 13 December (53).

14. With lines from 1 Peter 1:18–19, 'But with the precious blood of Christ, as of a lamb without blemish and without spot', Nicholson suggests the spirit could embrace God's example while the body was still unclean.

15. Nicholson's 'stripling clerk of a parish priest' is likely to have been Michael O'Leary, who was curate in Cahirciveen in 1844. Edward Fitzgerald was Parish Priest in 1844 (*Thom's* 264).

16. The line is from William Cowper's comic ballad 'The Diverting History of John Gilpin' (1782).

17. The women who returned from America had a great deal more autonomy because they usually returned with their own money.

18. On Easter Sunday, 23 March 1845, Nicholson compared the few bonnetless women in the church who witnessed the sermon about the resurrection with the lingering Marys at the cross: Mary, the mother of Jesus, Mary Magdalene, and Mary, the mother of James and Joses.

19. The Methodist minister was John Liddy of the Wesleyan Mission Station (*Thom's* 1845, 377).

20. Nicholson again quotes Matthew 25:35, 'I was a stranger and ye took me in'.

Chapter XX

1. Nicholson may be referring to Bible commentators: Adam Clarke (1762–1832), Matthew Henry (1662–1714) and Thomas Scott (1747–1821). Thomas H. Mason's photographs of Aran seaweed gatherers document the use of young girls as beasts of burden down to the 1930s. In her essay "The Real Molly Macree", Margaret MacCurtain discusses the difference between the idealized Irish colleen and the reality of life for girls in rural Ireland in the late nineteenth century.

2. Valentia Island was principally owned by the Rt Hon Maurice Fitzgerald, the Knight of Kerry, who had a lodge called Glanleam on the island (*Thom's* 1845, 155). Mrs Fitzgerald demonstrated the 'pattern of goodness' (Foster 537).

3. Cromwell built forts at the two entrances to Valentia Harbour in 1653, one of which was the star-shaped fort near the Valentia lighthouse (Pochin Mould 49). Catherine O'Connell spoke of seeing the remains of Cromwell's fort (151).

4. The lines may be from a version of the traditional song 'The Exile of Erin'.

5. The man Nicholson met had visited her home town of Chelsea, Vermont.

6. The little church on the hill was the Church of Ireland in Valentia, which was built on the road to the slate quarry in the early nineteenth century. The Roman Catholic church of Saints Darerca and Teresa was built in Chapeltown (Pochin Mould 120).

7. Nicholson thinks of the lines from 2 Timothy 3:15, 'And from a child thou hast

known the holy Scriptures'.

8. Fraser described the Sportsman's Hotel as a small inn favoured by anglers (345). Lady Chatterton mentions a Mr Quirk in connection with the Sportsman Hotel (271–2). This may be the Jerry Quirke who put up Nicholson without charge.

9. O'Connell's Derrynane hospitality was legendary and no more so than in the winter of 1844 and the spring of 1845, when there were constant visitors. 'He loved to show hospitality in a large way, and it flattered him to receive strangers from all parts of the world' (Gwynn 242). Had he been home, he was certain to have been a welcoming host to a woman who shared his commitment to abolitionism and his friendship with advocates of the cause in America.

10. There is no listing of a coast guardsman for the area in *Thom's*; however, *Thom's* 1845 lists a fleet of revenue cruisers, and inspection stations in the seventeen maritime counties (131–3).

11. Foster explained that there were squatters on the O'Connell estate because the rents were small and there were no evictions.

12. Nicholson witnessed the Shrove Tuesday Skellig tradition in Cork on Shrove Eve, 4 February 1845. James Beale's painting 'Skellig Night on South Mall 1845' documents that night.

13. Nicholson declines to speculate about O'Connell's politics on gender grounds. On the other hand, Jael is described as walking softly when she went to Sisera and drove a nail into his temple (Judges 4:21).

14. Nicholson describes the 'smooth underfoot' new road from Waterville through the Coomakestra Pass to Derrynane.

15. The original O'Connell house built by Captain John O'Connell at Derrynane dates from 1702; nothing of the original house remains. When Daniel O'Connell inherited the house in 1825, he added a south wing with a dining-room facing the sea and a sitting-room above it. He also added a library wing with a study on the ground floor (*Derrynane* 10–12). Erin Bishop describes extensive renovations: 'several sitting-rooms and bedrooms and turning of the back of the house into the front' (Bishop 55). Derrynane has been a museum since 1967.

16. O'Connell was in Dublin in the spring of 1845 when the Irish university question was being debated (MacDonagh 261). According to one of his biographers, O'Connell's health was broken by the winter of 1844 (Gwynn 241).

17. Currently, the O'Connell portraits and family portraits hang in the drawing-room and sitting-room of Derrynane. There are three O'Connell portraits including the one by J.P. Haverty where O'Connell stands in a Napoleonic pose with the Kerry landscape behind him. Another Haverty painting of O'Connell among his followers in the 1840s was a gift to Derrynane from its former owner Eamon de Valera (*Derrynane* 14). The portrait of Mary O'Connell with her youngest child Daniel Edward hangs in the dining-room. The Derrynane curator says that the painting described by Nicholson of a brother and sister swinging on a rope has disappeared.

18. The simple, white-walled chapel, on the style of the chapel in the ruined monastery at nearby Abbey Island, was added to the house in 1844 upon his release from prison by a grateful O'Connell (*Derrynane* 10). The first Mass in the chapel was celebrated on Christmas Day in 1844; however, Nicholson describes the

chapel as unfinished at the time of her visit. In his essay 'O'Connell – The Man', John J. Hogan describes the honoured place at Derrynane held by O'Connell's chaplain (286). Bishop says that by 1827 O'Connell was looking for a priest for Derrynane. Mary O'Connell's nephew served as chaplain in 1830; the *Catholic Directory* (1836) lists a Patrick O'Connell as parish priest (Bishop 155).

19. Chatterton suggests that Jerry Quirke's dwelling was the Sportsman Hotel (271–2). Since the Sportsman Hotel was located at Ballybrack, south-west of Lough Currane, it appears that Nicholson retraced her steps toward Cahirciveen when she left Derrynane.

20. Describing the woman dancing on the strand at Ballinskelligs Bay, Nicholson quotes Proverbs 17:22, 'A merry heart doeth good like a medicine'. The image stirred Brendan Kennelly, who used it in his poem 'My Dark Fathers':

> And yet upon the sandy Kerry shore
> The woman once had danced at ebbing tide
> Because she loved flute music – and still more
> Because a lady wondered at the pride
> Of one so humble.

21. Herodias was the wife of Herod Philip and mother of Salome. Herod Philip's half-brother Herod Antipas divorced his wife to marry Herodias. Nicholson alludes to Matthew 14:6, 'But when Herod's birthday was kept, the daughter of Herodias danced before them, and pleased Herod'.

22. Lady Chatterton wrote *Rambles in the South of Ireland during the Year 1838* (1839). Her objective was to write a book that would 'remove some of the prejudices' in the minds of people who were afraid to visit Ireland.

Chapter XXI

1. Nicholson refers to Genesis 50:10, 'And they came to the threshing floor of Atad, which is beyond Jordan; and there they mourned with a great and very sore lamentation: and he [Joseph] made a mourning for his father seven days'.

2. Frank O'Connor wrote a short story, 'The Long Road to Umera', on the theme of an old woman who yearned to be buried with her people.

Chapter XXII

1. Nicholson may have been walking on the road west of the Iveragh Mountains through the Ballaghisheen Pass towards Killorglin.

2. The new road through the mountain may have been the road through the Ballaghisheen Pass that goes between Waterville and Killorglin.

3. That children were frightened of Nicholson because they had never seen a woman with a bonnet is similar to a story told about people around Ballinamuck, Co Longford, in 1798, who thought that the high helmets worn by Hessian soldiers were part of their heads.

4. If Nicholson was heading for the Gap of Dunloe, she might have left the road at Boheesil; however, it sounds like she may have continued along the ridge by Lough Acoose on the western side of the Macgillycuddy Reeks and then turned east towards Kilgobnet and Beaufort.

5. The household of the abusive drinker was probably around Beauford.

6. Nicholson's new perils would be her walk through the Gap of Dunloe where tourists were advised to hire a pony and guide. Even were she so inclined, the five shillings for the pony would have been beyond her budget (Hall II, 183).

7. Fraser advised visitors to Killarney to acquaint themselves with the area in order to avoid 'the confusion arising from the conflicting and marvellous stories of waiters, ostlers, buglemen, boatmen and guides' (301).

8. Croker said the colour of the Purple Mountain comes from the purple stratum of slaty rock whose slivered fragments cover the upper parts of the mountain (119).

9. A number of streams empty into the Upper Lake of Killarney. One forms the Derrycunnihy Waterfall. Another flows under Lord Brandon's Cottage (Fraser 295). 'The virtuous woman who looketh well to the ways of her household' alludes to Proverbs 12:4, 'A virtuous woman is a crown to her husband', and to St Paul's Letter to Titus 11: 4–5 and Timothy 11:1–10.

10. Nicholson describes Lord Brandon's tower and garden with Proverbs 24:30–31, 'I went by the field of the slothful, and by the vineyard of the man void of understanding; And, lo, it was all grown over with thorns and nettles had covered the face thereof, and the stone wall thereof was broken down'.

11. Six miles from the Turk Waterfall was the lane that led to Hyde Cottage and the Derrycunnihy Waterfall (Fraser 294).

12. Nicholson alludes to Psalm 121:4, 'Behold, he that keepeth Israel shall neither slumber nor sleep'.

13. An astral lamp was contrived to give off an uninterrupted source of light.

14. Nicholson mentions brothers and sisters. Extant records indicate that she had two brothers but there is no record of any sisters.

15. Croker identified the Protestant rector of Hyde Park as Rev. Arthur Hyde, who welcomed visitors to cross through his gate to reach the Derrycunnihy Cascade (129–130).

16. Dinis is at the south-western end of Lough Laune.

17. Dinis Cottage is marked on the Ordnance Survey map of the Reeks. In 1844 a Mr Herbert planned to build a banquet hall for visitors on Dinis.

Chapter XXIII

1. Jonathan Walpole was the Agent to the Limerick Coach and Dingle Car Proprietor; his premises were located on Castle Street. There is a Walpole's Lane in Tralee.

2. The magistrates in Tralee in 1845 were Oliver Stokes, Esq, Thomas Collis, Esq, T. Barrow, and Pierce Clute, Esq.

3. Nicholson identified Walpole as a Scots Presbyterian; he is listed among the Protestants and Dissenters in Pádraic de Brún's 'Tralee Voters in 1835' (78).

4. Matthew 5:14, 'Ye are the light of the world. A city that is set on a hill cannot be hid'. Nicholson means that Christian colonies like Dingle which preach the Bible will be a light to the Irish and an example to the world.

5. The Protestant mission on Lord Ventry's estate would be the first of a chain of colonies that moved northward to the costal counties of Limerick, Clare, Galway, Mayo, Sligo and Donegal. The Dingle colony was located on Quay Lane

(Strand Street). Fifteen houses were built in 1840–2 at a cost of 450 pounds; ten houses were added. Houses and gardens were rented to colonists for 12 shilllings/year. The colony reached its peak in 1846 when there were 142 colonists in Ventry and 245 in Dingle. After Gayer died in 1848, the colony declined. By 1854, there were only 180 converts in the settlement. There is a photograph of 'The Colony' (1890) in the Lawrence Collection. A few of the original houses survive, especially those at the junction with Strand Street (Graham 39).

6. Nicholson alludes to Aesop's fable 'The Wolf in Sheep's Clothing' to describe the suspicion that Michael Devine, the parish priest of Dingle in 1844, might have had about her (*Thom's* 264).

7. In 1833, Lord Ventry appointed the Rev. Charles Gayer as his private chaplain and charged him with establishing a Protestant colony at Ventry. Lord Ventry built a church glebe house and school. By 1838, Gayer had 170 converts. Gayer was appointed Rector of Ventry in 1841.

8. The Methodist family were the family of Coastguardsman Thomas Jackson (Graham 39). Between 1840 and 1890 the coastguards and their families lived in Cooleen or Station Row in Dingle town. There were six houses, a watch house and a signal pole.

9. 'The bush though burning is never consumed' is Nicholson's paraphrase of Exodus 3:2, 'Behold, the bush burned with fire, and the bush was not consumed'. While the passage usually refers to the manifestation of the presence of God, Nicholson means that the Methodists' zeal does not diminish.

10. 'We do not worship images' refers to Leviticus 19:4, 'Turn ye not unto idols, nor make to yourselves molten gods: I *am* the Lord your God'. What converts mean is that they do not believe in the special powers of the Virgin Mary or the saints.

11. William Carleton described the practice of students doing lessons aloud, 'cheering and cheerful in the noise of friendly voices', in 'The Hedge School' (306–7).

12. The Roman Catholic priest turned Mission Society clergyman was Thomas Moriarty, known locally as Tomás an Éithigh, Thomas the Liar (Foley 57).

13. Nicholson does not identify the teacher; however, Mrs D.P. Thompson identifies a Miss Rae who was in charge of the sixty girls in the Irish Mission Society school in Ventry.

14. Nicholson visited the school run by the Presentation sisters in Dingle. She highly approved of their educational standards and the principles that informed the way that they educated poor children.

15. Nicholson describes the *leacht cuimhneacháin*, a memorial monument made of stones. Nicholson disapproved of such superstitions; however, she added her own stone to the marker.

16. Lady Chatterton identified the antiquarian priest as Father Casey of 'Muirmac', perhaps Murreagh in Kilmalkedar parish (I, 144–8, 187). *Thom's* (1844) lists a John Casey as parish priest of Keel-Dingle (264). There is a monastic site with St Brendan's Oratory at Kilmalkedar.

17. Lady Chatterton devoted a chapter of her Irish travels to the story of Piaras Feiritéar (Pierce Ferriter), Kerry poet, and to the origin of the place-name of Sybil

Head (I, 192–213). Poet and patriot, Feiritéar was the last Irish commander to fall to Cromwell's forces. Sybil Head was named for Sybil Lynch of Galway, who eloped with another Feiritéar. She drowned in a cave where she was hiding from her angry father (Lavelle 47).

18. Nicholson compares the Irish children to the young David.

19. Nicholson may have yearned to see Dunquin because Lady Chatterton praised its beauty from the summit of Mount Eagle (180).

20. Glin Castle was the demesne of John F. Fitzgerald (1791–1854) who was the Knight of Glin in 1844; the Knight of Kerry was Maurice Fitzgerald.

Chapter XXIV

1. Nicholson could have travelled on the Dublin Steampacket Company's paddle-wheel steamer *Garryowen*, the largest iron ship in its day (1834). The *Garryowen* did the Tarbert–Kilrush–Limerick run for twenty-five years. The trip took about three and a half hours (Ignatius Murphy 70). The *Limerick Reporter* (1841) quotes the fares as 2/6d for cabin and 1/6d for deck passage.

2. The ancient cathedral, St Mary's, founded by Donal Mór O'Brien in the late twelfth century, was damaged by the Cromwellians.

3. The Water Gate of St John's Castle was the one gate of seventeen that remained standing in 1760.

4. The Limerick Workhouse was opened on 20 May 1841 with accommodation for 1600 (O'Connor 262). If Nicholson's informant was correct, the workhouse was overcrowded in 1845.

5. Nicholson's impressions of Ennis, an 'ancient town going to decay', were shared by Fraser, 'modern additions straggle out along the public roads in long lines of cabins and detached houses, so that both the new and old parts of the town, suburbs, and outskirts are ill-defined, scattered, and do not present a single good street' (383), and by the contributor of the Ennis entry in *The Parliamentary Gazetteer of Ireland* who described its 'very shabby and even poor and disorderly appearance'.

6. The Franciscan monastery was Clare Abbey (Abbey of Saints Peter and Paul or Monasterium de Forgio). It was founded by Donal Mór O'Brien sometime before 1189. The ruins are visible from the Limerick–Ennis Road. The battle, known as the 'carnage of Clare', that Nicholson mentions is one of the battles fought between rival branches of the O'Brien family (Spellissy 109).

7. At the time Nicholson visited Ennis, the Church of Ireland church was the reroofed Franciscan Friary founded by Donnchad Cairbreach O'Brien in 1242. The new Church of Ireland church was built in 1871 and the Friary was returned to the Franciscans in 1969 (Garner 18, 20–1).

8. Lord Gort held the leases to the market town of Gort, which had 3627 people and 563 houses in 1837 (Lewis I, 666). He lived at Lough Cutra. Another large land-owner, Robert Gregory (1790–1847), owned 15,000 acres north of Gort. Gregory had a reputation as an improving landlord; however, the agricultural depression brought years of low corn prices and there was high unemployment among agricultural labourers.

9. There was a small inn at Oranmore (Fraser 365).

10. Once the Galway–Clifden road was complete in 1834, Bianconi developed a car service: 'One of Bianconi's well-appointed two-horse cars runs daily from Galway to Clifden in connection with the Dublin mail performing the journey in eight hours' (Fraser 421).

11. The Galway curate may have been E. Bourke, E.E. Maunsell or John Treanor (*Thom's* 1834, 313).

12. Nicholson noticed that the spread of the national schools in Ireland, founded in 1831, introduced a standard curriculum – reading, grammar and arithmetic – and literacy in English into the Irish countryside.

13. The policeman may have been the RIC Sub-Inspector Martin Clune (*Thom's* 1845, 518).

14. Nicholson's Oughterard schoolmaster shared some of the traits of William Carleton's Matt Kavanagh ('The Hedge School', 1830), but hedge schoolmasters were disappearing from the Irish countryside. When the Halls visited Galway in 1842, they remarked that there were far fewer hedge schools than there had been on an earlier visit (III, 260). The founding of the National School system started the process, but there were other changes in the culture of the Irish countryside. The 1833 Ordnance Survey project involved translating traditional place-names into English.

15. 'Full well they laughed and counterfeited glee' is line 201 of Oliver Goldsmith's 'The Deserted Village'.

16. Nicholson was near Lough Bofin, about four miles from Maam Cross.

17. Lewis says there were national schools in Moyrus parish at Ballinafad, Roundstone and Moyrus, and a private school in Timbole Bridge (II, 406).

18. John 14:1–2, 'Let not your heart be troubled. In my father's house there are many mansions', was one of Nicholson's favourite Bible passages.

19. Nicholson's route took her the ten miles from Maam Cross to Recess.

20. Police were stationed in Recess from about 1833. There were barracks located at the present site of Paddy Festy's (Mannion 45). The Halls identified a half-way house between Maam Cross and Clifden as Flyn's (III, 478).

21. The Lissoughter Quarry was located just north of the main road near the Recess Post Office. There were also quarries in Barnanoraun and Derryclare. In northern Connemara there were quarries at Streamtown and Cregg (Mannion 47).

22. In their conclusion to their *Ireland: Its Scenery and Character*, the Halls also spoke of the government's responsibility to support the development of Ireland's natural resources. 'In brief, the time is approaching – if it be not yet arrived – when the vast natural resources of Ireland may be, and will be, rendered available for the combined interests – interests that never can be otherwise than mutual and inseparable – of the United Kingdom' (III, 495).

23. Nicholson again alludes to Matthew 25:35, 'I was a stranger and ye took me in'.

24. The teaspoon is later lost and recovered (*Annals* 171–2). Mannion says that the Cummins of Tipperary came to the area to manage a staging house for Bianconi's Galway–Clifden car service. The Canal Stage between Recess and Ballinahinch was opposite to Michael and Bridget Nee's house in Derrynavglaun (58).

25. Red was the traditional colour of women's petticoats in Connemara. Little

boys were usually dressed in skirts in the west of Ireland until they went to school. Some believed boys so dressed were safe from the fairies.

26. There were special charms and prayers to protect against nightmares (O'Sullivan, *Handbook* 487).

Chapter XXV

1. Christ Church, located on Church Hill north-west of Clifden's market square, was built in 1810 (Robinson 44). It was replaced in 1853.

2. The two-storey stone building across from Christ Church is the Protestant school built in 1824 by the Diocese of Tuam. It was closed in 1956. When Nicholson says that the children were clothed by the society, she means the Connaught Home Mission Society which was founded in 1837 by the evangelizing Protestant Archbishop of Tuam, Power le Poer Trench (Villiers-Tuthill, *Clifden* 29).

3. In her history of Clifden, Kathleen Villiers-Tuthill says that the Catholic Archbishop of Tuam, John MacHale, kept the national schools out of his diocese (68). As Nicholson points out, there were private Roman Catholic schools in Clifden. Nicholson said McHale prohibited reading Scripture appertaining to lessons.

4. Nicholson probably climbed to a site north-west of the town where there is now a monument to the town's founder, John D'Arcy (1785-1832).

5. Nicholson describes the walls to the Gothic Clifden castle built by John D'Arcy. By 1845 the property had passed to D'Arcy's eldest son Hyacinth, who became rector of the Parish of Omey after the sale of his estate for famine-related debt. Robinson describes the remains of a 'marine temple of sea shells'; it is probably the 'fairy castle' Nicholson described (Robinson 47).

6. The lines are from Alexander Pope's 'An Essay on Man', *Epistle* I, l. 95.

7. The Third Order of Franciscans moved to Ardbear December 1837 and opened a free school for boys. The building was replaced in 1979 (Villiers-Tuthill 30-1).

8. May Day was celebrated to welcome the summer. The most popular custom was gathering spring flowers to decorate the household (Danaher, *Year* 88). The old lord in Nicholson's note was Lord Bantry.

9. One story of robbers on the Roundstone road was linked to the half-way house between Clifden and Roundstone, where the owners robbed and murdered passing packmen. When some of their victims surfaced in the lake, they were tried and executed (Robinson 56).

10. When Father Mathew visited Clifden in the summer of 1840, he told the people not only to give up alcohol but to be careful to 'govern their passions on all occasions' (Kerrigan 134).

11. Nicholson's hostess was a Mrs Moran.

12. The mission school was run by the Irish Home Mission.

13. William Crotty worked within the Athlone Presbytery (*Thom's* 1844, 376). Roundstone was built in the 1820s for Scottish fishermen by the Scottish engineer Alexander Nimmo. John Nimmo donated land for a Presbyterian church about 1840. The 'kirk', as it is called locally, was demolished in the 1930s; the remains of the graveyard are on Fuchsia Lane.

14. The graveyard is at the back of Gurteen Bay strand and is now protected by a rock wall.

15. Girls were used to transport heavy loads such as seaweed and turf well into the twentieth century. Thomas H. Mason includes a photograph of girls on Inishere carrying seaweed on their backs in his book *The Islands of Ireland* (Pl. 104).

16. The young man's story that Sir Walter Raleigh brought potatoes to Ireland and planted them at his home near Youghal, Co. Waterford in the later sixteenth century is a popular legend in Ireland. How the potato arrived in Ireland is a matter of speculation. What we do know is that potatoes were cultivated in County Wicklow by the 1640s (Zuckerman 19). Potatoes became a staple crop for the Irish because even a small plot of land could produce a substantial crop. By the nineteenth century, the rural Irish labourer was existing on a diet of potatoes.

17. The site of the old barracks is occupied by three houses next to the Roundstone post office.

18. One can see the remains of the half-way house at Derrycunlagh. Nicholson would have been travelling back to Clifden through the Roundstone Bog.

19. Nicholson would have been glad to leave the half-way house because it was a place with a reputation for heavy drinking (Robinson 56).

20. This may have been Ballinaboy or Ardagh where the road from the Roundstone bog would join the Ballyconneely road. When the woman describes her daughter as becoming 'dark' overnight, she means that she became blind. The Irish word *dall* means both blind and dark.

21. Nicholson's parting words were lines from the Epistle of St James, 'And one of you say unto them, "Depart in peace, be ye warmed and be ye filled"' (2:16).

22. In 1845, Nicholson received a grant of twelve testaments for distribution in the south and west from the Hibernian Bible Society (*Hibernian Bible Society Annual Report 1842–1849*).

23. Kindness to a 'stranger in a strange land' (Exodus 2:22) is a recurring theme in *Ireland's Welcome to the Stranger.*

24. The Church of Ireland curates in Clifden in 1844 included Mark Foster (Renvyle), Joseph Duncan and James Ashe (*Thom's* 1844, 312).

25. The Sub-Inspector at Clifden in 1845 was James Ireland (*Thom's* 1845, 518). Diamond Mountain (Binn Ghuaire) is south-east of Letterfrack in the Connemara National Park. While Park personnel ask walkers not to climb Diamond because of the erosion, it is considered an easy climb of about 1400 feet that takes about two hours. The climber is rewarded with a magnificent view of the Bens and the seascape of north Connemara (Lynam 14–15).

26. The school that so shocked Nicholson must have been in Letterfrack, where there was a police barracks. The district improved after the Famine when an English Quaker couple, James and Mary Ellis, moved to Letterfrack and gave employment to the local people.

27. The 'diamond' appearance of the mountain is caused by a 'satellite-granite intrusion' below its surface (Lynam 34). You can avoid the northern slope by a trail that takes the climber over rocky slabs. Lynam describes a cairn not a cave at the far end of the ridge.

28. The Halls found Tully a miserable place with neither tea nor bread when they visited the village in 1842 (III, 478).

29. Nicholson's 'certainly wiser' suggests the last lines of Coleridge's 'The Rime

of the Ancient Mariner': 'A sadder and wiser man/He rose the morrow morn'.

30. The ancient village was Claddaghduff. The huts Nicholson describes sound similar to the ones at Dooagh (Achill) illustrated in the Halls' *Ireland* (III, 404). The village lost most of its population during the Famine (Villiers-Tuthill 59).

31. Omey Island is separated from the mainland by a tidal stream. Today people can walk or drive across a marked route over the sand at low tide.

32. In the early nineteenth century three Omey townlands (Cartoorbeg, Gooreen and Gooreenatinny) were owned by the D'Arcy family of Clifden. Cloon and Sturrakeen were the property of the Martins of Ballinahinch (Robinson 52). The Martin townlands were on the eastern side of the island closest to the crossing.

33. Lady M was no doubt a Martin, perhaps the wife of Thomas Martin who was the son of 'Humanity Dick', the Martin known for founding the Society for the Prevention of Cruelty to Animals.

34. Nicholson probably went to Gooreenatinny to a house belonging to Hyacinth D'Arcy or one of the other D'Arcys of Clifden.

Chapter XXVI

1. Having visited the Clifden school run by the Diocese of Tuam and a school she described as the national school, Nicholson probably visited the private schools in Clifden run by Roman Catholics. She does not mention visiting the Franciscan school.

2. Chapters 18 and 19 of the Book of Revelations predict the fulfilment of the prophecy of Isaiah that the enemy will fall and that the anger of God will be fierce. As a Christian, Nicholson would have accepted that Mary was the mother of Jesus, but she would have rejected any special spiritual powers that Roman Catholic theology assigned to her.

3. There are reports of Lady Clare activities in Galway earlier in the spring of 1845 cited in the Outrage Reports for the county. The reports, however, place the events further south and east, in the Oranmore, Loughrea and Mount Bellew regions. In each case, a person dressed in female attire threatened the householder. In the case of the Loughrea episode, the householder was threatened with a pistol for buying land from which a family had been evicted. In the Mount Bellew region, persons trying to collect Poor Rates had to travel under police escort (March 17, 1845, Outrage Reports, Galway 11/487–29099). Martin Clune was Sub-Inspector of the Royal Irish Constabulary in Oughterard.

4. Fraser said there was a small Methodist meeting-house in the city (366). She ended up in the "leper's gallery" in St Nicholas's Collegiate Church. The south transept was galleried in 1561 (Killanin 286).

5. The number of Scripture-readers increased from 3 in 1841 to 49 in 1851 (Langan-Egan 75).

6. Nicholson's car would have changed horses in Tuam. The Halls passed up Tuam on their 1842 journey; it was 'no great loss for it is a dirty ruinous looking place' (III,415).

7. In 1844, Howe Peter Browne was the 3rd Marquis of Sligo. His residence was at Westport House.

8. Nicholson paraphrases 2 Corinthians 9:6, 'He which soweth sparingly shall

reap also sparingly; and he which soweth bountifully shall reap also bountifully'.

9. Monument erected to Lord Sligo's agent. Staff at Westport House suggest that the monument may have been the statue on the octagon to George Glendenning that was destroyed during the Troubles. The octagon now has a statue of St Patrick.

10. Nicholson would later praise Rev Patrick Pounden in *Annals of the Famine* for his work on behalf of Famine relief (116). Rev Pounden and his wife died working among the poor.

11. *Thom's* spells the name Smythe (276).

12. St Paul told the story of Ananias and Sapphira who pretended to give the proceeds from the sale of property to the Church but who held back a portion of the price.

13. Nicholson repeats the lines she used to describe Rev. Joseph Fisher's lack of charity tp praise the charity of the Westport Bible-reader's family.

14. The celebrated mountain is Croagh Patrick, site of the most famous pilgrimage in Ireland. The earliest mention of St Patrick's association with Croagh Patrick is in the seventh century Breviarium of Tíreachán (MacNeill 71).

15. Nicholson describes the annual Lughnasa pilgrimage up Croagh Patrick as taking place on the Friday before the last Sunday in July. In the late nineteenth century, the pilgrimage was moved to the last Sunday of July. *The Mayo News* (25 July 2001) reported that thousands were expected for the pilgrimage on July 29th.

16. Pilgrims gather at Murrisk for the climb (2510 feet, about three miles). The present route merges with Tóchar Phádraig, the old pilgrim trail. The ascent from the Westport side is more difficult.

17. When Nicholson meets the schoolteacher who tries, sensibly, to convince her not to try the climb the mountain alone, she thinks of Goldsmith's village schoolmaster, 'For e'en though vanquished, he could argue still' ('The Deserted Village', l. 122).

18. Nicholson was cutting it very close. She left at 2 pm for an ascent that takes about three hours. The sun set at 8:11 on 28 May 1845.

19. Nicholson wandered around in boggy land east and north of the Reek (Croagh Patrick), till she found the pilgrim's path. The steep, pebbly path that she describes is Casán Phádraig (Patrick's Path) which leads to the summit (MacNeill 81).

20. On a clear day, the view from Croagh Patrick takes in all of Clew Bay. Clare Island is at the mouth of Clew Bay, three miles from Louisburgh.

21. There was an old chapel on the summit where there was an altar. While the chapel has disappeared, pilgrims still say prayers on the site (MacNeill 81).

22. The earliest legends of St Patrick banishing demons from Croagh Patrick involve birds (MacNeill 73). Twelfth-century clerics Giraldus Cambrensis and the Cistercian Jocelin describe Patrick expelling snakes not birds.

23. The safer path was probably the path down to Murrisk where pilgrims relaxed in 'the old Patron Field' after their devotions (MacNeill 82).

24. There was a fair in Westport on 22 May 1845 (*Thom's*).

25. In *Women and Work in Ireland*, Mary Daly points out that women's income from the domestic textile industry peaked at the end of the eighteenth century

and collapsed early in the nineteenth century. That women continued such work was a measure of their lack of other employment opportunities (10–11).

Chapter XXVII

1. Mr Smith took the text of his sermon from the Second Epistle of Peter 3:11, 'Seeing then that all these things shall be dissolved, what manner of persons ought ye to be in all holy conversations and Godliness'.

2. Derbyites were disciples of Rev John N. Darby. Ordained in Wicklow in 1826, he resigned in 1827 and joined the Plymouth Brethren. See *Annals* 188.

3. Nicholson wanted to see Achill because of the Christian missionary colony at Dugort.

4. Nicholson later identifies the Newport Bible-reader as a Mr Gibbon.

5. Nicholson quotes from James 1:6, 'But let him ask in faith, nothing wavering: for he that wavereth is like a wave of the sea driven with wind and tossed'.

6. Mrs Savage was Susan Bole Savage (d 1856). Mr Savage was a coast guard turned hotel-keeper. During the the Famine, the Savages distributed relief on behalf of the Relief Committee of the Society of Friends (Hall III, 394). Everyone who visited the region had a good word for the Savages. Here again Nicholson turns to Matthew 25:35 to describe the Savages' hospitality.

7. The Rev Edward Nangle (1798–1866) established the Protestant Missionary Colony in Achill on August 1, 1834.

8. Like Nicholson, the Halls were favourably disposed towards Nangle and the colony before they visited in 1842. After meeting an orphan boy Nangle dismissed from the colony and three others produced by a Newport clergyman, the Halls questioned the Christian charity of the colony (III, 397).

9. The benevolent doctor was N. Adams. *Thom's* lists him as a Certificate Practitioner, Lying-in Hospital (*Thom's* 1845, 268).

10. The Achill Sound ferry crossed the quarter mile sound at low tide (Hall II, 394).

11. Edward Lowe was the curate at the Achill Mission (*Thom's* 1845, 312).

12. The Halls said the orphans' dining-room was the principal feature of the colony (III, 396).

13. The Halls' engraving of the Achill village of Dooagh shows the windowless, thatched stone structures that Nicholson called 'kraals' (III, 404).

14. Nicholson later identified the gentleman of respectability in England as the reformer and philanthropist Joseph Sturge (*Ireland's Welcome* 336).

15. The editor of a Christian paper may have been Joshua Leavitt (1794–1873), whose papers included the *Evangelist*, the *Journal of Public Morals*, and the *Emancipator*. There is no trace of the religious manuscripts that Nicholson thought she would get published; however, some of the material may have appeared in *Annals of the Famine* or in *Loose Papers*.

16. The remains of the deserted village of Slievemore on Achill follow the settlement pattern Nicholson describes.

17. Nicholson describes the rural custom of booleying, driving stock to summer pasturage on the mountainsides. Keem, Tawnaghmore and Bunowna were booley villages on Achill (Kingston 76).

18. The Halls reported that the government built a good road west of Keem (III, 405). Along the ridge of nearby Achill Head, there are deposits of purple quartzite Achill 'amethyst' (Buckley 206).

19. Nicholson quotes from Proverbs 15:1, 'A soft answer turneth away wrath'.

20. Having commented on the class differences she met in Ireland, her remarks about stinted servants on Achill reinforced the Halls' reports of a lack of Christian charity in the Achill colony.

21. Nicholson does not identify the reformed priest attached to the colony. He may have been a John Ródaigh who appears in an Achill folksong called 'Na Préachers', where he is accused of abandoning the true faith for 'a piece of the mountain with squinty Nangle'.

22. There was no second edition of *Ireland's Welcome to the Stranger*; however, Nicholson visited the colony again during the Great Irish Famine. Rev Nangle refused Nicholson's gestures of reconciliation (*Annals* 105).

23. When Nicholson returned to Newport during the Famine, she stayed with Mrs Margaret Arthur (*Annals* 12–13, 83–4).

24. Sir Richard Annesley O'Donnell had the reputation of being a resident, improving landlord. James Tuke reported that he employed nearly 1000 women at flax-making (9). On the other hand, his drivers evicted tenants. O'Donnell claimed ignorance of the episode; Nicholson's view was that landlords were responsible for those they employed (*Annals* 115). See Hall III, 383, 385–6.

25. The glen Nicholson describes may be a place called the Glen, formerly called the Alt (Kirby 27), located south-west of Knocknarea. Yeats refers to the mile-long, narrow Glen in his poem 'The Man and the Echo'.

26. Nicholson probably visited the Glencar waterfall. Yeats refers to the falls in 'The Stolen Child' and 'Towards the Break of Day'.

27. Bianconi had a boat/stage service between Sligo and Dublin. Nicholson may have gone from Sligo to Carrick-on-Shannon by boat and then met the Dublin car.

28. Fraser lists the 131-mile route from Sligo to Dublin (434).

29. Nicholson probably refers to the Royal Hibernian Academy of Arts (1823). Its premises at Lower Abbey Street were destroyed during the 1916 Rising (Craig, *Dublin* 286).

30. The mendicity institutes were voluntary associations formed in Dublin and in other towns to assist the poor with money, food and even accommodation. oakum-picking or other kinds of work were required of those receiving support. Schooling was provided for children. Mendicity institutes laboured with inadequate resources for the large number of women, children and elderly who sought their aid. The Poor Law of 1838, with its provision for the construction of union workhouses, replaced the private mendicity institutes (Connolly, *The Oxford Companion to Irish History* 357).

31. Sodom and the other 'cities of the plain' (Genesis 13:12) were located in what is now the southern portion of the Dead Sea.

32. Watch-towers were built at crossroads and on the outskirts of cities like Jerusalem to conceal or shelter sentries. Judah remained loyal to the House of David.

Chapter XXVIII

1. The tract deposit was the Religious Tract and Book Society for Ireland, which was located at 15 Upper Sackville Street (*Thom's* 309). The headquarters of the Hibernian Bible Society was located at the same address. Philip Dixon Hardy also distributed religious books and tracts. Joseph Sturge (1793–1859) was an English corn factor and philanthropist who supported abolitionism, temperance and peace organizations. A friend of Daniel O'Connell and Father Mathew, Sturge probably also supported Nicholson's later relief efforts.

2. Nicholson used the same phrase from Matthew 5:14 about the Dingle colony.

3. Nicholson alludes to Psalm 48:12, 'Walk around Zion, and go round about her: tell the towers thereof'.

4. Matthew 20:3, 'And he went out about the third hour, and saw others standing idle in the market-place'. Nicholson suggests that if she had had an easy time in Ireland, she would not have fulfilled her mission.

5. Nicholson's work with abolitionism informed her wider interest in social justice. Her time in Ireland – 1844–5, 1846–8 – would have overlapped with Frederick Douglass's visits to Ireland between 1845 and 1847. Both were friends of the Dublin Quakers Richard Davis and Hannah Waring Webb, so it is tempting to think they might have met in Ireland.

6. Nicholson planned to write *Ireland's Welcome to the Stranger* to encourage American readers to aid the Irish poor. She also wrote accounts of the Famine for *The Friend* and 'Ireland at the Present Moment' for *Howitt's Journal*.

7. Nicholson paraphrases Hebrews 13:1–2, 'Be not forgetful to entertain strangers for thereby some have entertained angels unaware'.

8. Nicholson's reference to 'the past winter of famine' places her time in Belfast after her *Ireland's Welcome to the Stranger* tour. She went to Belfast from Dublin by steamer on 6 July 1847. She went west after her Belfast visit.

9. Nicholson particularly admired the Belfast Ladies' Association for the Relief of Irish Destitution for their active efforts on behalf of the Irish poor. See *Annals* 7, 58–9.

10. Nicholson uses the lines from Mark 12:17 to say that she was speaking plainly about the political and socio-economic conditions of the Irish and advised 'Caesar' that there must be change. Nicholson wrote the lines after her relief efforts during the Famine. She returned to Ireland on 7 December 1846 and left on 4 September 1848.

11. 'The fiery furnace' is from the Book of Daniel 3:23. Shadrach, Meshach and Abednego choose martyrdom in the fiery furnace rather than deny their faith.

BIBLIOGRAPHY

Aldwell, Alexander. *Cork Directory 1844, 1845*. Cork: Aldwell, 1846.

Andrews, Hilary. *The Lion of the West: A Biography of John MacHale*. Dublin: Veritas, 2001.

'Asenath Nicholson', *The Friend*, Seventh Month (1855), 122–3.

Augustine, Father, O.F.M. *Footprints of Fr. Theobald Mathew O.F.M., Apostle of Temperance*. Dublin: Gill, 1947.

Beale, James. 'Skellig Night on South Mall' in *Illustrated Summary Catalogue of the Crawford Art Gallery*. ed. Peter Murray. Cork: Cork VEC, 1991.

Beecher, *Catherine. Letters to Persons Who Are Engaged in Domestic Service*, New York: Leavitt & Trow, 1842. pp.87-9.

Bianconi, M.O'C. and S.J. Watson. *Bianconi: King of the Irish Roads*. Dublin: Allen Figgis, 1962.

Bishop, Erin I. *The World of Mary O'Connell 1778–1836*. Dublin: Lilliput Press, 1999.

Brown, Stephen J. *Ireland in Fiction* I. Shannon: Irish University Press, 1969 [1915].

Buckley, Barbara, 'The Geology of Mayo' in *Mayo*, ed. Bernard O'Hara. Galway: The Archaeological, Historical and Folklore Society, 1982. pp.201-6.

Cambrensis, Giraldus. *Topographia Hiberniae*. Dublin: Celtic Society, 1848.

Carleton, William. 'The Irish Fiddler', *Tales and Sketches Illustrating the Character, Usages, Traditions, Sports and Pastimes of the Irish Peasantry*. Dublin: James Duffy, 1849.

—. *Traits and Stories of the Irish Peasantry*. Dublin: James Duffy, 1849.

Chatterton, Lady Georgiana. *Rambles in the South of Ireland During the Year 1838*. 2 vols. London: Saunders and Otley, 1839.

Class 4 Emerald. *Through the Eyes of Emerald: A Short History of Wicklow Town*. Wicklow: Class 4, 1999.

Coleridge, Samuel Taylor. 'The Rime of the Ancient Mariner', *Selected Poetry and Prose*. ed. Stephen Potter, London: Nonesuch Press, 1962. pp. 19-57.

Cleary, Jimmy. 'Wicklow Harbour', *Wicklow Historical Journal*, I, 3 (1990), 57–64.

Conlan, Patrick, O.F.M. *Franciscan Ireland*. Cork: Mercier, 1978.

Cooney, Dudley Levistone. *The Methodists in Ireland: A Short History*. Blackrock: The Columba Press, 2001.

The Cork Commercial Courier, Cork, 1845

Cork Examiner, Cork, 1845

Cork Post Office General Directory, 1844.

County and City of Cork Almanac. Cork: F. Jackson, 1843.

Cowper, 'The Diverting History of John Gilpin', 'On the Receipt of My Mother's Picture out of Norfolk', *The Poetical Works of William Cowper*. New York: Oxford University Press, 1934.

Craig, Maurice. *Dublin 1660-1860*. London: Cresset Press, 1952.

—, and Michael. *Mausolea Hibernica*. Dublin: Lilliput Press, 1999.

Croker, T. Crofton, ed. *Killarney Legends*. London: Henry G. Bohn, 1853.

—. *Popular Songs of Ireland*. London: George Routledge, 1886 [1839].

Crossman, Virginia, 'mendicity institutes', *The Oxford Companion to Irish History*.ed. S.J. Connolly, New York: Oxford University Press, 1998. p. 357.

Daly, Mary E. *Women and Work in Ireland. Studies in Irish Economic and Social History*. Dublin: Dundalgan Press, 1997.

Danaher, Kevin. *In Ireland Long Ago*. Dublin: Mercier Press, 1962.

de Brún, Pádraic. 'Tralee Voters in 1835', *Journal of the Kerry Archaeological and Historical Society*, XIX (1986), 143-8.

—. 'A Ventry Convert Group, 1842', *Journal of the Kerry Archaeological and Historical Society*, XIII (1980), 143–6.

Derrynane: A Short Guide to the Home of Daniel O'Connell. Dublin: National Parks and Monuments Service: Office of Public Works, 1980.

Donnell, Robert. *Thoughts on Various Subjects*. Louisville,KY: L.R. Woods, 1854.

Douglass, Frederick. *My Bondage and My Freedom*. New York: Dover Press, 1969 [1855].

Dowling, A. *Johnstown, Galmoy and Urlingford Parishes*. Freshford: Wellbrook Press, 1978.

Dublin Post Office Annual Directory and Calendar. Dublin: John S. Folds, 1844.

Durrell, Penelope and Cornelius Kelly, eds. *The Grand Tour of Kerry*. Allihies: Cailleach Books, 2001.

Elizabeth, Charlotte. *Letters from Ireland MDCCCXXXVII*. New York: John S. Taylor, 1843.

Evans, E. Estyn. *Irish Folk Ways*. London: Routledge Kegan Paul, 1957.

Everett, Nigel. *Wild Gardens: The Lost Demesnes of Bantry Bay*. Bantry: Hafod Press, 2000.

Foley, Patrick. *The Ancient and Present State on the Skelligs, Blasket Islands, Dunquin and the West of Dingle*. Dublin: An Cló-Chumann, 1903.

Foster, T.C. *Letters on the Condition of the People of Ireland*. London: Chapman and Hall, 1846.

Fraser, James. *A Handbook for Travellers in Ireland Descriptive of its Scenery, Towns, Seats, Antiquities, etc. with various Statistical Tables also an Outline of Its Mineral Structure, a Brief View of its Botany, and Information for Anglers*. Dublin: William Curry, 1844.

Friel, Brian. *Translations*. London: Faber & Faber, 1981.

Furlong, Nicholas. 'Life in Wexford Port 1600–1800' in *Wexford History and Society*. eds K. Whelan and W. Nolan. Dublin: Geography Publications. 1987.

Garner, William. *Ennis Architectural Heritage*. Dublin: An Foras Forbartha, 1981.

Goldsmith, Oliver. 'The Deserted Village', *Selected Works*. ed. Richard Garnett. Cambridge, MA: Harvard University Press, 1951. pp. 607–19.

Graham, Dan. 'Dingle Coast Guard Station', *The Kerry Magazine*, V (1994), 39.

Grant, Elizabeth Smith. *The Highland Lady in Ireland: Journals 1840–1850*. eds Patricia Pelly and Andrew Tod. Edinburgh: Cannongate Classics, 1991.

Gwynn, Denis. *Daniel O'Connell*. Cork: Cork University Press, 1947.

Hale, Thomas. 'Historical Address' in *Centennial Celebration of the Settlement of Chelsea, Vermont*. Keene, N.H.: Sentinel, 1884.

Hall, Samuel and Anna. *Ireland: Its Scenery and Character.* 3 vols. London: Hall, 1843.

Harrison, Richard S. *A Biographical Dictionary of Irish Quakers.* CorkCity Quakers: A Brief History. 1665-1939. Cork: Red Barn Publishing, 1991.

Healy, W., P.P., *History and Antiquities of Kilkenny County & City.* Kilkenny: P.M. Egan. 1893.

Henderson, Ebenezer. *Iceland, or the journal for a residence in that island during the years 1814 and 1815.* Edinburgh: Oliphant, Waugh and Innes, 1818.

Hibernian Society Annual Report 1842–1849. Dublin: Hibernian Bible Society, 1849.

Hogan, John J. 'O'Connell – The Man' in *Daniel O'Connell: Nine Centenary Essays.* ed Michael Tierney. Dublin: Browne and Nolan, 1948.

Hone, J.M. 'Asenath Nicholson', *Dublin Magazine,* IX (October–December 1934), 37–41.

Hore, Philip Elliot. *History of the Town and County of Wexford.* London: Elliot Stock, 1911.

'Individual Exertions: Mr. Bianconi', *The Dublin Penny Journal,* (8 September 1832), 87.

Inglis, Henry. *A Journey Through Ireland During the Spring, Summer and Autumn of 1834.* London: Whittaker and Co.,1838.

In Memoriam. William Goodell. Born in Coventry, New York, October 27, 1792. Died in Janesville, Wisconsin, February 14, 1875. Chicago: Guilbert and Winchell, 1879.

Jocelin [Jocelyn]. *The Life and Acts of St. Patrick. Dublin:* J. Blyth, 1809.

Kelleher, Margaret. 'Asenath Nicholson's Famine Annals' in *The Feminization of Famine.* Cork: Cork University Press, 1997.

Kennelly, Brendan. *Selected Poems.* Dublin: Allen Figgis, 1969.

Kerrigan, Colm. *Father Mathew and the Irish Temperance Movement.* Cork: Cork University Press, 1992.

Killanin, Lord and Michael V. Duignan. *The Shell Guide to Ireland.* 2nd ed. London: Ebury Press, 1967.

Kirby, Sheelah. *The Yeats Country. A Guide to Places in the West of Ireland Associated with the Life and Writing of William Butler Yeats.* 2nd ed. Dublin: The Dolmen Press, 1963.

Kohfeldt, Mary Lou. *Lady Gregory: The Woman Behind the Irish Renaissance.* London: André Deutsch, 1985.

Kohl, J.G. *Travels in Ireland.* London: Bruce and Wyld, 1844.

Langan-Egan, Maureen. *Galway Women in the Nineteenth Century.* Dublin: Open Air, 1999.

Lavelle, Des. *Kerry.* Dublin: O'Brien Press, 1986.

Lewis, Samuel, *A Topographical Dictionary of Ireland,* 2 vols. London: S. Lewis, 1837.

Limerick Reporter, 1841

Lincoln, Colm. *Steps and Steeples: Cork at the Turn of the Century.* Dublin: O'Brien Press, 1980.

Lynam, Joss. *The Mountains of Connemara: A Hill-Walker's Guide.* Roundstone: Folding Landscapes, 1998.

McCaffrey, Lawrence J. *Daniel O'Connell and the Repeal Year.* Lexington: University of Kentucky Press, 1966.

MacCurtain, Margaret. 'The Real Molly Macree' in *Visualizing Ireland. National*

Identity and the Pictorial Tradition. ed Adele M. Dalsimer. Boston: Faber, 1993.

MacDonagh, Oliver. *The Emancipist: Daniel O'Connell 1830–1847.* London: Weidenfeld and Nicolson, 1989.

Macintyre, Angus. *The Liberator: Daniel O'Connell and the Irish Party 1830-1847.* London: Macmillan, 1965.

MacNeill, Máire. *The Festival of Lughnasa.* 2nd ed. London: Oxford University Press, 1980.

Mannion, Karen, ed. *Chroí Chonamara, The Heart of Connemara: The History of Ballinafad, Recess and Bun na gCnoc.* Recess: BRB Community Council, 1998.

Mason, Thomas H. *The Island of Ireland.* 3rd ed. London: B.T. Batsford, 1950.

The Mayo News, 25 July 2001.

Maxwell, William. *Wild Sports of the West.* 2 vols. London: R. Bentley, 1832.

Miller, Kerby A. *Emigrants and Exiles: Ireland and the Irish Exodus to North America.* New York: Oxford University Press, 1985.

Moore, Thomas. *Irish Melodies.* London: J. Power, 1808-34.

Murphy, Maureen. 'Asenath Nicholson & the Famine in Ireland' in *Women & Irish History: Essays in Honour of Margaret MacCurtain,* eds Maryann Gialanella Valiulis and Mary O'Dowd. Dublin: Wolfhound Press, 1997.

Murphy, Ignatius. 'Pre-Famine Passenger Service on the Lower Shannon', *North Munster Antiquarian Journal,* XVI (1973–4), 70–83.

Murray, James. 'Health and Medicine in Galway' in *Galway: Town and Gown 1484–1984,* ed. Diarmuid Ó Cearbhaill. Dublin: Gill & Macmillan, 1984.

Musgrave, Sir Richard. *Memoirs of the Different Rebellions in Ireland.* 2 vols. 3rd ed. London: Marchbank, 1802.

The Nation, 10 June 1843.

The New York Directory. New York: J. Doggett, 1842-1845.

Nicholson, Asenath. *Annals of the Famine in Ireland.* ed Maureen Murphy. Dublin: Lilliput Press, 1998.

—.'Ireland at the Present Moment', *Howitt's Journal,* II (1847), 141–2.

—.Letter, *The Friend.* (1847), 212, 218.

—.*Lights and Shades of Ireland.* London: Houlston and Stoneman, 1850.

—.*Loose Papers or Facts Gathered During Eight Years' Residence in Ireland, Scotland, England, France and Germany.* New York: The Anti-Slavery Office, 1853.

—.*Nature's Own Book.* 2nd ed. Glasgow: William Brown, 1846.

—.'Pictures of the Present in Ireland', *Howitt's Journal,* III (1847), 111.

Nissenbaum, Stephen. *Sex, Diet and Debility in Jacksonian America: Sylvester Graham and Health Reform.* Westport, Conn: Greenwood Press, 1980.

O'Cahill, Donal. *Killarney: Land and Lake.* 8th ed. Dublin: The Clíona Press, n.d.

O'Connell, Catherine M. *Excursions in Ireland during 1844 and 1850 with a visit to the Late Daniel O'Connell, MP.* London: Richard Bentley, 1852.

O'Connor, Frank. *Leinster, Munster and Connaught.* London: Robert Hale,1950.

—.'The Long Road to Umera', *The Stories of Frank O'Connor.* London: Hamish Hamilton, 1953.

—. *A Short History of Irish Literature.* New York: G.P. Putnams, 1967.

O'Connor, John. *The Workhouses of Ireland: The Fate of Ireland's Poor.* Dublin: Anvil Books, 1995.

O'Donoghue, D.J. *The Poets of Ireland. A Biographical and Bibliographical Dictionary of Irish Writers of English Verse.* Dublin: Hodges Figgis & Co, 1912.

O'Faoláin, Sean. *King of the Beggars: Daniel O'Connell and the Rise of Irish Democracy.* New York: The Viking Press, 1938.

O'Gráda, Cormac. *The Great Irish Famine.* Dublin: Gill &Macmillan, 1989.

Ó hOgáin, Daithi. *Myth, Legend & Romance: An Encyclopaedia of Irish Folk Tradition.* London: Ryan Publishing, 1990.

O'Maolchathaigh, Séamus. *An Gleann agus a Raibh Ann.* 2nd ed. Baile Atha Cliath: An Clóchomhar, 1964.

O'Murchadha, Ciarán. *Sable Wings over the Lands: Ennis, Country Clare, and its Wider Community during the Great Famine.* Ennis: Clasp Press, 1998.

O'Súilleabháin, Seán. *A Handbook of Irish Folklore.* Hatboro, PA. Folklore Associates, 1963.

O'Sullivan, Maurice. *Twenty Years A-Growing.* New York: The Viking Press, 1933.

O'Sullivan, Sean. *Legends from Ireland.* London: B.T. Batsford, 1977.

O'Tuathaigh, Gearóid. 'Aspects of Nineteenth-Century Galway' in *Galway: Town and Gown 1484–1984.* ed Diarmuid O'Cearbhaill. Dublin: Gill & Macmillan, 1984.

The Parliamentary Gazetteer of Ireland, Adapted to the New Poor-Law, Franchise, Municipal and Ecclesiastical Arrangements, and Compiled with a Special Reference to the Lines of Railroad and Canal Communication as Existing in 1844–45. 3 vols. Dublin: A. Fullarton and Co, 1846.

Pochin Mould, Daphne D.C. *Valentia: Portrait of an Island.* Dublin: Blackwater, 1978.

Pope, Alexnder. 'Being the Prologue to the Satires', 'Epistle','An Essay on Man', I, l. 95. *The Oxford Anthologyof English Literature.* I. eds Frank Kermode and John Hollander. New York: Oxford University Press, 1973.

Praeger, Robert Lloyd. *The Way that I Went.* London: Methuen, 1947.

Robinson, Tim. *Connemara. Part 1: Introduction and Gazetteer.* Roundstone: Folding Landscapes, 1990.

Shakespeare, William. 'Julius Caesar,' 'Twelfth Night,' *The Living Shakespeare.* ed. O.J.Campbell, New York: Macmillan, 1949. pp. 702-41; 612-49.

Slater's 1846 Directory. London: Slater's, 1846.

The Southern Reporter. Cork, 1845.

Spellissy, Seán. *The Ennis Compendium from Royal Dún to Information Age.* Ennis: The Bode Gallery, 1995.

Swift, Jonathan. *Poems of Jonathan Swift.* ed. Harold Williams,Oxford: Clarendon Press, 1958.

Thom's Dublin Directory. Dublin: Thom's, 1844, 1845, 1846.

Thompson, Mrs D.P. *A Brief Account of the Rise and Progress of the Change in Religious Opinion Now Taking Place in Dingle, and the West of the County of Kerry, Ireland.* Seley: Burnside and Seeley, 1845.

The Tourist's Illustrated Hand Book for Ireland. London: John Cassell, 1853.

Thom's 1844. Dublin: Thom's, 1844

Thom's 1845 Almanac. Dublin: Thom's. 1845

Trench, Charles Chenevix, *The Great Dan. A Biography of Daniel O'Connell.* Dublin: Jonathan Cape, 1984.

Tuke, James H. *A Visit to Connaught in the Autumn of 1847*. 2nd.ed. London: Charles Gilpin and Co., 1848.

Villiers-Tuthill, Kathleen. *Beyond the Twelve Bens: A History of Clifden and the District 1860–1923*. 2nd ed. Dublin: Connemara Girl Publications, 1990.

—. *History of Clifden 1810–1860*. 2nd ed. Galway: *Connacht Tribune*, 1992.

Welch, Robert, ed. *The Oxford Companion to Irish Literature*. Oxford: Clarendon Press, 1996.

Wigham, Maurice J, *The Irish Quakers: A Short History of the Religious Society of Friends in Ireland*. Dublin: Historical Committee of the Religious Society of Friends in Ireland, 1992.

Wilde, Lady Jane Francesca. *Ancient Cures, Charms and Usages of Ireland*. London: Ward and Downey, 1890.

Woods, Christopher. 'American Travellers in Ireland before and during the Great Famine: a Case of Culture Shock' in *Literary Interrelations: Ireland, England and the World*. ed Heinz Kosok. Tubingen: 1987.

Yeats, Jack B. *Life in the West of Ireland*. Dublin: Maunsel, 1912.

Yeats, William Butler. *The Collected Poems of W.B. Yeats*. New York: Macmillan, 1951.

Young, Edward. 'The Complaint; of Night Thoughts on Life, Death and Immortality', *The Oxford Anthology of English Literature*. I. eds Frank Kermode and John Hollander. New York: Oxford University Press, 1973.

Zuckerman, Larry. *The Potato: How the Humble Spud Rescued the World*. Boston: Faber and Faber, 1998.

MANUSCRIPT SOURCES

The Annals of the South Presentation Convent, Cork.

Fitz McCarthy, Connie. 'Asenath Hatch Nicholson: An Unknown American Author.' Unpublished thesis. Southern Connecticut State College, 1975.

O'Flaithartaigh, Máirtín. 'Na Préachers.' Private collection.

Outrange Reports, 17 March 1845, Galway 11/287-29099. National Archives of Ireland.

Webb, Alfred. Journal. Irish Society of Friends Library, Swanbrook House, Dublin.

INDEX

INDEX OF PLACES

Abbeyleix, Co. Laois (Queen's), 157

Achill, Co. Mayo, 319, 321, 327, 330, 336

Achill Sound, Co. Mayo, 319, 320, 321, 331, 337

Alps, 261

America, 20, 23, 26, 27, 39, 45, 61, 72, 74, 75, ·77, 78, 84, 91, 95, 97, 98, 106, 107, 113, 118, 121, 125, 142,143, 154, 157, 171, 172, 206, 207, 221, 235, 251, 281, 282, 291, 294, 298, 324, 329, 331, 333, 336, 338, 339

Arklow, Co. Wicklow, 31, 32, 33, 34, 36, 39, 41, 44, 53, 168

Atlantic Ocean, 262

Avoca, 32, 36, 39, 40, 51, 167

Ballinasloe, Co. Galway, 115, 117, 119

Ballyarthur, Co. Wicklow, 43

Banagher, Co. Offaly (King's), 135, 141, 142, 145

Bandon, Co. Cork, 191, 198, 199, 211

Bantry, Co.Cork, 136, 191, 200, 201, 202, 204, 205, 220

Bantry Bay, Co. Cork, 204, 206

Bay of Ross, Co. Kerry, 235, 236-7

Belfast, Co. Antrim, 339

Bethel, ancient city north of Jerusalem, 176

Birmingham, England, 336

Birr, Co. Offaly (King's), 114, 115, 145

Blackwater River, 79, 84, 85, 88, 89, 333

Blackrock, Co. Cork, 183, 184

Blarney, Co. Cork, 184, 185, 186, 187

Bog of Allen, 27

Boston, MA, 226

Cahirciveen, Co. Kerry, 235, 242

Canada, 109

Cappoquin, Co. Waterford, 67, 78, 84, 89, 91, 92

Cashel, Co. Tipperary, 77

Castlebar, Co. Mayo, 319, 330, 331

Castlecomer, 56

Cavan, 339

Clare Castle, Co. Clare, 281-2

Clare Island, Co. Mayo, 313, 316, 317

Clifden, Co. Galway, 285, 288, 292, 293, 294-5, 296, 298, 299, 304, 305, 306, 307, 308, 310

Clonmel, Co. Tipperary, 77, 78-9, 91, 92, 170,277

Clontarf, 19,20-1

Cloyne, Co. Cork, 191,192

Connaught (province), 3, 11, 28, 30, 123, 126, 137, 154, 207

Connecticut, 171

Connemara, Co. Galway, 3, 132, 281

Connor Hill (Connor Pass), Dingle, 275

Cork (county), 8, 9, 111, 253

Cork, Co. Cork, 170, 177, 178, 180, 181, 182, 184, 185, 195, 198, 201

Cove (Cobh), Co. Cork, 184, 188, 194, 195

Croagh Patrick, Co. Mayo, 308, 314-17

Derrynane, Co. Kerry, 248

Diamond Mountain, Co. Galway, 293, 300-03, 304

Dingle, Co. Kerry, 269, 270, 271, 273, 274, 275, 279, 336

Dublin, Co.Dublin, 4, 5, 6, 9, 10, 11, 12, 17, 28, 19, 20, 21, 22, 25, 27, 29, 37, 44, 52, 53, 61, 77, 79, 96, 119, 131, 151, 156, 157,I 68, 160, 169, 178, 238, 250, 281, 299, 317, 319, 334, 323, 333, 334, 336, 341

Dungarven, Co.Waterford, 67, 78, 84, 91

Dunquin, Co. Kerry, 277, 278, 279

Durrow, Co. Laois (Queen's), 156

Eden, 39

England, 20, 28, 45, 54, 80, 84, 105, 116, 235, 254, 294, 313, 319, 324

Ennis, Co. Clare, 281-2

Enniscorthy, Co. Wexford, 168

Eyre Court, Co. Galway, 135

France, 319

Galway, Co. Galway, 113, 115, 120, 122,

123-4, 125, 126-31, 154, 283, 284, 285, 307, 310, 311, 312, 317

Grange, Co. Tipperary, 67

Glendaloch (Seven Churches), Co. Wicklow, 44, 46-51

Glengariff, Co. Cork, 201, 202, 205, 208, 211, 218, 219, 222, 223 ,226, 323

Gorey, Co. Wexford, 168

Gort, Co. Galway, 282-3, 284

Halifax, Nova Scotia, 109

Irishtown (Ringsend, Dublin), 30

Johnstown, Co. Kilkenny, 57, 60

Keem Mountains, Achill Island, Co. Mayo, 319, 324, 325

Kenmare, Co. Kerry, 220-22

Kerry (county), 3, 235, 245, 253, 265, 267, 268, 277, 278, 312

Kerry Mountains, 224, 229, 235, 239, 257, 261, 262

Kilbride, Co. Wicklow, 36, 44, 45

Kilcooley, Co. Kilkenny, 67, 74, 156

Kildare (county), 27

Kilkenny (county), 63, 75, 127, 143, 298

Kilkenny, Co. Kilkenny, 54, 55, 56, 58, 66, 90, 156

Killahester, Co. Wicklow, 41

Killarney, Co. Kerry, 112, 201, 222, 224-6, 227, 228, 229, 230-32, 234, 238, 263, 264, 265, 266, 267, 268, 271, 303

Killorglin, Co. Kerry, 235, 263

Killoyra, Co. Kerry, 258

Kingstown (Dun Laoghaire), Co. Dublin, 5, 9, 10

King's (county), 27

Knockmealdown Mountains, 78

LaTrappe, France, 81

Leinster (province), 144

Leitrim (county), 333

Lismore, Co. Waterford, 84, 88, 89, 90, 302

Limerick, Co. Limerick, 281

Liverpool, England, 5, 8, 10, 11, 54, 55

London, England, 35

Longford, Co. Longford, 333

Loughrea, Co. Galway, 115, 135, 136, 137

Mississippi River, 281

Munster (province), 144

New Birmingham, Co. Tipperary, 67, 71

Newbridge, Co. Kildare, 39

New England, 33, 45, 173, 226, 339

New York, New York, 1, 6, 7, 10, 17, 23, 33, 44, 52, 61, 62, 74, 79, 89, 104, 121, 122, 123, 131, 135, 136, 154 ,156, 172, 173, 181, 192, 209, 222, 225, 234, 246, 249, 252, 255, 256, 266, 281, 311, 324, 327

Niagara Falls, New York, 224

Newport, Co. Mayo, 319, 331

Omey Island, Co. Galway, 293, 304, 305-7, 333

Oranmore, Co. Galway, 115, 131, 132, 282, 284

Oughterard, Co. Galway, 286, 310-11

Parsonstown (see Birr), Co. Offaly (Queen's)

Rathdrum, Co. Wicklow, 39, 40, 168

Roscrea, Co. Tipperary, 97, 102, 105, 112, 113, 115, 151, 152, 153, 154

Roundstone, Co. Galway, 292, 295, 296-7, 298

Sahara Desert, 286

Samaria (region between Galilee and Judea), 86

Scotland, 319

Shannon River, 269, 280, 281

Siberia, 286

Skelligs Rocks, Co. Kerry, 253

Sligo, Co. Sligo, 319, 331, 333

Sybil Head, Co. Kerry, 277

Tara, Co. Meath, 66

Tarbert, Co. Kerry, 279-80

Thurles, Co. Tipperary, 67, 75, 76, 97, 119

Tipperary (county), 75, 78

Tralee, Co. Kerry, 269-71, 310

Tullamore (Queen's), Co. Offaly, 19, 22, 23, 25, 27, 29, 41, 54

Tully, Co. Galway, 293, 303-04, 309

Urlingford, Co. Kilkenny, 54, 57, 62, 64, 65, 66, 92, 95, 97, 98, 102, 113, 131, 151, 153, 154

Urlingford Spa, Co. Kilkenny, 67, 69

Ulster (province), 144

Valentia Island, Co. Kerry, 248, 249-50, 256

Ventry, Co. Kerry, 274

Vermont, 248, 250, 266

Washington, D.C., 39

Waterford, Co. Waterford, 170, 172, 176, 177

Waterville, Co. Kerry, 250

West Indies, 171

Westmeath (county), 333
Westport, Co.Mayo, 308, 312, 314, 317-18, 319, 321, 331
Wexford, Co. Wexford, 168, 170, 172, 175
Wexford, Co. Wexford, 168
Whiting-Bay, Co. Waterford, 84
Wicklow (county), 31, 33, 34, 35, 36, 37, 42, 52, 60, 161, 164
Wicklow, Co. Wicklow, 167
Windsor Castle, England, 68
Youghal, Co. Waterford, 84, 85
Zion, Jerusalem hill, 337

INDEX OF PERSONS

Aaron, 1
Abraham, Rt. Rev., Bishop of Waterford, 82
Adam, 16
Admas,Dr,Achill Colony curate, 321, 323
Aigin[Egan], Mary, Birr woman, 146-50
Albert, Prince, 68
Ananias, 133
Arthur, Margaret, Postmistress of Newport, Co. Mayo, 331
Bantry, Lord, 201, 208-09, 211, 214, 215-16
Barker, Sir William, Kilcooley, 75
Barrett, Mr, Achill friend, 323, 326, 328, 329, 330
Barrett, Mrs, Achill friend, 323
Barter, Dr Richard, hydropathic cure, St Anne's Cork, 187.
Belshazzar, 82
Bennett, Gordon, New York journalist, 192
Bianconi, Charles, Irish public transportation pioneer, 78, 84, 92, 177, 199-200, 285, 299
Brandon, Lord, 266
Burke, Mr, Methodist minister, Kilbride, Co. Wicklow, 44
Burke, Richard, flour-dealer, Thurles, Co. Tippperary, 97
Burke, Mrs, Thurles, 75, 76
Caesar, Gaius Julius, Roman general and statesman, 340

Cambrensis, Giraldus, Welsh geographer and historian, 101
Casey, Mrs, Killarney landlady, 223, 264
Charleville, Earl of, 27
Chatterton, Lady Georgiana, travel writer, 257
Cromwell, Oliver, Lord Protector of England, 74, 89, 112, 206, 250, 277, 281
Crotty, Rev. WIlliam, Presbyterian clergyman, Roundstone, Co. Galway, 297
Danker, Mrs, Cork friend, 184-5, 195, 198
Daughter of Herodias (Salomé), 257
David, King of Judah and Israel, psalmist, 278
Desmond, Prince of, 186
Devonshire, Lord, Lismore, Co. Waterford, 88, 89
Downer, Dr William, Roscrea apothecary, Co. Tipperary, 112
Elizabeth, Charlotte (Charlotte Browne Tonna), author, 58
Eve, 82
Felix, procurator of Judea, 196
Fisher, Mrs Ellen, Cork hotel-keeper, 179, 198
Fitzgerald, Mrs Thomas, friend in Cloyne, Co. Cork, 193-4
Fleming, C., Old English Temperance Hotel, Dublin, 13
Gayer, Rev. Charles, Dingle Colony, Co. Kerry, 272
Gayer, Mrs, 272
Gibbon, Mr, itinerant Bible-reader, Newport, Co. Mayo, 331
Goldsmith, Oliver, author, 53, 110, 173
Graham, Sylvester, American health reformer, 16
H, Miss, Dublin friend, 334
Hackett, Co. Wicklow rebel, 36
Hall, Anna Maria, Irish novelist and travel writer, 186, 187, 325
Harburton, Lady, founded schools for poor children, Dublin, 53
Hatch, Martha, AN's mother, 6
Hatch, Michael, AN's father, 1, 6
Herod (Antipas), ruler of Judea, 82
Howe, Rev., Baptist missionary, Cork, 179

Jacob, son of Isaac, 259
Jackson, Thomas, coastguardsman, Dingle, Co. Kerry, 272, 274, 277, 279
Jasson, Rev., Baptist missionary, Cork, 179
Job, 217
Joseph, son of Jacob, 167
Joseph of Arimathea, 63
Kane, Sir Richard, Baronet, Mount Melleray benefactor, 81, 82
Kane, Lady, 82
Kathleen, Glendalough guide, 49-50
Keane, William, gave AN ride from Roundstone, Co. Galway, 310
Kenmare, Lord, Killarney, Co. Kerry, 222, 228
Knight of Kerry (Maurice Fitzgerald), 280
Lowe, Rev. Edward, Achill curate, 321
Lucifer, 82
Luther, Martin, 44
M'Sweeney, Daniel, parish priest of Bandon, Co. Cork, 199
M, Lady (Martin), Omey Island, Co. Galway, 305
Mathew, Father Theobald, temperance reformer, 14, 26, 63, 64, 65, 72, 77, 91, 97, 107, 108, 110-11, 150, 169, 180-4, 185, 188, 191, 196-7, 199, 201, 209, 220, 295
M'Gloukin, Mickey, Cahirciveen, Co. Cork landlady, 242-4
McHale, John, Bishop of Tuam, Co. Galway, 293
Moran, Mrs, friend in Roundstone, Co. Galway, 298
Moore, Thomas, poet, 40, 48, 49
Moses, 196
Musgrave, Sir Richard, historian, 84, 86, 87-8, 91
Nangle, Rev. Edward, founder of the Achill Mission, Co. Mayo, 319, 321, 324, 326, 327, 330, 336-7
Nangle, Mrs, 326, 327-8, 329, 330
Nebuchadnezzar, king of Babylon, 82
Nevin, Lady, Co. Wexford, 172-3
Nicholson, Asenath, identified as "the American," 11, 44, 52, 80, 89, 95, 96, 103, 108, 109, 132, 153, 154, 156, 163, 172, 174, 186, 191, 230, 232, 236, 251, 262, 274, 284; identified as "the American stranger," 19, 20, 56, 59, 69, 71, 74, 88, 115, 152, 179, 228, 298: identified as "the stranger," 148, 195, 217, 225, 238, 247, 257, 260, 267, 268, 271, 282, 290, 320, 324, 337, 339
Nicholson, Mr, Sligo 331
O'Brien, King Donal Mór, Holy Cross Abbey, Thurles, Co. Tipperary, 75
O'Connell, Daniel, M.P., "The Liberator," 20, 26, 29, 52, 78, 84, 89, 90, 91, 98, 235, 248, 251, 253, 254, 255, 256
O'Connell, Maurice, Derrynane, Co. Kerry, 254, 256
O'Connolly, Mr., friend, Clonmel, Co. Tipperary, 177
O'Donnel, Sir Richard, landlord, Newport, Co. Mayo, 331
Old Nick (devil), 124
Ossian (Oisín), son of Fionn Mac-Cumháil, 34
King O'Toole, legendary figure, Co. Wicklow, 48, 49
Page, M, friend, Co. Wicklow, 166
Parnell, John, Co. Wicklow, 39
Pounden, Rev. P., Rector of Westport, 308, 312
Power, Maurice, M.D., 184-5, 189, 195
Power, Mrs, 185
Quirk, Jerry, hotel-keeper, Ballybrack, Co. Kerry, 256
Raheley, Maurice, lodge-keeper, Co. Kerry, 258, 259
Raleigh, Sir Walter, English courtier, navigator, 297
Rebecca, wife of Isaac, 3, 86, 112, 225
Rector of Kilbride (Rev. W. Daly), Co. Wicklow, 44, 45, 46
Rector of Hyde Park, Killarney (Rev. Arthur Hyde), Co. Kerry, 267
Ross, Lord (William Parsons), 115, 117, 177
Ruth, protagonist of the Book of Ruth, 3, 225
Ryan, M.V., Rev. D., Prior of Mount Melleray Abbey, Co. Waterford, 82
St. Bridget, 240
St. John, 162, 287-8, 298-9
St. Kevin, 48, 50-1
St. Mathew, 178, 217, 247, 296
St. Patrick, 47, 314, 316

St. Paul, 16, 196, 313
St. Peter, 319
Savage, R.R., hotel-keeper, Achill
    Sound, Co. Mayo, 319, 320
Savage, Mrs, 320-1, 330, 331
Scanlan, Methodist minister, Grainge,
    Co. Tipperary, 72
Scott, Sir Walter, author, 49, 226, 254
Sligo, Lord (Peter Browne), 312, 317
Smith, Rev. Presbyterian minister,
    Westport, Co. Mayo, 312, 317, 319
Solomon, 35, 74,105, 107, 266, 337
Steely, M, lodging house, Co. Galway,
    310
Sturge, Joseph, English corn factor,
    reformer, 336
Talbot, John, Roscrea Quaker, Co.
    Tipperary, 113
Timothy, recipient of St Paul's letters,
    16, 50
Vesey, Molly, lodging-house keeper,
    Achill, Co.Mayo, 319, 321-3, 328, 329
Victoria, Queen, 26, 27, 68, 181
Virgin Mary, 138-9, 218, 230,231, 243,
    309, 328, 333
Voltaire, Francois, French author,
    philosopher, 52
Walpole, Mr, Walpole's Hotel, Tralee,
    Co. Kerry, 269, 270-1, 279
Walsh, Mr, friend, Birr, Co. Offaly
    (King's), 145
White, Dr, Urlingford, Co. Kilkenny,
    98, 118, 119, 156, 158
Wicklow, Lady, 34, 35, 39, 53
Wicklow, Lord, 34, 39
Yankee Doodle, 74, 156

INDEX OF SUBJECTS

abbeys, Kilcooley, 67, 74, 156; Holy
    Cross, 67, 75-6; Mount Melleray, 67,
    76, 79-83, 98
absentee landlords, 45, 176
Achill missionary colony, 319, 328, 330;
    accomplishments of the colony,
    328; Achill Herald, 336-7; converts,
    269, 273, 274, 318, 325, 330, 339; lack
    of charity; Nangle and women in
    the Bible, 336, Nangle and Jesuits,
    328
alcohol, 16, 19
American(s), 16, 17, 21, 172-3, 176, 181,
    189, 191, 199, 200, 204, 246, 250,
    317, 327, 339
American Indians, 27, 68, 132
American wake, 61
Arab, 286
bagpipers, 65, 66
banshees, 1
Baptists in Ireland, 84, 95, 115, 117, 178,
    188, 330, 331; Baptist ministers,
    Waterford, 179; Castlebar, 331
baptism, 312
Battle of Arklow, 36
beggars, 14, 17, 19, 20, 25, 26, 27-8, 29,
    30, 41, 50, 54, 56, 57, 84, 85, 99,
    100, 107, 108, 118, 122, 171, 180, 185,
    186, 305, 307, 318, 319, 333, 339
Bible, 16, 20, 23, 62, 107, 115, 120, 123,
    126, 139, 141-2, 157, 160, 161, 162,
    165, 167, 169, 170, 203, 231, 259, 275,
    297, 315, 320, 329, 330, 336; Irish
    (language) Bibles, 160, 203, 233,
    245, 318; Douay, 162, 163, 165, 167,
    209, 223, 231, 233, 250; AN as Bible
    reader, 123, 126, 141-2, 160, 162, 163,
    178, 234, 240, 243, 287-8, 291, 305,
    309, 310; Bible readers (not AN),
    129, 165, 168, 296, 298, 300, 306,
    313, 319, 325
bog oak, 14, 298
bog(s), 29, 50, 61, 148, 175, 253, 266, 276,
    302, 304, 330
burial grounds, Roundstone, 297,
canal boats, 27, 54, 299
caoine, 267
caves, Cloyne, 194, Diamond, 302
Christian Brethren, 107
Church of Ireland, Rathdrum, 40,
    Roundstone, 297
class, 174
coast guards, 248,251,273
Connaughtmen, 112, 115, 123, 125, 127,
    135, 158,161; looking for work, 28,
    143, 144
Connemara, girl(s), 115, 132, 133, 283,
    290; hospitality, 281, 290,
    improved, 293, 307; robbers, 295
consumption, 310
dance, 10, 54, 60, 66, 102, 112, 165, 189,

248, 257, 288-9
Danes, 105, 280
Derbyite, 319
domestic violence, 264
dress, 54, 60, 65-6, 105, 128-9, 133, 161,
    206, 208, 276, 281; Connemara girl,
    133, 301; Quaker, 77; red petticoats,
    287, 291, 301, 311
education, 142, 143; by class,274-5; edu-
    cation of girls, 17, 212; indepen-
    dence, 86
ejectment, 246
emigration, 54, 61, 121, 174, 200, 226,
    234, 248, 275, 307; exile,250; Irish
    in America, 168-9, 252, 298, 317,
    338; result of eviction, 296,
    returned emigrants, 115, 121-2, 131,
    246, 268
employment, 20; lack of government
    encouragement, 289; women, 249,
    250, 256-7, 297, 301
English, 20, 78, 106, 122, 130, 152, 209,
    251; Englishman, 108, 177, 199, 236,
    237, 289; language, 125, 273
English government, 87, 98
Established Church, 15, 95, 123, 147
exhibition, Dublin, 14
faction, 54, 64
fairs, 54; Cahirciveen, 244, 245, 246;
    Newport, 331; Westport,317
fairies, 1, 78, 133, 151; fairies and red
    petticoats, 291
famine, 3, 57, 217; present famine, 339,
    340
fiddler(s), 54, 55, 66, 102, 289, 299
fishermen, 36-8, 55, 175
fisherwomen, 126
five talents (parable), 35
foot bathing, 141, 207, 238
fraud, 270-1, 335
funerals, 39, 77, 97, 109, 116, 224, 225,
    228, 258, 267, 115, 121-2, 131, 246,
    268
gaol(s), Cork, 191,195-6; Tullamore, 19,
    25; Wexford, 170
grants, 78
Good Samaritan, 10, 149
harp, 9, 56, 66
Hibernian Bible Society, 3, 299
hobgoblins, 78
holy wells, 50, 84, 86, 93, 170

holidays, Christmas, 302; Easter,246;
    May Day, 295; St John's Eve, 202;
    St Patrick's Day, 214, 234; Shrove
    Tuesday, 253
hunger, 21, 130, 178
hunting, 165, 253
idleness, 132;
Iliad, 160, 165
Independency, 44
Independent Church, 319
Irish cabins, 12-3, 19-20, 29, 34-5, 38,
    58, 66, 86-7, 101, 113-14, 119-20, 123,
    147, 148-50, 151, 162-3, 168, 200-01,
    212-13, 253, 266, 276, 305
Irish character, 93; courtesy of children,
    115, 117-18; generosity, 295; hospi-
    talit, 240-1, 253, 267, 268; knowl-
    edge of Americans, 125; reputation
    for idleness, 132; verbal skills, 118,
    127-8, 165
Irish language, 69, 85, 86, 125, 127, 203,
    213, 214, 236, 239-40, 242, 252, 276,
    291, 306, 324, 325
Irish servant girls, 57; going to Amer-
    ica, 121; in America, 58, 67, 249;
    remittances, 58; returned from
    America, 58, 59, 122, 131, 246
itinerants, 65
Jesuits, 328, 329
Judah's towers, 335
Kerryites: 235-6, 239, 245, 248; cunning-
    ness, 265, 277
kish, 57, 58
labourers,26, 28, 30, 33, 42, 112, 115, 130;
    travelling in search of work, 169;
    fear of reprisal if they tell the truth,
    332
Lady Clare (agrarian agitator), 308, 311
landlords, 296
Latin, schoolby scholars, 166, 223, 277,
    296
legends, Glendalough, 48-51; St Kevin,
    48; Cloyne cave, 194; Killarney,
    227; 'the little foxes', 11, 89
literacy, 202, 214, 273; literacy and con-
    verts,326, 329; literacy in Irish, 203,
    214
Luther's hymn ('A Mighty Fortress is
    Our God'), 44
market(s),124; Galway,125, 128;Roscrea,
    153

marriage, early, 221; abandoned wife, 287

Methodism in Ireland, 44, 67, 72, 73, 105, 117, 246, 273, 304, 311

military, Queen's regiment, 30; in Galway, 129

mines, 29, 41-2, 46, 72-3, 99

Dingle Mission, 329, converts 329

ninety-eight, 34, 36, 43

nunneries (convents), 75, 97, 170, 228; Blackrock, Co. Cork, 183; Cork, 180-1; Dingle, 274-5; Killarney, 228; Monkstown, Co. Cork, 184; Thurles, 97; Wexford, 170

'Old Hundred', 44

oppression, 174, 232, 272, 338

orphans, 116, 321, 323

Papists, 45, 274

Pharoah's frogs, 29

pigs, 15, 24, 25, 37, 38, 64, 67, 68, 87, 103, 113, 115, 123, 124-5, 132, 140, 142, 143, 152, 201, 214, 216, 229, 253, 276, 305, 306, 320

pilgrims, 94

piper(s), 288, 289

police, 271, 286, 296, 298, 300, 302, 303, 319; think AN is a Lady Clare, 308, 311

politics, 52-3

poorhouse(s), 13, 25, 40, 97, 108, 109, 171, 201, 280; diet, 13, 25; school, 25; Bantry, 201, 202; Dublin North Union, 5, 14-15; Roscrea, 108; Tullamore, 19, 25

Pope, 98

Popery, 44, 117, 218, 318, 319, 329

potatoes, 11, 13, 14, 21, 25, 33, 42, 58, 59, 61, 64, 67, 68, 71, 72, 87, 90, 94, 95, 99, 100, 101, 106, 107, 112, 113, 114, 117, 118, 119, 120, 121, 122, 123, 127, 132, 127, 138, 140, 141, 143, 146, 148, 149, 152, 155, 157, 161, 167, 168, 174, 175, 178, 179, 188, 202, 203, 207, 213, 216, 226, 230, 233, 238, 240, 242, 244, 246, 248, 249, 253, 256, 257, 259, 260, 264, 267, 284, 290; crop, 296; a curse, 297; digging, 143; fields, 304; lumpers, 106, 107, 114; planting, 306; ridges, 253; seaweed manure, 297, 301, 302, 303, 304, 305, 306, 307, 312; seed potatoes,

267; theft of potatoes 171

poverty, 19, 22, 36, 68, 80, 108, 110, 117, 168, 199, 200, 203, 205-6, 281, 300, 327, 335; poverty as a judgment, 205

prelacy, 44

Presbyterianism in Ireland, 44, 88, 271; Birr, 115, 117; Galway, 128; Roundstone, 297; Westport, 308, 312

priest(s), 37, 53, 56, 69, 77, 90, 123, 142, 183, 185-6, 188, 217, 218, 220, 269, 271, 272, 274, 277; and fairy belief, 291; turncoat priests, 297, 319, 329

prophecy, 20

proselytism, 269, 272, 274; soupers, 271, 273

Protestants, 12, 17, 20, 35, 39, 45, 51, 52, 56, 60, 71, 75, 84, 89, 93, 95, 97, 102, 104, 105, 106, 107, 113, 115, 117, 141, 150, 157, 161, 165, 166, 167, 169, 173, 174, 177, 181, 183, 184, 191, 192, 195, 197, 198, 199, 208, 211, 212, 218, 223, 230, 233, 246, 267, 271, 272, 274, 275, 285, 287, 293, 296, 310, 318, 323, 329, 339

Protestant clergy, 71

Quakers, 6, 77, 78, 84, 91, 92, 95, 113, 114, 154; White Quakers, 77

quarries, Achill Island, 319, 325; Recess, 281; Valentia Island, 249, 250

racism 281

tracts, 71, 188, 211, 222, 231, 235, 242, 243, 305, 306, 310, 323, 330, 331

rent, 120

Repeal, 20, 29, 52, 91, 98, 255

robbers, 295, 339

Roman Catholics, 35, 39, 51, 52, 53, 54, 56, 62, 74, 75, 76, 79-83, 84, 93, 94, 95, 97, 98, 103, 104, 105, 106, 115, 123, 141, 157, 160, 63, 165, 166, 167, 169, 173, 177, 181, 184, 191, 192, 195, 198, 199, 209, 212, 223, 230, 233, 250, 267, 271, 272, 293, 300, 310, 318, 320

Romanism, 285, 323

runaway match, 143, 227

school(s), 13, 15, 27, 37, 39, 54, 56, 66, 85, 97, 142, 160, 286; Achill, 319, 321, 323; Arklow 34-5; Blackarock, Co. Cork, 183; Clifden, 295, 300; Connemara, 287, 293; Dublin, 53; Glengariff, 211-12; Newport, 331; Roundstone, 296-7; Thurles, 75; Tullamore, 25; Tully,

304; Ventry, 274-5; Westport, 314; Wicklow, 168, 169, 170, 172;

Scotchman, 88, 271

servants, 13, 15, 16, 17, 35, 56, 63, 64, 65, 71, 73, 90, 99, 100, 103,1 04, 105, 107, 119, 137, 141, 146, 147, 153, 163, 173, 175, 191, 198, 226, 243, 272, 305, 308, 327, 329, 335

Shakers, 82

shamrock, 294

singing, 29, 63, 112, 117, 133, 154, 164, 165, 166, 220, 234, 253, 261, 265, 316

slavery, 23, 27, 98, 226; American slave-holder, 23; American slavery, 329, 331-2, 338; American slaves, 27, 72, 77, 97, 226

snuff, 171

staring, 125, 127, 132, 192, 207-08, 230, 238, 244, 248, 326

starvation, 334, 338

stirabout, 8, 15, 25, 108, 212, 281, 334

superstitions, 275 ,291

tea drinking, 15, 19, 56, 66, 108, 136, 139, 141, 148, 267, 321

temperance, 26, 44, 45, 53, 57, 64, 72, 73, 103,110, 112, 124, 68, 181, 182, 183, 196, 209-10, 220, 234, 261

textiles, 143

tithes, 106, 175

tobacco, 66, 77, 108, 117, 118, 127, 161, 171, 200, 207, 266, 303, 322

transportation (as a sanction), 25, 29

unemployment, 168, 175, 199, 201, 283, 335

vegetarianism, 16

Ventry Colony, 274

wages, Bianconi drivers, 78; cobbler,24; fruit-sellers, 17, 20, 29; labourers, 13, 20, 42, 48, 56, 72, 77, 78, 92, 98, 120, 130, 161, 175, 272; miners, 46, 73; servants, 105; quarry-workers, 249; seaweed gatherers, 256, 301; stone-breakers, 331; weavers, 318

wake(s), 54, 62-3

widow's mite, 3, 150